THE AGRARIAN DRAMA
The Leftists and the Rural Poor in India
1934-1951

The Agrarian Drama

The Leftists and the Rural Poor in India 1934-1951

AMIT KUMAR GUPTA

Issued under the Auspices
of
Nehru Memorial Museum & Library

MANOHAR
1996

First Published 1996

ISBN 81-7304-142-3

Published by
Ajay Kumar Jain for
Manohar Publishers & Distributors
2/6 Ansari Road, Daryaganj
New Delhi - 110 002

Laser-typeset by
Mudrit
D-33 Hauz Khas
New Delhi - 110016

Printed at
Rajkamal Electric Press
G.T. Karnal Road
Delhi - 110 033

To the memory
of the
martyrdom
of the
Ahalyas,
the Doddi Komarayyas
and the
Sheonath Passis

CONTENTS

FOREWORD

It gives me great pleasure to say a few words about this scholarly project, which was conceptualised and completed by Dr. A. K. Gupta — initially, as a fellow of the Nehru Museum; and later, as a Research Professor of the University Grants Commission — over the past few years.

Dr. Gupta has taken upon himself the daunting task of writing about three substantial segments of our recent past, each one of which constitutes a very considerable theme in itself. The nationalist struggle in India; the entry of our peasant communities into history as its 'subjects' rather than its 'objects'; and the growth of left movement; are themes on which there exists a substantial corpus of scholarly writing. Dr. Gupta has drawn these three themes together into an analytical narrative. This is a formidable exercise; and the fact that it rests substantially on original materials makes it all the more commendable.

Indeed, through drawing three discrete trajectories of our recent past into a composite historical analysis, Dr. Gupta has placed the scholarly community under a heavy debt. That his book is addressed as much to the professional historian as it is addressed to the intelligentsia in general imparts an additional significance to what Dr. Gupta has written.

I trust, therefore, that this book will get the wide readership which it so richly deserves.

Teen Murti House
New Delhi

Ravinder Kumar

PREFACE

Historiography has of late paid a good deal of attention to the movement of peasants in the colonial and contemporary India, from the time they attempted elementally at organising themselves to the days their mentors were busy ideologically in mobilising them. Howsoever enlightening and insightful, the outcome of such academic interest seems at the most to offer prosaically a series of disjointed accounts of diverse peasant struggles in different regions, and at various phases, without having much connection with one another, or falling into certain patterns, and consequently blurring somewhat their anti-colonial and anti-feudal significance. The piecemeal portrayals also reveal a carefree tendency for lumping all kinds of agitating peasants together in an one-dimensional way, despite the recognition that the peasants, or more qualifyingly, the actual tillers of the soil (*kisans*) in India, have always remained categorised from a socio-economic point of view. Although the categories could, and did combine at times in a common cause, some more determinedly for existential reasons than others, their motivations and objectives were never exactly the same, and often these turned out to be at variance with each other beneath the surface. The poor and better-off sections in rural society always have separate axes to grind, different aspirations to strive and divergent dreams to dream. The relative unconcern of historians so far for this differential trend among *kisans* is conspicuous particularly in their depiction of those class-based agrarian mobilisations which the left political activists tried to build up from the mid-1930s onwards. It has facilitated in a way even the creation of a dubiety over the leftists' commitment to the causes of the *kisan* masses, whether they genuinely wanted to orgainse the rural poor, or made a grand show of it to cover up the defence of the better-off *kisans*' interests. The suspicion has gone so far as to encourage some of the present-day radicals to try in the 1970s and 1980s a make-believe reappraisal of their predecessors.

A touch of historiographical dissatisfaction and a lot of lactic curiosity have led me, therefore, to enquire further into the ideology-oriented, and differentiation-based, leftist mobilisation of the toiling *kisans*. Since I wished to follow the mobilisational aspects of one region in relation to those of various others, I had to look for an all-India perspective, and take into account the panoramic overview of the Indian independence and left movements. The scope of my enquiry being rather wide, I knew that it demanded and extensive research, and that the result of such an exercise might hopefully bring a substantial fresh information into focus, and perhaps put a number of old facts in a new light. What I had not really anticipated was the findings' influencing me to visualise a theatrical representation of events — their dramatic unfolding heighteningly towards a climax. An element of drama was so emphatically emerging out of the research that I thought it my duty to try to convey a feel of it to the prospective readers, and decided therefore, to present the discussions on my enquiry in a dramatic format — arranging them in Acts and Scenes rather than in serialised chapters. As I had always found an "Introduction" or a "Conclusion" to be inadequate for studies of longer periods of rapidly changing scenario (which seem to deserve several "Introductions" and "Conclusions" for their readers' clearer appreciation), I felt somewhat relieved when the format of a drama afforded me the opportunity to use the "Setting" several times in the text in place of the "Introduction", and the utterances of the Raisonneur (the Chorus, or the *Sutradhar* or the *Vivek* in Bengali *Yatra* performance) at a number of points as my own views to replace the "Conclusion". It is, however, for the readers to judge whether these contrivances have in any way helped me in my presentation.

The gestation of this book is rather long, and spread over the phases of conceiving it, undertaking the research for it and then writing it out. In all these phases I have shared my concerns with Mr. Sumanta Banerjee whose sustained interest in my work has encouraged me throughout. I have also received encouragement from Professor Ravinder Kumar whose generous support proved always to be crucial for my work, and who has very kindly agreed to my request for writing a Foreword. I am highly obliged to them, as well as to Dr. Prabhu Mahapatra who cleared up my confusions over some of the economic issues. I would not have been able to collect the material for this study had I not received a Nehru Memorial Museum and Library Fellowship. Similarly, I could not have completed the writing of the book if the University Grants Commission had not allowed me to do so as its Research Scientist. I am deeply indebted to both these esteemed organisations for their magnanimity.

I would like gratefully to acknowledge the help that I received at the time of material collection from some of my young friends, notably Professor Kapil Kumar, Dr. P.C. Pradhan, Mr. K. Shivamohan Reddy and Dr. N. Balakrishnan, who translated into English the extracts from an important Tamil source. Late Mr. C.V. Subbarao did the same in respect of a considerable amount of Telugu material. Over and above, Subbarao had always found time for a fellow-inquirer — at a very busy stage of his short life — to attend to each of my queries, and search out details to meet any of my statistical requirements. I am also thankful to the staff members of the National Archives of India (New Delhi), the State Archives of Andhra Pradesh (Hyderabad), Bihar (Patna), Maharashtra (Bombay), Tamil Nadu (Madras), Uttar Pradesh (Lucknow) and West Bengal (Calcutta), the Nehru Memorial Museum and Library (New Delhi), the National Library (Calcutta), the Central Secretariat Library (New Delhi), the P.C. Joshi Archives or the Archives on Contemporary History (Jawaharlal Nehru University, New Delhi), the Communist Party of India Central Archives (Ajoy Bhavan, New Delhi), the Saraswatha Niketanam Library (Vetapalam, Prakasham District, Andhra Pradesh), the Ananda Bazar Patrika Library (Calcutta) and the Jugantar Office (Calcutta) for extending to me and a few of my friends all facilities for research.

My debt to the Nehru Memorial Museum and Library authorities increased heavily when they decided to bring out this book as one of their publications. The Deputy Director of the organisation, Dr. Hari Dev Sharma, and its affiliated Senior Fellow from the Indian Council of Historical Research, Dr. Maya Gupta, have read through the type-script between them, and suggested many improvements. Dr. N. Balakrishnan of the same orga-nisation and his colleagues have taken pains in checking some of the proofs, and getting the Index prepared and the cover design made. I would like to thank them all, and also record my appreciation of the promptitude with which Manohar Publishers and Distributors, New Delhi has succeeded in publishing the book. A special word of thanks is due to Sudhir Mathur and his "Mudrit" for labouring so hard on a hand-written script, and transforming it eventually into a computerised print-out of high order.

I am of course entirely responsible for the contents of this book. Any errors of fact, interpretation and presentation are unintended, but mine alone.

15 November 1995 AMIT KUMAR GUPTA

PROLOGUE

Leftism, or the left-wing political activity, which grew oppositionally to the governmental positions, and turned ideologically towards the radical social transformations, was bound to play a significant role in the rising of the colonial world on account of its peoples' two-fold sufferance at the combined hands of the colonialists and the native exploiters. Since the left-wing political activity was dependent on the mobilisation of the people, especially of the under-privileged among them, for experimenting with more equitable social orders, the leftists could not, however, make their presence felt on the Indian scene till the days of the countrywide anti-British mass agitations. They managed to surface in a flutter only when the Rowlatt Bills, the Non-Co-operation and the Civil Disobedience movements demonstrated the great strength of popular upsurge on the one hand, and the birth of a socialist state in Russia, as well as its survival against the heavy odds, raised sky-high hopes for socialism on the other. Their common inspirational fund appeared initially to have been drawn from abroad the rudiments of Marxist-Leninist precepts, which reached them — despite the British vigilance against such importation — through the occasionally smuggled in political literature. The manner their natural nationalistic opposition to the British Raj was sharpened with the help of some understanding of the world capitalist system that had generated imperialism, of the mechanism that had enabled the imperialist powers to subordinate the economies of the colonised countries to their own, of the symbiosis that existed between the colonialists and the native exploiters of people in the colonies — pointed clearly to the debt the Indian leftists owed to the Marxist-Leninist line of thinking. Marxism-Leninism was also writ large on the way they attempted at perceiving the social exploitation that prospered on the basis of class interests and contradictions within societies, committing themselves to the task of leading the vast masses of the downtrodden against their alien and native oppressors, contemplating the liquidation of all exploitative systems by setting up a *Majdoor-Kisan Raj* (the Rule of the Workers and the Peasants), and planning to win complete independence and socialism for the Indian people.

The kind of socialism that must be brought in India, and more so, the precise method of its bringing about under the colonial conditions, were the basic issues over which the Indian leftists — like their counterparts in the rest of the colonised world — could not agree. Would socialism be attained in graduation, by the piecemeal social engineering, and through a so-called "revolution by consent"; or dramatically in one massive sweep by the wholesale replacement of the wornout social order with a new one, and through a qualitative changeover by force? Would socialism in India be a "social democracy" (as opposed to the mere political democracy), gymnastically balancing the diverse pressure groups within the country; or a "dictatorship of the proletariat" (as reduced to the dictatorship of their party), steamrolling the road designed in its interest? Would the social liberation of the Indian people await their political independence from the Raj; or should the battles against imperialism, and against the collaborative native exploiters, be waged together? Could the anti-imperialist struggle of the multiplicity of classes, categories and communities be cohesively, but compromisingly, carried on under the prevailing bourgeoised leadership of the Indian National Congress; or should the mantle of leading it be taken over by such subaltern categories as the workers and the peasants to give the struggle a more socially advanced, though not necessarily cohesive, popular thrust? On these, and similar other questions, the Indian leftists differed very considerably among themselves, and while some — standing on the edifice of Marxism-Leninism — tried to find the answers either with the aid of the international Communist movement, or even without it, through reference to the ideas of Leon Trotsky and Rosa Luxemburg; the others searched for their's in various sources, ranging from the tradition of western liberalism to that of radical humanism, from the Fabian Socialist fundamentals to the teachings of Democratic Socialism, from the Christian Socialist thoughts to the Gandhian anarchist concepts. Consequently, the Indian left movement had turned into an acrimoniously divided camp, in which each of the participating groups vociferously contested the standing of the others, and claimed its own ordained path to be the only one for achieving the liberation of Indians, and the establishment of socialism in India. Despite all their divergences, extending from the ones of degrees to those of kinds, every left group or leftist organisation — whether it was the Communist Party of India (founded in 1925), or the Congress Socialist and later the Socialist Party (founded in 1934 and 1947, respectively), or the Royist League of Radical Congressmen and the Radical Democratic Party (founded in 1937 and 1940, respectively), or the All-India Forward Bloc (founded in 1939), or the Bolshevik Party of India (founded in 1939), or the Revolutionary Socialist Party (founded in 1940), or the Trotskyite Bolshevik-Leninist Party of India (founded in 1941), or the Revolutionary Communist Party of India (founded in 1942), or the Democratic Vanguard (founded in 1951) — was dedicated generally in its characteristic mode to the causes of both anti-imperialism and the toiling masses' emancipation. As emancipators, each of them pledged itself to take the side of the economically most differentiated, and the socially most degraded classes and categories — the workers in the industries and the toilers on the soil in particular. Simultaneously all of them — irrespective of their largeness or smallness, their sub-continental presence or localised existence — tried to think and act on an all-India scale, and endeavoured at formulating policies and programmes for the whole country rather than for its specific part or parts.

From an all-India point of view, the agricultural situation in the country varied substantially from region to region, in terms of climate, soil, irrigation, yield, cropping pattern, market facility, cultivation practice, and, of course, tenurial arrangement. The land administration also differed from the *Zamindari* to the *Rayatwari*, and then to the *Mahalwari* or the *Malguzari*, leading to the creation of both the permanently and temporarily settled *Zamindars* and *Taluqdars*, as well as the perpetually and periodically positioned tenant landholders, with intermediaries and sub-tenancies galore in between. What eventually came out of this melting pot of proprietary rights and tenurial arrangements, and through the permutations and combinations of a plethora of enactments affecting them, was a landed hierarchy of the *Zamindars* and *Taluqdars* (paying tax to the Government and receiving rent from the occupant tenants), the occupant tenants (paying rent to the *Zamindars* and *Taluqdars* in the *Zamindari* areas, and tax to the Government in the non-*Zamindari* areas), the sub-tenants (paying rent to the occupant tenants in all the areas) and the landless tillers (selling labour power everywhere, freely or in bondage, in exchange of subsistence). Simultaneously with such a process of developments flourished two important groups on the Indian agrarian scenario — the traditional providers of rural credit (the *mahajans*), who also started acting as the sellers of agricultural products and buyers of industrial goods, and the emergent landlords of unrecognised nature from among the occupant tenants, who succeeded in grabbing more lands than the others by tampering with the village records they previously maintained as revenue officials, by using their higher social and caste positions to exert a certain extortionist pressure, by practising in grain-loaning and in taking over the borrowers' plots as a means of recovery, and then putting most of their lands on rent (usually the produce one) to the sub-tenants of various sorts, including the sharecroppers. Since credit had been extremely low in the rural sector, and land alienation ordinarily very high, leaving aside its extraordinary height at times of natural disasters and market disorders, lands steadily flowed into the hands of the landlords of all descriptions, either directly, or *via* the *mahajans*. Landlordism, whether of the *de jure* or of the *de facto* variety, reigned supreme over the entire Indian countryside at the beginning of the twentieth century — in partnership with the usurious capital, and in connivance with the colonial authorities. Colonialism found in the feudal recipients of rent, not only the loyal supporters of its political domination, and the junior partners of its economic exploitation of the colony, but also the most dependable stumbling blocks to the growth of native capitalism in agriculture. For appending Indian economy to the British and the capitalist world economy, the colonial authorities did need to bring India's countryside into commodity-money relations, and, of course, to commercialise its agriculture; but only under their own firm control, and without allowing the indigenous capitalist class the scope, and the necessary gaining in strength, to guide agriculture expectantly on independent developmental, and resultantly anti-colonial lines. It was in the colonialist interest, therefore, that pre-capitalism existed with the commodity-money economy, that the traditional agrarian structure suitably adapted to the metropolitan industrial and financial needs, and spared somehow from an outright collapse. Consequently, under the feudal-colonial regime, took place a colossal concentration of land in the hands of the landlords, a sharp decline in the availability of land for the *kisan* masses, a general degradation of the peasant holdings, a continued stagnation in the agricultural output, a phenomenal rise in the agricultural debt, and a steady increase in the rank of the landless.

It would, however, be an exaggeration to suggest that the British authorities were not aware of the deepening agricultural crisis and all its ominous repercussions for them and their authority in the countryside, or that some germination of capitalism in agriculture had not been taking place in India — either uncertainly under a feeble change of the governmental mind, or naturally in the conditions of commercial and marketing activity. The Government was compelled to think in favour of converting landlords into capitalist entrepreneurs on the Prussian junker model, and as revealed in the *Report of the Royal Commission on Indian Agriculture* of *1927-28*, a few of them did appear on the scene. More importantly, however, an affluent section of the independent peasant proprietors, or the rich peasants, started producing systematically for the market, and engaging wage-labour for garnering profit. But none of these two kinds of elements was yet the significant feature in the countryside where the feudal exploitative relationship had been the most dominant, and the landlordism and usury the singularly oppressive over all the sections of rural society — rich and poor. It was, however, the poor, or the section of rural population on whom the feudal-colonial system had thrust upon the heaviest weight of poverty, that suffered the most, and that in effect was heard the least. Who, incidentally, were the rural poor in India in the 1930s and 1940s, and how poor did they appear to be? Since the poverty of the past generation does not usually prick the conscience of its progeny much, these issues have not been discussed sufficiently clearly with a certain empirical sophistry in the post-independence India, Pakistan and Bangladesh. The economic historians are, however, in a position — if they so desire — to vivify on a sub-continental scale the poverty of the rural poor in the 1930s and 1940s by using the data which has survived, and by constructing and reconstructing on them. Such a daunting exercise could possibly be undertaken by making enquiries into the actual consumption level of the rural people, and the level of their production assets. As consumption level might both be absolute (depending upon some minimum caloric standard) and relative (varying in regional, ecological and other agricultural contexts), and related to income, an index of rural poverty would be obtained by trying to arrive at a per capita income, consumption, and more specifically, caloric consumption of the rural populace. Another index could also be secured by exerting to find out the position of landholding (the concentration of landholding, the subsistence landholding and the landlessness, varying in regions), the state of inputs (investments in canals and irrigational works) and implements, including the animal or bullock power (their possession and the dispossession), the access to credit (the lack of it more perhaps than its absolute level) and the employment availability (the market facility for labour, and its scarcity). The census data (on castes for 1931, on scheduled castes and tribes for 1951 and on occupations for 1931, 1941 and 1951) could also indicate the economically rural poor at their convergence with the sociologically lower castes, as perhaps the labour migration data would impressionistically do so to a certain extent.

In case one finds out from all this that a particular *kisan* used to go to the coffee plantation during the agricultural off-seasons to work as a migrant wage labourer; hired on rent (with, or without a deed) a tiny unirrigated plot of an acre or two; procured a pair of bullocks and a few implements of agriculture; earned far below, and consumed much less than the per capita rural income and consumption, respectively; lived gaspingly with the help of a minimum (under the Indian conditions) caloric intake worth 616 grams of food grain per day;[1] groaned under the burden of certain debts he previously incurred at an exorbitant rate of interest, and which he had failed to repay even partially; shorn off any earthly valuable which he could mortgage for a fresh loan; belonged to a socially outcaste and religiously polluted community — the discovery shall, indeed, give the graphic portrayal of a rural poor and the extent of his poverty in India in the 1930s and 1940s. Such an impeccable model of standard rural poverty does help in bringing out the intricacies of operations of an exploitative agrarian apparatus, and their starkly obvious personified outcome. But does the model assist the historical enquirer in identifying those whom the leftists of the time were expected — as per their ideologies — to organise in the rural mobilisation, and in understanding how they shaped its various facets, and why? Can one meaningfully delineate any agitation or movement of unidentified, unspecified participants, and reflect their aspirations — collective, or otherwise? Did such participants carry tags on their backs to indicate their falling short of the model by certain centimetres, or their exceeding it by a few more, and justify a possible classification accordingly? Since they also did not carry similar tags showing who among them was holding what size of plot, and who happened to be plotless, any approximation of their class or category status on the basis of landholding becomes inconvenient. Even the attractive Leninist norm that those who had to sell their labour power "outside" — howsoever partially, and in graded proportions, over and above its employment in their respective holdings — could be classified into the different categories of the rural poor,[2] and a recent attempt at its quantified elaboration in

1. The National Sample Survey (1960-1) figure, cited in V.M. Dandekar and N. Rath *Poverty in India*, Pune, 1971, p.7.
2. Lenin hinted at this norm in 1898 in his *Development of Capitalism in Russia*, and later asserted it while introducing the Agrarian Thesis to the Second Congress of the Communist International held in 1920.

India,[3] is hardly likely to be of much use in view of the missing tags. The historical enquirer of the Indian rural poor's movement in the 1930s and 1940s is then left with no other alternative but to fall back upon the age-old, and the much used practice of trying to decipher the concerns felt, the demands made and the slogans raised by the participants in their mobilisational processes. If the slogans were raised against bondage, the demands made in favour of the wage increase, and for the higher price of agro-industrial products, one could suspect who might have been behind them. Identically, if the sharing of the produce-rent was questioned, the ejectments opposed and the tenurial security claimed, one could guess who might have been involved in these. Similarly, if in the circumstances of difficulty, the "no-rent" cry was raised, the re-payment of debts refused and the alienation of land resented, one could suppose who

3. Utsa Patnaik in her writings (articles in the *Economic and Political Weekly* and the *Journal of Peasant Studies* between 1971 and 1983, and a book, *Peasant Class Differentiation: A Study in Method with Reference to Haryana*, Delhi, 1987.) proposed a method of analysing peasant households by using a single index, namely, "the labour exploitation criterion" to measure the use of family labour in two ways: directly, in terms of the hire and sale of labour, and indirectly, in terms of the rent and lease of the plot. Since rent paid by a weak household, having insufficient land, constitutes surplus labour which is appropriated by the proprietor of the land, its payments could be converted into an equivalent value of "labour time" for calculating the balance of alienated labour and appropriated labour of a household in relation to the amount of its own labour on the land it holds. Landlords, capitalist farmers and rich peasants will be distinguished by a large positive value of their exploitation ratio (E), because they have a large component of appropriated labour and a negligible amount of family labour on their own lands. The value of E will in proportion be slightly positive, or slightly negative in the case of the middle peasant household, and clearly negative in respect of the poor peasant, who is dependent more on selling or alienating labour and less on working in his holding. The value of E will be strongly negative in the case of the agricultural labourer, who does not have a plot to labour, and who depends totally on selling his labour to others. In spite of such criticisms of the single indicator of exploitation as her leaving out other important relations through which a surplus can be appropriated, including the credit mechanism and the off-farm trades, or her messing up the variety of agricultural duties into a simplistic "labour time" of the kind assumed for capitalist production, Patnaik's endeavour is one of the remarkable scholarly attempts of the recent times at peasant class differentiation in India.

might have been affected. Likewise, if resistances were organised against the landlords' oppressions, battles fought with their goons and their official collaborators, and precious lives laid down, one could imagine who might have been in the forefront of all this, and with whose sympathy. The bondage and wage labourers, as well as the artisans and the "menials" or the low-caste *Dalit* "untouchables", the under-tenants and the share-croppers, the small or the marginal tenants in effect seem to have constituted the rural poor in India, embodied together the characteristics and the extent of rural poverty, and shared the Leninist norm of wholly, or partially in gradation, selling their labour power "outside". This composition apparently conforms to what the villagers themselves considered to be the poor in their midst, and it tallies also with what the leftists perceived to be the case, though they were unwilling to lay much stress on the low caste factor. It is, however, possible that all small peasants had not been as weak as they always appeared, especially during the post-second world war days of rising agricultural prices, or that the landholding capacity of some under-tenants and sharecroppers had not been as inconsequential as it generally looked, particularly where they continued to be present for a relatively longer length of time. But such examples were so rare, and so exceptional to the rule, that their existence could scarcely have affected the class and category relations under an overbearing feudal-colonial system in the Indian countryside.

The prevailing condition of rural poverty being alike all over the country, despite its varying levels; the suffering of the rural poor being similar throughout India, despite its difference in degrees; their subjection to the landlord-colonialist exploitation being the same on a sub-continental scale, despite its dissimilarity in local nuances; and the leftists' outlook being invariably all-Indian, despite their inability to operate in equal strength in every region; any review of the left-rural poor interaction and syndrome has to be an all-India affair even if it is not wholly perfect, nor entirely complete.

Act One
1934-39

THE SETTING

The uneasy serenity that reigned over the Indian countryside was broken rather rudely during the latter half of the first world war. The din had generally been made by some sections of the substantial land-holding peasantry — the emerging dissenters — against an overbearing Raj in the villages. Their clamour, in its proper perspective, was both a cause and an effect of the nationalist experimentation with anti-imperialist mass movement. It marked not only an impressive expansion of the Indian National Congress's social base, signifying considerable slackening of the hold of the British and their allies over rural society, but also opened up the prospect for the vast majority of *kisans* to assume a decisive role in the liberation of their country. Such a natural task in a predominantly agricultural India was, however, difficult for the *kisans* to undertake unless their multitudinous lower components — the suffering and the impoverished among them — joined in escalating the range and raising the level of the commotion. This did hardly happen in the 1920s, and the poor and the landless peasants were seldom seen to take an active part in the bustle, despite widespread disaffection among them. Barring some occurrences in the unusual wake of the Khilafat and Non-Co-operation movements, and in the mythical impendency of *Swarajj* (self-rule),[1] all other well-known agrarian agitations prior to the mid-1930s were produced and shaped mainly in the interests of the upper crusts of Indian peasantry. Their dominance over the proceedings was in fact writ large on most areas of the country, for instance, in Champaran (1917) for opposing the appropriations of the planters, in Kheda (1918) for suspending the collection of land revenue, in several parts of Bengal and Bihar (1920) for resenting the imposition of *Chowkidari* tax, in Satara (1920-1) for withstanding the upper caste *mahajan* (moneylender) and landlord opressions, in Midnapore

1. These were the Moplah, the Rampa, the Awadh, the Mewar, the Kanika-raj and the Darbhangaraj outbursts, or those sub-millenarian episodes which grew out of the poor and the landless peasants' desperations.

(1921-2) for protesting against the Union Board levy, in Guntur (1922-3) for organising a "no-tax" campaign, in Borsad (1925) for opposing a punitive police impost, in East and West Godavari (1927) for foiling a rise in revenue rates, in Bardoli (1928) for refusing to pay the land tax, and resisting the consequent confiscation of lands, and in Bilga (Jullundur, 1930) for following the example of Bardoli. The thrusts of the substantial peasant categories continued unabated throughout the Civil Disobedience movements (1930-3), and these hardly flagged ever thereafter. Nevertheless, the state of rural unrest in the 1930s could not remain the same, and it had undergone significant changes, first, during the period of the great Depression between 1929 and 1933, and then in 1934 — the year the left nationalists formed the Congress Socialist Party — and about the time the disarrayed Communists regrouped themselves to work among the toiling masses.

The Depression dislocated rural society through a catastrophic fall in prices of the agricultural products, a sharp decline in average net income per acre and a drastic reduction in the purchasing power of the peasantry. Unlike the inflation towards the end of the first world war, which had hurt the poor peasants in the main, and thereby contributed to their joining in some of the delirious enactments of 1920-1, the Depression adversely affected all categories of peasants everywhere. Those who had a surplus to sell, and who could be termed as the "rich" and the "middle" peasants, or as the affluent, suffered heavily from a dramatic dwindling of return from the market. Consequently, the prevailing cost of cultivation, especially the land revenues and water rates, turned out to be exorbitantly high for all self-cultivating peasant proprietors. That largely explained the keen interest the substantial peasants took in the Civil Disobedience movement, and the "no-tax" temper that they rapidly flew into, as well as the subsequent pleas they made persistently for reducing, revising and remitting the Government demands.[2] The fall in income during the Depression

2. The popularly held belief that the "worst affected" by the Depression were "the relatively better off" peasants who had "a surplus to sell" (Sumit Sarkar, *Modern India*, Delhi, 1983, p. 258), does not seem to be quite true. The truth approximately is that the Depression impaired the fortunes of all agrarian categories, including the landlords, and that it perhaps damaged the interests of the poor peasants more than those of the others.

also had a devastating effect on the tenants of various varieties. They were unable to pay the rent, and what was worse, they failed to raise loans for tiding over the difficult times. Apart from their being infinitesimal in number, the Cooperative Credit Societies were reluctant to make advances to desperate debtors. The professional *mahajans* or the village *banias*, too, were not in a position to give fresh loans because of their inability to recover the old ones. Simultaneously, it was not possible for the poor, and even the substantial peasants, to try to repay their past debts, which, with a 50 to 60 per cent fall in prices, had practically doubled in real terms. Thus the only borrowing they could manage, more in grains than in cash, was from the rich and the dominant landed sections under stringent stipulations. The *rayati mahajans* naturally became the controlling authority in the countryside, enforcing often the small cultivators to become sharecroppers in their lands. Protected occupancy tenants were forced to join the ranks of the tenants-at-will and the land prices slumped. The loss of land or of the hold over land was phenomenal everywhere, and in Bombay and the Central Provinces and Berar, for example, it led to the concentration of 72 per cent of the cultivated land in the hands of 29 per cent of the agrarian population.[3] The fortunes of agricultural labourers were also seriously jeopardised by the Depression, not so much through a fall in the wages, which had not really been very striking in comparison to the fall in prices, but because of a severe curtailment of employment opportunities. The surplus producers, who previously employed a number of hands for field activities, decided during the Depression to manage with only a few. They restricted the employment of *khetmajdoors*, fell back largely upon the family labour, stopped giving advances to labourers and reverted to wages in kind to save cash. Added to their perennial problem of seasonal and annual fluctuations in income, therefore, the agricultural workers had suddenly to confront with unemployment, worsened conditions of service and wages in coarse grains.[4]

3. D. Rothermund, *Indian Economy Under British Rule and Other Essays*, Delhi, 1983, p. 130.
4. All these ill-effects of the Depression on agrarian society in India have generally been corroborated by the findings of the economic historians of various schools.

Of course the poor peasants' sufferings had not received as much public attention as the substantial peasants' did. The small cultivators' gradual relegation to the ranks of the sharecroppers or the dispossessed, and the agricultural labourers to the levels of the destitutes, had in effect been put far behind the rich and the well-to-do peasants' difficulties in meeting the Government demands or raising the amount of *taccavi* (the advances by the Government). The "no-tax" slogan was louder than the "no-rent" cry — the hostility to reassessment operations clearer than the bitterness against eviction proceedings. All this was evidently due to a distinction between the nature of respective grievances of the substantial and the poor categories. While the "no-tax" represented a frontal attack on the Government, the "no-rent" embodied a resistance to the immediate social oppressors, and in the prevailing calculations of anti-imperialist mass mobilisation, the so-called "peasant nationalists" seemed infinitely more preferable and less distracting to the national leadership than the peasant non-conformists. But even then, some disconcerting incidents were taking place sporadically in the countryside from the days of the Civil Disobedience movements. It was natural for any suffering people to take advantage of a tumultuous situation for ventilating their own specific grievances. By joining the nationwide Civil Disobedience movements, though not as extensively and vociferously as perhaps the rich and the well-to-do peasants could manage, the poor peasants did make some of their points felt in a certain way. The acute problems of the *kisans* of Hissar, for example, were highlighted when they not only declined in April 1930 to pay rent, but also seized the crops of their landlords. In May 1930 the desperate poor peasants rose violently against the oppressive *mahajans* and *Zamindars* of Kishoreganj in Mymensingh, Bengal. The lower peasantry resorted in September 1930 to a series of hostile acts against the landlords in the Jat-dominated villages of Meerut and Bulandshahar, the United Provinces. A "no-rent" campaign and an agitation against eviction continued throughout 1931 in Rae Bareli. The landlord-tenant relations took an ugly turn in September 1931 in Puri, Orissa, and the tenants put up opposition against the *Zamindari* oppressions in Venkatagiri estate, Nellore, Madras province. There were anti-moneylender disturbances in Rohtak in December 1930, in Krishna and Guntur in September 1931 and in Jammu in October 1931. These and similar other occurrences were known more or less to all serious political observers. What was not known adequately, however, seemed to be the fact that the poor peasants' anxiety for resistance as the last resort, howsoever instantaneous and infructuous, did not really wane even when the Civil Disobedience movements turned moribund.

The poor peasants' ability to stand against their oppressors had often been reflected between 1932 and 1934 in a large number of happenings all over the country. A typical illustration was the manner in which the tenants forced the *Malguzars* at Jaijaipur (1932) and Janjgir (1933) areas of Bilaspur, the Central Provinces and Berar, to forgo rent and burn documents.[5] The tenants of *Istimrari* estates of Mewar (such as, Sathana, Shergarho, Masuda and Bagsuri) were involved in a "no-rent" campaign practically throughout 1932 in the face of severe repressions.[6] Tenants in a *tahsil* of Pilibhit, the United Provinces, resisted successfully a number of irregular dues collected by the *Zamindar*, over and above rent.[7] In Rae Bareli and Buland-shahar of the same province, the *Naib Tahsildars* and the police parties were resisted by the tenants when they tried to attach the *kisans*' properties for arrears of rent. The resistance led eventually to police firings, deaths and injuries.[8] The *kisans* were reported in Palamau, Bihar, to be opposing payment of rent and using force against the landlords' *amlas* (agents).[9] There were signs of unrest in some other parts of Bihar also, more specifically in Gaya and Purnea, and in Banka sub-division of Bhagalpur, the tribal peasants (of Santhal origin) refused loan repayment to the *mahajans*, as well

5. Home Poll. Fortnightly Reports for 1st half of January 1932 and 1st half of March 1932, File Nos. 18/1/32 and 18/3/32, National Archives of India (hereafter N.A.I.).
6. *Ibid.*, 1st half of February 1932, 2nd half of February 1932, 1st half of March 1932, 2nd half of March 1932, 1st half of April 1932, 1st half of June 1932 and 2nd half of September 1932, File Nos. 18/2/32, 18/3/32, 18/4/32, 18/6/32 and 18/9/32, N.A.I.
7. *Ibid.*, 2nd half of July 1932, File No. 18/7/32, N.A.I.
8. *Ibid.*, 1st half of July 1932 and 1st half of August 1932, File Nos. 18/7/32 and 18/8/32, N.A.I.
9. *Ibid.*, 2nd half of March 1932, File No. 18/3/32, N.A.I.

as rent payment to the landlords, on account of crop failure.[10] Peasants also declined to pay rent and repay debt at Laksam *thana*, Tripura, and at Babiganj of the same district about 100 indebted peasants attacked the house of a landlord-moneylender, killed his son, destroyed valuables and burnt documents.[11] A "no-rent" situation developed at Debra, Midnapore, in March and in parts of Rajsahi in April 1933 in Bengal. Peasants were reported to be resisting and "harassing" moneylenders in Contai, Midnapore, and in Tangail, Mymensingh.[12] In October 1933 the *kisans* in a body refused to pay rent to the landlords in Gopalpur, Assam. There were reports of considerable unrest in Tanjore, Madras province, and in Warangal, Hyderabad state, in 1933-4.[13] Tenants opposed high rent in the *Zamindari* areas of Nellore,[14] and their confrontation with the landlords actually led to riots, deaths and injuries in Krishna, Madras province, in June 1934.[15] Without citing any further illustration from other parts of the country, it could be said that the poor peasants in India were not wholly a weak, meek and fatalistically dispirited mass of humanity, and that in exigencies at a local level they were capable of fighting against oppressions and injustices. Like the rich and the well-to-do peasants, however, they needed political direction and ideological vision for making the most of their capabilities on a larger scale. In 1934 it seemed as if the poor peasants had met at last with their political mentors — those who would commit themselves unequivocally to their cause.

Although the Communists — theoretically the staunchest among the allies of the down-trodden — followed the nationalists on the agricultural scene as early as the latter half of the 1920s, their attempts at rural mobilisation through the Workers and Peasants Party (mainly in Bengal, the Punjab, the United

10. *Ibid.*, 2nd half of October 1933 and 1st half of November 1933, File Nos. 18/10/33 and 18/11/33, N.A.I.
11. *Ibid.*, 2nd half of October 1934 and 1st half of November 1934, File Nos. 18/10/34 and 18/11/34, N.A.I.
12. *Ibid.*, 1st half of March 1932 and 1st half of April 1932, also 1st half of May 1934, Files Nos. 18/3/32, 18/4/32 and 18/5/34, N.A.I.
13. *Ibid.*, 1st half of November 1933, 2nd half of November 1933 and 1st half of January 1934, File Nos. 18/11/33 and 18/1/34 N.A.I.
14. *Ibid.*, 1st half of February 1934, File No. 18/2/34, N.A.I.
15. *Ibid.*, 1st half of June 1934, File No. 18/6/34, N.A.I.

Provinces and Bombay) did not make much headway in the face of a repressive Government. Identically, a number of dedicated individuals among the nationalists (such as, N.G. Ranga, Indulal Yajnik, Swami Sahajanand Saraswati and Kalka Prasad), who remained active in the countryside with some concern for the exploited, and who imbibed socialist orientations during the decline of the Civil Disobedience movements, were also too distant from each other, and too much under the surveillance of both the Government and their Congress colleagues to make any advance. The formation of the Congress Socialist Party in May 1934, within the broad organisational framework of the Indian National Congress, was, therefore, significant as much for the probability of co-ordination among the left activists as for the possibility of the *kisan* consolidation to a greater extent. The C.S.P. not only supplied the splinter groups of left nationalists with a common platform, but it also provided the individual advocates of the *kisans'* welfare with a rallying point through its attractive agrarian programme. Even before the birth of the C.S.P. some of its leading exponents like Sampurnanand had elaborated their ideas on certain aspects of the agrarian situation. In his pamphlets, *When We Are in Power* in early 1930, and *A Tentative Socialist Programme For India* in April 1934, Sampurnanand called for the abolition of the *Zamindari* system (though personally he was in favour of compensating the *Zamindars*), long-term settlements and occupancy rights for all cultivators, control over rent by the legislature, moratorium on agricultural debts and redistribution of land on the basis of small farms (one-plough standard).[16] Such demands, reflecting mainly the viewpoints of the small peasant proprietors and poor peasants, were crystallised further, for instance, in the deliberations of the Bombay Socialist Group of 1934, who demanded abolition of the *Zamindari* and *Taluqdari*, establishment of state proprietorship over all lands, redistribution of land in a manner as to make each holding economically viable, revocation of all feudal and semi-feudal

16. *A Tentative Socialist Programme of India*, Sampurnanand, File No. 41/1/34 Poll. 1934, N.A.I.

levies and liquidation of arrears of rent and debt.[17] All these points were reiterated by the C.S.P. when it formally came into existence, and though its documents had not specifically discussed the problems of agricultural labourers and sharecroppers, they did mark an advance by stating that the *Zamindari* should be abolished without compensation,[18] that the uneconomic holdings must be exempted from rent and tax, and that the homestead of the peasant should be spared from attachment in the execution of money-decrees.[19]

The emergence of the C.S.P., with its insistence on the nationalisation of key industries and the abolition of *Zamindari*, raised consternation both in the Congress and the Government circles. While the Congress Working Committee decided on 18 June 1934 — as Jawaharlal Nehru felt at that time, for reassuring "various vested interests"[20] — to condemn all loose talks about confiscation of private property and class-war; the Government, who initially welcomed the formation of the C.S.P. as "a disruptive force within the Congress",[21] concluded thoughtfully soon thereafter to attack the C.S.P. as "an organisation of political gangsters" which had been set up to promote class war and confiscate property, or "seize power and acquire wealth by robbing others".[22] From another extreme position, the Communists were also critical of the Congress Socialists' "misleading role" of "hoodwinking the revolutionary masses", and of perpetuating the bourgeois Congress's ideological hold over the toiling people by raising sham socialist slogans.[23] This line of criticism was the natural outcome of an anti-Social Democratic "Third Period"

17. Narendra Deva, *Socialism and National Revolution,* Bombay, 1946, pp. 3-19.
18. *Constitution Programme and Resolutions of the First Conference of the All India Congress Socialist Party,* Bombay, 1934.
19. *Advance* (English daily), 21 October 1934.
20. Nehru to Gandhi, Allahabad, 13 August 1934, Home Poll. File No. 3/8/34, N.A.I.
21. Home Poll. File No. 7/22/34 of 1934, N.A.I.
22. *Ibid.*, File No. 39/23/34 of 1934, N.A.I.
23. *Ibid.*, File No. 7/7/35 of 1935, N.A.I.

stand[24] of the Sixth Communist International (1928) which jaundiced even the views of such guardians of the Communist Party of India as Rajani Palme Dutt and Ben Bradley. While Dutt found the birth of the C.S.P. to be "a manoeuvre of the bankrupt Congress leadership to conceal its bankruptcy and adapt its forces under a new 'socialist' coat of painting to the new [revolutionary] currents among the masses", [25] Ben Bradley discovered the C.S.P. to be "a new weapon" in the hands of the bourgeoisie for "deceiving" the masses.[26] What the Communists failed for some time to notice in their militant enthusiasm in 1934 was the fact that, despite various basic and subtle differences, they shared with the Congress Socialists under a colonial situation a common hostility against a symbiotic, as well as somewhat ambivalent, relationship between the Raj and the indigenous vested interests. It was in fact possible for both of them, particularly when the nationalist leaders wilfully played down the abuses of such a relations to formulate a programme of joint action in a number of areas, including the agrarian sector.

24. The "First Period" (1917-21), according to the Comintern, was a revolutionary phase — a situation in which the revolution was achieved in Russia with the prospect of similar achievements in other countries. When the prospect in effect could not come true, the Comintern favoured the "Second Period" (1922-7) — the phase in which the newly born Soviet Russia hoped to surmount its economic and security problems, posed by hostile capitalist countries, through understanding with the Social Democrats, especially those in the Governments of some of the anti-Communist states. This policy of coöperation did not eventually succeed, and the Social Democrats, not only refrained themselves from sympathising with the international Communist movement, but also deserted the working class consolidation in many European countries, notably in Germany against the Nazis. The setback led the Comintern to proclaim the "Third Period" (1928-33) — the phase of steadfast attention to the spreading of revolution without giving any quarters to the Social Democrats or elements of their ilk. Those who did not share the Communists' aggressive revolutionary zeal were dubbed as "counter-revolutionaries", and all Social Democratic Parties as "Social Fascists".
25. "Congress Socialism: A Contradiction in Terms", R. Palme Dutt, *Indian Forum*, October, 1934, File No. 1934/18, P.C. Joshi Archives, Jawaharlal Nehru University, New Delhi.
26. "What the Congress Socialists Want"? Ben Bradley, *International Press Correspondence*, Vol. 14, no. 63.

Although the Communists laid a doctrinaire stress on organising the working class rather than leading the peasantry, they had formulated clear views on the agrarian issues by 1934, and these resembled — at least in terms of immediate tasks — the Congress Socialist ideas. Like the Congress Socialists, they stood for the confiscation of all lands of the *Zamindars* and Princes without compensation, advocated the redistribution of lands among toiling peasants, demanded the annulment of all debts and arrears of taxes and invited the *kisans* to refuse to pay illegal levies to their landlords.[27] Additionally, the Communists called for an immediate nationalisation of the entire irrigation system, warned against the character of the rich (the "well-to-do") peasants, exhibited concern for the lot of the agricultural workers and reposed confidence on their revolutionary proletarian role in Indian conditions.[28] Importantly again, the C.P.I. asked its members to organise the *kisan* movement as the C.S.P. did,[29] and it planned for the formation of militant peasant committees to free *kisans* from "the oppressions of Anglo-Indian imperialism and its feudal allies" and to spearhead an all-Indian "no-tax, no-rent and no-debt campaign".[30]

Neither a proper countrywide organisation of the *kisans*, which the leftist parties keenly desired, nor the accomplishment of left unity in the countryside, which the circumstances actually demanded, came about till 1936. The delay in making the move was due mainly to the obduracy of the Indian Communists, who, under the dictates of a highly centralised international Communist movement, did not care to grasp the complexities of a colonial situation. Banned by the British authorities in July 1934, and bereft of much scope for open politics, the underground C.P.I. continued to harp on the Sixth Congress line — that of branding everybody as a reactionary who was not a

27. Abridged Draft of Political Thesis of the Central Committee, Communist Party of India (published in *International Press Correspondence*, Vol. 14, no. 40, July 20 1934), File No. 1934/42, P.C. Joshi Archives, J.N.U., New Delhi.
28. *Ibid.*, Also see the "Manifesto of the Anti-imperialist Conference" (held secretly in Bombay, October 1934), Home Poll. File No. 7/7/35 Poll. 1935, N.A.I.
29. Narendra Deva, *Socialism and National Revolution*, Bombay, 1946, pp. 3-29.
30. Abridged Draft of Political Thesis of the C.C., C.P.I., 1934, File No. 1934/42, P.C. Joshi Archives, J.N.U., New Delhi.

Communist, and every movement, howsoever popular, as counter-revolutionary if it was not led by them. This was amply demonstrated in the party's continuous denunciation of the Congress as a mere class organisation of the retrograde Indian bourgeoisie, the national movement as a mock fight against imperialism to serve only the interests of the capitalists and the landlords, the national leadership as entirely a capitulating one to both the British authorities and their Indian allies[31] and the prospect for setting up a bourgeois democracy in India as totally beyond the capabilities of the nationalists.[32] In their unflinching devotion to such flagrantly one-sided formulations, and in their fanciful expectation for the establishment of an "Indian Federated Workers' and Peasants' Soviet Government", following "the overthrow" of British rule,[33] the Communists did not realise how isolated they had become by persisting with their disparagement of the national movement, by refusing to participate in the Congress-led mass agitations, and, above all, by not being able at the same time to build any effective alternate anti-imperialist popular movement. The truth dawned on them only when the international Communist movement felt, primarily as a means of halting the menacing rise of Fascism in Europe, the need for shedding the sectarian prejudices of the Sixth Congress and for organising a *Fronte Populaire* of all the anti-Fascist and anti-imperialist forces. In the case of India, the Comintern was willing in 1935 to acknowledge the Congress as a joint platform against imperialism under a national-reformist leadership, who, despite its conciliatory approach, still represented the national opposition to British rule. The Comintern, therefore, urged the Indian Communists to come out of their seclusion and make use of the Congress as much as a forum for building up an anti-imperialist united front of all the progressive people, as for "exposing the tricksters of national reformism".[34] Such an united front within

31. "Manifesto of the Anti-Imperialist Conference" October 1934, Home Poll. File No. 7/7/35 Poll. 1935, N.A.I.
32. Abridged Draft of Political Thesis of the C.C., C.P.I., 1934, File No. 1934/42, P.C. Joshi Archives, J.N.U., New Delhi.
33. *Ibid.*
34. "Problems of the Anti-Imperialist Struggle in India", *International Press Correspondence*, Vol. 15, no. 10, 9 March 1935, Home Poll. File No. 7/9/35, 1935, N.A.I.

the Congress, it was hoped, would crystallise the revolutionary wing of the nationalist organisation "for the purpose of further developing the national liberation movement".[35] Soon after the formal acceptance of the *Fronte Populaire* line in its Seventh Congress (July 1935), the international Communist leadership asked the C.P.I. to build up a genuine anti-imperialist peoples' movement in India. For achieving this goal, the C.P.I. was told to follow a two-fold object: one, that of prosecuting the struggle against imperialism (British rule) by uniting all the anti-imperialist forces under the banner of the Congress (and by guarding against its vacillations), and the other, that of vigorously undertaking the toiling peoples' battles against their exploiters (the big bourgeoisie, the Princes, the landlords and the moneylenders) by forming a strong unity of the leftists.[36] Imperialists and the oppressors of the toiling masses were so interdependent and mingled up that popular struggles against them, according to the new thesis, became the two aspects of the same struggle. For the acceleration of this twin thrust, the C.P.I. was advised to work together with "all left-wing elements in the Congress", forget "mutual sniping and distrust" and forge unity on the basis of a minimum programme, i.e. complete independence for India, radicalisation of the Congress and organisation of mass struggles.[37] The same Rajani Palme Dutt and Ben Bardley, who condemned the C.S.P. in 1934, glorified it in early 1936 as the "grouping of all the radical elements in the existing Congress".[38] They not only persuaded the Indian Communists to join the C.S.P., but were reported to have also initiated the actual negotiations for it as early as August 1935.[39] The C.P.I. sent fraternal delegates to the second Conference of the C.S.P. in Meerut in January 1936,

35. "The Offensive of Fascism and the Task of the C.I. in the Struggle for Unity of the Working Class Against Fascism", G.Drimitrov, *International Press Correspondence*, Vol. 15, 20 August 1935.
36. "The Anti-Imperialist People's Front", Dutt and Bradley, *International Press Correspondence*, 29 February 1936, (a pamphlet by the C.P.I.), December 1936, available in Central Archives, Communist Party of India, Ajoy Bhavan, New Delhi.
37. *Ibid.*
38. *Ibid.*
39. "Communist Party in India", Minoo R. Masani, *Pacific Affairs* (English monthly), Vol. XXIV, March 1951, pp. 21-2.

and immediately thereafter the Communists were admitted into the C.S.P. as individual members through a decision of its National Executive.

Once the united front of the C.S.P. and the C.P.I. was somehow brought about, more as a by-product of external exigencies than through an appreciation of internal requirements, there was little apparent difficulty in their jointly venturing to organise the masses, more specifically the *kisan* masses. Locally the *kisans* were already being organised by the left activists or by their fellow-travellers. N.G. Ranga had set up the Andhra Provincial Ryots Association as early as 1928, and followed it up with the establishment of Andhra Zamindari Ryots Association. Swami Sahajanand had established the Bihar Provincial Kisan Sabha in 1929, and considerably increased its activities from 1933. In Orissa a Krushak Sangha came into existence in 1931, while in Bengal the Communists were rallying the *kisans* in 1928-9 through the Workers and Peasants Party in several districts, notably in Noakhali and Tripura, with the help of an adventurist Mukuleswar Rahaman.[40] Similarly, the Kirti-Kisan Party was engaged throughout the early 1930s in organising the peasantry in the Punjab, especially in Jullundur. In the United Provinces a Kisan Sangh started functioning from 1934 under the leadership of Purushottam Das Tandon, who had been working in the countryside since the early 1920s. All these organisational endeavours received a further boost with the birth of the C.S.P. In 1934 the C.S.P. workers and Yajnik became very active among the peasants in Maharashtra and Gujarat. The Karshaka Sanghams were formed in Malabar by early 1935 mainly at the initiative of the C.S.P. In April 1935 the South Indian Federation of Peasants and Agricultural Labourers was set up for organising peasants in all parts of southern India (Andhra, Tamil Nadu, Kerala and Karnataka).[41] The continuance of these and similar bodies in other parts of India, and the urgency the leftists felt for mobilising

40. I.B. Report on the Activity of the Bengal Provincial Kisan Sabha, 30 June 1939, File No. 333/39 Conf. Home Poll. Govt. of Bengal,1939, West Bengal State Archives, Calcutta.

41. "Charter of Peasants' Minimum Demands", The South Indian Federation of Workers and Peasants, Madras, 12 August 1935, Home Public, File No. 331/35, Pub., 1935, N.A.I.

the peasants all over the country, led eventually to the idea of uniting the *kisan* activities under a cohesive organisation on an all-India scale. The idea was taken up seriously by the C.S.P. at the time of its Meerut Conference, and a number of the *kisan* and C.S.P. leaders met on 15 January 1936 to discuss the subject, and decided to call an All India Kisan Congress with N.G. Ranga and Jayaprakash Narayan as conveners. On 11 April 1936 (when the Congress met for its Lucknow session) a conference of the representatives of *kisan* organisations and other *kisan* workers took place in Lucknow, and an All India Kisan Congress (to be named soon afterwards as the All India Kisan Sabha) was launched. The A.I.K.S. was to function as a common body of all categories of peasants — "rich", "middle" and "poor" — who suffered under the feudal, colonial system. However, as the A.I.K.S. would effectively be run by the leftists — the egalitarians who stood ideologically by the oppressed — it was expected to lay stress on the causes of the rural poor.

The point worth noticing is the remarkable manner in which the aspirations of the rural poor, the agitations of the peasants and the activities of the left had all converged on one single development, namely, the birth of the C.S.P. Howsoever much one disliked the Congress Socialists' amateurish involvement with vague and mixed up radicalism,[42] it would be hard to deny the C.S.P. of its rightful claim to have performed a historic role, first, by providing all kinds of leftists with an open arena to operate; secondly, by giving effect to a "united front" with the Communists, and then by raising the level of the *kisan* movement through the organisation of the A.I.K.S., thereby giving a new hope to the poor peasants in general.

Between the formation of the C.S.P. and that of the A.I.K.S., the rural poor often interacted with the leftists, and exhibited a willingness to respond to their exhortations. Even in 1934 the Government was disturbed to notice the presence of the Communists and the Congress Socialists on the agrarian scenes of

42. The C.S.P. had, for example, been dismissed sometimes as "the motley crowd of Marxists, Fabians, Gandhians and orthodox Hindus". S. Gopal, *Jawaharlal Nehru : A Biography, 1889-1947*, Vol. 1, Delhi, 1981, p. 188.

the U.P., Bombay, Madras, North-West Frontier and Assam.[43] There were reports from Tripura and Noakhali of the poor peasants' agitation in March 1935 with the slogan: "whose is the plough, his is the land".[44] Much of it seemed to be the spill-over of the movement in these two Bengal districts that was started as early as 1931 by Mukuleswar Rahaman, who had a close link with the Communist leaders in Calcutta, "Bankim Mukherji and Abdul Halim and Company".[45] In June 1936 the Krishak Samiti of Mukuleswar Rahaman (who had been imprisoned in 1933 on the garbled charges of "dacoity and arson") set up parallel courts at Lakshmipur, Noakhali, under the leadership of Mohammed Fazlullah (*alias* Chunu Mian), a right hand man of Mukuleswar. Fazlullah's courts settled up, for some time, all disputes in the locality, and the villagers practically stopped going to the British law courts.[46] In April 1935 the left activists successfully rallied poor cultivators of Tangail, Mymensingh, for a time, to boycott the *mahajans* and oppose land sales for arrears of rent.[47] In the same month in Rajputana, the authorities of Sikar Thikane, Jaipur, faced violent opposition from the lower Jat peasantry, who acted under the influence of the left political activists.[48] The Communists, the Kirti Kisan Party and the Zamindara League (Akali) were believed to have spread in August 1935 considerable agrarian disaffection in Hoshiarpur district, as well as in Kapurthala and Malerkotla states.[49] The left-dominated Karza Committees, created originally to plead for the liquidation of agrarian debts, also appeared in 1936 to have played a leading role in organising the poor peasantry in certain parts of the Punjab.[50] The Congress Socialists

43. N.C. Hallet's note on Communist activities, 12 March 1934, and views of the Provincial Governments, Home Poll. File No. 7/11/34, 1934, N.A.I.
44. Home Poll. Fortnightly Report for 2nd half of March 1935, File No. 18/3/35, N.A.I.
45. I.B. Report on the Activity of the Bengal Provincial Kisan Sabha, 30 June 1939, File No. 333/39 Conf. Home Poll. Govt. of Bengal, 1939, West Bengal State Archives, Calcutta.
46. *Ibid.*
47. Home Poll. Fortnightly Report for 1st half of April 1935, File No. 18/4/35, N.A.I.
48. *Ibid.*, 2nd half of April 1935.
49. *Ibid.*, 1st half of August 1935, File No. 18/8/35, N.A.I.
50. *The New Age* (English monthly), Vol. IV, no. 1, June 1937, p. 6.

(like N.G. Gore) and the left *kisan* leaders (like Yajnik) undertook relief work among peasants in some areas of Maharashtra, Kanara and Gujarat (Kolaba, Dharwar, Satara, East Khandesh, Kaira and Surat), which were subjected between 1934 and 1936 to extreme hardship on account of drought and crop failure. Simultaneously, they felt compelled to raise some of the burning problems of the poor peasantry, namely, their acute indebtedness and their sufferings at the hands of the landlords, rich peasants and *mahajans.* The Government revenue officials added to the poor peasants' miseries by taking invariably the side of the oppressors.[51] The leftists in fact used this opportunity for enquiring into the conditions of the Maharashtra peasantry, and demanded (through the Maharashtra Peasants Enquiry Committee) the abolition of the *Khoti* system and the conferment of occupancy rights on the long-standing tenants.[52] This in effect heralded an anti-*Khoti* agitation, and in January 1936 the cultivators at Chari (Kolaba) objected to the higher rental demands of the *Khots* and refused to till their lands.[53]

In the United Provinces the Congress Socialists and their allies were busy organising the *kisans* throughout 1935,[54] and although they failed to get their main resolution on the *Zamindari* abolition (without compensation) passed at the Provincial Kisan Conference in April 1935, they did manage to raise the demands for the reduction of rent and issue of rent .receipts, the moratorium on debts and arrears of rent, and the end of *nazrana* (presentation) and *begar* (forced labour).[55] In June 1936 the leftists were able, in the Political Conference of Sirsa in Allahabad district, to carry their resolution on various *kisan* demands, including the prohibition of ejectment for inability to pay rent and the occupancy status for the tenants-at-will with rights of

51. Reports on the Agrarian Situation, Bombay, Home (Special) Department, Files No. 800(53), Parts II and III, 1934-6, Maharashtra State Archives, Bombay.
52. Home Poll. Fortnightly Report for 1st half of June 1936, File No. 18/6/36, N.A.I.
53. *The New Age* (English monthly), Vol. IV, no. 1, June 1937, p. 6.
54. Home Poll. Fortnightly Report for 2nd half of April 1935, File No. 18/4/35, N.A.I.
55. I.B. Report on the Proceedings of the Provincial Kisan Conference, U.P., Allahabad, April 1935, File No. 1935/49, P.C. Joshi Archives, J.N.U., New Delhi.

mortgage and sale.[56] The mood of the *kisans* in Pratabgarh, following the District Kisan Conference in September 1936, according to the provincial Government, had the possibility of "degenerating into no-rent campaign of the former days".[57] There were reports of a "no-rent" call to the tenants in the *Zamindari* estates in Cachar,[58] and of worsening landlord-tenant relations in the coastal Orissa, following the Provincial Kisan Conference in Puri in November 1936.[59] In southern India the Congress Socialists were active in the rural areas of Malabar, and Ranga continued his campaign against the *Zamindari* oppressions in Ganjam and Chittoor.[60] Throughout 1935 his South Indian Federation of Kisans and Agricultural Workers advocated the causes of the small peasants, the *zamin-rayats* (in the *Zamindari* areas) and the sub-tenants of the *Jenmis*, *Kanamdars* and *Mirasdars*, along with those of the field-hands.[61] At the same time, Ranga organised marches of peasants in November 1936 in Guntur, Krishna and Kurnool,[62] and later in November 1936 in West Godavari, Trichinopoly and South Arcot to represent their grievances to the local authorities.[63]

However, the leftist organisers of *kisans* in 1935-6 were perhaps most active in Bihar under the leadership of Swami Sahajanand. They articulated peasants' grievances by undertaking whirlwind tours in the countryside, and by addressing to innumerable gatherings of *kisans*. Denouncing the oppressions of the *Zamindars* and their *amlas* (retainers), and predicting the extinction of the *Zamindari*, the Swami and his followers often dwelt upon the miseries of the rural poor,[64] the burdens of

56. Home Poll. Fortnightly Report for 2nd half of June 1936, File No. 18/6/36, N.A.I.
57. *Ibid.*, 1st half of October 1936, File No. 18/10/36, N.A.I.
58. *Ibid.*, 2nd half of October 1936, N.A.I.
59. *Ibid.*, 2nd half of November 1936, File No. 18/11/36, N.A.I.
60. *Ibid.*, 1st and 2nd halves of July 1935, File No. 18/7/35, N.A.I.
61. "Character of Peasants' Minimum Demands", the South Indian Federation of Workers and Peasants, Madras, 12 August 1935, Home Public, File No. 331/35 Pub., 1935, N.A.I.
62. Home Poll. Fortnightly Report for 2nd half of November 1935, File No. 18/11/35, N.A.I.
63. *Ibid.*, 2nd half of November 1936, File No. 18/11/36, N.A.I.
64. *Ibid.*, 2nd half of January 1935, File No. 18/1/35, N.A.I.

irregular exactions, the insecurities of the tenants[65] and the problems of the landless labourers.[66] Their campaigns sometimes resulted, not only in the *kisan* marches to the district officials and provincial legislators for voicing their demands,[67] but also in organised resistance on a small scale. A typical example of such resistance took place early in 1936 in Tikari estate in Gaya. After evicting tenants of certain plots on the ground of outstanding rent, the Tikariraj tried to take away the crop that had been raised. The ousted peasants, supported by most of the villagers, opposed the move, surrounded the *khalihan* (barn) where the crop was stored, and guarded it to prevent its seizure by the *amlas*.[68] In Patna district some tenants of Silao village raised a hue and cry in June 1936 when their lands had overnight been brought under the *Zamindar's* personal possession. Almost a similar situation developed about the same time in Gaya district and involved, once again, the Tikariraj which had dispossessed some tenants of their lands at Sunda village. When the raj's men came to till these lands, the evicted peasants — led by "some fifteen women" — stubbornly obstructed them.[69] In the interior of Patna a police officer was detained in July 1936 by "a mob of rioters" or tenants whose lands had been declared as *nilami*.[70]

The united front of the Congress Socialists and the Communists doubtlessly encouraged the fighting propensities of the rural poor — the small and poor peasants, the sharecroppers and the agricultural labourers. They also provided these sections with an organisation, and consequently with a political leadership, as well as with some definite direction. So far as the rural poor were concerned, the leftists had thus created a situation in which, in the Gramscian term, "a matching of the thrust from below with orders from above"[71] was feasible. But neither the

65. *Ibid.*, 1st half of June 1936, File No. 18/6/36, N.A.I.
66. *Ibid.*, 2nd half of July 1936, File No. 18/7/36, N.A.I.
67. *Ibid.*, 2nd half of March and 1st half of April 1936, File Nos. 18/3/36 and 18/4/36, N.A.I.
68. *Ibid.*, 1st half of February 1936, File No. 18/2/36, N.A.I.
69. *Ibid.*, 2nd half of June 1936, File No. 18/6/36, N.A.I.
70. *Ibid.*, 2nd half of July 1936, File No. 18/7/36, N.A.I.
71. Antonio Gramsci, *Selection From the Prison Notebook*, London, 1971, p. 188.

C.P.I.-C.S.P. alliance nor the A.I.K.S., as a body, was devoted solely to the causes of the rural poor. The C.S.P. in fact wanted to build up a broad *kisan* movement of all categories — "rich", "middle" and "poor" — without bothering too much about the existence of contrary interests among them. Of course, at a theoretical plane, it vaguely apprehended the "rich" peasants' bid for "annexing" the *kisan* organisation, and stressed, therefore, as an antidote, on the "struggling" peasants' participation in the movement.[72] But in practice the C.S.P. directed most of its energies almost instinctively towards developing a "separate" or a distinct class organisation of the *kisans*,[73] which in reality amounted to a coalition of various peasant components. In contrast, the C.P.I. seemed to be more conscious of the categorisation of peasant society in India, and more knowledgeable about the characteristics that distinguished the rich, the better-off and the poor peasants from each other.[74] It was also clear in its view that the A.I.K.S. should not become "the land appropriators' organisation", but remained an instrument primarily in the hands of the "toiling producers" — the multitude of peasant cultivators "whether as owners or tenants or as both".[75] At the same time, however, the C.P.I. felt that in an anti-feudal and anti-usurer campaign, under a colonial set-up, "all classes of cultivating peasants" should be included into an organisation for fighting their common enemies.[76] In other words, the C.P.I., like the C.S.P., contemplated the A.I.K.S. as an organisation of all peasant categories. Only it was not quite certain, with its orthodox predisposition towards the wage-earners, about the agricultural labourers — whether to include them in the A.I.K.S., or to affiliate them with the trade-unions, or to form a separate

72. *The Congress Socialist* (English weekly), 18 June 1936.
73. "Swaraj Kiun Aur Keise" (Hindi pamphlet), Dr. Rammanohar Lohia's Presidential Address at the Second Bihar Provincial Congress Socialist Conference, 5 December 1936. Also see the "Faizpur Thesis" or the Resolution passed in the Third All India Congress Socialist Party Conference, Faizpur, 23-25 December 1936, *The Congress Socialist*, 9 January 1937.
74. "The Madras Peasantry and Platform of Struggle", P. Sundarayya, *The New Age* (English monthly), October 1937, Vol. IV, no. 5, pp. 186-91.
75. *Ibid.*, April 1937, Vol. III, no. 11, pp. 416-7.
76. *Ibid.*, October 1937, Vol. IV, no. 5, pp. 186-91.

organisation of their own.[77] In course of time the C.P.I. eventually reconciled itself to the generally accepted opinion that the *khetmajdoors* were, after all, the tillers of the soil like the *kisans*, though the poorest among them, that their problems were "more in common with the lower peasantry than with the workers",[78] and that they were found to be the natural constituents of the A.I.K.S. — "the organisation of the exploited masses in the countryside".[79] Considering the fact that the basic task before the peasantry in India was to confront the torturous dominance of the imperialist-landlord-usurer combination, and also the fact that the contradiction between the landlords-usurers and all the other categories of peasants was more fundamental (or "primary" as it was said) than the internal bickerings among themselves, both the C.S.P and the C.P.I. — instinctively and consciously — opted for preparing the A.I.K.S. as a fighting machine for the entire peasantry. There was no other alternative in colonial India for the leftists but to promote a multi-class platform of peasants of all hues — from the vacillating to the stubborn, just as the nationalist leadership had little choice except projecting the Congress as the multi-class organisation of anti-imperialist elements of all sorts — from the compromising to the unwavered. Like the Congress, in a certain way, the A.I.K.S. also suffered from some of the disadvantages of its being a multi-class organisation — notably through the greater influence the substantial and powerful members were alleged to have exercised on its proceedings.[80]

The hands of the substantial or the rich and the better-off peasants were apparent from the programme that the A.I.K.S. had worked out for itself even at the outset. Apart from raising the common demands of *kisans* of all categories, such as the

77. *Ibid.*, pp. 190-1. Also the issue of April 1937, Vol. III, no. 11, pp. 416-7.
78. *Ibid.*, Vol. IV, no. 5, October 1937, pp. 186-91.
79. Presidential Address of Swami Sahajanand, 3rd Session of All India Kisan Sabha, Comilla, 11-14 May 1938, M.A. Rasul, *A History of the All India Kisan Sabha,* Calcutta, 1974, pp. 29-30.
80. Although the multi-class character of the Congress was proclaimed by its radical critics as the root cause of the shortcomings of the national movement, a similar characterisation of the A.I.K.S. has not yet been acknowledged by them to be a handicap for the *kisan* movement.

abolition of landlordism without compensation, the cancellation of arrears of rent and revenue, the reduction by 50 per cent of rent, revenue and water tax, the declaration of five years' moratorium on all agrarian debts, the grant of immunity from attachment of minimum holdings for failure to pay rents, debts and taxes and the ending of *begar* and illegal exactions, the A.I.K.S. emphasised in its Kisan Manifesto of August 1936 on some of the slogans typically favourable to the village rich, namely, the introduction of a graduated tax on agricultural incomes above Rs. 500 (per annum) in place of land revenue, the lowering of the freights upon the transport of agricultural commodities, the stabilisation of prices of agricultural products at the 1929 (pre-Depression) level through necessary adjustments of exchange and currency policy, the bringing to book of all those officials (in Public Works Department, Excise, Revenue, Railways and Police) who compelled peasants to give them bribes on various counts and the vesting of the administration of communal, grazing and forest lands in the village *Panchayats*. The A.I.K.S. also demanded facilities for state marketing, supplies of seeds and fertilisers and insurances against cattle deaths and fires.[81] Despite some tilt in favour of the better-off *kisans*, the A.I.K.S. did nevertheless manage to represent the interests of the poor peasants. Its Kisan Manifesto, for example, insisted on full occupancy rights for all kinds of tenants, desired immunity from arrest and imprisonment for inability to pay debts, rents and revenues, suggested the transfer of unoccupied lands of the Government and those of the landlords to the landless *kisans* for cultivation on cooperative basis and demanded the fixation of minimum wage for the agricultural workers, as well as their coverage under the Workmens' Compensation Act.[82] Consequently, in spite of its preoccupation with the general grievances of various grades of peasantry against the Government, landlords and *mahajans*, the A.I.K.S. and its provincial units took up from time to time, and from place to place, the poor

81. The All India Kisan Manifesto, 21 August 1936, *Indian Annual Register*, N. Mitra (Ed.), 1936, Vol. III, pp. 293-6.

82. *Ibid.*

peasants' causes, and led them to resist the acts of oppression. This was not remarkable in any way, and it merely conformed to the radicalism the left leaders so loudly proclaimed.

The leftists' interaction with the rural poor had been crystallised in a series of actual encounters they waged locally through the A.I.K.S. against their avowed common adversaries. The battles were initially fought between 1937 and 1939, coinciding with a chain of significant developments that took place on the national scene. The first in line was the adoption, under the persistent leftist pressure, of an Agrarian Programme by the Congress at its Faizpur Session in December 1936. Although the A.I.K.S. had already submitted its Kisan Manifesto to the Congress,[83] and the C.S.P. members pleaded for its acceptance *in toto*, the Faizpur Congress substantially amended the *kisan* demands by shelving the more militant and drastic slogans (such as, the abolition of all forms of landlordism without compensation or the transfer of landlords' lands to cultivators or the right of all peasants to bear arms to chase away ostensibly their human and animal torturers), keeping some of the concrete issues vague (such as, the substitution of "50 per cent reduction" in rent and revenue by "substantial reduction", and the "minimum" wage of the agricultural labourers by a "living wage"), and even hesitating on widely acclaimed measures (such as, the acceptance of a "moratorium" on agricultural debts for the time being on condition that a special tribunal would look into them, or the counterbalance of a desire to oppose ejectment for arrears of rent with a reluctance to prevent arrest and imprisonment for inability to pay). Consequently the Agrarian Programme passed at the Faizpur Congress left "much to be desired" in the opinion of the leftists[84] who felt "defeated" when they failed, even with the blessings of the Congress President, Jawaharlal Nehru, to get the A.I.K.S. affiliated to the Congress as a body.[85] Yet, despite all its weakness, the Faizpur Congress Agrarian Programme did

83. Swami Sahajanand's statement on behalf of the All India Kisan Committee, August, 1936, *The Congress Socialist* (English weekly), Kisan Supplement.
84. *The Communist* (cyclostyled), a central organ of the C.P.I., Vol.1, no. 14, February 1937, Central Archives, Communist Party of India, Ajoy Bhavan, New Delhi.
85. *Ibid.*

signify the growing influence of leftism in national politics, as well as the nationalist recognition of the importance of the *kisan* movement. Simultaneously, the Programme committed the Congress publicly to the task of fulfilling many of the immediate *kisan* demands which the A.I.K.S. voiced, namely, the exemption of uneconomic holdings from taxation, curtailment of irrigation charges, reduction of rent and revenue, abolition of feudal dues and forced labour, annulment of arrears of rent and "fixity of tenure... of all tenants".[86] All these commitments, whether meant seriously or not, considerably improved the Congress image in the eyes of the common man and woman, and also enabled the Congress candidates to get the support of the newly enfranchised substantial peasants about a month later (in February 1937) in the elections for introducing Provincial Autonomy under the Act of 1935.

The election results were on the whole favourable to the Congress, empowering it to form ministries in eight provinces (Bombay, Madras, the U.P., the C.P. and Berar, Bihar, and Orissa by the middle of 1937, in N.W.F.P. in September 1937 and in Assam in September 1938), and to act as formidable opponents in the rest (the Punjab, Sind and Bengal). Both as a ruling and as an opposition party, the Congress was supposed to function on all agrarian matters in accordance with the Faizpur Programme. It was mainly on the issue of the agrarian reforms — their implementation or otherwise by the Congress ministries and legislators — that the gulf between the rightists and the leftists widened within the Congress. Similarly, it was the attitude to be assumed towards the landlords and *mahajans* — an approach of softened disapproval or one of hardened distrust — that caused a rift in the Congress-A.I.K.S. relations. Between 1937 and 1939 an estrangement also crept into the "united front" that the leftists somehow managed to put up, and the growing apprehension of a Communist take over of the C.S.P. had in fact led most of the prominent Congress Socialists in a National Executive meeting in Bombay in May 1939 to plan the wholesale expulsion of the Communists from the party.[87]

86. The Congress Agrarian Programme, Faizpur Session, 27-28 December 1936, *Indian Annual Register*, N. Mitra (ed.), Vol.II, p.206.

87. Asim Kumar Chaudhuri, *Socialist Movement in India*, Calcutta, 1980, p.77.

When the situation seemed thus to be taking acrimonious turns, over the agrarian scenario and around the nationalist-leftist postures, came the disturbing intervention of the second world war. India was dragged into it by Britain in September 1939 without caring for the opinion of its people, and the Congress provincial ministries resigned in protest against the British impudence. It was against this backdrop of Provincial Autonomy, starting with the Faizpur Programme and ending in the outbreak of the war, that the rural poor fought many of their battles under the leftist political guidance. Their engagements were so numerous, and spread over such a multiplicity of geographical, administrative and cultural terrains, that it would simply be impossible to try to discuss all of them or most of them. The plausible alternative could only be an attempt — howsoever feeble — at their appreciation by examining some of the specimens. Such specimens of struggles of the village poor (the small or poor peasants, the sharecroppers, and the agricultural and bonded labourers) with which the leftists and the A.I.K.S. had been involved between 1937 and 1939 were waged often over a combination of burning questions, of which one proved invariably to be more central than the others. It would be convenient, therefore, to discuss the agitations in accordance with the issues that dominated their proceedings, such as the rack-rentings and landlord oppressions (including *begar* and illegal levies), the sharing of crops and defence of forest rights, the insecurity of tenures and eviction from lands, and the wages and bondages.

SCENE I

Bondage and Wage Labourers

The left activists in Andhra were perhaps the first among Indian radicals to mobilise the agricultural labourers and give clear expressions to their grievances. This, however, they did by organising the *khetmajdoors* in separate unions with linkages in the Kisan Sabha. By the middle of 1937 they actually succeeded in raising the basic slogans of the agricultural workers, such as the minimum wage of Rs. 10 a month, a eight hour day and one paid holiday a week.[88] At the beginning of 1938 the leftists were able not only to establish agricultural labourers' unions in five districts of Andhra, but also to lead victorious strikes on the issue of wages at Mukkamela (West Godavari), Verullapada (Krishna) and several other places in Nellore. At Verullapada the entire small peasantry joined hands with the agricultural labourers in their agitation against the rich and powerful landlords. Despite all attempts on the part of the opponents at breaking their strike through terror and the use of force, the agricultural labourers succeeded in exacting a satisfactory settlement in April 1938.[89] However, the achievement in Andhra had hardly been repeated elsewhere in India. On the contrary, a similar attempt at the landless labourers' agitation in Bihar, under the aegis of the Kisan Sabha, ended practically in a disaster. The agitation started in September 1937 in the eastern part of Patna district and among the *Musahars* (belonging to a *Harijan* or *Dalit* caste) in Tirhut over the demands for increased wages and improved conditions of work.[90] Soon after it gathered momentum, the movement seemed to have gone out of hands of the local Kisan

88. "The Madras Peasantry and Platform of Struggle", P. Sundarayya, *The New Age* (English monthly), October 1937, Vol. IV, no. 5., pp. 186-91.
89. Report of N. Prasada Rao on Andhra, *National Front* (English weekly), 24 April 1938.
90. Home Poll. Fortnightly Report for 1st half of September 1937, File No. 18/9/37, N.A.I.

Sabha leaders. The embarrassment was caused apparently, by a short-living Khetihar Majdoor Sangh — an organisation that had been set up in 1937 by some Bihar Congressmen, including Jagjivan Ram, at the instance of Rajendra Prasad. Its sole aim was to disrupt the following of the leftist-led Kisan Sabha by playing "landless labourers against raiyats".[91] The Sangh's vituperative campaign in fact led some of the agricultural workers to come into violent clashes with their direct employers — the substantial peasants. There were armed conflicts between them and the rich *kisans* in July 1938 at Mal Salami and Chandi, leading to bloodshed. Reports of identical incidents soon followed from four other villages of Patna district,[92] and the agitation had thereafter been crushed by the authorities in the name of maintaining law and order. The whole affair so glaringly revealed a chink in the multi-class consolidation of *kisans* that the Bihar Provincial Kisan Sabha leaders grew hesitant for some time to take up another fight on behalf of the agricultural labourers. Although its leaders continued to talk of the demands of the "rural proletariat", their main effort throughout 1938-9 was somehow to harmonise relations between the substantial peasants and their hired hands. They tried to explain the "involuntary" exploitation of the *khetmajdoors* by the landholders in terms of the latter having scarcely any alternative, under the strain of rack-renting, but to minimise the cost of cultivation even at the expense of the wage-earners.[93] They appealed to the substantial *kisans* to consider the *khetmazdoors* as their own "kith and kin" who should be given their due,[94] and exhorted both the sections to realise "the great and growing need for their united front".[95]

The confusion in Bihar could have been cleared by the leftists not so much by glossing over the contradiction between the rich peasants and the agricultural workers as by highlighting the exploitation of those who employed labour most in the countryside, or by

91. *Ibid.*, 2nd half of August 1937, File No. 18/8/37, N.A.I.
92. *Ibid.*, 2nd half of July 1938, File No. 18/7/38, N.A.I.
93. Swami Sahajanand's Presidential address at the 3rd session of A.I.K.S. Comilla, 13 May 1938, *National Front* (English weekly), 22 May 1938.
94. *Ibid.*
95. Resolution on Agricultural Labour, 4th session of the A.I.K.S., Gaya, 9-10 April 1939, M.A. Rasul, *A History of the All India Kisan Sabha*, Calcutta, 1974, p. 59.

actually directing the combatant wage-earners to the doorsteps of the *Zamindars* — the oft-repeated "main or common enemy" in agrarian society. Such a tactical move might have taken away the bite from the substantial peasants' hostility, and even earned for the *khetmajdoors* the sympathy of other categories, as it did at Verallapadu in Krishna, and Palayur in Tanjore.

In Perulam area of Tanjore district a *Mirasdar*, K.P. Ganapathi Subramania Ayyar, owned extensive lands in Kalikundi, Palayur, and several other villages, and employed a large number of Adi-Dravidas (*Dalits*) as *Pannayals* (farm-hands) on very low *varams* (wages of paddy). The continued disaffection among the farm-hands over the amount of *varam* soon attracted the attention of the local Congress Socialists. It was at this point that the *Punnaiyals* felt, following the distress caused by a flood in the region in November 1937, that their *varam* for the year 1938 should be paid at an increased rate three months in advance (i.e. in March) of the usual time (i.e. June). The issue was taken up by the leftists in a series of meetings, and the agricultural labourers placed it before the *Mirasdar* as a demand. The *Mirasdar* not only refused to consider it, but also asked his agents to remove the paddy from the threshing floors. Tensions mounted up and a strike of the field-labourers started in March 1938. The strike, which lasted for about a week, proved so effective that the *Mirasdar* had to come to a compromise in the presence of the revenue officials, by promising to increase the amount of *varam* and to pay it next month (April). But, instead of acting in accordance with the agreement, he planned an act of retaliation in collusion with the police. On 28 April 1938 the *Mirasdar's* hirelings and some policemen (who were brought to investigate a trumped-up theft case in the locality) jointly attacked the Adi-Dravida *cheri* (quarters) at Palayur village. They arrested the Adi-Dravidas who resisted, beat up the rest, broke their shacks, molested their women and looted their belongings. The assault created such a terror that a sizable number of the Adi-Dravidas actually fled from the place, leaving the *Mirasdar* free to import labour from outside.[96] It necessitated a fresh long

96. M. Marimuthu's petition to the District Magistrate, Tanjore, 30 April 1938, Public General Department, G.O. No. 404 of 4/3/1939, Tamil Nadu State Archives, Madras.

struggle on the part of the left activists, and a lot of sympathy and support of other peasant categories, to move the Home minister of the Congress ministry in Madras to enquire into the incident, secure the release of the arrested Adi-Dravidas, censure the policemen who sided with the *Mirasdar*, stop him from importing labour and compel him to settle the *varam* accounts — though regrettably at the old rate. Judging by the sufferings the agricultural labourers had to undergo, the outcome did not mark a resounding victory in their favour. However, the experience of the struggle generated in them a consciousness of their rights, as well as a hostility towards "the existing state of affairs".[97]

Unlike the Adi-Dravidas, the *Regars* (agricultural labourers) in Ajmer-Merwara hardly received any political guidance in their autonomous attempt at resistance against the *Khewatdars* (landlords). The tension developed at Saradhana village in October 1938 over the *Regars'* opposition to illegal exactions, especially to the demand of *Kolvi* — a kind of house-tax on the shanties the wage-earners set up in portions of the landlords' lands. The dispute led to a strike that the landlords eventually managed to break with the help of the Commissioner, Ajmer-Merwara.[98] In comparison, the Bhil agricultural labourers in parts of the Panch Mahals district (Gujarat) fared better, under the leadership of the Gujarat Kisan Sabha, against their landlord-*mahajan* employers. Following meetings in which the *kisan* leaders like D.M. Pangarkar spoke, the Bhil labourers of Ankleswar *taluk* struck work early in March 1939.[99] They demanded cancellation of some outstanding debts and a minimum wage of four annas a day with two meals.[100] They defied all kinds of pressures and actual acts of coercion, threatened the likely deserters in their own ranks with a heavy

97. Confidential Report of the Sub-Divisional Magistrate, Negapatam, to the District Magistrate, No. 21, 16 August 1938, *Ibid.*
98. Home Poll. Fortnightly Report for 2nd half of October 1938, File No. 18/10/38.
99. Report on the Kisan Sabha activities, district-wise, Broach and the Panch Mahals, Government of Bombay, Home (Special) Department, File No. 800(53)-BC of 1939, Maharashtra State Archives, Bombay.
100. Home Poll. Fortnightly Report for 1st half of March 1939, File No. 18/3/39, N.A.I.

fine,[101] and succeeded in forcing a favourable settlement. Similar incidents of struggle on the part of agricultural workers, whether successful in attaining their limited objectives or not, took place at the village and *taluk* levels in many other parts of the country. Comparatively, the expressions of unrest, and of solidarity among the bonded labourers — the most desperately placed strata in rural society — were understandably few and far between.

Despite its formal disapproval by the authorities, and its perfunctory abolition in some forms by law, the debt bondage — "somewhat akin to slavery" — was in vogue, according to the official admission in September 1939, in numerous parts of rural India.[102] The circumstances leading to the bondage of labourers or farm-hands were the same in all areas where it prevailed under such denominations as *Bhaghela* and *Jeethagadu* in some parts of Hyderabad and Andhra, *Gothi* and *Khambari* in north Tamil Nadu, *Kamiauti* or *Kami* in Bihar, *Guti* and *Bahabandhi* in Orissa and similar other categorisation in the rest of India. Invariably a field-worker, who eked out a precarious existence, was forced by a situation beyond his control to borrow money from a landlord or a rich peasant under a contract to work in the debtor's field and household with (as in the cases of most bonded labourers, such as the *Bhaghelas*,[103] the *Kothias*, the *Halis*, the *Gutis*), or even without (as in the cases of the *Jeethagadus* in Warangal and the *Rajwarris* in Gaya, Patna, Munghyr and Palamau) payment of wages till the debt was deemed to have been cleared. In some systems, such as, *Guti*, *Gothi* and *Bahabandhi*, a period of service was fixed for repayment after which the borrower could be free to serve elsewhere. Sometimes he received during his servitude food and loin cloth, over and above cash wages which the employer kept

101. The Bhil *Panch* decided to impose a fine of Rs. 5/- on any Bhil who would resume work before a settlement.

102. N.M. Joshi's question in the Central Legislative Assembly, Home Judicial, File No. 19/14/39 Judl. N.A.I.

103. *Bhaghelas* in Warangal were paid in any one of the following ways in the early 1930s: (a) Rs. 2½ to Rs. 5 per month, (b) food and Rs. 20 per year, (c) one meal a day plus 12-30 *seers* of *jowri* per month. (Home Public, File No. 32/3/35 Pub. of 1935, N.A.I.)

for adjustment against the loan.[104] In practice, however, a destitute bonded labourer — often a low-caste or an outcaste — was never able to repay his debt. On the contrary, his debt in fact continued to mount by the accrual of compound interest, binding him and his family perpetually to his employer. Apart from a few instances like that of the *Bhaghelas*, whose debts were wiped off after their deaths, most other types of bonded labourers had to shoulder their burdens of debts from generation to generation. The bonded labourer and the family, including the women members, had always to be at the beck and call of his employer, attending to all kinds of agricultural and domestic duties. They were often subjected to indignities, abuses and physical tortures, and in many cases certain penal clauses were attached to the bonds they contracted.[105] The impact of bondage was so crippling, and it rendered the bonded labourer so disabled that he and his family could hardly ever think of dissent of any kind. Political activists, whether of the nationalist or the leftist variety, were seldom found to have taken much interest in his lot. Consequently, one rarely came across illustrations of resistance on the part of the bonded labourers, and the agitations of the *Nankars* in Mymensingh district of Bengal and Sylhet district of Assam, as well as those of the *Halis* in south Gujarat, were such exceptional happenings.

Like the *Malas* and *Madigas* in Andhra of Madras province, the *Nankars* were *Dalit* cultivators who had been attached to the landlords' estates in the districts of Mymensingh in Bengal, and Sylhet in Assam. They were given tiny strips of lands to till for their livelihood, without any right emanating thereof, on condition of giving free labour (unlike the *Malas* and *Madigas* who received some semblance of wages) on specified days in a month, as domestic servants and field-hands, as well as on all festive and special occasions. Additionally, they were called upon to act as doorkeepers and night watchmen, and *lathials* (*lathi* or stick-weilding retinues) to discipline the defiant *rayats*. Being untouchables, they had no right to get the services of village artisans, such as the potters, the barbers and the

104. Home Judicial, File No. 19/14/39 Judl. of 1939, N.A.I.
105. *Ibid.*

washermen, or to come near the temples and kitchens of the gentry, although their services were utilised for all work of hard labour in Hindu worship, including the carrying of images of gods and goddesses for immersion. In 1937 some local Kisan Sabha leaders of Mymensingh like Rabi Niyogi, Hemanta Bhattacharya and Jiten Sen — the "outsiders" — articulated for the first time at Sherpur the long accumulated Nankar sentiment against exploitation and injustice. Early in 1938 the *Nankars* of about 50 villages met at Taragarh to formulate their demands which they presented in writing to the *Zamindars*, the Government officials and other official and non-official bodies. Their charter called for abolition of the *Nankar* system, the fixation of fair rent and the granting of occupancy status on the lands occupied by the *Nankar* cultivators. The *Nankars* were, however, willing to perform all duties during the festive occasions, provided their right to enter the temples and present offerings to the images was conceded.[106] All through the months of July, August and September 1938 the newly organised *Nankars*, supported by a large section of the lower peasantry, such as the *Hridi Kshatriyas*, pressed their demands and negotiated with the *Zamindars* and the local officials. The *Zamindars* declined to consider all pleas of the *Nankars* and decided to teach them a lesson by bringing at Sherpur some hired notorious characters from outside, and by arming them to the teeth. The *Nankars* also prepared for the worst and started taking out semi-armed processions from village to village. Tension mounted by the beginning of October 1938, particularly during the days of *Durga Puja*. The much apprehended skirmishes, however, did not actually take place and the *Zamindars'* enthusiasm for the use of force dwindled in the face of the aggressive and determined posture of the *Nankars*.[107] From October 1938 the *Nankars* stopped giving free labour to the *Zamindars* and their agitation continued throughout 1939-40. For all practical purposes, the *Nankar* system ceased to operate in Mymensingh any longer. Such, however, was not exactly the

106. Pramatha Gupta, *Je Sangramer Shes Nei* (Bengali), Calcutta, 1971, pp. 58-9.
107. Home Judicial, File No. 19/14/39 Judl. of 1939. N.A.I.

case with the *Nankars* in Sylhet district where they were unable to break their shackles even after a spell of vociferous agitation. Encouraged by the local Kisan Sabha activists, the Sylheti *Nankars* demanded, like their counterparts in Mymensingh, the abolition of the system and the tenancy right over the lands under their occupation. The campaign was launched from the Bhatipara *Zamindari* in the west to the Mahakali *Zamindari* (Badarpur) in the east, and from Banghi Kunda in the north to Prithimpasa in the south of Sylhet district, and for a time it seemed that the Sylheti *Nankars* would also come out of the humiliating rut they were in. But the agitation suffered a set back when the Congress Coalition Government refused to safeguard the *Nankar* interest in its Sylhet Tenancy Act of 1939, mainly on account of opposition of the landlord elements within the ministry.[108] The setback — though dampening — did not altogether put an end to the movement, for it continued intermittently in the area, both before and after the partition.

Like the *Nankars*, but on a larger and more impressive scale, the *Halis* in south Gujarat began their agitation first at Lavet of Mongrol *taluk* in Navasari district of Baroda state. It came in the wake of an intense sharecroppers' and tenants'-at-will movement in Mongrol *taluk* early in 1938, and received the sympathy and support of all segments of the poor peasantry. The *Halis*, on both sides of the Tapti, in Baroda state and in Surat and Broach districts, were the Dubla bonded labourers of the landlords, *mahajans* and rich peasants, known as the *Dhaniamas*. Their number was generally believed to be more than one lakh and a half. It was said that every well-to-do farmer in this region desired to secure a few *Halis*, by lending several hundred rupees to them in their hours of difficulty, just as he liked "to purchase a pair of bullocks".[109] Inspired by the example of the poor peasants at Lavet, the *Halis* — under the leadership of the

108. Biresh Misra, "Kisan Struggle in the Surma Valley" in Biresh Misra, Pranesh Biswas and Achintya Bhattacharya, *Struggle of the Surma Valley Peasantry*, All India Kisan Sabha Golden Jubilee Series, no.5, New Delhi, 1986, pp. 7-9.

109. "Halis: The Serfs of Gujarat", Sumant B. Mehta, *National Front* (English weekly), 13 March 1938.

local Kisan Sabha — struck work in April 1938, demanding the abrogation of their past debts and the abolition of the *Hali* system. Their brave defiance of the hirelings of the masters so impressed the other categories of peasants that these "little rebellions" of the serfs became "the united front of small tenants and agricultural workers".[110] Consequent to a joint rally of peasants on 22 May 1938, the Naib Sabha of Baroda state had to visit Lavet for settling matters with the representatives of *kisans* on the one side and those of the landlords and *mahajans* on the other. In the settlement reached on 23 May 1938 it was decided to abolish the *Hali* system, and the landlords-*Sahukars* agreed to engage the Dublas as daily wage-earners, and not as *Halis.* However the agitation had to be renewed in June 1938 when the landlords-*sahukars* flouted the agreement of 23 May and insisted on re-payment of debts, as well as the observance of the *Hali* contract, which the Dublas flatly refused. Both sides took the dispute to the district court of Kathore, and the *Halis* resorted to strike once again. Despite the physical force used by the opponents, the *Halis* continued their strike resolutely, and it soon spread from Lavet to the whole of Mongrol *taluk.* From Mongrol its impact was felt among the *Halis* throughout Navasari, Surat and Broach districts.[111] Meanwhile in the thick of the battle in December 1938 came the verdict of the district court declaring the practice of *Hali* as illegal. The announcement, which was greeted with joy, had left the landlords and the *sahukars* with no other alternative but to accept defeat, and engage the Dublas on a daily wage of four annas.[112] The success of Mongrol greatly encouraged the *Halis* in Surat district to commence their battle for emancipation. It started in Mandavi *taluk* in the beginning of 1939, and spread quickly to Bardoli[113] where so many rich peasant nationalists of 1928 *satyagraha* (non-violent civil resistance) had drastically reversed their position to become the opponents of the *Hali satyagrahis* (non-violent civil resisters). Although the *Dhaniamas* were upholding a demonstrably lost

110. "Lavet Makes a Little History", Indulal Yajnik, *ibid.*, 19 June 1938.
111. *Ibid.*, 24 July 1938.
112. *Ibid.*, 25 December 1938.
113. Home Poll. Fortnightly Report for 1st half of March 1939, File No. 18/3/39, N.A.I.

cause, they nevertheless decided to continue their counter-checking the Dublas throughout the second half of 1939. There was news of strikes by the *Halis* from different parts of Surat and Broach, and about 500 *Halis* at Mota, Bardoli *taluk*, were reported to have struck work in August 1939.[114]

114. *Ibid.*, 1st half of August 1939, File No. 18/8/39, N.A.I.

SCENE II

Sharecroppers

The rising of the *Halis* at Lavet, and later in the contiguous areas, was, however, the off-shoot of an intense struggle of another variety, namely, the one that had already been launched at the beginning of 1938 by the sharecroppers and the tenants-at-will belonging to such depressed communities as the Dublas, Dhodias and Kolis. This agitation for a fair share of crop or a bearable rent in kind also began first at Lavet, and then spread to other areas. Like the sharecropping contracts in all other parts of the country, those at Lavet also provided apparently for an equal division of crops between the proprietors of land and the cultivators who tilled it on year-to-year basis, but acquired no tenurial right. In reality, however, the division of crops (50 : 50) was inequitably favourable to the rentiers, bestowing on them profit without labour — and also practically without investment. Under the sharecropping system, the landlords seldom supplied seeds, agricultural implements and cattle to the cultivators. The sharecroppers had to arrange for these themselves and then labour to earn one-half share. The rentiers' share of the crops or the produce-rent had always been higher than the cash-rent, except in the period of the great Depression. In the post-Depression days the produce-rent rose several times higher than the cash-rent, and it continued to be so, particularly steeply, from 1939 and throughout the war period of rising prices. While the landlords thus profited from sharecropping in every way, the sharecroppers suffered economically even at the best of times. It was noticed that if the expenditure on seeds and manure and the cost of cultivation (mainly the labour charges for the sharecropper and his family members at the prevailing rate of wages) was deducted from the market value of one-half share of the produce per acre, an unencumbered sharecropper was left actually with some small loss.[115] The deficit used to increase manifold if the sharecropper was encumbered (which happened invariably to be the case) and compelled to pay back at least partially — in cash or kind — the previously incurred loans. Without exception, he was also subjected stringently to various illegal feudal exactions, which his landlord would most ingeniously devise, for all social occasions, for maintaining the crop accounts, for measuring the grains, for providing safety and security to the tiller, so on and so forth. To all these should be added his difficulties in reaching the market for his produce, his lacking in holding power and his being forced to sell the crops soon after harvesting when the prices were low. (The landlords could afford to wait for a few months to take advantage of the price fluctuations.) The small cash that he derived from the market and the portion of grains that he retained for family consumption (if he was raising food crops) did not carry the sharecropper much further, especially if he had to spend on births, marriages, illnesses and deaths in his family. So, in about five to six months after the harvesting, he was forced to stand before the landlord-*sahukar* with folded hands for taking loans afresh.

Living year after year under this depressing situation, the sharecroppers at Lavet gradually became somewhat exasperated. They were, therefore, ready to respond to the overtures made to them by the Kisan Sabha workers operating from Surat and Navasari. In February 1938 the lower peasantry at Lavet, under

115. It has been calculated in Bengal on the basis of prices existing during 1934-8 (the years of agricultural recovery after the Depression) that if the expenditure on seeds and manures (Rs. 3-14), the one-half share to the landlord (Rs. 13-6) and the wages at the current rate for agricultural labour (of the sharecropper himself and his family members for such field operations as ploughing, sowing, harvesting and threshing — coming altogether to Rs.13-8) were deducted from the total value of the produce per acre (17 maunds of rice and straw worth Rs. 30-10), the sharecropper would be left with some small loss (2 annas). This computation, attempted by a revenue official, has been cited in Adrienne Cooper, "Sharecroppers and Landlords in Bengal, 1930-50: The Dependency Web and Its Implications", *Journal of Peasant Studies* (Special Issue on Sharecropping and Sharecroppers, ed. T.J. Byres), Vol X, nos. 2 and 3, Jan.-April 1983).

the guidance of the Kisan Sabhaites like Ramjibhai Choudhury, and local activists like Chandubhai, raised its voice against the half-crop sharing system and refused to give the landlords any portion of the crops (grains, as well as cotton). When the landlords' goons tried to use force, the *kisans* resisted them with the call "defend your crops", and took the entire produce to their barns. To the landlords' threat of evictions and issue of court notices, they prepared grimly "to hold" their lands[116] and received spontaneous popular support in the region. On 27 March 1938 an unprecedented crowd of 7,000 peasants gathered at a meeting at Lavet to express their solidarity with the *kisan satyagrahis.*[117] In April 1938 the contest swung in favour of the agitators when the landlords-*sahukars* were forced to accept from them one-third crop share.[118] But the struggle was not over, and both the sides approached the Naib Sabha of Baroda state for its intervention. In the prolonged negotiations, the *kisans* (represented by D.M. Pangarkar) insisted on doing away with the practice of sharing crops altogether, demanded fixation of fair rent in cash and withdrawal of all eviction notices.[119] The landlords-*sahukars* opposed these moves tooth and nail, and the state Government apparently sided with them. That the authorities were in league with the landlords became very clear when an attempt was made to break the *kisan* rally on 3 July 1938. It was followed by the arrest of Kisan Sabha workers (like Ramjibhai Choudhury) and externment of leaders (like Yajnik and Pangarkar) from the areas, and later the arrest and conviction of Pangarkar for two months. Lavet was besieged by policemen and the entire Mongrol *taluk* had turned into "a veritable concentration camp".[120] In the face of such repression it was difficult for the *kisans* to continue the struggle uncertainly for

116. When the landlord of Mandan village, one Kharsedji Mancherji, won early in 1938 an eviction suit against his tenants, they refused to give up the land. The landlord thereafter brought the police, who had to arrest two sharecroppers and face a hostile crowd of 400 demanding their release.
117. *National Front* (English weekly), 24 April 1938.
118. *Ibid.*, 19 June 1938.
119. *Ibid.*
120. Dinkar Mehta's report, *The Congress Socialist* (English weekly), 16 October 1938.

long. Negotiations began and a settlement had somehow been reached in February 1939, by which the sharing of crops as a system was retained throughout Mongrol, but at a substantially reduced rate[121] (approximately 1½ for landlords and 2½ for *kisans*), the eviction notices were withdrawn and the arrested were freed.

The sharecroppers' determined struggle in Mongrol gave a fresh impetus to the *Choudras* (sharecroppers) of Surat, especially of Mandavi *taluk*, who had already expressed their grievance against the customary sharing of crops (50 : 50) with the landlords as early as July 1937.[122] They strongly felt then that they should get two-thirds share for themselves, but did not take any effective step to back up their demand. This, however, they eventually took in July 1938, after witnessing the developments at Lavet, and following the advice of the Kisan Sabha leaders (Yajnik and Pangarker in the main). The sharecroppers of Mandavi refused to give either one-half crop shares or to repay old debts to the landlords-*sahukars*. Instead, they offered the landlords one-third, clarifying not to concede even a grain later if it was not accepted. The landlords-*sahukars* replied by instituting a large number of law-suits against the cultivators for non-payment of rent, and bringing in the police through their influence on the local officialdom. Armed with decrees from the law courts in their favour, and assisted by the police, they tried to attach the crops or recover their one-half shares. The *kisans*, on their part, decided to meet force with force, raising the pattern of resistance to a militant height that had not been attained in Mongrol. A series of clashes followed in the second half of 1938 during which the *Choudras* had beaten up the landlords and their men when they came to forcibily remove the crops, obstructed the police in the execution of decrees in the landlords' favour and snatched away from the landlords' possession their one-half share.[123] The

121. *National Front* (English weekly), 12 March 1938.

122. Reports on the Kisan Morchas, Mandavi and Bulsar *taluks*, Govt. of Bombay, Home (Special) Department, File No. 1019 of 1940-1, Maharashtra State Archives, Bombay.

123. A note on kisan agitation in Mandavi taluk, Surat, 10 July 1939, Govt. of Bombay, Home (Special) Department, File No. 800(53)B. Pt. III, 1939, Maharashtra State Archives, Bombay.

Government of Bombay, headed by a Congress ministry which promised to protect the *kisans'* interests, then came forward in the defence of the landlords-*sahukars* on the plea that "if the leaders or supporters of the movement [of the sharecroppers] attempt to disseminate class hatred and ideas involving the use of organised and unorganised violence", it must take preventive measures.[124] The measures soon turned out to be the Collector's notification threatening the "recalcitrant" *kisans* with ejectment, the District Magistrate's order prohibiting meetings and demonstrations in the region under Cr.P.C. Section 144, the large scale arrests of *kisans* on the charges of robbing crop shares and assault,[125] the despatch of police reinforcements to Mandavi, and finally, as well as significantly, the mobilisation of the locaL Congress for counteracting the Kisan Sabhaites. The Mandavi *kisans*, who could not quite measure up the Congress ministry's affection for the landlords-*sahukars*, were clearly no match for the organised violence of the Government. Their ability to resist wilted under severe pressure, and the movement gradually petered away. By March 1939 Mandavi appeared to be quiet again after a quick storm.

The storm nevertheless was not entirely blown over Surat, and its effect could still be felt in Pardi and Bulsar *taluks* throughout 1939. In Pardi (Pardi Mahal) the relations between the landlords-*sahukars* and the sharecroppers were seriously disturbed over the sharing of crops. The issue came particularly to the forefront on account of a shortfall in rains in 1938-9 and the consequent crop failure. The trouble started when 13 sharecroppers of Paria, Pardi, were sentenced to one year's rigrous imprisonment for obstructing the landlords in the removal of crops. The *kisan* leaders like Thakorebhai K. Patel and Bujaji Vicaji — the "outsiders" — succeeded in mobilising the Dhodia sharecroppers against their Bania, Anvil and Rajput landlords, and in organising an impressive meeting on 30 April 1939 to commence the cultivators' campaign for holding all crops. The occurences ran on familiar lines, namely, the issue of court decrees in favour of the landlords, the

124. *Ibid.*
125. Home Poll. Fortnightly Reports for 2nd half of December 1938 and 1st half of January 1939, File Nos. 18/12/38 and 18/1/39, N.A.I.

clashes between the *kisans* and the landlords' men over the removal of crops, the burning of the *kisans*' huts and the felling of the landlords' trees, the assaults on the *kisans* and their arrests by the police. As it happened in Mandavi, the local Congress, led by its President, Premshankar, opposed this movement of the sharecroppers and sided with the landlords and the law-enforcing authorities.[126] Despite all endeavours of the landlords-*sahukars*, and the support they received from the police, the officials and the local Congress, the sharecroppers' agitation could not altogether be halted even by the end of 1939. In fact in the latter half of 1939 it was found to be spreading in other areas of Surat, notably in Bulsar *taluk*, with Bodhai village as the centre.[127]

The sharecroppers also agitated under the leadership of the leftists in other parts of the country, irrepressibly in the Punjab and Bengal, but also in a small way in the *Istimrari* areas of Ajmer-Merwara, and in Sind. In Ajmer-Merwara grew up a campaign in favour of a more equitable division of the produce between the *Istimrardars* (the landlords) and their tenants-at-will, for the cultivators there had to part approximately with two-thirds of the crops as rent and other feudal exactions. At Deoli the *kisans* even thought of taking away the entire crop from the threshing floors to their homes, without giving the landlords any share. The *Istimrardars* naturally raised a hue and cry over the move which prompted the authorities to take preventive measures, including the arrest of two leading agitators — Indra Dutt *Swadhin* and Rajendra Kumar.[128] Matters took a more noisy turn in Sind where the landless Haris cultivated the *Jagirdars*' lands as sharecroppers under the *batai* arrangement, or on the basis of paying one-half share of the crops as rent. The *Jagirdars* or landlords (2,000 in number) held about 71 lakhs of acres against approximately 15 lakhs of acres possessed by the peasant

126. A note on kisan agitation in Mandavi taluk, Surat, 10 July 1939, Govt. of Bombay, Home (Special) Department, File No. 800(53)B.PT.III, 1939, Maharashtra State Archives, Bombay.
127. *Ibid.*
128. Home Poll. Fortnightly Report for 1st half of June 1938, File No. 18/6/38, N.A.I.

proprietors or the *Topedars.*[129] Much of these 71 lakhs acres of the *Jagirdari* lands was tilled by the Haris, who thereby constituted the most important agricultural work force in the province. Like the fate of the sharecroppers everywhere, the Haris' one-half share of crops was invariably siphoned off through various kinds of feudal levies imposed by the *Jagirdars.* Besides, without having any tenurial right, they were subjected to a continuous process of ejectments. Some Congress Socialists like Jamshed Mehta and Narayandas Bechar took the initiative in organising the Haris under the Sind Hari Party — a body affiliated to the All India Kisan Sabha. The party held a conference of 500 Haris drawn from a radius of 50 miles in Karachi, and on 26 April 1937 it organised a march to represent to the Government their demands for the allotment of some lands on reasonable terms, as well as for full one-half share of the produce without levies of any kind.[130] In October 1937 the Haris from Tande Jam undertook a spectacular march covering nine miles to Hyderabad for demonstrating before the Collector. The reason behind their agitation was the arrest of some of them by the police on the landlords' charge of unauthorised removal of crops from the fields.[131] The Haris, in fact, commenced a *satyagraha* and succeeded in obtaining the release of the arrested. On 18 December 1937 the Sind Hari Party held another conference at Hyderabad to put forward to the authorities the Haris' claims for land, some tenurial right on plots they had occupied and the landlords' strict adherence to the equal distribution of crops.[132] Their agitation continued spasmodically in the subsequent years also, but practically without any result, except the vague promise of "sympathetic consideration" from the successive ministries of Hidayatullah and Allah Bux. The situation in western Punjab was, however, far more serious than Ajmer-Merwara and Sind, and also more rewarding from the *kisan* point of view.

129. Mushtaq Ahmad, *Government and Politics in Pakistan*, Karachi, 1963, pp. 197-8.
130. *The All India Kisan Bulletin*, 30 April 1937, Central Archives, Communist Party of India, Ajoy Bhavan, New Delhi.
131. Home Poll. Fortnightly Report for 1st half of June 1938, File No. 18/6/38, N.A.I.
132. *Ibid.*, 2nd half of December 1937, File No. 18/12/37, N.A.I.

With the completion of irrigation projects like Head Sulemanki and Sutlej Valley Canals between 1922 and 1928, vast tracts of arid lands of Montgomery and Multan districts of the Punjab were turned cultivable for the ample production of wheat, cotton and oil seeds. At the time of allotting these lands on lease, the Government invited tenders and selected the highest bidders as the lessees. The tender-holders, in their turn, distributed these lands among the landless peasants (mostly Muslims) on the *batai* arrangement, or on produce-rent at the rate of one-half share of the crops. The *batai* cultivation became so much in vogue that in course of time 79.3 per cent of the cultivated land in Montgomery and 74.4 per cent in Multan was tilled by the sharecroppers or under-tenants. In the early 1930s, following the Depression, the tender-holders or the landlords (both individuals and companies) tried to maximise their profits by insisting on the sharecroppers' paying a number of irregular levies (such as, Anna *Thaba*, *Malba Khata*, *Jhajari*, *Pakhi*, etc.), and on their giving labour without payment. It had been shown that, after meeting all the exactions from one-half share, and repaying some of his previous crop loans, the sharecropper was eventually left hardly with one-fourth of the gross produce.[133] The sharecroppers of Nili-Bar — the colony area between the Ravi and the Sutlej and a part of Chunan *tahsil* of Lahore district — were the first to act for the redressal of their desperate situation. Noticing the signs of unrest among the Nili-Bar cultivators, the leftist Punjab Kisan Sabha — which enjoyed greater support among the substantial peasants than the poor ones, and whose support-base was stronger in the central region (Amritsar, Lahore, Jullundur and Ferozepur) than in the western part (Montgomery and Multan)[134] — became active for the first time in organising the *batai* peasants. The Sabha deputed a number of *kisan* activists (Jalwant Singh, Wadhwa Ram, Ram Singh, Waryam Singh, etc.), under the direct supervision of its President, Baba Jawala Singh, to tour the area, hold rallies of the *kisans* and take an

133. Master Hari Singh, *Punjab Peasant in Freedom Struggle,* Delhi, 1984, p.282.
134. Bhagwan Josh, *Communist Movement in Punjab*, Delhi, 1979, pp. 121-4.

under-tenants' deputation to the Revenue minister (Sunder Singh Majithia) in the Sikander Hayat Khan ministry for representing their grievances. Demanding an equal division of crops on the fields, the abolition of *begar* and irregular levies, and the fixation of a fair price for fodder, about 25,000 sharecroppers of Nili-Bar struck work on 20 May 1937 and refused to pick cotton or sow wheat. The strike was so complete and its impact so unnerving that the tender-holders were compelled to make a compromise in the month of May itself through the mediation of the District Commissioner. They accepted the half and half division of crops on the field, promised not to insist on the payment of levies and agreed to the fixation of fodder price payable by the cultivators.[135]

The success of the Nili-Bar under-tenants so encouraged the *batai* cultivators in the surrounding localities that most of them wanted their landlords to give effect to the terms of the Nili-Bar agreement of May 1937. The cultivators of about 20 villages in Talamba *thana* (Multan) had struck work for nearly a month to extract in September 1938 the gains of the Nili-Bar struggle.[136] The sharecroppers of various *chaks* in Montgomery district also asked for the concessions accorded to the *kisans* of Nili-Bar.[137] Staking similar claims, the cultivators of 15 *chaks* in Khanewal *tahsil* (Multan) went on strike under the leadership of the Kisan Sabhaites.[138] In this case also the tender-holders and the Government came to terms with the cultivators by giving concessions. Side by side their attitude of reasonableness, the landlords and the authorities also hit back, unleashing the forces of repression on the agitators. The police often made *lathi* charges for breaking the *kisan* rallies and arrested the Kisan Sabhaite "outsiders" for fomenting troubles and spreading "the

135. Master Hari Singh, *Punjab Peasant in Freedom Struggle*, Delhi, 1984, pp. 281-2.
136. *Kirti Lahar*, 7 August and 8 September 1938, cited in Bhagwan Josh, *Communist Movement in Punjab*, Delhi, 1979, p. 131.
137. Home Poll. Fortnightly Report for 2nd half of June 1938, File No. 18/6/38, N.A.I.
138. *Ibid.*, 1st half of October 1938, File No. 18/10/38, N.A.I.

Communist influence".[139] The landlords also organised a Zamindar Association to oppose the *batai* peasants' agitation, hired *goondas* to attack the *kisans* and informed the police of the whereabouts of the *kisan* leaders.[140] This policy of concession and coercion did eventually help the authorities in restricting the developments to a manageable limit.

Sharecropping being practised over 25 per cent of its total cultivated lands,[141] Bengal was expected, on the lines of Gujarat and the Punjab, to become a hotbed of the sharecroppers' agitation. There were in fact reports of clashes between the *Bargadars* (sharecroppers) and the *Jotedars* (rich tenants with considerable lands or *jotes*, who profited as much by giving lands to sharecropping as by lending money and grains to tillers) in Tripura and Noakhali over the repayment of crop loans,[142] in Faridpur over the *Bargadars*' claim for some tenurial rights,[143] in Bogra, Dinajpur, Birbhum, the 24-Parganas and Midnapore over the measurement of shares[144] and the replacement of one *Bargadar* in a plot by another.[145] The authorities, who had previously found the *Bargadars* to be submissive generally, were struck by the change the leftists had brought about in their demeanour, especially in the 24-Parganas and Midnapore — where they exhibited unmistakable signs of "political consciousness".[146] Curiously enough, the sharecroppers in Bengal — unlike their counterparts in Gujarat — did not raise between 1936 and 1939 their class demand for an alteration in the

139. *Ibid.*, 1st half of February 1939, File No. 18/2/39, N.A.I.
140. Master Hari Singh, *Punjab Peasant in Freedom Struggle*, Delhi, 1984, p. 284.
141. Exactly 24.9 per cent according to the Ishaque Commission of 1944-5, H.S.M. Ishaque, *Agricultural Statistics by Plot to Plot Enumeration in Bengal, 1944-1945*, Calcutta, 1946, Part I.
142. Home Poll. Fortnightly Report for 2nd half of December 1937, File No. 18/12/37, N.A.I.
143. *Ibid.*, 2nd half of April 1938, File No. 18/4/38, N.A.I.
144. *Ibid.*, 2nd half of February 1939, File No. 18/2/39, N.A.I.
145. *Ibid.*, 1st half of July and 2nd half of December 1939, File Nos. 18/7/39 and 18/12/39, N.A.I.
146. "A Brief Summary of Political Events in the Province of Bengal", Home Poll. File No. 148/41-Poll (I), 1941, N.A.I.

proportion of crop shares, or the two-thirds of the crop share for themselves.[147]

The only noticeable exception was the movement of the *Tanka* peasants of north Mymensingh which challenged the exploitative basis of sharecropping, without raising, of course, the formal demand for the two-thirds crop share. *Tanka* was a produce-rent which the cultivator had to pay in a quantity fixed between him and the landlord. *Tanka* lands were originally jungle tracts, cleared and made cultivable by the landless peasantry. The landlords thereafter allowed the peasants to cultivate these lands on the basis of annual sharecropping contracts, but conceded not even a semblance of occupancy right. In the 1920s the *Tanka* peasants had to give their landlords usually four to six maunds of paddy for cultivating a plot of 1¼ acres, yielding 15 to 20 maunds.[148] The quantity of paddy was often fixed every year through open bidding, i.e. whoever promised the maximum would receive the land. As a result, the produce-rent increased sharply in the 1930s, and a cultivator in 1936-7 had to give seven to 15 maunds of paddy for a plot of 1¼ acres. The market rate of paddy at this point of time was Rs. 2 and 4 annas a maund, and the cash rent for a non-*Tanka* plot of the same size varied from Rs.5 to Rs.7 a year. So a *Tanka* peasant was forced to pay annually in monetary terms Rs.11 to Rs.17 — more than what an ordinary *rayat* paid.[149]

The landlords gained enormously through the *Tanka* arrangement, and the *Zamindars* of Susang alone collected under this head about two lakh maunds of paddy from the sharecroppers. In Susang the *Tanka* peasants came largely from the Hajong tribe, who belonged to the terrains of the Garo hills. Apart from the Hajongs, the Muslim peasants formed a substantial section of the *Tanka* sharecroppers in Susang, as well as at Kalmakonda, Nalitabari, Haluaghat and Sree Bardi. It was the Muslim peasantry who first resented the oppressive burdens of the *Tanka* under the leadership of Moni Sinha — a newly

147. It is said that in the 1920s in Jessore the sharecroppers raised for the first time the call for a two-thirds share or the *tebhaga* in Bengal. The call was forgotten thereafter for long, till it became the battle-cry in 1946.

148. *National Front* (English weekly), 8 January 1939.

149. Moni Sinha, *Jeeban Sangram* (Bengali), Dacca, 1983, p. 46.

released Communist detenu and trade-union worker — who hailed ironically from the *Zamindar* family of Susang. The resistance actually started in November 1937 in a meeting at Dasal village, and it soon spread over to numerous other villages through the exertions of the Kisan Sabha activists. Under Moni Sinha's guidance, the *Tanka* peasants refused to give the landlords the agreed amount of paddy and demanded the abolition of the *Tanka* system, the grant of occupancy rights in their favour and the permission to pay rent in cash.[150] The hostility on the part of the landlords and the presence of the police in the affected areas could not, however, stem the progress of the agitation. By the beginning of 1938 the *Zamindars* were in fact found to have collected only a negligible portion of their contracted share of crops. The intensity of the movement eventually compelled the Fazlul Huq ministry in Bengal to order in 1938 for the survey operations in the area under the police stations of Kalmakonda, Durgapur, Haluaghat, Nalitabari and Sree Bardi to determine the production of paddy per acre. The survey findings led in 1939 to a sizable decrease in the *Tanka* peasants' burden, reducing their crop rent to half the total produce, and in some cases even less. The *Tanka* peasants thus registered by the end of 1939 a partial victory, without, of course, being able to achieve their main objective — the abolition of the *Tanka*. Consequently, the fight against the *Tanka* did not end in 1939, it was to be renewed again after some respite.

Though not so much concerned with the fundamentals of sharecropping, the *Bargadars* in north Bengal did resist the unjust exaction of their landlords. At the leftist instance, they started an agitation against the *Hattola* (also called *Gandi*) or the levy imposed by the landlords and *Ijaradars* (usually the *Jotedars* who took contracts from the *Zamindars*) on the proceeds of the weekly markets or fairs (*hats* and *bazaars*) held on the village lands under their control. *Hat* was a regular feature of Bengal's rural economy[151] where miscellaneous items from paddy, rice and vegetables to utensils, cloth and cattle

150. *National Front* (English weekly), 8 January 1939.
151. According to the official findings in 1940, about 6,000 *hats* were held regularly in undivided Bengal.

were sold and bought. The *Tola* or *Gandi* was collected from the well-to-do businessmen (who sold costly items) and the poor peasants (who sold few seers of rice or vegetables) at certain high rates in cash (for the perishable goods), as well as in kind (for the non-perishable ones). The levy fell particularly heavily on the poor peasants who were also harassed by all kinds of extra demands of the *Zamindars'* and the *Ijaradars'* men. It had been a sore point with them for long, and their discontent was expressed in the looting or breaking of *hats* — the news of which appeared sometimes in the Government records of the 1920s and 1930s, not only in Bengal but also in Orissa. In fact an agitation against the *Hattola* was organised first in Angul area of Cuttack, in the first half of April 1939.[152]

In north Bengal the issue came up at the District Kisan Sabha Conference of Jalpaiguri, held on 27 June 1939 at Mainadighi, where a resolution was passed against the *Hattola.*[153] Soon the local Kisan Sabha launched an agitation in the *hats* against *Tola* at Boda, Debiganj and Pachagarh. Kisan volunteers led processions, convened meetings and resorted to picketings at the *hats.* The *Zamindars* and *Ijaradars,* on their part, lodged complaints with the police and brought the Government officials and the Sub-Divisional Officer on the scene, but could not stop the defiant peasants. The success in Jalpaiguri encouraged the *kisans* in Cooch Behar, Dinajpur and Rangpur to start agitating in their respective areas. A climax was reached in October 1939 in the famous *Kalir Mela* (Goddess Kali's Fair) at Dumduma, Atwari *thana,* Dinajpur, where 900 trained peasant volunteers demonstrated with sticks and red flags against *Zamindar* Madhav Dutta's exorbitant *Lekhai Kharach* or charges for his writing receipts for all sales of domestic animals in the fair. Armed policemen were called at the site to maintain law and order, and the district authorities promulgated Section 144 Cr. P.C. in the locality. To avoid direct confrontation with the police, the *kisan* leaders gave a call for the boycott of the fair and decided to

152. Home Poll. Fortnightly Report for 1st half of April 1939, File No. 18/4/39, N.A.I.

153. Ranajit Das Gupta, "Krishak O Rajniti : Jalpaiguri, 1938-40" (Bengali), *Parichaya* (Bengali monthly), November 1983, pp. 57-8.

hold a parallel fair — a *Dasher Mela* (Fair of the People) — a short distance away within the jurisdiction of Jalpaiguri district. The move brought the *Zamindar* to his senses and a settlement with the agitators was reached by bringing down the *Lekhai Kharach* of Rs. 2 for a cow and Rs. 6 for a buffalo to annas 2 and annas 4, respectively. By December 1939 the *Hattola* ceased practically to exist in most parts of Jalpaiguri and Dinajpur (though it continued in Rangpur), and the Kisan Sabha's position among the peasants was "established".[154] Unlike the opposition to the *Tanka* system in Mymensingh, the anti-*Hattola* campaign in north Bengal was not merely a sharecroppers' affair. Along with the *Adhiars* (the sharecroppers), other sections of rural society, such as the well-to-do and rich peasants, and even the village *banias* participated in it against the *Zamindari* and *Jotedari* expropriation. In forging this anti-feudal unity of the various categories lay the credit and the strength of the Kisan Sabha in north Bengal — the venue of some of the most determined struggles of the rural poor.

154. Report of the Bengal Kisan Movement, 1939-40, 23.2.40, Appendix-D, *Annual Report of All Kisan Sabha, 1939-40*, Central Archives, Communist Party of India, Ajoy Bhavan, New Delhi.

SCENE III
Anti-Evictions

Apart from the *Hattola* and *Tanka* agitations, the sharecroppers in Bengal had to fight, almost without any break between 1937 and 1939, against their dispossession, or eviction from the lands they tilled. The machination that a *Zamindar* or a *Jotedar* invariably laid was to proceed against the sharecropper — whom he wanted to throw out — in a court of law, accusing him of non-payment of rent, and to obtain an order, declaring the plot in question to be allowed to become *Khas* or the landlord's own. As the sharecropping contracts were made orally, and the records of rent (often fictitiously entered against the name of an illiterate *kisan*, and legalised by obtaining his thumb impression on them) were kept by the landlords, the sharecropper had practically no chance of defending himself in a civil suit, especially when the court, the revenue officials and the police were in league with the landlords. The manoeuvring was apparent to all, including the British civilians — the so-called *mai-baaps* (the parents of the people) — who, however, had little intention to prevent its operation despite their knowledge that "the law allows it [dispossession] and the civil courts give effect to it, so that there will of necessity be cases of hardship, if not oppression — pure and simple".[155] The plot of land naturally did not remain *Khas* for long, for it required some investment, even if small, for its cultivation. Soon it was reverted to the sharecropping arrangement with another *kisan* on a highly increased amount of *salami* (charges for the new contract) and payment of the *nazraṇa* (presentation to the landlord). The *Bhagchasis*' (sharecroppers') resistance against *uchchhed* (eviction) and over the *Khas*, usually on a small scale under the

155. Report of Commissioner (A. Graham), Presidency Division, to Secretary, Home Dep., Govt. of Bengal, 24 November 1939, Home Poll. Conf. File No. 333/39 of 1939, West Bengal State Archives, Calcutta.

leadership of the local Kisan Sabhaites, was widespread in most parts of Bengal. Only when a situation went really out of control was it mentioned in official reports. There were a number of cases in December 1937 in Tipperah and Noakhali in which the *Bargadars* clashed with their landlords, after being accused of "looting" the crops they raised on lands turned into the *Zamindars' Khas.*[156] Similar developments occurred in Jalpaiguri and Birbhum[157] in 1938, and in April 1939 the sharecroppers in Kishoreganj, Mymensingh, stubbornly resisted the landlords' "concerted move" to dispossess them.[158] In July 1939 the *Bhagchasis* in several places in Midnapore obstructed, some times "in open violence", the landlords' attempts at the transfer of their lands to others.[159]

However, the agitations over converting *bhag* lands into *Khas* were more serious, and certainly more numerous, in the 24-Parganas. They started in 1937 and continued, under the guidance of the Communists and other leftists, till the end of 1939. In August 1937 the "outside" political activists were believed to be inciting cultivators to forcibly plough lands held in *Khas* by the landlords.[160] A month later, the *Samiti* (the local branch of the Kisan Sabha) started organising the *kisans* evicted by the Port Canning (*Zamindari*) Company in Sandeshkhali, Canning and Haroa *thanas* of the Sundarbans region. On 27 October 1937 the Bengal Provincial Kisan Sabha brought 1,000 such dispossessed peasants from the affected areas to Calcutta for presenting their grievances to the Government. A meeting was also held on that day at Shraddhananda Park where Swami Sahajanand and Subhas Chandra Bose addressed the peasants.[161] In November 1937 the B.P.K.S. planned a *satyagraha* against evictions in certain villages

156. Home Poll. Fortnightly Report for 2nd half of December 1937, File No. 18/12/37, N.A.I.
157. *Ibid.*, 2nd half of July and 2nd half of November 1938, File Nos. 18/7/38 and 18/11/38, N.A.I.
158. *Ibid.*, 2nd half of April 1939, File No. 18/4/39, N.A.I.
159. *Ibid.*, 2nd half of July and 1st half of August 1939, File Nos. 18/7/39 and 18/8/39, N.A.I.
160. *Ibid.*, 1st half of August, 1937, File No. 18/8/37, N.A.I.
161. Note by the Special Branch, Police, on Bengal Provincial Kisan Sabha, Calcutta, 3 July 1939, Home Poll. File No. 333/39 Conf. West Bengal State Archives, Calcutta.

of Sandeshkhali and Canning. Two volunteers (Pulin Bhattacharya and Nural Huda) sent from Calcutta were, however, arrested for inciting peasants against the landlords. They were later tried by the Sub-Divisional Officer, Alipore, and sentenced to one year's rigorous imprisonment. In the face of strict official vigilance, the *kisan* agitation in Sandeshkhali and Canning could not make much headway. But such was not precisely the case in Haroa — where the evicted peasants of Uchildah and Minakhan rallied against the landlords when some of their resumed lands were auctioned. In April 1938 the B.P.K.S. again brought the evicted *kisans*, mainly from Uchildah and Bhangur, to Calcutta for persuading the members of the Bengal Legislative Assembly to take up their cause.[162] Despite the strong feeling it raised, the B.P.K.S.-led agitation was generally restrained in the 24-Parganas, and without any direct confrontation either with the landlords or with the Government officials and the police. But a splinter group of leftists under Soumyendra Nath Tagore, who broke away from the B.P.K.S. in March 1938, advocated a more militant and violent form of peasant agitation in Hasnabad, Bijpur and Sagar *thanas*, and became active in Sandeshkhali, Canning and Haroa also. The activities of this group[163] between September 1938 and May 1939 resulted often in isolated cases of peasants' refusal to pay *bhag*, their forcibly removing paddy from the *Khas* lands and their clashes with the landlords' agents. The most serious of all these occurred in February 1939 when the *Naib* (manager) of Sir Daniel Hamilton's estate, along with some others, had severely been beaten up by Tagore's followers, and two guns were taken away from the *cutcherry*.[164] Disdainful of the compromising approach of the Congress Socialists, and critical

162. *Ibid.*

163. Soumyendra Nath Tagore, who was closely associated with the Communist movement from the mid-1920s, organised his followers into a group in 1935 — known as the Ganabani group (named after its mouthpiece, *Ganabani*). In March 1938 the group adopted the name, the Communist League of India, and later in the late 1940s it turned into the Revolutionary Communist Party of India.

164. Note of Intelligence Branch, Police, on Bengal Provincial Kisan Sabha, 30 June 1939, File No. 333/39, Conf. Home Poll. Dept. Govt. of Bengal, West Bengal State Archives, Calcutta. Also Home Poll. Fortnightly Report for 2nd half of February 1939, File No. 18/2/39, N.A.I.

of the pseudo-revolutionism of the "Congress Communists",[165] Tagore and his adherents challenged — in a certain way — the position of the B.P.K.S. in south 24-Parganas. Consequently, the B.P.K.S. was forced to assume a posture of militancy in the region, revitalise its propaganda machinery and concentrate on the battles already waged. The situation at Uchildah soon reached violent proportions over the *Khas* disputes, resulting in August 1939 in the death of a *darwan* (door-keeper) of the Port Canning (*Zamindari*) Company.[166] The district authorities sent a police force into the area and imposed Section 144 Cr.P.C., banning the meetings of the Kisan Sabha at Uchildah and the neighbouring villages. The measures failed to check the rising temper of *kisans*, and by December 1939 their clashes with the landlords' men were turning into open conflicts with the police.

Like the *Bhagchasis* in Bengal, more particularly in the 24-Parganas, the under-tenants in west Punjab, or the *batai* cultivators in Montgomery and Multan, had to confront with ejectments in 1938-9. Normally the landlord in the Punjab, as everywhere else in India, ousted a sharecropper mainly to extract from the new incumbent various levies at a higher rate. To this motivation were added in 1938-9 two special circumstances which contributed to an increase in the number of ejectments in western Punjab. One was the Government decision soon after the Nili-Bar settlement of May 1937, to split up some of the colony lands into smaller lots to attract more investors from among the rich peasants who could till and manage the land themselves. After the auction, at the time of occupation, the new lessees often found that their lands were being cultivated by the under-tenants. As they wanted to till their own lands, the rich peasants had no alternative but to try to eject the sharecroppers. The *batai* peasants, on their own part, had no intention to deliver the lands to the new tender-holders, and thus a contest began early

165. This expression was used by Tagore's Communist League of India in its "Political Line adopted at the 2nd Party Congress", *Red Front*, No. 2, March 1940, File No. 1940/5 and 1/2 8. P.C. Joshi Archives, J.N.U., New Delhi.

166. Home Poll. Fortnightly Report for 2nd half of August 1939, File No. 18/8/39, N.A.I.

in 1938 as much to the discomfiture of the Punjab Kisan Sabha as to the delight of the Unionist ministry. The Kisan Sabhaites first tried to dissuade the rich peasants from submitting tenders, and in this they did not naturally succeed. Once their persuasions failed and a conflict ensued, it must be pointed out to the credit of the Punjab Kisan Sabhaites — who had been known for their substantial peasant sustenance[167] — that they sided with the under-tenants in a steadfast manner. The other circumstance that led to fresh frictions between the tender-holders and the under-tenants was born out of the widespread notion that if a *batai* cultivator continued to cultivate a plot consecutively for six years, he would be entitled to some tenurial rights. The idea gained currency on account partly of the Kisan Sabha's propaganda in favour of the *batai* cultivators' interests, and partly because of the landlords' apprehension of some likely tenurial re-arrangement in the Punjab in consequence generally of a hue and cry for land reform during Provincial Autonomy. The B.G. Kher ministry of Bombay had, in fact, proposed in early 1938 in its Bombay Small Holders' Relief Bill that a tenant, who was in possession of a piece of land continually for six years, might be entitled to some right on it.[168] To insure themselves against such impending calamity, the lessees in western Punjab decided to shift their under-tenants by interchanging the plots occupied by them. Although the procedure did not result in any actual dispossession of the *batai* cultivators, it did produce for them a certain discontinuity and displacement, and also led them to believe in the veracity of the rumour. They, therefore, resented the landlords' move and opposed it wherever they could. At Suchan village of Montgomery in February 1939, for example, the landlords' attempt at interchanging the plots severely disturbed their relations with the under-tenants and led eventually to a violent clash, resulting in the death of one and injuries to nine.[169]

167. Bhagwan Josh, *Communist Movement in Punjab*, Delhi, 1979, p. 145.

168. See subsequent p.68 and f.n. 181.

169. Home Poll. Fortnightly Report for 2nd half of February 1939, File No. 18/2/39, N.A.I.

The anti-eviction agitation, like the demand for the *batai* on the field itself, also started first in Nili-Bar in February 1938 when the under-tenants refused to give up their plots to the new lessees.[170] The refusal soon grew into a movement against ejectments, and by March 1939 it engulfed substantial parts of Montgomery and Multan. Forcible attempts at eviction were also met with force, and complaints of attacks and counter-attacks were lodged with the police. On several occasions the armed police had to be despatched from the district headquarters to the countryside, apparently to prevent "breach of peace",[171] but actually to help in giving effect to ejectments. The situation took a serious turn on 12 April 1939 when the police assistance was sought in Chak Number 451 near Burewala, Multan, for ejecting the *batai* tenants from certain lands re-leased to the new grantees. Hundreds of peasants gathered to resist the police, offer *satyagraha* and court arrest.[172] The authorities retaliated by detaining a large number of *kisans* and the Kisan Sabha activists, prosecuting and convicting them. Despite a big under-tenants' conference at the village Basti-khel Mohariwala, and the exhortations of the leftist leaders like Munshi Ahmad Din, the agitation could not be continued in the face of the Government onslaught.

Almost similar was the outcome of the anti-eviction agitation at Ghalla Dher (Mardan district), North-West Frontier Province — one of the most intense of all such occurrences in the entire northern part of the country. The small cultivator tenants of Ghalla Dher were accused by Nawab Hamidullah Khan of Tora — an important feudal chief — of occupying some of his lands without proper tenurial title. The *kisans*, who had never been conscious of the intricacies of legality, felt that their occupation was valid since they were tilling the land hereditarily for long, and were paying rent. When the Nawab took the matter to the court of law the peasants energetically contested it. At the instance of the local Congress Socialists, they had already been resisting the Nawab's plans for imposing various illegal levies on them. The court proceedings, however, did not eventually go in

170. *Ibid.*
171. *Ibid.*, 1st half of March 1939, File No. 18/3/39, N.A.I.
172. *Ibid.*, 2nd half of April 1939, File No. 18/4/39.

their favour, and — as it happened so often — the Nawab managed to obtain an ejectment order. In June 1938 he sent some of his men to take possession of the lands which were then being cultivated by the tenants. Sensing resistance from the tenants, he had asked beforehand for police protection against "unlawful and forcible" cultivation of his lands. The police, therefore, arrived in full force to assist the Nawab's men in the name of maintaining "law and order".[173] The Ghalla Dher tenants resolved to start a *satyagraha* on 15 June — the day the Nawab's men and the police reached the village — and continued it till August 1938. The police attempts at breaking the *satyagraha* often resulted in scuffles and jostles, leading to numerous cases of injuries, including those to women and children. Arrests of the *satyagrahis* were made in batches, and whenever a batch of arrested persons were escorted to Mardan, a large crowd of villagers accompanied them up to the prison gates.[174] Altogether 253 persons were held, including 19 Congress Socialists and their leaders, N. Akbar Ali Shah of Nowshera and M. Abdur Rahim Popalzai of Peshawar.[175] They were arrested for organising unlawful assembly, disturbing the peace and inciting the tenants against the landlord. Eventually 11 of them had been sentenced to two years' rigorous imprisonment, 160 to 6 months' and the rest were released on personal bond.[176] The Congress Premier of North-West Frontier Province, Dr. Khan Saheb, who visited Ghalla Dher during the *satyagraha*, did not feel any qualm about its ruthless suppression or about upholding a feudal magnate's prerogative to dispossess his long-standing tenants. Branding the agitation as a deliberate obstruction to the processes of civil law, and as one engineered by the Congress Socialists, the Frontier Congress ministry approved of all police actions, even the

173. Speech of Dr. Khan Saheb, 5 November 1938, *N.W.F.P. Legislative Assembly Debates*, 1938, Vol. IV, p. 242.
174. Home Poll. Fortnightly Report for 2nd half of July 1938, File No. 18/7/38, N.A.I.
175. Speech of Dr. Khan Saheb, 4-5 November 1938, *N.W.F.P. Legislative Assembly Debates*, 1938, Vol. IV, p. 244.
176. Home Poll. Fortnightly report for 2nd half of September 1938, File No. 18/9/38, N.A.I.

excesses, and refused the Congress Socialist leaders (Acharya Narendra Deva, M.R. Masani and Munshi Ahmad Din) permission to visit Ghall Dher.[177] The Ghalla Dher peasants thus lost their battle — apparently a hopeless one in view of the hostility of a "friendly" Government — but succeeded in setting up for others an example of stubborn anti-eviction resistance.[178]

The anti-eviction agitation also flared up in Gujarat, Maharashtra and Kanara district of the province of Bombay. In May 1938 the landlords in Dhanduk *taluk* of Ahmedabad distirct forcibly dispossessed the poor peasants from their lands which they had occupied for long.[179] The landlords' actions were believed to have been pre-emptive for by-passing certain provisions of the Bombay Small Holder's Act VIII of 1938. Apparently these provisions offered the peasants — who held plots continuously for six years — some occupancy right, provided they had all through paid their rent regularly.[180] The stiff opposition that the tenants managed to put up against these attempts at eviction, and the B.G. Kher ministry's re-affirmation of the new Act,[181] eventually dampened the landlords' enthusiasm for ejectment. Almost identical was the position in Karwar *taluk* in Kanara district where the *rayats* encountered the landlords through a method of social and economic boycott. Hundreds of them met at Ghadasi on 12 July and decided that if a landlord ejected any of the tenants, his lands would neither be cultivated nor taken up by other cultivators. And, in case such a landlord tried to cultivate the land of the ejected *rayat* himself, no one among the other *rayats* and agricultural labourers would labour for

177. Speech of Dr. Khan Saheb, 4-5 November 1938, *N.W.F.P. Legislative Assembly Debates*, 1938, Vol.IV, p. 244.
178. *National Front* (English weekly), 2 October 1938.
179. I.K. Vyas, President, Dhanduk Taluk Congress Committee, to K.M. Munshi, Minister for Law and Order, 28 April 1938, Home (Special) Department Govt. of Bombay, File No. 918-A of 1938, Maharashtra State Archives, Bombay.
180. District Superintendent of Police, Ahmedabad, to Secretary, Home Dept. Govt. of Bombay, Home (Special) Dept. File No. 918-A of 1938, Maharashtra State Archives, Bombay.
181. Circular No. S.D. 1737, Home Dept. Poll. Govt. of Bombay, 7 July 1938, *ibid.*

him.[182] The tenant-landlord friction over ejectment had sometimes led to physical violence, as it did in September 1939 between the Maratha *Khots* and their Kunbi tenants in Khed *taluk* of Ratnagiri district.[183]

Almost on the same pattern, the tenants — at the instance of the leftists — met the land-grabbing challenges in Tamil Nadu of Madras province, and were even involved in direct confrontation with the police. The sample of a number of such conflicts was the Malamanjari incident that took place in September 1939 in Papanasam *taluk* of Tanjore district. A *Mirasdar* at Malamanjari village, Abdul Qadir Rawther, wanted to evict some of his tenants whose lands he intended to use for his own farming. As a counter-move, the *rayats* appealed to the Sub-Judge's court at Kumbakonam against this attempt at dispossessing them on the ground of their long occupation of the plots — actually since the days of their forefathers. The Sub-Judge granted an injunction in their favour under the Tenancy Act I of 1908 (as amended by Act XVIII of 1936). The injunction so infuriated the *Mirasdar* that he promptly lodged a complaint with the police, charging some of the *rayats* with theft, damage and destruction of his personal effects in the village.[184] The intention was to implicate them in false criminal cases with the help of the local police. When the police party came to the village to teach the *rayats* a lesson on the pretext of making "enquiries", it was surrounded by an angry mob of about 300 persons. Threatened and attacked by the mob, the police party resorted to firing before beating a hurried retreat.[185] The frustrated *Mirasdar* had no alternative but to abandon his scheme for the time being.

It was the issue of eviction again that caused between 1936 and 1939 considerable commotion among the *kisans* in the U.P., more

182. Weekly Confidential Report, District Magistrate, Kanara, No. c. 96, 20 July 1938, *ibid.*
183. District Superintendent of Police to District Magistrate, Ratnagiri, No. B/171/194, 27 September 1938, *ibid.*
184. District Magistrate, Tanjore, to Chief Secretary, Govt. of Madras, No. 5756, 5 September 1939, Public (Gen. Dept.), G.O. No. 32 of 1940, Tamil Nadu State Archives, Madras.
185. District Superintendent of Police, Tanjore, to Inspector General of Police, Madras, 5 September 1939, *ibid.*

particularly in Gorakhpur and Banaras. There the problem grew over the *Taluqdari* and *Zamindari* management of their *Khudkasht* and *Sir* lands. The *Khudkasht* lands were those which the landlords enjoyed exclusively, without giving these on rent to the tenants, and by getting them cultivated through the employment of agricultural labour. Further, the landlords possessed the *Sir* lands which they were supposed to cultivate themselves, or with the help of the *khetmajdoors*, but which they could also let out to the tenants. The tenant of a plot of *Sir* land did not acquire any tenurial right over it, and thus remained a tenant-at-will perpetually under the threat of ejectment to make room for a higher bidder. As his name was deliberately kept out of all records, the tenant-at-will, or the *Shikmi Kashtkar* in local parlance, was often ejected by the landlord as a trespasser on the *Sir* land. Previously the cases against trespassing were to be brought within a period of 12 years. In 1926, under the Agra Tenancy Act III, the time limit for lodging complaints against the tresspassers was reduced to three years. So every three years the landlords would go for evicting their unrecognised *Shikmi Kashtkars* from the *Sir* lands through civil actions, and even get payment for damages (four-times the rental value).[186] The landlords found the entire procedure to be so effective that they made use of it in their *Khudkasht*, too. They started giving the *Khudkasht* lands to the landless tillers on rent, and later on brought cases against them for "conspiracy to take forcible possession" of the *Khudkasht* and evicted them by obtaining court orders. Besides, in all such cases over the *Sir* and *Khudkasht* the landlords invariably secured injunctions of the courts, prohibiting the tillers from touching the standing crop.[187] The steady regularity with which a large number of cases for dispossession were brought before the civil and revenue courts that it caused eventually a legal pandemonium by the mid-1930s,[188] and attracted some public attention, especially of the Congress Socialist activists. The leftists and the Kisan Sabhaites,

186. Legal Expert to Revenue Secretary, 10 August 1938, Revenue Dept. U.P. Govt. File No. 475/38, U.P. State Archives, Lucknow.
187. Note by V.N. Mehta, Junior Member, Board of Revenue, Banares, U.P. *ibid.*
188. Premier (Pant) to Mehta, Board of Revenue, 7 August 1938, *ibid.*

who spearheaded the over-all Congress campaign for a fresh tenancy legislation in the U.P., also highlighted the urgency for granting some occupational right to the tenants over the *Sir* lands.[189] By the beginning of 1938 — when the newly installed Congress ministry under Govind Ballabh Pant was planning its tenancy legislation — the leftists had already succeeded in bringing the issue of the *Shikmi Kashtkars'* insecurity to the forefront.[190] That the Pant ministry would not be able to disregard the point altogether was apparent to the *Zamindars* and *Taluqdars*, and they lost no time in launching a two-fold ejectment operation to defend the *Sir* — their "birth right" as they saw it.[191] By the middle of 1937 they vastly increased the pace of dislodging the *Shikmi Kashtkars* from the *Sir*, and simultaneously tried to turn as much of the *Rayati* land into the *Sir* or *Khudkasht* as possible by ousting the long-standing small tenants. The conversion of the *Rayati* land into the *Sir* or *Khudkasht* was generally put into effect by fraud, backed up by force. The fraud was practised by tampering records with the help of the village *Patwaris* (revenue assessors) — by preparing a false document in contravention of the *kisan's* hereditary occupational rights, and obtaining his thumb impression on it. As rent receipt was hardly ever issued, it had not been difficult at all to get a decree against the tenant on the ground of non-payment of rent. With a court order in hand, and with the abetment of the local police, the landlords' armed goons went on the rampage to secure ejectment.[192] Although all this seemed somewhat easy to begin with, the landlords soon ran into difficulties when the poor peasants dared to stand up to them under the leadership of the Kisan Sabha. They raised slogans against the malpractices of the landlords and the *Patwaris*, demanded rent receipts and

189. Home Poll. Fortnightly Report for 2nd half of April 1937, File No. 18/4/37, N.A.I.
190. *Sangharsh* (Hindi weekly), 17 January 1938.
191. Nawab Sir Yusuf used the expression in the U.P. Legislative Assembly, see *Sangharsh* (Hindi weekly), 12 December 1938.
192. Dr. Biswanath Mukherji, "Gorakhpur Me Zamindar-Kisan Samvandh", *Sangharsh* (Hindi weekly), 1 January 1939.

obstructed the *Zamindars'* men from occupying their lands.[193] There were reports of social boycott of the *Zamindars* and their agents from certain parts of Unnao and Gorakhpur.[194] On 1 May 1938 about one lakh peasants demonstrated in Fyzabad in front of the Congress minister, Rafi Ahmad Kidwai, protesting against evictions by the *Zamindars* for turning the *Rayati* land into the *Sir*.[195] News of clashes between the *Zamindars* and the tenants were often heard from various parts of the eastern division of the province.[196] The situation rapidly worsened in Gorakhpur where the *Zamindars* were alleged to have engaged "bad characters" to overawe their tenants.[197] The agitation against forcible eviction was fiercest in Maharajganj *tahsil* of Gorakhpur where some tenants actually lost their lives while resisting the *Zamindari* onslaughts.[198] Battle also raged high in Padrauna *tahsil* of Gorakhpur and in Chandauli *tahsil* of Banaras. In Chandauli the *kisan* activists decided to fight even after being discouraged and censored by the District Congress.[199] In all these places *kisans* also faced the usual modes of official repression — assault, arrest and detention. But their struggle under the banner of the Kisan Sabha was not entirely in vain, and the authors of the Tenancy Act of 1939 had to take some of their complaints into account. The Act served the *kisans'* cause by restricting the extent of the *Zamindars' Sir* lands. It stipulated that if a landlord was assessed more than Rs.25 a year as per the local rates, his *Sir* land would cease to remain the *Sir*. It stated further that if the landlord possessed more than 50 acres as the *Sir* and some of it was let out, then the *Sir* land beyond 50 acres would no longer remain the *Sir*.[200] Also, the Act did not provide the landlords with any

193. *Ibid.*
194. Home Poll. Fortnightly Report for 2nd half of January 1938, File No. 18/1/38, N.A.I.
195. *Sangharsh* (Hindi weekly), 6 May 1938.
196. Home Poll. Fortnightly Report for 1st half of May 1938, File No. 18/5/38, N.A.I.
197. *Ibid.*, 2nd half of June 1938, File No. 18/6/38, N.A.I.
198. Statement of Mohanlal Gautam, M.L.A., *Sangharsh* (Hindi weekly), 10 October 1938.
199. *National Front* (English weekly), 2 October 1938.
200. Act XVII of 1939, the United Provinces, Sections relating to the *Sir*.

means to turn the *Rayati* lands into the *Sir*. As regards the tenurial rights of the *Shikmi Kashtkars*, the Congress legislation declared those on lands ceasing to be the *Sir* as hereditary tenants.[201] But the rest of them on lands continuing to be the *Sir* could remain in occupation for five years, following which the landlord might take it over on the ground of his personal use. Thus the *Shikmi Kashtkar* was left exposed by the Act of 1939 to eviction at the interval of every five years.[202] The reason behind the Pant ministry's allowance of such periodical evictions was its loyalty to a powerful section of the traditional rural gentry, whom it preferred to differentiate as "small Zamindars", or those who paid less than Rs. 25 a year as per the local rates, or possessed less than 50 acres of the *Sir*. What was astounding, however, seemed to be the affection that the champions of the *Shikmi Kashtkars* or the leftists showed towards those "small *Zamindars*". The Socialist ideologues sometimes even thought aloud that the *Shikmi Kashtkar* must be given some occupational right, but not by wholly depriving the lawful owner of the *Sir*[203] or that the "small *Zamindars*" "should not come to harm" over the *Sir* question.[204] It was no wonder, therefore, that the tenants-at-will on the *Sir* failed in their struggle to achieve what they justifiably deserved.

Like the agitation over the *Sir* lands in the U.P., the *Bakasht* movement in Bihar was caused by regular eviction of cultivators from the lands of similar classification, and under almost identical situation. As it was in the case of the *Sir*, the landlords exercised direct control over the *Bakasht* which they could give on rent either in cash or in kind, to landless peasants for cultivation. The *Bakasht* was different from the *Zirat* (which was the landlords' own *Khas* land, cultivated through the employment of wage labour or by the sharecroppers as in the *Khudkasht* in the U.P.), as well as from the *rayati* (which was given on rent to tenants having protected right of occupation as in the U.P.), though in the popular understanding of Bihar it had sometimes been mixed up with the *Zirat* in the fashion the *Sir* was confused with the *Khudkasht* in the U.P. Strictly from the legal

201. *Ibid.*, sections 6 and 9.
202. *Sangharsh* (Hindi weekly), 23 May 1938.
203. *Ibid.*, 14 February 1938.
204. *Ibid.*, 23 May 1938.

point of view, however, the *Bakasht* varied from the *Sir* in one important respect, i.e. a short term tenant or a tenant-at-will on the *Bakasht* could obtain some occupational right over his holding which his counterpart was unable to acquire on the *Sir*. The Bengal Tenancy Act of 1885 (which operated in Bihar) had conceded the occupational right to the tenant on the *Bakasht* if he had occupied his holding continuously for 12 years or more. Although this right was hardly ever claimed in practice before the mid-1930s, either because of the blissful ignorance on the part of its claimants, or on account of the landlords' alacrity in shifting tenants at short intervals, the eventual knowledge of its existence greatly encouraged the *Bakasht* cultivators. That they must uphold the legitimacy of their position had, in fact, rendered their movement in Bihar far more powerful and extensive than the *Sir* cultivators' agitation in the U.P.

To the ranks of the periodically evicted, harassed and aggrieved *Bakasht* cultivators were added in the early 1930s a large number of dispossessed *Rayati* tenants, whose lands had also been brought into the category of the *Bakasht*. This happened during the calamitous days of the Depression when a lot of *Rayati* holdings were sold up on account of the tenants' failure to pay rent, and the purchasers — invariably the landlords — turned these into the *Bakasht* mainly to earn more profit through sharecropping, with the additional advantage of not conceding any tenurial right to the cultivators. The former tenants, whether retained as sharecroppers on the lands or ousted altogether from them, deeply resented the loss of their lands, as well as of the status, having been pushed down from the position of occupational tenants to that of tenants-at-will. There was also a feeling among them of being let down as clients by the *Zamindars*, who in their role as patrons, should have aided them in their hour of difficulty by remitting dues, rather than take improper advantage of their distress by bringing in suits for arrears. It was the moral tenor — the strong sense of having altogether been wronged — that convinced the *Bakasht* peasants of the justification for complaint against the *Zamindars*. They had, therefore, little hesitation in taking to the agitational course when some of their leaders gave out a call.

The agitation over the *Bakasht* commenced originally on a low key in June 1936, first in Munghyr (Barahiya Tal) and then in Gaya (Reora and Mahijawan), with a tendency to spread in other districts like Patna, Shahabad and Saran. It was started mainly at the initiative of local leaders like Karyanand Sharma of Munghyr and Jadunandan Sharma of Gaya, and the activities were confined to meetings and demonstrations, highlighting the evicted peasants' grievances. Occasionally the agitators went in deputations to the district authorities and pressed for the restoration of their *Bakasht* tenancies and recognition of their occupational status under the Act of 1885. While the Government officials were content to treat these activities with indifference, the *Zamindars* took a serious exception to them and decided to adopt strong-arm methods against the "recalcitrant" *kisans.* The *kisans* and their leaders could not withstand in 1936 the *Zamindari* offensive, and by the end of the year their movement appeared to have "fizzled out".[205] In actuality, however, the *kisan* agitators halted to find out effective means for counteracting the onslaught of the *Zamindars,* as well as to receive the support and guidance of the Bihar Provincial Kisan Sabha. Although the Bihar Provincial Kisan Sabha was not prompt enough to own up the movement,[206] its President — Swami Sahajanand Saraswati — lost little time in encouraging it or undertaking whirlwind propaganda trips in its favour in the Bihar countryside. His guidance was also decisive in the agitators' adopting the technique of *satyagraha* as an answer to both the *Zamindari* reaction and the official inaction. The *satyagraha* of peasants (usually squatting or sitting indefinitely) was to take place on lands from which they had been ejected, and on which they had raised or likely to raise their crops. The *satyagrahis* or the *kisan* volunteers were asked to conduct themselves peacefully and to remain within the non-violent limits. While offering *satyagraha* in defence of lands and crops, women were given a

205. Agrarian Trouble in Barahiya Tal Area, Monghyr, Govt. of Bihar, Home Poll. Dept. (Special), File No. 42 (111)/1938, cited in Rakesh Gupta, *Bihar Peasantry and the Kisan Sabha, 1936-1947,* New Delhi, 1982, p. 193.

206. Being aware of the pro-landlord stance of the Bihar Congress, and reluctant to risk its hostility, the Bihar Provincial Kisan Sabha did not formally assume the leadership of the *Bakasht* movement till its Conference at Waini in December 1938.

prominent part to play, accompanied by children and old men. The motive was to cause embarrassment to the police and the landlords' men who would be roundly condemned if they used force in removing women, children and the infirm from the scene of *satyagraha.*[207] The *kisans* and their leaders — whether of the pro-Communist variety in Munghyr or of the pro-Socialist type in Gaya — were to desist from upholding false tenurial claims, coining offensive slogans and avoiding troubles with the police.[208] The attitude was clearly one of moral protest of the clients against the misdemeanour of their patrons. Because of their good intentions, however, the peasant protestors had not fully realised at the beginning that the nature of their protestation — whether it would run on the non-violent lines or go berserk — did not really depend upon them. If the landlords decided to crush the impudent lowly people physically, and their *amlas* and *gomastas* (agents) let loose a reign of terror in the villages, with the help of a sympathetic administration and a friendly police, the *kisans* would eventually be left with no alternative but to resort to *lathis* — their only instrument of self-defence — and raise the cry "*Lathi Hamara Zindabad* " (long live our sticks). Even Swami Sahajanand had openly to give consent to "the defensive use of force" against the *Zamindars* and their agents.[209] Thus peace was in no way guaranteed in the Bihar countryside if the *Bakasht* agitation was resumed. And at the same time the *kisans* could not be held back from going ahead with the agitation once the technique of land *satyagraha* was accepted and the sanction of top leaders like Swami Sahajanand obtained.

In 1937 the *Bakasht* agitation flared up once again in Munghyr and Gaya, and then extended towards Patna, Shahabad and Champaran. It was renewed in Barahiya Tal of Munghyr,

207. Although the police and the landlords' men had shown little scruple in using force against women, children and old men, they nevertheless conceded their discomfiture off and on. Home Poll. Fortnightly Report for 2nd half of July 1939, File No. 18/7/39, N.A.I.

208. All this is apparent from a survey of the statements, speeches and writings of the *kisan* leaders involved in the struggle, as well as from the issues of the *Janta* (Hindi weekly ed. by Rambriksh Benipuri) of 1939.

209. Home Poll. Fortnightly Report for 1st half of December 1937, File No. 18/12/37, N.A.I.

following a *kisan* conference at Sheikhpura on 27 and 28 February. The conference generated some tension in the area, and the *kisans* in about a dozen villages opposed their landlords, who were known to be "particularly oppressive".[210] The landlords, on their part, complained to the local authorities of the removal of crops from the *Bakasht* lands by the troublesome cultivators. The unrest in Barahiya Tal soon led to the arrest of Karyanand Sharma and his 19 associates, and to their detention till June 1937. Instead of restraining the agitation, however, the arrests inflamed it further, and resulted in stubborn, continuous *satyagraha* in the villages, and to — what the landlords termed as — the widespread "looting" of crops (which really meant the ejected peasants' refusal to part with their crops).[211] The situation was deteriorating so fast that the alarmed Congressmen in Bihar, who were all set for forming a provincial ministry under the Act of 1935, decided to intervene. Their intervention was prompted partly by a desire to defend the interests of the Bhumihar Brahmin landlords — the long-standing supporters of the Congress,[212] and partly by an anxiety for demonstrating the willingness to stand by the *kisan* underdogs, in accordance with the Faizpur Agrarian Programme.

At the political conference held at Jammui in the middle of March 1937, where the chairman of the reception committee (Kalika Prasad Singh, M.L.A.) roundly condemned the "looting" of crops, a small body was formed to enquire into the Barahiya Tal agitation and bring about some settlement between the *Zamindars* and the *kisans*. The Congress-appointed enquiry committee, headed by Babu Rajendra Prasad, devised shortly a compromise formula (known as the Prasad Award) on the principle that the position prevailing before 1936 — the year the agitation broke out — should again be reverted to the satisfaction of both the parties.[213] The implication was that the *Rayati* lands made *Bakasht* after 1935 were to be rescinded and restored to their cultivators, and that there should not be any further attempt

210. *Ibid.*, 1st half of March 1937, File No. 18/3/37, N.A.I.
211. *Ibid.*, 1st half of April 1937, File No. 18/4/37, N.A.I.
212. *Ibid.*, 1st half of March 1937, File No. 18/3/37, N.A.I.
213. Rakesh Gupta, *Bihar Peasantry and the Kisan Sabha, 1936-1947*, New Delhi, 1982, pp. 133-4.

at turning the *Rayati* into the *Bakasht* in future. Simultaneously, the Prasad Award upheld the *Zamindars'* right to select the plot to be given to a cultivator, as well as to determine the terms under which it could be given. Consequently, the *Zamindari* practices of not keeping a cultivator for long at one plot, and not issuing him a rent receipt — so as to prevent him from acquiring any occupational right — were unequivocally endorsed. Although the Award raised some hopes of reinstatement for those who lost their *Rayati* lands recently, it neither protected the bulk of the *Bakasht* peasants from periodical evictions, nor offered them any prospect of acquiring occupational rights in the future. Despite their misgivings, the *kisan* protestors were nevertheless willing to give the Award a fair trial, and their spokesmen came before the arbitration committees which were set up on its recommendation. It was, however, the *Zamindars* in the Tal area who made a mockery of the Award and torpedoed the settlements which were negotiated, and sometimes achieved. Reluctant to return to the position of 1935, some landlords like Badri Narayan Sinha flatly refused to abide by the Award. Others, who were persuaded to come to some agreements, looked for pretexts to break them as early as the ensuing cultivating season of 1937-8. Even a visit by the Bihar Congress Premier, Shri Krishna Sinha, to the area did not eventually bear any fruit.[214] By the summer of 1938 the *Zamindars* and the *kisans* turned back to their original position confronting each other, primarily because of the Provincial Congress's failure to bring its *Zamindari* following around.

Meanwhile the agitation continued to disturb certain parts of Gaya and Patna. The peasants' protest in Jehanabad sub-division of Gaya led in April 1937 to the raiding by the landlords' men into their villages, the raping of their women and the burning down of their huts. In retaliation, the *kisans* also hit back, and waylaid and killed a *Zamindar*.[215] Attacks on the *kisans* and acts of reprisal by them also affected peace in Patna where a

214. Home Poll. Fortnightly Report for 1st half of November 1937, File No. 18/11/37, N.A.I.

215. *Ibid.*, 2nd half of April 1937, File No. 18/4/37, N.A.I.

Patwari lost his life in a scuffle.[216] At Soubhadra village in Gaya took place a serious clash in July 1937 when the agitating cultivators were faced with the *Zamindars'* gun-totting *amlas.*[217] Towards the end of 1937 the physical clashes between the *kisans* and *Zamindars'* hirelings became more frequent in both Gaya and Patna. The storm-centre in Patna was Barh sub-division, and in Gaya the Arwal area — where the pitch of the agitation turned so intense (especially at Kudrasi village) that a Special Magistrate had to be sent there along with a party of Gurkha Military Police.[218] Barahiya Tal in Munghyr once again blazed up, and the peasants in some parts of Shahabad, Champaran and Saran were also reported to be joining the fray.

In the following year in 1938 the *Bakasht* movement in Bihar attained its increasingly high stature. The Barahiya Tal area, Sheikhpura and Lakhisarai in Munghyr; Arwal, Reora, Masuda and Dumaria in Gaya; Sasaram, Muriar and Babna in Shahabad; Pandoul, Dekuli and Raghopur in Darbhanga; Chandi, Paijna and Masaurhi in Patna; Tirhut, more particularly Ramnagar estate, in Champaran; Lalganj and Mahua in Muzaffarpur and Ambari in Chhapra were some of the important venues of the agitation with a number of secondary sites scattered over other districts.[219] Picketing in the landlords' threshing floors and *satyagraha* on the *Bakasht* lands started at Arwal in Gaya as early as January 1938.[220] It assumed a formidable proportion by the summer of 1938 under the leadership of Jadunandan Sharma, and at the instance of local leaders like Sheo Shankar Bharati and Malaya

216. *Ibid.*
217. *Ibid.*, 2nd half of July 1937, File No. 18/7/37, N.A.I.
218. *Ibid.*, 1st and 2nd halves of December 1937, File No. 18/12/37, N.A.I.
219. Apart from Rakesh Gupta, *Bihar Peasantry and the Kisan Sabha, 1936-1947*, New Delhi, 1982, which deals essentially with Munghyr, and Stephen Henningham, *Peasant Movements in Colonial India, North Bihar, 1917-1942*, Australian National University, 1982, which examines exclusively the happenings in Darbhanga, detailed studies have not yet been made of the *Bakasht* movement in other important areas, including Shahabad. The historians' neglect of south Bihar, especially of Gaya — the most convulsive of all the places — is particularly surprising.
220. Home Poll. Fortnightly Report for 2nd half of January 1938, File No. 18/1/38, N.A.I.

Krishna Brahmachari.[221] Agitation at Sheikhpura and in Barahiya Tal of Munghyr was renewed when the *rabi* (winter) crop came up for harvesting in March 1938. In October 1938 commenced a *satyagraha* there, and its reverberations were felt at Bakribazar and in Begusarai.[222] In June 1938 the *Bakasht* peasants were reported to have refused to hand over their lands in Tirhut of Champaran, and revealed a hostile demeanour against Ramnagar estate.[223] Similar information about the peasants' resistance was received from Sasaram in Shahabad.[224] An agitation also broke out at Reorah of Gaya in October 1938 with the threat of a widespread *satyagraha*. The *satyagraha* eventually started there on 22 December 1938 and resulted in the arrest of Jadunandan Sharma and his three associates.[225]

The agitation in 1938, as it was — to a certain extent — in 1937, could not remain peaceful in the face of the unbridled use of force by the *Zamindars*. The *kisan* resisters were encouraged by their leaders to organise village defence parties and arrange for some "alarm system" as a precaution against sudden onslaughts by the *Zamindars'* retainers.[226] They were also advised to take recourse to what Swami Sahajanand had described as "*Kushti-Koshta, Patki-Patka*" (wrestling or the use of force).[227] Consequently, the use of force started playing an important role on the agrarian scene, and the magnitude of violence considerably increased. A serious clash, for example, took place over the *Bakasht* lands between the *kisans* and the *Zamindars'* men on 18 February 1938 at Kesrai village near Daudnagar of Gaya, resulting in some deaths.[228] A number of "minor riotings"

221. *Ibid.*, 2nd half of May 1938, File No. 18/5/38, N.A.I.
222. *Ibid.*, 2nd half of October 1938, File No. 18/10/38, N.A.I.
223. *Ibid.*, 2nd half of June 1938, File No. 18/6/38, N.A.I.
224. *Ibid.*, 2nd half of July 1938, File No. 18/7/38, N.A.I.
225. *Ibid.*, 2nd half of December 1938, File No. 18/12/38, N.A.I.
226. Speeches of Swami Sahajanand, *ibid.*, 2nd half of May 1938, File No. 18/5/37, N.A.I.
227. Swami Sahajanand's speech in Deo, Gaya, 11 November 1938, *ibid.*, 1st half of November 1938, File No. 18/11/38, N.A.I.
228. *Ibid.*, 2nd half of February 1938, File No. 18/2/38, N.A.I.

were reported from Champaran,[229] Patna and Munghyr.[230] Disturbances were also reported to have taken place in Sasaram, and violence flared up in Gaya on 4 July 1938 when a confrontation between the *kisans* and the *Zamindars' amlas* at Masaurah village, Nawdah police station, left one dead and several seriously injured.[231] The district authorities noted in October 1938 four cases of agrarian riots in Muzaffarpur over the *Bakasht* lands.[232] A riotous situation developed in Munghyr on 19 November 1938 when the landlords' party attacked a *kisan* procession in Barahiya Tal.[233] Clearly the circumstance had undergone a drastic change, and the righteous indignation the *Bakasht* peasants felt in 1936 over their landlords' misdeeds was turning in 1938 into a fierce defence of lands and crops. In the heat that the encounters generated, the *kisans* and their leaders also could not continue any longer with their uncertain confidence in the pro-landlord provincial Congress leadership. In the latter half of 1938 in fact the growing estrangement of relations between the Kisan Sabha and the Congress came into the open.

The Bihar Provincial Congress Committee, who had been urged as early as February 1937 by the influential High Command members "to prevent the continuous mischief that the Swami [Sahajanand] was doing",[234] came into conflict with the leftists and the Kisan Sabhaites at the time of the provincial elections, and over the issue of aligning with the *Zamindars*. Later, Swami Sahajanand's removal from the All India Congress Committee without giving him any chance to explain his position, and the directive early in 1938 prohibiting the Congress members from addressing the Kisan Sabha meetings,[235] further widened the rift. In 1938 the Provincial Congress created a special Kisan Branch to counteract the influence of the Kisan Sabha in the countryside,

229. *Ibid.*, 1st half of June 1938, File No. 18/6/38, N.A.I.
230. *Ibid.*, 2nd half of June 1938.
231. *Ibid.*, 2nd half of October 1938, File No. 18/10/38, N.A.I.
232. *Ibid.*
233. *Ibid.*, 1st half of December 1938, File No. 18/12/38, N.A.I.
234. Patel to Prasad, 12 February 1937, File no. 11/37, Rajendra Prasad Papers, N.A.I.
235. *Sangharsh* (Hindi weekly), 17 January 1938.

and to mediate between the landlords and the *kisans* for settling agrarian disputes.[236] Such one-sided conciliatory moves at the height of the agitation over the *Bakasht*, and that, too, without any open criticism of the conduct of the *Zamindars*, damaged the Congress-Kisan Sabha relations beyond repair. The attempt of Congressmen like Bepin Bihari Verma and Narayanji at an intervention in the disputes in Gaya in June 1938,[237] and the strong reactions they evoked among the *kisans*, was a notable example. Still the Congress persisted with its plan of "neutralising" the Kisan Sabha through "accords" between the landlords and the peasants,[238] and the Kisan Sabha consequently hardened its attitude and started talking in terms of "opposing the Congress-*Zamindar* alliance". Both the *kisans* and their leaders already had, as mentioned earlier, some misgivings about the pro-landlord nature of the Prasad Award of mid-1937. Early in 1938 they publicly accused the Bihar Congress ministers of collaborating with the *Zamindars* by flouting the interests of the cultivators.[239] Apparently the leftist accusation was not unfounded, for the Congress in Bihar in fact had entered into an understanding with the *Zamindars* in December 1937,[240] and committed its ministry to the task of dealing with the *Bakasht* agitation on the lines of the Congress-*Zamindar* agreement. The outcome of all this was the introduction of the *Bakasht* Restoration Bill in 1938 in the Bihar provincial legislature and its eventual passage as an Act. As expected, especially in the light of the Prasad Award, the enactment piously proposed to return to their original tenants those *Bakasht* lands which had been sold up between 1929 and 1936. But it would be done only if the original tenants paid to the landlords within a period of five

236. Poll. and Special Dept. Govt. of Bihar, Fortnightly Report for 1st half of February 1938, Bihar State Archives, Patna.
237. Home Poll. Fortnightly Report for 2nd half of June 1938, File No. 18/6/38, N.A.I.
238. *Ibid.*, 2nd half of July 1938, File No. 18/7/38, N.A.I.
239. A Report on the Provincial Kisan Conference, Baichwara, 22-23 January 1938, *ibid.*, 2nd half of January 1938, File No. 18/1/38, N.A.I.
240. The Congress-*Zamindars* Agreement was signed in private on 13 December 1937, following prolonged negotiations, and the personal intervention of Patel. *The Congress Socialist* (English weekly), 22 January 1938.

years half the auction price of the holding, as well as the legal costs. Besides, the Act refused to touch at all (a) those *Bakasht* lands which had been brought under direct cultivating control of "petty" *Zamindars* whose annual income fell short of Rs. 5,000 and (b) those which had already been given away by the landlords to other "new" tenants. It was found soon after the legislation that the landlords had often succeeded in showing substantial portions of their *Bakasht* lands as already "settled" with the new tenants, or under the control of their own persons whom they disguised as "petty" *Zamindars*. To make matters difficult, the *kisans* were not in a position to pay half the auction price of their *Bakasht* lands, and could not afford even to manage paying the legal costs. What was worse, they had little documentary evidence in their possession to prove that specific plots remained under their occupation at the time of auction. Documentation was entirely the preserve of the landlords, who, as it was the case in the U.P., manipulated the records with the help of the *Patwaris*. The Congress ministry's measure, therefore, was ineffectual in restoring the *Bakasht* lands to their original tenants. Designed primarily to help the *Zamindari* circumvention, it was also not meant to be so. Thus the Kisan Sabha was right in saying that the Congress ministry sacrificed "the vital interests of the *kisans* in order to placate the *Zamindars*",[241] or in encouraging demonstrations at various places to criticise the ministry.[242] Far from bringing down the *kisan* temper, the Bihar Congress ministry's piece of legislation inflamed it further and led in 1939 to outbursts of hostility not only between the *kisans* and the *Zamindars* — a vigorous renewal of the old feud — but also between the Kisan Sabha and the all powerful Government under the Congress — an engagement in a new contest of obvious unequals.

The *Bakasht* agitation in Bihar reached its peak during the first half of 1939, between the months of January and August. Apart from continuing with their stubborn resistance against ejectments in Barahiya Tal in Munghyr and at Reorah in Gaya, the peasants

241. Home Poll. Fortnightly Report for 2nd half of April 1938, File No. 18/4/38, N.A.I.
242. *Ibid.*, 1st half of October 1938, File No. 18/10/38.

in 1939 also extended their movement to Amwari in Saran; Dumoria, Mahijawan and Masuda in Gaya; Lagar in Munghyr; Muriar, Betri and Bargaon in Shahabad; Ghosrawan in Patna, and Deokli and Raghopur in Darbhanga. The *satyagraha* in Barahiya Tal was organised by Karyanand Sharma and his associates (like Panchanand Sharma and Anil Mitra) through largely attended *kisan* meetings (such as the ones held at Repura and Maharam Chak) and some training imparted to the would be *satyagrahis* at Lakhisarai. The *satyagraha* began in April 1939 and continued till a climax was reached at the beginning of May — on the days fixed for a massive *kisan* demonstration in Munghyr town. Fearing some disturbance, the district authorities decided to prevent the peasants from pouring into the town, and arrested a number of their leaders, including Karyanand Sharma. Eventually the agitating peasants were persuaded to return to their villages on the promise that the authorities would look into their grievances sympathetically. The promise was hardly kept by the district officials, except that they prevailed upon the Arbitration Committee to expeditiously give its findings on the disputes. The findings ran on the familiar lines of the Prasad Award, conceding occupancy rights to the *Bakasht* cultivators only in 800 *bighas* out of a disputed 14,000 *bighas*.[243] It was a meagre outcome, indeed, but howsoever much the *kisans* disliked it, and resented the pro-landlord stance of the Arbitration Committee, they could do precious little while most of their leaders and activists were in jail, and when the officials were pre-determined to uphold the decisions of the Committee. Thus the Barahiya Tal agitation had to be suspended on 6 May 1939, for the time being of course, on a clear note of despondency. Such, however, was not the case at Reorah where the *satyagraha* forced the District Collector to intervene in the disputes personally, and not through the setting up of an Arbitration Committee. Following investigations, he decided to allot four-fifths of the disputed lands to the tenants, allowing the *Zamindars* to retain only one-fifth.[244] The *kisan* gains amounted

243. Rakesh Gupta, *Bihar Peasantry and the Kisan Sabha, 1936-1947*, New Delhi, 1982, p. 220.
244. Home Poll. Fortnightly Report for 1st half of February 1939, File No. 18/2/39, N.A.I.

to about 1,000 *bighas* and the *Zamindars* got approximately 200 *bighas*. Besides, the district authorities also agreed to release all those who were arrested at Reorah, including Jadunandan Sharma.[245]

The intensity of the struggle in Barahiya Tal and the success of the Reorah peasants, in terms of concrete gains, greatly encouraged cultivators in other parts. Reorah also showed the *kisans* the way to, and the necessity for, seizing the standing crops on the disputed *Bakasht* lands. So far the *kisan satyagraha* was offered mainly to prevent the *Zamindars* from occupying their lands, or taking away the crops. The agitators usually left the crops on the fields, and even when — on very rare occasions — they harvested, the crops were kept at a common yard with a view to settling the landlords' accounts, and not carried away to their homes. When Jadunandan Sharma asked the peasants during the Reorah *satyagraha* about the state of the standing crops, the *kisans* replied that these were getting wasted on the fields. Sharma promptly advised them to harvest the crops for their own consumption, rather than leaving these for rats and pigs. "Satisfy your hunger first" was the slogan he raised, and the *kisans* responded by cutting the crops and carrying these to their homes.[246] The *Zamindars* and the police raised a hue and cry over such "looting" of crops, but were unable in practice to stop it. The seizure of crops in fact became hereafter the chief feature of the *Bakasht* movement throughout 1939, signifying the rising tide of *kisan* militancy in Bihar.

Following the example of Reorah, Gaya, a *satyagraha* commenced in January 1939 at Muriar (Sasaram sub-division), Shahabad, by defying all prohibitory orders of the local authorities.[247] The *kisans* of Amwari in Saran, under the leadership of Rahul Sankrityayana, organised their *satyagraha* in February 1939.[248] It was continued without a break, despite the arrest and conviction of Rahul, till July 1939 when negotiations started with

245. *National Front* (English weekly), 14 May 1939.
246. *Ibid.*
247. Home Poll. Fortnightly Reports for 1st and 2nd halves of January 1939, File No. 18/1/39, N.A.I.
248. *Ibid.*, 2nd half of February 1939, File No. 18/2/39, N.A.I.

the *Zamindars.*[249] The *kisans* of Deokli and Raghopur in Darbhanga resorted to *satyagraha* in March 1939 following the *Zamindar's* refusal to accept any arbitration.[250] The local leader, Jamuna Karji, was arrested along with Surya Kanta Singh and Uma Kanta Missir in connection with the struggle and sentenced to eight months' imprisonment. Two months later, *satyagraha* began at Masuda, Mahijawan and Majhwa in Gaya on a fairly large scale. About 100 persons were arrested at Mahijawan, including the local organiser, Sheo Shankar Bharati. At Majhwa the number of arrested persons rose to 35.[251] The *satyagraha* struggle became intense about this time at Lagar, Gogri *thana* in Munghyr, where a number of local *kisan* activists were detained.[252] The *kisans* of Ghorasan in Patna launched their *satyagraha* on 28 July, spearheaded by a band of 24 women.[253] In Gaya the *kisans* of Dumaria followed the examples of Masuda and Mahijawan — the two places where 22 and 50 persons, respectively, were arrested in August 1939.[254] In Shahabad the *Bakasht* cultivators adopted the *satyagraha* model of Muriar at Betri on 14 July 1939. The pattern of Betri was soon taken up at Bargaon of the same district — where about 80 arrests were made in the month of August.[255] In August again, the *kisans* of Pandoul in Darbhanga staged a *satyagraha* against the ejectments carried out by the Darbhangaraj, and about 70 persons were taken into custody there in the first 20 days of the agitation.[256]

Not only the pitch of the agitation was the highest in 1939, the number of violent incidents during the year also became the largest — far exceeding the occurrences of 1937 and 1938. The extent of violence should be apparent if some incidents are

249. *Ibid.*, 1st half of July 1939, File No. 18/7/39, N.A.I.
250. *Ibid.*, 1st half of March 1939, File No. 18/3/39, N.A.I. At Raghopur the *kisans* secured through arbitration some of the disputed lands in August 1939.
251. *Ibid.*, 2nd half of July 1939, File No. 18/7/39, N.A.I.
252. *Ibid.*, 1st half of July 1939.
253. *Ibid.*, 1st half of August 1939, File No. 18/8/39, N.A.I.
254. *Ibid.*
255. *Ibid.*, 2nd half of August 1939.
256. Stephen Henningham, *Peasant Movements in Colonial India, North Bihar, 1917-1942*, Canberra, 1982, p. 162 and *National Front* (English weekly), 13 August 1939.

cited as specimens. In February 1939 an attempt at forcible crop cutting led at Amwari in Shahabad to an armed clash between the *Zamindars* and *kisans.*[257] On 12 March the *Zamindars'* party attacked a *kisan* meeting in Gahlaur, Sikandra *thana* in Munghyr and seriously injured a *kisan* activist. Almost under similar circumstance, and about the same time, the *Zamindars'* men and the cultivators fought with arms at Suara, Nokha *thana* in Shahabad.[258] Approximately 100 *kisans* with *lathis* confronted in April 1939 the police and the *Zamindars* in Barahiya Tal, Munghyr, to prevent the threshing operations. In the same month took place the looting of the *Zamindars' cutcherries* in a number of places in Gaya and Darbhanga.[259] Early in May 1939 about 100 tenants with *lathis* stormed a *Zamindar's cutcherry* at Rani Pakri in Champaran, and the landlord's establishment survived only at the armed intervention of the police led by the Sub-Divisional Officer.[260] There were armed conflicts in July 1939 between the landlords and the tenants at Warsaliganj and Obra (Aurangabad) in Gaya, and riots at Sikaria and Darigaon (Sasaram) in Shahabad.[261] Innumerable such skirmishes were reported from various places in Darbhanga.[262] There were instances of violence on the same line during July 1939 at Masuda, Bhalua, Aganda and Mahijawan in Gaya; Warisnagar in Darbhanga and Chak Yusuf in Munghyr.[263] In the first half of August the landlords' *amlas* used fire-arms to kill two *rayats* at Leukaha, Tirhut, following a serious clash.[264] On 8th of the same month a pro-landlord *tahsildar* was murdered by the tenants in Mohama, Shahabad district.[265] Not only the pro-landlord *tahsildars*, but also the loyal and the "new" tenants had to face the wrath of the agitated *kisans.* At Hasua in Gaya, for example, a riot broke out

257. Home Poll. Fortnightly Report for 2nd half of February 1939, File No. 18/2/39, N.A.I.
258. *Ibid.*, 1st half of March 1939, File No. 18/3/39, N.A.I
259. *Ibid.*, 2nd half of April 1939, File No. 18/4/39, N.A.I.
260. *Ibid.*, 1st half of May 1939, File No. 18/5/39, N.A.I.
261. *Ibid.*, 1st half of July 1939, File No. 18/7/39, N.A.I.
262. *Ibid.*
263. *Ibid.*, 2nd half of July 1939.
264. *Ibid.*, 1st half of August 1939, File No. 18/8/39, N.A.I.
265. *Ibid.*, 2nd half of August 1939.

in July 1939 between the "new" and the "old" tenants, and a "new" tenant lost his life in a fracas at Pakribarwan in the same district.[266]

Once the *kisans'* fight against the landlords started turning into a confrontation with the Congress ministry, the authorities went all-out to counter the *Bakasht* movement. Committing itself to the protection of the *Zamindari* interest in private, and consequently snapping all its links with the Kisan Sabhaites in public, the ministry decided upon a policy of carrot and stick for dealing with the agitators. The carrot was dangled through the appointment of arbitration committees, the mediation of the district officials and the actual grant of concessions on occasions — both nominally (as it was in Barahiya Tal) and substantially (as it was at Reorah). It was, however, the use of the stick that the Government heavily relied upon. Apart from deploying a large number of policemen, the authorities often sent Mounted Military Police and Armed Reserve Police to most centres of agitation. Sometimes the Gurkha soldiers were brought into the troubled areas for breaking up stubborn resistance.[267] There were indiscriminate arrests of the *kisan satyagrahis*, and several hundreds of them were behind the bars by May 1939.[268] By September 1939 the number of detained persons increased to about 600.[269] Many of those arrested were tried on criminal charges and convicted. Even those who could not be framed were also detained and treated as ordinary criminals. Demanding the status of political prisoners (which, indeed, was their true position), four *kisan* leaders (Rambriksha Brahmachari, Shri Jagannathji, Karyanand Sharma and Anil Mitra) undertook lengthy hunger strikes in jails. Although violence erupted off and on, mainly under the *Zamindari* provocations, the *Bakasht* agitators never even dreamt of waging armed struggle of any kind. Mentally, they were not inclined as a rule to go beyond the limits of land *satyagraha*. Consequently, the police and the

266. *Ibid.*, 1st half of July 1939, File No. 18/7/39, N.A.I.
267. *National Front* (English weekly), 14 May 1939.
268. *Ibid.*
269. Stephen Henningham, *Peasant Movement in Colonial India, North Bihar, 1917-1942*, Canberra, 1982, p.163.

military did not face much difficulty in breaking their defences or steamrolling their opposition. The Congress ministry's attempts at blending doses of concession with tons of coercion seemed to have had their desired effect. In mid-September in fact the Government was relieved to note that the campaign had "become much less pronounced".[270] With the outbreak of the second world war, the stress on internal security and the introduction of a more authoritarian style of governance, following the resignation of the Congress ministry in October, the agitation over the *Bakasht* lands in Bihar reached practically a moribund stage by the end of 1939.

Howsoever delirious, long-lasting and glorifying, the *Bakasht* agitation in Bihar remained on the whole an exclusive struggle of the dispossessed short-term tenants or tenants-at-will. Their demands scarcely went beyond the restoration of lost tenancies or the regularisation of fragile tenures. As a result, despite a clear expression of over-all rural sympathy for their cause, they failed to involve various other agrarian categories in their movement. They might have been able to extend it far and wide had their leaders chosen to resist simultaneously such *Zamindari* excesses as the negation of the villager's rights over forests, lakes and pastoral lands, or the extraction of *begar* (forced labour) and illegal *abwabs*[271] which adversely affected almost all sections of village society. Some of the leaders of the *Bakasht* movement tried to rally their followers, to begin with, on the common ground of opposition against the *Zamindari* oppressions. A pro-Communist Karyanand Sharma, for example, organised a demonstration in Barahiya Tal against the enforcement of *begari* by the *Zamindars*, and presented on 6 April 1936 to the Collector of Munghyr a memorial signed by a thousand *kisans*.[272] Such activities, which could have been

270. *Ibid.*.
271. Bihar Provincial Kisan Sabha listed innumerable kinds of illegal actions by the *Zamindars* and the tortures they practised on the entire village community in the various districts of Bihar. See for details, Awadheshwar Prasad, Sinha, *Kisan Sabha Aur Kashtkari Kanoon Samsodhan* (Hindi), 1935.
272. Rakesh Gupta, *Bihar Peasantry and the Kisan Sabha, 1936-1947*, New Delhi, 1982, p. 192.

pursued more energetically, were, however, relegated to the background once the excitement overtook the *Bakasht* agitation. It was particularly unfortunate at a time when the resistance against the *Zamindari* excesses was growing in certain other parts of the country, of which the Bihar leaders could not have altogether been ignorant.

SCENE IV

Against Landlords

The excesses the landlords committed on rural society, over and above the extraction of their rental due, or the crude manifestations of their social exploitation in the countryside, were by no means confined to the *Zamindari* or *Taluqdari* regions. These were practised, almost in equal proportions, by those magnates and intermediaries in most other parts of the country who had grabbed in course of time vast tracts of land through legal and illegal means, and rented them out to tenants of all sorts. Although they differed in their nomenclatures, and to an extent in jurisdictions, the *Jenmis*, the *Mirasdars*, the *Deshmukhs* and the *Deshpandes*, the *Khotedars*, the *Istimrardars*, the *Jagirdars*, the *Malguzars*, the *Biswedars* and the like identically subjected the rest of the village populace to their persistent demand for *begar*, enhanced rent and illegal levy, and claimed proprietary right over community lands, lakes and forests. Though the poorer, and consequently, more vulnerable sections groaned endlessly under the feudal pressures, no category of cultivators escaped the stranglehold — not even the richest among the substantial ones. Whenever, therefore, an attempt was made to resist the feudal oppressions, there emerged the possibility of a joint front of the *kisans* of various stratas. Being aware of this advantage, and committed ideologically to the abolition of landlordism, the leftists and the Kisan Sabhaites did try sometimes to build up anti-feudal campaigns. One such campaign seemed feasible, with the prospect of a countrywide dimension, on the issue of the enhancement of rent by the landlords.

The point was taken up in Bengal where a "no-rent" agitation at Memari in Burdwan, and an opposition to rack-renting in Contai and Tamluk sub-divisions of Midnapore took place towards the end of 1937.[273] Similar resistance against the

273. Home Poll. Fortnightly Reports for 2nd half of November and 2nd half of December 1937, File Nos. 18/11/37 and 18/12/37, N.A.I.

enhancement of rent developed in Noakhali in December 1938[274] and at Daspur in Midnapore in February 1939, and in the following month in Arambagh of Hooghly, as well as in some parts of Dinajpur, Malda and Rajsahi.[275] But none of these really took off the ground, and — apart from generating "a no-rent mentality"[276] — these had not grown into a movement affecting other parts of the province. The outcome was not very different in two other provinces of eastern India, namely, Assam and Orissa. In Assam the Surma Valley Kisan Sabha spearheaded a "no-rent" campaign in north Sylhet at the beginning of 1938.[277] It assumed serious proportions in Bhatipara *Zamindari* by the end of the year, necessitating the deployment of armed police there.[278] The Bhatipara *kisans* continued their battle throughout the first half of 1939 under the leadership, among others, of Karuna Sindhu Roy — the lone Communist member in the Assam legislature — and faced repressive acts of the *Zamindar* and the Government, including 26 arrests by the police.[279] By the latter half of 1939, however, the agitation gradually petered away, without much reverberation in the rest of Sylhet or in the neighbouring areas.

In Orissa a vociferous "no-rent" agitation started in the middle of 1937 in Kanika estate of Balasore,[280] and at the beginning of 1938 in the estates of Khallikote and Attagada of Ganjam, under the leadership of the Congress Socialists.[281] The high rent demands were also opposed by the tenants in Chousathipara and Sukinda estates of Cuttack in the latter half of the year.[282]

274. Special Branch note on Bengal Provincial Kisan Sabha, 3.7.89, File No. 333/39 Conf. Home Poll. Govt. of Bengal, 1939, West Bengal State Archives, Calcutta.
275. Home Poll. Fortnightly Report for 2nd half of March 1939, File No. 18/3/39, N.A.I.
276. *A Brief Summary of Political Events in Bengal During the Year 1938*, Home Dept. Govt. of Bengal, Calcutta, 1939.
277. Home Poll. Fortnightly Reports for 2nd half of March and 1st half of April 1938, File Nos. 18/3/38 and 18/4/38, N.A.I.
278. *Ibid.*, 1st half of December 1938, File No. 18/12/38, N.A.I.
279. *Ibid.*, 2nd half of April 1939, File No. 18/4/39, N.A.I.
280. *Ibid.*, 1st half of July 1937, File No. 18/7/37, N.A.I.
281. *Ibid.*, 2nd half of January and February and 2nd half of June 1938, File Nos. 18/1/38, 18/2/38, and 18/6/38, N.A.I.
282. *Ibid.*, 1st half of November 1938, File No. 18/11/38, N.A.I.

But the more serious incident in Orissa took place in the first quarter of 1939 when 5,000 Munda Lutheran Christian *kisans* in the Bolangir area stubbornly resisted the sudden and sharp rent increase by the Gangpur princely state. Led by one Nathaniel Munda, and apparently without any direct involvement of the leftists, the tribal *kisans* confronted the state and the Government officials on 24 April 1939 and faced the indiscriminate police firings, resulting in numerous deaths and injuries. The agitation was thereafter quelled as much with the help of the local Lutheran Church as by the unleashing of the forces of repression.[283] The "no-rent" temper was not much in evidence in northern and central parts of India, barring some instances in Ajmer-Merwara and Patiala. Plagued by the high rentals, the tenants in most of the estates of Ajmer-Merwara refused at the beginning of 1939 to pay their customary dues.[284] Almost on the same lines, the *kisans* of the *Biswedari* villages in Patiala state agitated against the high crop rental demands of the landlords throughout 1939 and forced the Maharaja to appoint an Enquiry Committee to go into the complaints of over-assessment.[285] Although the peasants' resentment against the *Khotedars* and the *Khoti* system was mounting all the time,[286] there was little organised resistance in Maharashtra against the landlord's exorbitant demands for rent. The only exception seemed to be the case of Kolaba district where B.R. Ambedkar's Independent Labour Party gave in December 1938 a call to the tenants in a number of villages to stop paying high rent to the landlords.[287] The Kisan Sabhaites in Gujarat were also too preoccupied with a "no-tax" contest between the substantial cultivators and the state

283. Biswamoy Pati, *Resisting Domination: Peasants Tribals and the National Movement in Orissa, 1920-50*, New Delhi, 1993, pp.126-128.
284. *Ibid.*, 2nd half of February 1939, File No. 18/2/39, N.A.I.
285. Mridula Mukherjee, "Communists and Peasants in Punjab : A Focus on the Muzara Movement in Patiala, 1937-53" in *The Indian Left : Critical Appraisals*, Bipan Chandra (ed.), New Delhi, 1983, pp. 402-4.
286. Home Poll. Fortnightly Reports for 2nd half of November 1937, 2nd half of June 1938 and 2nd half of January 1939, File Nos. 18/11/37, 18/6/38 and 18/1/39, N.A.I.
287. *Ibid.*, 2nd half of December 1938, File No. 18/12/38, N.A.I.

authorities in Manasa,[288] and with the remission of revenue in the drought affected parts,[289] to take up the tenants' grievance over rent for a showdown with the landlords. Only in Surat in the latter half of 1938 did they organise a *kisan* agitation, demanding reduction of rent, and witholding its payment.[290] Unlike western India, the situation in the southern parts of the country seemed to be somewhat different, especially in the Malabar region.

The lease-holders or the tenants of all sorts in Malabar and in Kasargad *taluk* of South Kanara district were subjected for long to the excessive charge of rentals by the landlords, or the *Jenmis* — the original *Rayatwari Pattadars* (holders of a legal tenure)— who had acquired large amounts of lands through various questionable means. Under the leadership of the Congress Socialists, most of whom subsequently turned Communists, the local Kisan Sabha or the Malabar Karshak Sangham prepared for an anti-*Jenmi* agitation since its inception. By 1938 the agitation gathered considerable momentum in Chirakkal, Kottayam, Kurumbranad, Wallurvanad, Ponnani, Wynaad and Kasargad *taluks* through the activities of the peasant volunteers, the village-level propaganda work and the social boycott of the *Jenmis,* and culminated into a full-fledged "no-rent" campaign.[291] When the *Jenmis* tried to attach the property of the non-paying tenants, the *kisans* put up stiff resistance[292] and even clashed with the police.[293] The rent collection by the *Jenmis* being paralysed, the authorities feared heavy loss of revenue[294] and retaliated by prosecuting a large number of agitators, reinforcing the local

288. *Ibid.*, 1st half of April 1938, File No. 18/4/38, N.A.I.
289. *Ibid.*, 2nd half of February 1939, File No. 18/2/39, N.A.I.
290. *Ibid.*, 2nd half of October, 2nd half of November and 1st half of December 1938, File No(s) 18/10 to 18/12/39, N.A.I.
291. "Activities of the Communist Party among the Peasants in Malabar" Central Intelligence Bureau Report of 30.4.41, Home Poll. File No. 7/9/4 Poll. (1) of 1941, N.A.I.
292. Home Poll. Fortnightly Report for 2nd half of October 1938, File No. 18/10/38, N.A.I.
293. "Activities of the Communist Party among the Peasants in Malabar", Central Intelligence Bureau Report of 30.4.41, Home Poll. File No. 7/9/4 Poll. (1) 1941, N.A.I.
294. Home Poll. Fortnightly Report for 1st half of November 1938, File No. 18/11/38, N.A.I.

police and setting up additional police stations.[295] Despite all these measures, the "no-rent" movement continued unabated throughout the first half of 1939, and it was not let up till the Congress ministry in Madras was constrained in the middle of 1939 to appoint a Malabar Tenancy Enquiry Committee for reviewing the agrarian situation. As it was in Malabar, the tenants in the *Zamindari* areas of the Andhra region, more particularly in Venkatagiri (Nellore), Challapalli (Krishna) and Mandasa (Visakhapatnam), complained often of high rent and of harshness in its collection. Although the point was raised in a big way in Mandasa in September 1938, and a "no-rent" campaign con-templated in February 1939 in certain places of Chittoor,[296] the *kisans* and their leaders did not actually go all-out for starting one. The anti-*Zamindari* agitation of the Andhra peasants of all categories — the well-to-do and the poor, as well as of the agricultural labourers — heightened not so much on the question of high rent as it was on the issue of the landlord's bulldozing their traditional rights over the community lands, lakes and forests.

The confrontation between the tenants and the *Zamindar* in Kalipatnam (West Godavari) took place over a stretch of marshy land, resembling a lake. The spot abounded in fishes, and the tenants — who were also fishermen — enjoyed the right of fishing there for long. Since the late 1920s the *Zamindar* of Kalipatnam had an eye on this marshy land which he wanted to reclaim, and pledged to settle with the local landless ones. With the help of the Irrigation Department, he managed by the middle of 1938 to reclaim about 4,000 acres, and started measuring these for sale at high prices — and not for distribution to the landless as originally assured. The tenants opposed this move as much for the *Zamindar's* going back on his promise as for his violating the villagers' joint claim over the rent-free common land, especially for his flouting their age-old right of fishing. As their petitions and deputations to the Sub-Collector, Narsapur, in

295. "Activities of the Communist Party among the Peasants in Malabar", C.I.B. Report of 30.4.41, Home Poll. File No. 7/9/4 Pol. (1) of 1941, N.A.I.
296. Home Poll. Fortnightly Report for 1st half of February 1939, File No. 18/2/39, N.A.I.

July 1938 did not help, the *kisans* launched in October 1938 an agitation under the leadership of the leftists "from outside".[297] Characteristically, the police and the local Government officials sided with the *Zamindar*, and the Andhra Provincial Congress Committee disowned the movement for its being "Socialist-inspired".[298] The agitation nevertheless continued and reached its peak in March 1939 when the *kisans* and their leaders undertook *satyagraha* to prevent the transfer of newly sold plots to their buyers. The authorities sent reserve police parties to Kalipatnam, imposed Section 144 Cr. P.C. and ordered *lathi* charges on the demonstrators. During the six days of *satyagraha* (6 to 12 March 1939) 80 persons were arrested, including 28 women,[299] on the charges of rioting and causing the breach of the peace. While the *satyagraha* was on, T. Prakasam — the Revenue minister of Madras — visited Kalipatnam and urged the agitators to suspend their agitation. The *satyagraha* was eventually called off at the intervention of the Madras Premier, C. Rajagopalachari, and the arrested persons were released. The Congress ministry asked the Collector of West Godavari to enquire into the rights of the villagers and settle the issue with the help of the representatives of both the parties — the *Zamindar* and the *kisans*.[300]

As it was in Kalipatnam, the anti-*Zamindari* trend in Challapalli (Krishna) also started mainly as a protest against the landlord's encroachment on the community *lanka* lands (used primarily for grazing) and forest *banjar* lands. In September 1937 the *Zamindar* of Challapalli sold away 1,400 acres of forest *banjar* lands lying beside Challapalli, Mangalapuram and Ramanagaram which the inhabitants of these villages used for collecting firewood and similar other purposes. Soon an agitation was conducted intermittently against the *Zamindar* by the Divi Taluk Kisan Sabha, and it came to a head in 1939 when the *Zamindar* and his officials first tried in May to cultivate grazing lands at Potarlanka and Gajulanka, and then actually sold in August

297. *Ibid.*, 1st half of March 1939, File No. 18/3/39, N.A.I.
298. *Zamin Ryot* (English weekly), 21 October 1938.
299. Home Poll. Fortnightly Report for 1st half of March 1939, File No. 18/3/39, N.A.I.
300. *Ibid.*, 2nd half of March 1939, File No. 18/3/39, N.A.I.

some forest *banjar* lands at Mangalpuram.[301] The *Zamindar's* attempts at grabbing the *Inam*[302] and forest lands also caused considerable unrest among the tenants in Mandasa (Visakhapatnam) and prompted the Kisan Sabha-led marches (*jathas*) in September 1938 to demand, among other points, the restoration of the villagers' right over the community lands and forests.[303]

Interference with the forest rights often sparked off commotions in the countryside, particularly among those who were heavily dependent on the forest products, such as the poor peasants and the agricultural workers. The *kisans* of Khariar estate (Sambalpur) and Bissam Cuttack (Koraput), Orissa, stridently resented in April 1939 the *Zamindars'* imposition of a number of cesses.[304] In Ratnagiri district of Maharashtra a dispute over the forest rights resulted in May 1938 in an outbreak of physical violence. At Natu village of Khed *taluk* the Mahar peasants (mostly agricultural labourers) had felled trees in the nearby forest to rebuild their cottages before the onset of monsoon. The *Khotedars*, who claimed jurisdiction over the forest and did not recognise anybody else's right to use it, accused the Mahars of theft and complained to the Magistrate. Armed with a search warrant issued by the Magistrate, and accompanied by a police party, the *Khotedars* and their hirelings raided the Mahar locality. The Mahars, under the influence of the Independent Labour Party of Ambedkar, resisted the raiders, and many were injured in the clash that ensued.[305] The district authorities later arrested 18 leading Mahars on the charge of rioting, but not a single person among the *Khotedars'* men, and convicted the *kisans* to various terms of rigorous imprisonment in the face of some public criticism. The assertion of the forest rights of the *kisans*, as against the *Zamindars'*, led sometimes to more serious consequences, as it did in Drug in the Central Provinces.

301. *Zamin Ryot* (English weekly), 11 August 1939.
302. Home Poll. Fortnightly Report for 1st half of April 1939, File No. 18/4/39, N.A.I.
303. *Zamin Ryot* (English weekly), 23 September 1938.
304. Home Poll. Fortnightly Report for 1st half of April 1939, File no. 18/4/39, N.A.I.
305. Report of the District Superintendent of Police, Ratnagiri, no. 75 of 25 May 1938, Home (Sp) Dept. of Bombay, File No. 927-B of 1938, Maharashtra State Archives, Bombay.

The trouble in Dondi-Lohara *Zamindari* of Drug district started over its *Diwan's* high-handedness in the management of forests under its jurisdiction. He imposed a grazing fee (*rahdari*) on the forest lands, and prohibited the felling of trees in the forests or collection of wood therefrom, except by the timber merchants and contractors on high payment. The *kisans* and other villagers, who had long been exercising their right to the forest lands, found the prohibitory orders to be unjust and harsh. In January 1938 a clash took place when the landlord's *Dafadars* (forest guards) tried to prevent the *kisans* from taking away the grass they had collected from the forest for their cattle.[306] This incident and similar others forced the peasants of the area to think in terms of asserting their rights over the forest lands. In Sarju Prasad, a "young and inexperienced pleader of Balod" and a Congress Socialist, they found a mercurial leader. An agitation commenced with so much of noise and popular support that the startled *Zamindar* and the district authorities approached the senior Congressmen of the area to control Sarju Prasad.[307] Apparently, Sarju proved to be rather "uncontrollable" for the political bosses,[308] and the agitation under his leadership continued to grow. Meetings were held and processions organised against the prohibitory order and the grazing fee, and Sarju steadily built up an atmosphere of forest *satyagraha*. The peasants of the neighbouring *Zamindaris*, such as Khujji and Pannabaras in Drug, and Uprora in Bilaspur, also felt encouraged by the example of Dondi-Lohara to reaffirm their forest rights.[309] Following some half-hearted attempt at an arbitration on the part of the district authorities, the *kisans* of Dondi-Lohara started their forest *satyagraha* under Sarju Prasad on 7 May 1939. About 4,000 persons participated in it by cutting down trees at 11 points for five days. The *satyagraha* came to a halt on 11 May

306. Home Poll. Fortnightly Report for 2nd half of January 1938, File No. 18/1/38, N.A.I.
307. *Ibid.*, 1st half of February 1938, File No. 18/2/38, N.A.I.
308. The Congress leaders in Drug, as well as in Raipur, disowned Sarju Prasad and the movement. On his part, Sarju Prasad was publicly critical of the local Congress throughout, and issued later a pamphlet against it.
309. Home Poll. Fortnightly Report for 1st half of November 1938, File No. 18/11/38, N.A.I.

when many of the agitators, including Sarju Prasad, were arrested and prosecuted.[310] Although Sarju Prasad was thus forcibly shifted from the scene, the agitation did not altogether die out. The Dondi-Lohara *kisans* found a new leader in Narsingh Prasad Agarwal, who led them to resume the *satyagraha* on 26 July 1939. Special armed policemen were rushed to the spot by the authorities and a large number of arrests made.[311] Narsingh Prasad was arrested, prosecuted and sentenced to nine months' imprisonment. Thirteen of his followers were also convicted simultaneously for six months in jail.[312] Still the *kisans* managed somehow to continue the fight by refusing to pay the grazing fee, by socially ostracising all the *Zamindars'* men and by cutting trees from the forests off and on.[313] Their mood of defiance in fact persisted throughout the rest of the year 1939.

Neither the opposition to rack-renting, nor the insistence on community rights, however, could be as effective in bringing about the anti-landlord *kisan* solidarity as the fight against feudal exactions of labour and levy would. Over and above their being more blatantly irregular modes of social exploitation than rent, or even systematised grabbing of land, the practices of *begar* and *abwabs* heaped crippling indignities on individuals without distinction, and perhaps those belonging to the substantial and rich agrarian categories resented these more than did the poorer ones. There were numerous instances all over the country where most of the peasants of a locality expressed their resentment, or actually stood up against the feudal exactions. The main resolution that the attending 2,000 *kisans* passed in the Puri District Kisan Conference in Orissa demanded in April 1937 the abolition of illegal levies collected by the *Zamindars*.[314] The *kisans'* meetings in Ganjam in September 1937 called for an end of the system of *Vetti* (forced labour or *begar*) and *rasad* (supply

310. *Ibid.*, 1st half of May 1939, File No. 18/5/39, N.A.I.
311. *Ibid.*, 2nd half of July 1939, File No. 18/7/39, N.A.I.
312. *Ibid.*, 1st half of July 1939.
313. *Ibid.*, 2nd half of August 1939, File No. 18/8/39, N.A.I.
314. *Ibid.*, 2nd half of April 1937, File No. 18/4/37, N.A.I.

of various articles and provisions free of charge).[315] Similar slogans against *rasad* and *begar* had unequivocally been raised in March 1938 in Bilaspur of the Central Provinces.[316] The district officials in Bengal were struck at the beginning of 1938 by the extent of agrarian discontent over the *abwabs* and accordingly reminded the *Zamindars* of Dinajpur[317] and Rajsahi[318] of the necessity for extreme caution. The tenants of several districts in Bengal were found to be combining under the Krishak Samiti or Kisan Sabha for stopping the payment of *taheri, parbani* and other *abwabs* to the *Zamindars.*[319] Disaffection was rife on the issue of *begar* in the *Istimrari* areas of Ajmer-Marwara, and many felt that it might "result in bloodshed".[320] It was expected to be so, for refusal to *begar* meant manhandling of the *kisans,* seizure of their carts and bullocks and subjecting them to various other forms of persecution, including throwing them out of the village.[321] Irregular exactions also prompted the tenants in Hazara district of N.W.F.P. to lodge innumerable complaints to the Deputy Commissioner, Haripur, against their landlords.[322] Although the cry against the *Malba* (a levy to raise funds for the use of the village headmen in entertaining the revenue and police officials on tour) rent the air in the Punjab, especially in Amritsar, Ludhiana and Hoshiarpur,[323] the tenants in Patiala, Una *tahsil* of Hoshiarpur and the Nili-Bar belt of west Punjab often raised their voice against the imposition of irregular *abwabs* by the landlords. The *kisans* in Patiala refused altogether "to pay the *Biswedars* anything over and above their share of the crop".[324]

315. *Ibid.*, 2nd half of September 1937, File No. 18/9/37, N.A.I.
316. *Ibid.*, 1st half of March 1938, File No. 18/3/38, N.A.I.
317. *Ibid.*, 2nd half of January 1938, File No. 18/1/38, N.A.I.
318. *Ibid.*, 1st half of March 1938, File No. 18/3/38, N.A.I.
319. *Ibid.*, 1st half of April 1938, File No. 18/4/38, N.A.I.
320. *Ibid.*, 2nd half of April 1938.
321. A.C. Lothian, Chief Commissioner, Ajmer-Merwara, to Secretary, Home Dept. Govt. of India, No. 53-A/37-III, Mount Abu, 19 April 1938, Home Public, File No. 24/1/38, Public, N.A.I.
322. Home Poll. Fortnightly Report for 1st half of April 1939, File No. 18/4/39, N.A.I.
323. *Ibid.*, 1st and 2nd halves of July 1938, File No. 18/7/38, N.A.I.
324. Master Hari Singh, *Punjab Peasant in Freedom Struggle*, Vol.2, New Delhi, 1984, p. 242.

The *Zamindari* and the *Jagirdari* exactions of *begar* and *abwabs* were, however, the severest in the U.P., equally in its eastern and western parts. The *kisans'* resentment on these two counts was very widespread, though the continuance of both seemed as much an economic requirement for the landlords as a matter of their prestige. Reports of the killing of a *Chamar* in July 1939 for his refusal to undertake *begar*,[325] or of an attack by the *Zamindar's* men, armed with guns, spears and *lathis*, on the tenants for their opposition to *begar*,[326] or of beating up all the peasant opponents to *begar* and *abwabs*,[327] were quite common. It was also well-known that the U.P. *Zamindars* wanted, in the name of protecting themselves and their *karindas* (agents) from the "murderous attacks" of the *kisans*, but actually for systematic extraction of *begar* and *abwabs*, to set up a common private army. In the Oudh *Zamindars'* Conference held in Lucknow on 28-29 May 1938 they in fact passed a resolution in favour of the formation of a Volunteer Corps for "self defence", having "a distinctive uniform and emblem".[328] The plan did not mature eventually, for the Pant ministry found it too medievalist and potentially dangerous to be encouraged in any way. At a lesser scale, but likewise, the exactions by the *Jenmis* (such as, *Vasi* and *Nuri*) caused considerable disaffection among the peasants in Malabar and resulted in their *jathas* against the landed magnates like Venagayil Nayanar, Kurukkattidathil Nayanar and Kurumathur Nambiyar in the latter half of 1938.[329] The arbitrary feudal imposts were similarly contributory to the *kisan* unrest in Venkatagiri (Nellore) and Challapalli (Krishna) *Zamindaris*. But,

325. Home Poll. Fortnightly Report for 1st half of July 1938, File No. 18/7/38, N.A.I.
326. *Ibid.*, 1st half of August 1938, File No. 18/8/38, N.A.I.
327. Note on the Zamindar of Pali, Lalitpur Sub-Division, Jhansi, by S. Ross, Parliament Secretary, Govt. of U.P., 16 October 1937, Home Police File No. 472 of 1937, U.P. State Archives, Lucknow.
328. Report on the U.P. Zamindar's Conference, Lucknow, 28-29 May 1938, Police Dept. File No. 179 (20)/38, U.P. State Archives, Lucknow.
329. K. Gopalankutti, "The Integration of Anti-Landlord Movement with the Movement Against Imperialism: The Case of Malabar, 1935-39", *The Indian Left : Critical Appraisals*, Bipan Chandra (ed.), New Delhi, 1983, p. 204.

despite the prevalence of strong sentiments and occasional outbursts against these, the problems of *begar* and *abwabs* had not received the kind of serious attention of the leftists they really deserved. Consequently, one hardly comes across between 1936 and 1939 any strong anti-*begar* and anti-*abwab* movement, except the one that took place in Munagala (Krishna) in 1938.

Munagala Pargana in Krishna district, comprising 23 villages and 19 hamlets, and covering about 110 square miles, originally belonged to the state of Hyderabad. It became a part of British India in 1802, following which a *Zamindari* was created there under the Permanent Settlement. Situated on the border of the Nizam's territories and surrounded by the areas of Nalgonda district, Telengana, the Munagala *Zamindars* enjoyed a favoured frontier area's treatment from the British authorities. They had, therefore, little difficulty in running their *Zamindari* as whimsically and tyrannically as they liked. The age-old accumulated tensions between the *Zamindars* and the tenants came into the open visibly for the first time in the early 1930s, between 1931 and 1933. The exposure came in the wake of the first Zamin Ryot Conference held under the aegis of the Congress in Munagala in 1930 and the stir that it caused among the local peasants. The *Zamindar* (Nayani Venkata Ranga Rao) disliked the effect that the conference had on his tenants, and as a manifestation of his displeasure, he imposed "fines" on those peasants who took part in it, and harassed them in all possible ways, e.g. pounding their cattle, forfeiting their agricultural implements and even forcing them to sell their lands.[330] All these, and the atrocities that were generally being perpetrated by the *Zamindar* for long, attracted the attention of the Andhra Congress leaders in course of time, and prompted Nellore Venkatarama Reddy, the founder of the *Zamin Ryot* weekly, to visit Munagala in 1933 in connection with the Andhra Provincial *Zamin Ryot* Association's survey of the conditions of *rayats* in the *Zamindari* areas. The survey report was later published in

330. Venkateswara Rao Tatavarti, *Munagalla Pargana Praja-Udyama Charitra* (in Telugu, or History of the People's Movement in Munagala Pargana), Munagala, 1981, pp. 16-17.

the *Zamin Ryot* issue of 25 January 1935, revealing the various modes the *Zamindar* of Munagala used in exacting forced labour and other services from the villagers. The sympathy with which the world outside Munagala heard their case, greatly enthused the *kisans* of the *Zamindari*, and encouraged them to search ways and means for the redressal of their grievances, especially over *Vetti* (forced labour) and *Vettichakiri* or *Vettipani* (forced services). Some of the Congressmen who visited Munagala in 1937 (including the Congress Socialists-turned Communists like C. Rajeshwar Rao) noticed the growing peasant unrest there on these two issues, and wanted to take steps for giving it an organised shape. The West Krishna District Congress in fact formed a committee (dominated by the leftists) in June 1938 to enquire into the Munagala affair. Its report, which was completed by the beginning of August 1938, brought out the sufferings of *kisans* to the full, as well as their anxieties for offering resistance. It discussed how the *Zamindar* forced the villagers to give *Vetti* for digging his *motabaris* (wells with stairs), building the school under his management and cultivating his *Kamatham* (or *Khas*) lands. He similarly compelled everybody to give *Vettichakiri* to him and his agents — the village traders to send free supplies, the washermen and the barbers to render free services and many others to serve in his household without any charge.[331] Deviations from *Vettichakiri* or semblances of refusal were severely punished, either by imposing "fines" on the culprits or by torturing them physically. The *Zamindar* also collected irregular levies on all conceivable grounds and demanded *mamul* (a kind of *nazrana*) for any act that required his assent in the most far-fetched manner. Even for repairing his own hut one had to get the *Zamindar's* permission by making an adequate payment.[332] Over and above all these, the *Zamindar* charged his tenants high rent (perhaps the highest among all the Andhra *Zamindaris*), usurped jurisdiction over the *Inam* and grazing lands and evicted tenants whenever he wished. He also encouraged his men to behave like the Maratha marauders, and

331. *Ibid.*, pp. 40-8.
332. *National Front* (English weekly), 9 July 1939.

snatch those valuables away from the villagers which caught their eyes.[333]

Following the publication of the report in August 1938 and its circulation, the situation in Munagala took sharp and rapid turns. N.G.Ranga and Indulal Yajnik — the renowned Kisan Sabha leaders — came to Munagala at the invitation of the left-dominated West Krishna District Congress and addressed a number of meetings. Their visit was followed by the founding of a Rayat Sangham in Munagala, which held its first general body meeting of 4,000 members on 21 September 1938, and which affiliated itself formally to the Krishna District Rayat Sangham.[334] By the closing months of 1938, the Rayat Sangham had succeeded in setting up 40 village level branches, organising bodies of volunteers (*Bala Sanghams*), highlighting the peasants' grievances over *Vetti, Vettichakiri* and feudal levies, and raising the slogan: *Maku Vaddu ee Zamindari Pondu* ("We do not want the *Zamindars*").[335] At the beginning of 1939 an uproarious agitation was well on its way in Munagala under the leadership of the leftists like Ranga Rao, N. Prasada Rao and V.S.L. Prasad. The peasants of Munagala practically stopped giving to the *Zamindar* not only *Vetti, Vettichakiri* and the irregular levies, but also started withholding the rent. At the call of the Sangham they even commenced socially boycotting the *Zamindar* and his employees. At Kaluvakova village the agricultural workers struck work for sometime at the *Zamindar's* refusal to pay the wages originally agreed upon. Despite the *Zamindari* pressure brought upon the strikers, through the Congress leaders like A. Kaleswara Rao,[336] the strike continued unabated, and it was called off only when the District Collector intervened early in January 1939 and persuaded the landlord to make the

333. N. Prasada Rao, *Andhralo Rayatu Udyamam* (in Telugu, or Peasant Movement in Andhra), Hyderabad, 1946.
334. Venkateswara Rao Tatavarti, *Munagalla Pargana Praja-Udyama Charitra* (in Telugu, or History of the People's Movement in Munagala Pargana), Munagala, 1981, chapter 4.
335. *Ibid.*
336. N. Prasada Rao, *Andhralo Rayatu Udyamam* (in Telugu, or Peasant Movement in Andhra), Hyderabad, 1946.

payments.[337] In January 1939 itself the provincial Congress Committee began mediating between the *Zamindar* and the *kisans* of Munagala, resulting in an award given by its General Secretary, Gottapati Brahmaiah. By the award, the *kisans* were required to suspend their agitation and resume paying rent to the *Zamindar*. The *Zamindar* was asked, on his part, to pay for the labours and services he would requisition, make a proper survey to fix rent afresh and give up his encroachments into the common lands.[338] Although the *kisans* paid Rs.30,000 of the total rent they withheld (Rs. 90,000),[339] the *Zamindar* showed little inclination to observe his part of the understanding. Rather, he assumed an aggressive posture and directed his hirelings to beat up the agitators. By April 1939 the Sangham and the C.S.P. renewed the *kisan* agitation with vigour and prepared elaborately for a showdown, culminating in a *satyagraha* for 17 days. The *satyagraha* began on 2 June 1939 from Nandigudem with roughly one volunteer from each family in the village,[340] and it continued in the face of brutal police assaults, injuring 35 persons. In the course of the *satyagraha* 354 persons were arrested, of whom four were convicted for one year and 72 for six months. A "Munagala Day" was observed in Krishna district and other parts on 11 June 1939 to protest against the repressions, and the pressure of public opinion mounted on the Government for its immediate intervention. Although the local Congressmen scrupulously stayed away from the *satyagraha*, and some among them like P. Venkatasubbayya actually condemned it, the Madras Congress ministry, nevertheless, decided to make a move and bring about a settlement. T. Prakasam, the Revenue minister, visited Munagala along with the *kisan* leader, Ranga, and prevailed upon the agitators to suspend their *satyagraha* from 18 June 1939 on the guarantee that the Government would

337. *Zamin Ryot* (English weekly), 13 January 1939.
338. Venkateswara Rao Tatavarti, *Munagalla Pargana Praja Udyama Charitra* (in Telugu, or History of the People's Movement in Munagala Pargana), Munagala, 1981, chapter 4.
339. *National Front* (English weekly), 9 July 1939.
340. N. Prasada Rao, *Andhralo Rayatu Udyamam* (in Telugu or Peasant Movement in Andhra), Hyderabad, 1946.

ensure the implementation of the Brahmaiah award.[341] Prakasam, however, could not make much progress as the Congress ministry resigned soon thereafter. But one of the last acts that the ministry did perform was the release of all the Munagala prisoners, except four.

341. *National Front* (English weekly), 9 July 1939.

THE RAISONNEUR'S MONOLOGUE

Unlike the heroic struggle of the *Bakasht* peasants in Bihar, and the determined fight of the *Halis* and the sharecroppers in south Gujarat, the Munagala peasant's agitation was neither spectacular nor extensive by any standard. And yet, paradoxically, without being fully aware of it themselves, the leftists were able in Munagala to register a political advance which they could not equal elsewhere between 1936 and 1939. They succeeded in a certain way there in building up, on the strength primarily of the poor peasants and agricultural labourers, the anti-feudal consolidation of various peasant categories — one of their avowed main tasks in the agrarian sector under a colonial-feudal regime. The peasant solidarity, the Communists strongly felt, was their immediate concern against "Imperio-feudalism",[342] on which would depend the realisation of their goal, namely, the "agrarian revolution" or the introduction of a fundamental change in the agrarian economic relationship, by abolishing landlordism and usury (thus freeing peasants from the grossest modes of exploitation), and by vesting ownership of land in its actual tillers.[343] Seen in this light, the leftists and the Kisan Sabhaites appeared to have achieved, in the limited context of Munagala, the unity of the peasant masses on a fairly sound basis — not so much by harping on rack-renting, nor by over-bidding for the agricultural labourers' wages, as by highlighting *Vetti, Vettichakiri* and the feudal levies. The understanding among the different kinds of poor peasants, who, more or less, shared the same economic plight, had often been witnessed in the battle arena itself. It was seen, for example, in the sympathy the sharecroppers

342. *The Communist* (cyclostyled), the central organ of the C.P.I., Vol. 1, No. 15, March 1937, Party Documents, C.P.I., Ajoy Bhavan, New Delhi.
343. P.C. Joshi's article on the Kisan Movement and the Comilla session of the A.I.K.S., *National Front* (English weekly), 5 June 1938.

felt for the *Halis* in south Gujarat, or the support the small tenants gave to the *Nankars* in Mymensingh, Bengal, or the encouragement the agricultural labourers provided to the poor peasants in Kanara district, Bombay province, by refusing to till their snatched away lands for the landlords. Contrarily, instances of similar cooperation between the poor and the substantial peasants — those markedly unequals in economic terms — were very rare, indeed. In fact, apart from the short-lived combination of the well-to-do peasants and the petty shop-keepers with the *Adhiars* against the *Hattola* of the *Ijaradars* in Jalpaiguri, Bengal, such solidarity, as it was demonstrated in Munagala, had not been attained in any other part of India. Consequently, once the *kisan* solidarity was attained to an extent, it had not been proved difficult for the leftists to rouse in Munagala their anti-landlord slogan: *Maku Vaddu ee Zamindari Pondu.* The Munagala *kisans'* voice against the *Zamindars* — the principal targets in the agrarian revolution — seemed more natural, and certainly more relevant than the propagandist far-cry against the *Zamindari* in Bihar and the U.P. (*"Zamindari Pratha Nash Karo*"),[344] or the *Khotedari* in Maharashtra ("Abolish *Khotedari*"), or. the *Malguzari* in the C.P. ("Destroy *Malguzari*").[345] Like all other agitations, the Munagala peasants' movement was, in the leftist parlance, essentially a "partial struggle" (to battle against the ill-effects of a system), but it had shown — with the participation of most segments of village society — the prospect of its becoming an embryonic "total struggle" (to fight against the system itself).

That the Munagala experience was valid by their own theoretical standard, and that it could or should shape the future of agrarian politics in India, had hardly been realised by the leftists. Little evidence of such realisation in fact was available in their political literature of the time which took note of the affair rather cursorily along with many others. Not only Munagala, very few of the numerous agrarian struggles (with the exception

344. Home Poll. Fortnightly Report for 1st half of April 1939, File No. 18/4/39, N.A.I.

345. *Ibid.*, 2nd half of November 1937, File No. 18/11/37, N.A.I. for both the provinces.

of the *Bakasht* because of its sheer militancy) had adequately been analysed in the leftist and *kisan* circles. These had, of course, been reported in the weeklies run by the left political parties and groups and in the bulletins issued by the A.I.K.S., but without much effort to draw lessons from them or exchange notes of the agitators of one area with those of another. As a result, one notices some communication gap among the leftist-led *kisans* in various parts of the country, fighting practically for the same causes under almost similar circumstances. The *Bargadars* and their mentors in north Bengal, for instance, did not know much of the successes and failures of the movements of the *Choudras* in south Gujarat or the *batai* cultivators in western Punjab, and, therefore, had not felt particularly inspired or despaired by the happenings outside Bengal. The coordination of a specific variety of struggles — the first step towards orchestrating a conglomeration of such struggles in future on a national or sub-continental scale — was very difficult, indeed, for any all-India organisation, howsoever long-standing, socially grass-rooted and programmatically justified its position might have been. Barely four years old, the A.I.K.S. was not really in a position to work that wonder, and despite its endeavours to organise *kisans* all over the country through publications, reports, meetings and conferences, all the agitations of the rural poor that it had led till 1939 remained localised, fragmented and disjointed from each other. Even the most formidable among these — the *Bakasht* movement in Bihar — was confined to exclusive pockets in some localities, and whether the Congress Socialists failed in particular in their strongholds to conduct it "properly" or not,[346] the struggle did neither spread far and wide enough to meet the challenges of repression, nor rally the diverse agrarian categories to force the hands of the authorities.

The fact was that the A.I.K.S. could not give its undivided attention to the causes of the rural poor, and as a multi-class organisation of the peasantry, it was also not in a position to do so. Under the influence of the well-to-do and the substantial categories, it had often to take up — simultaneously with the

346. Sahajanand Saraswati, *Mera Jeewan Sangharsh* (Hindi), Patna, 1952, p. 522.

interests of the poor peasants — issues of high assessments, remissions in times of difficulty, exorbitant rates for canal water, arbitrary taxes like the *Chowkidari*, remunerative prices for such cash crops[347] as sugarcane, cotton, groundnut and jute, and similar other questions. Some of the local agitations that it had built up on these points were, to an extent, hostile to the Government, and, therefore, exhibited an anti-imperialist temper. A situation was thus developing very fast in which the *kisan* movement on the whole appeared distortedly to be running on two indistinct parallel anti-imperialist and anti-landlord lines, as if the burden of fighting an obdurate Government had fallen on the shoulders of the substantial peasants as much as the responsibility for resisting the oppressive landlords rested on the backs of the poor ones. It was the political task for the makers and designers of the A.I.K.S. — the Congress Socialists and the Communists — to dispel the distortion, and assert that anti-landlordism and anti-imperialism together formed only one bold line of struggle for the entire peasantry in colonial India. The fulfilment of the task depended not so much on picking up the grievances of *kisans* of all sorts and launching "partial" battles galore over every one of them, as on highlighting the major agrarian objective (namely, the intensification of the struggle against colonialism by attacking the landlords and usurers, and through the distribution of land among the tillers) and giving priority to those partial ventures in which the multitudinous rural poor held the key positions, and which had the maximum possibility of being linked with it. That the A.I.K.S. could not bring many of its movements out of their local isolation, failed to integrate even some of them into a pattern or patterns, and wavered on occasions between the commitment to the poor and the care for the substantial and the well-to-do, were all due largely to its leftist leaders' inability to live up to their political responsibilities. Their inability again was

347. Sometime the rural poor, i.e. poor peasants and sharecroppers, were also involved in agitation over the cash crop pricing, especially of jute and sugarcane. A note of such involvements has been taken in Act two, Scene I.

more on account of a lacking in confidence in the objective rather than of any lapse in understanding it. The leftists, more particularly the Communists, knew what they were talking about in the name of agrarian revolution, but did not seriously entertain the belief that it could at all be accomplished in the near future. The slogans like "abolish landlordism and usury" and "give land to the tiller" were raised because they seemed politically attractive, and perhaps ideologically sound, and not because they were realisable at a reasonable rate. What was beyond the immediate reach was often considered not worth the hustling and bustling — even by those devoted to the ideals of radical social transformation.

Compared to their sin of not believing in themselves, the other failings of the leftists were rather small and ordinary — not unusual in the new-comers breaking a fresh ground for themselves. Howsoever much they desired to be identified with the rural poor, and shared the *kisans'* hopes and sorrows, the leftists could not often rise above either the ideological rigidities ingrained in them or the interests of the classes to which they belonged. The rich peasant background of many of the Congress Socialist activists in Maharashtra, who dominated the Kisan Sabha proceedings in the region, was partly responsible for the rather subdued state of the rural poor there in comparison with the agitating well-to-do. In fact the most ebullient champion of the poor peasants in certain parts of Maharashtra seemed only to be B.R. Ambedkar's Independent Labour Party — not so much for its commitment to radicalism, as for its concern for the welfare of one community — the Mahars. Like the Congress Socialists in Maharashtra, the Communist *kisan* organisers — who belonged to the substantial category of peasants — were no less class-conscious in the Punjab. Except some specific areas in the west, the Punjab Kisan Committee or Sabha was too engrossed generally in upholding the peasant proprietors' causes to think of the tenants-at-will or the agricultural labourers. None could, however, equal the record of the Congress Socialists in eastern U.P., who, true to the rentier character, openly sympathised with the "small *Zamindars*" over the issue of the *Sir*. Some of the Bihar Kisan Sabha leaders were also disproportionately anxious to convince the "petty *Zamindars*" of their desire to maintain "amicable" relations with them.[348] Along with such occasional exhibition of loyalties to their classes of origin, a strong, doctrinaire approach also interfered with the leftists' line of thinking, and the case of the Communists typified the trend. To them, the revolutionary potentialities of the peasants were axiomatically inferior to those of the industrial workers,[349] and their role in a popular struggle — whether it was occurring in a predominantly agricultural country or in an industrial nation — could only be supplementary to the "vanguard" role of the working class. The mobilisation of the peasantry, including the poor and the landless, thus being thought to be lower in order than the organisation of the workers, the *kisan* movement did not receive in the Communist circles the importance that it really deserved. Even those of its members who preferred to work on the *kisan* front, went about the task of rallying the peasants without much guidance from the above, and certainly with little innovation to stimulate them. The earlier criticism by perceptive observers like Munshi Premchand that the leftists in India, out of a lack of genuine interest in the *kisans* and fear of hard work, had not carefully studied the circumstances of the peasantry which their Chinese counterparts did under Mao Zhe Dong as early as 1927,[350] seemed still to be relevant, to an extent, after four years of organised *kisan* activities. Their attempt, for

348. A Note on the All India Kisan Sabha Conference, 9 & 10 April 1939, Gaya, Home Poll. Dept. (Special), Govt. of Bihar, File No. 217/1939, Bihar State Archives, Patna.
349. The industrial workers, having "nothing to lose but their chains", and everything to gain, would throw their lot unhesitatingly in a revolutionary movement, irrespective of its successes or setbacks. The peasants, on the other hand, being passionately attached to their occupied lands, or to the prospect for such occupation, would hesitate to join the revolutionary movement, lest they forfeited — in the case of any reverse — whatever they possessed, and hoped to possess.
350. Premchand was probably the first in India who took public note of "one political leader of our neighbour, China" (Mao Zhe Dong), and of his labours on the Chinese peasant question, as reflected in the Hunan Report of 1927 — almost six years subsequent to the event — in a brief editorial in his *Hans* of 28 June 1933, see Amit Kumar Gupta, "Marxbad-Leninbad, Premchand aur Mao", *Tisri Duniya* (Hindi monthly), April 1982, Vol. 2, No. 3, New Delhi.

example, at understanding the class differentiation of the Indian peasantry was based more on the obedient acceptance of the broad Marxist stereotypes, namely the rich, the middle, and the poor peasants and the agricultural labourers,[351] rather than on the appreciation of their applicability in the Indian context, especially in view of the overlapping nature of such categories in it. In rural society in India a rich peasant often acted as a *mahajan*, particularly for loaning grains, and the so-called middle peasant, who did manage to balance his expenditures with earnings, worked sometimes also as a landholder-cum-sharecropper. Similarly, a poor peasant, holding a few acres of land, served frequently as a sharecropper, and even as an agricultural labourer, to earn his miserable livelihood. Likewise, a sharecropper supplemented his income by working as an agricultural labour, and it was not extraordinary to find a field-hand venturing to take a tiny plot on sharecropping. Besides, every village had its army of artisans — the potter, the barber, the carpenter, the washerman, the blacksmith, and the village menial — who was with or without any land, who tilled his land part-time or left it to the sharecropper, and whose economic situation differed from extreme poverty to comparative ease. Also, there were differences of mental attitude, not only between the rich and the poor peasants, but also among the poor peasants themselves. A small cultivator who possessed an infertile bit of land, claimed greater prestige than a sharecropper, and a sharecropper — whether he owned his implements and cattle or not — considered himself socially superior to a *khetmajdoor*, irrespective wholly of their belonging all together to almost the same economic level. The social and political thinking processes of each category were, therefore, highly complex and verily mixed up, and to make matters worse, they were widely exposed to the strong influences of castes, communities and religious beliefs. It was quite possible for a Muslim sharecropper or a scheduled caste Hindu *khetmajdoor* to feel, or imagine his

351. Presidential Address by Muzaffar Ahmad, Mymensingh Krishak Conference, 24 February 1938, M. Ahmad, *Krishak Samasya* (in Bengali), Calcutta, 1954, pp. 52-3.

feeling, for some common bond of unity with a rich peasant, a landlord and a *mahajan* of his own community or caste. The leftist *kisan* activitists, armed barely with a four-fold Marxist class categorisation of the peasantry, and without making any allowance for its overlappings, were not really in a position to deal effectively with such complexities. Their simplistic preconceptions not only left them ill-equipped to tackle unpredictable social and political behaviours, but also to follow even the predictable ones, such as the conduct of the middle peasants. The middle peasants, who were said to have possessed moderate holdings "to make two ends meet"[352] (varying between five to 10 acres of widely different quality), did not appear to have followed a line of action different from the ones adopted by the rich or the poor peasants. They might have had a separate existence arithmetically, but little characteristic social or political claims of their own. In accordance with their economic comforts or discomforts, they either lined up with the substantial and the well-to-do or joined the poor *kisans* — sided more in fact with the latter than with the former. Unlike the countries in the West and some other parts of the world, the articulated political entity of the middle peasant was a myth that the Communists first initiated in India in the late 1930s, in order to cling to the Marxist class differentiation of the peasantry, and which the social scientists elaborated in the recent times, mainly for their liking for alluring imported concepts.[353] Neither the *kisan* agitations of the time, especially those under discussion here, had revealed the discernible voice of the middle peasants, nor the more down-to-earth among the Indian Marxists had heard any such cry.[354] It was not necessary for the leftists to think at all

352. *Ibid.*

353. According to Hamza Alavi, the middle peasants, unlike the weak and meek poor peasants, are "the most militant elements of the peasantry" and "a powerful ally of the proletarian movement". See his "Peasants and Revolution" in Kathleen Gough and Hari P. Sharma (eds.) *Imperialism and Revolution in South Asia*, London, 1973, pp. 291-337. The view is an approximation of what Eric R. Wolf has observed in his *Peasant Wars of the Twentieth Century*, London, 1971, pp. 291-3.

354. P. Sundarayya, "The Madras Peasantry and Platform of Struggle", *The New Age* (English monthly), Vol. IV, no. 5, October 1937, pp. 186-91.

about the middle peasants — the faces in the crowd of the substantial cultivators or that of the poor *kisans*.

The only people among the peasants whom the leftists were doctrinally inclined to give credit for some reliable militancy, were the agricultural labourers, primarily because of their pauperised, landless and wage-earning character. That was the reason why some of the leftists were keen on affiliating the *khetmajdoors* with the trade-union movement of the industrial workers, or putting the "agrarian proletariat" in the revolutionary company of the "industrial proletariat". That was also the reason why the leftists spoke, in mechanical conformity with their ideology, of placing the agricultural labourers in the "forefront" of the multi-class *kisan* movement,[355] despite the prevalence of a serious contradiction between the substantial peasants and the agricultural labourers — the employers of wage-labour and the suppliers of it — or the exploiters and the exploited. Howsoever much the leftists tried to gloss over the class contradiction by saying, as Swami Sahajanand did, that the rich peasants' exploitation of the *khetmajdoors* was primarily due to their being expropriated in turn by the landlords,[356] it was clearly not possible to unite the rich *kisans* and the *khetmajdoors*, or to make the Aesopian wolf and the sheep to drink from the same spot by the stream, without their being led into the common struggles against landlordism and usury, and without their having learnt by experience the mutual advantages of such joint enterprises. Only through their sustained fighting capability, and uncompro-mising approach to the grimly fought common battles, could the *khetmajdoors* emerge as the natural forerunners of the *kisan* movement. But, involved as they were between 1936 and 1939 in the partial struggles only, and rather diffident in launching the united movements of the entire peasantry, the leftists' longing

355. Presidential Address by Muzaffar Ahmad, Mymensingh Krishak Conference, 24 February 1938, in M. Ahmad, *Krishak Samasya* (in Bengali), Calcutta 1954, pp. 52-3.

356. Swami Sahajanand's Presidential Address at the 3rd session of the A.I.K.S., Comilla, 13 May 1938, *National Front* (English weekly), 22 May 1938.

for a proletarian lead in the *kisan* movement remained as remote — and as faint — as their slogans of ringing the death-knell to landlordism and usury, or of distributing land to the tiller.

Neither their laxity in the striving for programmatic targets, nor their rigidity in the observance of doctrinal rituals could eventually deter the leftists from making significant progress within the limits they seemed to have set for themselves — the confines of the partial struggles. The Communist and the Congress Socialist *kisan* activists of 1936-9 were undoubtedly the first among the rural political organisers of all lines — rightists or leftists — who championed the causes of the rural poor, among others, in a systematic and highly politicised manner. Their splintered and emotionally-charged predecessors of the early 1920s and early 1930s lacked the strength of ideology, the political will and the organisational skill that came with it. Their successors, in their turn, tried to construct — cautiously at times and recklessly at others — upon the very edifice that was built in 1936-9, irrespective of its high or low quality. To ignore, or not to remember, the role of the Communists and the Congress Socialists in mobilising the poor peasants in the late 1930s is to deprive the pioneers of their rightful due — the recognition they so appropriately deserve.[357] The performance of the pioneers, however, was greatly facilitated by the post-Depressionary agrarian circumstances in India, and by the way the peasant masses — already drowned in their miseries — desperately wanted to clutch at any straw. They were willing to listen to whosoever sympathised with their lot — and in whatsoever manner — whether it was a conservative Purushottam Das Tandon in the U.P., or an adventurist Mukul-eswar Rahaman in Bengal, or a balladeer Duggirala Bala-ramakrishnayya in coastal Andhra. Thus, when the left-minded persons came forward and the leftists decided to take the field with the promise — almost messianic — of founding a golden

357. Many still believe, as did the author of this book till recently, that the Indian Communists in the past (i.e. before 1947 in particular) "neglected" the organisation of the landless and the poor peasants. See Sumanta Banerjee, *India's Simmering Revolution : The Naxalite Uprising*, London, 1984, p. 60.

kingdom in the style of a semi-mythical Soviet Russia,[358] the rural poor in many parts of India immediately responded, veered round the flamboyant would-be deliverers and heard their angelic voices in amazement. Although the membership figure of the A.I.K.S. did not show any category-wise break up, the very fact that it swelled rapidly within two years of its formation to 5,46,800[359] was indication enough of the rural poor's participation in it. Besides, the massive peasant rallies that the Kisan Sabha succeeded in holding, even in areas where it was insufficiently organised (such as, the one of 10,000 on 27 December 1937 at Morkha in the C.P., or the other of 15,000 on the Kisan Day, 1 September 1937, in Cuttack in Orissa) were also suggestive of the very considerable involvement of the small and poor peasants — "the backbone" of the Kisan Sabha by the admission of its leaders.[360] The response sometime was so overwhelming that the limited number of the *kisan* activists — those opting for the less revolutionary work among the peasants than the more revolutionary task among the workers — could not cope with it. At places they were literally dragged by the poor *kisans* into assuming leadership. The experience of Moni Sinha, a Calcutta-based trade-unionist, who was persuaded by the *Tanka* peasants to lead their movement in Mymensingh — his native place in East Bengal[361] — was a case at hand. Apart from their known egalitarianism and the trumpeted ideological position, the leftist *kisan* leaders and activists had nothing else really that could attract the poor peasants. Economically, most of them belonged either to the class of urbane petty bourgeoisie, especially the professional sections, or to the rich peasants and the rentiers. This was true, for instance, as much of Swami Sahajanand and Rahul Sankrityayana of Bihar, of Bankim Mukherji and Abdulla Rasul of Bengal as of N.G. Ranga and P. Sundarayya of Andhra, E.M.S. Namboodiripad and A.K. Gopalan of Kerala, or of Indulal

358. Speeches of Swami Sahajanand and Jadunandan Sharma, Home Poll. Fortnightly Report for 1st half of May 1938, File No. 18/5/38, N.A.I.
359. M.A. Rasul, *A History of the All India Kisan Sabha*, Calcutta, 1974, p. 22.
360. Swami Sahajanand's Presidential Address, 3rd A.I.K.S. Conference, Comilla, 11-14 May 1938, *ibid.*, p.29.
361. Moni Sinha, *Jeeban Sangram* (Bengali), Dacca, 1983, pp. 44-5.

Yajnik and D.N. Pangarkar of Gujarat, as well as of their numerous counterparts at the provincial and district levels. Socially, they belonged more to the urbane intelligentsia than to the typified agrarian society, and in the rural setting they invariably turned out to be "the outsiders" in their mentality and value-judgement — even after originating from the villages or growing out of the rich peasant background. Despite their being "the outsiders" in the countryside (which was how the British bureaucracy so aptly described them in the official records), and the chances, therefore, of their becoming unacceptable in the village lifestyles, the leftist idealogues and organisers in practice not only not encountered any difficulty, but had actually been welcomed by the peasant masses. Neither the idiosyncratic hostility that the cultivators were known sometimes to have felt for the non-cultivators, nor the difference that prevailed between the low castes and the high castes, nor the disagreement that existed among the followers of one creed with those of another — really stood in their way, and proved to be the stumbling block.

The foregoing review of the rural poor's agitations between 1936 and 1939 does not contain a single instance where the communalist and casteist tendencies were formidable enough to disrupt the rural poor's mobilisation, or frustrate their leftist leaders' exertion. The reason for this uninhibited trend in the countryside, as well as for the warmth shown there to the leftists, lay evidently in the aspirations of the poor peasants to withstand their social and economic sufferings — the urges that had put all other considerations into the background.[362] With an enthusiastic audience in the rural poor, therefore, the leftist "outsiders" so monopolised the initiative in their agitations — wherever they occurred — and so dominated their proceedings, that one would be inclined, in the limited Indian experience of

362. In the light of the experiences of the *kisan* movement of 1936-9, it is difficult to appreciate the present day criticism that the leftists, especially the Communists, in the past did not take the alarming implications of the communalist and casteist tendencies as seriously as they ought to have. Why should the Communists and the Congress Socialists bother themselves too much when they had not really been threatened by these?

1936-9, to uphold the Wolfian assertion about the poor peasants' depending invariably and decisively upon the help of "the external powers" or "the outsiders" for all their political actions.[363]

In fact the leftist hold over the Kisan Sabha-led agitations of the poor peasantry was so complete between 1936 and 1939 that it allowed little scope for those initiatives to come into play which originated from the "autonomous domain" of "subaltern politics".[364] There is hardly adequate evidence (except an insipid one of the *Regars'* in Ajmer-Merwara, and a meteoric another of the Munda tribals in Gangpur) to contend that the poor peasants had, on their own, wanted to decide the manner their struggles should be conducted, or the way departures must be made — to suit the local conditions — in the line of action prescribed by the leftists. There was no noteworthy attempt on the part of the *kisans* at defying their leaders, and no serious misunderstanding with their mentors, except a fleeting discomfiture at Reora, Gaya, in the middle of 1939 over the re-distribution of *Bakasht* lands recovered from the *Zamindars*. The sudden ultra-revolutionary advocacy of Jadunandan Sharma, the Gaya Supremo, for collectivising these lands,[365] or short of that, dividing them equally among the landless, instead of restoring them to their original holders as per the very objective of the *Bakasht* agitation, threatened to rake up dissensions among the peasants.[366] Sharma, however, could not go very far, and the Kisan Sabha soon resolved the matter by refusing to flout the agreed programme, and by returning the lands to those from whom they were snatched away. The outcome, or the rectification, eventually

363. "Poor peasants and landless labourers are unlikely to pursue the course of rebellion unless they are able to rely on some external power .... Where such external power is present, the poor and the landless labourers have latitude of movement, where it is absent, they are under near-complete constraint". Eric Wolf, *Peasant Wars of the Twentieth Century*, London, 1971, pp. 290-1.

364. Ranajit Guha (ed.), *Subaltern Studies I : Writings on South Asian History and Society*, London, 1982, p. 4

365. *National Front* (English weekly), 7 May 1939, Vol. II, no. 13.

366. The Government officials tried to project these as bickerings between the high and the low castes. Home Poll. Fortnightly Report for 1st half of May 1939, File No. 18/5/39, N.A.I.

increased the *kisans'* confidence in their leaders rather than diminishing it in any way. The credibility of the left political activists seemed thus to be so high, and their ideological outpouring so stirring, that the rural poor did not mind being carried away by them and leaving the burden of decision-making generally to the leftists' care. Functionally also, under the pyramidical formation of the Kisan Sabha, they were left practically with very little alternative. The A.I.K.S. was headed by the All India Kisan Committee, or the central body that sought to coordinate the activities of the provincial branches. The Provincial Kisan Sabhas, on their part, grew out of the District (sometimes Sub-Divisional), the *Taluk* (sometimes the *Thana*) and the Village level Kisan Committees. Both the A.I.K.C. and the Provincial Kisan Committees were packed with the left politicians who belonged mostly to the classes of urban petty bourgeoisie and rentiers. The composition of the District and the Sub-Divisional Committees was not much different, except that a sprinkling of the upper peasantry's representation was often found in them. The rural poor could squeeze their nominees only into the *Taluk* or the *Thana* and the Village Committees (also known as the "Primary Committees"). But even these were so overwhelmed by the directives of the educated, petty bourgeois District and Sub-Divisional leaders that they enjoyed hardly any opportunity for originating a move or taking a crucial decision. The "Primary Committees" in effect functioned as the sounding boards or the means of communication between the leftist leadership and the masses at the grass roots. The leftists were yet to realise the importance of, and the urgency for, creating local leadership, or generating local initiative. Seldom had they tried to constitute, over and above their rather narrow branch of a local Kisan Sabha, a broad body of all the *kisans* of a certain locality for conducting some specific agitation within its limits. Such a body of *kisans* was essential, as the events proved later on, as much for involving the inhabitants of the area as for encouraging their own leaders. Failure to do this, especially the inability to gear up the *kisan* leaders on the spot, could lead to grave setbacks if the reputed, and the apparently irreplaceable initiators of the movement were removed abruptly from the scene. The *kisan* agitations nearly collapsed with the arrest of Karyanand Sharma in Munghyr, the externment of D.N. Pangarkar from Mongrol *taluk* of Navasari district in Baroda, the conviction of N.Akbar Ali Shah and M. Abdul Rahim Popalzai at Ghalla Dher in Mardan district of N.W.F.P. and the imprisonment of Sarju Prasad and Narsingh Prasad in Dondi-Lohara in Drug district of the C.P. It should, however, be remembered that the battle fronts — the actual fields of action — produce their own heroes and heroines, who are capable of taking a lead, or giving a thrust. To the astonishment of the leftist ideologues, and irrespective of all their patronising gestures or the lack of these, the leaders among the *kisans* were being born in every agitation in the countryside — out of the ranks of the small peasants, the sharecroppers and the agricultural labourers. That they would influence from time to time the making of the decisions about themselves, especially after they got themselves adjusted to the sparklings of the ideology and the ways of the ideologues, was almost a certainty.

Although the rural poor had not shown much of an autonomous audacity, they did nevertheless reveal in all the left-dominated partial struggles a determination to resist their exploiters and persecutors. The readiness with which they rallied round the leftists, and followed the Kisan Sabha lead, wherever it had been given, was in itself symptomatic of their inherent, abiding militancy or their "consciousness of insurgency"[367] — as some preferred to term it. It was their militant demeanour that prompted them to vigorously take up and try the various techniques of struggle the leftists thought fit to employ, such as taking deputations to the civil authorities and public bodies, making approaches to the courts of law, organising the *kisan* marches or *morchas* to the administrative centres and offering frontal resistance to the oppressors and their henchmen. The leftists and the *kisan* leaders were generally very anxious to keep the methods of frontal resistance, or face to face engagements, within peaceful bounds, and without any involvement in violent law and order situations. Their concern

367. Ranajit Guha, *Elementary Aspects of Peasant Insurgency in Colonial India*, London, 1983, p. 15.

for maintaining peace, and their enthusiasm for non-violence, stemmed largely from an apprehension for losing control over the forces they intended to harness, as well as from a lack of clarity as to the revolutionary situation they were pledged to bring about. Besides, the over-all nationalist strategy of "non-violent non-cooperation" being proved rather effective against the Raj, it seemed convenient for them — and also in order with the fashion of the day — to borrow from it in their fight against the landlord-usurer combination. The borrowing resulted in the use of the *satyagraha*, or the "land *satyagraha*" in the leftist terminology,[368] as the most important and frequently employed technique of the evicted poor peasants' frontal resistance. The *batai* cultivators, the field-hands and the bonded labourers also took often to "non-cooperation", and "struck" work or refused to serve during the sowing and harvesting seasons. The spirit of non-cooperation also prevailed over such methods as the social ostracisation or the total boycott of the *kisans*' opponents in the villages, and, on rare occasions, over the refusal to pay irregular levies and to give gratuitous labours and services. The militant *kisans* unhesitatingly participated in all these modes of struggle and succeeded in raising them at certain places, especially the land *satyagrahas*, to a very high emotional pitch. The ferment that some of these *satyagrahas* produced was followed, logically and almost spontaneously, by the more determined and more aggressive forms of encounters. The *kisans*' defence of their right to stay on the lands they tilled, in the face of their antagonists' unbridled use of physical violence, led them sequentially to defend their only property — the crops they had raised — and their personal safety and security. Whether the leftists fully grasped it or not, the poor peasants knew by their very living the extent of violence that enforced the quietude in the countryside. They had, therefore, little illusion as to the character their resistance was bound eventually to assume. Their leftist leaders also could not disregard the violent realities for long, and unwilling to beat a retreat, they had to agree to the *kisans*' use of force by stating publicly that non-violence was,

368. *National Front* (English weekly), 2 October 1938.

after all, not their *deota* (god).[369] The semi-armed clashes over lands and crops were more numerous in Bihar than in any other part of India, and the militancy of the rural poor reached its unintended climax in the *Bakasht* movement, as the leftist political and tactical advance reached its unknowing maximum in the agitation in Munagala. The Munagala and the *Bakasht* were the utmost limits to which the leftists and the rural poor could travel together in 1939, and not any further beyond, for the Communists and the Congress Socialists — the guiding angels — were reluctant either to experiment with armed resistance or to elevate and escalate the partial struggles.

Within the limited sphere of partial struggles, however, the joint record of the leftists and the poor peasantry was impressive on the whole. Apart from their growing rapidly in stature, as well as in the belief in themselves, they fought shoulder to shoulder many a battle against very formidable, well-entrenched enemies. The landlords-usurers not only received the support of the colonial regime and the protection from its bureaucracy, police and judicial machinery, but they also enjoyed the affection generally of the much acclaimed nationalist politicians. Barring few isolated admirers of socialism (Nehru, for instance), and a few liberals among the ministers (Prakasam, for example), the Congress leaders at the central, provincial and district levels — whether in Drug or Surat or Krishna — and the Congress ministries in all the eight provinces under them — whether it was Dr Khan Saheb's in N.W.F.P. or G.B. Pant's in the U.P. or B.G. Kher's in Bombay — were wholly unsympathetic, if not always hostile, towards the interactions between the leftists and the rural poor. Despite the awesome strength of the opponents, and the direct and indirect help they managed to get from those in power, including the defenders of the Faizpur Agrarian Programme, the poor peasants under the leftists did not fare too badly against them. In fact the battles they won outnumbered the contests they lost, and even in the beaten ones their inspirational gains from fighting together were by no means negligible. If the agricultural labourers lost in some cases, as the

369. Swami Sahajanand's speech at Deo, Gaya, 11 November 1938, Home Poll. Fortnightly Report for 1st half of November 1938, File No. 18/11/38, N.A.I.

Musahars in Patna and the Regars in Ajmer-Merwara did, they won a number of others at Verullapadu and Kaluvakova in Krishna, Mukkamela in West Godavari, Perulam in Tanjore and Ankleswar in the Panchmahals. The sharecroppers' defeat in Mandavi in Surat was more than compensated by the victories of their counterparts in Mongrol *taluk* in Baroda, in Nili-Bar in Lahore, and in Jalpaiguri. The loss the evicted peasants suffered at Ghalla Dher in Mardan or in some parts of Montgomery and Multan was balanced, to some extent, by the success of the *Tanka* peasants in Mymensingh and of the *kisans* of Papanasam in Tanjore. The anti-eviction battles that the *Sir* and the *Bakasht* peasants waged in the U.P. and Bihar, respectively, did not go waste altogether, and produced certain concrete legislative and material gains. Bonded labourers registered signal victories in Mymensingh and in Baroda, and so did the "no-rent" campaigners in Malabar and Patiala. An anti-*Zamindar* fight was lost in Dondi-Lohara in Drug, but a similar one was won in Kalipatnam in West Godavari, and another in Munagala in Krishna was in sight of a moral victory. What was of real consequence, however, had been lying portent — not in the number of successes of the leftist-led poor peasants, nor in the number of their failures — but in the political strength their successes and failures collectively represented, and in the prospect its utilisation offered for the future. Clearly by 1939, the rural poor had made their presence felt somewhat conspicuously on the national scenario, as much by their opposition on divergent issues to the landlords-usurers, as by their confrontation with the abettors of their opponents — the police, the officials and the ministries. If the acts of confronting the Raj in the countryside, and of challenging there its beneficiaries and promoters, were in any way indications of genuine aversion for imperialism — which they certainly were — the poor peasants did seem to emerge, consciously for the first time, as potentially a very powerful anti-imperialist force. The coming into being of their potentiality depended largely on its wilful recognition by other anti-imperialist contingents, and hinged decisively on the leftist policies and practices.

Act Two
1940-45

THE SETTING

The outbreak of the second world war had further bolstered up anti-imperialism in India, and added a certain new dimension to it. The fact that Britain eventually fumbled into an armed contest, which would debilitate and preoccupy the British for long, was enough in itself to encourage all the Raj's opponents. Despite the chorus of condemnation against the Fascists, or even some far-cry of sympathy with the British, Indians generally were interested in securing some political advantage out of Britain's predicament. While a few wanted to curry favour with the British by joining them at their hour of crisis, others pressed them for a price for the Indian support, namely, the concession of a national Government during the war, and a free India thereafter. A number of them even flexed their muscles for a physical confrontation with an overbearing Raj at its troublesome worst. All these attitudes stemmed essentially from a straightforward characterisation of the war, that it was an imperialist one, being fought by the imperial powers for a major redistribution and readjustment of their old and new spoils. If that, indeed, was the true character of the war, and which did seem to be so to many in 1939-40, then the interest of the subject people could be served best only by exploiting the difficulty of the British, and forcing as much leverage out of them as perhaps was possible. There, of course, were certain ponderings over the complexity of the circumstance, some qualms about the justification of placing the imperialists and their worst kind — the Fascists — in the same grade, or about the sagacity of playing down the anti-Fascist content of an imperialist war. The uneasiness had in fact been betrayed in the Congress anxiety for knowing the British "war aims", for finding out — in case it was envisaged to set up "a new world order" on the principles of democracy

— whether Indians should at all obtain a rightful place in it.[1] The British unwillingness, however, to convince Indians of any lofty cause they were fighting for, or to make some commitment on India's political future, over and above their reluctance to share power with Indians at the centre, did by no means help to articulate the anti-Fascist propensities of Indian people. Rather, the British obduracy, the arrogance with which they subjected India to their own war — with scant regard for the Indian sensibilities — had caused the public attention in India to slide away from anti-Fascism, and concentrate almost entirely on anti-imperialism. In the context of 1939-40, therefore, an all-out opposition to the Raj once again appeared to be a first priority to most Indians, barring, to an extent, those who depended upon the colonial system for their present fortunes, and also those who leaned heavily on the British for their future gains.

As staunch anti-imperialists, the Indian left — the Communists and the Congress Socialists — naturally felt easy at the way popular feelings had been turning against the British authorities over the issue of the war. The phoney combat, which the imperialist powers had tried to avoid by appeasing the Fascists, and in which they joined as a last resort to safeguard their own severely threatened interests, seemed to the leftists to be bearing a predominantly imperialist character. Their surmise was further reinforced when Soviet Russia — the spectre over the imperialists and the Fascists alike — concluded a non-aggression pact (on 29 August 1939) with the Nazi Germany, who could not possibly take on all at one time, to steer clear apparently from an imperialist imbroglio, or "a second imperialist war" as the Communists termed it.[2] The character of a war, however, might change for all concerned, or appeared to have changed even for a particular people, on account of a certain drastic alteration in the circumstances. Till such a dramatic shift took place, and

1. The Congress Working Committee Resolution, 14 September 1939, M. Gwyer and A. Appadorai (eds.), *Speeches and Documents on the Indian Constitution, 1921-47*, London, 1957, pp. 484-7.
2. "The Proletarian Path", File No. 1940/48, P.C. Joshi Archives, J.N.U., New Delhi.

its implications examined, the leftists in India, excepting a few, were at the ready not only to jump into the anti-imperialist bandwagon, but also to drive it to their chosen course. The attitude towards the war was so fundamental for them that their entire functioning within the colonial framework between 1940 and 1945 was moulded almost singularly by it. It had been more so with such of their avowed concerns as for the welfare of the peasantry in general, and the emancipation of the rural poor in particular, in view specially of the dominance of inter-depending imperialist oppressors and feudal exploiters in the countryside. Consequently, any alteration later in the leftist perception of an ever-changing war scenario — their understanding or misunderstanding of a subsequent twist and a turn on the battlefront — was bound to affect profoundly the cause of the radical agrarian transformation that they so stoutly stood for. Taking all this into account, and enjoying the obvious advantage of hindsight, one could conveniently review the interactions between the leftists and the rural poor in the war period in three discernible phases. While they were moving jointly in the first phase (1940-1) to take a step forward, the second phase (1942-3) saw them resiling from it, and the third (1944-5) found them again to be readying themselves for another lunge.

SCENE I
1940-41

In 1940-1 the Communists were perhaps the most vociferous advocates of an anti-imperialist national struggle among the left forces in India, and certainly the most ardent of them all in exhorting the *kisan* masses to play an important role in it. This fact had been overlooked, and also forgotten, so flagrantly later on,[3] that some elucidation of it is needed called for putting the record somewhat straight. According to the Communist understanding in 1940, India could neither remain neutral in the "imperialist war", nor support Britain in it by any chance, and "to do either would mean betrayal of the national movement".[4] What Indians had been historically obliged to do instead was to denounce as "traitors" all those who talked of supporting the Allies, or of cooperating with the Government for defence,[5] and "to make revolutionary use of the war crisis" for achieving their freedom.[6] By the "war crisis" the C.P.I. meant both the existential crisis for Britain and the "revolutionary crisis" within India where, during the pendency of the war, the destruction of provincial autonomy, the establishment of the Ordinance Raj, the repression

3. The adverse public reaction to the C.P.I.'s position in 1942, and its consequent isolation during the "Quit India" movement, had left such an overwhelming mark on the political observers and historians (including those apologetic apologists of the Communists themselves) that they invariably tend to judge the Communist activities in the war period almost entirely by the post-1942 developments (which have been discussed in some detail in Scene II of this Act), and without paying much heed to the pre-1942 occurrences.
4. The C.P.I. Politbureau Resolution of November 1939 was elaborated by the beginning of 1940 into a policy statement, entitled, "The Proletarian Path". It is available in File No. 1940/48, P.C. Joshi Archives, J.N.U., New Delhi
5. "The impending Agrarian Crisis and Our Tasks", Central Committee, C.P.I., Circular No. 59, 25 June 1940, Central Archives, Communist Party of India, Ajoy Bhavan, New Delhi.
6. "The Proletarian Path", File No. 1940/48, P.C. Joshi Archives, J.N.U., New Delhi.

of civil liberties and the acute economic exploitation, as well as the squeezing of all Indians (including those belonging to the national bourgeoisie) for financing the contest, would drive the people steadily to the path of revolt. The deepening of the crises should produce in due course a phase of "glorious possibilities", which the Communists thought to be their bounden duty to utilise. The utilisation, in the opinion of the C.P.I., was dependent upon the rallying of forces of national revolution in direct confrontation with the forces of British imperialism, or the harnessing of the nationalist revolutionaries for "armed insurrection" and "conquest of power".[7]

For a determined bid for state power, the Communists contemplated an intensification of the workers' and peasants' agitations, by resorting to strikes in major areas of industry and transport, as well as to "no-tax" and "no-rent" campaigns in the villages. Once the administration was thus rendered paralysed simultaneously in the urban and rural sectors, they wanted to launch an attack on the imperialist state apparatus, by over-running the police posts and storming the military positions with the help of bands of militant activists (the "national militia" as they were termed) on an extensive scale. The Communists anticipated a widespread tumult to effect cracks within the army, desertions of the Indian soldiers and their joining hands with the revolutionary masses. Following the destruction of the Raj, the political parties and other bodies representing the victorious populace were expected to form a provisional revolutionary Government, which in its turn would summon a Constituent Assembly — elected on the basis of adult franchise — to frame the constitution of free India.[8] They also desired the Constituent Assembly to function as an organ of the "people's power" to fulfil the basic demands of the national democratic revolution, namely, the establishment of a democratic republic, the formation of the people's army, the abolition of landlordism, the cancellation of the agricultural debts, the eight-hour limitation of the workers' daily labour, and the guaranteeing of living wage for them. The Communists were in favour of achieving the goal of national democratic revolution by upholding the

7. *Ibid.*
8. *Ibid.*

unifying traditions of the Indian National Congress, by isolating its vacillating Gandhian leadership, and by transforming the national movement into a proletarian-led mass upsurge against the foreign rule. To them, the battles against the British and their collaborators, against splitting the Congress, as well as against its compromising leaders, were part and parcel of the same anti-imperialist struggle.[9]

Unlike the earlier phase ending in 1939, the C.P.I. did not lay in 1940 any particular stress on the nurturing of a united left front. Although they hoped for the other leftists to play a prominent role in the crusade against imperialism, and also in weaning the Congress away from the Gandhian fold, the Communists seemed too keen to direct the entire enterprise to their ordained "proletarian path" by themselves, regardless of the possibility or impossibility of performing such an instant marvel in their limited strength and standing. If not wholly utopian, the Communist plan of 1940 — the echo of the Leninist call during the first world war in Russia for "turning the imperialist war into a civil war" — smacked certainly of "adventurism", a critical epithet they had used liberally in 1939 for attacking other fellow socialists' attitude towards the war.[10] Adventurism nevertheless was so rampant in 1940, and the spectacle of the Allied reverses offered such crudely romanticised potentialities, that no one — much less the revolutionists and militants — could remain wholly unaffected by it. Excepting the numerically sparse Royists, or the League of Radical Congressmen led by M.N. Roy, who were entitled to the claim of some originality for viewing the war even in 1940 as essentially an anti-Fascist popular one, and, therefore, for favouring support to the British war-efforts, much against the rising tide of populism,[11] all other leftist organisations of varying strength and

9. *Ibid.*
10. Second War Circular of the C.S.P., December 1939, issued by Jayaprakash Narayan, Gen. Secy., in Vinode Prasad Singh and Sunil Mishra (eds.), *Samajbadi Andolan Ke Dastabej*, 1934-52 (in Hindi), Delhi, 1985, p. 236.
11. See V.B. Karnik, *M.N. Roy: Political Biography*, Bombay, 1978; for Roy's views on the war in April 1940, and the Resolution of the League of Radical Congressmen, Meerut, October 1940, on p. 452 and pp. 457-8, respectively.

character assumed more or less similar high-strung adventurous postures, without, of course, being able to lay bare their respective positions as daringly, and exhaustively, as perhaps the Communists did. Few illustrations, howsoever implicit in their significance, should be sufficient to indicate the prevailing mood of Quixotic dare-devilry among the leftist political parties. The Forward Bloc, whose Supremo, Subhas Chandra Bose, was enamoured of the Fascist successes in the war, and who foresaw an impending British collapse in 1940, pleaded for an all-out offensive against the supposedly moribund Raj, and forcing it with the help of the Citizens' Volunteer Corps to give up power to the provisional national Governments at the centre and in the provinces.[12] The "Anushilan" group of Marxists, who formed the Revolutionary Socialist Party in March 1940 after breaking away from the C.S.P., on the ground that the latter had "surrendered to Gandhism",[13] and faltered to face the British, also toyed with the idea of a War Council at the head of a network of secret societies in Lucknow to spearhead "the anti-imperialist national democratic revolution".[14] The Communist League under the guardianship of Soumyendranath Tagore, a breakaway group of the C.P.I., which in April 1943 turned into the Revolutionary Communist Party of India, wished to work for the violent overthrow of British rule, the establishment of a provisional revolutionary Government and the founding of a democratic republic of workers and peasants to mark the attainment of the bourgeois democratic phase of the Indian revolution.[15] The Bolshevik Party, which was formed in 1939 by another group of Communist dissidents, did not really lag far behind others in its anticipation of a massive anti-imperialist revolutionary movement, carried on by the toiling masses for blowing up the Raj. Following the overthrow of the rule of the imperialists and the feudal elements, it foresaw the establishment of a "democratic

12. Bose's Nagpur Address, Second Session of the All India Forward Bloc Conference, 18 June 1940, and Bose's Statement in *Forward Bloc*, 29 June 1940, in Subhas Chandra Bose, *Crossroads*, Calcutta,1962, pp. 318-23.
13. Jogesh Chandra, Chatterji, *In Search of Freedom*, Calcutta 1967, pp. 527-8.
14. "Origin of R.S.P.", Buddhadev Bhattacharya, *The Call*, March-April 1981, Calcutta, Vol. XXXI, Nos. 3-4, p. 16.
15. Soumyendranath Tagore, *Revolution and Quit India*, Calcutta, 1946.

dictatorship of the proletariat and the peasantry".[16] The Bolshevik-Leninist Party (Trotskyite) likewise felt the urgency for capturing power, convening a revolutionary Constituent Assembly and setting up a workers' and peasants' Government.[17]

In the heady days of early 1940, when most of the leftists exuberantly messed up thus the realities and the unrealities of the situation, the C.S.P. seemed to have felt compelled to keep its cool, and restrain the belligerency of the rank and file. The C.S.P. was, however, the first among the left political parties to take a very aggressive stand on the issue of war, and in a manner that had additionally been the most uncompromising. As early as September 1939 (barely a week after Britain joined the war) it not only objected to the blatant British act of dragging a reluctant India into the "imperialist war", in which neither Germany nor Britain deserved any sympathy whatsoever, but also took it to be a kind of Hitler-like assault of the Raj on Indian sensibilities, which all self-respecting Indians could not but resist forthwith.[18] Refusing to bargain India's freedom for its support to the British war-efforts, mainly because such haggled independence would hardly be equivalent to a truly attained one, the C.S.P. was in favour of launching a determined offensive against the Raj without any loss of time. Indian people, in its view, did not really require much time to prepare for the confrontation, for their national pride had been hurt to such an extent by the British on the war-issue that they would readily respond to the call for action. [19] The C.S.P.'s energetic ascent to the dizzy height of militancy in September 1939, however, was as dramatic as its hurried descent two months later in November 1939. Failing miserably to change the A.I.C.C. war-resolution into a battle-cry for freedom at Wardha in October 1939, the

16. Draft Programme of the Bolshevik Party of India, Party Documents, Central Archives, C.P.I., Ajoy Bhavan, New Delhi.
17. Satyabrata Ray Chaudhuri, *Leftist Movements in India,1917-47*, Calcutta, 1977, p. 232.
18. First War Circular of the C.S.P., September 1939, issued by Jayaprakash Narayan, Gen. Secy., in Vinode Prasad Singh, and Sunil Mishra (eds.), *Samajbadi Andolan Ke Dastabej, 1934-52* (in Hindi), Delhi, 1985, pp. 227-30.
19. *Ibid.*

Congress Socialists abruptly discovered their own limitation — that they were not strong enough to fight the British imperialism alone, and that, for this purpose, they had no alternative but to fall back upon the Congress. Unlike the Communists, who thought about wresting the initiative within the Congress from the Gandhian leaders, the Congress Socialists in effect agreed to follow them devoutly all the way, except, of course, trying to keep the Congress on the rails of popular struggle.[20] Consequently, by the beginning of 1940, the C.S.P. had to continue to procrastinate over the moves that the Congress leadership made from time to time (such as, its refusal to cooperate with the British in the war, and its calling upon the provincial Congress ministries to resign) in the fond hope that it was moving eventually towards a show-down, "even if slowly".[21] The battle between the Congress and the Raj being "inevitable",[22] the Congress Socialists found it convenient to wait and watch, and "not to hurry".[23] Their persistence with patience was rewarded ironically in October 1940, not by the bang of an animated Congress-led mass movement against the Raj, but by the whimper of an under-played *satyagraha* by individual Congressmen and women. The Individual *Satyagraha's* object was to voice anti-war views, in violation of the war-time Government restrictions, by individuals specially selected for the purpose. It was clearly a device to make the Congress presence felt all over, and to give the militant popular feeling a symbolic vent, without providing the Government with any substantial ground for a severe crack-down.[24]

20. Second War Circular of the C.S.P., December 1939, *ibid.*, pp. 230-6.
21. *Ibid.*
22. Speeches of Acharya Narendra Deva at Fyzabad, Kanpur and Aligarh on 12, 13 and 14 November 1939, respectively, *Sangharsh* (Hindi weekly), 19 November 1939.
23. Rammanohar Lohia's speech at the U.P. Kisan Conference, Mathura, 17 December 1939, *ibid.*, 20 December 1939.
24. The courting of arrest by individual Congressmen and women, nominated initially by Gandhiji, and later by the Congress committees at various levels, reached its peak in June 1941 with the detention of nearly 20,000 persons. It, however, rapidly petered out by October 1941 when the authorities released most of the prisoners.

Both the Communists, who flared for action, and the Congress Socialists, who froze to inaction, had nevertheless a common stake in the countryside — among the *kisans* whom they jointly rallied from 1936 to 1939. Between themselves they seemed on the whole to agree to the view that the war situation was going to dislocate the price-structure of agricultural products, and adversely affect the dwindling fortunes of *kisans*. To ensure cheap supply of raw materials for the war, the British authorities would try to control the agricultural prices by imposing import restrictions on a variety of items. Such restrictions, which were actually introduced in the first half of 1940, should obstruct the primary producers from obtaining higher prices for their produce, but would not prevent the middlemen and speculators from raising prices in the markets through manipulations. The *kisans*, who lacked the holding power, excepting a small minority of the rich and the affluent among them, were already known for their selling freshly harvested crops when the prices had not yet picked up, and also for buying grains — after consuming in several months what they retained for themselves — when the prices had really reached their peak. This syndrome of the average *kisan's* low-selling and high-buying was likely to be accentuated further during the war-years, owing as much to the half-hearted interventionism of the Government as to the manipulating stratagem of grain-dealers. Almost similar tendencies would operate practically the same way in the marketing of industrial and consumer products, subjecting the *kisan* and his family to exorbitantly high prices for essential com-modities, such as clothes, cooking and kerosene oils, utensils, matchboxes and tilling implements. Worse still would be *kisans*' inability to get any return from their commercial or cash crops on account of the major buyers' — the European countries' — joining the war one after another, and dropping thereby from India's export list. Those, who still had not joined the war, did find maritime transport difficult because of it, and looked for suitable substitutes, as the U.S.A. was trying to do for a replacement of jute. In fact in the six months between 20 December 1939 and 13 June 1940 the prices of some important commercial crops in India showed, as per their opening rates in Bombay market, a steady decline:[25]

ground-nut	29%
ground-nut oil-cake	49%
linseed	37%
cotton seed	9.5%
jute	26%

The leftists of all hues appeared on the whole to have foreshadowed in 1940 the onrush of a severe agrarian crisis in India — perhaps "more devastating" than of the time of the great Depression.[26] Most of them also anticipated the unfolding of the agrarian crisis to coincide with the crumbling of the British power in the war. If that was likely to be the scenario, what should they do to perform their immediate, as well as distant political tasks? The Congress Socialists were in favour of enlivening the *kisan* movement by holding British imperialism responsible for the inflationary trends, and by preparing the peasantry for "no-tax" and "no-rent" campaigns as constituents of a large nationwide civil disobedience movement.[27] The Communists also thought about explaining that the agrarian crisis was not the outcome of any natural calamity, but the effect of the war imposed on *kisans* by an alien Government.[28] They intended further to make extensive use of *kisan* marches and "no tax", "no rent" campaigns as preparations for a national upsurge.[29] Both of them decided to harp on such general agrarian items as remission of rents and land revenues, moratorium on debts and interests,

25. "The Impending Agrarian Crisis and Our Tasks", Central Committee, C.P.I., Circular No. 59, 25 June 1940, Central Archives, Communist Party of India, Ajoy Bhavan, New Delhi.
26. *Ibid.*
27. Second War Circular of the C.S.P., December 1939, issued by Jayaprakash Narayan, Gen. Secy., in Vinode Prasad Singh, and Sunil Mishra (eds.), *Samajbadi Andolan Ke Dastabej, 1939-52* (in Hindi), Delhi, 1985, p. 234.
28. "The Impending Agrarian Crisis and Our Tasks", Central Committee, C.P.I. Circular No. 59 of 25 June 1940, Party Documents, Central Archives, Communist Party of India, Ajoy Bhavan, New Delhi.
29. "Proletarian Path", File No. 1940/48., P.C. Joshi. Archives, J.N.U., New Delhi.

remunerative prices for agricultural products, fixation of prices for the manufactured items which *kisans* commonly used, and opposition to the war-recruitments, war-levies and war-loans for mobilising the peasantry — the upper crust of it more perhaps than its base. The base, or the multitudinous rural poor, could effectively be raised if more fundamental issues were taken up, as it had been done between 1936 and 1939, such as their wages and greater crop-shares, and their freedom from bondages, forced labours and feudal exactions. The strong linkages between the indigenous exploiters and the imperialists — those who squabbled among themselves for spoils in different parts of the world — were, after all, a lot easier to convey to the peasant masses than the complicated connections in the price structure, the imperial Government and a remote war. Much depended really upon the panoramic overview that one had taken of the anti-imperial and anti-feudal movements as they stood in India in 1940, and the possibilities he or she had seen during the war of their supplementing and complementing each other. Seen in this light, the C.S.P.'s perception was found on the whole to be characteristically more nationalistic than socialistic. Despite their anxiety for maintaining a separate organisation of *kisans*, taking up *kisans*' "day to day economic demands",[30] and encouraging *kisans* to resist oppressions,[31] the Congress Socialists preferred to give the attainment of independence, or the united struggle for "democractic revo-lution" a clear priority over the struggle for "social revolution", or the opposition to the exploiters within Indian society, as if the two were distinctly separate thrusts which could never be driven on rewardingly together even up to a certain point. In their view the success of the national movement depended singularly on the unity of the democratic forces, coming from all classes of the people, including the peeved exploitative ones, and therefore, they must exercise extreme caution, "for if we impose social revolution on democratic revolution, it will break the unity

30. *Sangharsh* (Hindi weekly), 12 August and 9 September 1940.
31. *Ibid.*, 26 August 1940.

of the democratic forces".[32] Still the Congress Socialists expected the process of democratic revolution to draw the *kisan* masses in spite of its lacking in social content, mainly because of the *kisans*' growing realisation that the social changes in their interest could take place only after the country was freed from foreign domination.[33] Nowhere did their leaders try to explain how they came to know what *kisans*, especially the more numerous poor *kisans*, were actually realising, and why should the democratic unity suffer in quantity and quality if a certain social content of it attracted innumerable poor *kisans*, and distracted some numerable landed interests.

The Communists, on their part, were in favour of imparting social content into the democratic, or, in their terminology, the "national democratic" revolution to put forward "the revolutionary slogans as the slogans of the entire national movement", and build it up — with the widest possible participation of the toiling masses — as "the people's movement".[34] To achieve this end in the countryside, and to guarantee the maximum possible *kisan* participation in the nationalist struggle, therefore, they felt it necessary to continue simultaneously with their work for the "agrarian revolution", or for the introduction of fundamental changes in the agrarian relations by ending the feudal stranglehold of the landlord-usurer-colonialist combine, and by vesting ownership of land in the tiller. To them, anti-imperialism and anti-feudalism were aspects of the same popular struggle against the colonial system, each attracting its own warriors from the ranks of the other. Of the two main slogans of the agraian revolution, namely "abolish landlordism" and "give land to the tiller", the Communists were prepared in 1940 for raising the first, and backing it up with the militant action against the oppressions of landlords and the police.[35] They were also favourabley disposed towards raising the second slogan, and wished to give an

32. *Ibid.*, 10 December 1939.
33. Narendra Deva's statement on the Independence Day, *ibid.*, 28 January 1940.
34. "Proletarian Path", File No. 1940/48, P.C. Joshi Archives, J.N.U., New Delhi.
35. *Ibid.*

intermediary call to the peasants "to hold the crop", to refuse to pay part of it as rent, and to resist by all means its confiscation.[36] The potentiality of the new slogan was so radically tempered, and its "no-rent" implication so wide in sweep, that it alarmed the guardians of law and order as soon as it had been conceived.[37] In comparison with the C.S.P.'s hesitancy, the C.P.I. was confident that the agrarian scenario would become the storm-centre of anti-imperialist trial of strength, that the mass of *kisans* should play a leading part in it, and that — to ensure their role — the Communist *kisan* organisers "must dig themselves in".[38] Even then, whether they felt confident or diffident, the C.P.I. and the C.S.P. together were really in a position in 1940 to lead the rural poor to the path of resistance all over the country, commit the All India Kisan Sabha to day-to-day struggles against feudal exploiters, "end the economic power of those parasites of imperialism, and shake the political might of the British Government in the land".[39] Other left parties and groups had little base among *kisans*, they were either totally absent from the scene (such as the Bolshevik Party, the Bolshevik-Leninist Party and the League of Radical Congressmen), or peripherally present in certain pockets (such as, the Forward Bloc in small stretches of the Central Provinces and Bihar, the R.S.P. in a few localities of north Bengal, and the Communist League in a tiny spot of south-west Bengal).

In their espousal of the rural poor's causes, the Communists, the Congress Socialists and their allies in the All India Kisan Sabha, however, had to suffer in 1939-40 from two noticeable handicaps — one external to their joint venture, and the other internalised in its everyday working. Externally, the leftists and the rural poor both were subjected to the draconian restriction of civil liberties that the Raj had imposed on the Indian people in the name of war-time exigency. The day India was committed to

36. "The Impending Agrarian Crisis and Our Tasks", Central Committee, C.P.I., Circular No.59 of 25 June 1940, Party Documents, Central Archives, Communist Party of India, Ajoy Bhavan, New Delhi.
37. Home Poll. Fortnightly Report for 1st half of July 1940, File No. 18/7/40, N.A.I.
38. "Proletarian Path", File No. 1940/48 P.C. Joshi Archives, J.N.U., New Delhi.
39. Political Resolution, 5th Session of the A.I.K.S., Palasa, March 1940, in M.A. Rasul, *History of the All India Kisan Sabha*, Calcutta, 1974, p. 66.

war (3 September 1939), the authorities announced their intention to formulate the Defence of India Rules, "expedient for... the maintenance of public order", over and above the defence of British India.[40] The D.I.Rs., drawn on the lines of the Defence of India (Criminal Law Amendment) Act of 1915 and the War Regulations in the United Kingdom, were promptly framed and hurriedly passed by the end of September 1939 as the Defence of India Act. The Act empowered the central Government to make rules for all conceivable subjects, and conferred upon it wide and drastic powers over civil life in India while the war lasted. The authorities could prohibit or regulate public meetings, fairs and processions; prevent the use of uniforms and flags; censor messages and stop publication of news; restrict movement of people in specified areas; detain them for contravening the rules under the Act; and, if necessary, bring them for trial before the specially created tribunals.[41] Consequently, any act or speech in public, whether it directly concerned the British war-efforts or not, might be construed as an offence, and proceeded against. Howsoever much they tried to be ready for "emergencies",[42] and blend "open" works with the "secret",[43] the agrarian agitators were certain to face immense difficulty in evading internment, externment and detention, with or without trial, and in conducting meetings, rallies and processions. These external blocks could become more stumbling if the internal cohesion was threatened by some discord. Internally, the leftist consolidation on the *kisan* front was already under strain on account of unseemly mutual bickerings between the C.S.P. and the C.P.I.

It all started with the tendency of those Communists who were members of the C.S.P. to function as a well-knit group, as perhaps

40. N. Mitra (ed.), *The Indian Annual Register*, July-Dec. 1939, Vol. II, p.21.
41. Low Francis (ed.), *The Indian Year Book, 1940-41*, Vol. XXXVI, pp. 502 and 892.
42. Second War Circular of C.S.P., December 1939, issued by Jayaprakash Narayan, Gen. Secy., in Vinode Prasad Singh, and Sunil Mishra (eds.) *Samajbadi Andolan Ke Dastabej, 1934-52* (in Hindi), Delhi, 1985, p. 237.
43. "The Impending Agrarian Crisis and Our Tasks", Central Committee, C.P.I., Circular No.59 of 25 June 1940, Party Documents, Central Archives, Communist Party of India, Ajoy Bhavan, New Delhi.

some of the anti-Communists similarly did under the guidance of Minoo Masani and Asoka Mehta,[44] and press upon the party their own ideological predilections. The fact was that the Communists considered the C.S.P. as an open platform of broad left unity, or a kind of mass organisation, and therefore, they were anxious — particularly when their own party continued to remain illegal — for making the best use of it, and try persistently and ingeniously to control it.[45] There was nothing unusual about such expansionist conduct, for any political group that joined the mass organisation — whether a trade-union, a Kisan Sabha or a cultural association — adopted, more or less, the same behavioural pattern, including the Congress Socialists themselves, without, of course much success *vis-a-vis* the Indian National Congress. What irked the Congress Socialists most was not the presence of a separate Communist bloc among them, but its being able — through means fair and not so fair — to establish control over the C.S.P. units in the south,[46] in the Punjab in substance,[47] and in attaining some position of strength in other places. The Communist challenge within the C.S.P. surfaced alarmingly for the Congress Socialists at the party's Lahore Conference in April 1938 when the Communist members put up a separate draft thesis for adoption, and a panel of their own names for election to the National Executive. Although both were narrowly defeated, the Congress Socialists had to confront the Communist bid for a take-over, and begin a fight to prevent it. It was in this context that they raised a row over the Communist "plan of work" in the C.S.P. (May 1938), discovered the "Communist plot" against it (September 1938) and accused the Communists of "infiltration" into the organisation stealthily in the guise of a "Trojan horse".[48] The Communists retaliated by physically taking over those local units of the C.S.P.

44. Sajjad Zaheer's oral history transcript, no. 298, pp. 92-3, Manuscript Section, Nehru Memorial Museum and Library, New Delhi.
45. B.P.L. Bedi's oral history transcript, no. 270, pp 109-10, *ibid.*
46. M.R. Masani, *The Communist Party of India*, London, 1945, p. 69
47. B.P.L. Bedi's oral history transcript, no.270, pp. 105-6, Manuscript Section, Nehru Memorial Museum and Library, New Delhi.
48. M.R. Masani, *The Communist Party of India*, London, 1945, pp. 67-9.

in which they dominated, and by accusing the Congress Socialists of anti-Marxism, social-reformism, adventurism and Menshevik opportunism in turn. The Communists and the Congress Socialists were thus steadily falling apart from the end of 1938 to the end of 1939, though Jayaprakash Narayan — one of the leading Congress Socialists and the General Secretary of the C.S.P. — tried benignly to postpone the process. In April 1940 came the final break when the National Executive of the C.S.P. directed its provincial units to ask for the resignation of Communist members, and in default of which, to expel them from the party.[49] The eventual break, and all the unpleasantries which preceded it, had already corroded the C.P.I.-C.S.P. joint enterprise in the trade-union and student movements. That they should be able to do the same to the *kisan* movement was, therefore, a foregone conclusion.

Handicaps notwithstanding, the prospect of the poor *kisans*' agitation in India, which — in the ultimate analysis — depended more on the agitated than on the agitators, was far from unsatisfactory. Obviously, the war-time inflationary trends, from which *kisans* would hardly benefit as producers, but suffer heavily as buyers, barring, of course, the well-to-do among them, was destined to add to their prevailing burden of misfortunes. Similarly, the distress of the agricultural labourers would certainly accentuate on account of their inability to maintain the precarious balance between the low wages (having little prospect of a rise, if at all) and the steep upward movement of the prices in general.[50] Apart from the economic pressure that invariably contributed to peasant militancy, as it clearly did in the previous phase of economic deflation, a certain desire for self-assertion, a kind of belief in themselves, seemed to have come over the poor peasants, the sharecroppers and the agricultural labourers. The experience of the numerous partial struggles they waged at the instance of the leftists, between 1936 and 1939, was responsible for the subtle change in their disposition. The memories of the little advances they made in

49. Resolution, National Executive, C.S.P., 1940, in Vinode Prasad Singh and Sunil Mishra (eds.), *Samajbadi Andolan Ke Dastabej, 1934-52* (in Hindi), Delhi, 1985, p. 193.

50. "Economic Effects of War", a write-up by R.D. Bhardwaj, 1940, Central Archives, Communist Party of India, Ajoy Bhavan, New Delhi.

such engagements far outlasted the agony of the ground they lost, or they were used to losing. Resultantly, they were more conscious than before of their social exploitation, and more willing than ever to resist all its manifestations, provided the torch-bearers — the enlightening ideologues — showed them the way. A sample survey of the happenings on the *kisan* front, those which involved the rural poor and the leftists, should bear this out to some extent. Together they waged in 1940-1 battles against repressions of the authorities, oppressions of the *Zamindars* and other landlords and evictions from lands they tilled, simultaneously with fights for their customary rights over forests and tanks, their share of crops, living wages and freedom from bondages.

The uncertainties of employment and the pangs of hunger so gripped the agricultural labourers in 1940-1 that they seemed to have concentrated almost all their energies on the search for food rather than on their right to fight for higher wages. This was apparent from the way they acted under the influence of the Communists and the Congress Socialists in the southern part of India. On 15 September 1940 a considerable number of agricultural labourers surrounded the Sub-Divisional Officer of Tenali, Guntur, demanding employment and food.[51] A similar crowd of them was reported to have waited upon the Senior Sub-Divisional Magistrate at Gundivada, Andhra.[52] The leftists also organised "hunger-marches" in Malabar, as well as in Salem, Ramnad, Chingleput and Trichinopoly districts of Tamil Nadu. Their frequency increased so much by July 1941 that the authorities started dubbing them as "routine" in the province of Madras. "Hunger-marches" from villages went to the *Tahsildars* and Sub-Divisional Officers to represent their sufferings on account mainly of the phenomenal rise (twice the price of the previous year) in the price of rice. The "marches" were common in the south, as well as in the east, where one such "march"

51. Home Poll. Fortnightly Report for 2nd half of September, 1940, File No. 18/9/40, N.A.I.

52. Government of Madras, Public (General) Dept., D.O. No. P4-a23 of 20.12.1940, Fortnightly Report for 1st half of December 1940, Tamil Nadu State Archives, Madras.

created a furore at Habiganj, Assam, in December 1941.[53] In Malabar the local Karshak Sanghams, under the Communist guidance, embarked upon a novel and a highly original method of consumer resistance by the agricultural labourers. They enquired into the prices that *kisans* received for their paddy, calculated the price of one seer of rice at that rate, and then added to it one anna to the rupee. The amount arrived at was recommended to the "hunger-marchers" as the proper price to be paid for rice, and they were encouraged to go to the grain shops in a body while marching on, or returning from a march, and buy their supplies.[54] The exercise of force hidden in such consumer resistance came to the open in the "hunger-marches" in some divisions of Krishna, West Godavari and East Godavari districts of Andhra. Claiming that they had not received their seasonal customary advances, the marching labourers demanded free doles of grains from their employers under the threat of "looting".[55] The threat created so much panic among the well-to-do landholders and the rich peasants, that the authorities were pressurised by them to unleash terror upon the agitators and prosecute five or six of their leaders.[56] Almost an identical situation developed a little later in Rangpur, Bengal, where the Communist-led "hunger-marchers" demanded in April 1941 paddy advances from the village rich.[57] About 200 persons were reported to have stormed into the house of a local *mahajan* at Gopikantapur, Birbhum, in July 1941 to demand paddy loans.[58] The agricultural labourers in Nadia went a step further, and had actually "extorted" advances of paddy from their prospective

53. Home Poll. Fortnightly Report for 2nd half of December 1941, File No. 18/12/41, N.A.I.
54. Extract from cyclostyled Party Circular in Malayalam, no.37 of the Kerala Branch of the C.P.I., Home Poll. File No. 7/9/41 Poll(1) of 1941, N.A.I.
55. Government of Madras, Public (General) Dept., D.O. No. P4-19, Fortnightly Report for 2nd half of September and 1st half of October 1940, Tamil Nadu State Archives, Madras.
56. Home Poll. Fortnightly Report for 2nd half of April 1941, File No. 18/4/41, N.A.I.
57. *Ibid.*
58. Home Poll, Fortnightly Report for 1st half of July 1941, File No. 13/41, West Bengal State Archives, Calcutta.

employers.[59] The looting of grains and grain shops had already started in Tamil Nadu as early as October 1939,[60] and in Andhra, notably in East Godavari district, by June 1940.[61] Widespread in different parts of Madras province in the second half of 1940, and throughout 1941, the cases of looting had also been reported from eastern India. Orissa, for example, reported a sharp rise in the theft of paddy and utensils,[62] and paddy-looting was believed to be quite common in Hooghly and Midnapore districts of Bengal.[63] There were also reports of large scale paddy-looting from Khulna and Basirhat sub-division of the 24-Parganas,[64] as well as from many parts of Chittagong Division of Bengal in December 1941.[65] By January 1942 reports of looting of *hats* (weekly fairs or *bazaars*) started piling up from the 24-Parganas, Mymensingh and Rajsahi districts of Bengal.[66] Whether they were directly involved in all such cases of brigandage or not, the left activists might have indirectly supported them. Their involvement in the agitations of the Dublas and Dhodias, however, was wholly direct and unequivocal.

The agitation of the Dubla field-hands was an on-going one from 1938-9 against the notorious *Hali* system of bonded labour in certain parts of Surat and Broach districts.[67] They were demanding, under the guidance of Gujarat Kisan Sabha, the abrogation of their past debts which had been instrumental in turning them into the *Halis*, and the abolition of the *Hali* system altogether, as well as the recognition of their right to

59. Home Poll. Fortnightly Report for 1st half of June 1941, File No. 18/6/41, N.A.I.
60. Public Dept. Government of Madras, G.O. No. 1719 (MS), Confidential, Tamil Nadu State Archives, Madras.
61. Home Poll. Fortnightly Report for 1st half of June 1940, File No. 18/6/40, N.A.I.
62. Biswamoy Pati, *Resisting Domination : Peasants, Tribals and the National Movement in Orissa, 1920-50*, New Delhi, 1993, p. 149.
63. Home Poll. Fortnightly Report for 1st half of June 1941, File No. 18/6/41, N.A.I.
64. *Ibid.*, 2nd half of October 1941, File No. 18/10/41, N.A.I.
65. *Ibid.*, 1st half of December 1941, File No. 18/12/41, N.A.I.
66. *Ibid.*, 2nd half of January 1942, File No. 18/1/42, N.A.I.
67 See Act I, Scene I, pp. 44-6.

work as free wage-earners. The *Dhaniamas* or the landlords, *mahajans* and rich peasants, in their turn, had refused to make any concession to the Dublas, in spite of the long-drawn strikes of the *Halis* practically throughout the second half of 1939. The beginning of 1940 witnessed not only a continuation of the *Hali* strikes, but also the expression of massive support the Dublas received from the rest of the local landless and sharecropping peasantry. Meetings and processions were held in their favour, spearheaded by such leaders as Yajnik, Pangarkar, Thakorebhai and Vicaji. The unrest, which was confined in the past to Bardoli *taluk* in the main, had extended in the first quarter of 1940 to Olpad, Chorasi and Mandavi *taluks.*[68] Some compromise had, however, been effected in March 1940 through the mediation of the local Congress, by which the *Dhaniamas* agreed not to press the Dublas for the repayment of old debts, and to engage them for the present at fixed daily wages in cash.[69] The issue nevertheless was not settled, and it lingered on for some more time in south Gujarat, especially in Broach. South Gujarat was also the scene of the struggle of the Dhodia agricultural labourers, and it started originally over a piece of land some of them possessed at village Paria of Pardi Mahal. When a *mahajan*-landlord tried to grab the land, the Dhodias resisted, and the consequent clash resulted in the arrest and conviction of 13 persons. It was for the defence of the Dhodias that Thakorebhai, Pangarkar and Yajnik reached the village, and addressed their first meeting there on 30 April 1939. The sustained propaganda of these Kisan Sabha leaders soon awakened the Dhodias, and inspired them to demand for the advances and higher wages. Thakorebhai in fact distributed among them a leaflet detailing the minimum rates of wages that the Kisan Sabha had decided on 28 February 1940 for all the agricultural labourers in Gujarat.[70] The *sahukars*-landlords retaliated by deciding to bring field-hands from outside to work

68 Report of the District Superintendent of Police, Surat, 21.3.40, Home (Sp.) Dept., File No. 1019 of 1940-1, Maharashtra State Archives, Bombay.

69. *Ibid.*

70. Home (Sp.) Dept. Note 20.3.40, File No. 800(53) BV of 1939-41, Maharashtra State Archives, Bombay.

on their lands. Over this question of importation of labour, commenced thereafter a series of clashes between the Dhodias and the landlords' hirelings, leading to physical fights, police cases and even *kisan*-police confrontations.[71] The agitation, which also spread over Bulsar *taluk*, suffered a setback in May 1940 with the internment of Yajnik and Pangarkar in Ahemedabad and Surat towns, respectively, and it gradually wilted under the repressions of the authorities from June onwards. The case of the Dhodias was perhaps the lone instance in the whole of 1940-1 in which the agricultural labourers actually fought in an organised manner for a wage-increase. Otherwise, they and their leaders were content most of the time in raising the issue, without fighting for it, as they did, for example, in the Bhandara District Kisan Conference at Mahagaon, the Central Provinces, in January 1940,[72] in the *kisan* "marches" in the province of Madras in October 1940,[73] in the *kisan* "march" at Thesra, Kaira district, in January 1940[74] and in the Maharashtra Kisan Confer-ence at Dhulia, West Khandesh, in May 1941.[75]

Compared to the resistance of agricultural wage-earners, the sharecroppers' struggle seemed to have excelled as much in number and territorial extent as in voicing the basic slogan. The sharecroppers of south Gujarat, for example, especially of Pardi Mahal, Chikhli Mahal and Bulsar in Surat district, and Kalol in the Panch Mahals district, raised the issue of sharing crops straightaway, without any beating about the bush. Apart from keeping one-half of the crops for themselves, the *sahukars*-landlords invariably retained a considerable portion of tillers' share either as repayment of some loans they had already been

71. Report of District Superintendent of Police, Surat, 21.3.40, Home (Sp.) Dept., File No. 1019 of 1940-41, Maharashtra State Archives, Bombay.
72. Home Poll. Fortnightly Report for 1st half of January 1940, File No. 18/1/40, N.A.I.
73. *Ibid.*, 2nd half of October 1940, File No. 18/10/40, N.A.I.
74. C.I.D. Report, 16.1.40, Home (Sp.) Dept., File No. 1019 of 1940-1, Maharashtra State Archives, Bombay.
75. Report of the District Superintendent of Police, West Khandesh, 10. 5. 41, Home (Sp) Dept., File No. 800(53)-B(1), 1941, Maharashtra State Archives, Bombay.

alleged to have taken, or as deduction of certain other charges, such as, for pasturage, for the safe-keeping and measuring of grains etc. The inequality of division had hit the *kisans* very hard when crops failed in 1938-9 on account of scarce rainfall, and the Government was forced to suspend partially the collection of revenue in about 40 villages.[76] Placed in such difficult circumstances, the sharecroppers refused to give the crop-shares to the landlords, who promptly began taking recourse to the court proceedings. As a result, by the first quarter of 1940, a powerful agitation developed in the area among the "misguided" sharecroppers at the instigation of "outside leaders" like Thakorebhai, Vicaji, Pangarkar and Yajnik.[77] Large rallies were held and processions were taken out, demanding two-thirds crop-share for tillers and one-third for landlords.[78] Singing songs and wielding *lathis* (sticks), *kisans* participated in the demonstrations in large numbers and displayed a solidarity not witnessed in this region ever before.[79] Soon the inevitabilities followed one after the other — clash with the landlords' goons, appearance of the custodians of law and order on the scene, externment of the *kisan* leaders from the affected area under Rule 26 of the D.I.R., prohibition of demonstrations and meetings there under Sec.144 Cr. P.C. and arrest of 26 persons. The authorities, who took the agitation to be "patently Communist in its instigation", were determined to quell it expeditiously.[80] Although smouldering throughout the second half of 1940, and the news of sharecroppers' meetings still trickling in as late as 1941,[81] the agitation was practically over by June 1940 with a few nominal gains, such as the withholding of the landlords'

76. Report of District Magistrate, Surat, 21 March 1940, Home (Sp.) Dept., File No. 1019 of 1940-1, Maharashtra State Archives, Bombay.
77. Report of the District Superintendent of Police, Surat, 21.3.40, *ibid.*
78. *Ibid.*
79. *Ibid.* The atmosphere was almost as high-strung and heady as that of the *Tebhaga* movement in Bengal (1946-47) which south Gujarat wholly anticipated in its miniature form six years earlier.
80. Note of Secretary, Revenue Dept., 2.5.40, Home (Sp.) Dept., File No. 800 (53) - BV of 1939-41, Maharashtra State Archives, Bombay.
81. *Ibid.*

crop-share in some cases, and certain landlords' agreeing under duress to scale down the produce-rent a little.

The crop-share or the produce-rent seemed also to have generated a strong undercurrent of tension between the tenants-at-will and their landlords in Tamil Nadu. That it had not taken the shape of an open agitation, in the manner it did in south Gujarat, was due perhaps to the "organisational weakness" of the left *kisan* activists in Tamil Nadu,[82] as compared to those in other parts of Madras province. The sensitive nature of the situation could nevertheless be felt from the citation of a simple incident — typifying many such others — that occurred in Trichinopoly district in the middle of 1940. The Pallars of Lalgudi *taluk* cultivated annually the lands of the Brahmin *Mirasdars* on the basis of sharing the crops — not in the usual equal proportions, but by surrendering 60 per cent of gross yield to the landlords and retaining 40 per cent for themselves. Meeting all the cultivating expenses (for seeds, manure, bullocks, implements etc.) from their share, the Pallars were left eventually with about 20 per cent of the gross yield[83] — a quantity too inadequate to support even the barest of livelihood. Consequently, they readily rallied round one M.K. Gupta, "a professional agitator from the Justice Party",[84] who was bent upon plaguing the Brahmin landlords. He exhorted the Pallars to refuse to cultivate the lands till the *Mirasdars* agreed to raise the annual crop-sharing arrangement more equitably, or scale down the rent. Gupta and a few of his associates started addressing the meetings of the Pallars in April, and by June 1940 — with the approach of the sowing season — the agitation picked up some momentum. The *Mirasdars* could neither search out new sharecroppers nor import agricultural labourers from outside. They were, however, bailed out of their difficulty by the friendly authorities, who promptly clamped Section 144

82. *Annual Report of the A.I.K.S.* 1939-40, p. 33.
83. Collector, Trichi, to Secretary, Public Dept., Government of Fort St. George, 20 June 1940, Public (Gen.) Dept., File No. G.O.N. 1466 of 27.7.40 Tamil Nadu State Archives, Madras.

Cr.P.C. in Lalgudi to deal with the prevailing "lawlessness".[85] Gupta fled from the scene at the very sight of the police, and the district authorities faced little difficulty in containing the Pallars soon in a ham-handed manner.

Although the condition of the Santhal *Bataidars* in Purnea district of north Bihar was similar to that of the Pallars in Trichinopoly, if not worse, the issue of crop-share had as such hardly dominated their line of action or agitation in 1940-1. Lands were leased to the Santhal *Bataidars* by the *Maliks* (substantial tenants of *Zamindars* like the *Jotedars* of Bengal) on yearly *adhi-batai* at oral terms, or on payment of half the gross produce as rent. The *Bataidars*, who provided all the inputs in labour and kind, were subjected by the *Maliks* to various types of illegal exactions or *abwabs*, from *salami* (charges for the contract) to *laogi* (charges for guarding the crops), from *peechhla* (charges for weighing grains)) to *turi* (the last layer of grains on the threshing floor), over and above *begari* (unpaid labour) on every conceivable count. Deducting *adhi-batai* and the *abwabs* from their share, the Santhal sharecroppers in Purnea used to receive, even by generous official calculations, "about one-third of the produce".[86] Despite such open loot from their share of crops, which was directly and immediately responsible for sharecroppers' precarious state of existence, the Santhal *Bataidars* had neither seriously questioned the sharing arrangement, nor brought to the fore their demand for a reduction in produce-rent. They did, however, wage an impressive battle of their own mainly around the tenurial

85. Notes of the Public (Gen.) Dept., Government of Madras, of 23.9.40 and 7.11.40, *ibid.*

86. N.P. Thadani, Collector of Purnea, "Report on the Agrarian Trouble in Dhamdaha and Dharahara Police Stations of Purnea District", Political and Special Dept. Government of Bihar, File No.120(1), n. 39, p. 51, 1940, cited in Anand Chakravarti's "The Unfinished Struggle of Santhal Bataidars in Purnea District, 1938-42", *Economic and Political Weekly*, Vol.XXI, no. 42, 18 October 1986, p. 1854. In Chakravarti's own opinion this was an over-estimate, since the exactions on account of *adhi-batai, laogi* and *peechhla* alone reduced twenty seven and a half seers from every maund the sharecroppers received (p. 1855).

right to stay on the lands they tilled (to be taken up in this scene a little later), but curiously enough, without highlighting the injustice involved in the tilling system itself. The reason behind this exceptional behaviour was partly the urgency they felt for standing against the *Maliks'* determination to throw them out of their lands, and partly the prospect they saw in their resistance for acquiring some occupational right. What, however, seemed to be more baffling was the fact that the issue of sharing crops did not spark off any significant move for agitation in Bengal, where sharecroppers happened to be most numerous, and the Communist *kisan* agitators most vociferous. Had the question not been a heavily pressing one for the sharecroppers, and the leftists not been aware of its gravity, the relative quietude over it would have been understandable. Contrarily, however, the *Bargadars*, or *Bhagchasis* or *Adhiars* of most parts of Bengal — as it was natural for them — were not only very sore about the mode of crop-sharing, but also anxious for bringing about an urgent change in the arrangement. They were known for sometime in certain areas of Jessore district to have clamoured for the two-thirds share of the crop.[87] Their concern was also reflected in the anti-*Jotedar* outcry over the crop-share at Thakurgaon, Dinajpur, in February 1940.[88] In Tamluk, Midnapore, the *Bhagchasis* demonstrated against the *Jotedars* in March 1941, demanding "more than one-half share of the crop".[89] In Khulna the *Adhiars* insisted in December 1941 on passing over to the *Jotedars* "only one-third of the crop share".[90] The justification of such demands was already known to the Government, as well as to the public, through the publication in 1940 of the findings of the Land Revenue (Floud) Commission of 1938, who took pity on the *Bargadars'* plight,

87. Ranajit Das Gupta, "Krishak O Rajneeti: Jalpaiguri" (in Bengali), *Parichaya*, November 1983, p. 72.
88. Home Poll. Fortnightly Report for 2nd half of Feburary 1940, File No. 18/2/40, N.A.I.
89. Home Poll. Fortnightly Report for 2nd half of March 1941, File No.13141, West Bengal State Archives, Calcutta.
90. Home Poll. Fortnightly Report for 2nd half of December 1941, File No. 18/12/41, N.A.I.

and recommended a two-thirds share of crops in their favour. The left-dominated B.P.K.S., who knew, or supposed to have known the sharecroppers' anxiety all along, also felt encouraged by the Commission's stand to recognise in its 4th Conference at Panjia, Jessore (8-9 June 1940), the *Bhagchasis'* claim to a two-thirds share. Yet the leftists, even the Communists, did hardly talk about agitating for the two-thirds share immediately before, or long after the Panjia Conference till September 1946 — after withholding the march of history for six long years — when they dramatically called for a struggle for the *Tebhaga* (the two-thirds share). This wavering over such a vital point was inexplicable, except perhaps in terms of the leftist, or the Communist reluctance to go against the interest of the urbane *Bhadralok* middleclass, who had links with the countryside only as the rentiers of the sharecropped lands, and from whose ranks emerged most of the highpriests of radicalism in Bengal. The leftists' hesitancy nevertheless was confined to the sharing of crops, without affecting much their otherwise steadfast commitment to the sharecroppers' overall welfare. That was the reason why they could be credited in 1940-1 with the organisation of two forceful sharecroppers' agitations in Bengal, namely, the *Hattola* and the *Adhiar*.

The *Hattola* agitation or the resistance to the *Jotedars'* levy on the weekly *hat* (market) proceeds was a continuing one since its signal success in Dinajpur and Jalpaiguri in 1939. The cause was taken up at the beginning of 1940 in various village *hats* of Rangpur and the *gajan melas* (fairs held on the *Chaitra Samkranti*) of Burdwan.[91] The agitation in Rangpur soon gathered momentum, and the *Jotedars* and *hat*-proprietors felt so much intimidated that the district authorities had to arrest some "ring leaders".[92] Matters came to a head on 21 June 1940 in Tushbandhav *hat* where about 60 *kisan* volunteers not only persuaded all the stall-owners and vendors not to pay *Tola*,

91. Confidential File No. W-325/40 of 1940, Government of Bengal, Home Dept. Poll. Branch, West Bengal State Archives, Calcutta.
92. Home Poll. Fortnightly Report for 1st half of June 1940, File No. 18/6/40, N.A.I.

but also surrounded the local *Zamindar's* house, following an altercation. The agitators dispersed only after the arrival of the police party, and its resorting to blank fires.[93]

In August, the Rangpur District Kisan Sabha demanded a total abolition of *Hattola*, and enlisted more than 2,000 *kisan* volunteers to agitate all over Rangpur.[94] Despite widespread repressions and large scale arrests under the D.I.R., the movement continued in Rangpur till about November 1940.[95] The agitation meanwhile had spread from Rangpur and Burdwan to Jessore and the 24-Parganas, notably in Hingalganj *hat* in July 1940,[96] and then to Khulna.[97] In Jessore it continued successfully in Chaknagar and Kathalitola *hats*, Dumaria,[98] and by the middle of 1941 it assumed a serious proportion in Noapara *hat*.[99] Thereafter the Government seemed to have managed to contain the *Hattola* agitators by taking action against most of the leading among them under the D.I.R.

Unlike the *Hattola* resistance, in which the *Bargadars* were joined by various sections of rural society, including the village shopkeepers, the *Adhiar* agitation was exclusively a movement of the sharecroppers with a more extensive sweep — surpassed only by the *Tebhaga* of 1946-7.[100] The agitation started during the harvesting season of 1939-40 almost simultaneously in Dinajpur and Jalpaiguri — the scenes of the *Hattola* outcry of 1939. Encouraged by their success in the *Hattola*, the *Adhiars* decided to give expression to their long pent up feelings against the *Jotedars* over the issue of crops — not their sharing, but

93. Home Poll. Fortnightly Report for 1st half of July 1940, File No. 30/40, West Bengal State Archives, Calcutta.
94. Home Poll. Fortnightly Report for 1st half of August 1940, File No. 18/8/ 40, N.A.I.
95. *Ibid.*, 2nd half of November 1940, File No. 18/11/40, N.A.I.
96. *Ibid.*, 2nd half of July 1940, File No. 18/7/40, N.A.I.
97. *Ibid.*, 1st half of September 1940, File No. 19/9/40, N.A.I.
99. *Ibid.*, 1st half of June 1941, File no. 18/6/41, N.A.I.
100. That the agitation affected, in some way or the other, certain pockets of Rangpur, Rajsahi, Khulna, Jessore, Dacca and Midnapore, apart from the two major centres in Dinajpur and Jalpaiguri, has not yet been fully appreciated by the historians of the *kisans* in Bengal, or by the over-enthusiastic observers of Bengali left-wing politics.

their stacking before sharing. In accordance with the sharecropping terms, the harvested crops were taken to the *Jotedars' Khamars* (yards), or kept in their *Kholans* (granaries) till they were actually divided. The stacking of paddy in *Jotedars'* yards or granaries afforded them with an opportunity for dictating terms to the *Adhiars* at the time of division of crops, through all kinds of fraudulent practices in weighing and measuring, and by deducting the illegal exactions and heavily charged paddy loans from the sharecroppers' share, whether they agreed to it or not. The sharecroppers, who invariably resented the arrangement, and took it to be primarily responsible for many of their woes, had nurtured over time a strong desire to move against it, and take the crops to their own yards instead of the *Jotedars'*. Out of this urge was born the main slogan of the *Adhiar* movement: *Nijo Kholane Dhan Tolo* (stack paddy in your own granary). Subsequently three more slogans were added to it,one against irregular exactions of the *Jotedars* (namely, *Baje Adaya Bandho Karo* or stop illegal levies), and the others against exorbitant rates of interest (50 per cent or more) that the *Jotedars* charged on paddy loans (namely, *Karjo Dhaner Sud Kamao* or lessen interest on paddy loans, and *Beej Dhaner Sud Nai* or no interest on seed grains). The severity of interest on these loans had been analysed by the district officers, according to whom the *Jotedars* lent at a time when the price of paddy reached its peak, and deducted re-payment when it came down to its lowest. Consequently, observed an official: "A Jotedar lends one maund of paddy in May when the price is Rs. 2 per maund. At 50 per cent interest he expects Rs. 3 back about July. By July the price of paddy has dropped to say Re. 1 and the *Adhiar* must return 3 maunds of paddy to cover Rs. 3. He, therefore has to pay 2 maunds of paddy as interest on 1 maund (i.e. 200 per cent instead of original 50 per cent) for a period of 2 to 3 months".[101]

By January 1940, Thakurgaon of Dinajpur became the focal point of the *Adhiar* movement, which soon extended to Boda,

101. W.A.B. Price, Superintendent of Police, Rangpur, to A.D. Gordon, Inspector General of Police, D.O. No. 1308 of 6/7 April 1941 Home Poll. File No. W325/41, West Bengal State Archives, Calcutta.

Debiganj and Pachagarh of Jalpaiguri,[102] and Kalia of Jessore.[103] At Thakurgaon, where *Bargadars* were reported to have "misappropriated", or forcibly taken away the harvested crops to their own yards,[104] 45 persons were arrested, and the arrest warrants had been issued against 150 others.[105] The total number of arrested persons in Jalpaiguri was about 300 at the beginning of March 1940.[106] Both in Jalpaiguri and Dinajpur a series of tripartite talks were held among the district officials, the representatives of the *samitis* and those of the *Jotedars*, but none of these succeeded in bringing about any settlement.[107] Meanwhile the agitation had spread over several parts of Rajsahi and Mahishadal of Midnapore,[108] Rangpur, notably at Dimla, as well as Pabna.[109] In a village in Pabna the *Adhiars* — like their counterparts in south Gujarat — were believed to have socially boycotted the *Jotedars.*[110] Matters took a serious turn in Nilphamari of Rangpur and Tamluk of Midnapore where the sharecroppers in March 1941 started stacking paddy in their own yards.[111] Similarly in Manikganj, Dacca, the *Bargadars* refused to carry crops to the *Jotedars' kholans,*[112] and in Khulna

102. Ranajit Das Gupta, "Krishak O Rajneeti: Jalpaiguri" (in Bengali), *Parichaya,* November 1983, p. 66
103. Home Poll. Fortnightly Report for 2nd half of January 1940, File No. 18/1/40, N.A.I.
104. *Ibid.,* 2nd half of Feburary 1940, File No. 18/2/40, N.A.I.
105. *The Communist* (cyclo), 32. Vol. II. no.8, April 1940, Party Documents, C.P.I. Central Archives, Communist Party of India, Ajoy Bhavan, New Delhi.
106. Home Poll. Fortnightly Report for 1st half of March 1940, File No.18/3/40, N.A.I., and also *The Communist,* (cyclo), Vol. II, no.8, April 1940, Party Documents, Central Archives, Communist Party of India, Ajoy Bhawan, New Delhi.
107. Ranajit Das Gupta, "Krishak O Rajneeti: Jalpaiguri" (in Bengali), *Parichaya,* November 1983, p. 67.
108. Home Poll. Fortnightly Report for 2nd half of July 1940, File No. 18/7/40, N.A.I.
109. *Ibid.*, 1st half of September 1940, File No. 18/9/40, N.A.I.
110. Home Poll. Fortnightly Report for 2nd half of December 1940, File No. 30/40, West Bengal State Archives, Calcutta
111. Home Poll. Fortnightly Report for 2nd half of March and Ist half of April 1941, File Nos. 18/3/41 and 18/4/41, N.A.I.
112. *Ibid.*, 1st half of October 1941, File No. 18/10/41. N.A.I.

they took away the harvest to their own yards.[113] Despite the extensive use of the D.I.R. and Section 144 Cr.P.C., the Government did not seem to have succeeded even by the beginning of 1942 in stamping out the *Adhiar* movement altogether.

Like the sharecroppers, the tenants-at-will or the under-tenants were also active in 1940-1 in resisting evictions from, and claiming some rights on, the lands they tilled, but unlike the previous years of 1938-9 — when such endeavours produced agrarian agitations of consequence — they had somehow not been able to repeat their performances. The difference was perhaps due to a change in the circumstances in which the landlords regained their self-confidence under the protective cover of a distinctly authoritarian, war-worried Government, who, devoid of popular backing, expected to lean more heavily on landlordism than the elected provincial ministries ever did. With the recovery of the landlords' morale, therefore, the task of the poor peasants was to become more difficult, their mobilisation more disjointed, and defence more vulnerable. Irrespective of the handicaps, nevertheless, they did manage to take up the cudgels wherever they were forced to do so in the stout vindication of their fragile status. In Thana district of Maharashtra, for example, the tenants-at-will had to fight back in July 1940 when their landlords began an offensive, and dispossessed them with the help of legal processes. Having never received receipts for rent, it was impossible for the *kisans* to prove that they had paid rent regularly. At that point the landlords, armed with rent decrees, came to take possession of lands at Shirgaon village, Kalyan *taluk*, and a serious clash followed on 3 July 1940 between the landlords' hirelings and the under-tenants. It led to the beating up of all the landlords' men, the arrival of the police on the scene and the arrest of the *kisan* resisters.[114] Exactly a similar clash took place in November 1940 in Bakharganj, Bengal,

113. Home Poll. Fortnightly Report, for 2nd half of December 1941, File No. 13/41, West Bengal State Archives, Calcutta.

114. Deputy Superintendent of Police to Superintendent of Police, Thana District, 4 July 1940, Home (Sp.) Dept., File No. 918-A, Maharashtra State Archives, Bombay.

under almost similar circumstances when the landlords obtained possession of lands in execution of rent decrees. They then tried to induct new entrants into the holdings which the dispossessed *kisans* stubbornly resisted till the local police had broken their backs by using force.[115] The repeated attempts of the Haris of Sind in 1940 at clinging precariously to the lands they cultivated had failed likewise in the face of the *Jagirdar*-police combine.[116] Almost identical was the outcome of another agitation in Nili-Bar colony of the Punjab, where the under-tenants had successfully resisted the tender-holders or the lease-holders in 1937. Soon after the commencement of war, and sensing the hardened official attitude towards agitationists of all varieties, the tender-holders decided to take the initiative in evicting *kisans* from their respective plots. The opposition of *kisans* took the form of a land *satyagraha* (in which a number of them courted arrest), as well as the shape of a delegation to the Revenue minister for pleading their case.[117] Neither the *satyagraha* nor the delegation led by Daya Singh, Secretary, Punjab Kisan Committee, however, could make much headway. Like the Nili-Bar under-tenants, the tenants-at-will at Bhatipara and Rankeli of Slyhet, Assam — who were already known in 1939 for their opposition to the *Zamindars* — also had to struggle hard to resist the *Zamindari* attempts at ejecting them from their lands. Taking advantage of the over-all war-time situation, the *Zamindars* tried to dispossess *kisans* by the sheer use of force — with the help of a large number of *lathials* (*lathi* or stick-weilding retinues) — and settle lands in their

115. Home Poll. Fortnightly Report for 1st half of November 1940, File No. 18/11/40, N.A.I.
116. *Annual Report of All India Kisan Sabha*, 1939-40, p. 13.
117. *Ibid.*, p. 17.
118. Home Poll. Fortnightly Reports for the 1st and 2nd halves of January 1940, File No. 18/1/40, N.A.I. These tillers were mainly the immigrant Bengali Muslim *kisans*, who had entered into the Brahmaputra and the Surma (Cachar and Sylhet) Valleys of Assam from the contiguous east Bengal districts. Much to the resentment of the local peasants, they came in increasing numbers since the first world war. By 1940 they had found a champion of their cause in Maulana Abdul Hamid Khan (Maulana Bhasani), who organised them in Goalpara on a distinct communal line.

place with the agricultural hands imported from Bengal.[118] The evicted peasants were, therefore, caught up in a situation in which the *batai* cultivators in west Punjab (Multan and Montgomery districts) had been entangled in, namely, to fight on the one hand the landlords' *lathials*, and to frighten away on the other the new settlers on the scenario. Meetings were held, litigations undertaken and violent clashes occurred over the forcible occupation of lands. The conflicts, which spread over to Jalalpur,[119] continued to cause the district authorities some anxiety throughout the latter half of 1940. In January 1941 in fact the Government decided to move additional police contingents into Sylhet to contain the agitation at Bhatipara and Rankeli.[120] It was through the use of force — the arrests and detention of the leading agitators — that the Government officials were able by the middle of 1941 to bring about certain uneasy compromises between the tenants and the landlords.

The major centres of bitter anti-eviction struggle, namely those in the eastern U.P. and Bihar, continued also to be active in 1940-1, though not as extensively and passionately as they were in 1938-9. The controversy about the *Sir* lands in the U.P. had only partially been resolved by the much talked about Tenancy Act which the Congress-led U.P. legislature passed in 1939. The tenants-at-will or the *Shikmi Kashtkars* were still exposed to eviction by the landlords from the *Sir* lands at an interval of every five years. What was worse, however, appeared to be the vast scope for manipulation that the measure had provided to the village *Patwaris* (revenue officials) in recording who among the *Shikmi Kashtkars* rented which land, and for how many years. Consequently, when the Act was actually put into operation, coinciding with the outbreak of the war and the exit of the Congress from office, the *Zamindars* and *Taluqdars* had little difficulty in tampering with the *Patwaris'* records, and in throwing out *kisans* from lands on the ground either that their names did not figure in the records, or that the records showed their lands to be due for resumption (after five years) by the landlords. Taking advantage of the "D.I.R. Raj", the *Zamindar-*

119. *Ibid.*, 2nd half of April 1940, File No. 18/4/40, N.A.I.
120. *Ibid.*, 1st half of January 1941, File No. 18/1/41, N.A.I.

Patwari combination became so emboldened as to increase the *Khudkast* (*Zamindars'* own lands) by ousting tenants — in violation of the Tenancy Act of 1939 — even from the *rayati.* [121] As a result tenants, who had been tilling specific plots for generations, suddenly discovered that their names were missing from the *Patwaris'* records.[122] Ejectment of *kisans* from their lands, therefore, never really stopped, and it in fact assumed serious proportion in Gorakhpur and Banaras districts. There were reports of some articulation of the *kisan* grievances from Unnao,[123] and of considerable outburst of anger from Munshiganj in Rae Bareli.[124] The *Shikmi Kashtkars* were also known to have put up stiff opposition against evictions in Maharajganj and Padrauna *tahsils* of Gorakhpur.[125] That these did not lead to a powerful movement in 1940-1 was due to the leftists', especially the Congress Socialists' perception of political priorities — their anxiety for joining the Individual *Satyagraha* in preference to leading the poor peasants against the assaults of the *Zamindars.*[126] This issue of priorities not only relegated the *Sir* cultivators' cause to the background, but also brought to the fore the tensions prevailing between the Congress Socialists and the Communists. Their estrangement, which was becoming apparent in the *kisan* movement all over India, turned particularly sour in the U.P. and Bihar — the acknowledged strongholds of the Congress Socialists. The two clashed openly in March 1941 at the Bihar Provincial Kisan Conference at Dumraon, Shahabad, where the Congress Socialists wanted to merge the *kisan* movement with the nationalist mobilisation, for giving anti-imperialism a clear precedence over anti-feudalism; and the Communists wished to retain the separate existence of the Kisan Sabhas for performing the anti-feudal and anti-imperial

121. *Sangharsh* (Hindi weekly), 7 April 1941.
122. *Communist* (English monthly, printed), Vol. II, no. 15, January 1941.
123. Home Poll. Fortnightly Report for 2nd half of February 1940, File No. 18/2/40, N.A.I.
124. *Sangharsh* (Hindi weekly), 13 January 1941.
125. *Communist* (English monthly, printed), Vol. II, no. 15, January 1941.
126. *Ibid.*

tasks of the one and the same struggle.[127] The difference of opinion soon led both the factions of the Kisan Sabhaites — the Communist one under Jamuna Karji, and the Congress Socialist one under Rambriksh Benipuri — to launch a propaganda campaign against each other for rallying their respective supporters.[128] A split in the B.P.K.S seemed imminent in June 1941, when Awadheshwar Prasad Sinha, the Congress Socialist President of the A.I.K.S., accused the Communists of destroying the *kisan* movement for their own ulterior gains.[129] It finally came at the beginning of July 1941 in Calcutta where the Central Kisan Council decided to recognise the faction led by Jamuna Karji as the real B.P.K.S.[130]. The Congress Socialists in the Kisan Council, headed by Awadheshwar Prasad, protested against the decision and left the A.I.K.S. for all practical purposes. From 1941 onwards, therefore, the Bihar *kisan* movement — one of the forerunners in the whole of India — presented a picture of deepening leftist disunity, with the official B.P.K.S. functioning under Karji, the Congress Socialists operating under Benipuri outside it, and in its opposition in the main, and the Forward Blocists under Sheel Bhadra Yajee acting inside it, though wavering between the Communists and the Congress Socialists. The disappearance at this juncture of some of the important *kisan* leaders of Bihar had further confounded the confusion. Under the D.I.R. Swami Sahajanand Saraswati and Rahul Sankrityayana were arrested in March 1940, Jadunandan Sharma in June 1940 and Karyanand Sharma in September 1940. Disarrayed thus the leftists were not exactly in a position to take up the evicted *Bakasht* peasants' banner as energetically, and determinedly, as they had done before in 1937-9. This need not, however, give one the impression that the leftists in 1940-1 had neglected the *Bakasht* issue and failed to revive the

127. *Sangharsh* (Hindi weekly), 24 March 1941.
128. Home Poll. Fortnightly Reports for 2nd half of March and 2nd half of April 1941, File Nos. 18/3/41 and 18/4/41, N.A.I.
129. Awadheshwar Prasad Sinha's letter to Provincial Kisan Sabhas, *Sangharsh* (Hindi weekly), 9 June 1941.
130. Home Poll. Fortnightly Report for 1st half of July 1941, File No. 18/7/41, N.A.I.

movement which entered into a stalemate at the end of 1939, or that the *Bakasht* agitation had come altogether to "an end", and "ceased" to exist by January 1940.[131] There were in fact enough indications to show that in the first phase of the war the *Bakasht* movement had been continuing in various pockets of Bihar, though understandably on a low key.

There were reports of a revival of the *Bakasht* agitation in Barahiya Tal, Munghyr, as early as February 1940.[132] On 16 February 1940 the *kisans* of Bikram, Patna, were involved in a serious clash with the *Zamindars*' hired gangs over the harvesting of crops on the *Bakasht* lands. The landlords' men fired at the demonstrating *kisans*, killing two and injuring ten, including two women. A similar violent incident also took place at Paijnia village of Mokamah, Patna, resulting in the deaths of two (one on each side) and injuries to many. Agitation also seemed to have commenced at Damari, Gaya, by the second half of February 1940.[133] Throughout March 1940 Barahiya Tal and Paijnia remained stormy, forcing the landlords to secure a portion of the harvested *rabi* crops only with the help of the police and the district officials.[134] Meanwhile the agitation was starting afresh in areas like Masaurhi, Patna, and at certain places in Darbhanga district where Ramnandan Mishra was believed to be active.[135] The situation deteriorated fast in Gaya and Patna, and serious clashes were reported from Bhadokhara in Gaya, and Marachi of Mokamah in Patna. In both the cases the authorities despatched armed police under a Magistrate.[136] All the known leaders meanwhile were seen to be preparing for

131. Stephen Henningham, *Peasant Movement in Colonial India, North Bihar, 1917-42*, Australian National University, 1982, pp. 165 and 248, fn. 94 of chapter 6. Rakesh Gupta also appears to be in agreement with Henningham when he states that there was no *Bakasht* agitation "during the first phase of the war", *Bihar Peasantry and the Kisan Sabha, 1936-47*, 1982, p. 228.
132. Home Poll. Fortnightly Report for 1st half of February 1940, File No. 18/2/40, N.A.I.
133. *Ibid.*, 1st half of February 1940.
134. *Ibid.*, 1st half of March 1940, File No. 18/3/40, N.A.I..
135. *Ibid.*
136. *Ibid.*, 2nd half of March 1940.

launching the *Bakasht* campaign in full swing — Sheel Bhadra Yajee in Patna, Jadunandan in Gaya, Ramanandan in Darbhanga,[137] Karyanand Sharma in Munghyr and Dhanraj Puri in Champaran.[138] However, the detention of some of these key figures, backed up by other repressive measures, appeared to have halted the progress of the agitation. But it reappeared dramatically in January 1941 in Bhagalpur where the *Bakasht* peasants started harvesting crops forcibly at Sonbarsa, and the authorities responded by rushing police reinforcement there.[139] The instance of Sonbarsa was followed later at Baragaon of the same district and at Makdampur and Ismailpur of Gaya, leading to the arrest of the so-called "crop looters".[140] Shahabad was also affected in September 1941 when the *Bakasht kisans* joined those well-to-do and rich peasants who were protesting against a steep increase in rent by the Dumraonraj.[141] In fact the Dumraon peasants jointly threatened to undertake a *satyagraha* against the landlord in December 1941. While the Dumraon *satyagraha* did not eventually take off the ground, an agitation over the *Bakasht* lands broke out at Sikandra in Munghyr and at Saidpur in Bhagalpur. At Banaili in Munghyr it took a violent turn when the *Zamindars'* men used fire-arms freely in a clash.[142] The *Bakasht* agitation thus continued intermittently till Swami Sahajanand called in April 1942 for its suspension, after his release from Hazaribagh jail, in the B.P.K.S. Conference at Sherghati, Gaya.[143]

Simultaneously with the revival of the *Bakasht* movement, and for the redressal of almost similar grievances as those of the *Bakasht* peasants, the Santhal *Bataidars* started an intense agitation in Purnea district of north Bihar. It was localised in the

137. *Ibid.*, 1st half of April 1940, File No. 18/4/40, N.A.I.
138. *Ibid.*, 2nd half of May 1940, File No. 18/5/40, N.A.I.
139. *Ibid.*, 2nd half of January 1941, File No. 18/1/41, N.A.I..
140. *Ibid.*, 1st and 2nd halves of July 1941, File No. 18/7/41, N.A.I.
141. *Ibid.*, 2nd half of September and 1st half of November 1941, File Nos. 18/9/41 and 18/11/41, N.A.I.
142. *Ibid.*, 1st half of December 1941, File No. 18/12/41, N.A.I.
143. *Ibid.*, 1st half of April 1942, File No. 18/4/42, N.A.I.

Dhamdaha revenue circle, or the police stations of Dhamdaha, Rupauli and Dharahara — where chunks of reclaimed forest lands of the estate of the Darbhangaraj had been rented out to tenure-holders or powerful occupancy *rayats*, known as the *Maliks*. These *Maliks*, on their part, gave lands for actual cultivation to sharecroppers — the *Bataidars* belonging to the Santhal tribe — on the usual orally committed sharecropping terms. The long suffering Santhal *Bataidars* might have indefinitely continued to suffer the feudal exploitation of the *Maliks* had it not been for some amendments the Congress ministry in Bihar effected in 1937 and 1938 in the provincial Tenancy Act of 1885. The amendments, and the discussions on them, highlighted two facts, one that an under-tenant, who had continuously held land for twelve years, would be deemed to have acquired the right of occupancy in the land, and two, that the landlords were obliged to issue receipts for rent, irrespective of its payment in cash or in kind. The ignorant Santhal *Batidars* came to know of both these facts from some of the non-conformist anti-*Zamindari* Congress workers in the district like Dhaturanand Choudhury, and a few sympathetic district officials like C.H. McNeill, the Sub-Divisional Officer, and Rameshwar Singh, the District Magistrate.[144] More importantly, they were able to comprehend the vital link between the rent receipt and the prospect for occupancy right, and consequently to raise before the *Maliks* in mid-1939 a clamour for receipts for the shared crops. The *Maliks* promptly retaliated either by forcibly setting up new *Bataidars* in place of the existing ones, or by instituting cases of criminal trespass against the original *Bataidars*. Faced with evictions, and bereft of any rent receipt to justify their occupation, the Santhal *Bataidars* were compelled to fight the *Maliks* through violent means. They started gathering on the disputed lands with bows and arrows, and defending their occupational right by force. As expected, the gatherings led to skirmishes, injuries, deaths, police interventions, arrests and criminal proceedings for rioting. There were also instances

144. Anand Chakravarti, "The Unfinished Struggle of Santhal Bataidars in Purnea District, 1938-42", *Economic and Political Weekly*, Vol. XXI, no. 42, 18 October 1986, pp. 1848-58.

where the Santhal *Bataidars* had reaped and stored the crops, but refused to give the *Maliks* their share without proper receipts.[145] In the midst of such turmoil throughout 1940 and the early part of 1941 the authorities — despite their dislike of the Santhali lawlessness and sympathy for the *Maliks* — did attempt to bring about some settlement between the *kisans* and the tenure-holders. But the negotiations had broken down over the *Maliks*' refusal to issue rent receipts to the *Bataidars* unless the latter conceded a two-year limit to all future *Batai* settlements, or, in other words, accepted the *Maliks*' right to evict the *Bataidars* at two years' interval.[146] It was like taking one's life to prove that he or she had been living, and the Santhal *Bataidars* could not be expected to agree to such an amazing proposal. They flatly refused, and in consequence the *Maliks* never actually issued rent receipts, howsoever much the Government tried to make out that they had successfully been persuaded to do so.[147]

A significant aspect of the Santhal *Bataidars*' commotion in Purnea was its thin — rather non-existent — linkage with either the left politics or the B.P.K.S. Although Swami Sahajanand visited the area sometime before the occurrences in 1938, and the Government presumed "the Communists and other leftists from Bhagalpur" to be behind the Santhal *Bataidars*,[148] there was little evidence to prove that the Communists and the Congress Socialists played any significant role. The catalysts behind the defying Santhal attitude, namely the Congressite Dhaturanand Choudhury, the serving Sub-Divisional Officer and the transferred District Magistrate, were interested in the case out of juridical and humanitarian considerations, and as exceptions to the general run of the pro-*Malik* District Congress and

145. Home Poll. Fortnightly Report for 1st half of March 1940, File No.18/3/40, N.A.I.

146. Anand Chakravarti, "The Unfinished Struggle of Santhal Bataidars in Purnea District, 1938-42", *Economic and Political Weekly*, Vol. XXI, no. 42, 18 October 1986, p. 1858.

147. Home Poll. Fortnightly Report for 1st half of July 1940, File No. 18/7/40, N.A.I.

148. *Ibid.*, 2nd half of October 1940, File No. 18/10/40, N.A.I.

District administration. The real leaders of the movement were the Santhals themselves, including their chief negotiator Dulla Tudoo — a primary school teacher. The agitators' use of *digga* (drum) to transmit messages to the community at large, and their formations with bows and arrows at a spot or spots were reminiscent of typical *hools* (Santhal rebellions) of the long past, and indicative of a certain degree of autonomous activity. Similar occurrences, but generating more distinct autonomy of action among the poor *kisans* of the so-called tribal vintage, had taken place in 1940-1. One could cite at least two examples to illustrate the point, both over the dispossession of lands, one among the Gonds of Adilabad in Hyderabad state early in 1940, and the other among the Savaras in the Agency tracts (between Andhra Pradesh and Orissa) in the first half of 1941.

The Gond rising in Adilabad district, known popularly as Babijheri revolt after its place of occurrence, or Komaram Bhimu's revolt after its legendary leader, was a product of the dual process of alienation of lands and stringent conservation of forests. The Gonds, whose settlement in the area continued undisputed for centuries, were rudely shaken when the Nizam's Government replaced in 1875 the traditional tribal land revenue system by the permanent settlement, leading to the emergence there of non-tribal revenue officials-cum-landlords like the *Deshmukhs* and *Deshpandes* in place of the *Mokashis* (chieftains) and *Sarpatlas* (village elders). The subsequent opening of coal mines in Kottagudem, the laying down of railway lines from Kazipet to Nagpur and the construction of highways further exposed the region to the outside world, and led to an increase in demand for the forest produce, and consequently in the Government expectation of profit from it. Almost simultaneously, the Government attracted the predatory landlords from the neighbouring Karimnagar district to come to the area in the expectation for profitable cotton cultivation, by giving them *patta* (title-deed) over as much land as they could make use of. It also resolved to bring, side by side, more and more forest lands as reserve forests, under the strict conservancy regulations. The tribal *kisans*, who were uncertain about the significance of a *patta*, and who, anyway, had been prevented from obtaining it through the machinations of the *Patwari*-landlord combine, suffered heavily by both these measures. They lost their lands in the valley to the landlords, and lands in the forest to the Government reserve. Caught in this predicament, a group of dispossessed Gonds, Kolams and Naikpodus settled down at Babijheri in Asifabad by clearing the forests and cultivating lands for about five years. Suddenly in 1940 they were asked by the state authorities to evacuate Babijheri on the ground that it had been declared a part and parcel of Dhanoa state forest. When they refused to evacuate at the instance of Komaram Bhimu, their huts were set on fire by the forest guards. Bhimu, who at a certain stage of his life was in touch with the fugitive followers of Alluri Sitaram Raju,[149] sought justice by petitioning to the revenue and forest officials, and visiting Hyderabad to plead for the title-deed of the lands the Gonds occupied. But all his efforts were in vain and he had later been arrested, along with some others, for putting up resistance against eviction. Released on bail, Bhimu and his associates continued to defy the eviction orders and came into clashes with the forest guards. Eventually they were confronted with a party of one hundred policemen, and in the violent conflict that followed on 1 September 1940,

149. Komaram Bhimu belonged to a family at Sankepalli village, Asifabad, which lost its lands to a local moneylender. Following his father's death, Bhimu and his brothers shifted to Surdapur, where they reclaimed forest land and began cultivation. However, at the time of harvesting, a *Pattadar* claimed the crops on the basis of a title-deed to the land. In the quarrel over the crops, Bhimu was reported to have killed the *Pattadar* and fled. An absconding Bhimu roamed about many places in search of a livelihood, and served for sometime in the tea-gardens of Assam as a labourer. It was in the Assam tea-gardens that Bhimu learnt to read and write, and also came into contact with some of the run-away participants of the Rampa rebellion of Alluri Sitaram Raju, 1922-4. Later, on his return to Adilabad, Bhimu worked as an attached labourer and created quite a sensation by successfully representing his employer in a land dispute before the revenue officials. It was an astounding feat for a labourer, and the fellow Gonds rightly took pride in his achievement. Thereafter Bhimu and his brothers came to Babijheri, cleared the forests and settled down as cultivators. This sketch of Bhimu's whereabouts has been taken from a review in the *Srajna* (a Telugu periodical), no. 150, April 1984, of SURA, *Porata Vartamanamlo Komaram Bhimu* (Komaram Bhimu in the Contemporaneity of Struggle), Hyderabad, 1983.

Bhimu and eleven others were killed fighting on the spot. The battle was lost, but the legend of Bhimu and Babijheri grew and became an integral part of the Gond folklore.[150]

If the fire in Bhimu was kindled by any chance through his acquaintance with Raju's absconding associates, it was smouldering throughout among the people Raju operated as a rebel, namely, the Savaras in the hilly and forest-covered Agency tracts. It was the Savara tribe who followed Raju during the Rampa rebellion in 1922-4, and repeated the performance, under the leadership of Harideo, in 1931. On both the occasions the Savaras were defeated by the British forces, but not crushed, and their indomitable spirit remained more or less intact. Economically, however, the Savaras — handicapped as they were with their primitive agricultural methods and weak market relations — could not recover even in the mid or the late 1930s from the debacle they had faced during the Depression years. Heavily in debt, they lost their lands steadily all the time to the *sahukars* and merchants from the plains — the *Pandus*. Having been reduced to the state of wage and bondage labourers, and reaching practically the end of their tether, they dramatically demanded in January 1941 for the cancellation of all debts and the ejectment of all the *Pandus* from the Agency tracts. The demands were followed soon by a spurt of "lawlessness", occasioned by some *Pandus*' killing two Savaras, and by their raping a Savara woman.[151] The angry Savaras attacked the *Pandu* houses and shops, and forcibly occupied those fields and properties which they had lost to the *Pandus*. The authorities rushed into the affected area 300 armed policemen, used force indiscriminately and stamped out the commotion after detaining approximately 600 Savaras.[152] The leftists and the Kisan Sabhas had little to do with either the Savara outbreak or the Babijheri rising. It was in fact doubtful if they had at all taken any note of the Babijheri incident when it happened. The Savara outbreak, however, was not entirely missed, and the Andhra Communists

150. *Ibid.*
151. *Communist* (English monthly, printed), Vol. III, no. 5, July 1941.
152. *Ibid.*

urged the Savaras in their organ *Swatantra Bharat* for giving it the shape of a movement: "Let not this revolt become a temporary outburst, organise it" [153]

Whether they were tribal cultivators like the Savaras and Gonds, or non-tribal tillers like the small peasants, the under-tenants and the agricultural labourers, the poor *kisans* — living in the vicinity of jungles — invariably encountered identical forest-related problems. Most of these complications were caused by those landlords and local authorities who exercised their jurisdiction over forests by ignoring the *kisans*' traditional right to make use of the forest land and the forest produce. Such problems in the Dondi Lohara *Zamindari* of Drug in the Central Provinces had culminated in 1938-9 into a long-drawn agitation of the poor *kisans*. Sarju Prasad, who had led that agitation, and suffered imprisonment on account of it, reappeared on his release in Dondi Lohara early in 1940.[154] Soon he was found to be active among the *kisans* in an attempt to rally them against the *Zamindari* orders, prohibiting collection of fire-wood and imposing a grazing fee on the forest lands. In his speeches Sarju Prasad was as critical of the *Zamindari* as of its promoters — the orthodox district Congress and the oppressive local Government.[155] Despite the official warnings against his activities,[156] Sarju Prasad continued "to foment trouble" with a fair amount of success, especially in connection with the grazing fee (*rahdari*).[157] His anti-grazing fee propaganda also seemed to have affected some of the neighbouring localities, such as the Matin *Zamindari* in Pendra.[158] A similar tension was reported to be building up throughout 1940 in Talcher state in Orissa, over harsh forest management among other agrarian issues.[159] In

153. *Ibid.*
154. Home Poll. Fortnightly Report for the 1st half of January 1940, File No. 18/1/40, N.A.I.
155. *Ibid.*, 2nd half of March 1940, File No. 18/3/40., N.A.I.
156. *Ibid.*, 1st half of May 1940, File No. 18/5/40, N.A.I.
157. *Ibid.*, 1st half of April 1940, File No. 18/4/40, N.A.I.
158. *Ibid.*, 1st half of May 1940, File No. 18/5/40, N.A.I.
159. Biswamoy Pati, *Resisting Domination : Peasants, Tribals and National Movement in Orissa, 1920-50*, New Delhi, 1993, p. 151.

Venkatagiri of Nellore in Andhra, the *kisans'* gathering of fire-wood in the *Zamindari* forest, in defiance of a civil court decision against it, led to considerable commotion. The authorities had to send the Reserve Police to contain the situation, and make a number of arrests.[160] The confrontation between the agitating *kisans* and the police, however, assumed violent proportions in Mandasa of Visakhapatnam in Andhra, where the resistance against the forest dues and prohibitory orders was acclaimed in the leftist circles as "one of the most heroic" of such struggles.[161] In a village near Palasa (the venue of the A.I.K.S. Conference, 1940), belonging to the *Zamindari* of Mandasa, a strong police contingent arrived on 1 April 1940, under a Deputy Superintendent of Police and a Joint Magistrate, to put a stop to the "unauthorised" collection of fire-wood and the alleged felling of trees in the forests. The police arrested seven leading figures of the forest agitation in Mandasa, and faced an angry crowd of about 300 at the time of leaving the place. The mob managed to free the prisoners forcibly, though five of them were captured again. In the struggle that followed, the policemen fared badly, and they had to beat a hurried retreat after firing indiscriminately. The police firing resulted in the deaths of five and critical injuries to four.[162]

Politically a more far-reaching encounter over forest land, however, had taken place in the eastern part of Chirakkal and Kottayam *taluks* of Malabar, where *punam* cultivation was in vogue. Under the *punam* arrangement a poor *kisan*, often a landless one, sought the permission of the *Jenmi* or the landlord for taking on rent a piece of his forest land, cleared the allotted plot, and then cultivated it. Although the rent of the forest land ought to have been very low, it was not actually so, and over and above its payment, the *Jenmi* invariably charged the *kisan* a number of irregular levies. The *punam* cultivators' sufferings eased a bit in 1938-9 when K.P.R. Gopalan organised them for

160. Home Poll. Fortnightly Report for 2nd half of April 1940, File No. 18/4/40, N.A.I.

161. *Annual Report of the A.I.K.S.*, 1939-40, pp. 23-4.

162. Home Poll. Fortnightly Reports for 1st and 2nd halves of April 1940, File No. 18/4/40, N.A.I.

demanding better treatment from the *Jenmis.* Consequently in the following year, their rents were reduced to an extent, evictions stopped and requests for clearing plots liberally granted.[163] Next year, subsequent to the Government onslaught on the Communists for the "anti-imperialist war" stand, the *Jenmis* felt encouraged to resume their extortionist pressures. The lead was taken by the *Jenmi* of Ellaranji, Korakkathidam Nayanar, who refused either to give forest lands to the *punam* cultivators or renew their annual lease of plots, unless they agreed to pay enhanced rents and all the irregular levies. The *kisans* and their leaders had to fight back, and in February 1941 they not only declined to pay high rent for lands already under occupation, but also started "encroaching" upon fresh forest lands. The *Jenmi* promptly secured the help of the authorities, and commenced, in collaboration with the police, a reign of terror in Ellaranji. For three months his residence was turned into a camp of the Malabar Special Police, who arrested a large number of persons, including 13 "ring leaders",[164] and registered criminal cases against 40. Although the policy of repression seemed somehow to have prevailed over the *punam kisans,* their struggle echoed practically all over Malabar. Demonstrations and meetings were held in their support in most parts, especially in Calicut, Walluvanad and Kurumbanad *taluks,* and a massive anti-*Jenmi* movement began unfolding itself.

That an anti-*Jenmi* or anti-landlord storm had been rising in Malabar and its neighbourhood by the beginning of 1941 was apparent from the numerous rallies and *jathas* the Karshak Sanghams organised, demanding reduction of rent in kind, cessation of all malpractices in measuring it, cancellation of its arrears and immunity of the standing crops from attachment if arrears had not been cleared. The Sangham volunteers moved from place to place to ensure that the *kisans'* crops were not attached, and that, if necessary, *Jenmis'* men and the court *peons* chased away.[165] There were some signal victories of the *kisans*

163. *Communist* (English monthly, printed), Vol. III, no. 6, August 1941.
164. Central Intelligence Bureau Report of 30.4.41, Home Poll. File No. 7/9/41 Poll (I), N.A.I.
165. *Communist* (English monthly, printed), Vol. III, no. 6, August 1941.

in their anti-landlord campaigns. One such case was that of the *Jenmi* Kalliat Nambiar, who insisted on all his tenants' renewing their leases so as to enable him to charge them "renewal" fees. He expected to collect a tidy sum out of this, and promised the local authorities of the contribution of a part of it to the war fund so that he could count on them if his tenants resisted. The Sangham did resist, not only by raising a furore over the issue, but also by urging every tenant to convey individually to the landlord his or her inability to pay the renewal fee. The *Jenmi* panicked at this demonstration of solidarity and determination, and gave up his plan eventually.[166] Another case was related to the *Jenmis* of Hosdurg in Kasargad *taluk*, or to be more precise, of Kayyur village. Although Kasargad *taluk* belonged administratively to South Kanara district, it was adjacent to Chirkkal *taluk* of north Malabar, with an overwhelming majority of Malayalam-speaking people, having the same culture and society that prevailed throughout Malabar. However, being a part of South Kanara or Karnataka — where Rayatwari system was in operation — the *Jenmis* of Hosdurg enjoyed the legal status of tenants, and not of *Zamindars*. The garb of tenants, or of the so-called "substantial *rayats*", had proved to be advantageous to the *Jenmis* of Hosdurg as it reduced the position of their *de facto* tenants into that of *de jure* under-tenants, having little occupancy right, and suffering perpetually from threats of ejectments and rent enhancements.[167] Matters came to a head early in 1941 when the *Jenmis* of Hosdurg decided as a cohesive group to move, following the Government attempt at cracking down the Communists in Malabar, for harvesting the crops sown by the under-tenant *kisans* on the plea that they had evicted the former under-tenants, and had replaced them with the new ones.[168] As a counter-move, the Sanghams sent their volunteers

166. E.M.S. Namboodiripad, *Selected Works,* Vol. II, Calcutta, 1985, p. 210.
167. The protection — howsoever inadequate — that the Malabar Tenancy Act of 1930 had provided to the tenants in Malabar *vis-a-vis* the *Jenmis* was not available to the *kisans* of Hosdurg. As a result, the main demand of the Karshak Sanghams in Kasargad at this point was for bringing Hosdurg under the purview of the Malabar Tenancy Act of 1930.
168. E.M.S. Namboodiripad *Selected Works,* Vol.II, Calcutta, 1985, p. 212.

to protect the standing crops, oppose the *Jenmis*' hirelings and assist the *kisans* in harvesting. In the confrontation that took place in Hosdurg, and more specifically at Kayyur village in February 1941, the *Jenmis* sought and received the services of the police in intimidating and beating up *kisans*, and arresting some of their leaders. Despite the repressions, however, the landlords were able neither to grab the crops nor to eject the *kisans*, and they had to be content with the *status quo*, as their counterparts in Malabar were compelled to remain over the *punam* lands and the renewal of leases.

Anti-landlordism was in evidence in other parts of the country as well, though not as intensely as it had been in Malabar. Voices were stridently raised against landlords in Maharashtra, for example, and the *kisan* meetings in Thana, Nasik and Kolaba districts often discussed the withholding of rent to landlords if it was not substantially reduced.[169] In the first session of the Maharashtra Kisan Conference in May 1941 were raised the slogans, "down with the landlords" and "end the landlords' illegal exactions", as well as the demand for restoration of lands from the clutches of the *sahukar*-landlords.[170] The *sahukar*-landlords drew similar attention of the *kisans* in south Gujarat, and about 600 poor peasants (sharecroppers and agricultural labourers) marched in February 1940 from Wankas in Pardi Mahal to Vapi, shouting anti-*sahukar*-landlord slogans.[171] An identical march of the *kisans* from all the *Zamindari* estates of Ganjam in Orissa was organised in January 1940 to protest before the Collector against the oppressions of the landlords[172], though the compromising "substantial *rayats*" in Khallikote and Attagada estates decided not to participate in it.[173] However, a bitter conflict between the *Zamindar* and the *kisans* over

169. Home Poll. Fortnightly Report for 2nd half of April 1940, File No. 18/4/40. N.A.I.
170. Home (Special) Dept., File No. 800(53)-B(I) of 1941, Government of Bombay, Maharashtra State Archives, Bombay.
171. *Ibid.*, File No. 1019, p. 4, Maharashtra State Archives, Bombay.
172. Home Poll. Fortnightly Report for 1st half of January 1940, File No. 18/1/40, N.A.I.
173. *Ibid.*, 2nd half of January 1940, N.A.I.

enhancement of rent, and distrainment for it, could not be avoided in Parlia-khemedi of Ganjam in 1940-1.[173a] The left political activists also planned for a "no rent" campaign in coastal Orissa, but it had to be abandoned on account of the ravages of flood in Balasore and Cuttack in July 1941.[174] Despite the setback, the anti-landlord feeling was reported to be running very high in Kanika, Aul and Dompara *Zamindaris*,[175] as well as in Madhopur estate.[176] The *kisans* and their leaders in fact remained preoccupied throughout with the problem of the *Zamindari* oppression, and the proceedings of the Orissa Provincial Kisan Conference in Cuttack in June 1941[177] amply bear this out.

Resentment against the *zulm* of the *Maliks* and *Zamindars* appeared to have grown in volume in the N.W.F.P.,[178] western U.P.[179] and Bihar,[180] and it led to frequent frictions in certain parts of Bengal. The *kisans* in Rajsahi, for example, stood up against the *Zamindari* "highhandedness",[181] complained against the *Zamindars*' "malpractices" to the district authorities[182] and raised a cry for the abolition of the *Zamindari* system.[183] The tension at Hodal Narayanpur (Patrasayer) in Bankura, Bengal, over the *Zamindari* extraction of illegal dues from *kisans* was settled only after the landlords had been persuaded to "refund"

173a. *Ibid.*, 1st March 1940 and 1st January 1941, File Nos. 18/3/40 and 18/1/41, N.A.I.

174. Biswamoy Pati, *Resisting Domination : Peasants, Tribals and National Movement in Orissa, 1920-50*, New Delhi, 1993, p. 148.

175. *Ibid.*

176. Home Poll. Fortnightly Report for 1st half of November 1941, File No. 18/11/41, N.A.I.

177. *Ibid.*, 1st and 2nd halves of June 1941, File No. 18/6/41, N.A.I.

178. *Annual Report of the A.I.K.S.*, 1939-40, p. 7.

179. *Sangharsh* (Hindi weekly), 26 August 1940.

180. Home Poll. Fortnightly Report for 2nd half of December 1941, File No. 18/12/41, N.A.I.

181. *Ibid.*, 1st half of April 1940, File No. 18/4/40, N.A.I.

182. *Ibid.*

183. *Ibid.*, 2nd half of April 1941, N.A.I.

the amount.[184] Extraction of illegal dues by the *Zamindars*, particularly by Tirthanath Bose, the *Zamindar* of Kaigram, was responsible in May 1940 for a *kisan* outburst in the Monteswar-Memari region of Burdwan, Bengal.[185] The pattern was repeated later at Bidhi-Chandrapur,Burdwan, where *kisans* forced *Zamindars* to issue receipts for all illegal exactions, and agree to adjust the amounts against the rent.[186] An identical disturbance was reported from Gangajalghati, Bankura, Bengal, where *kisans* agitated against the Searsol estate *Tahsildar's* refusal to issue rent receipts, and his penchant for taking *kisans* to the court on the ground of non-payment of rent.[187] Some "rumblings" of "no-rent" were heard towards the end of 1940 in Hooghly and Mymensingh,[188] and the reports of the *Zamindar-kisan* clashes received from Faridpur, Bengal.[189] Such clashes over the *Zamindars*' attempts at turning the *rayati* lands into *Khas* were also reported from Sandeshkhali and Canning, the 24-Parganas, Bengal.[190]

The anti-*Zamindari* and the "no rent" agitation that involved a sizable number of the rural poor, and continued for a longer duration in Bengal during 1940-1, had taken place in the Amta-Uluberia region of Howrah district. A substantial part of land in this region had been settled by the *Zamindars* on the *Kut Khamar* tenancy arrangement, under which the rent of a holding was determined annually by appraising its value and the value of crops standing on it at the current market rates. These were

184. Townsend, Commissioner, Burdwan Division, to the Chief Secretary, Government of Bengal, 31 July 1940, Home Dept. File No. W325/40, West Bengal State Archives, Calcutta.
185. Townsend, Commissioner, Burdwan Division, to Additional Secretary, Government of Bengal, File No. 247C of 24.5.40, *ibid.*
186. Home Poll. Fortnightly Report for 2nd half of June 1941, File No. 13/41, West Bengal State Archives, Calcutta.
187. *Ibid.*, 2nd half of July 1940, File No. 30/40.
188. Home Poll. Fortnightly Report for 2nd half of November 1940, File No. 18/11/40, N.A.I.
189. Home Poll. Fortnightly Report for 1st half of December 1940, File No. 30/40, West Bengal State Archives, Calcutta.
190. *Ibid.*

calculated on the spot by the *Zamindars' Gomostas* (employees) in consultation with some of the leading tenants of the village, and the money figure thus arrived at, was divided and one half of it charged as rent.[191] Although the system appeared to be a cash-rent version of kind-rent *Bhag chas* variety, or share-cropping, it was in effect financially more burdensome for the cultivator because of the inclusion in rent the ever-increasing yearly value of plots. The only redeeming feature that somehow had emerged out of it in course of time was the practice among the revenue officials of showing the *Kut Khamar* tenancies in the settlement records. About 2,000 acres of land had in fact been shown in the settlement records as *Kut Khamar* in Amta alone. As a result an anomalous situation developed in 1940 in which the *Kut Khamar kisan*, who should have received some occupational right by virtue of his being mentioned in the settlement records, was treated as an over-paying under-tenant with all the hazards of an insecure annual contract. The anomaly might have had helped the *kisan* at an early stage when he was making a fallow land arable, and when its precarious yields were spared from the permanent liabilty of a uniform annual money-rent. But once the land had been developed with its normal production of crops, the *Kut Khamar* turned as much disadvantageous to the *kisan* as it was advantageous to the landlord.[192] The usual disadvantage of the *kisan* increased manifold in actuality because of the manipulations the *Gomostas* were known to have carried out in the accounting, and the social pressure they succeeded in bearing upon the village elders to agree to it. Soon a situation was reached in which *kisans* started failing to pay the high rent in time, and thus exposing themselves to the cancellation of their annual tenancies. The leftist-led *kisan* agitation in Howrah began in these circumstances in 1939-40, demanding the abolition of *Kut Khamar*, and for its replacement by a regular rent system. The landlords doggedly opposed the move because of the substantial loss of

191. Note by A.C. Hartley, District Magistrate, Howrah, Feburary 1941, Revenue Department L.A. Branch, File No. 10R-3/4/B, June 1941, West Bengal State Archives, Calcutta.

192. *Ibid.*

profit it would entail, and because of their loss of power over *kisans*, who, under the regularised money-rent, should automatically acquire a certain occupational right. A "no-rent" campaign, therefore, began by the beginning of 1941 in the Amta-Uluberia region,[193] and it assumed alarming proportions at the end of the year, particularly at Jhinkura and Jaypur,[194] despite the attempts of the district officials at bringing about an understanding. While the landlords refused to negotiate till the *kisans* paid the rent and cleared the arrears, the *kisans* pointed out the frequent failures of their crops, and insisted upon the remission of the amount in default. The remedial step that they and their leaders thought of, and towards which even the district officials were favourably disposed of,[195] namely, the regularisation of the *Kut Khamar* tenancies under section 112 of the Bengal Tenancy Act, as it was done previously in the case of the *Uthbandi* tenancies,[196] also could not be given any concrete shape. The Revenue minister, B.P. Singh Roy, who himself happened to be a big landlord, was naturally opposed to such regularisation and appeasement of *kisans*, and advocated instead a policy of "inaction", to be backed up by a blending of soft and harsh official attitudes towards the agitators.[197] The *Kut Khamar kisans'* agitation, therefore, persisted throughout 1941, becoming "acute" sometime,[198] and easing up to an extent at another.[199]

The question of rent and its remission, in view especially of drought and crop failure in certain parts of Andhra, led to a series of anti-*Zamindari* outbursts. In Venkatagiri was organised

193. Home Poll. Fortnightly Report for 2nd half of March 1940, File No. 18/3/40, N.A.I.
194. *Ibid.*, 1st half of December 1940, File No. 18/12/40, N.A.I.
195. *Ibid.*
196. The *Uthbandi* holdings in Nadia and Murshidabad were similar in character to those of the *Kut Khamar*, and these were regularised under section 112 of the Bengal Tenancy Act as early as 1923-4.
197. B.P. Singh Roy's note of 2.6.41, File No. 10R-3/41, Revenue Dept. L.R. Branch, West Bengal State Archives, Calcutta.
198. Home Poll. Fortnightly Report for 1st half of January 1941, File No. 18/1/41, N.A.I.
199. *Ibid.*, 2nd half of January 1941.

a campaign on the slogan "no crop, no rent", and in the nearby Perimedi estate grew an opposition against the use of force for collecting rent. In Bobbili, Tekkali, Baruva and Uddanam Chikati *Zamindaris* of Visakhapatnam, numerous small local struggles were launched against the landlords' refusal to remit rent, or their moving the courts of law for the recovery of arrears.[200] Simultaneously in Krishna district was revived the agitation against the landlord in Munagala — the scene of joint struggle of the *kisan* masses in 1939. Following the *Zamindar's* reluctance to give effect to the Brahmaiah award, and to discontinue with the practice of *Vetti* and *Vettichakiri*,[201] as well as the continued detention of four of their leaders, including N. Prasada Rao, the Munagala peasants were left with no other alternative but to resume their resistance. It led to outcries in meetings and demonstrations, and by September 1940, to clashes with the *Zamindar's* men, and the consequent imposition for sometime of Section 144 Cr.P.C. on the locality.[202] The situation did not seem to improve much even after the intervention of the District Collector, and his offer of arbitration.[203] In the latter half of 1941 the Sangham in Munagala also prepared itself for going to the Munsiff's court to enforce the Brahmaiah award on the *Zamindar*.[204]

As it had already been revealed in the case of Munagala agitation, the poor *kisans*' protestations against the *zulm*, irregular levy and rack-renting by landlords — the ills common to all peasant categories — received the sympathy, and sometimes the support of the more substantial and well-to-do

200. *Annual Report of the A.I.K.S.*, 1939-40, p.23.
201. See Act I, scene IV, pp. 105-6. Also Amit Kumar Gupta, "The Leftists and the Munagala Agitation, 1938-39", *Economic and Political Weekly*, 10 June 1989, pp. 1295-6.
202. Fortnightly Report for the 1st half of September 1940, Government of Madras, D.O. No. P.4-17, Public (General) Dept. Tamil Nadu State Archives, Madras.
203. Home Poll. Fortnightly Report for 1st half of September 1940, File No. 18/9/40, N.A.I.
204. Venkateswara Rao Tatavarti, *Munagalla Paragana Praja Udyama Charitra* (History of the Peoples' Movement in Munagala Pargana), Munagala 1981, chapter V.

kisans. The emergence of similar solidarity seemed possible in 1940-1 among the *kisans* engaged in the production of cash crops, especially sugarcane and jute, *vis-a-vis* the owners of sugar and jute mills, their middlemen and their protectors — the omnipotent Government. Cultivation of crops like sugarcane and jute was more a cash receiving device than a purely surplus accumulating one on commercial lines. The small producers and poor *kisans* found it useful for paying rentals, re-paying money-debts and buying essential items, and therefore, fitted it conveniently to their cultivating time and space. Structured by monetary advances, planted to cater to the needs of the industries and intervened by a plethora of middlemen, who included the landlords and the *mahajans,* their raw products reached the gates of the sugar and jute mills at prices dictated by the mill-owners — the sugar capitalists of the U.P. and Bihar, and the jute manufacturing houses of Bengal. Besides, the peasants' produce of both sugarcane and jute was also subjected to the buyers' and their agents' false gradings, under-weighments and high commissions.[205] Such a relationship of dependence and extortion between the tillers and the mill-owners in a semi-feudal rural setting was quite in order under colonialism, and the authorities' only concern had been to ensure that its balance remained more or less untilted. Some tilting nevertheless did take place during the great Depression when the prices of sugarcane and raw jute tumbled down for successive years from 1930 to 1932. Factories paid "absurdly low prices for the sugarcane",[206] and the average net income from jute per acre came drastically down. Following the post-Depression agricultural recovery, the prices crashed again in 1936-7 on account of over-production from consecutive bumper crops. The Government response to this exigency was to try to fix up minimum fair prices for the products, as well as to contain the extent of their cultivation. While the first was imposed to a

205. Shahid Amin, *Sugarcane and Sugar in Gorakhpur: An Enquiry into Peasant Production for Capitalist Enterprise in Colonial India,* Delhi, 1984, pp. 204-5.
206. Memorandum by the U.P. Government for the Sugar Conference in Delhi, 10-12 July 1933, *ibid.*, p. 208.

certain limit on the sugar mill-owners, and which the jute manufacturing houses invariably succeeded in turning to their favour, the second measure could only be given some effect to the growing of jute, without its being made applicable to the cultivation of sugarcane. Neither the attempts of the Congress ministries in the U.P. and Bihar at fixing a minimum price for sugarcane, nor the policy of the Bengal Government to restrict jute cultivation was, however, proved really to be effective in the inflationary war-time situation of 1940-1. Seeing the steady rise in commodity prices, the sugar mill-owners held their stock in the hope of selling it at higher prices. The artificial shortage thus created not only suited their interest, but also led to a panic-stricken situation in which the sugarcane-growers rushed to the mills with their produce in increasing quantities. The mill-owners refused to buy their crops unless its fixed price was reduced from annas 7-9 *pies* to annas 5-9 *pies* per maund, and even threatened to close their mills. The U.P. and Bihar Governments had reluctantly to agree to reduce sugarcane price first to annas 6-3 *pies*, and then to annas 5-6 *pies* per maund in May 1940,[207] leaving the sugarcane-growers in their provinces in the lurch. The fate of the jute cultivators was no different, suffering especially as they did from the vicissitudes of an export-oriented market.The climate of war and its actual outbreak led to a boom in the jute market, giving the manufacturing houses an opportunity to corner fabulous profits in 1939-40. The *kisans* did hardly get any share of it, for they had sold their crops before the price could reach its peak. In the following year, i.e. 1940-1, when they expected a higher price for their crops, the Government decided to restrict jute cultivation more stringently. What had been worse was the sudden fall in prices in 1940 owing to the war-time difficulties of transporting Indian jute, and the resultant closure of the American market to it. Meanwhile the jute cultivators' clamour for the fixation of a fair price for their product, which the Government hesitantly fixed at Rs.7 per maund at the beginning of 1940, had had no effect whatsoever. Faced with the slump, and the shyness of the mill-owners, the cultivators were forced

207. *Ibid.*, pp. 233-4.

to sell their crops at as low a price as Rs. 2½ per maund, and even then they failed to market more than half their produce.[208] The authorities neither enforced the price of raw jute that they themselves fixed, nor devised any other method to rescue *kisans* from the disaster.

The agitation of the sugarcane and jute cultivators grew mainly over the issue of fair prices for their crops. Unlike the jute-growers, whose crops passed through an elaborate hierarchy of agents, and who, therefore, had no direct contact with the mill-owners, the sugarcane-growers used often to deliver their product directly at the gates of the mill-owners. Consequently, they could give vent to their ire straightaway against the direct exploiters, which they often did by denouncing the mill-owners for their "policy of lust",[209] or even by attacking mills and beating up the employees, as it happened in Hordoi in March 1940.[210] In Bihar *satyagrahas* were contemplated before the sugar mill gates, and the Kisan Sabha leader, Jamuna Karji, was believed to be preparing for such "courting of arrests" in January 1941 in Motihari of Champaran district.[211] Eventually, however, the sugarcane-growers' discontent took the shape of protestations against the Government decision to reduce the prices of their crops, and developed as an anti-Government agitation. In a meeting in Patna on 2 February 1940 the Bihar Provincial Kisan Sabha held the Government responsible for the sugarcane cultivators' plight.[212] Mohanlal Gautam, the C.S.P. leader, was reported to be "instigating" anti-Government agitation in several districts of the U.P., and the Collector of Gorakhpur appeared to have encountered hostile *kisan* deputations.[213] The sugarcane-growers held a rally in Muzaffarpur on 3 January 1941, and marched in a procession to the District Magistrate to press for

208. Of the raw jute production of 1,25,62,000 bales (1 bale= 5 maunds) for 1940-1, about 61,50,000 were expected to be consumed in total, leaving approximately a surplus of 64,12,000 bales.

209. *Sangharsh* (Hindi weekly), 9 December 1940.

210. Home Poll. Fortnightly Report for 2nd half of March 1940, File No. 18/3/40, N.A.I.

211. *Ibid.*, 1st half of January 1941, File No. 18/1/41, N.A.I.

212. *Ibid.*, 1st half of February 1940, File No. 18/2/40, N.A.I.

213. *Ibid.*, 1st half of January 1941, File No. 18/1/41, N.A.I.

higher sugarcane prices.[214] On the same day at Munshiganj, the Rae Bareli District Kisan Conference vociferously demanded a fair sugarcane price.[215] By March 1941 the sugarcane cultivators in the U.P. and Bihar were reported to be raising anti-Government slogans,[216] and in April 1941 the Government decided to use its iron hands. Leading leftist agitators in the U.P., predominantly the Congress Socialists, were detained under Rule 26 of the D.I.R.[217] The similar method was used in Bihar to remove from the scene the prominent Communist leaders of the sugarcane cultivators.[218] These arrests practically left the sugarcane-growers leaderless, and by the middle of 1941, their agitations in the U.P. and Bihar showed signs of waning.

In Bengal, where the jute cultivators were hardly able to reach their direct exploiters, they expressed dissatisfaction mainly against the Government, and marginally against the middlemen. In addition to the demand for a fair price for their crops, the jute cultivators had another major issue to fight for, namely, the withdrawal of the Government scheme to restrict jute cultivation. From their point of view, the scheme — which the Government ostensibly adopted as a safeguard against any drastic fall in raw jute prices — was in effect putting an embargo on the poor *kisans'* ability to raise cash. The Hooghly District Kisan Samiti strongly protested against the Government's restrictive policy on the ground that it was undermining the interests of the poor *kisans.*[219] The Samiti also organised a signature campaign on printed petitions to the Government for the abandonment of the jute restriction scheme.[220] The *kisans* of Howrah district met at Guptipara in March 1941 to demonstrate against the restriction

214. *Ibid.*
215. *Sangharsh* (Hindi weekly), 13 January 1941.
216. Home Poll. Fortnightly Report for 1st March 1941. File No. 18/3/41, N.A.I.
217. *Ibid.*, 2nd half of April 1941, File No. 18/4/41, N.A.I.
218. Report on Bihar Agrarian Situation, Home Poll. File No. 31/1/41 Poll(I), N.A.I.
219. Letter from Tushar Chatterji. *Ananda Bazar Patrika* (Bengali daily), 6 February 1940.
220. Home Poll. Fortnightly Report for 2nd half of April 1941, File No. 13/41, West Bengal State Archives, Calcutta.

of jute cultivation.[221] Similar protest meetings were held at various places in Rajsahi,[222] at Baduria in the 24-Parganas[223] and at Daspur in Midnapore.[224] The widespread resistance to the restriction was further stimulated by a certain amount of class conflict among the jute-growers. Somewhat differently from the sugarcane cultivators of the U.P., who included the substantial and poor *kisans* — mostly of the small producers variety, the jute-growers in Bengal also included the *Jotedars* and a large number of the *Bargadars.* The attempts at implementing the scheme of restriction invariably revealed the *Jotedars* to be keeping all their lands earmarked for jute to themselves (as *Khas* for cultivation through the agricultural labourers), giving very little to the *Bargadars* on sharecropping. The sharecroppers naturally resisted such "unreasonable" *Jotedari* monopolisation in the whole of north and north-east Bengal, especially in Jalpaiguri, Dinajpur and Rangpur.[225] The demand for the fixation of a minimum price for raw jute, however, appeared to be more widespread than the issue of restricted cultivation, and it continued throughout the year 1941 to be the slogan of all categories of jute cultivators of Bengal alike. They considered Rs. 8 per maund on the whole as a fair price, though the Rangpur District Kisan Samiti was in favour of fixing it at Rs. 10 per maund.[226] Despite the repressive measures of the Government, their agitation persisted on the anti-Government lines, and through a certain underground network, in Rangpur, Pabna, Dinajpur and Jalpaiguri, and extended to Barisal, Hooghly, Howrah, Jessore, the 24-Parganas and Birbhum.[227]

Although anti-Government in their direction, the sugarcane and jute cultivators' agitations neither raised the peasantry's over-all struggle against imperialism to any fierce new height,

221. *Ibid.*, 1st half of March 1941, West Bengal State Archives, Calcutta.
222. *Ibid.*
223. *Ibid.*, 2nd half of April 1941, West Bengal State Archives, Calcutta.
224. *Ibid.*, 2nd half of March 1941, West Bengal State Archives, Calcutta.
225. *Ibid.*, 2nd half of December 1940,and also 1st and 2nd halves of February 1941, West Bengal State Archives, Calcutta.
226. *Communist* (English monthly, printed), Vol. III, no. 1, February 1941.
227. *Ibid.*, Vol II, no. 15, January 1941.

nor combined it — as their leaders dreamt of — with a possible anti-imperialist mass upsurge, following the interlude of Individual *Satyagraha*.[228] Their agitations nevertheless were indicative of the fact that the ground was being prepared for the direct and face to face confrontations between the rural poor, as well as the peasantry as a whole, and the imperialist rulers of India. Acute tensions had already been built up in the countryside with the peasantry's enthusiastic response to the Kisan Sabha's call for "Na Ek Pai, Na Ek Bhai" (not a single *pai* to the war fund, and not a single recruit to the British army),[229] and the authorities' retaliation by detaining, mostly under Rule 26 of the D.I.R., the *kisan* activists and leaders for showing even the slightest inclination to oppose the British war-efforts. Still the anti-war *kisan* propaganda continued unabated in various parts of the country, especially in areas like the Punjab — where the Government always searched among *kisans* for the richest haul of recruits. At the fair in Sri Anandpur Sahib in Hoshiarpur in March 1940 a gathering of 8,000 heard the *kisan* leaders speaking against war and imperialism.[230] A large number of the Communist *kisan* activists were in fact arrested in the Punjab for their anti-war activities, including for "the tampering with the sepoys' loyalties" to the British army.[231] There were also unmistakable signs in the rural sector of the Kisan Sabhas' preparations for a showdown with the Government. Their volunteer corps, which had come into existence in various regions in the late 1930s, were being reorganised and reinforced in 1940-1. The *kisan* leaders in Burdwan, Bengal, were reported in May 1940 to be collecting money and paddy "with a view to supporting volunteers..., should a civil disobedience movement be declared".[232] Krishna Benode Roy of Jessore, Bengal, was believed similarly to be campaigning for the overhaul of the

228. Home Poll. Fortnightly Report for 1st half of January 1941, File No. 18/1/41, N.A.I.
229. M.A. Rasul *A History of the All India Kisan Sabha*, Calcutta, 1964, p. 72.
230. Home Poll. Fortnightly Report for 2nd half of March 1940, File No. 18/3/40, N.A.I.
231. *Ibid* , 2nd half of June 1940, File No. 18/6/40, N.A.I.
232. Conference of the Krishak Samiti, May 1940, Home Dept., Government of Bengal, File No. W325/40 of 1940, West Bengal State Archives, Calcutta.

Kisan Volunteer Corps, keeping "the impending struggle against the British" in view.[233] The Karshak Sanghams in Kerala in the same vein had instructed all the local branches to raise their auxiliary volunteer units, arrange for the volunteers' physical and political training and hold their meetings at regular intervals. Each volunteer was put in charge of 20 families in a locality, to whom he was to explain the Sangham activities twice a week. Volunteers were also asked to give effect to a "rice dole" system, under which they collected rice from the families under their charge, and put the collection to the local office once a week.[234] Almost on an identical pattern volunteer units were being organised in Tamil Nadu on the basis of a well-laid out "training programme."[235] These attempts at organising the peasantry, particularly its lower ranks, were not without the accompanying "incidents", or acts in defiance of the authorities. A typical such incident occurred at Haroa in the 24-Parganas, Bengal, where one "outsider" *kisan* agitator (Sudhangshu Dutta) was arrested by an armed police party on 15 October 1940. At the time of effecting the arrest, the policemen were surrounded by a mob of 300 *kisans*, and threatened with dire consequences. In the scuffle that followed, the policemen fired at the mob and wounded some of its members. On its part, the mob succeeded in snatching the fire-arms of the policemen and rescuing the prisoner. Thereafter the policemen were severely beaten, injured and chased away. Later on arrived the police reinforcements, who set up camps at Haroa, tortured the villagers, and arrested about 50 persons,[236] without being able to recover either the prisoner or the fire-arms. Though isolated and small, the Haroa-like frayings of the poor *kisans*' anti-imperialist temper were by no means uncommon in other parts of the country. What, however, had been unparalleled, and pregnant with possibilities, was the rural poor's vanguard action against imperialism in Malabar.

233. *Ibid.*
234. Extract from Circular No.14, Central Intelligence Bureau Report of 30.4.41, Home Poll. File No. 7/9/41 Poll., N.A.I.
235. Report of Central Intelligence Officer, Madras, 5.1.41., Home Poll. File No. 129/41 Poll(I), N.A.I.
236. Brief Summary of Political Events in Bengal, 1940, Home Poll. File No. 129/41 Poll.(I), N.A.I.

Subsequent to the outbreak of the war, and in accordance with the leftist opposition to an "imperialist" conflict, the *kisan* leaders of Chirakkal convened a Taluk Kisan Conference on 15 September 1940 to discuss their agitational course of action. The planned conference coincided with the call of the Kerala Provincial Congress Committee to observe 15 September as a day of protest against the brash British refusal to accommodate the Congress views on the governance of India during and after the war.[237] Despite the orders of the District Magistrate of Malabar, prohibiting meetings and demonstrations on the 15th, about 2,000 *kisans* gathered for a conference at Morazha, and came into a clash with the police in which one notorious Inspector and two constables were killed. Skirmishes between the police and the *kisan* masses also took place in Kottayam *taluk*, at Mattanur where a constable died, and in Tellicherry where two *kisan* volunteers were shot dead. Repression was soon let loose in the villages of Chirakkal and Kottayam *taluks*, leading to arrests, searches, beatings and intimidations.[238] The official terror in fact pursued the Sanghams wherever they had led *kisans* to some sort of resistance. It eventually reached Kasargad *taluk*, where *kisans* — more particularly the poorest sections among them — were engaged in a struggle against the *Jenmis*. Kayyur village — which was the scene of the under-tenants' agitation over the harvesting of crops in February 1941 — received the authorities' special attention. The police visited Kayyur on 26 March 1941, searched for the agitators and "absconders", beat up the villagers and arrested four *kisan* volunteers. The raid was believed to be a measure to forestall a *kisan* demonstration against the Raja of Neelaswaram, scheduled for 30 March. The police atrocities so infuriated the villagers that they decided to hold a protest meeting at Kayyur, and on the 28th — the day the meeting was due — a procession of

237. The protest was a part of the countrywide outcry over the Viceroy's "August Offer" of 1940, which turned down the Congress proposals for the national Government of India (of various political parties under the aegis of the British) during the war, and for the grant of Indian independence after the war.

238. A.K. Gopalan, *In the Cause of the People: Reminiscences*, New Delhi, 1973, pp. 142-3. Also see Home Poll., File No. 7/9/41, Poll (I), N.A.I.

about 150 *kisans* met a police Sub-Inspector on the way, chased and killed him.[239] Another policeman, who took refuge in a village official's house, was attacked and stabbed.[240] On the 29th arrived at Kayyur a police force from Mangalore under an Assistant Superintendent of Police, but it did not dare to step into the village. It entered the village next day (the 30th) only after the arrival of a platoon of Malabar Special Police headed by the District Magistrate of Malabar and the Deputy Inspector General from Mangalore. The entry was followed by such reprisals as house-breakings, physical tortures and molestations of women. Practically all the inhabitants of Kayyur (about 4,000), and almost 40 per cent of the neighbouring village Padakkad fled and hid themselves in the forests. Of the numerous arrested, 65 *kisans* were charged with murder and violence, and committed to the Sessions Court, South Kanara, for trial. Meetings and processions were banned in the entire area under Section 144 Cr.P.C.,[241] and on 25 April 1941 the authorities declared the Malabar Karshak Sangham and its affiliated bodies as "unlawful associations".[242]

The act of violence at Kayyur, and the police atrocities preceding and succeeding it, as well as the trial and conviction of the *kisan* prisoners, attracted the attention of the Indian people, in some form or the other, for more than two subsequent years. The *kisan* accused were acclaimed generally as popular heroes, and the Government and the police as perpetrators of the worst kind of oppression. At the inspirational level, therefore, the happenings at Kayyur seemed to have contributed to the intensification of anti-imperialist feelings among Indians in general, and among *kisans* in particular. The Communists' claim in public that "Kayyur went down before the reign of terror, but wrote a glorious chapter in the *kisan* annals of India,"[243] was

239. *Communist* (English monthly, printed), Vol. III, no. 6, August 1941.
240. Central Intelligence Bureau Report on the "Activities of the All Malabar Peasants' Union", April 1941, Home Poll. File No. 7/9/41 Poll(I), N.A.I.
241. *Ibid.* See also *Communist* (English monthly, printed), Vol. III, no. 6, August 1941.
242. *Ibid.*
243. *Communist* (English monthly, printed), Vol. III, no. 6, August 1941.

substantially true. But no less true apparently was their introspection into the incidents in private, or their inner-party discussions over it in confidence. While everybody agreed with the Kerala Provincial Committee of the C.P.I. that the violent acts at Kayyur were "defensive actions", and that these took place "spontaneously" when the population was "up against police repression", the Politbureau of the party questioned the extent to which the Communists should go along with spontaneity. "Acts done spontaneously, without consideration to the strength of the party and its links with the masses in a particular place," it felt, "really do more harm than good to the party". To substantiate its finding, the Politbureau pointed out the demoralisation of the people of Kayyur after the incidents, instead of their being "steeled and embittered" as the Kerala P.C. thought, their fleeing to the forests, their surrendering to the police without much resistance, clearly indicated that the Communist and the *kisan* organisations had not yet taken firm roots. The central party leadership, however, acknowledged the initiative and the bravery of the "vanguards" who retaliated against the police excesses, and met violence with violence; but wondered whether the brave acts of "the few" would really help in building a mass movement, if they were not planned, and the *kisan* population mentally not prepared for withstanding their repercussions.[244] The critical points thus raised by the Communist ideologues were theoretically incontrovertible, and good Communists should have awaited the ideal situation — the complete politicisation of the local peasantry and the establishment of a sound organisation to match it — before venturing at all to jump into any fray. Perhaps the Kasargad Communist activists by themselves would have preferred to wait, had it not been for the Kayyur *kisans'* impatience for autonomous actions, as well as for the absence at Kayyur of a worldly wise and restraining village party committee. Even then the outcome on the whole was far from being unsatisfactory, considering the fact that a model circumstance for a Communist-

244. Party Letter, No. 43, 1 July 1941, Party Documents, Communist Party of India, Central Archives, Ajoy Bhavan, New Delhi.

led anti-imperialist rising did not develop anywhere in India in 1940-1, nor did the Communists manage to demonstrate hitherto their ability to bring it about. The Kayyur incidents marked in their limited, small way the culmination of the three radical trends in agrarian politics, namely, the unity of *kisans* against landlords (the *Jenmis*), their actual engagement in a bitter anti-landlord struggle and their straightforward confrontation with the imperial authorities. In other words, the Kayyur outburst represented in miniature the rare, conscious combination of the direct anti-feudal and anti-imperialist thrusts of the *kisan* struggle. Such an amalgam being the fond hope — the avowed object — of the Communists and the leftists on the *kisan* front, the Kayyur incidents seem to represent politically the highest point that they could attain in 1940-1.

THE RAISONNEUR'S MONOLOGUE

If Kayyur was the farthest that the leftists and the rural poor could manage to go together, would it not then be right to say that they had, more or less, been successful in their joint ventures in 1940-1? The answer must take into account not only what they had done, and wanted to do, but also the circumstances that conditioned their doings and undoings. The circumstances for the left political agitators appeared in retrospect to be both favourable and unfavourable to an extent. These were favourable because of the deepening war-time crisis on the agro-economic front — almost as much as the leftists had foreshadowed it — and where desperation might have led their following increasingly to the chartered path of agitation. The chartered path, namely, the simultaneous continuation of the anti-imperialist and the anti-feudal struggles, or the pursuance of the twin objects of the "national democratic" and "agrarian" revolutions, did not seem in 1940-1 as clear as it was during the preceding years of 1934-9. The outbreak of the war, and Britain's troubles over it, had brought the anti-imperialist tasks ahead of the anti-feudal duties, and the most intolerant of feudalism among the Indian left — the Communists — recognised it more than the others. The confusion came about the method to be adopted for galvanising the struggle against imperialism — whether to make use of the anti-feudal battles for rallying the innumerable *kisan* warriors face to face with imperialism (as the Communists contemplated), or to restrain their hostility towards feudalism for paying undivided attention to freedom from the imperialist rulers (as the Congress Socialists wished). The divergence of the Congress Socialists' and the Communists' perceptions, and more so, the obsession for gaining petty political advantages over each other, were bound to affect the anti-imperialism they fostered together, especially when the modicum of popular Government had practically been revoked and the country passed already over to the "D.I.R. Raj". Howsoever wavering and compromising in their dealings with the Raj and its feudal allies, the provincial Congress ministries tried to uphold, even if uncertainly, some semblance of civil liberties, and thereby, provided the leftists and the rural poor with a certain space between 1937 and 1939 to take their breath. Denied of this breathing space in 1940-1, the Congress Socialists and the Communists, notwithstanding their spacious professions, were not really expected to go very far, or work out any wonder. That they were able to keep the embers of the past agrarian agitations alive, and even kindle new ones — with more militant prospects in view — speaks favourably of their steadfast attachment to the cause of the rural poor's social and political emancipation. The victories and defeats, the credit and the debit sides, did not actually count in such trials of strength; what mattered had been the fighting spirit that was being raised in the Indian countryside — the willingness of the *kisan* masses to resist both their immediate and remote oppressors.

The bulk of the *kisan* masses — the poor peasants, the sharecroppers and the agricultural labourers — who had fought some of their battles in 1936-9 under the leftist guidance and had gained substantially in self-confidence, showed little hesitation in 1940-1 in responding to the call of their mentors — the middle class ideologues and activists from the urban centres, or the so-called "outsiders". Whether it was the resumption of the old struggles (such as, the *Halis*' and the sharecroppers' in south Gujarat, the *Hattola* resisters' in Bengal, the *Sir kisans'* in the U.P., the *Bakasht* peasants' in Bihar, the anti-*Zamindari* in Munagala and Venkatagiri, Andhra Pradesh, as well as in Malabar, Madras, and in Bhatipara and Rankeli, Assam, and the forest-dwellers' agitation in Dondi-Lohara, the C.P.), or the commencement of the new ones (such as, the *Adhiars'* and the *Kut Khamar* tenants' in Bengal, the *punam* cultivators' in Malabar, the anti-eviction in Kasargad, the Dhodia agricultural labourers' in south Gujarat, the under-tenants' in Thana, the Pallars' in Lalgudi, Trichinopoly, the jute and sugarcane-growers' in Bengal, Bihar and the U.P., the "hunger" marchers in various parts of the country), they veered round the leftist "outsiders" and the Kisan Sabhas, faced the landlords'goons and the authorities' police, and suffered beatings, arrests and imprisonments. Not all the rural poor's struggles were led by the leftists, who, with limited organisational strength, and under the surveillance of the "D.I.R. Raj", could not possibly have reached all the nooks and corners of the countryside. They were scarcely able, for instance, to establish contacts with those who lived on the fringes of rural society, and in the difficult terrains, such as the tribal *kisans*. Ever since the spreading of the nationalist and the leftist politics in the rural sector, therefore, the tribal *kisans* were perhaps the only ones who could display an autonomy of collective action. The Babijheri rising, the Savara outbreak and the Santhal *Bataidars'* agitation were shining examples of such heroic autonomous endeavours, and they resembled so closely with the Kisan Sabha-led agitations that the common man and woman, and even the authorities, mistook them to be leftist-inspired. All the tribal agitations, however, were not autonomous, and the left political activists succeeded sometimes in contacting and organising the tribal *kisans*, as they did, for illustration, in the anti-*Zamindari* Santhal outbursts in Palamau in September[245] and in Dumka in November 1940.[246] Likewise, all the leftist agitations were not altogether devoid of evidences of *kisans'* wresting some autonomous initiative at certain stages, and forcing the hands of their leaders. The numerous cases of social brigandage, the frequent clashes with the *sahukars'* and landlords' hirelings, the sharecroppers' recurring refusals to give crop-shares to landlords and a series of confrontations with the police, particularly for freeing the arrested *kisan* leaders — notably in Mandasa, Visakhapatnam, in April, and at Haroa, the 24-Parganas, in October 1940 — were indicative of this trend. The culmination of it was seen in the vanguard *kisan* actions at Kayyur, or the incidents which the Communist central leadership criticised in private as products of spontaneity.

Were the Communists and other leftists in a position at all in 1940-1 to repeat in different parts of the country the Kayyur

245. Home Poll. Fortnightly Report for 2nd half of September 1940, File No. 18/9/40, N.A.I.

246. *Ibid.*, 2nd half of November 1940, File No. 18/11/40, N.A.I.

incidents — the rare conjunctions of intense anti-feudal and anti-imperialist tendencies? If the leftist activities were seen in the over-all political perspective of India in 1940-1, they did not appear to be capable of producing such performances on their own — solely by themselves. Howsoever much the leftists dreamt grandoisely of isolating the vacillating Gandhian leadership in the Congress, transforming the national movement into a proletarian-led mass upsurge and completing the "national democratic revolution" in India, they were not placed at any vantage point yet either to pilot the Congress, or to lead the heterogeneous multi-class nationalist formation. Even their intrinsic ability to influence the Congress's decision-making, or to exert pressure on its decision-makers, was severely limited after Subhas Chandra Bose's ouster from the Congress Presidentship in April 1939, and Jawaharlal Nehru's reluctance to make common grounds with him at that point. Under these circumstances, the leftists were not really capable of giving a radical twist to the anti-imperialist struggle in India, and of raising it to an uncompromising, militant height. Until and unless the nationalists in the Congress, and their Gandhian leaders, of their own accord, adopted consciously an attitude for creating a "do or die" situation in the country, and asked the British threateningly to "quit India", it was difficult for the leftists to go on repeating Kayyurs. However, had the Congress stopped hesitating, and being dilatory, and passed unflinchingly its memorable August resolution in 1941, instead of in 1942, the outcome of India's campaign for independence might have been different with the whole-hearted support of all the leftists, including the battle-ready Communists, the massive participation of the rural poor, and the enactment of Kayyurs all over the country. That it did not happen the way it should have was, indeed, a historic tragedy.

SCENE II
1942-43

The influence the leftists exercised in 1940-1 over the *kisan* movement in general, and the initiatives they tried to take during the "D.I.R. Raj" phase in rallying the rural poor in particular, were rudely disturbed at the fag end of 1941 by the dramatic reversal of posture by the most militant among them. Diametrically opposite to their belief in the "imperialist" character of the war, and the anti-imperialist prospect that it heralded before them, the Communists came abruptly, and almost anti-climactically, to the conclusion on 13 December 1941 that the character of the war had been "fundamentally transformed".[247] Quite obviously if the war ceased to remain what it was before, and the advantages it offered did not appear to be as true as they had once been, the leftists and the *kisan* masses must act differently to fit themselves into the altered situation. What, however, did happen on the war front in 1941 that indicated such a drastic change in the circumstances, and compelled the Communists to think in terms of a radical transformation in the character of the war? The historic occurrences that absorbed the Communists' attention were Hitler's "thunderingly surprise" (to borrow an expression of Jawaharlal Nehru) invasion of Soviet Russia on 22 June 1941, the British and the American declarations of their support to the Soviet Union against Germany soon thereafter, and the conclusion of a Soviet-British agreement in July 1941 for concerted action against Germany.[248] That Hitler

247. "The All People's War Against Fascism and Our Policy and Tasks", Resolution of the Politbureau, C.P.I., 13 December 1941, Party Letter No. 156 (Cyclo.), 15 December 1941, Party Documents, Central Archives, Communist Party of India, Ajoy Bhavan, New Delhi.

248. Sometime later was signed the Soviet and United States agreement, after the U.S. had formally joined the war in December 1941, concerning "the principles applying to mutual aid in the prosecution of the war against aggression".

would eventually flout the Soviet-German non-aggression pact, after being relieved somewhat of his military preoccupations on the western front, and invade the Soviet Union at his own relatively free time, was a possibility which no one had ever ruled out. It had also not been possible to do so in view of Hitler's record against the Communists, his rabid ideological hostility towards Communism and his pet pan-German quest for expansion in the East. But that he would engage himself in a bout with Soviet Russia before forcing Britain and its allies to take on knock-out counts was not really anticipated, or considered a certainty. The Nazi invasion of Soviet Russia was, therefore, startling, to say the least, and it evidently marked a substantial change in the war situation, which even later on proved to be decisive. Whether a substantial change in the course of the war could be called a fundamental or qualitative one depended on who viewed the events, and from what position. The views of those who were organically connected with the Soviet Union in a monolithic Third International would not be similar to the opinions of others who did not belong to it, but who, nevertheless, admired the Soviet socialist experimentation.

To the participants of the international Communist movement, which was known to have been dominated as much by Bolshevik pre-possessions as by Russian national interests, the attack on the Soviet Union — the citadel of socialism — introduced a qualitative change in the war, and hence called for a world-wide endeavour to defend the only socialist country on earth, strengthen the hands of all those combatants (most important of whom was the imperialist Britain) already in combat with Germany and its collaborators, and undertake a crusade against the aggressor of the Soviet people — Fascism. From the Communist International viewpoint, the call for such a crusade was not only logical and theoretically justifiable, but also easy for its upholders in politically free, and chimerically independent, non-colonial countries to pay heed to it. It was, however, not exactly so for the Communists in the colonial countries where they had already been in the thick of their peoples' struggles for independence, and where the war-weariness of the colonial powers seemed to have promised such popular struggles some prospect of success. Would the Communists in the colonies give precedence to the internationalist anxieties of the clanhood over the nationalist concerns of their people, and retire from the anti-imperialist battle-fields within the homelands to join even their sworn enemies for the anti-Fascist defence of a distant Soviet Union? In case they were reluctant to do so, or felt hesitant to fall in line, had they really much chance to withstand the pressure of the Communist International, headed by the Soviet Union, and represented by such cohorts as the Communist Party of Great Britain, for enforcing conformity? The heart-searchings of the C.P.I. over the colonial Communists' dilemma continued for six long months, and the pros and cons of the issue debated among its leaders and members, both in detention and in the hiding. That the party had been unwilling to give up its anti-imperialist standing in the nationalist movement, freshly reinforced since the beginning of 1940, was made abundantly clear within a month of the invasion of Soviet Russia. In July 1941 the Politbureau of the C.P.I. issued a policy statement on the Soviet-German war, stating that the only way the Indian people could help in a "just" war in support of the Soviet Union was by fighting all the more vigorously for their own emancipation from the imperialist yoke. The freedom of people the world over could be achieved, according to it, not by harbouring the illusion that the British and the American support would "bring Soviet victory and a new world," but "by waging a ceaseless struggle to expose the imperialist war-crimes of the British and American rulers.... . Reliance on the people, on the working class, and not on the imperialists, this is the core of a true internationalist policy... . They are false internationalists and deceivers of people who say that we can side with the Soviet or win the war of the people by aiding the British Government's war efforts."[249] Very few Communist Parties of the world had expressed at such a sensitive point their views so daringly in contravention of the dictates of the international Communist movement as the C.P.I. appeared to have done. The insistence of the C.P.G.B., the self-appointed guardian of communism in colonial India, on the C.P.I's rallying round the

249. *Communist* (English monthly, printed), Vol. III, no. 6, August 1941.

British Raj to secure the victory of the Soviet Union, whether the Indian people attained independence or not, did not seem to have moved the party much. Even Rajani Palme Dutt's assertion that the interests of the colonial peoples of India and Ireland were bound up with the victory of the Soviet Union over the Nazis, and that such a victory was so absolute and unconditional that it did not depend on any future step "their rulers promise or concede",[250] had not really helped. For, in October 1941 the Central Committee of the C.P.I. reiterated its stand that by continuing the anti-imperialist struggle only the Indian people should be able to contribute to the Soviet Union's, and the world people's resistance against Fascism. It rejected the thesis that the inner contradictions of the imperialist powers had forced Britain and the U.S. to take the Soviet Union's side, and that, therefore, the Indian people must strengthen the hands of these powers. Rather, it unambiguously condemned those (like the C.P.G.B.) who wanted to assist the Soviet Union, or win the popular struggles in India entirely by aiding and abetting the British war-efforts as "false internationalists", "misguiding" the Indian people.[251] The C.P.I.'s position in October 1941 was, more or less, similar to the Congress's view, expressing solidarity with those peoples who were subjected to the Fascist aggressions, and asserting that only a free and independent India should be able to help "the larger causes" of the war.[252] It was also not very different from the C.S.P.'s opinion that one ought not to be carried away by those "who are exploiting the proletariat's sympathy for the Soviet Union", rather he or she should work for the revolutionary upheaval that the war was likely to bring in its trail.[253] The persistence with which the C.P.I. wanted to follow the goal of "national democratic revolution"

250. *Labour Monthly* (English monthly), September 1941, p. 381.
251. Party Letter, Central Committee, 30 October 1941, no. 53, Party Documents, Central Archives, Communist Party of India, Ajoy Bhavan, New Delhi.
252. Resolution, The Congress Working Committee, Bardoli, 23 December 1941, P. Sitaramayya , *History of the Indian National Congress,* Vol. II, Bombay, 1947, p. 310.
253. Narendra Deva, *Socialism and National Revolution,* Bombay, 1946, pp. 149 and 153-4.

during the war, and the firmness in which it refused to concede the vantage point where such an upsurge could take off the ground, and the left and the nationalist forces rally together, were given up a month and a half later at the speed of a blitz. These convictions were also thoroughly denounced by the same Politbureau which was responsible for them, as manifestations of "narrow bourgeois nationalism", and as "utterly wrong" since July 1941 when Britain came to the help of the Soviet Union.[254]

In their newly acquired wisdom, the leaders of the C.P.I. felt in December 1941 that the moment Hitler invaded the Soviet Union, and Britain and the U.S. rushed to its defence, the world of imperialism was divided sharply into two opposing camps in relation to the only socialist state in existence "in a manner as it had never happened before". Imperialist powers, who had hitherto been uniformly hostile to Soviet Russia, were now turned either into its friends or its enemies. This marked a qualitative change in the character of the war in which the friends of Soviet Russia were pitted against the enemies of it, the forces of progress ranged against the armies of reaction. In the new situation Britain could no longer be accused of continuing an "unjust" imperialist war, for it had already taken the side of the proletarian state in a "just" war against the reactionary aggressors. From the point of view of proletarian internationalism, therefore, the second world war ceased from July 1941 to remain "imperialist", and had become a "people's" one instead, in which the proletarians — the Communist Parties of all the countries — irrespective of their "national and local conditions", must defend the Soviets and the twenty four years' of socialism there. If the war had thus changed its character — necessitating the raising of one slogan (anti-Fascism), the fighting on one front (the world front of peoples against Fascism) and targeting on one enemy (Hitler-Fascists) — the main tasks of the "imperialist war" phase should not be relevant or valid any longer in the "people's war" stage, howsoever much the nationalists in India resented it. "Developing mass struggles

254. "The All People's War Against Fascism and Our Policy and Tasks", Politbureau Resolution, 13 December 1941, Party Letter No. 56, 15 December 1941, Party Documents, Communist Party of India, Central Archives, Ajoy Bhavan, New Delhi.

against the war, in order to achieve the immediate overthrow of the British Government, can not be our slogan for the present situation", the Politbureau of the C.P.I. continued, "for that would mean splitting the world front against Fascism, and its sabotage".[255] The new tasks of the Communists, according to it, should consist in bringing Indian people into the world front against Fascism, launching a "people's war" movement for popularising the great significance of the war, and putting "the full weight of India and her resources... on the side of the progressive forces"[256]. In other words, "the practical policy in India", in the opinion of the Politbureau, was to cooperate with the British Raj in all its war-efforts, to pressurise the Congress to give up its call for "conditional support" to the British — "an opportunistic bourgeois nationalist bargain" for crumbs of political power — to persuade it to withdraw all the anti-British moves, including the Individual *Satyagraha* and the boycott of legislatures, to ask it to make up with the Muslim League for the sake of popular unity, and, most importantly, to organise country-wide campaign for "rousing the people in favour of the Soviets", or to link India up with the anti-Fascist movement all over the world.[257]

The C.P.I's political somersault, or its complete turn about, from the posture of deadliest confrontation with British imperialism to the position of friendliest cooperation, or collaboration with it, and that, too, within a short span of seven weeks between the roaring and the mewing, was most astounding — almost inexplicable even today. Granting that ideological subtleties, as well as oddities, could dawn on individuals in a certain instinctive flash, or within a surprisingly short length of time, the dramatic reversal of the C.P.I.'s stand on the war from the "imperialist's" to the "people's" — could be understood only in terms of the "orders from outside",[258] or the commands of a stern, overbearing Third International. The inter-

255. *Ibid.*
256. *Ibid.*
257. *Ibid.*
258. Acharya Narendra Deva, "The War: Imperialist or People's?", *Samajbadi Andolan Ke Dastabej* (Hindi), Vinode Prasad Singh, and Sunil Mishra, (eds.) Delhi, p. 252.

national Communist movement was built up in so excessively centralised a manner, between the 1920s and the 1940s, that it hardly permitted any of its components to disagree with the policy once adopted or stated. The situation naturally turned worse at the time of the war, when even the scope of discussing a policy for adoption did not exist, such as it was on the occasion of the Hitlerite aggression on Russia. In case it had existed by some miracle, the views of the Communists from the colonial countries on an essentially European development would most probably not matter much, as it really did not matter even on the issue of colonialism — their direct and immediate concern. On the colonial question and its various ramifications, the leaders of the Third International had habitually assumed from the beginning an air of superiority over their colonial comrades, since the pioneers of Communism in the colonial countries suffered from certain obvious material and theoretical handicaps. Consequently, the Communist Parties in the colonies found it particularly difficult to depart or deviate from the political lines dictated to them by the leaders of the Third International.[259] It was in fact practically impossible for the C.P.I. to do so because of its relatively limited organisational strength in proportion to the vastness of India, and comparatively lesser stature in the massive Indian national movement. At no stage, therefore, did the C.P.I. show any inclination to question or defy the fiats of the arbiters of Communism from abroad, and it had preferred to suffer silently instead, when such dictates proved to be both misleading and injurious. It was only between July and December 1941 — a period of six months — that the C.P.I. for the first time in its history felt like a non-conformist, and desired to act on its own.[260] That its leaders could not go

259. A Sino-centric Mao Zhe Dong had succeeded, between 1929 and 1943, in warding off the orthodox Chinese Communists' and the Communist International's accusations of "peasant mentality" and "peasant guerillaism" either by taking refuge in the conventional Marxian verbosity, or by maintaining long, inscrutable silence.

260. After going through the available literature on the subject, the author tends to think that the C.P.I.'s six-monthly experiment with non-conformism was perhaps guided by Dr. G. Adhikari, the central figure of its underground organisation in 1941, and a Marxist of distinct original thinking.

any further, and felt overwhelmed at the prospect of being isolated in the Communist world, or marooned by the helmsmen of the Third International, clearly indicated a lack of faith in themselves — a trait not uncommon in the European Communist Parties, but quite common in their colonial counterparts.[261] To the C.P.I.'s diffidence — which could only be shed with extraordinary courage — was perhaps added some of its leaders' anxiety for relief from the endless wanderings in the underground and continual sufferings in the prisons. By February 1941, the police had already rounded up as many as 480 prominent Communists,[262] and the number of them detained without trial could well be over a thousand in October 1941. It was natural for the hard-core of the Communist detenus, who could not forget their long prison days in connection with the Lahore or Meerut Conspiracy cases, to be too enthusiastic for coming out of the detention camps on any ideologically arguable ground.[263] The weariest among those in the underground also felt the same way for seizing some good opportunity to come into the open. One can not entirely rule out in this context the rumour current in the anti-Communist circles of a communication from Harry Politt, the C.P.G.B. leader, to the C.P.I. through the good offices of Sir Reginald Maxwell, the Home Member of the Government of India, which was believed to have finally clinched the C.P.I.'s stand in favour of the "people's war".[264] Whether or not Politt had actually sent such a communication to

261. Even an old-timer like Ho Chi Minh, who was building a "nationalist" Vietnamese Communist movement in 1941-2, had to think first of explaining his strategy to Moscow and obtaining Moscow's approval before embarking fully on it. He in fact started on his Moscow mission through China in July 1942, was caught by the Kuomintung soon thereafter, and kept in captivity till the spring of 1943.
262. The Central Legislative Assembly Debates, Delhi 1941, p. 121, cited in Satyabrata Ray Choudhuri, *Leftist Movements in India, 1917-47,* Calcutta, 1977, p. 126.
263. A "Jail Document", believed to have been written by the Communist leaders in Deoli Detention Camp, and drafted originally by B.T. Ranadive, was circulated in the autumn for adopting a "people's war" position.
264. M.R. Masani, *The Communist Party of India : A Short History,* London, 1954, p. 80.

the C.P.I. leaders, threatening the party's excommunication from the international Communist movement if it refused to fall in line, and guaranteeing — on behalf of the British Government — the release of the Communist detenus and the legalisation of the party if it did, all these three factors, namely the fear of excommunication, the possibility of legal functioning and the probability of the prisoners' release, might have played their respective roles in the making of the Communist mind in India in December 1941.[265] An "All People's War Against Fascism" was declared thereafter by the Indian Communists, without any further loss of time, and to spearhead it they selected P.C. Joshi as their party's newly found ideologue in place of the hitherto acclaimed Dr. G. Adhikari. The Raj, however, took its own time to reciprocate, bargaining with Joshi for about six months, legalising the C.P.I. on 23 July 1942, and releasing the prisoners in batches haltingly after that.

Apart from the minuscule Bolshevik Party of India, none of the major left groups either appreciated the *volte face* of the C.P.I., or felt inclined to follow its example. The Trotskyite Bolshevik-Leninist Party remained firm in its opposition to the "imperialist" war, and the Revolutionary Communist Party of India also did not budge from a similar position.[266] The Forward Bloc's ebullience for resisting the British and their war, which swelled after Subhas Chandra Bose's disappearance from Calcutta in January 1941, had not in any way ebbed by the Hitlerite invasion of Soviet Russia. The Revolutionary Socialist Party continued to hold in the main that the Soviet Union's alliance with the Allies had not changed the character of the war, and

265. The Soviet Union's abject failure initially to stem the tide of Nazi invasion had considerably shaken the abiding Communist faith in its military capabilities. Even the non-conformists like Dr. Adhikari seemed to have felt "jittery" in November 1941, and to have reluctantly conceded that perhaps Soviet Russia would not be able to save itself without the Anglo-American help. (From a personal discussion with Professor Arun Bose, a member of the C.P.I. Central Committee in 1941-2, in Calcutta on 27 December 1990). The fear was likely to have some demoralising effect on the non-conformists *vis-a-vis* the advocates of the "people's war".

266. Home Poll. File No. 226/42 - Poll (I) of 1942, N.A.I.

that India could help the Soviet Union only after achieving its own independence.[267] The C.S.P., who did not believe that an imperialist war could change its character in the age of capitalism, pointed out that both the Fascist Germany and the imperialist Britain being capitalist countries, their contest could hardly benefit the colonised people. The emancipation of people in the colonies could only come through the destruction of capitalism, for which they were continue to launch assaults on "the centre of finance capitalist domination in Britain" and on the British power in India.[268] The C.S.P. refused to view the German-Soviet Russian conflict as anything but an escalation of the imperialist war, and declined to attach any radical significance to it, except that the patriotic Russians were fighting their aggressors to save their fatherland, but not for the sake of the emancipation of humanity, nor for the creation of a new world order, which, after all, could not really be undertaken in the company of the imperialists. The Congress Socialists in fact saw no indication of any basic change in the war situation that could turn the conflict into a "people's war",[269] and therefore, they preferred to persist with their "Waiting for Godot" (whose appearance was expected throughout the Samuel Becket play), or for a Congress call to challenge the Raj in India. The Radical Democrats or the Royists, who held on to their anti-Fascist war stand long before the Communists were compelled to think about it, and who should have been the Communists' natural allies in a "people's war" in India, were ironically denounced by the C.P.I. as the subservient "agents" of the British Government, and the "disrupters" of the

267. The R.S.P. thesis on the Russo-German War, ***Intensify National Struggle** : On the Revolutionary Defence of U.S.S.R.*, Calcutta, 1941.
268. "Fight the Battle for World Peace in India", a leaflet issued by Jayaprakash Narayan, Achyut Patwardhan and Rammanohar Lohia, Home Poll. File No. 3/52/43-Poll(I) of 1943, N.A.I.
269. Acharya Narendra Deva, "The War : Imperialist or Peoples?" ***Samajbadi Andolan Ke Dastabej*** (Hindi), Vinode Prasad Singh, and Sunil Mishra, (eds.), Delhi, 1985, pp. 238-53.
270. "The All People's War Against Fascism and Our Policy and Tasks", Politbureau Resolution, 13 December 1941, Party Letter No.56, 15 December 1941, Party Documents, Central Archives, Communist Party of India, Ajoy Bhavan, New Delhi.

popular movements in the country,[270] and hence it refused to have any truck with them. Consequently at the beginning of 1942, the C.P.I.'s position in the left movement in India had turned out quite expectedly, and also by its own anticipation,[271] to be one of virtual isolation. There would, however, have been little cause of regret for its members, had this isolation not affected, or "disrupted" those social and economic movements of the people which were acknowledged to have sustained anti-imperialism among the masses.

Indications were there in the new document itself which enunciated an "All People's War Against Fascism" that the C.P.I. would wish to continue its fight for the social and economic causes of the toiling masses, as well as for the political rights of all the Indians. Simultaneously with its all-out campaign in support of the anti-Fascist war, the party wished to work for India's "complete" independence, a national Government at the centre, the release of all political prisoners and the restoration of civil liberties. It resolved to demand for the recognition of the workers' unions, acceptance of their right to strike and a 25 per cent rise in their wages. Similarly, it reiterated its determination to stand for fulfilling some of the *kisan* demands, controlling the prices of daily necessaries, remitting land revenue in the flood and scarcity affected areas, and resisting "all forcible levies", including the "war levies".[272] Although it refrained scrupulously from mentioning the "agrarian revolution", and did not repeat the usual battle-cry against the landlords-usurers, nor raised the slogan of "land to the tiller", the C.P.I. could — had it so desired — still give expression to the rural poor's abhorrence for the feudal exactions and the bondages, and their craving for an increase in the wages and the crop-shares. A survey of the agrarian scene from 1942 to 1943, especially of the activities of the poor peasants, sharecroppers and agricultural labourers, however, did give the impression that the C.P.I. activists were more interested there in suspending the anti-feudal struggles in favour of the "people's war" — at least for the time being —

271. The C.P.I. apparently knew how bitter a pill its "people's war" was for the nationalistically inclined to swallow. *Ibid.*
272. *Ibid.*

than in prosecuting them as dourly as the circumstances would permit. Likewise in these two years, perhaps in a greater degree than in the previous years of 1940-1, the Congress Socialists exhibited more anxiety for resisting the "imperialist" war than for fighting the peasantry's anti-feudal battles in the rural sector. The feudal exploitation and the exploited rural masses had in effect been conveniently forgotten (of course, with an assurance of remembering them again after the Soviet Union's victory or India's attainment of independence, whichever would come earlier) in the heated theoretical controversy that was foisted upon the *kisan* movement over the issue of the "people's war" versus the "imperialist war". The way the controversy rocked the *kisan* movement could be understood from the example of Bihar, where the pro-Communist and pro-Swami Sahajanand activists were coming into wordy duels with the Forward Blocists (led by Sheel Bhadra Yajee) and the Congress Socialists (led by Rambriksh Benipuri) as early as January 1942.[273] Swami Sahajanand, who had turned an anti-Fascist in Hazaribagh Central Jail, was believed to have encouraged from the prison the debate in the Bihar Provincial Kisan Sabha.[274] While the anti-Fascists pleaded in Champaran district for the *kisan* cooperation with the police to safeguard the security of the villages, the anti-imperialists there asked the villagers to be ready for a "Kisans'-Labourers' raj", [275] expecting a British collapse in the war "in a few months".[276] Parallel to the exhortations of Rambriksh Benipuri, Awadheshwar Prasad and Shyamnandan Singh in Muzaffarpur in March 1942, urging *kisans* not to help the British war-efforts, ran the elocution of the recently released Swami Sahajanand, Mathura Prasad Mishra and Jadunandan Sharma in Gaya, asking *kisans* not only to do the opposite,[277] but also to join the army if they were "properly paid".[278] Meanwhile Japan's

273. Home Poll. Fortnightly Report for 1st half of January 1942, File No. 18/1/42, N.A.I.
274. Home Poll. File No.2/9/4 Poll (I) of 1942, N.A.I.
275. Home Poll. Fortnightly Report for 2nd half of January 1942, File No. 18/1/42, N.A.I.
276. *Ibid.*, 2nd half of February 1942, File No. 18/2/42, N.A.I.
277. *Ibid.*, 2nd half of March 1942, File No. 18/3/42, N.A.I.
278. *Ibid.*, 2nd half of April 1942, File No. 18/4/42, N.A.I.

entry into the war on the side of the Axis powers on 7 December 1941, and the spectacular advances of its armies through the Philippines, Indo-China, Malaya and Burma in the subsequent five months (by May 1942) raised the controversy to a higher pitch, leading the "people's war" group to think in terms of popular resistance at the village level against a possible Japanese invasion of India, and the "imperialist war" group to get ready for taking the advantage of an imminent fall of British rule in India, following the humiliating British defeats in Hongkong, Singapore, Manila and Rangoon. Both urged the baffled *kisans* to organise the village defences, not for protecting themselves from the landlords' men and the police, but for either resisting the "Japanese Fascists", or dealing a "death blow" to the Raj,[279] and they often came into physical clashes with each other, such as the one that took place at Sherghati in Gaya, in the first week of April 1942.[280] The intensification of the Congress Socialists' and Forward Blocists' campaign for an impending anti-British mass agitation[281] was matched by the stepping up of the Communists' and their allies' propaganda for an immediate anti-Japanese resistance movement.[282] To press their respective points of view upon *kisans*, two corresponding provincial conferences were simultaneously held in the first half of June 1942, at Bedaul in Muzaffarpur, by the former, and at Bihta in Patna, by the latter.[283] Almost all in the two camps were equally keen to remind *kisans* of their commitment to a future "Kisan-Majdoor Raj",[284] but none seemed to have the necessary time, and the seriousness of purpose to lead *kisans* to wage new battles or continue with the old ones. In his enthusiasm for

279. *Ibid.*, 1st half of March and 2nd half of April 1942, File Nos. 18/3/42 and 18/4/42, N.A.I.
280. *Ibid.*, 1st half of April 1942, File No.18/4/42, N.A.I.
281. *Ibid.*, 2nd half of April and 2nd half of June 1942, File Nos. 18/4/42 and 18/6/42, N.A.I.
282. *Ibid.*, 1st half of May and 2nd half of June 1942, File Nos. 18/5/42 and 18/6/42, N.A.I.
283. *Ibid.*, 1st half of June 1942, File No.18/6/42, N.A.I.
284. *Ibid.*, 1st half of April and 1st half of July 1942, File Nos. 18/4/42 and 18/7/42, N.A.I.

concentrating popular attention on anti-Fascism, even the dedicated Swami Sahajanand was unwilling "to dissipate" the *kisan* energies in fights over the *Bakasht* lands.[285]

The Bihar story, more or less, was repeated elsewhere in India, and the Communist and the Congress Socialist *kisan* workers in the Punjab were reported in March 1942 to have confronted each other rather "fiercely".[286] In a show of strength, the opposing groups held in May 1942 parallel conferences in the C.P. and Berar — a pro-"people's war" one in Amraoti (presided over by Yajnik) and an anti-"imperialist" one in Betul (under the presidentship of the Forward Blocist, R.S. Ruikar).[287] The Communists and their allies dominated the third Gujarat Provincial Kisan Conference in Bulsar (6 and 7 June 1942) but seemed to have encountered stiff resistance from their opponents in Ahmedabad.[288] The Congress Socialists generally fared better than their rivals in Maharashtra and the U.P. and their anti "imperialist" campaign among the Oriya *kisans* appeared to have picked up when Pandit Ramnandan Mishra undertook a propaganda tour of Orissa.[289] Similarly, the "people's war" group enjoyed a certain edge over their adversaries in the *kisan* movement in Bengal and the Surma Valley of Assam, as well as perhaps in some parts of Madras province. In fact the entire *kisan* movement throughout the country was thoroughly dismembered by the middle of 1942 — an outcome of the process that had originated in the Central Kisan Council meeting of the A.I.K.S. (12-13 February 1942) in Nagpur. It was there that the Communists won a Pyrrhic victory over their critics (who included a friendly Yajnik, apart from the hostile Ranga and Yajee) by outvoting them on the issue of the "people's war",[290] and bringing thereby the rift in the *kisan* organisation into the wide open. Not realising what they had done, the Communist

285. *Ibid.*, 2nd half of April 1942, File No. 18/4/42, N.A.I.
286. *Ibid.*, 2nd half of March 1942, File No. 18/3/42, N.A.I,
287. *Ibid.*, 1st half of May 1942, File No. 18/5/42, N.A.I.
288. *Ibid.*, 1st half of June 1942, File No. 18/6/42, N.A.I.
289. *Ibid.*, 1st half of July 1942, File No. 18/7/42, N.A.I.
290. Party Letter No. 6, 24 March 1942, Party Documents, Central Archives, Communist Party of India, Ajoy Bhavan, New Delhi.

kisan leaders also raised in Nagpur the slogan: "Death to the Japanese Fascist Invaders",[291] though by their own admission in the provinces they had been more active (like Bengal and Andhra Pradesh), the *kisan* neither understood the anti-Japanese slogan,[292] nor in any way was "impressed" by it.[293] The breach in the A.I.K.S. from the top to the bottom, and that, too, over such high national and international issues which went far above the *kisan's* low-down head, meant in effect the cessation of all agrarian agitations. Barring some stray and nominal acts here and there, the rural poor's struggle against their oppressors and exploiters suddenly came all over the country to a stand-still in 1942-3. Of the few sporadic occurrences in the first half of 1942, the most pregnant one politically, was scheduled to take place at Cannanore in Malabar.

The tiny town of Cannanore had by the late 1930s turned into a prosperous handloom centre, producing good clothing material. There were about 8,000 handlooms in 1940, owned by approximately 150 entrepreneurs, where more than 15,000 persons had been employed.[294] The employees came mostly from the outlying villages, especially from those belonging to the strom-centres of anti-*Jenmi* agitation — Chirakkal and Kottayam *taluks*. Although the handloom industry in Cannanore enjoyed a boom in 1940-1, it suddenly faced a crisis with the beginning of the Pacific war and the Japanese bombing of Rangoon. Dramatically its market in Ceylon, eastern India and Burma collapsed, following the large scale cancellation of orders already made for the products, and resulting in the closure of a substantial number of looms. By the second week of January 1942 about 7,000 handloom workers lost their jobs,[295] and a cloud of distress and unrest quickly enveloped Cannanore. Precisely at this point came the Communist-led Chirakkal and

291. *Ibid.*
292. Sunil Sen, *Agrarian Struggle in Bengal*, 1946-7, Calcutta, 1972, p. 30.
293. Political Letter, Andhra Report, 4 September 1942, Party Documents, Central Archives, Communist Party of India, Ajoy Bhavan, New Delhi.
294. District Magistrate, Malabar, to Chief Secretary, Madras Government, D.O. Conf.17 January 1942, Public (General) Dept., G.O. No. 722, of 3.3.1942, Tamil Nadu State Archives, Madras.
295. *Ibid.*

Kottayam Taluk Kisan Committee's call for a *kisan* demonstration, on 18 January in Cannanore, to air their anti-Fascist views, as well as to protest against the detention of some of their leaders without trial. The fact the *kisan* demonstration was to be held in Cannanore, where the disgruntled handloom workers would join hands with their vociferous brethren from the villages, and both of them belonging to the same series of villages, thoroughly unnerved the district authorities. The way the preparation for the rally went on, leaflets distributed and peasant *jathas* moved about the countryside, convinced the District Magistrate of Malabar of a deliberate Communist plan for a joint *kisans*-workers' rising. "It would be easily seen that this [the demonstration] is an attempt to bring together the peasants who have their grievances against the *Jenmis*, and the mill-employees who have their grievences against their employers", he recorded, and feared that if such unruly mob of aggrieved peasants and workers was allowed to be collected in Cannanore, "it would get out of control", and "resort to violence".[296] The District Magistrate's contention was confirmed by the local merchants and shopkeepers, who feared a looting of the *bazars*,[297] and the rally due on the 18th, therefore, was promptly prohibited under Section 144 Cr.P.C. The move, and the police arrangement that backed it up, so dampened the spirit of the organisers of the rally that they took quite some time to recover. It was only on 22 February 1942 that they managed eventually to hold an innocuous anti-Fascist *kisan* meeting at Kottayam, and passed certain mildly worded "people's war" resolutions. Although the incident ultimately produced a mole out of a mountain, it did, in its context, bring out the consternation with which the Raj viewed any possible collaboration — howsoever modicum — between the urban or semi-urban and the rural poor, and thereby signifying — even if somewhat indistinctly — a situation that the leftists of all varieties might have profitably explored. In the controversy that was raging over anti-Fascism versus anti-imperialism no one seemed to have taken any interest in 1942 in the possibilities the petty Cannanore development had offered.

296. *Ibid.*
297. *Ibid.*

The other agrarian agitations in the first half of 1942, or the semblances of them in reality, were few and far between. A *kisan satyagraha* against the high-handedness of the Dumraonraj in Bihar apparently fizzled out in January 1942,[298] and the attempts of Jamuna Karji at its revival later on did not produce any significant result.[299] In Bengal the *Kut Khamar* tenants were reported to have resumed their agitation for the occupancy status in March 1942 at Amta in Howrah.[300] About the same time an agitation of the *Bhagchasis* was brewing in Tamluk, Midnapore, as well as in certain parts of Murshidabad, against the *Jotedars* over the sharing of crops.[301] In Pabna it took a serious turn in June 1942 when the *Bargadars* objected to the *Jotedars*' practice of taking the entire crop to their yards for "safe-keeping", prior to its division.[302] News of some opposition to pay rent to the landlords came from the 24-Parganas in Bengal,[303] and parts of the U.P.[304] Acts of social brigandage on a small scale, such as the ransacking of *hats* (as in the 24-Parganas, Bengal),[305] or the looting of grain carts (as in a number of places in Tamil Nadu),[306] also appeared to have taken place. In the midst of such nibblings at agitation, the only act that had persisted for sometime, and also with a certain political fall-out, was the C.P.I.'s move for saving the lives of the doomed Kayyur accused. It may be recalled that 65 *kisans* were charged with the murder and violence that took place at Kayyur in Kasargad *taluk* on 28 March 1941. Of those prosecuted, the Sessions Judge of south Kanara convicted 18 to various terms of imprisonment, and sentenced four (Abubacker, Madthil Appu, Koyith-athil Chirukanthan and Potabara Kunhambu Nair) to death. The death sentences raised a furore in Malabar, especially

298. Home Poll. Fortnighly Report for 1st half of January, 1942, File No. 18/1/42, N.A.I.
299. *Ibid.*, 2nd half of February, 1942, File No. 18/2/42, N.A.I.
300. *Ibid.*, 1st half of March 1942, File No. 18/3/42, N.A.I.
301. *Ibid.*
302. *Ibid.*, 1st half of June, 1942, File No. 18/6/42, N.A.I.
303. *Ibid.*
304. *Ibid.*, 1st half of July 1942, File No. 18/7/42, N.A.I.
305. *Ibid.*, 1st half of January 1942, File No. 18/1/42, N.A.I.
306. *Ibid.*, 1st half of July 1942, File No. 18/7/42, N.A.I.

because of the Sessions Judge's admission in his verdict that in a mob violence like that of Kayyur — in which so many participated — it was difficult to identify the actual killer, and that the guilty might not have at all been produced before the court.[307] The harshest sentence on the four young *kisan* activists, who had a record of heroic struggles in their locality,[308] was clearly not the outcome of legal impartiality, but the result of the Raj's wrath on those who tried to defy it with impunity, and by whose destruction it wanted to set an example before the restive rural masses. On the issue of the Kayyur judgment, and more specifically, for the lives of the four condemned, the Communist *kisan* leaders and workers were able to build up a stir, first in Malabar, and then gradually in many other parts of the country. Meetings were organised, resolutions passed and amounts of money collected throughout 1942 and the early part of 1943. Although the campaign was often lost in the din of the "Quit India" movement (from August 1942 to March 1943), it never really died down, and even picked up a certain tempo between January and March 1943. The movement, however, could not save the four Kayyur vanguards, whose appeals to the Madras High Court and the Privy Council, and a mercy petition to the Governor-General, did not produce any favourable result, and who were hanged in Cannanore Jail — to the anguish of their countrymen — on 29th March 1943, a day after the second anniversary of the Kayyur incidents.[309] Their martydrom and the flutter it had caused within the country and outside,[310] to an extent, repaired — in the gloomy secluded days of the "people's

307. *People's War* (English weekly), 16 August 1942.
308. All the four semi-literate *kisans* came from the rural poor background. They had been taking part in the *kisan* movement since 1938, and remained active in the anti-*Jenmi* agitation in Kasargad *taluk* in 1940-1.
309. Report prepared by the Home Dept., Government of India, for an answer to the question (No. 38) of Raja Yuvaraj Dutta Singh in Central Legislative Council, July 1943, Home Poll. File No. 8/15/43 Poll (I) of 1943, N.A.I.
310. It was mourned widely in most parts of India, including the observance of a special day in the martyrs' honour and the setting up of a Kayyur Dependents' Fund in India, as well as in Britain, "with the blessings" of Edward Thompson, J.B.S. Haldane, R.W. Sorenson and William Gallacher. Viceroy's private and secret letter to the Secretary of State for India, 20 September 1943, Home Poll. File No.7/15/43-Poll(I) of 1943, N.A.I.

war" — the C.P.I.'s already tarnished patriotic credentials. Besides, the martyrs' announcement from the shadow of the gallows that they "felt proud to die" for the cause of the motherland, and that they wished their comrades to do the same for the "national cause",[311] was indicative of the frontal role the rural poor might have played at the height of anti-imperialist confrontation, provided, of course, they were mobilised into it through day to day anti-feudal struggles. So far as the rural poor and the leftists were concerned in the second half of 1942, two issues, namely, the attitude of the "people's war" group towards the most tempestuous of all anti-imperialist outbursts in India since 1857 — the "Quit India" movement, or the "August Kranti" (as the Congress Socialists termed it) — and the question of the *kisan* masses participating in it in full force, assumed considerable political significance. In a certain way, the two appeared to have not only been somewhat interwoven, but also capable together of producing a disconcerting note in the seemingly orchestratic course of events.

The war-time spoiling of the leftists for an anti-imperialist show-down in India had so abruptly been offered a free play in August 1942 that most of them were caught napping, leaving their limited forces largely unmarshalled. The fact was that apart from Gandhiji (who had assumed an uncharacteristic combative posture in the summer of 1942), no one really grasped the mood of the Indian people — their belief in the immediate German and Japanese victories in the war, their anticipation of an imminent collapse of the Raj, (both of which seemed well on the way with the fall of Singapore on 15 February, Rangoon on 8 March and the Andamans on 23 March 1942), their witnessing the British preparations for a "scorched earth" retreat[312] from eastern India, and their observing the inhuman way Indians were abandoned in Malaya and Burma at the time of "successful" British retreats. The mood was worsening because of the Indians' disdain for the obstinate Churchillian refusal to accommodate a

311. "Message from the Kayyur Heroes", *People's War* (English weekly), 3 January 1943.

312. It was called the "Denial Policy" in the British official parlance.

national Government at the centre, despite Stafford Cripps's exercise in good wishes during his mission to India in March-April 1942, their experience of the foreign Allied soldiery in India, who, with minor exceptions, behaved like an arrogant occupational army, and, above all, their suffering in the inflationary conditions, under the pressure of food shortages, and at the hands of the profiteers and "black-marketeers". Narendra Deva was perhaps right when he observed that in 1940 the leaders wanted to challenge the Raj but the people remained unprepared, and that in 1942 the people had become ready for the fight but the leaders developed cold feet.[313] Even Narendra Deva's own party, the C.S.P., who had avoided anti-feudalism for concentrating undivided attention on the anti-imperialist front, and waited indefinitely for the Congress to give the lead, was not organisationally prepared enough to join the fight planfully, and systematically. The position of the Congress organisation did not seem any better, in spite of the British after-thoughts about its clandestine preparations, or its so called "fifth columnist" activities, to justify the Raj's unbridled use of force.[314] Nobody in fact knew for certain that between 14 July 1942 (the day the Congress Working Committee adopted the "Quit India" resolution at Wardha) and 8 August 1942 (the day the A.I.C.C. ratified the resolution in Bombay) the British authorities had already planned a full-scale war on the Congress, with the prior approval of the War Cabinet, [315] as early as 16 July 1942,[316] and that the "zero-hour" of their massive assault had been fixed at 5 a.m. on 9 August 1942.[317] It was hardly necessary for any body to know, except perhaps Gandhiji, for the "Quit India" resolution was essentially an accommodation of views of

313 Narendra Deva's speech in the A.I.C.C. meeting, Bombay, 8 August 1942, *The Hindustan Times*, 9 August 1942.

314 R. Tottenham's "Congress Responsibility for the Disturbances, 1942-3", N. Mitra (ed.), *Indian Annual Register*, 1942, Vol. II, Chapter III, and T. Wikenden's Report on the Disturbances of 1942-3, P.N. Chopra (ed.), *Quit India Movement: British Secret Report*, Faridabad, 1976.

315. N. Mansergh, *The Transfer of Power*, 1942-47, Vol. II, London, 1971, No. 257, p. 378.

316. *Ibid.*, No. 272, pp. 394-5.

317. Home Poll File No. 3/15/42 of 1942, N.A.I.

those Congress leaders who foresaw an Allied defeat, and those who refused to visualise such an outcome, and that, too, after agreeing to take the Allies' side if the British withdraw from India, and let the "glow of freedom" release the energy of millions to "immediately transform the nature of the war".[318] The spirit of the resolution in fact was more of "cooperation" than of "threat",[319] more of a bargain counter than of a declaration of independence, and far from ruling out negotiations, it actually anticipated them in all earnest.[320] The motivator of the whole move, Gandhiji himself, had no premonition of the storm of popular protest breaking out too soon, certainly not before "two or three weeks",[321] or prior to his being able to chalk out a programme of action, and build up the "tempo".[322] That the movement started precipitately, and with unparalleled ferocity, was due as much to the Government policy of savage repression as to the popular conviction in the Raj's approaching doomsday, and to the popular response to the two of Gandhiji's watchwords, namely, "we shall either free India or die in our attempt", and "consider yourself a free man or woman, and act as if you are free".[323] If a vast number of people in colonial India started believing themselves to be free, the official repressions would simply flare them up to instantaneous fury. That was exactly what had happened after the Government rounded up the Congress leaders in the early hours of 9 August 1942.

With the acknowledged leaders behind the bars all over India, the conducting of the popular fury fell upon the shoulders of the younger and more volatile groups of political agitators, who

318. The "Quit India", Resolution, 8 August 1942, *The Hindustan Times*, 9 August 1942.
319. Jawaharlal Nehru's speech in the A.I.C.C. meeting, Bombay, 8 August 1942, *ibid.*
320. Gandhiji expected to wait upon the Viceroy and plead with him for the acceptance of the Congress demand. See Gandhiji's speech in the A.I.C.C. meeting, Bombay, 8 August 1942, *ibid.*
321. Abul Kalam Azad, *India Wins Freedom*, New Delhi, 1959, p. 42.
322. Gandhiji's speech in the A.I.C.C. meeting, Bombay, 8 August 1942, *The Hindustan Times*, 9 August 1942.
323. *Ibid.*

urged the people to expedite the Raj's end in accordance with their own interpretation of what the Congress leaders and Gandhiji had in mind till the 9th August crackdown. Consequently, in the midst of the fusillade of protests (processions, meetings, strikes and *hartals*) and the breaking loose of the official repressive forces (tear-gassing, lathi-charges, arrests and firings), beginning in the urban and semi-urban centres, and then spreading rapidly to the countryside, came into force a mass mobilisation of a special kind. Although some of the important C.S.P. leaders, who managed to evade arrest, and whose rank and file, as well as those of the Forward Bloc, played a prominent role in the upheaval, did attempt at providing an overall leadership by forming "the Central Directorate of the Indian National Congress", and issuing "instructions" from "the A.I.C.C. Office,"[324] the "Quit India" movement had begun almost on its own, assumed some sort of an autonomous, "un-Gandhian" character, progressed as a loose constellation varying in time and space, and gave birth to its own local heroes and heroines. The movement caused ripples in most parts of India, but raised crescendos in Bombay and western Maharashtra, Gujarat and certain parts of the C.P., Mysore state and a few pockets of Andhra, eastern U.P. and Bihar, Bengal and Orissa, and reached a shrilly high pitch in Hasan, Shimoga, Satara, Ashti-Chimur, Ghazipur, Azamgarh, Ballia, the whole of north and central Bihar, Midnapore and Talcher. Caught between the acts of pulling down the Raj (sabotaging communications and transport, destroying police stations and the Government offices, looting treasuries and food depots, setting up parallel civil and judicial administrations) and the acts of keeping it up (indiscriminate arrests and firings, torturing men and violating women, imposing collective fines and burning villages, using air force planes for reconnaissance and repeated machine-gunning), the writ of the British practically stopped running in many places for days and weeks, and in specific spots for months and years. The conflagration, however, had to encounter barriers building up in the Indian situation itself — the political articulation of

324. The part played by the C.S.P. and the Forward Bloc in the "Quit India" movement deserves a lot more attention than it has so far received.

separatism since 1941 (following the Pakistan Resolution of the Muslim League) was one which kept aloof the Muslim community generally, the war-time rise in prices of grains was another which seemed to have so benefited the substantial peasants in some areas (notably in the Punjab, western U.P. and Tanjore delta) that they did not take much interest in the agitation. And yet another — more significant from the point of view of the rural poor — was the hostility towards the "Quit India" movement of those who might have been at its forefront, had it, by any chance, taken place one year earlier.

True to their anti-Fascist "people's war" policy, and in their exaggerated alarm over an impending Japanese invasion of India (which, incidentally, was shared almost by everyone, including the Congress and the British Government), the Communists were in favour of concentrating all their energies on the defences of India, by rallying popular "voluntary" support to the British war-efforts. Considering "Britain's war" to be "our war", they wanted to encourage recruitment to the army, step up industrial production, help in the air-raid precautions and form Citizens' Armies for the protection of the cities, towns and villages.[325] Their anxiety for national defence was so great, and the urge for stopping the Japanese invaders so compelling that about 300 of them joined the British guerilla training camps in June 1942.[326] Within their policy framework, therefore, the Communists felt that the "Quit India" movement was giving "a pernicious direction to the anger of the people", destroying "the defence capacities of the nation", and weakening it through chaos "to fall under the axe of the Fascists [the Japanese]".[327] At an hour when the defence of India was of supreme importance, and the Raj not being in the mood to tolerate any undermining of it, the

325. *Forward to Freedom* (a booklet), 1942, Central Committee, C.P.I., Party Documents, Central Archives, Communist Party of India, Ajoy Bhavan, New Delhi.

326. "Fragments From A Guerilla's Diary", Rajbans Kishen, *People's War* (English weekly), 2 August 1942.

327. Political Resolution of the Enlarged Plenum Session of the Central Committee, C.P.I., 15-23 September 1942, Party Documents, Central Archives, Ajoy Bhavan, Communist Party of India, New Delhi.

C.P.I. foreshadowed — in the event of the Congress agitation — the wholesale arrest of the Congress leaders and the unleashing of the forces of repression. So the party pleaded with the Congress not to leave the Indian people "leaderless, and at the mercy of the mad bureaucrats",[328] tried to further dilute the "Quit India" resolution by moving amendments,[329] and asked its 12 members in the A.I.C.C. to vote against the resolution.[330] Thereafter, believing that the existence of the nation to be "hanging in the balance",[331] the C.P.I. denounced both "the blitz of brutal repression" by the imperialist bureaucracy,[332] and "the sabotage" of the defence of "their own country" by "the deluded patriots".[333] By trying to raise, therefore, the alternative slogans for the release of the national leaders, for the national unity (meaning, of course, the Congress-League unity at the top) and for the setting up of a national Government at the centre to organise national defence, the Communists not only refused to join "the blind patriots", but also opposed the forces of "disorder, anarchy", and the tendencies to commit "national suicide".[334]

The Communist opposition to the "Quit India" movement was effective to an extent in the areas where they wielded some influence, and among the social categories they professed to have specially been committed to. In Kerala, for example, the Communists claimed that on account of their efforts the movement was on a low key, without any imposition of collective fine or any incident of police firing, and that the cases of "sabotage" and *lathi*-charge turned out to be negligible.[335] Although their successes were far less, and the odds against

328. From "Yes, Fight, But Whom and How?" *People's War* (English weekly), 26 July 1942.
329. Amendments were moved by Dr. K.M. Ashraf, Sajjad Zaheer and S.G. Sardesai in the A.I.C.C. meeting, Bombay, on 7 August 1942.
330. *Hindustan Times* (English daily), 8 August 1942.
331. "All Together", P.C. Joshi, *People's War* (English weekly), 23 August 1942.
332. *Ibid.*, 16 August 1942.
333. *Ibid.*, 23 August 1942.
334. Political Resolution of the Enlarged Plenum Session of the Central Committee, C.P.I., 15-23 September 1942, Party Documents, Central Archives, Communist Party of India, Ajoy Bhavan, New Delhi.
335. E.M.S. Namboodiripad, "A Short History of Peasant Movement in Kerala", *Selected Writings*, Vol.II, Calcutta, 1985, p. 219.

them far more than in Kerala, the Communists did manage to strike a jarring note in other parts the country, and to exercise — even if weakly — a restraining influence on those who were used to listening to them. Their standing in the trade-union front also resulted in minimising the effect of the "Quit India" movement on the organised industrial labour. Apart from some initial minor responses in Kanpur, Bangalore, Poona and Ahmad-nagar, and the two lengthy major strikes in Ahmedabad and Jamshedpur, of which the latter was rumoured to have been encouraged by the Tatas themselves,[336] the working class did not whole-heartedly join the movement. Important industrial centres like Bombay and Calcutta were not seriously affected. The protagonists of the "Quit India" movement in Bengal in fact admitted that the Communists, and also the Royists, had practically prevented them from organising "labour strikes" in the province.[337] The story was almost similar in Madras, barring a few stray labour incidents in Coimbatore, and the South Indian Railwaymen — under the influence of the Communists — not only disregarded the call of their leader, V.V. Giri, for joining the movement, but also spoke against it in their conference of August 1942 in Tiruchirapalli.[338] The assertion of the Communists that they had succeeded in keeping intact the line of communication in the whole of the South Indian Railway, most of the Assam Bengal Railway, up to the Assam border, and enough of Grand Peninsular Railway, to maintain the flow of the Allied supplies from the Bombay port,[339] was not wholly unfounded. As it was with the industrial labour, the influence of the Communists had also been known to be considerable

336. Vinay Bahl, "Attitude of the Indian National Congress Towards the Working Class Struggle in India", *Congress and Classes : Nationalism, Workers and Peasants*, Kapil Kumar (ed.), New Delhi, 1988.

337 "Report of the Struggle For Independence in Bengal, August-September 1942", by the Council of Action, Bengal Provincial Congress Committee, Home Poll. File No.3/81/43 - Poll(I), 1943, N.A.I.

338. David Arnold, "Quit India in Madras : Hiatus or Climacteric?", *The Indian Nation in 1942*, Gyanendra Pandey (ed.), Calcutta, 1988, p. 211.

339. "Communist Reply to Congress Working Committee Charges", in *War and National Liberation : C.P.I Documents, 1939-45*, P. Bandhu and T.G. Jacob, (eds.), New Delhi, 1988, p. 255.

among the organised peasants, and their voice in the All India Kisan Sabha seemed no less decisive in 1942 than their opinion in the All India Trade Union Congress. Were they able, therefore, to affect the peasantry as much as they did the industrial labour?

Judging by the manner the "Quit India" movement set aflame the countryside in Gujarat, eastern U.P., Bihar, Bengal and certain parts of Orissa — precisely some of those areas where the leftists had been active throughout — as well as in western Maharashtra and parts of Mysore state, the Communists did not seem to have done too well on the *kisan* front. In fact the exhortations of their allies like Yajnik, President, A.I.K.S., and Sahajanand Saraswati, General Secretary, A.I.K.S., and Jadunandan Sharma, President, Bihar Provincial Kisan Sabha, in the late August 1942 on the "people's war" lines, condemning violence, sabotage, looting and "goondaism" let loose by the "Quit India" movement,[340] had not made much of an impact. Peasantry in the rural storm centres appeared generally to have welcomed the movement, took an active part in it and gave it the shape of a multiple civil rising. However, the peasantry in India — like its counterparts all over the colonised world — was not homogeneous, and its various components had been used to the viewing of situations in varying lights, and in consonance with their respective socio-economic aspirations. Although the substantial peasants in certain places had turned rather lukewarm towards the movement on account of their relative prosperity during the war years, they had participated in the upsurge in large numbers in other regions, and often played the decisive role there. It was the substantial *Patidar* and Anavil Brahmin peasantry who dominated the movement in the Gujarat villages, whether in Kheda and Mehsana, or in Surat and Navasari, and also whether wholly on their own, or partly in conjunction with others.[341] In eastern U.P. (Azamgarh, Ghazipur and Ballia) the substantial peasantry, and even the landed gentry belonging to the upper castes (such as Brahmins, Bhumihars

340. M.A. Rasul, *History of All India Kisan Sabha*, Calcutta, 1974, pp. 84-7.
341. David Hardiman, "The Quit India Movement in Gujarat", *The Indian Nation in 1942*, Gyanendra Pandey (ed.), Calcutta, 1988, pp. 77-104.

and Rajputs), commanded over the entire proceedings.[342] The story was not very different in Bihar (in Shahabad in particular, and the whole of north and central Bihar in general) where the happenings were predominated by those who emerged from the ranks of substantial peasants and "small landlords".[343] Again in Satara, where the movement continued in the underground till the beginning of 1946, and revealed some egalitarian streaks, the mainstay was the non-Brahmin, middle caste substantial peasantry.[344] Orissa also followed the same pattern of substantial peasant domination, despite considerable participation of the tribal *kisans*, who, in their turn, responded sometimes to the call of the socially privileged leading figures among them, such as the *Mustajars* (the village headman who collected rent for the estate, and enjoyed rent-free lands) of Malkangiri.[345] Midnapore in Bengal (Contai and Tamluk sub-divisions to be exact) was apparently the only example where the *Jotedar*-substantial peasant combination could not hold on to its sway over the agitation in spite of all endeavours, and it had soon to give way to the convulsive reflex actions of the poor peasants, and consequently to a relatively militant and radical popular temper.[346] Like those of their own category in some parts of the country, the substantial and the well-to-do *kisans* in eastern U.P., Bihar, Gujarat, Maharashtra, Bengal and Orissa had also found the war-time credit and grain shortages to their pecuniary advantage, and therefore, faced no particular difficulty in meeting their rent and tax obligations. Clearly a sense of desperation, or

342. Gyanendra Pandey, "The Revolt of August 1942 in Eastern U.P. and Bihar," *ibid.*, and also the author's discussion with Dr. Chandan Mitra, who had investigated extensively into the movement in Ballia, in New Delhi on 27 August 1990.
343. Gyanendra Pandey, "The Revolt of August 1942 in Eastern U.P. and Bihar", *ibid.*, as well as Stephen Henningham, *Peasant Movement in Colonial India, North Bihar, 1917-42*, Canberra, 1984, p. 193.
344. Gail Omvedt, "The Satara Prati-Sarkar", in *The Indian Nation in 1942*, Gyanendra Pandey (ed.), Calcutta, 1988, pp. 223-59.
345. Biswamoy Pati, "Storm Over Malkangiri: A Note on Laxman Naiko's Revolt, 1942", *ibid.*, pp. 185-201.
346. Hitesranjan Sanyal, "The Quit India Movement in Medinipur District", *ibid.*, pp. 19-69.

the economic pressure, had not induced them to spring into action and spearhead the "Quit India" movement. What probably was decisive with them had been their belief in the certainty of the Raj's collapse, as well as in the surety of the Congress's coming into power. Broadly they had supported the Congress most of the time, felt secured by its policies, programmes and utterances and interacted with its office-bearers at the district, sub-division and village levels. If the Congress was to rule after the fleeing of the British, they must side with it to ensure their future, establish their nationalist credential, assert their say in the state of affairs and mould the subsequent situations as much to their advantage as perhaps possible. With the advantage of hindsight of development in India's post-independence political economy, one could say that the substantial peasantry seemed to have remarkably been justified in the initiative they took in 1942. It was not despair but hope, not the "stifling" of their "soul" but the prospect in an independent India that led them to head the "Quit India" movement. Even the landlords, in search of some shelter in a future regime, reacted favourably to the nationalist hightide, either by staying significantly neutral (as the Maharaja of Darbhanga did), or by supporting the Congress (as some other Bihari *Zamindars* tried to do),[347] prominently through "youngmen from the *Zamindari* castes".[348] Moments of national euphoria seemed to offer as good a chance for escape to some as an opportunity for self-advancement to many others.

No furore, much less a conflagration, could take place in the Indian countryside without the active or the supportive participation of the multitude of rural poor in it. By discouraging their anti-landlord demeanour, and by segregating the anti-feudal content of their characteristic form of struggle against imperialism, one ought not to have expected the *kisan* masses to join the "Quit India" movement whole-heartedly, or to come to its forefront. The poor did nevertheless take part in it, not as an

347. Stephen Henningham, *Peasant Movement in Colonial India, North Bihar, 1917-1942*, Canberra, 1984, pp. 183-5.

348. Gyanendra Pandey, "The Revolt of August 1942 in Eastern U.P. and Bihar", in *The Indian Nation in 1942*, Gyanendra Pandey (ed.), Calcutta, 1988, p. 149.

organised category, but as an irregular formation, and left their unmistakable marks of militancy on the occurrences, despite a certain uneasiness about following the lead of their expropriators (the usurious and labour-employing peasant proprietors), or making common cause with their oppressors (the landlords and the *mahajans*). They hesitantly watched the way the movement broke out, suspiciously observed the initial setbacks the Raj suffered, haltingly joined the battle later at its thickest hour, especially in the mob attacks on the police posts, the railway stations, the post offices and other Government buildings, and started retiring uncomfortably from the scenes of actions the moment the British Government appeared to have wrested back the initiative. The observation that "the poor and the low caste people" began taking part in the revolt last, and started withdrawing from it first[349] was perhaps correct in the main. But their trail was discernible in all the affected areas in some form or the other. In Orissa the landless labourers and the tribal and poor peasants were believed to have been active in Cuttack, Dhenkanal and Koraput.[350] In Gujarat the *adivasi kisans* and the rural toiling masses, belonging to such castes as Baraiyas and Patanvadiyas, did participate in the movement in certain places of Surat, Navasari and Broach districts.[351] Though "under-represented" in southern Maharashtra, the *Dalits*, the poor peasants and the labourers had taken some significant part in it.[352] The joining of the "small occupancy peasants" and the *Bhagchasis* in the movement in Midnapore, Bengal, was not only substantial, but also responsible for opening up a dual front — one against the British Government, and the other against "the internal adversaries".[353] In eastern U.P. the District Magistrate of Azamgarh, R.H. Niblett, recorded the rebels'

349. Stephen Henningham, *Peasant Movement in Colonial India, North Bihar, 1917-42*, Canberra, 1984, p. 182.
350. Biswamoy Pati, *Resisting Domination: Peasants, Tribals and National Movement in Orissa, 1920-50*, New Delhi, 1993, pp. 164, 175 and 179.
351. David Hardiman, "The Quit India Movement in Gujarat", in *The Indian Nation in 1942*, Gyanendra Pandey (ed.), Calcutta, 1988, pp. 97-101.
352. Gail Omvedt, "The Satara Prati-Sarkar", *ibid.*, pp. 243 and 246.
353. Hitesranjan Sanyal, "The Quit India Movement in Medinipur District", *ibid.*, pp. 32 and 65.

approaching Madhuban, not only with *lathis* and spears, but also with "plough-shares, hammers, saws and spades".[354] Although their number (by the low-caste denomination) in the lists of those "convicted" and "killed in firings" in the "trouble spots" of Azamgarh and Ghazipur was considerably small,[355] the rural poor, the "untouchables" and others might have participated in considerable numbers when "the established authority had completely collapsed".[356] The trend became clearer in north Bihar where "the lower status groups" in rural society and "the improverished villagers" joined the movement in its later stage in search of questionable economic gains.[357]

The search for questionable gains assumed greater significance in the background of war-time inflationary conditions, and the scarcity of credit and grain in 1942. The vast section of rural producers, who had not only not benefitted from shortages of products and rises in their prices, but actually suffered immeasurably from buying grains and procuring bare necessaries at the sky-high market, or the "black market", happened to be the agricultural labourers, as well as the sharecroppers and poor peasants, whose meagre family consumption reserve of grains invariably dwindled by the summer in a normal year. Seeing the Raj collapsing in the first flush of the rebellion, and believing in the cry that rent the air, namely, "Angrez Bhag Gaya" (the English have fled), hordes of disorganised semi-destitutes went for snatching away whatever little they could lay their hands upon. The starving agricultural labourers in particular, as the Communists witnessed in Andhra, felt the shaking of the Government authority — the loosening of its grip on the affairs — and lost no time in pouncing upon the "opportunities".[358] When law and order temporarily subsided, the looting and

354. R.H. Niblett, *The Congress Rebellion in Azamgarh*, Allahabad, 1957, p. 13.
355. Gyanendra Pandey, "The Revolt of August 1942 in Eastern U.P. and Bihar," in *The Indian Nation in 1942*, Gyanendra Pandey (ed.), Calcutta, 1988, pp. 150-2.
356. *Ibid.*, p. 152.
357. Stephen Henningham, *Peasant Movement in Colonial India, North Bihar, 1917-1942*, Canberra, 1984, pp. 97-101.
358. Andhra Report, 4 September 1942, Political Letter, Party Documents, Central Archives, Communist Party of India, Ajoy Bhavan, New Delhi.

arsoning took over, and the distinctions between the professional criminal gangs and the deprived *kisan* groups disappeared. In Bengal, for example, the statistics of dacoities or robberies showed a phenomenal rise during the volatile months of the "Quit India" movement in comparison with the corresponding months in the previous year:[359]

Months	*1941*	*1942*
August	74	124
September	59	187
October	102	200
November	65	236

Such a development was bound to take place in a tumultuous situation in which hardly any familiar activist or ideologue was there — from the Communist, the Congress Socialist and the Forward Blocist ranks — to organise and guide the rural poor on the lines of radical agrarian risings. Consequently, the incidents of loot and arson started piling up, and properties affected were mostly of the Government, and very scarcely of the landlords, moneylenders and affluent peasant proprietors. Barring some stray cases, such as attacks on the *cutcherries* of Banailiraj in south Bihar, and Grant estate in Sonabarsa and Jamui *Zamindari* in north Bihar,[360] Sukhinda estate in Orissa and Mahishadalraj in Tamluk, Bengal, as well as some "seizures

359. Home Department, File No. 182/43-Police (C) of 1943, N.A.I.
360. Stephen Henningham, *Peasant Movement in Colonial India, North Bihar, 1917-1942,* Canberra, 1984, p. 254 and footnote 55. Also Home Poll. Fortnightly Report for 1st half of April 1943, File No.18/4/43, N.A.I.
361. Hitesranjan Sanyal, "The Quite India Movement in Medinipur District", *The Indian Nation in 1942,* Gyanendra Pandey (ed.), Calcutta, 1988, p. 63.

of grains",[361] and a few acts of aggression on moneylenders in the Panch Mahals and on the Parsi liquor-dealers-cum-landlords in south Gujarat,[362] but practically none in eastern U.P. and Maharashtra, private properties and social relations had not only not been under much strain during the "Quit India" movement, but these were also kept by the leaders deliberately and scrupulously outside its purview.[363] As a result the village "riff-raff" or the so-called "criminal elements" were allowed to practise their looting and arsoning spree strictly on the Government properties, and whenever they crossed the Rubicon, by robbing *mahajans* and hoarders, and ransacking the grain stocks of landlords and the well-to-do, which they sometimes did in Midnapore between October 1942 and July 1943, a sharp contradiction developed within the movement, and it collapsed following the resentment and obstruction of its propertied participants.[364] The Communist leadership in Andhra — who watched the occurrences from a safe, unconcerned distance — were surprised to see how quickly the panic-stricken rural propertied classes turned their faces from the Congress to the Government at the slightest instance of the labouring "rowdies'" attack on their properties (such as it happened at Bhimavarnam and Palacole in West Godavari and Tenali in Guntur).[365] Looting and arsoning of the Government offices and railway stations were galore in those regions where the "Quit India" movement had particularly been explosive, from Bhagabanpur and Bhimeswari in Contai to Sutahata and Nandigram in Tamluk, Jambusar and Amod in Broach to Songadh and Mandavi in south Gujarat, from Madhuban and Tarwa in Azamgarh to Sherpur and Moham-madabad in Ghazipur, Bithura Road and Bansdih in Ballia to Madhubani in Darbhanga and Begusarai in Munghyr, Shirvade and Bhosegaon in Satara to Eram Basudevpur

362. David Hardiman, "The Quit India Movement in Gujarat", *ibid.*, pp. 98 and 101.
363. Interviews of Satara activists, D.G. Deshpande and Dhanvantari in Omvedt, Gail, "The Satara Prati-Sarkar", *ibid.*, pp. 247 and 261, footnotes 31-2.
364. Hitesranjan Sanyal, "The Quit India Movement in Medinipur District," *ibid.*, p. 64.
365. Andhra Report, 4 September 1942, Political Letter, Party Documents, Central Archives, Communist Party of India, Ajoy Bhavan, New Delhi.

and Dhamnagar in Balasore. Some of the rural poor participants of the movement who did not join the loot, and who might not have felt the urge for playing any active role in the movement, were caught up in the vortex of state repression, suffered terribly and retaliated in vengeance. When the forces of repression were let loose in the countryside to suppress the movement, the police, the police informers and the army found easier targets among the poor than among the affluent, whose huts they burnt, women they ravished and men they tortured, often to death. The sufferers had to hit back by eliminating their torturers whenever or wherever they could, by attacking police parties, and even by challenging the army pickets. Their ire fell particularly on the policemen — whom they knew from their experience to be hoodlums under the Government pay, and mercenaries under the landlord-usurer patronage — and also on the police stations, the bastions, in their eyes, of the colonial authority and feudal oppression. The *thana* and the *Thanedar* received the maximum attention of angry villagers in most of the areas affected by the "Quit India" movement, and, under the circumstances, it could not have been otherwise even by the slightest margin.

Not all the rural masses, however, joined the movement, and many among them in fact stayed away from it. Had they not done so in their majority, and had the leaders of the upsurge not shuddered at their revolutionary potential, the history of the "Quit India" movement would have been written very differently, indeed. It was among the broad sections of the rural masses that the Communist activists and their allies had succeeded, to an extent, in exercising a restraining influence, not as much by their slogan of the "people's war" as by their symapathetic posture on the distress of the people, and bringing out thereby the lack of the socio-economic content in the "Quit India" movement. In Madras they were able to highlight such issues like high prices, low wages and food shortages to underscore the limited scope of the August rebellion.[366] Their attempts at drawing popular attention on the fast deteriorating food

366. Arnold David, "Quit India in Madras : Hiatus or Climacteric? ," in *The Indian Nation in 1942*, Gyanendra Pandey (ed.), Calcutta, 1988, p. 211.

situation in the country, especially in Bihar, Orissa, Assam and the C.P.,[367] and their organising "hunger marches" in several districts of Bengal, notably in the 24-Parganas, Malda and Rangpur,[368] had partially neutralised the impact of the "Quit India" movement in the countryside. In Bihar the Kisan Sabhaites also started talking about the problem of the ***Bakasht*** lands, the commutation of the produce-rent into cash, as well as of the difficulty of the sugarcane-growers.[369] By the end of 1942 in fact some of the prodigal *kisan* sons started turning back from the unknown terrains of the "August Kranti" to the known plains of the anti-*Zamindari*, and decided to rejoin the Bihar *kisan* movement.[370] Although the majority of the local Kisan Sabha at Putputia, Tamluk, resolved to join the movement in Midnapore by discarding the view of its Communist leader (Bhupal Panda),[371] there were other instances, in which the complicity of the local Communists could not entirely be ruled out, where some categories of the rural masses demonstrably refused to take part in it. One such refusal took place in Shahabad, where the Triveni Sangh — a body representing the backward cultivating castes like Koeris, Kurmis and Ahirs — decided to support the Government war-efforts and oppose the Congress.[372] But the more serious one occurred in Kheda, where a 10,000 strong crowd, belonging mostly to such lower castes as Baraiyas and Patanvadiyas, decided not to support the movement.[373] The pattern was the same in Mehsana district of Baroda, and the "subordinate peasantry" generally in central and northern Gujarat was found in 1942 to be "extremely hostile" towards the Congress.[374] Also in places where the agricultural labour was

367. Home Poll. Fortnightly Reports for 1st and 2nd halves of January 1943, File No. 18/1/43, N.A.I.
368. *Ibid.*, 2nd half of March 1943, File No. 18/3/43, N.A.I.
369. *Hunkar* (Hindi weekly), 20 December 1942 and 7 February 1943.
370. Letters of such prodigal sons could be found in Swami Sahajanand Saraswati Papers.
371. Hitesranjan Sanyal, "The Quit India Movement in Medinipur", *The Indian Nation in 1942*, Gyanendra Pandey (ed.), Calcutta, 1988, p. 44.
372. Gyanendra Pandey, "The Revolt of August 1942 in Eastern U.P. and Bihar", *ibid.*, p. 152.
373. David Hardiman, "The Quit India Movement in Gujarat", *ibid.*; p. 100.
374. *Ibid.*, p. 102.

"organised", which happened to be the case in certain parts of Andhra, "no looting had taken place".[375] However, a substantial part of the rural poor in India had neither been "organised" by the Kisan Sabhas, nor influenced by the Communists, and whose apathy towards the movement, therefore, could perhaps be explained through a reference to the over-all approach of the so-called radicals among its leaders — the Congress Socialists. Their conviction that the national revolution would have to precede a social one, and their strategy, therefore, not to alienate the rightist Congressmen "by measures exacerbating class hostility",[376] not to scare away the feudal and the rich peasant supporters of the Congress, in actuality prevented them from offering any advanced agrarian programme to the rural poor, and consequently, from inspiring the rural masses to come forward. Despite the Communists' exercising some hold over the industrial labour, and their influencing the rural poor at certain places, the petering out of the "Quit India" movement in the face of a cruelly coercive Government was not so much because of the C.P.I.'s "treachery" and "betrayal", of which one has heard so much in the Congress Socialist circles, but because of the signal failure of the "August Revolutionaries" themselves to devise any clear revolutionist plan of action, or at least to try to rise above the monotony of acts of sabotage, "raid" and political dacoity. That the fire continued to flicker in Satara and Midnapore for long — more to the discomfiture of the Raj than to the dislocations of its war-efforts — was due entirely to the exertions of the locally reared up stokers, with or without their acceptance of the C.S.P.'s suzerainty.

Between August 1942 (the month the "spontaneous revolt" flared up) and March 1943 (the time it seemed to have died down) the rural poor's voice was almost wholly drowned in the din of the "Quit India" movement, except for some dis-

375. Andhra Report, 4 September 1942, Political Letter, Party Documents, Central Archives, Communist Party of India, Ajoy Bhavan, New Delhi.
376. M.V. Harcourt, "The Quit India Movement, August 1942 : The Case Study in Militant Indian Nationalism", M.A. Thesis, University of Western Australia, 1967, p. 67, cited in Stephen Henningham, *Peasant Movement in Colonial India, North Bihar, 1917-42*, Canberra, 1984, p. 258.

organised, minor expressions of unrest here and there. The supporters and critics of the "August Kranti" being too busy to think of the peasant masses, the unrest was expressed invariably in the form of social brigandage. In the south, where a famine-like condition was fast developing in Bellary, Anantapur, Chittoor, Cuddapah, Visakhapatnam, Tinnevelli, Nellore and Kurnool, the frequent looting of grains and grain-carts on the highway had sometimes been extended to attacks on the Reddys' shops in the villages.[377] Police action against such attackers resulted on occasions in direct collisions with the villagers, as it did at Soma in Chittoor, where a police party in January 1943 was resisted, the police arms taken away and the arrested persons freed.[378] There was a spate of dacoities in Kolaba district in western India,[379] and a serious clash between the police and the Bhils took place in the Panch Mahals district in February 1943 when a hamlet was raided for arresting the "criminals".[380] In the north the poorer categories in the Punjab also grew restive over a sharp rise in the prices of wheat, following its extensive procurement by the Government for feeding the army.[381] Paddy looting became quite common in parts of Bengal,[382] and crimes against "private properties" increased steadily in Orissa.[383] In Gunupur *taluk*, Koraput district, the Savaras in large bands were reported to be forcibly taking away paddy from the fields.[384] The only occurrence of some political and ideological significance was the endeavour of Swami Sahajanand in November 1942 to raise the *Bakasht* issue, and to incite *kisans* of Gaya to harvest by force the crops standing on the *Bakasht* lands.[385] The Swami and his lieutenants believed, and quite rightly so it seems, that the Kisan Sabhas — irrespective

377. Home Poll. Fortnightly Reports for 1st half of October 1942 and 2nd half of March 1943, File Nos. 18/10/42 and 18/3/43, N.A.I.
378. *Ibid.*, 1st half of January 1943, File No. 18/1/43, N.A.I.
379. *Ibid.*
380. *Ibid.*, 1st half of February 1943, File No. 18/2/43, N.A.I.
381. *Ibid.*, 1st half of January 1943, File No. 18/1/43, N.A.I.
382. *Ibid.*, 1st and 2nd halves of January 1943.
383. *Ibid.*, 2nd half of March 1943, File No. 18/3/43, N.A.I.
384. *Ibid.*, 1st half of December 1942, File no. 18/12/42, N.A.I.
385. *Ibid.*, 2nd half of November 1942, File no. 18/11/42, N.A.I.

of the political struggle against Fascism, or in support of the British war-efforts — should not lose time in launching the economic or agarian struggles, for which primarily these were created.[386] The Communist *kisan* activists, who had already reached the height of their obsession with the "people's war", were in no mood to listen to the views of Sahajanand and his followers, and "the two sides started drifting apart".[387] The drifting began so acrimoniously that the office of the Swami-run weekly, *Hunkar*, the mouthpiece of the Bihar *kisan* movement, had to be separated from the Kisan Sabha establishment.[388]

In their unseemly haste for bolstering up the British defences in India, and thereby hoping to stop the Japanese Fascists, the C.P.I. leadership had by March 1943 practically given up the avowed path of agrarian revolution, and stepped into the alley of agricultural reformism. As it had already directed the industrial workers to "minimise" stoppages, "irrespective of what the boss or the bureaucrat does",[389] as well as the strikes, and avoid making "exaggerated demands" in order to step up production for war,[390] the Central Committee of the party similarly urged the entire peasantry to concentrate on "grow more food" as the only measure for its own, as well as for the nation's survival.[391] "Patriotism demands of the kisan to grow more food ... to feed

386. Swami Sahajanand Saraswati, "Samajvadi Yudh Aur Jana Yudh", *Hunkar* (Hindi weekly), 3 January 1943, and "Kisan Sabha Aur Rajneeti", *Hunkar*, 10 and 17 January 1943.
387. Arvind N. Das, *Agrarian Unrest and Socio-Economic Change in Bihar, 1900-80*, Delhi, 1983, p. 180.
388. Home Poll. Fortnightly Report for 1st half of December 1942, File no. 18/12/42. N.A.I.
389. "Unity of Action", a pamphlet issued by the Central Committee, C.P.I., May 1943, Party Documents, Central Archives, Communist Party of India, Ajoy Bhavan, New Delhi.
390. "Production Policy and Trade Union Tasks", Resolution passed in the Enlarged Plenum of the Central Committee, C.P.I., 22 September 1942, in *War and National Liberation:* C.P.I. *Documents, 1939-45*, P. Bandhu, and T.G. Jacob, (eds.), New Delhi, 1988, pp. 84-93.
391. "The Wayout of the Crisis", Report of the Enlarged Plenum of the Central Committee, C.P.I., Central Archives, Communist Party of India, Ajoy Bhavan, New Delhi.

the army, to feed the worker who makes goods for the army, and for the people".[392] To enable the *kisan* to play "the key role in the defence of his country", the Communist activists on the *kisan* front were, therefore, asked to give utmost priority to the "grow more food" campaign, and rally all-round support in its favour.[393] Of course, they were asked also to talk against the "speculative prices of food stuffs",[394] the "vast hoarding of foodgrains" and "blackmarketing", and to ponder over ensuring the peasants "a reasonable minimum price", or introducing "control rates" and "ration shops" for the daily necessaries.[395] All these utilitarian precepts in 1943 were, however, meant primarily for attracting the attention of the Government, and if necessary, for pressurising it to their acceptance. But what the Communists meant for the *kisans*, and offered them as the "main plank" of their agrarian programme was the "grow more food", with such fringe benefits as the tillage of the cultivable waste "at nominal rates", *taccavi* loans, cheap irrigation facilities, seeds, manure and moratorium on rents, debts and attachments "during the war".[396] When "grow more food" thus pushed out anti-landlordism from the Kisan Sabhas,[397] forcing them even to appeal to landlords for the use of fallow lands, such as it was in certain parts of Bengal and Kerala,[398] and at a time when the disarrayed non-Communist left in the "Quit India" movement day-dreamt of grain-lootings in the countryside to turn automatically into actions "to wrest power from the alien

392. "Unity in Action for National Defence and National Government", Resolution passed in the First Congress of the C.P.I., Bombay, May 1943, Party Documents, Central Archives, Ajoy Bhavan, New Delhi.
393. *Ibid.*
394. "Hands Off People's Food", a pamphlet by B.T. Ranadive, Bombay, 1942, Party Documents, Central Archives, Communist Party of India, Ajoy Bhavan, New Delhi.
395. "The Food Crisis and Our Tasks", Resolution of the Central Committee, C.P.I., 19 February 1943, in *War and National Liberation : C.P.I. Documents, 1939-45*, P. Bandhu and T.G. Jacob (eds.), New Delhi, 1988, pp. 114-21.
396. *Ibid.*
397. Swami Sahajanand Saraswati, *Inaugural Address*, 8th Session of the Bengal Provincial Students' Conference, Mymensingh, 1 June 1945, p. 9.
398. E.M.S. Namboodiripad, *Selected Writings*, Vol. II, Calcutta, 1985, pp. 222-3.

authority",[399] the rural masses were left throughout 1943, and for the first time in the history of their mobilisation since 1936, with no prospect for resuming their own battles against colonialism, but with all the sufferings of an economic breakdown — deprivation, destitution and starvation. As expected in such devastating circumstances, social brigandage — the only form of autonomous action that the rural poor easily take to — continued unabated.

The war-time shortages of essential commodities, especially of foodgrains, following the stoppage of rice imports from Burma and south-east Asia, and the procurement of supplies in large quantities by the military authorities for their troops in India, north Africa and Middle East, as well as by the United Kingdom Chamber of Commerce, had resulted in an unprecedented soaring of prices. The price of rice in Bengal, for example, which was Rs. 6 per maund in January 1942, rose to Rs. 14½ in January 1943, Rs. 24 in April 1943, Rs. 32 in June 1943 and Rs. 38 in August 1943 when price control was introduced. In September and October 1943 the "blackmarket" price of rice in Calcutta was Rs. 40, and in *mofussil* anywhere between Rs. 50 and Rs. 100.[400] Though not so staggeringly high as in Bengal, the price of rice, and also those of wheat, barley and jowar, rose alarmingly all through 1943 in most parts of the country, including the Punjab and western U.P. Prices of sugar, cooking oil, kerosene, coal, matchbox, paper, cloth and almost each item of the machine-made products started spiralling simultaneously. Whether the prices rose on account, as the Communists tried to make out, mainly of the speculative hoarding and profit-eering, and the bureaucratic failure to impose "controls",[401] or, as the Congress Socialists believed, primarily

399 . "Hunger Strikes the Land", Congress Bulletin, Bombay, 16 December 1942, Home Poll. File No. 3/1/43-Poll (I) of 1943, N.A.I.

400 . "Who Lives If Bengal Dies", a pamphlet by P.C. Joshi, November 1943, Party Documents, Central Archives, Communist Party of India, Ajoy Bhavan, New Delhi.

401. "Hands Off People's Food", a pamphlet by B.T. Ranadive, Bombay, 1942, Party Documents, Central Archives, Communist Party of India, Ajoy Bhavan, New Delhi.

because of the Government spending by issuing and circulating a limitless amount of paper currency,[402] which had later been calculated to have increased from Rs. 2,300 million in 1939 to Rs. 12,100 million in 1945,[403] or due to both the sets of factors, the worst sufferers in agrarian society were not those who could hold some stock for higher prices in the market, but precisely those who could not, and rather who ended up by buying foodgrains at high market rates. The exorbitant prices practically destroyed the rural credit and the wages in grains, and thereby caused dire distress to the agricultural labour in particular. In the southern *taluks* of Berar in April 1943, the labourers were reported to be working for a mere handful of jowars.[404] It was calculated by the district *kisan* leaders in Amraoti that the weekly income of a local landless labourer's family, consisting of four persons , was Rs. 2-8-0 in December 1942, the same as it had been in 1941, while its minimum expense had gone up to Rs. 4-10-0 , which in 1941 used to be Rs. 1-11-6.[405] In Bihar and Andhra the agricultural labourers were found to be clamouring for the wage increase in kind, as their earnings "could not keep pace with the rise in the prices".[406] The landless labourers in Bengal were the hardest hit from the beginning of 1943,[407] and the "dramatic fall" in the price-wage exchange rates against them, between 1939 and 1943, has now been revealed in recent researches.[408] The condition of *khetmajdoors* and "small peasants" was similar in Orissa, and the officials in north Balasore had

402. Congress Bulletin, Bombay, 16 December 1942, Home Poll. File No. 3/1/43-Poll(I) of 1943, N.A.I. Rammanohar Lohia was thought to be propagating this point of view later in July 1943. See Home Poll. Fortnightly Report for 2nd half of July 1943, File No. 18/7/43 , N.A.I.
403. Sumit Sarkar, *Modern India, 1885-1947,* Delhi, 1983, p. 406.
404. Home Poll. Fortnightly Report for 1st half of April 1943, File No.18/4/43, N.A.I.
405. *People's War* (English weekly), 10 January 1943.
406. Home Poll. Fortnightly Report for the 2nd half of June and 2nd half of August 1943, File Nos. 18/6/43 and 18/8/43, N.A.I.
407. "Food Grains Storage in India", Department of Food, Government of India, New Delhi, 1944, p. 11, Home Pub. File No. 199.44-Pub (C) of 1944, N.A.I.
408. Amartya Kumar Sen, *Poverty and Famines: An Essay in Entitlement and Deprivation,* Oxford 1981, pp. 63-7.

been struck by "the utter indifference of the wealthier classes to the conditions of the poor", and their lack of "compunction" at the time of removing stocks of paddy and rice from "the distressed areas to places outside".[409] Pressed back to the wall, and without any help from any quarters, the poor in rural society took naturally to robbery, by defying the "Quit India" taboo on touching the "private properties", and by concentrating on the loot of the foodgrains. There were cases of looting of paddy-carts and cloth shops in Chittoor and Kurnool,[410] and mainly of grains in Chingleput, Guntur and Malabar.[411] In Trichinopoly and South Arcot villages the police had to open fire repeatedly on the hordes of grain looters, injuring many.[412] So many cases of paddy looting were reported from the Bengal districts, and frequently so from Bankura,[413] that the Home Department in New Delhi felt outraged by the discovery that "more dacoities occurred in 1942 than in 1940 and 1941 put together", and that the figure of early 1943 had "beaten all previous records".[414] The Governor of Bengal, Sir John Herbert, was compelled, therefore, to explain to the Viceroy that most of the dacoities being grain looting, he hoped to see "a drop in dacoities" with the improvement in the provincial food situation.[415] Grain looting was widespread in Bihar, especially in Madhubani, Buxar and Sasaram,[416] and often the *Zamindar's* men, carrying rent collection, were waylaid. When a landlord or a *Parganait* in the Santhal Parganas was robbed of the amount he collected, and injured, a police party arrived at the tribal village to round up the suspects. The villagers resisted with bows and arrows, and even in the face of some police firings,

409. Home Poll. Fortnightly Report for 1st half of May 1943, File No. 18/5/43, N.A.I.
410. *Ibid.*, 1st half of April 1943, File No. 18/4/43, N.A.I.
411. *Ibid.*, 1st half of June 1943, File No. 18/6/43 N.A.I.
412. *Ibid.*
413. *Ibid.*, 1st half of April 1943, File No. 18/4/43, N.A.I.
414. Note by W.H.S. Smith of 3 March 1943 on Dacoity Figures in Bengal, Home Department, File No. 182/43 - Police(C) of 1943, N.A.I.
415. Sir John Herbert to Linlithgow, 19 June 1943, *ibid.*
416. Home Poll. Fortnightly Report for 1st half of May 1943, File No. 18/5/43, N.A.I.

compelled the party "to run for lives of its members".[417] Looting of granaries, notably of the Dhenkanalraj in Malapara,[418] was reported from Orissa, as well as from Assam. The chain of robberies by the dispossessed, however, had spasmodically been broken by few of their more politicised acts, in which the local *kisan* activists, especially of the Communist variety, were caught up in some way or the other. Despite their opposition to the looting of the grains and "food riots",[419] unlike the Congress Socialists, who sniffed in these the smell of the "next" violent rebellion,[420] the local Communist and pro-Communist activists could not altogether shut themselves up in the liberalist shell from their intimate constituency of the rural poor. Resultantly in August 1943, they were seen in East Godavari to be articulating the agricultural labourer's demand for higher wages, and launching successfully a strike in Amalapuram *taluk*.[421] On 14 September 1943 they even succeeded in organising a conference in Guntur, which more than 5,000 agricultural labourers attended to raise their various grievances.[422] The Communist *kisan* activists were also found in Bodokimedi estate of Ganjam district to have made in July 1943 a scathing attack on the *Mustajars* — the rent collecting middlemen of the estate — who exacted forced labour to get their rent-free lands cultivated.[423] Further they resisted in December 1943, as members of the Punjab Kisan Sabha, the lessees' attempts at ejecting the under-tenants from lands in the Haveli Project *Chaks* in Jhang and Multan districts.[424] The Communist activists also threatened the Bettiah estate in Bihar in September 1943 with an agitation if it refused to settle — in

417. *Ibid.*, 2nd half of April 1943, File No. 18/4/43, N.A.I.
418. Biswamoy Pati, *Resisting Domination : Peasants, Tribals and National Movement in Orissa, 1920-50*, New Delhi, 1993, p. 175.
419. "Report on the Food Crisis" by P.C. Joshi for the C.C. meeting, February 1943, Party Documents, Central Archives, Communist Party of India, Ajoy Bhavan, New Delhi.
420. Home Poll. Fortnightly Report for 1st half of June 1943, File No. 18/6/43, N.A.I.
421. *Ibid.*, 2nd half of September 1943, File No. 18/9/43, N.A.I.
422. *Ibid.*, 2nd half of September 1943.
423. *Ibid.*, 2nd half of July 1943, File No. 18/7/43, N.A.I.
424. *Ibid.*, 1st half of December 1943, File No. 18/12/43, N.A.I.

contravention of the spirit of "grow more food" — its large tracts of wasteland with local *kisans.*[425] In Bengal they continued to organise "hunger marches" of peasants, and commenced to undertake the anti-hoarding and profiteering campaign.[426] They made a similar move in the U.P.,[427] and advised the peasantry in the coastal Orissa not to allow paddy and rice, which had been requisitioned, or levied by the Government, to leave their villages.[428] By October 1943 their anti-levy stance seemed ominously to be assuming the posture of an agrarian agitation,[429] and it spread alarmingly from Orissa to other parts of the country. In their concern for paddy, rice and other foodgrains, as well as for the unhoarding, controlling and rationing of "people's food", the Communist revolutionaries — who had chosen, with some peripheral exceptions, to suspend agrarian revolutionism — were at their reformist best in the worst of the party's times in 1943. If not the first, the Communists and their rank and file in the Kisan Sabhas were the foremost among those who applied themselves to the search of ways and means for ameliorating a desperate food situation. "Food crisis" loomed large before their eyes as early as September 1942, and the Central Kisan Council, A.I.K.S., emphasised in its meeting in Bombay on the need for involving the transport companies for the speedy transport of grains in the provinces, for registering the godowns of wholesalers in foodgrains, and for forming public bodies to deal locally with the prices and supplies of foodgrains.[430] The Communists diagnosed the hoarding of foodgrains by the profiteering monopolist grain-dealers, and the "bankrupt" food policy of the Government to be the main factors responsible for the food crisis.[431] When prices started rising, the

425. *Ibid.*, 1st half of September 1943, File No. 18/9/43, N.A.I.
426. *Ibid.*, 2nd half of April 1943, File No. 18/4/43, N.A.I.
427. *Ibid.*, 1st half of October 1943, File No. 18/10/43, N.A.I.
428. *Ibid.*, 2nd half of August 1943, File No. 18/8/43, N.A.I.
429. *Ibid.*, 2nd half of October 1943, File No.18/10/43, N.A.I.
430. Report on the A.I.K.S. Central Kisan Council meeting in Bombay, 24-7 September 1942, *People's War* (English weekly), 4 October 1942.
431. "The Food Crisis and Our Tasks", Resolution of the Central Committee, C.P.I., 19 February 1943, *War and National Liberation: C.P.I. Documents, 1939-45*, P. Bandhu and T.G. Jacob (eds.), New Delhi, 1988, p. 114.

Government took it initially as a sign of prosperity, and permitted "unbridled profiteering" till a situation of scarcity developed. Faced with scarcity, it tried to control prices "half-heartedly", resulting in the situation to drift further as much by its reluctance to unearth hidden stocks as by its encouragement to grain purchasers' and contractors' fleecing the peasant producers of their reserves at the lowest possible price.[432] With many of the peasant producers' surrendering all their grains to the dealers, the small traders' failing to stay in the market, the grain-stocks' stealthily flowing out of the provinces, and the distribution systems' tumbling down altogether — leading often to the rotting of grains for want of transport — created a national malady of very acute nature. Apart from the panacea of "grow more food", the prescription of the Communists included the formation of broad-based "people's food committees", from the provincial to the village levels, and the organisation of "volunteer corps" or vigilant squads to search out secret stocks, prevent clandestine exporting of food stuff from one place to another, and manage the distribution points or the grain shops.[433] They also planned for highlighting the issue through food conferences, setting up consumers' cooperatives and organising relief work in the areas in distress. The Communist activists and the Kisan Sabhaites were active on these lines in most regions, but more so in the C.P. and Berar,[434] in Bengal and Bihar,[435] in Assam and Orissa,[436] and in Madras and the U.P.[437] Although the local officials frequently accused the Communist activists of politically

432. "Report on the Food Crisis" by P.C. Joshi for the C.C. meeting, February 1943, Party Documents, Communist Party of India, Central Archives, Ajoy Bhavan, New Delhi.
433. *Ibid.*
434. Home Poll. Fortnightly Report for 2nd half of January 1943, File No. 18/1/43, N.A.I.
435. *Ibid.*, 1st half of March and 2nd half of April 1943, File Nos. 18/3/43 and 18/4/43, N.A.I.
436. *Ibid.*, 2nd half of July, 2nd half of September and 2nd half of October 1943, File Nos. 18/7/43, 18/9/43 and 18/10/43, N.A.I.
437. *Ibid.*, 2nd half of July and 1st half of October 1943, File Nos. 18/7/43 and 18/10/43, N.A.I.

"exploiting" the critical food situation,[438] they nevertheless recognised sometimes the "good work" the Communists were doing generally,[439] and even predicted that if the Communists succeeded in continuing with such "good work", they would "emerge from the war with greatly increased influence".[440] The prediction was put to some test in Bengal where a great famine struck in 1943, and devastated its rural populace — especially the poorer section of it.

Whether the great famine of 1943 in Bengal was caused mainly by "the failure of exchange entitlement" (FEE), meaning the widening of gap between a sudden "upsurge" in rice prices and a fall in the wages in absolute terms, and signifying thereby the people's inability to buy rice at the contrived "tripling" of its market rate,[441] or substantially by the "food availability decline" (FAD), implying shortages of rice, following the cessation of its import from Burma, and increase in its export to such British defence posts as Ceylon,[442] and to such deficit areas as Travancore and Cochin,[443] as well as by the "scorched earth" steps of an invasion-phobe Government for removing "surplus" rice from the coastal districts, and incapacitating boat transport in the delta areas, there has not been much difference of opinion of late as to its being excessively destructive and singularly "man-made", or its being thrust by the conduct of some upon the destiny of all others. The human responsibility for the

438. *Ibid.*, 2nd half July and 2nd half of August 1943, File Nos. 18/7/43 and 18/8/43, N.A.I.
439. *Ibid.*
440. *Ibid.*, 2nd half of September 1943, File No. 18/9/43, N.A.I.
441. See Amartya Kumar Sen, "Famines as Failures of Exchange Entitlement", *Economic and Political Weekly*, Special Number, August 1976, "Starvation and Exchange Entitlements: A General Approach and its Application to the Great Bengal Famine", *Cambridge Journal of Economics*, No.1, 1977. Also his *Poverty and Famines: An Essay in Entitlement and Deprivation*, Oxford, 1981, pp. 63-70.
442. Boudhayan Chattopadhyaya, "Panchasher Manwantarer Karjya Karan Sandhane" (In Search of the Circumstances and Causes of the Famine of 1943), *Samskriti O Samaj* (Bengali), Vol. I, no. 1, April 1983, Niharranjan Ray Centre for Studies in National Integration, Calcutta.
443. J.N. Uppal, *Bengal Famine of 1943 : A Man Made Tragedy*, Delhi, 1984, p. 170.

ravages ranged very widely from the colonial authorities' distinct disinterest in food for India, in macabre contrast with their planning food in advance for Britain, to the casual unconcern and criminal ineptitude of those in charge of governing India and Bengal; from the monopolistic grain-dealers and war-time food contractors, who, by their extraordinary capacity for hoarding, had created the steepest imaginable "blackmarket" of foodgrains for the common humanity, to the large producers (the rich and the well-to-do peasants), who held back stocks to take advantage of the soaring prices. The blame must also be shared by the affluent consumers, who apprehensively accumulated more grains than they normally needed; by the landlords, rich peasants and moneylenders, who stopped — at the first sign of food scarcity — employing wage labourers, patronising artisans and advancing loans, especially in kind; and by all those, who, for the sake of self preservation and escape, abandoned field-hands, old and infirm relations, and even deserted their own families — hapless wives and children.[444] For a comprehension of the enormity of famine destruction, however, one hardly needs to take into account the whole sweep of the havoc it caused; instead, a mere reference to the computations of mortality should suffice. It was the contemporary non-official calculation of 3.5 million deaths during the famine and its aftermath, over and above the normal mortality, made by Professor K.P. Chattopadhyaya of Anthro-pological Department of Calcutta University early in 1944,[445] rather than the official calculation of 1.5 million deaths, made by the Famine Inquiry Commission on Bengal in 1945,[446] that has been upheld by the findings of recent researches. The findings varied from 3 million deaths[447] to 3.8 million

444. Paul R. Greenough, *Prosperity and Misery in Modern Bengal : The Famine of 1943-1944*, New York, 1982, pp. 207-25.

445. *Ananda Bazar Patrika* (Bengali daily), 20 February 1944.

446. Famine Inquiry Commission, *Report on Bengal*, Calcutta, 1945, Chapter I, Para 7, pp. 109-10.

447. Amartya Kumar Sen, "Famine Mortality : A Study of Bengal Famine of 1943", in *Peasants in History : Essays in Honour of Daniel Thorner*, E. Hobsbawm (ed.), New Delhi, 1981.

deaths,[448] and did not include the vast number of those who survived death by hair-breadth, and continued to linger on as the physically wrecked, or as the living dead. Who, however, suffered most in the "man made", devastating famine of 1943 in rural Bengal? Clearly those who not only had no land, but also had no control over it in any way — the agricultural labourers, the paddy-huskers, the fishermen, the village artisans and menials. In absolute terms, by far the largest group of famine-affected people belonged to the category of "agricultural labourers",[449] and the percentage of the worst victims was the highest among the fishermen.[450] Of the number of approximately 1.1 million destitutes, the agricultural labourers formed the bulk, followed closely by the artisans and menials.[451] Those who possessed some lands (such as the peasant cultivators of medium and small varieties) survived comparatively easily, by selling and mortgaging their holdings, and clinging desperately to their thinning stocks of grains. The advantage of possessing some crops or shares of paddy even tilted the scale of precarious survival in favour of the sharecroppers. The sufferings of the *Chuhandars* (small tenant cultivators) and *Adhiars* (share-croppers), who formed the bulk of the agricultural society in Jalpaiguri, for example, though very serious, indeed, were not as bad as those of the agricultural labourers and petty artisans.[452] But those who suffered slightly less relatively also underwent extremely severe economic deterioration throughout the famine period, either by losing land, or by selling utensils, agricultural implements, craft tools and cattle. Between mid-April 1943 and mid-April 1944 about 7,11,000 acres

448. Based on *Sample Survey of the After-Effects of the Bengal Famine of 1943*, Indian Statistical Institute, Calcutta, 1946, and the unpublished mortality data collected by the I.S.I. under the guidance of Professor P.C. Mahalanobis. See Paul R. Greenough, *Prosperity and Misery in Modern Bengal : The Famine of 1943-44*, New York, 1982, pp. 305-9.

449. Amartya Kumar Sen, "The Great Bengal Famine", *Poverty and Famines: An essay in Entitlement and Deprivation*, Oxford, 1981, p. 73.

450. *Sample Survey of the After-Effects of the Bengal Famine of 1943*, Indian Statistical Institute, Calcutta, 1946, p. 17.

451. "Bangali Kothay Cholechhe" (Whither Bengal), by Kshitish Prasad Chattopadhyaya, *Parichaya* (Bengali Monthly), Poush 1352 (November 1945), Vol. XV, no. 6, pp. 357-69.

452. *People's War* (English weekly), 2 January 1944.

out of 26.68 million acres of paddy land, which was approximately 3 per cent of the whole of it, had been sold out.[453] The figures indicated a three-fold increase over those of 1942, and implied that the sellers of land were mostly poor peasants,[454] or those who had less than two acres. Another 5,10,000 families were believed by the Bengal Provincial Kisan Sabha to have been forced to mortgage their lands with the moneylenders and rich peasants.[455] The loss of land, and the loss of agricultural implements and cattle, had resulted in the downward shifting of earning and ranking, from the categories of poor peasants and sharecroppers to the category of agricultural labourers. Such decline from independent cultivation of some sort to agricultural labour of the barest minimum seemed to have occurred in the cases perhaps of as many as 2 million peasants and their families.[456] It was no wonder, therefore, that the abundant availability of agricultural labourers, despite the high rate of mortality among them, kept the cultivating operations more or less intact in Bengal during the famine period, and resulted towards the end of 1943 in the production of the largest rice crop in history. Paradoxically, however, the record *aman* (winter) crop of more than 9 million tons in 1943 was the greatest proof of the agricultural labourers' weak economic position — their ever swelling vast number, and the consequent depreciation in the exchange value of their labour. If this happened to be one effect of the loss or the sale of the peasant cultivators' paddy lands, the other result was the passing of these lands into the hands of the non-cultivators and the rich peasants — their new purchasers. The non-cultivators, mostly the *Jotedars* who settled their freshly acquired lands with the *Bargadars*, and the rich peasants who extended their cultivating areas and increased their moneylending deals, turned out to be

453. *Sample Survey of the After-Effects of the Bengal Famine of 1943*, Indian Statistical Institute, Calcutta, 1946, pp. 28-9.
454. "Bangali Kothay Cholechhe" (Whither Bengal), by Kshitish Prasad Chattopadhyaya, *Parichaya* (Bengali monthly), *Poush* 1352 (November 1945), Vol. XV, no. 6, pp. 357-69.
455. Memorandum of Bengal Provincial Kisan Sabha to the Government of Bengal on Rahabilitation, Calcutta, October 1945.
456. *Ibid.*

the real gainers in 1943-4. The "man-made" famine not only not touched them, but also provided them with opportunities to grab land at a negligible price, and to profit by selling stocks at the "blackmarket".

Although the famine seemed to have taken Calcutta by storm in July 1943 and sent shock-waves through the provincial bureaucracy and the urban and semi-urban populace, it really began ten months earlier in October 1942 when the "new beggars" — not the nagging "professionals" — but the dignified "householders-turned-destitutes" started appearing on the streets of Calcutta.[457] That a calamitous situation was developing in the countryside, and that the landless section suffering most acutely "throughout the province", had already been known to the local officials in January 1943.[458] By March 1943 reports of starvation deaths and suicides started pouring into the district headquarters, as well as news of selling children and handing over women to the prostitute-mongers.[459] It became apparent towards the end of June 1943 that the destitutes could no longer bear the pangs of hunger by clutching on to their village homes. So by the beginning of July 1943 started the "great influx" to the towns and the city of Calcutta in search of food.[460] Urbanity in Bengal looked, somewhat shamefacedly and callously, to the "procession of skeletons"[461] — to those who had not been "accustomed to begging".[462] From July to December 1943, during the "worst phase of the famine",[463] it was starvation deaths all around, especially in the city streets,[464] sometimes

457. Editorial, *Ananda Bazar Patrika* (Bengali daily), 13 October 1942.
458. "Food Grains Shortage in India", Department of Food, Government of India, 1944, p. 11, Home Pub. File No. 199/44-Pub(C) of 1944, N.A.I.
459. Home Poll. Fortnightly Report for 2nd half of March 1943, File No. 18/3/43, N.A.I.
460. "Food Grains Shortage in India", Department of Food, Government of India, 1944, p. 24, Home Pub. File No. 199/44-Pub(C) of 1944, N.A.I.
461. *Ananda Bazar Patrika* (Bengali daily), editorial, 22 July 1943.
462. Home Poll. Fortnightly Report for 2nd half of August 1943, File No. 18/8/43, N.A.I.
463. "Food Grains Shortage in India", Department of Food, Government of India, 1944, p. 25, Home Pub. File No. 199/44-Pub(C) of 1944, N.A.I.
464. *Ananda Bazar Patrika* (Bengali daily), 28 July, 30 November and 2 December 1943.

recorded as more than 100 a day in Calcutta alone, and of course, many more indifferently left unrecorded.[465] A cursory glance at the contemporary newspapers should give an idea of the colossal loss of lives among the rural poor at various places[466] — about 50 per cent of the total number of agricultural labourers having perished in Noakhali,[467] 59,000 in Munshiganj,[468] 83,000 in Mymensingh and 33,000 in Barisal.[469] In December 1943 it was believed by the Government officials[470] that the most destructive phase of the famine had passed away, presumably with the harvesting of the record-breaking *aman* crop.

Confronted with the gravest of perils, the rural poor in Bengal conducted themselves differently at two different stages, first desperately, and almost single-handedly, struggling for existence between October 1942 and June 1943, and then, while losing the struggle for existence, resignedly surrendering to death between July and December 1943. Although separate in characteristics, one stage was born out of the other, and the surrender during the famine followed only in the face of a rout. If this basic point was not kept in view, any observer would tend to underplay the Bengali rural poor's desperate bid for survival, highlight their "uncomplaining surrender to death" — in sharp contrast with the hungry European (the French and the English between the 17th and the 19th centuries) poor's proclivities for "violent expropriation" of food — and try to explain their "fatalism" and "passivity" in the light of the traditional Bengali social norms and behavioural patterns in dealing with the "crises".[471] To lay stress on the second stage, without much attempt at exploring the first, or to emphasise

465. See *Jugantar* (Bengali daily), issues of October and November 1943.
466. *Ibid.*
467. *Ananda Bazar Patrika* (Bengali daily), 21 December 1943.
468. *Ibid.*, 3 December 1943.
469. *Ibid.*, 28 December 1943.
470. "Food Grains Shortage in India", Department of Food, Government of India, 1944, p. 25, Home Pub. File No. 199/44-Pub(C) of 1944, N.A.I.
471. This is exactly what Paul R. Greenough has done in his otherwise excellent study of the Bengal famine, *Prosperity and Misery in Modern Bengal: The Famine of 1943-44*, 1982, pp. 11, 59 and 267-75, and also what the urbane Bengali intelligentsia always imagined uncomfortably to be the whole truth.

upon the rural poor's capitulation to death, without taking sufficient note of their urges for living, would not only reduce the whole truth almost by half, but also deny them of their normal, virile longing for life, and their glory in spontaneously fighting for it. The fight had to be spontaneous between October 1942 and June 1943, for the nationalists were mostly in jail, the Congress Socialists on the run after the "Quit India" movement, the Communists in a compromising position with the Raj, and none practically had been there to mobilise the hungry against hunger. Even spontaneity was not free-flowing in the aftermath of the savage repressions of 1942, in the overbearing presence in Bengal of the British and American soldiery and in the demoralising effect of the Japanese air raids. Despite all this, the looting of grain shops and grain stores was rampant in the countryside, and petty crimes increased by leaps and bounds.[472] Dacoities proliferated throughout the *mofussil* till June 1943, especially in Dacca district,[473] and the official crime records (which were not exhaustive by any stretch of imagination) had borne enough evidence of the trend. The picture should be apparent if the six-monthly dacoity figures of 1943 were compared with those of the previous year:[474]

Months	*1942*	*1943*
January	108	342
February	135	406
March	161	611
April	158	720
May	128	928
June	144	927
Total	834	3,934

472. *Jugantar* (Bengali daily), 10 January 1943.
473. *Ananda Bazar Patrika* (Bengali daily), 13 July 1943.
474. Home Dept. File No.182/43 - Police (C) of 1943, N.A.I.

The authorities in Bengal felt that these dacoities were "virtually cases of grain looting due to serious food shortage [they loathed to call it a famine yet] in many parts of the province", and saw little chance of their abating unless the food situation dramatically improved.[475] They were, of course, proved to be entirely wrong, for the dacoity figures did start dropping — not on account of any dramatics in the food situation — but simply because the famished dacoits no longer had the physical capacity for dacoities from July onwards. They clearly had lost the battle for life, and therefore, were getting ready for their surrender to death. At this point began their long treks to the urban centres, with begging bowls in hands, instead of the sickles, and their dying in the city and town streets. While queing for death in the urban and suburban locales, the rural poor did not try any more to loot the shops, attack the rich, start widespread food riots and create grave law and order situations. Whether or not, the fatalism ingrained in them, and the "last streak" of an ancient civilisation kept within themselves,[476] had been responsible for their restrainment, one did notice, as the Famine Inquiry Commission had done in 1944, certain serious limitations to their assuming an aggressive posture. There was practically nobody to direct them into violent acts, and they themselves came from so many diverse areas that some solidarity on their part for concerted violent acts had practically been impossible to achieve. What, however, seemed crucial in this regard was their being "reduced to a state of debility which prevented vigorous action",[477] and led invariably to an unending stupor. The passivity of the dying in effect was the product of their total and utter helplessness — both physical and mental. At this hour of extreme helplessness, whosoever offered a helping hand, and expressed some gesture of genuine sympathy, was bound to touch the hearts of the sufferers — the famine victims. The Communists in Bengal appeared to have done so, not by organising agitations among

475. Sir John Herbert, Lt. Governor of Bengal, to Linlithgow, Viceroy, 23 August 1943, *ibid.*
476. Bhowani Sen, *Rural Bengal in Ruins*, Bombay, 1945, p. 17.
477. Famine Inquiry Commission, *Report on Bengal*, Calcutta, 1945, part I, Chapter IX, p. 68, para 13.

the famine-stricken — the opportunities of which they had already spurned away in their obsession for the "peoples' war" — but by organising relief, raising relief funds, drawing the attention of the whole country to the ravages in Bengal, and above all, marching a fresh troop of young cadres into the Bengal countryside.

The Communists and the Kisan Sabhaites in Bengal first tried their hands at relief work in October 1942 when a cyclone had hit (on the 16th) Midnapore and the 24-Parganas districts, affecting an area of 4,000 square miles and killing about 10,000 human beings.[478] As a significant non-official attempt at meeting the situation, Bengal Provincial Kisan Sabha had set up a Cyclone Relief Committee under the leadership of its General Secretary, M.A.Rasul, appealed to the public for funds and offered some relief to the cyclone-affected.[479] It drew upon this experience again 8 months later by organising a People's Flood Relief Committee, with the novelist, Tarashankar Bandyopadhyaya, as President and Niren Roy as Secretary during the Damodar and the Ajoy floods on 17 July and 4 August 1943 which inundated the districts of Burdwan and Hooghly, and jeopardised the lives of 2,50,000 people.[480] About a month later, on 29 September 1943, the Communists convened a meeting of the representatives of its various mass organisations and sympathisers at the Indian Association Hall, Calcutta, and formed a broad-based People's Relief Committee, with Nausher Ali as President, Niren Roy and Choudhury Moazzem Hussain as Joint Secretaries and Kshitish Prasad Chattopadhyaya as Treasurer. The P.R.C. sprang into action almost immediately after its birth, established branches in most of the districts and began a vigorous drive for funds and relief materials,as well as a campaign for focussing public attention on the famine victims. Both in the collection of funds and in the highlighting of the distress, the Indian People's Theatre Association (which had

478. Sugata Bose, *Agrarian Bengal : Economy, Social Structure and Politics, 1919-47,* Cambridge, 1986, p. 248.
479. Susnata Das, *Fascibad Birodhi Sangrame Abibhakta Bangla* (Undivided Bengal in Struggle Against Fascism), Calcutta, 1989, pp. 223-4.
480. Paul R. Greenough, *Prosperity and Misery in Modern Bengal: The Famine of 1943-44,* Oxford, 1982, p. 129.

already made its appearance in Bengal in March 1943) came strongly in support of the P.R.C. through the performances of its singers, dancers, actors and actresses in various parts of India. The Women's Association for Self Defence (*Mahila Atmaraksha Samiti*), which came into existence in April 1942, similarly assisted the P.R.C. in articulating public opinion, raising funds and collecting articles for relief. Of course, the staunchest supporters of the P.R.C. were the district Kisan Sabhas, who tried to build up squads of volunteers (*Krishak Vahinis*) to reinforce the relief work — at least 10 of them in each village, 30 in each union, 210 in each sub-division and 500 in each district.[481] From October 1943 the *kisan* and the P.R.C. volunteers started running gruel kitchens, distributing grains, supplying clothes and blankets, simultaneously with keeping watch on the newly harvested *aman* crops and guarding them against the hoarders.[482] By the end of 1943 the P.R.C. had managed to supply the countryside with Rs.1,50,000 worth of relief articles, and distribute 2,000 maunds of rice,[483] over and above its running 167 gruel kitchens.[484] The effort clearly was woefully inadequate, and fell short of the extent of relief provided by other moneyed and the financial capital-backed voluntary agencies, such as the Marwari Relief Society, and the Bengal Relief Committee of Syama Prasad Mukherjee. But the importance of the Communists' or the P.R.C's relief work lay not so much in its quantum, but in its dispersal throughout the length and breadth of the province, in its becoming a movement in itself, and in the enthusiasm that it generated among the famine-stricken. An artist-turned P.R.C. volunteer, Chitta Prasad, recalled how the destitutes in a small village in Midnapore implored him and his associates: "Why don't you come here more often? It fills our hearts with new hope".[485]

481. Susnata Das, *Fascibad Birodhi Sangrame Abibhakta Bangla* (Undivided Bengal in Struggle Against Fascism), Calcutta, 1989, p. 223
482. *People's War* (English weekly), 3 October and 5, 19 and 26 December, 1943.
483. *Ibid.*, 5 March 1944.
484. Saroj Mukherji, *Bharater Communist Party O Amra* (Communist Party of India and We), Calcutta,1986, Part II, p. 178.
485. *People's War* (English daily), 2 January 1944.

The new hope, however, flickered most when the P.R.C. excelled all other agencies in providing medical relief to the famine-ravaged. With the help of such public-spirited medicalmen as Dr. Amiya Bose, Dr. Narayan Roy and Dr. Moni Biswas, the P.R.C. had set up an elaborate organisation of medical relief under the overall supervision of Dr. Bejoy Kumar Basu in the immediate post-famine phase of widespread epidemics — of cholera, malaria and smallpox. (It should be remembered that much of the total number of mortality in the Bengal Famine — as it was found to be the case with most of the famines in India — was owing to epimedics, to which the famine-stricken had invariably become the easiest prey). Dr. Basu, who was a member of the Congress-sponsored Indian Medical Mission to the war-torn China in 1938, had the essential experience, and the attitude to lead the P.R.C.'s combat against the diseases on the rural front. Medical units were promptly formed, dispensaries started, doctors and medical students enlisted and the *kisan* and youth volunteers mobilised. Help was secured from the well-known laboratories, stocks of quinine procured and vaccines against cholera, typhoid and smallpox collected. By the middle of January 1944 the P.R.C. medical teams were in the thick of the battle against epidemics, and they had succeeded in vaccinating more than two lakhs of people in the villages.[486] The targets were, however, so difficult to reach that the P.R.C. and Dr. Basu had to think about requisitioning the support of the entire medical fraternity in Bengal. By the beginning of March 1944 they had succeeded in constituting a widely based Bengal Medical Relief Coordination Committee, consisting of the representatives of various health organisations, ambulance corps and pharmaceutical companies, under the chairmanship of Dr. Bidhan Chandra Roy, to give them the necessary support.[487] Side by side, the P.R.C. continued its drive for funds, asking people all over India to contribute whatever little they could afford, for "one rupee saves one life from malaria, one anna makes one life immune to cholera, four annas save one cholera victim, and Rs. 3,400 keep one medical

486. *Ibid.*, 23 January 1944.
487. *Ibid.*, 5 March 1944.

squad going for three months".[488] By the beginning of 1944 about 50 medical squads of the P.R.C. were functioning in 500 villages, running 14 medical centres, and treating approximately 2,000 patients daily.[489] The P.R.C.'s capacity for stepping up medical relief increased immensely by the beginning of June 1944, when it managed to set up 73 medical centres, covering 21 districts of Bengal.[490]

The famine relief work of the Communists, and its humanistic aspect, impressed almost everybody in Bengal, including the retrospective anti-Communist chronicler of the Indian National Congress.[491] The villagers were generally appreciative of it, and the rural poor or the famine-victims in particular seemed to have been greatly touched by it. They were moved by the sincerity of the new, young "outsiders", by the social non-conformism (in eating food prepared by the low-caste peasants, or in sleeping in the outcastes' huts) of those belonging to the *Bhadralok* (gentry) category, and by the "outsiders'" adapting themselves to the rural ways of raw life. Many of these young, new "outsiders" did depart from the villages at the end of the relief work, leaving behind memories of their abounding good will. Some continued to come back to the scenes of their activity from time to time, and renewed contacts with those whom they served. Few even stayed in the villages to give their humanitarian acts a political and ideological direction, and facilitate afresh — as it has been observed by some — the Communist "leadership entry" into the rural Bengal.[492] Interacting with the villagers, they appeared to have not only revamped the organisation of the Kisan Sabhas,[493] but also kept the sparks of peasant militancy

488. The P.R.C.'s appeal for funds, *ibid.*, 30 April 1944.
489. P.C. Joshi's article, *ibid.*, 12 March 1944.
490. *Ibid.*, 11 June 1944.
491. Amales Tripathi, "Bharater Swadhinata Sangrame Jatiya Congress, 1908-47" (National Congress in India's Struggle for Independence), *Desh* (Bengali weekly), 19 November 1988, pp. 63-4.
492. Jnanabrata Bhattacharya, "An Examination of Leadership Entry in Bengal Peasant Revolts, 1937-47", *Journal of Asian Studies*, Vol. XXXVII, no. 4, August 1978, pp. 611-34.
493. The Organisational Letter of Provincial Kisan Council, Bengal, 1 June 1944, cited in Susnata Das, *Fascibad Birodhi Sangrame Abibhakta Bangla* (Undivided Bengal in Struggle Against Fascism, Calcutta, 1989, p. 223.

flying in 1944-5, either by raising voices against hoarding and "blackmarketing" of essential commodites, or by denouncing the profiteer-police-bureaucracy combine. That the Communist movement survived in Bengal at that point, got eventually over its amnesia of popular struggles, succeeded in gathering some momentum later on, and was found to be actually "kicking" in the post-independence era, especially in the 1960s and 1970s — was due crucially to the historic appearance in the countryside of the unacknowledged, and heretofore unsung, P.R.C. volunteers — those stethoscope-slinging, rice bag-pulling and gruel kitchen-managing urbane, petty bourgeois youth.

THE RAISONNEUR'S MONOLOGUE

The years 1942 and 1943, which witnessed the hightide of anti-imperialism in India, and a violent nationalist tumult at its crest, also marked, ironically enough, the lowest ever ebb in the mobilisation of the rural poor — the powerful components of popular upsurge whom the leftists were rallying since 1936. As it has already been noted, the explanation for this anomalous situation was apparent in the over-all approach of the leftists themselves, in their renunciation of resistance against feudalism in rural society, and in their reluctance to link it up with anti-imperialism — the necessary pre-condition for a successful national democratic revolution. The attitude of the Congress Socialists, who tried heroically to live up to their anti-imperialist credentials, was based on their scare of the disruption that any fight with feudalism might cause to the multi-class nationalist consolidation, and on their obvious preference for playing the role of nationalists — in the expectation of winning the landlords-*mahajans*' approval — to the acting as socialists in the conviction for enlisting the rural masses' support. Similarly, the attitude of the Communists, who attempted energetically at proving their anti-Fascist rather than the anti-imperialist credentials, was founded on their anxiety for the safety of the Nazi-invaded Soviet Russia, and on their giving priority to the tasks of "people's war" against Fascism than to the duties towards a joint anti-imperialist and anti-feudal struggle. Never before had an extraneous factor, such as the Hitlerite invasion of Russia, or an internal actuality, such as the dubious disposition of the landlords-*mahajans*, proved to be so decisive, and so disconcerting in the history of the Indian national movement. Whosoever gained and lost at this peak of the turmoil among the contending parties, i.e. the leftists, the nationalists, the landlords-*mahajans* and the Raj, and, of course, in whatever degree and depth, the conspicuous sufferers throughout these two years in all respects were the rural poor — the agricultural labourers, the sharecroppers, the small peasants and the artisans. The war-time soaring prices, the hoarding and "blackmarketing", the scarcity and famine had found their easiest victims among the poor in the countryside. What was worse, the rural poor's mentors had not only deserted them to fend for themselves, but also withdrawn unilaterally from all anti-feudal contests, leaving them in effect at the mercy of the D.I.R.-backed, regrouped and reassured rural exploiters. Most of the agitations launched in the previous year (such as the sharecroppers' in Gujarat, the *Adhiars*' and the *Kut Khamar* tenants' in Bengal, the anti-*Jenmi* in Malabar, the Munagala peasants' in Andhra and the *Sir kisans*' in the U.P.) were discontinued, and those freshly thought of (such as the workers' and *kisans*' in Cannanore of Malabar, the sugarcane and jute-growers' in Bihar and Bengal, the *Bataidars*' in Jhang and Multan of the Punjab, the agricultural labourers' in Andhra, the *Bargadars*' in Bengal, the *Bakasht* peasants' in Bihar and an anti-*Mustajari* one in Ganjam of Orissa) abruptly given up. Not that those who in the recent past activated the *kisan* masses to resist exploitation and defy repression had all of a sudden departed bag and baggage from the rural scene. The guiding angels were still very much there, ever ready to show the rural poor their ordained path, but managed — after all their exertions — to create confusion by asking them, as the Congress Socialists did, to join their class adversaries in the name of fighting an oppressive Raj, or by exhorting them, as the Communists did, to join their ruthless alien rulers on the plea of fighting the invisible Japanese Fascists. The confusion over selecting a friend out of the two foes was further confounded by the bickerings among the leftist ideologues and activists themselves — the quarrels of the Congress Socialists with the Communists, and those of the Communists with the Rangaites, the Swamites and the Yajnikites. The perplexed *kisans* did not really know when to resist, whom to resist, with whose assistance, and for what gains.

In such a topsy-turvy world of theirs, the rural poor had no alternative but to stick to those grim lessons which they learnt by their lives of sufferings, namely, to endure gnashing their teeth, and at the tether's end, to take to robbery and looting, and when even that was no more feasible, to beg and die. Acts of freebooting, secretly planned and excuted by small groups of men, women and children, in various parts of the country — particularly in the southern and eastern parts — were the only autonomous moves that the rural poor could make on their own in 1942-3. It was social brigandage again, and the ransacking of the Government properties, which characterised their brief and limited participation in the "Quit India" movement. Their participation could not but be limited when none seriously tried to mobilise them, and some clearly were opposed to their mobilisation. While the Congress Socialists did not make any special attempt at leading them, lest it should raise class issues to the detriment of an imaginary rural class consolidation; the Communists did try to dissuade them from joining, lest it should paralyse the administration in the interior and jeopardise the anti-Fascist war-efforts. And yet the *kisan* masses in certain areas took part in the movement, not because they saw in it the furtherance of their class interests and aspirations — as the rural rich justifiably seem to have seen — but because they could not help it, partly on account of their being sucked into the vortex, as so many other elements in Indian society had been, and partly owing to their spotting in the tottering of the Raj some opportunities for brigandage. Consequently, their association with the "Quit India" movement was bound to be somewhat brief, coinciding precisely with the short period which began by stirring the popular belief that the Raj had fallen, and which ended by discovering the rude reality that it had not. Depredation also dominated their desperate bid in 1943 for survival in the worst of the food crisis in India, before, of course, succumbing rather tamely to the great famine in Bengal, and famine-like conditions in Orissa and certain other parts of the southern peninsula. It is difficult to imagine what else they might have done, since they were left wholly to themselves by the Communists, who were not interested in organising them in convulsive outbreaks, except leading relatively safe "hunger marches" to the Government officials, as well as by the Congress Socialists, who, relying fatalistically on the hungry people's spontaneity of actions against the Government, did not actually bother to come out of their underground shelters to stand beside them. Social brigandage, as a form of autonomous or semiautonomous peasant reaction to the socio-economic sufferings, was rather old-fashioned, indeed, even by the Indian standard, and scarcely innovative. Taking recourse to it as late as in the uproarious 1940s, and that, too, as in the shape of innumerable, unconnected and scattered "cases" of dacoities — in no way comparable to such coordinated acts of depredation as those of the Savaras or the Santhals — did not speak very highly of the quality of consciousness and the level of leadership among the rural poor after about a decade's experience in agitational politics. It seemed to be rather paradoxical, for, despite their reclining very heavily on their leftist mentors and the "outsider" ideologues, and the left political parties' unconcern for stimulating local leadership among them, the peasant masses did produce their heroes and heroines among them, to an extent, between 1934 and 1941, and as it would be seen later, to a large extent, between 1944 and 1951. Their political consciousness and confidence in themselves, once aroused, also never really flagged, except in 1942-3, and appeared to have grown in degree at all other times. Perhaps the position of the rural poor in 1942-3 was not as enigmatic as one feels allured to make it out today. Probably their material condition had been too feeble, their economic deprivation too staggering, and the desertion by their friends, philosophers and guides too demoralising to inspire in them any autonomous initiative of top quality. Besides, in an age of fast communications and acrimonious ideologies, at the juncture of war-time emergency and vigilance, and in the plains and easy terrains — not in the distant hills and jungle tracts — the scope for autonomous action of any kind was certainly very narrow. It must have been rendered narrower by the interferences and obstructions of hierarchical societies, of political parties — of the Congress Socialists and the Communists themselves.

It was not possible for the leftists, who professed to champion the cause of the rural poor, to continue to neglect them indefinitely for long, especially after the blowing over of the "Quit India" movement, or the survival of the Soviet Union in the war. Being in the "open", and not in jails and under surveillance like their Congress Socialist counterparts, the Communist *kisan* activists were in a better and freer position to make amends for their desertion of the rural poor by shifting the objectives from "grow more food" to offer relief to the famine-victims, from the anti-Fascist resistance to the fight against hoarders and "black marketeers". Almost similarly, and despite their handicaps in the underground, the Congress Socialists also tried to atone for their sins by coming closer to the *kisan* masses in the few places still under the left nationalist domination.

SCENE III
1944-45

While the Communists continued to maintain an unsavoury peace with the British Raj, the Congress Socialists remained at an unequal war with it throughout the post-"Quit India" movement period till the release of the Congress prisoners in June 1945. They saw no useful alternative to fighting the British authorities, and therefore, favoured its continuance from the underground, and if possible, by adopting guerilla tactics.[494] Apart from the silver-lined fact that the C.S.P refused to give up its uncompromisingly aggressive posture, however, nothing much really came out of the token resistance of a defeated army of stragglers, except occasional lootings of the Government funds, stray acts of sabotage,[495] some propaganda against peasants' selling stocks to the Government and encouragement to minor food riots, without being able to organise a single "big one".[496] These hardly left any mark on the rural poor's mind, but some other activities did to a certain extent in places where the flames of "August Kranti" still burnt, such as Satara in Maharashtra and Midnapore in Bengal. Although the local activists in none of these two places were strictly under the control of the C.S.P. — the rebellious Patri Sarkar in Satara being only nominally under its guidance, and the Tamluk Jatiya Sarkar and the Kanthi Swaraj Panchayat in Midnapore being free even from such a formality — all the three, more or less, followed the same pattern, and conformed to a similar line of

494. "To All Fighters for Freedom", Jayaprakash Narayan's second letter, August 1943, *Samajbadi Andolan Ke Dastabej* (in Hindi), Vinode Prasad Singh and Sunil Mishra (eds.), Delhi, 1985, pp. 274-7.
495. Home Poll. Fortnightly Report for 1st half of November 1943, File No. 18/11/43, N.A.I.
496. Communist Reply to the Congress Working Committee Charges, December 1945 in P. Bandhu and T.G. Jacob (eds.), *War and National Liberation, C.P.I. Documents, 1939-45*, New Delhi, 1988, p. 274

action, to which the C.S.P. leadership either reluctantly relented, or did not show enough aversion to relenting. In Midnapore, for example, the Tamluk Jatiya Sarkar and the Kanthi Swaraj Panchayat, which functioned throughout 1943 and the first half of 1944,[497] not only organised relief for the cyclone and flood victims, ran dispensaries and grappled with the precarious food situation, but also tried to stop the movement and the sale of grains to the Government contractors,[498] seize stocks of the affluent land-holders and grain-dealers and punish "black-marketeers" with heavy fines.[499] The Sarkars also collected by intimidation both money and grains from the rich — the *Zamindars*, the *Jotedars* and the businessmen — and their demands in individual cases rose as high as Rs. 40,000 in cash and 500 maunds in rice.[500] The anti-feudal undercurrent beneath such activities often encouraged the *kisan* masses to loot paddy, resist the *Zamindari* rent collection, and even rob the collected amount in broad daylight, as it happened notably at Sutahata, Tamluk, in January 1944.[501]

Temper against feudal exploitation had identically been aroused in Satara through the activities of the Patri Sarkar, which operated from the beginning of 1943 to the end of 1946, without paying much heed to Gandhiji's call for surrender. Beside undertaking such reforming measures as denouncing untouchability, enforcing prohibition, banning prostitution, simplifying marriages (known as inexpensive "Gandhi weddings") and cleaning villages, the Sarkar fought vigorously against the scarcity of food grains, looted the Government grain stores, seized the affluent peasants' stocks, prevented the courts' confiscation orders on lands from being executed, got disputed lands tilled

497. The Sarkars were wound up, and the leaders and the activists surrendered to the Government in answer to Gandhiji's call (on 1 August 1944) to them for doing so.
498. Home Poll. Fortnightly Report for 2nd half of March 1944, File No. 18/3/44, N.A.I.
499. Hitesranjan Sanyal, "The Quit India Movement in Medinipur District", Gyanendra Pandey (ed.), *The Indian Nation in 1942*, Calcutta, 1988, pp. 54-60.
500. *Ibid.*
501. Home Poll. Fortnightly Report for 2nd half of January 1944, File No. 18/1/44, N.A.I.

with the help of volunteers and guarded the crops on the fields.[502] It also endeavoured to "control *sowcars*" or *mahajans* by lowering the rates of interest,[503] and by forcing them to restore the mortgaged lands to the destitute widows and craftsmen.[504] Chastising the criminals and village toughs, who often acted as the landed magnates' hired goons, it tried to curb sexual exploitation of women by severely punishing the rapists — most of whom belonged to the categories of rich peasants, *mahajans* and landlords.[505] Even in a few isolated cases, it was reported to have given away some of the absentee landlords' lands to the landless, and assumed increasingly an anti-landlord and anti-*sowcar* position in 1945.[506] Sending a shock-wave through the rural rich, and consequently, spreading influence among the rural poor in the interior of the Maratha districts like Sholapur, Ratnagiri, Poona and Kolaba all through the year 1945,[507] the Patri Sarkar did leave an impression on the posterity as to its being "a power at the village level that was more on the side of the poor and toilers than any previous state power".[508]

The C.S.P. leadership was not alone in relenting, voluntarily or involuntarily, to the expression of anti-feudal inclinations of the local "August revolutionaries", the C.P.I. leaders also had to do the same in respect of alike tendencies of their cadres, who began rehabilitating themselves in the countryside. The Communist-led Kisan Sabha in Andhra was the first to resume popular resistance to the *Zamindari* excesses in Venkatagiri, Nellore, as early as the beginning of January 1944.[509] The dispute

502. *Free Press Journal's* reports of 5 and 6 October 1945, Home Poll. File No. 98/45-Poll(I) of 1945, N.A.I.
503. *Ibid.*
504. Gail Omvedt, "The Satara Prati-Sarkar", in Gyanendra Pandey (ed.), *The Indian Nation in 1942*, Calcutta, 1988, p. 248.
505. *Ibid.*, pp. 246-7.
506. *Ibid.*, pp. 248 and 254.
507. Home (Sp.) Department, File No. 50 I(a) of 1945-6, Maharashtra State Archives, Bombay.
508. Gail Omvedt, "The Satara Prati-Sarkar", in Gyanendra Pandey (ed.), *The Indian Nation in 1942*, Calcutta, 1988, p. 248.
509. Home Poll. Fortnightly Report for 1st half of January 1944, File No. 18/1/44. N.A.I.

arose over a sudden increase by the *Zamindar* in the fees for the collection of fire-wood and the grazing of cattle in lands which were deemed to be his. The resentment against this arbitrary increase, which was to the detriment of all, including the poor, led soon to its wholesale defiance, and to a full-scale anti-*Zamindari* agitation. The negotiated settlement that the District Collector tried to bring about in March 1945 appeared to have failed to satisfy the contesting parties.[510] Not being sure of success in a direct physical confrontation with the *kisans*, the *Zamindar* decided thereafter to take the matter to the civil court, and to allow the *status quo* to continue in the mean time. Almost similar *Zamindari* high-handedness resulted in June 1944 at Kanbhaipur, Kaira, in an agitation of the under-tenants, who refused to till lands in protest against the *Zamindar's* unilateral increase in rent.[511] Seeing large stretches of land uncultivated, the alarmed authorities pressurised the *Zamindar* to come to some understanding with the local Khedut Sangh. Such enforced settlement was, however, not reached in the dispute over the produce-rent between the landowners-cum-landlords and their tenants-at-will at Mannargudi in the rice-rich district of Tanjore, where the local officials — true to their salt — sided with the feudal exploiters. Matters, which actually started in April 1944,[512] came to a head in June 1944 when the tenants-at-will, at the instance of the local Kisan Sanghams, refused to take up lands for cultivation, except on better terms,[513] and became involved in a number of minor clashes with the landlord's men. Seeing the flare up, the authorities prepared themselves elaborately for "rigorous measures" against the Communist *kisan* activists of the area, and provided the landlords, and their imported labour from outside, with full police protection.[514] Even then the agitation at Mannargudi did not show any sign of a let up,[515]

510. *Ibid.*, 1st half of March 1945, File No. 18/3/45, N.A.I.
511. *Ibid.*, 2nd half of June 1944, File No. 18/6/44, N.A.I.
512. *Ibid.*, 2nd half of April 1944, File No. 18/4/44, N.A.I.
513. D.O. No. P. 4-11, 7 June 1944, Public (G) Department, Government of Fort St. George, Tamil Nadu State Archives, Madras.
514. Home Poll. Fortnightly Reports for 1st and 2nd halves of June 1944, File Nos. 18/6/44. N.A.I.
515. *Ibid.*, 2nd half of October 1944, File No. 18/10/44, N.A.I.

and it in fact continued in full force in March 1945,[516] rising to a high pitch in August 1945 over the externment of two of its leaders from the area.[517]

Mannargudi had its echoes in certain other parts of the country, such as in Ganjam district of Orissa, where the Communist *kisan* workers led the under-tenants in June 1945 against the *Mustajars*,[518] in Gorakhpur and Banaras, eastern U.P., where they rallied the *Sir kisans* against the "large scale ejectment proceedings" initiated by the *Zamindars*,[519] and in Jalpaiguri, Bengal, where they seemed to be "inciting" the *Adhiars* against the *Jotedars*.[520] The newly awakened militancy of the Communists on the *kisan* front, however, was reflected best in the Shovna area of Khulna district, Bengal. In the heydays of the "grow more food" campaign, about 15,000 *bighas* of water-logged lands at Kadamtala, Balabuna and Badurgachha villages were reclaimed through the joint efforts of the local Samiti and the *Zamindar*.[521] These lands were settled with the landless peasants for making them arable on the understanding that the *Zamindar* would not eject the tillers if they paid him one-half share of the crops. With the approach of the harvesting season in 1944, however, the *Zamindar*, Rai Bahadur Sailendra Nath Ghosh, was found to be planning ejectment of the tillers from the reclaimed lands, negotiating fresh lease for these with others, and bringing in *lathials* from Faridpur to take possession of the crops by force.[522] The Samiti, under the leadership of Bishnu Chatterjee, swiftly went into action, rallied 3,500 *kisans* on 27 December 1944, and harvested all the crops in the presence of the *Zamindar's lathials* and the authorities' police force, who

516. *Ibid.*, 2nd half of March 1945, File No. 18/3/45, N.A.I.
517. *Ibid.*, 1st half of August 1945, File No. 18/8/45, N.A.I.
518. *Ibid.*, 1st half of June 1945, File No. 18/6/45, N.A.I.
519. *Report on the General Administration of the United Provinces*, Lucknow, 1945, p. 21.
520. Home Poll. Fortnightly Report for 2nd half of March 1945, File No. 18/3/45, N.A.I.
521. *People's War* (English weekly), 16 January 1944.
522. *Ibid.*, 3 June 1945.

did not dare to challenge the enraged *kisans*.[523] Such massive *kisan* action, in the face of the *Zamindari* hirelings and the *Sarkari* policemen, reminded one of the *Bakasht* peasants' delirious defence of their crops in 1938-9. Curiously enough, despite the repeated anti-*Zamindari* and anti-fedual clarion calls of Swami Sahajanand and Jadunandan Sharma, notably in Tirhut and Gaya,[524] and barring a minor agitation against the Dumraonraj in Buxar,[525] the hitherto turbulent Bihar countryside remained more or less placid throughout 1944-5. The reason behind such unusual quietude could not wholly be the misty gloom that the official repressions and the nationalist frustrations had cast over it in the post-"Quit India" movement days. Partly, and perhaps decisively, the brewing up of dissension among the builders of the *kisan* movement there did also contribute.

The Communists, who had controlled the Bihar Provincial Kisan Sabha since the beginning of 1943 with the blessings of Swami Sahajanand, were seen between 1944 and 1945 to be falling clearly apart from him and his followers. Initially when the Swami, like Yajnik, resented (in the A.I.K.S. Central Council meeting in Bombay) in August 1943 the C.P.I.'s use of the Kisan Sabha solely as a platform for preaching its own brand of politics, or for imposing on *kisans* its exclusive doctrinaire slogans, without even paying a lip service to the *kisan* causes,[526] the Communists tried to assuage his feelings through a formal recognition of the separate existence of the Kisan Sabha, independent of the C.P.I, and by the promise of sparing the Sabha from being utilised as their propaganda vehicle.[527] At the beginning of 1944, however, especially in the wake of a highly successful Bezwada Conference of the A.I.K.S., the Communists seemed to have shed all their apologetic pretensions towards the Swami, and they were seen to be openly and bitingly critical

523. *Ibid.* The issue was later put by the District Magistrate of Khulna before an Arbitration Committee for settlement.
524. Home Poll. Fortnightly Reports for 1st and 2nd halves of October 1944, File No. 18/10/44, N.A.I.
525. *Ibid.*, 1st half of December 1944, File No. 18/12/44, N.A.I.
526. Report of Intelligence Bureau, Home Ministry, Government of India, September 1943, Home Poll. File No. 7/23/1943, N.A.I.
527. *Ibid.*

of him the moment he aired his views in favour of the resumption of *kisan* agitations. They believed the Swamiji was being ultra-revolutionary primarily to cover up his inability "to recover from the shock of the post-9 August 1942 repressions".[528] Sahajaṇand, on his part, attempted at currying favour with the Congressmen of all sorts, particularly in Bihar, in the false hope of bringing them into the Sabha, and neutralising with their help the Communist influence over it.[529] He appeared suddenly to have forgotten altogether how little the Congressmen — generally sympathetic towards the landlords — shared his concern for the well-being of the rural poor. There were even rumours that Swami Sahajanand was contemplating either of disengaging the Bihar Provincial Kisan Sabha from the Communist-dominated A.I.K.S., or of setting up a separate organisation of *kisans* with the help of the Congress.[530] The rupture finally came in March 1945 when Swamiji, the President of the A.I.K.S, found the Communists to be going back on their word, and propagating their controversial line on the "Pakistan" issue[531] among *kisans*. In anger he suspended his General Secretary (Bankim Mukherji), the entire central office of the A.I.K.S., the whole of the B.P.K.S. and some district committees in Bengal for using the Kisan Sabha to achieve the Communist political ends, and the Central Kisan Council, in retaliation,

528. *People's War* (English weekly), 26 March 1944.
529. Home Poll. Fortnightly Reports for 1st and 2nd halves of February 1945, File No. 18/2/45, N.A.I.
530. *Ibid.*, 1st half of March 1945, File No. 18/3/45, N.A.I.
531. The C.P.I. believed, on the basis of the Soviet Union's example, that India — being a multi-lingual and multi-national country — should establish a genuinely democratic and voluntary federation of peoples in which the nationalities should have the right to secede. The belief did not allow the party to become averse to the concept of Muslims' seceding from the rest of India, if they so desired, and consequently to the creating of a kind of Pakistan under the Muslim League banner. This line of thinking resulted in the Communists' searching , between 1942 and 1946, for the "progressives" in the League ranks, their equating the League's role with that of the Congress so far as opposition to imperialism was concerned, and their demanding for an anti-British joint front of the League and the Congress.

censured him for all these highly "irresponsible acts".[532] The break-up had adversely affected not only the *kisan* movement in Bihar, but also the political standing of the Communists all over the Indian countryside. Isolated from the nationalist public opinion, they were already facing some obstruction on the *kisan* front from their opponents, as well as the erstwhile allies. The Congress-led Gram Seva Sangham had in fact threatened in 1943 to undermine their position in Malabar, though unsuccessfully at the end.[533] The Kirti Kisan group in the Punjab was fighting the members of the C.P.I. ceaselessly in 1943 for a hold over the Punjabi *kisans*.[534] Unlike Yajnik, whose departure from the A.I.K.S had halted the progress of the *kisan* movement in Gujarat, but who nevertheless did not wilfully challenge the position of the Communists, Ranga and his Ryots' Association had put up the stiffest and the longest opposition to the Communist activists in Andhra from January 1944 onwards.[535] In an unfavourable situation like this, where friends were becoming scarcer and foes more numerous, only the rank sectarians among the Communists could think of parting company with Swami Sahajanand and his followers. That the Communist *kisan* leaders and workers chose exactly to do so, despite warnings from some of the front-ranking among them,[536] betrays more their pride in the conquest of the Kisan Sabha organisational structure than their concern for unitedly organising the *kisan* masses. Unitedly, or not, the poor in the rural sector could still be

532. *People's War* (English weekly), 18 March 1945.
533. Home Poll. Fortnightly Reports for 2nd half of July and 2nd half of October 1943, File Nos. 18/7/43 and 18/10/43, N.A.I.
534. *Ibid.*, 2nd half of September and 2nd half of November 1943, File Nos. 18/9/43 and 18/11/43, N.A.I.
535. *Ibid.*, 1st half of January and 2nd half of September 1944, and also 1st half of January and 1st half of March 1945, File Nos. 18/1/44, 18/9/44, 18/1/45 and 18/3/45, N.A.I.
536. E.M.S. Namboodiripad and P.C. Joshi felt that "the general tendency of our comrades is to popularize party policy and build up party organisation and to palm them off as Kisan Sabha policy and Kisan Sabha organisation. This is one of the factors which scares non-party patriots...and leads to ... frictions between Swamiji and ourselves. We must fight this sectarian tendency." See E.M.S. Namboodiripad's "Bezwada Session of A.I.K.S.: What Next?", *Party Letter* (printed), Vol. IV, no. 7, 31 May 1944, Party Documents, Central Archives, Ajoy Bhavan, New Delhi.

mobilised even with a sectarian approach, and this happened to be true to an extent in 1944-5 in the case of the agricultural labourers.

The Kisan Samitis' espousal of the agricultural labourer's demand for higher wages in Bengal, and the agitation they were able to build up there in the various districts in 1944-5, led to some increase in the *khetmajdoors'* daily income. It rose from the average rate prevailing all over Bengal, i.e. 8 to 10 annas a day with one meal, to daily Rs. 2 without a meal in Midnapore, Rs. 2½ in Chittagong and Rs 2 in Tippera.[537] The demand for higher wages was also the central issue over which the Communist *kisan* activists succeeded in organising the agricultural labourers in some of the Andhra districts. The outcome was a spurt of confrontations between the labourers and their employers in a number of places, notably in the Amalapuram area of East Godavari, where a clash in May 1944 resulted in the death of one, and injury to some others.[538] Almost similarly over the clamour for a wage-rise, the *kisan* agitators were successful in organising the agricultural labourers in Chingleput district, Tamil Nadu, and leading their strikes gainfully in the first half of 1945.[539] In the same vein the Communists (spearheaded by P.T. Punnose and Verghese Vaidyan) managed to mobilise the agricultural labourers of Kuttanad, Travancore — the majority of whom came from such outcastes as Pulayas and Parayas. Their struggle for higher wages, as well as for social justice, continued practically throughout 1944, and geared up in the process the Karshaka Tozhilali Sanghams with 6,000 members.[540] A more serious, far-reaching, and also a more long-lasting Communist-led agitation, however, unfolded itself in Thana district of Maharashtra, among the Worlis who uniquely combined in themselves the wage and bondage labour, as well as the sharecropping serfdom.

537. Home Poll. Fortnightly Report for 1st half of June 1945, File No. 18/6/45 N.A.I.
538. D.O. No. P.4-11, 8 June 1944, Public (G) Department, Government of Fort St. George, Tamil Nadu State Archives, Madras.
539. Home Poll. Fortnightly Report for 1st half of August 1945, File No. 18/8/45.
540. *People's War* (English weekly), 22 April 1945.

The Worlis were the majority among the 1,50,000 strong *Adivasi* inbabitants of the hilly, forest tracts in Umbergaon, Dahanu and Palghar *taluks* of Thana district in Maharashtra. They in fact constituted 55 per cent of the total population in Umbergaon and Dahanu, and owned at one time most of the lands of the entire region. Following the advent of British rule in the area, the Worlis lost in about 80 years or so almost all their lands to the *sowcars*-landlords, who infiltrated the place from outside under the protection of the Raj, and systematically expropriated — with the connivance of its local officers, police and law-courts — all that the tribal *kisans* possessed. In the main the land-grabbing was effected either through unscrupulous practices in lending money to the Worlis, or by forcibly obtaining their thumb impressions on specially designed land deeds. Besides, at the time of the first survey settlement, the revenue officials, who were heavily bribed, transferred to the *sowcars*-landlords a lot of lands without the Worlis' knowledge. Times of scarcities and famines also compelled the Worlis to part with their lands for paltry sums of money, or small amounts of grains. The extent of expropriation and land alienation was so much that by the 1930s the Worlis were left with 6.8 per cent and 2.2 per cent of the total cultivated lands in Dahanu and Umbergaon *taluks*, respectively.[541] After robbing the Worli of his land, the *sowcar*-landlord usually settled him as a tenant-at-will, by dividing the plot into two parts, retaining the more fertile one for personal cultivation, or as a *Khas*, and giving the less fertile one to the tenant on sharecropping basis, provided the tenant tilled the *Khas* without remuneration. Since sharecropping had been made conditional on the free tilling of the *Khas*, and its ploughing, reaping and harvesting to be undertaken first, the arrangement was appopriately described as a serf-tenure, and the Worli serf — in his role of a sharecropper — received the same raw deal that sharecroppers and under-tenants everywhere got from their landlords, namely, the curtailment of his share by using fraudulent weights, deducting grain loans (*Khavatis*) at

541. D. Symington, Report on the Aboriginal Hill Tribes of Bombay, Bombay, 1939, cited in S.V. Parulekar, *Revolt of the Varlis*, Bombay, 1947, pp. 4-6.

50 per cent interest and charging various feudal levies. He and his family also had to offer all kinds of free services to his landlord, supplying fire-wood, bringing water, carrying milk and working as domestic servants. The *sowcars*-landlords, who owned extensive grass lands, and took lease of forests from the Government, engaged the Worlis in the dry season as labourers for cutting grass and felling trees at the lowest possible wages. The Worli was thus a serf, a sharecropper and a wage-labourer, all rolled into one, and in a slight turn of luck he could also become a bonded labourer for life. This status he would earn by borrowing some cash from the *sowcar*-landlord at the time of a certain need (usually on the occasion of a marriage ceremony), and by agreeing to repay it with interest through hard labour for a stipulated long period. The number of bonded labourers, or the "marriage slaves" as they were popularly called, seemed to have been quite numerous.[542] The pitiable circumstances of the Worlis, who lived and suffered barely 80 miles away from the city of Bombay, could not have wholly been missed either by the authorities or by the political workers. Yet, only a philanthropic organisation, initiated by the ex-Prime Minister of Bombay, B.G. Kher, in 1940 — the Adivasi Seva Mandal — took a reformist interest in the Worli uplift by calling for changes in their modes of life, challenging superstitions, spreading education and offering medical services. However well-meaning and civilising, the Mandal could not make much headway in ameliorating the condition of *Adivasi* life, primarily because of its reluctance to touch any of the basic ills that plagued the Worlis — the serfdom, the low wages and the bondages — lest the powerful *sowcars*-landlords should raise a hue and cry against it. In consequence, the conditions not only remained the same in kind, but actually deteriorated by degrees during the inflationary war years.

It was the highest price for the meanest necessaries of life against the lowest possible daily wage (one anna a day)[543] that finally broke the silence in the forests of Thana. In November 1944 the Worlis of Umbergaon *taluk* refused to fell trees and

542. *Ibid.*, pp. 6-17.
543. *Ibid.*, p. 30.

cut grass unless the *sowcars*-landlords increased their wages to annas 12 a day.[544] The strike, an autonomous action on the lines of the agitation of Santhal *Bataidars* of Purnea in 1940-1, and similarly encouraged by a sympathetic individual, K.J. Save, a Government appointed Assistant Backward Class Officer, continued for more than six weeks, in which 3,000 *kisans* participated under the leadership of Mahiya Dhangada and Deodhekar.[545] The resistance eventually fizzled out when the local authorities pressurised Save to desert the Worlis, the Mandal turned too anxious to persuade them to resume work, and none came forward to take their side.[546] The strike did not succeed, but the Worlis learnt their lessons in unity and struggle, and attracted the attention of the leftists. Unlike their neglect of the Santhal *Bataidars*, the Gonds and the Savaras in the early 1940s, the leftists, or to be more precise the Communists, lost no time in inviting 15 Worli representatives from Umbergaon to the Maharashtra Kisan Sabha Conference at Titawala near Kalyan on 7 January 1945,[547] and rushing in volunteers into the area under the guidance of young Mrs. Godavari Parulekar, who lived with the *kisans* from February 1945, propagated ideology among them, and inspired them to stand up against the brow-beating *sowcars*-landlords through her own example.[548] The Worli response to Godavari and company was instantaneous, and it crystallised at the Umbergaon Taluk Kisan Conference held on 23 May 1945 — the day the Worli liberation was said to have commenced. The large gathering of *kisans* (5,000 according to the Communist sources, and 2,500 in the opinion of the Government officials) decided to abolish serf-tenure and forced labour, and resolved not to cultivate the private lands of the *sowcars*-landlords unless they paid a daily wage of 12 annas, and not to render them any free service. Within a day of the

544. *Ibid.*, p. 31.
545. *People's War* (English weekly), 24 June 1945.
546. Leslie J. Calman, "Congress Confronts Communism, Thana District, 1945-47", *Modern Asian Studies*, Vol. 21, no. 2, 1987, pp. 332-3.
547. *People's War* (English weekly), 4 February 1945.
548. Leslie J. Calman, "Congress Confronts Communism, Thana District, 1945-47", *Modern Asian Studies*, Vol.21, no. 2, 1987, pp. 333-4.

conclusion of the Conference, its resolutions were orally communicated to each *kisan* family in the *taluk*, and forced labour and free services were stopped in Umbergaon in a few weeks. In the month of June 1945 itself — the month the rainy season had set in — the institution of serf-tenure collapsed, with the *kisans* bluntly refusing to cultivate the *Khas* without the wages, and the *sowcars*-landlords agreeing, under the pressure of circumstances, to concede to the demand. Close on the heels of such momentous developments in Umbergaon, came the upheaval in Dahanu *taluk* where the problem of debt-slavery, or "marriage slavery", was most acute. Before Godavari and her associates could manage to reach Dahanu from Umbergaon, and organise the *kisan* movement there, the Worlis started gathering on their own, and following such meetings at Akharmal and Narpud early in September 1945, which were attended by thousands, processions had been taken out in all parts of the *taluk*. As they marched along, the processionists stopped at the doors of the landlords' houses, called out the debt-slaves by their names to join them, and about 3,000 men and women came out of their bondage to follow the processionists.[549] Thus in a short span of four months the Worli *kisans* won memorable victories, by uprooting serf-tenure, ending forced labour and emancipating the debt-slaves. They wanted to go further, and in the first week of October 1945 — when the season for cutting grass approached — the Worlis, under the banner of the Kisan Sabha, declined to work unless Rs. 2½ were paid for cutting 500 pounds of grass. On the *sowcars*-landlords' refusal to pay the amount, began a strike in both Umbergaon and Dahanu *taluks*, and not a single Worli was available for grass-cutting. Various retaliatory measures against the strikers, such as lodging false complaints against them and their leaders in the criminal courts, stopping *Khavati* advances to *kisans* and pressurising the district authorities for the suppression of the strike, having failed, the *sowcars*-landlords hatched an ingenious plot to so contrive the law and order situation as to lead to a Worli-police clash. They spread the rumour through their hirelings that Godavari was due to hold

549. *People's War* (English weekly), 29 October 1945.

an important meeting at Talawada village in Umbergaon *taluk* at the midnight of 10 October 1945 where each Worli must be present, preferably with *lathis*, sickles and axes to counter any possible landlord attempt at causing disturbance. Simultaneously they informed the police that a violent and armed mob was scheduled to collect at Talawada with the intention of launching surprise murderous attacks on the lives and properties of landlords.[550] The trick worked with remarkable ease, for the Worli *kisans* took the rumoured call for the meeting to be true — not knowing that Godavari was actually lying ill at that very point in Kalyan[551] — and started gathering at the appointed place throughout the night. Before the Kisan Sabha organisers could comprehend what really was happening, the police, as anticipated, arrived on the scene in full force in the night itself. Presuming the gathering to be violent, and panicking at its large number (nearing 30,000), the police commanded it to disperse, and on refusal, opened fire on it repeatedly between the morning and the afternoon of the 11th. The firing seemed not only "indiscriminate", but also unprovoked, for there was no evidence at all of the Worlis' turning violent in any way, either before or after the attacks, or of a single policeman being hurt in the whole gory episode.[552] Despite the death of five among them, and injury to many more, the defiant Worli *kisans* refused to leave the unfurled red flag at the venue, and disperse, till their Kisan Sabha leaders addressed them. On being informed of the tragic development, Kamalakar Ranadive, the Communist activist from Khatalwada, had to hurry through 12 miles to reach Talawada, and inform the waiting *kisans* of the deception they were subjected to.[553] It was only after hearing him at about 3 p.m. — subsequent to their gathering for 15 long and trying hours — that the Worlis finally left the scene for their homes, in a dejected mood, of course, but feeling steeled as they had never felt before.

550. S.V. Parulekar, *Revolt of the Varlis*, Bombay,1947, pp. 43-5.
551. Godavari Purulekar, *Revolt of the Warlis*, New Delhi, 1986, All India Kisan Sabha, Golden Jubilee Series, 1936-86, no. 1, p. 17.
552. Statement of the Adivasi Seva Mandal, *Bombay Chronicle*, 25 October 1945.
553. S.V. Parulekar *Revolt of the Varlis*, Bombay, 1947, p. 45.

The Worli *kisans*' steadfast attachment to their cause was apparent from the manner they continued the struggle against all odds, and in spite of every act of official repression. On 13 October 1945 came the banning of meetings, processsions and assemblies in the whole area under the D.I.R. Two days later (on 15 October) six Communist leaders of the Worlis (including Godavari) were externed from Thana district, followed by the arrest of more than 100 *kisans*,[554] the merciless beatings of suspected agitators and the total terrorisation of the entire populace, forcing a sizable section of it to take refuge in the forests.[555] And yet the *kisans* persisted with their wholesale refusal to undertake grass-cutting work, stuck to their demand for wage increase, clamoured for the release of their arrested brethren, and insisted on the withdrawal of the Communist leaders' externment. Such indomitable resistance was bound to produce some results — the authorities' rescinding the externment order on 25 October, the landlords' acquiescing in the wage increase and the police's freeing *kisans* held on trumped up charges. Hardly had any victory of the rural masses over the feudal-bureaucratic alliance been more obvious and sweeping in India than that of the Worlis of *Thana* — the backwater of both the *kisan* and the left movements. Rumblings were also being clearly heard throughout 1944-5 in another such backwater — in the Telengana countryside of Hyderabad state — but nobody seemed to have the sensitised hearing to catch and spot these till they became explosive in July 1946.

What appeared to be taking place in the rural Telengana at this point was an articulation of popular disapproval of the authorities' forcible war-time "levy" of grains. The "levy" on grain producers at an arbitrarily low price was an essential part of the Government policy of insurance against the scarcities from 1943, and finding the measure to be contrary to their pecuniary interests, *kisans* generally resented it. The resentment, however, had not exactly been vociferously expressed, except

554. Leslie J. Calman, "Congress Confronts Communism, Thana District, 1945-47", *Modern Asian Studies*, Vol. 21, no.2, 1987, p. 336.
555. S.V. Parulekar, *Revolt of the Varlis*, Bombay, 1947, p. 48

such sporadically mild protests as in Midnapore in Bengal,[556] in certain parts of Andhra,[557] and in specific areas of Surat in south Gujarat.[558] In comparison, the protest was more distinct in Telengana where the Nizam's Government introduced the "levy" in October 1943 by fixing a quota per acre, and by purchasing the "levied" grains through a state-controlled Hyderabad Commercial Corporation. The actual collection of the "levy" was left to the local officials at a price lower than the rate prevailing in the surrounding British-Indian territories. Consequently, the "levy" prompted some smuggling of grains from Telengana, and it also led soon to large scale falsification of crop returns, misrepresentation of lands producing crops and various irregularities in the weighing of procured grains. The landlords in Telengana invariably succeeded, with the help of their position of power, and in collusion with the rural officialdom, in lessening their burden of the "levy", and in increasing it disproportionatley on the peasantry. The "levy" in fact deprived the substantial peasants of the profits from their surpluses, and the unsubstantial ones of the food for their subsistence. In retrospect at a later stage, the Revenue and Police minister of Hyderabad state conceded that the village officials compelled the poor peasants, having barely enough for family consumption, to part with half their stock of grains. He further confirmed that the "levying" process was dominated by the landlords and other influential persons of "good castes", who evaded it with the connivance of the village officials. In many cases, he also felt, the peasants did not even receive the money the authorities spent as price.[559] The *kisans*' grievances against the "levy" soon attracted the attention of the local Communist activists, who in 1944 decided to raise their voice in opposition to the injustices and malpractices

556. Home Poll. Fortnightly Report for 2nd half of March 1944, File No. 18/3/44, N.A.I.
557. *Ibid.*, 2nd half of October 1944, File No. 18/10/44, N.A.I.
558. *Ibid.*, 1st half of November 1944, File No.18/11/44, N.A.I.
559. Report to H.E.H. The Nizam's Government on the Communist Agitation in Hyderabad State, W.W. Griegson, Revenue and Police Member, 5.12.46, Proceedings, Ministry of States, Government of India, File No. 15 P (S), 1947, N.A.I.

involved with its collection.[560] The protestation over the "levy" issue, which threatened to assume the proportion of a campaign in 1945, was, however, a mere flicker of the conflagration that was being aflame to blaze Telengana.

560. Amit Kumar Gupta, "The Communists and the Outbreak of the Telengana Rising, May 1944-February 1947", in Amit Kumar Gupta (ed.), *Myth and Reality: The Struggle for Freedom in India, 1945-47*, New Delhi, 1987, pp. 463-4.

THE RAISONNEUR'S MONOLOGUE

In 1944-5 the rural poor and the leftists, especially the Communists, despite all their sectarianism, seemed to be inclined once again, after years of their marooned and mired existence, for taking a joint stride forward. Any taking off bid, or poising to get in motion, has a certain grandeur about it, and much of such grandeur in 1945 was stolen clearly by the determined Worli *kisans*. Their craving for emancipation, their rising in unexceptionable unison and their great urgency for forging ahead like a disciplined army (who hardly turned violent at any stage) — were perhaps unparalleled in the history of the Kisan Sabha movement. And so also were the high degree of their success, the phenomenal speed of their achieving it and the loyalty with which they followed their mentors. The Worli *kisans'* crowding around the red flag on 11 October at Talawada in the face of police firings, their refusal to disperse on that day until the leaders came and addressed them, and their compelling the authorities soon thereafter to withdraw the externment order on some of the leading "outsiders" — were proofs of the faith they had placed on the Communist *kisan* activists. The faith apparently was not misplaced in any way, and Godavari and her associates did rise to the occasion, identify precisely the issues of the Worli struggle, and inspire the *kisans* to undertake it, even with the probability of its leading to a headlong clash with the landlord-bureaucracy combine. It was not easy for the Communists — howsoever safely positioned in the obscurity of the Thana forests — to do all this, and stick to the Worlis within the banal but yet unbroken "people's war" framework. What Godavari and her fellow Kisan Sabhaites, however, could not manage to do was to keep pace with the speed at which the *kisans* succeeded in spreading the agitation among themselves, and in taking such bold, autonomous initiatives as in Dahanu *taluk* over the issue of bondage. Nobody realised it better than the Communist *kisan* activists, who admitted that the role of the

Kisan Sabha in the upsurge was "less important", and "secondary" to the role played by "the Varlis themselves".[561] It was the *kisans*' exercise of autonomy in an age of ideologues and ideologies, operating, of course, along the Communist-charted route, that rendered the Worlis' to become one of the outstanding peasant struggles in India.

561. S.V. Parulekar, *Revolt of the Varlis*, Bombay, 1947, pp. 41-2.

Act Three
1946-51

THE SETTING

With the quietening of the guns on the front and the bombers in the sky, and following the clearance of the mushroomed atomic clouds over Hiroshima and Nagasaki, the post-war world in 1946 appeared to have drastically, and intractably changed. While Germany, Italy and Japan lay demonstrably prostrate in the battlefield, France and Britain — who managed to survive by hair-breadth, and staggered precariously out of it — were committed agonisingly for some time to the exclusive nursing of their own wounds. Those who arose upright from the ashes and dusts of the arena were the United States and the Soviet Union, the former to reorganise the world capitalist system, and resuscitate the wounded and the fallen, and the latter to carve out a niche in eastern Europe for a parallel socialistic system. The birth-pang of another socialistic state could also be felt in China where the civil war resumed with renewed vigour. What, however, seemed to be most distinctive was the phenomenal rise of an anti-imperialist fervour among the colonised people, whether they were Iraqis or Syrians in west Asia, Egyptians or Lybyans in north Africa, Ghanaians or Guineans in west Africa, Argentinians or Chileans in south America. The intensity of feeling also heightened in south-east Asia, where Vietnamese and Indonesians furiously resisted the restoration of the French and the Dutch regimes. Indians were similarly expected to shake the entire edifice of colonial rule in south Asia by their imminent tearing off the shackles of bondage. The whole of the world, including Britain itself, realised that a war-ravaged, exhausted metropolitan country would not be able to hold India even for a short time, and that the final confrontation between the Indian people and the Raj could far exceed the earlier one in August 1942, and perhaps go beyond the bulldozing capacities of a restless army, a tense police and an over-stretched civilian "steel frame".

The recruitment of Britons in the Indian Civil Service seemed to have receded rapidly before their enlistment for the military services, and the British entry into the cadre had practically stopped at the height of the war in 1943. Besides, the sparsely populated I.C.S. as a cadre — a minority of whom only were loyal Europeans (numbering 587) alongside a majority of potentially "unreliable" Indians (numbering 614) — had already been so greatly harassed by such crisis management duties as holding the prices, ensuring the supplies, hunting the "fifth columnists", sounding the air-raid signals and enforcing the "black-outs", over and above its ever increasing daily executive and judicial chores, that it was not in a position in the mid-1940s to carry on for long without being turned into a wreck. The picture that the Indian military personnel presented (in the army, navy and air force) in 1946 was even worse with its European elements hankering for demobilisation — for an opportunity to go home — rather than staying on indefinitely in India, and with its Indian elements growing restive over the pay and the discriminatory treatment meted out to them, especially in the wake of the popular outcry in November 1945 over the issue of the Indian National Army, or the Red Fort trial of their comrades-in-arms who "deserted" to the side of Subhas Chandra Bose's national Government in exile. The condition of the police was also not quite comforting to the authorities, for its rank and file felt aggrieved on account of inadequate salaries, sub-standard rations and bossy hierarchical misbehaviours. Their coming in touch with certain left political activists, and attempts at some form of trade-unionism in Bihar, Bengal, Assam, Madras and Bombay in the first half of 1946,[1] culminated in March 1947 into a full-scale police "mutiny" in Bihar (notably in Gaya, Munghyr and Patna) that was suppressed only with the help of the army, and that, too, after the spilling of an amount of blood.[2] Only a mummified

1. Home Poll. Fortnightly Reports from January to June 1946, File Nos. 18/1/46 to 18/6/46, N.A.I.
2. Report of the Chief Intelligence Officer, Bihar, 5 April 1947, Home Poll. File No. 7/4/47 Poll (I) Secret, 1947, N.A.I. It is a pity that the police "mutiny", led by Ramanand Tiwari, did not receive the degree of historians' attention that it truly deserved.

arch-imperialist like Winston Churchill, the leader of the British War Cabinet, refused to see what even an unfeeling Wavell, the penultimate Viceroy, seemed to have seen in the post-war Indian scenario, and later recorded: "Our time in India is limited, and our power to control events almost gone. We have only prestige and previous momentum to tread on and they will not last long".[3]

The position clearly was that the second world war had in its sequel brought about a change in the old colonial order, and opened up the possibility of a new one. It was no longer practicable for a war-weary country like Britain to bear the burden of ruling over an unruly colony, such as the vast Indian sub-continent, and yet overdraw all the geo-political, military and economic advantages from it. In the face of stubborn Indian opposition, the systematised use of India's economy — to further Britain's global trade interests — had also become inconvenient, if not impossible. Supplying the bulk of India's imports had already slipped out of the British to the American hands, and India's "Sterling Debts" to Britain (on account of its "governance") was liquidated to meet the cost of British war supplies from India. The cost of Indian supplies did not stop there, it in fact forced Britain to become indebted to India for about 3,300 million pound — the famed "Sterling Balance". India was no more a protected field for the expatriate entrepreneurship, and for the civil and military careers of Britons. To hold India even then by the sheer use of force — for the sake of imperial glory only, if not for anything else — was wholly unrealistic in view of the steadily dwindling strength of a run-down Raj. Its revival would have necessitated such massive doses of reinforcements in men, money and material, and so much care, as Britain was incapable of undertaking in its prevailing state of economy. Besides, why should capitalism in Britain permit an enormous investment that was not only downright bad, but frankly and utterly ruinous? The classical

3. Wavell, *The Viceroy's Journal*, Oxford, 1973, p. 368.

form of colonialism, which had so hysterically been upheld by the Churchillians, thus being rendered demonstrably untenable, would the British colonialists give up their colonial advantages from India without trying, howsoever feebly and day-dreamingly, to find a way-out, particularly when the blue-prints epitomising such a way-out dangled all the time before their eyes?

The blue-prints for economically subjugating a people and a country, without correspondingly shouldering the loads of direct administration, were being drawn up in a number of places from the beginning of the twentieth century. Nowhere else had such endeavours been more successful than in Latin America — whether in its industrially germinating constituents like Mexico, Chile, Brazil, Argentina, Bolivia and Uruguay, or in its agriculturally contained portions like Guatemala, Honduras, Nicaragua, El Salvador, Costa Rica and Panama (the so-called "Banana Republics") — the region that the monopoly capitalists of the United States completely dominated. The domination was effected by seizing the Latin American foreign trade, manipulating land leases, credits and loans, extracting immunities of the U.S. imports and capital investments from taxation, foisting upon the people all sorts of puppet regimes and *juntas*, and founding the American military bases in their support. There was no reason why in certain colonised countries (especially those of multifarious social character) similar puppetry could not suitably be enacted, the colonialist effect maintained, and the onus for it shrugged off. A land and its diverse people could still be satellitecally placed, economically expropriated and militarily utilised, even after conceding to them political independence, if their diversities were somehow accentuated, and thereafter perpetuated, through the propping up of ineffectual and obliging ruling cliques. The possibility that the Indian nationalists might not be willing to play into the hands of the puppeteers, despite all the lure for political power, and the certainty that an internally sagging Britain could not again be in a position to dictate the world market, and assume the role of a world power, did not perhaps wholly dissuade the incorrigible romantics among the arbiters of British economic destiny from running their imagination to a wild neo-colonialist riot.[4] In terms of practical politics also Britain had little to hope against all odds, but to make a bid for safeguarding its favourable economic relations in the future, expectantly either with a loosely united, and pretendingly independent, Indian dominion of the disparately set forces, or with the artificially disunited, and seemingly freed, Indian dependencies of exaggerative divergences. Both these alternatives hinged for their realisation upon the successful playing up of the pluralities, and some of the contrarieties of the Indian people — a method which was likely to pay the British as much rich dividend in their tactical retreat from India as it certainly had done in their keeping aloft the standard of the Raj.

Of all the distinctions among Indians that the Raj had tried to magnify and make use of (such as between the British Indians and the States' people, the "martials" and the "non-martials", the tribals and the non-tribals, the urbanites and the non-urbanites, the Brahmins and the non-Brahmins), those between the followers of two long co-existing religions, Hinduism and Islam, or between the Hindu majority and the substantial Muslim minority, proved to be the most effective. On almost all of the public matters, the Raj had succeeded in subtly setting the one against the other, by acknowledging the Muslim League as the only representative body of the Indian Muslims, by casting

4. This, more or less, seemed to have been the general leftist perception in India in the immediate post-independence days, and it lingered on for quite sometime even thereafter. However, the recent historical researches on the subject in India and abroad, based quasi-imaginatively on the stereotyped administrative records of the Governments and papers of political dignitaries, have not so far corroborated it, though more discerning among their conductors did notice the British "illusion" of remaining a "world power" to have considerably influenced their decision to divide and quit. (See Partha Sarathi Gupta, "Imperial Strategy and the Transfer of Power" in Amiṭ Kumar Gupta (ed.), *Myth and Reality: The Struggle for Freedom in India, 1945-47*, New Delhi, 1987, pp. 42-3). The perception, by circumstantial evidence, seems so strong even today that it may still be well worth fresh enquiries into the British political economy of the latter half of the 1940s, as well as into the British capitalists' world views and strategies, on the basis of analyses of the files of British economic and financial ministries, the papers of the captains of British industries and the literature produced by their spokesmen.

doubts on the nationalist credentials of a "Hinduised" Indian National Congress, and by using the League as a political force to counter-balance the Congress. The way at the initial stage of the war the Raj utilised the League's demand for a separate homeland of the Indian Muslims (Pakistan) to thwart all constitutional negotiations with the Congress, the manner in which it allowed the League practically through the backdoor (in the absence of the Congress from the legislative scene on account of the "Quit India" movement) to take over some of the provincial ministries, and the sardonic pleasure with which its bureaucracy noted the spreading of the League's sphere of influence among Muslims with the aid of intrigues and dispersal of official patronages[5] — all seemed to point at the careful building up of a backlash that could retard the progress of the anti-imperialist movement. What, however, appeared to be the worst from an anti-imperialist standpoint — and contrary to the great nationalist expectations — was not that the League had been benefiting from the exercise of some political leverage under the Raj's shadow (which ended any way in North-West Frontier Province and Bengal, and continued precariously in Sind and Assam when the Congress M.L.As decided to return to the legislatures in 1945), but that its emotive scheme of a Pakistan for the Indian Muslims — the panacea for all their ills — had fast been attracting a very considerable following. The perplexed nationalist leaders did hardly know how to cope with the rising of a separatist tide, whether to blockade its way altogether, or to turn it accommodatively towards the main current. Their indignant, self righteous desire to do away with communalism simply through its denunciation, their criticism of the retrograde feudal leadership of the League and reluctance to understand the minority misgivings — howsoever substantiated or fabricated — failed palpably to stem the flow. Their fumbling about a strategy for winning over the Muslim masses, persistence

5. The elation of Cunningham, the N.W.F.P. Governor, at the League's success in the Frontier by-elections of 1943 is a pointer. See Baren Ray, "Pakhtun National Movement and Transfer of Power in India", in Amit Kumar Gupta (ed.), *Myth and Reality: The Struggle for Freedom in India, 1945-47,* Delhi, 1987, p. 239. Also see Sumit Sarkar, *Modern India, 1885-1947,* Delhi, 1983, p. 409.

with the speaking in Hinduistic idioms (such as, *Vande Mataram, Ram Rajya, Satyagraha*) and hesitancy in dealing strongly with the aggressive Hindus — allowed the League enough space for putting up politico-religious contrivances. It in fact had little difficulty in raising the bogey of a "Hindu Raj", imagining "Islam in danger" under its threats, and propounding the theory that Hindus and Muslims constituted two incompatible "nations". The educated Muslim middle classes and business interests readily supported the League's line, hoping that the severance of a part of the Indian sub-continent would spare them from the unequal competition with the long-standing and overbearing Hindu business houses and professionals. To this prospect of Muslim hegemony over jobs and business activities in a specified region, was added the Muslim peasantry's anxiety in the Punjab and Bengal for some relief in a future Pakistan from the Hindu *Bania* and *Zamindari* exploitation. Truly or fancifully, the League's support-base among the Indian Muslims had broadened so dramatically by 1946 that it afforded its Supremo, M.A. Jinnah, to assume — with unflinching British support — an increasingly obdurate bargaining posture *vis-a-vis* the Congress. Jinnah's growing obduracy was apparent as early as July 1944 when he set Gandhiji's belated initiative for a Congress-League rapprochement at naught, and refused to budge — even at the risk of jeopardising the unexceptionable claim for independence of all, including Hindus and Muslims — from his obsessive demand for a wholesome Pakistan (comprising of the Muslim majority provinces of Sind, the Punjab, Baluchistan, North-West Frontier, Bengal and Assam in their entirety). The situation seemed to have been tailor-made for dreaming neo-colonialist dreams, and their dreamers in Britain perhaps thought they could use it for creating either a disjointed, weak Indian federation, or two mutually distrusting, unstable states to their ulterior advantage. Howsoever distressing to the common man and woman, and disconcerting for their hopes and aspirations, the Pakistan issue was to dominate the Indian political scene throughout the second half of the 1940s, and particularly from August 1946 when the League's "direct action" for winning away Pakistan marked a new high in the inter-communal riots in Calcutta. It was in this backdrop of the communal tangle, the foreseeable termination of the Raj, and plausibly, the romanticisation of a future British stewardship in India, that the leftists and the rural poor staged in 1946-7 a memorable leap forward — the culmination of their taking off bid since 1945.

The mental preparation for the leap was fairly even so far as the rural poor had been concerned, mainly because they — like many others — could somehow sense the forthcoming closure of the Raj, its replacement by certain indigenous agencies, and the anti-feudal prospect that such transition might offer. The process, however, was not so evenly with the leftists, who could smell the Congress's preference for a negotiated settlement with the Raj — following the ice-breaking, and yet abortive, Simla Conference of June-July 1945 — rather than for a freshly fought out *fait accompli*, and felt uncertain whether any new wave of anti-feudalism, and even of anti-imperialism, would make much headway if the Congress had already set its eyes singularly on the negotiations, and brushed aside all ideas of agitational diversions. The tendency of the leftists in 1946, therefore, was to try to dissuade the Congress from its attempts at negotiations with the Raj, to turn it to the ways of "revolutionary struggle of the masses" (which "really" could put an end to imperialism in India),[6] and to remind it of the potentiality of the revolutionary fire (which "alone" could burn down "the edifices of imperialism, together with the edifices of communalism and feudalism").[7] Whether they were the Congress Socialists or the Forward Blocists, the Revolutionary Socialists or the Revolutionary Communists, the Bolsheviks or the Democratic Vanguards, their exhortations followed, more or less, the same line, and despite the anxiety for launching the "militant class struggles",[8] and championing the causes of the peasants' and workers' "class organisations",[9] they had still to look up to the

6. Narendra Deva, "The Common Man and the Congress", *Janata* (English weekly), 10 February 1946.
7. Jayaprakash Narayan's Sattement, *ibid.*, 26 January 1947.
8. *Programme and Post-War Revolution*, Draft Manifesto of the All-India Forward Bloc, Bombay, 1946, p. 46.
9. Narendra Deva, "The Common Man and the Congress", *Janata* (English weekly), 10 February 1946.

Congress on account either of their lingering linkage with it, or of the peripheral existence of their own. In spite of its isolation during the post-1942 phase, the C.P.I. was perhaps the only leftist party of some influence and significance, unlike the Radical Democratic Party of steadily paled insignificance, which could take a distinctly different position. Ironically, its very seclusion in effect seemed to have helped it to gain by 1945 an unprecedented organisational strength, due as much to the freedom to function in the "open", as to the opportunity to operate in a field relatively cleared of the Congress and the C.S.P. The total membership of the C.P.I. increased from 4,464 in 1941 to "well over 30,000" by the end of 1945,[10] with the control over the All India Trade Union Congress of nearly 5 lakh members, and the All India Kisan Sabha of 8 lakh strong. Its claim to have grown into the "third" largest political party in India, after the Congress and the League,[11] was perhaps not wholly absurd. The C.P.I. was also not formally obliged to maintain any connection with the Congress, following the differences it had since 1942, and the charges of anti-nationalism and anti-Congressism it faced, leading to the "resignation", as well as the "removal" of its representatives from the Congress in December 1945.[12] Even after its thus being freed from the burden of ties with the Congress, and placed at the vantage-point for signalling the masses towards some radical alternatives, the C.P.I. leadership did hardly show signs of its commitment to the "national democratic revolution" that it stood for, and of its determination to wrench any fresh initiative. Rather, it seemed to be quite content with its three years' habit of treating popular struggles lukewarmly, and with its newly bloated proportion of the party and mass organisations. In the narcissistic appreciation of their own strength, and in the exaggerated expectation of

10. "Communist Reply to the Congress Working Committee Charges", Bombay, December 1945, in P. Bandhu and T.G Jacob (eds.), *War and National Liberation, C.P.I. Documents, 1939-1945*, New Delhi, 1988, p. 271.

11. *Ibid.*, p. 353.

12 Resolution of the Congress Working Committee Meeting, Calcutta, 7-11 December 1945, N.N. Mitra (ed.), *Indian Annual Register*, 1945, Vol.II, p. 102.

their partnering the Congress and the League in a final settlement with the Raj, the Communist leaders raised the slogan of the "Congress-League-Communist Unity".[13] Their clamour for the formation of such a "joint front" became necessary also as a replacement for the outmoded policy of the "united front", whose fundamental dictum was to prosecute the anti-imperialist struggle in India under the aegis of the Congress, and which had, therefore, turned obsolete with the ouster of the Communists from it. What was interesting about the new "joint front" had not merely been the Communist leaders' appearing to be more agreeable to the negotiations with the Raj than to the renewal of the popular resistances against it, but their simultaneously betraying an elitist concern for recognition as at par with the counterparts in the Congress and the League, as well as for the achievement of Congress-League-Communist entente through agreements among the leaders at the top, or "from above", unlike the assiduous building up of the united front in the past among the ranks, or from "below". It was, however, the militant and the enthusiastic Communist ranks, not the Communist leaders — the district and the local committees, and not the Politbureau and the Central Committee — the field-workers, and not the policy pronouncers — that seemed really to have turned at this point the fortunes of the Communist movement in India.

Apparently the Communist rank and file, and their local front-runners, who were vigorously active since the blowing over of the "Quit India" movement, and relentlessly tried to attract the common man and woman, had by the latter half of 1945 managed to overcome most of the inhibitions and prohibitions of the erstwhile "peoples' war" policy. They were now anxious for making use of "any political agitation" which might arise on the national, agrarian and trade-union fronts, irrespective of its magnitude and intensity. Some of the close observers had in fact been struck by the readiness with which the Communists tried to recover their lost grounds, and by their remarkable

13. "Communist Reply to the Congress Working Committee Charges", Bombay, December 1945, in P. Bandhu and T.G. Jacob (eds.), *War and the National Liberation, C.P.I. Documents, 1939-1945,* New Delhi, 1988, p. 382.

survival of the "quandary" that the expulsion of the Communist representatives from the Congress was expected to produce.[14] The way the Communists led — in the context of the rising prices — such memorable strikes as the tramway workers' in Calcutta in September 1945, the press workers' in the C.P. and Berar in October 1945, the Kesoram Cotton Mill workers' pottery workers', and the Braithwaite factory workers' in Calcutta in December 1945, and the Birla mill workers' in Gwalior in January 1946, to name only few, the manner they threatened to lead the all-India strikes of the railway workers and the postal employes in December 1945, and the ease with which they rode thereafter on the crest of the unprecedented industrial actions all over the country,[15] were expressions enough of their pent-up militancy — of their impatience with the reformist excursions. Almost similar, though vastly more stirring in its popular sweep, was the Communists' espousal of the causes of anti-imperialistic urban outbursts — in Calcutta over the Red Fort trial in November 1945, in Calcutta again on the Rashid Ali Day in February 1946, in Bombay, Karachi and Madras about the same time in connection with the Royal Indian Navy revolt and the working class rising in support of it, in many parts of the country (including Lahore, Ahemedabad, Agra, Kanpur, Patna and Madurai) in protest against the Calcutta-Bombay-Karachi firings, and in Allahabad on the "ration-cut" issue that sparked off the popular fury of 80,000. The official policy of the Communist movement in India, however, still did not undergo any radical

14. "A Note on the Communist Infiltration in Indian Politics, with special reference to recent civil disorders in Bombay, Calcutta, Karachi, Madras and Lahore", 28 February 1946, New Delhi, a secret report prepared by the Home Dept., Government of India, Home Poll. File No. PR 1/103/46 of 1946, N.A.I.

15. The following table should bear out the enormity of the situation:

	1945	*1946*
Disputes	820	1,629
Workers Involved	7,47,530	19,61,948
Man-days Lost	40,54,499	1,27,17,762

(From: *The Indian Labour Year-Book, 1950-51*, p. 175.)

change, for, while the unmistakable proofs of its rank and file participation in the tumults forced the Raj to seriously contemplate (in the meeting of the provincial Governors) "the reimposition" of ban on the C.P.I.,[16] and when the ordinary party members and their sympathisers desperately felt the need for organising the advancing and the barricading masses, and leading them for the "final assault" on imperialism,[17] the Central Committee preferred not to take their note, remained stubbornly unmoved and continued to lag far behind the events.

It was not that the heat generating below ceased altogether to rise above and touch the surface, nor that the militancy of the cadres failed wholly to confront the moderation of the top brass within the C.P.I. and try to effect a change in the party line. Even in December 1945 the advocates of the militant opinion within the Central Committee did question the sagacity of carrying on "the understanding of the war-period to the post-war world", living on "the illusion of peaceful development", and expecting too much from the social democratic leadership of the British Labour Party, "which could not but trail" eventually the imperialist bourgeoisie in Britain. They also succeeded in impressing upon the party the urgent need for "reformulating" its strategy, "rousing the people directly for asserting independence", and making "a united plan of final bid for power".[18] Blowing hot and cold for some time, the moderate party leaders, however, managed in the Central Committee meeting of August 1946 to twist the radical slogan of "a united bid or assault for power" in such a way as to mean it to be an endeavour for realising their pet call for the "Congress-League-Communist joint front" *vis-a-vis* the British authorities. Simultaneously, they were able to force upon the party cadres their fancied scheme for channelising "the unprecedented

16. "A Note on the Communist Infiltration in Indian Politics etc.", Home Poll. File No. PR 1/103/46 of 1946, N.A.I.
17. "Prastut Hao" (Get Ready), an editorial by Somnath Lahiri, *Swadhinata* (Bengali daily), 15 February 1946.
18. "The New Situation and Our Tasks", Resolution of the Central Committee, 16 December 1945, Central Archives, Communist Party of India, Ajoy Bhavan, New Delhi.

features of mass revolutionary upsurge" into a united move for independence under the auspices of the "joint front".[19] But the August Resolution of 1946, though it marked some sort of victory of the moderates, was in reality not wholly a moderate document, and the militants had not failed totally to secure in it a few of their basic points. They persuaded the Central Committee, for instance, to acknowledge the great popular urge for "the liquidation of imperialist rule" in India, and to invoke the spirit of revolutionism within the party so that it "boldly leads all popular struggles, develops the initiative and the fighting capacity of the masses".[20] Such a moderate-militant tussle at the leadership level resulted only in the party's practising a very anomalous political strategy — the curious amalgam of revolutionary fervours and reformist tactics, of engineering "popular upsurges" and befriending "compromising" bourgeois leaders[21] — which ran on till the militants in the C.P.I. challenged the moderates' position in the middle of 1947, and clashed recklessly over the vexed characterisation of Indian independence.

Irrespective of what was happening at the apex of the C.P.I., the Communist activists among the *kisans* in the countryside displayed perhaps as volatile a tendency as their comrades in the trade-union front or on the urban scene had done, and certainly preceded them all by taking an earlier start. The alacrity with which their Kisan Sabhas tried — in the wake of famine and famine-like conditions — to take over the village food committees, which the authorities originally had set up to boost the distribution processes, turn them into instruments against the hoarders and "blackmarketeers" of food grains, surround at times the dishonest traders' godowns and landlords' barns, demand the dispersal of grains thus seized at the "controlled" rates and on short-term loans, organise the agricultural labour on the basis of demands for minimum wages, and resist the Government's inequitous grain levy on the cultivators — seemed

19. "For the Final Assault", Resolution of the Central Committee, August 1946, Central Archives, Communist Party of India, Ajoy Bhavan, New Delhi.
20. *Ibid.*
21. *Ibid.*

already to have energised and enlivened the rural poor in many parts of the country. A fighting mood was gradually being built up in the rural sector for over two years, and an examination of some of the agrarian agitations that had surfaced in 1946-7, and raised storms in certain corners of the horizon, would bear out that they had actually been gathering momentum since 1944-5.

SCENE I
1946-47

The momentous occurrence of the year 1946 — which in its sequel resulted in the most significant of the peasant outbreaks in India — took place early in the month of July in the Telengana region of Hyderabad state, or more accurately at Kaduvendi village of Janagaon *taluk* in Nalgonda district. Frustrated by his failure to snatch away a 6-acre plot of the widowed washer-woman, Ailamma, at Palakurthi village, and incensed by the resistance the *kisans* had put up on her behalf, the landed magnate of the locality — the Visunuri *Deshmukh* Ramachandra Reddy of Janagaon — planned a retaliatory murderous attack on some of the leading resisters. On 4 July 1946 his hired hoodlums invaded the homes of these leaders at the neighbouring Kaduvendi village, and after being fought back and chased away, they took shelter in the *Deshmukh's* fortress-like *garhi* or residence. The *kisans*, armed with lathis, slings (*wadishela*) and agricultural implements, and raising slogans, followed them there. The *Deshmukh's* men then opened fire on the crowd, killing Doddi Komarayya on the spot, and injuring four others.[22] Infuriated by the firing, the mob surrounded the place, captured the culprits, and prepared for setting the *garhi* on fire. A large contingent of the local police arrived at that very moment, and rescued the *Deshmukh* and his family by dispersing the angry gathering. Thereafter, and immediately before the cremation, Komarayya's dead body was taken out by the villagers in a rupturous procession, and people hurried from distant places to take part in it,[23] Soon Komarayya's martyrdom was widely

22. "Note dated 1 February 1947 on the Situation in Nalgonda District", Hyderabad State C.I.D., Proceedings, Ministry of States, Poll. Dept. Govt. of India, File No. 15-P(S)/47 of 1947, N.A.I.

23. P. Sundarayya *Telengana People's Struggle and Its Lessons*, Calcutta, 1972, pp. 36-7.

mourned in noisy meetings and delirious demonstrations, and within a few weeks it opened up the flood-gates of popular fury against the landlords and the state police, inundating several villages of Nalgonda (notably in Janagaon, Suryapet, Bhuvanagiri and Hazurnagar) and certain parts of Warangal and Karimnagar districts.[24] Apparently the 4th of July 1946 heralded the Telengana *kisan* masses' historic undertaking of the struggle for transforming a predominantly feudal society, and completing the tasks of an agrarian revolution. But did the saga really commence at that precise juncture, in that specific manner, and as spontaneously as it seemed to have done? A peep into the objective conditions in which the "docile" and "mild" Telugu peasantry in Hyderabad state[25] lived, and the subjective urgings they felt, and to which they so readily responded, should further clarify the position.

Telengana, which formed practically one-half of the formidable (in extent, population and economic viability) Indian state of Hyderabad,[26] was governed — in the name of the hereditary ruling family — by a traditional aristocracy that derived its strength from the prevailing feudal social order. One should not, however, consider the Nizamshahi Hyderabad to be an epitome of medievalism, devoid of all modernistic traits. On the contrary, it was endowed with a fairly advanced system of railways, communications and administrative apparatus under the charge of an apparently forward-looking bureaucracy, whose members — the products of the British Indian universities — were familiar with the developmental processes of political economy. Much of Hyderabad's economic activities were, therefore, moulded by the bureaucrats, whether it was the founding of some infrastructural base for industrialisation through a virtual state monopoly in transport and energy (1875-919), or the bestowal of institutional and financial state support for the industrial undertakings of various sorts (1920-39), or the

24. *Ibid.*, p. 39.
25. A note by T.B. Creagh Coen, Deputy Secretary, Ministry of States, 11 January 1947, Proceedings, Ministry of States, Poll. Dept., Govt. of India, File No. 15 P(S)/47 of 1947, N.A.I.
26. In area, population and the number of people speaking a language (Telugu) Telengana constituted roughly the half of the Nizam's territories.

promoting of a structural change from the engineering and chemical-based industries, under a state-planned economic develop- ment (1940-48). Despite the bureaucratic concern for rapid industrialisation under the state patronage, the over-all industrial growth in Hyderabad state by the latter part of the 1940s was quite limited. In the official euphoria over the structural change, the artisanal industries were sadly neglected, and allowed to suffer from mounting indebtedness, resulting in the artisans' being reduced to the position of wage-earners and landless agricultural labourers.[27] Although some of the small scale industries — especially those producing petty consumer items — showed indications of progress, the agro-processing units like the oil, rice and flour mills did not do well at all, and many of them suspended functioning in the lean times of agricultural production. In the corporate sector, which consisted of the heavily state-financed (through the Government-managed Industrial Trust Fund) joint stock companies to operate single units with large capacities (such as in mining, metallic, engineering, ceramic and chemical, forest and agro-based industries), and where the bureaucracy laid most of its emphasis, failed to register any spectacular growth, and resultantly, to render Hyderabad "any less backward" than the rest of India.[28] Since private entrepreneurs had not shown much initiative in investment, and preferred to depend almost wholly on the Government support, the liberal state-financing eventually led to a situation where the assets sunk in big companies had no relation to their returns, and the amounts of loans advanced to them often far exceeded the paid-up value of their capital. Nothing practically was done to stop such large scale sinking of capital, or the Government funds, primarily because its beneficiaries were those who ran the Government, namely, the bureaucracy-aristocracy combine. The bureaucracy in Hyderabad

27. S. Kesav Iyengar, *Rural Economic Enquiries in Hyderabad State, 1949-51*, Hyderabad, 1951, pp. 526 & 556.
28. C.V. Subbarao, "Hyderabad: Social Context of Industrialisation, 1875-1948", unpublished monograph, Indian Council for Social Science Research, New Delhi, 1990, pp. 94-6.

had in fact emerged from the aristocracy, and the holding of key positions in the civil service depended as much on education and aptitude as on parentage, creed, status of the family in social hierarchy, the land it owned and controlled. The ministers and civil servants were not only the agents of the ruling aristocracy, but also the members of the ruling class itself — with all the stakes in the defence and maintenance of its feudal base. They were interested, of course, in broadening and strengthening the material basis of the feudal society, but not in upsetting and undermining it in any way. Consequently, their experimentation with the state enterprise in industrialisation failed to bring the historic factors into play — the capitalist class did not take its birth, the agricultural surplus did not boost up industrial development, and the industrial investment did not seem profitable to land-rent, moneylending and agrarian trade. The feudal social structure and its milieu, which invariably constrained industrial growth, both on the demand and the supply sides, still reigned supreme. The Nizam's Government was overwhelmingly dependent yet on revenues from land, custom on crop export and excise, and his autocratic rule rested almost entirely on the political support of the landed magnates.

The landed magnates were such feudal elements as the *Jagirdars* and others (namely, the *Ijaradars, Matkadars, Samsthandars*) in the *Jagirdari* areas[29], and similar semi-feudal components like the *Deshmukhs* and *Patel-Patwaris* in the *Diwani* areas.[30] Of the total land in the state, 30 per cent was *Jagirdari*, 60 per cent *Diwani* and 10 per cent *Sarf-e-Khas* or the Nizam's personal estates. The cultivation in *Sarf-e-Khas* was done mainly through the hired and bonded labourers under the direct supervision of the state officials. Although in theory the *Jagirdars* and other intermediaries were not the legal proprietors of the *Jagirdari* lands, in practice they behaved as owners of the estates, treated cultivators as tenants, collected rent and

29. These were the areas where the *Jagirdars* collected land revenue on behalf of the Government, or acted as intermediaries between the state and the cultivators.
30. These areas were directly under the Government land revenue system.

other cesses from them, maintained armed retainers and enjoyed certain judicial, police and even minting powers.[31] The tenantry consisted of the occupancy tenants (*Shikmidars*, who held land as long as they paid rent) and tenants-at-will with some prospect (*Assami-Shikmidars*, who paid rent, and who — as regular rent-payers — were entitled to *Shikmidari* rights after 12 years), but mostly tenants-at-will without any prospect whatsoever (*Kouludars*, who paid the annual rent in advance for a tenure of one year or two years). Tenancies were auctioned to *Assami-Shikmidars* and *Kouludars* in accordance with their ability to bid (known as the *Gundu Guttalu* system), and records were messed up to hoodwink the Nizam's Government as to the exact amount collected from the tenants. All tenants were subjected to high tax[32] and irregular exactions, and the tenants-at-will exposed to periodic evictions. The conditions of the *Jagirdari* areas were generally disorganised, lands remained unsurveyed, rent receipts and *pattas* withheld and primary facilities (of health, education and communication) denied.[33]

Administratively, the situation was better in the *Diwani* lands under the direct control of the state, though the condition of the majority of cultivators was essentially the same. In these lands all the peasant proprietors — the so-called and the real — were *Pattadars*, having obtained their *patta* directly from the state. Being owners of large holdings, some of the *Pattadars* rented out lands to various categories of occupancy tenants, such as the *Shikmidars* and *Pot-Pattadars* (who took a part of the *Pattadars'* lands on condition of paying the proportionate revenue to the state), and tenants-at-will like *Assami-Shikmidars* and *Kouludars*. Apart from these, there were the *Ijara* tenants,

31. The *Jagirdars* of Gadwal and Wanaparthi, for example, had authority to mint coins.
32. The Nizam's Government conceded that the assessments charged by the *Jagirdars* were "far higher" than those charged in the neighbouring *Diwani* villages. See Report by W.V. Griegson, Revenue and Police Member, 5 December 1946, Proceedings, Ministry of States, Poll. Dept. Govt. of India, File No. 15 P(S)/47 of 1947, N.A.I.
33. Suravram Pratapa Reddy, *Jagirulaloni Sthitigatulu* (in Telugu, meaning "Conditions in Jagirs"), Hyderabad, 1941, pp. 1-26, available at Saraswatha Niketanam, Vetapalam, Prakasam District, Andhra Pradesh.

or those who cleared and occupied forest lands in the hope that the reclaimed plots would be allotted to them. Tax was collected from them, without issuing any receipt, and the cultivation in these lands had hardly been shown in the Government records. Consequently, the *Ijara* tenants were thrown out with the help of the revenue officials whenever the landlords wanted to grab these lands.[34] Among the *Pattadars*, the *Deshmukhs* and the *Patel-Patwaris* assumed the position of landed magnates in the *Diwani* lands. Originally revenue farmers (*Deshmukhs*) and the tax collectors (*Patel-Patwaris*), they lost their jobs when the Nizam's Government decided in the 1860s to collect the dues in the *Diwani* areas direct from the cultivators. The latter, however, had not entirely been divested of their official duties, and they were still entrusted with the responsibility for maintaining the village records. As a compensation, the *Deshmukhs* and the *Patel-Patwaris* were given lands, as well as state pensions. By using their influence and knowledge as revenue-farmers, by manipulating survey records which they themselves had created and conserved, and by dictating the settlement operations, the *Deshmukhs* managed to take away as much good land as possible. Once they possessed large tracts of land, and started letting these out at exorbitant rent,[35] they grew in power and position and became eventually the arbiters of rural society. As arbiters they extracted a number of irregular levies from the villagers, and collected *Nazrana* and *Mamul* (a kind of bribe) on every possible plea. The yield from these squeezings was very considerable, and it formed — according to popular belief — about one-third of their total

34. The Communist Party booklet (in Telegu), *Conditions of Telengana and the Deshmukhs' Exploitation in Nalgonda and Warangal*, no publication details, 1945(?), available at Saraswatha Niketanam, Vetapalam, Prakasam District, Andhra Pradesh.
35. The Nizam's Government confirmed that the *Deshmukhs* were "rack-renting those to whom they sub-let their own occupancy holdings." (Report by W.V. Griegson, 5th December 1946). The Hyderabad State C.I.D. also spoke of "undoubted rack-renting" by the *Deshmukhs* and *Patels*. (Note by the Hyderabad C.I.D. of 14 February 1947.) Proceedings, Ministry of States, Poll. Dept., Govt. of India, File No. 15 P(S)/147 of 1947, N.A.I.

income. Their land grabbing also continued side by side their ever expanding position of dominance, and with the support and assistance of the state revenue and police officials. They forcibly seized lands on any pretext, be it defaulting in the payment of rent and loan instalments, or irregular levies, or fines imposed for reluctance to give free services.[36] Their looting in land was so prolific that by the 1940s they monopolised 60 to 70 per cent land in certain districts, and individually held at times 40,000 acres (Visunuri Deshmukh), 1,00,000 acres (Kalluri brothers), and even 1,50,000 acres (Jana Reddy Pratapa Reddy).

Underneath the variety of tenurial arrangements, and between the *Jagirdars* and the *Bhaghelas* and *Jeetagadus* (bonded labourers), or the *Deshmukhs* and the *Malas* and *Madigas* (hereditarily attached *Harijan* or *Dalit* field labourers), there lived in Telengana diverse categories of rural population. From the socio-economic point of view, these categories could broadly be identified as the substantial or rich peasants, the poor peasants, the agricultural labourers and artisans, and the sprinkling of petty village shopkeepers. The rich peasants in Telengana were discernible among the *Pattadars* and *Shikmidars* — the independent family producers and wage labour-hirers — who used their surplus for a profit through lending[37] and selling in the market. Few of the *Shikmidars*, and most of the *Assami-Shikmidars* and *Kouludars* — whose meagre plots failed to ensure their subsistence without undertaking wage labour — were poor peasants. The agricultural labourers, who had no land whatsoever, and the artisans, who followed some trade to eke out a precarious existence, belonged to the landless part of rural society. Together, and reduced practically to the same level under conditions of indebtedness, loss of lands and

36. K. Balagopal, "Telengana Movement Revisited", *Economic and Political Weekly*, 30 April 1983, Vol. XVII, no. 18, pp. 709-12.

37. The substantial peasants — following the footsteps of the landed magnates — stepped into the rural moneylending business in a big way in the 1930s, which had previously been monopolised by the professional *sahukars* (*Komtis*). They, however, always dominated the grain-loaning, charging in the 1930s a 50 per cent interest on foodgrains and 100 per cent interest on seed-grains.

low wages, the landless and the poor peasants constituted the great multitude in the Telengana countryside.[38] Having little worth while property, land and crop to offer as security for loans incurred, they were ever exposed to bondages during hard times, or times of expensive social obligations (festivals, marriages, illnesses and deaths). Peasants of all categories, the rich, the poor and the landless had, however, one common factor — all of them had suffered, in some way or the other, at the hands of their feudal tormentors. The *Jagirdari*, *Deshmukhi* and *Patel-Patwari* stranglehold on the rural Telengana, which grew over a carefully laid system of tenurial denials, rack-rentals, irregular exactions and periodic evictions and dispossessions, was forcibly sustained with the help of institutionalised practices of *Vetti* (forced labour) and *Vettipani* or *Vettichakiri* (enforced services). The practice of *Vetti* had emerged through the ages as a measure against the exodus of agricultural labourers and artisans (the potter, the washerman, the barber, the blacksmith etc.) from their villages at times of famine and scarcity. It was thought that petty grants of land would tie them to their villages, and accordingly the artisans received tiny plots from the rent-free *Inam* lands and the village common lands (*gramanattam*) at the reduced rate of regular land tax, and some of the labourers and the *Dalit Malas* and *Madigas* got bits and pieces from the lands of their proprietors. In return, the artisans had to serve the village community, and the labourers — those who had thus attached themselves — their respective proprietors. Such labour (*Vetti*) continued perpetually without any payment, and became applicable to all those under bondage for incurring or inheriting loans from their landlords. Beside this, in the *Jagirdari* areas the *Jagirdars* customarily exacted in the characteristic feudal fashion all kinds of unpaid services from anybody domiciled in his *jagir*. The practice was borrowed in course of time by the landed magnates, and introduced in the *Diwani* area, too, under the name *Vettichakiri* or *Vettipani* — the most elaborate arrangement for extorting free services from the entire

38. S. Kesav Iyengar, (i) *Economic Investigations in Hyderabad State, 1929-30*, Vol.1, Hyderabad, 1931, p. 20, and (ii) *Rural Economic Enquiries in Hyderabad State, 1929-51*, Hyderabad, 1951, p. 55.

rural population, including the rich peasants and the village shopkeepers. The Nizam's Government extended it further in 1927 by issuing orders that services to the touring state officials in the villages were obligatory to all the villagers.[39] The orders did mention of payment for such compulsory services, but the feudal beneficiaries of *Vettichakiri* were opposed to creating any precedent for payment, and the officials were only too eager to abide by their opinion. So *Vettichakiri* was claimed not only by the *Jagirdars, Deshmukhs, Patel-Patwaris,* but also by all the state officials. It included the performance of domestic jobs, acting as retainers, supplying of provisions, procuring of concubines (*adabapas*) and labouring in the fields. Even houses were built, gardens laid and sugar and oil mills constructed with the help of *Vettichakiri*. The villagers had to be at the beck and call of their exploiters, quite often to the neglect of their own agricultural work. *Vettichakiri* was invariably backed up by the ill-treatment of the peasants, their being abused and beaten, and their womenfolk insulted and violated.[40]

Approximately from the post-first world war years the Telengana rural society began experiencing an economic phenomenon that was capable of changing its circumstances to a large extent. It was the spreading of commercial agriculture, especially the cultivation of oilseeds (groundnut and castor), for catering principally to the needs of the industrial West, and exporting the bulk to Britain and the United States. Aided by the state's providing for the infrastructural facilities (the improvements in trade mechanism and transport, as well as the supplies of seeds and fertilisers), and supported by the export demand for the produce, the cash crops soon incorporated the rural economy of Telengana into the world market. The profitable price of the oilseeds encouraged almost everybody to

39. In 1922-3 the state Government started a detailed survey and assessment of land with a view to fix the land tax afresh. The operation involved extensive movements of the revenue and police officials in the rural areas, and consequently necessitated the carrying of their luggage, and arranging for their food, shelter and other facilities.

40. D.V. Rao, *Hyderabadu Samsthanamlo Vettichakiri* (Forced Labour and Services in Hyderabad State), Bezwada, 1946, pp. 1-28, Saraswatha Niketanam, Vetapalam, Prakasam District, Andhra Pradesh.

take to their cultivation, and it brought certain uneven changes in the over-all cropping pattern, acreage and output. Recent studies, however, have failed to establish clearly any direct relationship between movements of prices and the growth rates in acreage and output, either across crops or across different periods.[41] While in the worst days of falling prices, at the time of the great Depression, the acreage and the output seemed even to have increased, the price recovery in the post-Depression period, or its sky-rocketing during the inflationary war years, did not — contrarily — show their significant growth. From the economic viewpoint of peasants generally, barring, of course, the small number of the rich ones who possessed the rare strength for rolling on investments, commercialisation had not brought the improvement that was expected of it. True, the peasants tried to make good any drastic fall in their income (such as it was in the Depression days) by "producing a larger quantity than before",[42] but the advantages of price recovery had not accrued to them, mainly on account of a built-in pressure to sell the produce soon after its harvesting at a low price. The pressure accentuated, ironically, with the expansion of the market economy, under which the landlords — the traditional grabbers of lands on any pretext — grabbed more and more lands (including the "dry" lands where oilseed cultivation was possible) for cultivating the profitable cash crops, and for preventing others from occupying them. The increase in lands in the landlords' hands did lead to an increase in the area of cultivation, but also to an increase in demand for cultivators and labourers, and therefore, to an increase in tenancies.[43] The proportion of tenants-at-will to the total number of tenants

41. C.V. Subbarao, "Hyderabad: Social Context of Industrialization, 1875-1948", unpublished monograph, Indian Council for Social Science Research, New Delhi, 1990, Appendix 7B, p. 132.
42. A.I. Qureishi, *Economic Development of Hyderabad*, Vol.1, Rural Economy, Bombay, 1947, p. 257.
43. Between 1931 and 1945, there had been a very considerable increase in the number of tenants. The proportion of protected tenants to the total number of cultivators increased from 32 per cent in 1931 to about 45 per cent in 1945. See *ibid.*, p. 133.

increased leaps and bounds to 78 per cent in 1948-9.[44] The extension of tenancies seemed to have taken place only at the expense of their quality, or, in other words, most of the tenants engaged had no protection whatsoever, and they merely swelled the existing crowd of thoroughly insecure tenants-at-will. The deteriorating condition of tenancies, coupled with the dramatic fall in the real income during the deflationary years (1929-34), as well as in the inflationary years (1939-40), resulted in an astounding rise in rural indebtedness. According to the inhabitants in the investigated villages in 1950, the total amount of their debts increased by 43 per cent between 1931 and 1939, and by 83 per cent between 1939 and 1950.[45] The indebtedness of the peasantry was responsible directly for alienation of land, and at times for its selling at ridiculously low prices.[46] The official figure of land changing hands in the surveyed villages in 1948-9, i.e. 7 per cent of the total,[47] did not seem to represent even a fraction of the over-all picture. Alienation of land through the court decrees on formal debts was hardly an important mode the Telengana landlords adopted for land acquisition. To them, the occupation of land on the basis of informal debts (recorded, or misrecorded, on bits of papers), through forcible evictions with the help of sheer muscle-power and the conniving local police and revenue officials, was not only the least time-consuming, but also the most convenient. The commercialisation of agriculture within a powerful feudal set up, therefore, reinforced the landlord- moneylender stranglehold over the rural Telengana, and did not slacken it in any way — intensified the feudal exploitation and oppression instead of diminishing them to any extent. It was not that commercialisation did not benefit at all certain categories of the peasantry other than the landlords, nor that the semi-capitalist contradiction had not developed

44. S. Kesav Iyengar, *Rural Economic Enquiries in Hyderabad State, 1949-51*, Hyderabad, 1951, p. 55.

45. *Ibid.*, p. 436.

46. Ravi Narayan Reddy had recorded in his book, *Heroic Telengana*, New Delhi, 1973, p. 5, how a poor peasant sold his entire holding (of 2 acres of "wet" land) to him for a paltry sum of Rs. 25.

47. S. Kesav Iyengar, *Rural Economic Enquiries in Hyderabad State, 1949-51*, Hyderabad, 1951, p. 116.

between the labour-employing and moneylending rich peasants on the one hand, and the landless and the marginally landholding labourers on the other.[48] But the way the rich peasants had been prevented by the landlords from acquiring fresh plots, obstructed from sharing in the facilities (in fertilisers and seeds) offered by the Government, compelled to the performance of *Vetti-chakiri*, forced to the paying of various kinds of irregular exactions and subjected to the landed magnates' approval even for engaging labourers — all emphatically bore out their more fundamental contradiction with the architects of the feudal order. The divisioning of the rural Telengana was immensely wider, and also intensely sharper, into the camp of the feudal and semi-feudal landed magnates and that of the rest of the population, including the rich peasants, than its breaking into the following of the rich peasants and that of the poor peasants and agricultural labourers. The outcome of such line-ups, however, depended largely on those who could make revolutionary use of them, or on those subjective elements who could take radical advantage of the prevailing objective situation.

As it seemed to have happened, most of the radical elements in Telengana merged themselves with the Communist movement during its aggressive "imperialist war" phase (1939-41). The C.P.I., which had managed to set up a branch in Hyderabad state in 1939, was found one year later to be attracting not only the socialistically-oriented political workers, but also the nationalists — and even some of the staunchest among them. The patriotic content of its "proletarian path" in 1940, and its anxiety for a trial of strength with the British authorities, synchronising with the rising temper of the nation, had drawn towards it all those who felt disenchanted with the dispirited ploddings of the Congress leadership. Thus along with a group

48. For a highlighting of this aspect, see Pavier Barry, *The Telengana Movement, 1944-51*, New Delhi, 1981, and Thirumali, Inukonda, "Aspects of Agrarian Relations in Telengana 1928-48", unpublished M.Phil. dissertation, Centre for Historical Studies, Jawaharlal Nehru University, New Delhi, 1979, of course, with their respective slants.

of radical intellectuals (the "Comrades' Association")[49], came into the Nizam State Communist Party a number of participants in the Gandhian movements (from among the members of the Andhra Maha Sabha[50] in Telengana and the Maharashtra Parishad[51] in Maratha-wada) and the defiant young men of a local nationalistic variety (the student protestors of the *Vande Mataram* agitation)[52]. Together they contributed richly to the growth of the Communist influence and organisation in Hyderabad generally, and in Telengana in particular. Coming sizably from a rural background, they found in 1940 the party's understanding of the war-time agrarian crisis to be true, and its anxiety for mobilizing the crisis-ridden peasantry to be to their liking. The Telengana Communists' enthusiasm for organising *kisans* led eventually to the conversion of the Andhra Maha Sabha into a regional Kisan Sabha. Originally they planned to form a Kisan Sabha of their own in 1940, but abandoned the idea when the Nizam's Government threatened them with a ban. Thereafter the Communists decided to work within the A.M.S. (where some of their members had already been playing leading roles), and use it as an instrument for work in the rural

49. In the late 1930s a group of socialist ideologues, including the Urdu poet, Makhdoom Mohiuddin, formed the "Comrades' Association" in Hyderabad city.
50. Starting in 1922 as an association for upholding the cause of the Telugu language and culture in Hyderabad state, Andhra Jana Sangham had turned into Andhra Maha Sabha in 1930. It soon grew into a powerful semi-political organisation, representing moderate nationalist and Gandhian viewpoints, and acting as a cementing force behind the various sections of the Telugu-speaking people in Hyderabad.
51. Andhra Maha Sabha's equivalent in Marathawada.
52. The agitation of the students started in October 1938 over the prohibitory order on singing the patriotic anthem, *Vande Mataram,* in the Osmania University hostels. The agitators also refused to put on the Muslim dress (as per the custom of the University) and demanded facilities for learning Sanskrit and their mother-tongues (Telugu, Marathi and Kannada). The agitation continued for about two months, and a large number of students were rusticated from the University, as well as from other colleges and schools.

areas.[53] On its part, the A.M.S. had always taken note of some of the agrarian issues, including the one of landlord oppression, though mainly from the point of view of the landholding *Pattadars.* Often it expressed its concern for the high rate of land and water taxes, the difficulty in obtaining agricultural loans, and the need for good seeds and agricultural facilities. The demands for a reduction in land tax and the revision of the land tax system were made in the A.M.S. conferences of 1940 and 1941. The sufferings of the people under the *Jagirdars* and the urgency for abolishing the practice of forced labour were discussed in the conferences of 1942 and 1943. For the first time the problems of the tenants-at-will were voiced by the A.M.S. in 1944 (11th conference in Bhuvanagiri), and in 1945 (12th conference in Khammam) the doors of the A.M.S. were opened to agricultural labourers and poor peasants of all sorts.[54] The character of the A.M.S. in fact was changing perceptibly from 1940 when the Communists proceeded to establish their ascendancy over it. Following the election of their representative, Ravi Narayan Reddy, as the President of the A.M.S. in 1941 (8th Conference at Chilkur), there began a contest for controlling the Sabha between the youthful radicals and the veteran moderates. Although the moderates wrested the leadership in 1942, they were unable to retain it for very long. The contest was finally decided in favour of the Communists with the election of Ravi Narayan Reddy as President for the second time in 1944, and with the departure of the moderates from the organisation in a huff. The Communists and their supporters meanwhile had transformed the A.M.S. into a *kisan*-based mass organisation by recruiting a large number of members from the rural areas, by reducing the membership fee from Re. 1 to annas 4 in 1941 —

53. Barry Pavier, *The Telengana Movement, 1944-51,* Delhi, 1981, p. 82. It should also be noted in this connection that the A.M.S. had by this time a distinguished record of working for social regeneration, cultural progress and administrative and political reforms. By associating themselves with it, the Communists also hoped to share in its reputation and goodwill.

54. C. Rajeshwar Rao, Arutla Ramchandra Reddy and Y.V. Krishna Rao, *Bhuswamya Vidhanam Raddukai Rayatulu Veerochito Tirugubatu* (Heroic Peasant Rebellion for the Abolition of the Feudal System), Vijayawada, 1973, part I, chapter IV, pp. 23-5.

and then to anna 1 in 1944,[55] and by initiating agitation on all the pressing agrarian issues.

Committed to the avowed ideal of agrarian revolution, and to the task (of the "united front" days) for fighting the imperialist-feudal alliance, the Telengana Communists took naturally to the path of anti-feudalism from the beginning. The slogans of the "imperialist war" phase, namely, that of resistance to the oppressions of landlords,[56] or waging day to day struggles against the feudal exploiters,[57] reinforced their anti-feudal tendency, and boosted their opposition to the landlords. What, however, seemed valid to the central Communist leaders in the "imperialist war" phase, did not remain so in their eyes in the "people's war" period, and therefore, the C.P.I. sacrificed between early 1942 and the mid-1945 all the anti-feudal, as well as the anti-imperialist, agitations at the alter of anti-Fascism. Curiously enough, the Telengana Communists had managed somehow even during these years, and contrary to the stand of the central leadership, to continue with their mobilisation against the landlords. Not being rated very high ideologically in the Indian Communist circles,[58] the new converts' lack of understanding of a policy-change had perhaps been treated lightly by the high-priests in Bombay. It could also be a deliberate act of surreptitious defiance on the part of the Telengana ranks, who had already been impressed[59] by the manner some of their Andhra comrades were trying to keep the embers of

55. Ravi Narayan Reddy, *Heroic Telengana*, New Delhi, 1973, pp. 19 and 21. In 1944-5 the A.M.S. had a Standing Committee, district and *taluk* committees and innumerable village committees with more than 1,00,000 members from the villages.
56. *Proletarian Path*, 1940, File No. 1940/48, P.C.J. Archives, J.N.U., New Delhi.
57. Political Resolution, 5th Session of the A.I.K.S., Palasa, March 1940 in M.A. Rasul, *History of All India Kisan Sabha*, Calcutta, 1974, p. 66.
58. Ian Bedford, "The Telengana Insurrection", unpublished Ph.D. thesis, Australian National University, Canberra, 1967 (microfilm at the N.M.M. & L.), p. 211.
59. Ravi Narayan Reddy, *Heroic Telengana*, New Delhi, 1973, p. 37.

anti-*Zamindari* agitation burning in Munagala,[60] and who felt like emulating the example. Whatever was the circumstance, it would not be easy to dismiss the Telengana Communists' claim in retrospect to their revolutionary militancy *vis-a-vis* the central policy of reformism.[61] The situation turned out to be more congenial for the Communists in Telengana by the end of 1945 and soon thereafter, when the C.P.I. started talking at the national level again of "the village parasites and British toadies",[62] of the "landlord oppression",[63] and of the anti-landlord categories, including the rich peasants and the "new capitalists in the village."[64] This was more or less what the Telengana Communists were already doing, namely, attempting at an anti-landlord understanding among all classes of cultivators, and calling upon the "small landholders" to sympathise with the causes of the poor peasants and agricultural labourers.[65] They, however, remained conscious of the fact that the mainstay of their strength had clearly been the rural poor — the poor peasants and the agricultural labourers. They were, therefore, persistently vocal in favour of the rights of the tenants-at-will, and against their evictions.[66] They also continued to raise from time to time the slogan for giving land to the landless, and demanded increase in the wages of the bonded and agricultural labourers (for example, 40 seers of jowar in a month for a *Bhaghela* to 90 seers) and improvements in the working conditions (namely, 8 hours work in a day, and 30 holidays in a year).[67] That the Communists succeeded in building up an

60. Munagala in Krishna district was adjacent to the Nizam's territories in Nalgonda.
61. D.V. Rao, "Telengana Armed Struggle and the Path of Indian Revolution", *Proletarian Path* (monthly), Calcutta, November 1973, p. 8.
62. "On the New Political Situation", Resolution, Central Committee, C.P.I., 16 December 1945, Party Documents, Central Archives, Ajoy Bhavan, New Delhi.
63. Election Manifesto, C.P.I., *People's Age* (English weekly), 13 January 1946.
64. "On the New Political Situation", Resolution, Central Committee, 16 December 1945.
65. D.V. Rao, *Hyderabadu Samsthanamlo Vettichakiri* (Forced Labour and Services in Hyderabad State), Bezwada, 1946, 16 December 1945.
66. *People's Age* (English weekly), 22 December 1946.
67. *Ibid.*, 10 November 1946.

anti-landlord common front in Telengana was evident from the speed with which their agitation against *Vetti, Vettichakiri* and the irregular levies developed.

The discontent over *Vetti* and *Vettichakiri* had been brewing long before the Communists appeared on the political scene in Telengana. There were cases of isolated *kisan* agitation on these issues in different localities for brief periods, but the *Jagirdars* and *Deshmukhs* always succeeded in breaking the resistance. The A.M.S. took up the question for the first time in its second conference at Devarakonda (1931), and this inspired the petty shopkeepers in certain areas to stop unpaid supply of provisions to the landed magnates. The act of defiance, however, did not last for long, and the A.M.S. continued to discuss the issue without any further consequence. It was in 1940 that the A.M.S. under the Communist leadership launched an anti-forced labour and services campaign. A "week" against *Vettichakiri* was observed, and the A.M.S. activists, including its President, Ravi Narayan Reddy, went on extensive tours in the countryside to arouse public opinion. In 1941-2 took place a series of demonstrations against the *Deshmukhs* of Cherukapalli and Chandupalli (Nalgonda). In 1943 the campaign picked up in Suryapet (Nalgonda) and Khammam (Warangal), and extended from *taluk* to *taluk*. Two successful agitations were waged in 1944, one in Janagaon (Nalgonda) against the Visunuri *Deshmukh*, Rama Chandra Reddy, and another at Manukotaluka (Warangal) against *Deshmukh* Cheralapalem Gopala Rao. Another massive struggle followed soon in Warangal *taluk* where *Vettichakiri* practically ceased in about 40 villages.[68] By 1945 the movement against *Vetti* and *Vettichakiri*, under the guidance of the A.M.S., engulfed most parts of Nalgonda, Warangal and a small part of Karimnagar districts. It also succeeded in putting an end to the collection of irregular levies at many places, and among the suffering notables were the Kalluri *Deshmukh* in Madira (Warangal), Pingali *Deshmukh* at Malkalagudem

68. D.V. Rao, *Hyderabadu Samsthanamlo Vettichakiri* (Forced Labour and Services in Hyderabad State), Bezwada, 1946, pp. 1-28.

(Warangal), the Visunuri *Deshmukh* and the Koduru brothers in Janagaon (Nalgonda) and Dupalli Rama Reddy in Bhuvanagari (Nalgonda).

The A.M.S. was in great demand in the rural Telengana, and the *kisans* came to its leaders with invitations to open branches (*sanghams*) in their villages.[69] Having championed some of the popular causes, the Communists could not shrink away from taking up the others, especially when the people themselves were so keen. The movement against the feudal oppressions (*Vetti*, *Vettichakiri* and the irregular exactions), therefore, turned naturally towards a resistance against the feudal expropriations (evictions and dispossessions). The resistance against evictions grew precisely in those areas where the anti-forced labour and services movement had raised its head. It sprang up in Janagaon (Nalgonda) when the inhabitants of Mundraya village in the middle of 1944 opposed the attempts of the *Deshmukhs* (the Koduru brothers) to forcibly occupy some lands. They were joined in their fight by people from the neighbouring villages under the banner of the A.M.S. The struggle, however, failed eventually, and the *Deshmukhs* not only had their way with the help of the police, but also managed to get the leading agitators arrested on trumped up criminal charges.[70] Nevertheless, the illustration of Mundraya was emulated by the peasants in the rest of Janagaon, Bhuvanagari and Suryapet. The Pusukuri *Deshmukh* Raghav Rao's endeavours to drive away the Lambadis (tribal peasants) from their lands at Dharmapuram, Janagaon (Nalgonda), were frustrated collectively by all categories of *kisans*. At Edavelli village, Suryapet (Nalgonda), Jana Reddy Pratapa Reddy's efforts to eject the tenants-at-will were successfully neutralised. In a similar fashion the *kisans* counteracted the landlords' attacks on their lands and crops at Batavolu, Huzurnagar (Nalgonda), Mallacheruru, Huzurnagar

69. Arutla Rama Chandra Reddy, *Telengana Porata Smruthulu* (Memoirs of the Telengana Struggle), Vijayawada, 1981, pp. 31-5.

70. Arutla Rama Chandra Reddy and G. Gopala Reddy were arrested along with 20 others on charges of attempted murders. The sensational trial (Palakurthi Conspiracy Case) of the accused continued for about one year, and in the middle of 1945 they were all released.

(Nalgonda), Thimmarapuram (Warangal), Desaipet (Warangal), Papukullu, Illendu (Warangal), and many other places.[71] The agitation against fresh ejectments raked up the tragic memories of the past ones, and led those dispossessed in the last 20 years or so to hope for the return of their lost holdings. The clamour of the vast landless peasantry for the possession of lands was already known to the Telengana Communists, and they had taken particular note of the peasants' "land thirst" in their book on the Janagaon peasants' movement, entitled, *Janagama Prajala Veerochito Poratalu.*[72] At the height of anti-eviction agitation, therefore, they anticipated the emergence of the issue of the seizure and distribution of land to a certain extent.

Both kinds of resistances (against the feudal oppressions, and against the feudal expropriations) were generally meant to be peaceful, and the Communists and the A.M.S. members had not shown much violent intention. Each act of resistance led to their arrests, and to criminal proceedings against them. They fought all these arduous legal battles to the best of their ability, and often came out of them unscathed. They usually tried to seek redress by referring disputes over lands to the local state officials. They resented the pro-landlord corrupt officialdom as much as they appreciated the fair play of some good officers.[73] The Communist leader and the President of the A.M.S., Ravi Narayan Reddy, took up the issues of forced labour and services, "levy" grains[74] and evictions with the Nizam's Government in Hyderabad, and personally discussed matters with the Revenue and Police minister at least twice, in November 1944 and

71. P. Sundarayya, *Telengana People's Struggle and its Lessons,* Calcutta, 1972, pp. 28-34, and P. Venkataramanaya, *Warangallu Zilla Rayatu Poratalu* (Peasants' Struggle in Warangal District), Bezwada, 1946, pp. 1-16.
72. D.V. Rao, "Telengana Armed Struggle and the Path of Indian Revolution", *Proletarian Path* (English monthly), November 1973, Calcutta, p. 11.
73. There were instances in Warangal district where conscientious officials earned the approbation of the local Communists. The Nalgonda Communists, in fact, were disappointed at the transfer of Abdul Alam — an impartial Munsiff — from Suryapet.
74. See Act Two, Scene III, p. 271.

January 1946.[75] The case of Ailamma's lands at Palakurthi village, Janagaon (Nalgonda) — which received some public attention by the end of 1945 — was characteristic of the cautious Communist approach. Ailamma, the widowed washer-woman, who wanted to get her lands cultivated through others, had to seek the Visunuri *Deshmukh's* permission, and received it after paying him some bribe. At the time of harvesting the Visunuri *Deshmukh* demanded a further amount which Ailamma could not afford. She then contacted the local A.M.S., whose volunteers came forward to help her in the harvesting. The *Deshmukh* promptly complained to the police claiming Ailamma's holdings to be his own, and alleging that the A.M.S. volunteers were forcibly taking away his crops. The police lost no time whatsoever in reaching the spot, arresting and torturing five Sabha members. The Communists and their followers then created some commotion over the issue, and forced the district authorities to institute an enquiry into the case. The enquiry officers (an Assistant Deputy Superintendent of Police and a Circle Inspector) were so influenced by the *Deshmukh* that their report in December 1945 went against Ailamma, stating that the lands belonged to the *Deshmukh*. Meanwhile the arrested A.M.S. members raised a hue and cry over the tortures they suffered, and demanded an enquiry. The enquiry into the allegations of torture by the Superintendent of the District Police was also influenced by the *Deshmukh*, and the findings in January 1946 dismissed the charges brought by the arrested persons. The Communists and the A.M.S. did not relent, they took the case thereafter to a court of law, and won in February 1946 a resounding legal victory. The arrested A.M.S. members were released and Ailamma's right over her lands vindicated.[76]

The right of Ailamma, however, would not have been protected at all had the *kisans* not defended her crops against the *Deshmukh's* men so determinedly and forcefully for such a long

75. The Communist pamphlet, *Conditions of Telengana and Deshmukhs' Exploitation in Nalgonda and Warangal*, no publication details, 1946(?), pp. 1-52, available at Saraswatha Niketanam, Vetapalam, Prakasam District, Andhra Pradesh.

76. *Ibid.*

time. It had not always been possible for the resisters against ejectment and land-grabbing to avoid the use of force. While facing the hirelings of landlords, *kisans* were compelled sometime to use force much before the occurrence of the case of Ailamma. In the defence of the *Kouludari* rights in Janagaon (Nalgonda), the Lambadis had to resort to it as early as January 1945.[77] Force was used at Edepalli, Suryapet (Nalgonda), when Jana Reddy Pratapa Reddy's musclemen came to take possession of some lands, and were beaten back. The villagers of Batavolu, Huzurnagar (Nalgonda), repulsed the landlord's hirelings by the use of force. Throughout 1945 similar incidents happened at Alipuram *Jagirdari* (Warangal), Brahmankotta (Warangal), Nasikull (Nalgonda), Malkalagudem (Nalgonda) and several other places. The incidence of violence increased during the harvesting season, and the peasants had to defend their crops against being looted by the landlord's men. It was at the beginning of 1946 when the police and revenue officials came to take away forcibly the "levy" grains that the villagers of Akunoor and Machi Reddy Palli put up a strong resistance with whatever arms they could lay their hands upon. Later, after the resistance was broken, the police tortured the villagers, raped their women and destroyed their properties.[78] Irrespective of the disposition of the Communists, therefore, armed clashes were taking place in Nalgonda and Warangal fairly regularly. The arms used were invariably very petty — *lathis*, slings, sickles and other agricultural implements. Women made use of brooms, stones, utensils and chilli powders. Once the battle had begun, entirely because of the enthusiasm generated through their political campaigns, the Communists were left hardly with any other alternative — either they proved themselves true to their causes and their following, or they retraced their steps and got obliterated from the *kisans'* vision. Though none wanted the destruction of the Communist movement that they had built in

77. A note on the situation in Nalgonda District, Hyderabad State, C.I.D., 1 February 1947, Proceedings, Ministry of States, Government of India, File No. 15P(S)/1947, 1947, N.A.I.

78. D.V. Rao, "Telengana Armed Struggle and the Path of Indian Revolution", *Proletarian Path* (English monthly), November 1973, Calcutta, p. 12.

Telengana upon their sacrifice, many hesitated in escalating the fight for fear of inviting repressions. It was the Nalgonda District Committee of the Telengana Communists who took the initiative in acknowledging the state of war prevailing in the countryside. By taking a cue from their Andhra comrades,[79] the Communists in Nalgonda and other places had in the meantime set up in the middle of 1945 a volunteer corps of the A.M.S., composed primarily of "agricultural labourers, poor peasants and middle peasants".[80] Towards the end of 1945, the Nalgonda District Committee decided to arm the volunteer corps with *lathis* and raise the slogan: "resist the goondas of the landlords with sticks in your hands".[81] Then at the beginning of 1946, after enquiring into the incidents of Akunoor and Machi Reddy Palli, and seeing the militant temper of the *kisans*, the Committee further decided to resist by using force not only against the landlords, "but the police as well".[82] The arrival at both these decisions, in effect, committed the Communists in Nalgonda district to the cause of armed struggle,[83] and turned the *Chitti* (petitioning) Sanghams

79. During the "Quit India" movement, and after, the Andhra Communists organised volunteer crops to defend themselves from the attacks of the *goondas* (rowdies) incited by their detractors.
80. D.V. Rao, "Telengana Armed Struggle and the Path of Indian Revolution". *Proletarian Path* (English monthly), November 1973, Calcutta, p. 12.
81. Arutla Rama Chandra Reddy, *Telengana Porata Smruthlu* (Memoirs of the Telengana Struggle), Vijayawada, 1981, pp. 60-1.
82. D.V. Rao, "Telengana Armed Struggle and the Path of Indian Revolution", *Proletarian Path* (English monthly), November 1973, Calcutta, p. 12.
83. Communists in other districts, i.e. Warangal and Karimnagar, continued to ponder over the issue for some more time. D.V. Rao had claimed that while the Nalgonda District Committee, representing "the revolutionary trend", took the initiative, the Communists in other districts preferred to follow "the liberal reformist" line. (*Ibid.*, pp. 8-11.) The fact that the rising — so far as the participation of the Communists was concerned — occurred mainly in Nalgonda district gives credence to Rao's contention. The British residents in Hyderabad (A.C. Lothian and C.G. Herbert), the Revenue and Police minister (W.V. Griegson) and the Hyderabad State C.I.D. noted this fact and described the rising of 1946-47 as "Nalgonda kisan disturbances, engineered by the Communists". (Proceedings, Ministry of States, Govt. of India, File No. 15P(S)/47, 1947, N.A.I.) P. Sundarayya's narrative of events also conveys an impression that the rising at its first phase was predominantly a Nalgonda affair. (*Telengana People's Struggle and its Lessons*, Calcutta, 1972, pp. 35-52.)

into *Gutappa* (*lathi*-weilding) Sanghams. Thus by the middle of 1946 some Communists at certain places were willing to play in Telengana the game that they had started, and on the lines their peasant supporters preferred.

Armed and unarmed popular struggles were so mixed up throughout 1945 and the first half of 1946 that it would be difficult to indicate a specific date or an incident as the starting point of the Telengana armed rising. It was not clear — even from the vantage-view of the Communists — when exactly the cadres took to arms, and whether their District Committee's decisions were made to give the activists a lead, or merely to ratify the steps they had already taken. However, a point of no return (to unarmed struggle) was reached, certainly in Nalgonda district in July 1946 (as it has previously been noted) in connection with the happenings at Kaduvendi village, and following the fall of the Telengana *kisans*' first martyr — Komarayya. After Komarayya's martyrdom, almost everything seemed to have changed in Nalgonda, and "changed utterly".[84] Meetings were called, red flags hoisted, village committees set up, defence squads formed, semi-armed bands marched and full-throated slogans raised, sounding the death-knell of landlordism. Landlords generally fled the villages, and those who remained were socially ostracised. Most of their henchmen were caught, tried by the village committees, and suitably punished. At a village adjacent to Kaduvendi the *kisans* seized for the first time 200 acres from the landlord, and restored these through the village committees to their rightful owners.[85] By August 1946 the Nizam's state administration completely collapsed in the affected areas of Nalgonda, Warangal and Karimnagar, and a parallel rebel Government, run on "the lines of the Patri Sarkar", was established.[86] The state officials stopped

84. This was how W.B. Yeats expressed the Irish mood following the martyrdom of rebels in April 1916 in his poem, "The Easter Rising".

85. D.V. Rao, "Telengana Armed Struggle and the Path of Indian Revolution", *Proletarian Path* (English monthly), November 1973, Calcutta, p. 13.

86. Note on Nalgonda District, Hyderabad State C.I.D., 1 December 1947, Proceedings, Ministry of States, Govt. of India, File No. 15P(S)/47, 1947, N.A.I.

going inside the rebel areas, and the policemen took refuge mostly into the precincts of their stations. The months of September and October 1946 were in fact full of hostile demonstrations against the police *zulm*,[87] and whenever the police parties dared to go out for arresting the A.M.S. members, they were confronted with the armed gatherings of 200 to 300 persons. Simultaneously, the villagers used some ingenious system of signalling to forewarn their leaders against the raiding police parties. Even attacks on police stations were often feared, though these actually did not take place.[88] The Communists and the A.M.S. members appeared dramatically to be in full command of the situation under the over-all guidance of the District Committee of Nalgonda. Their programme of actions included:

(a) the guaranteeing of free justice to all by the village committees,
(b) the trying of the oppressive landlords by special courts,
(c) the returning of all irregular exactions, in grain and in cash, by the landlords, and finally, as well as, most importantly,
(d) the restoring to the *kisans* their "illegally" taken away (including those taken away through manipulations of "legal" procedures) lands by the landlords.[89]

Lands thus seized from the landlords, and restituted to their original occupiers, amounted by the beginning of 1947 to about 3,000 acres.[90] Nalgonda clearly had shown the way, but the

87. The Police minister of the Nizam's Government had to concede later that the local policemen always acted in Telengana in a *zabardast* (oppressive) manner, and regarded themselves "too big for their boots". Report by W.V. Griegson, 5 December 1946, *ibid.*

88. Fortnightly Reports of the Hyderabad Residency (from the Resident to the Secretary, the Crown Representative) for the months of September, October, November and December 1946, *ibid.*

89. D.V. Rao, "Telengana Armed Struggle and the Path of Indian Revolution", *Proletarian Path* (English monthly), November 1973, Calcutta, p. 13.

90. Amit Kumar Gupta, "Communists and Telengana Rising, May 1944-February 1947", Amit Kumar Gupta (ed.), *Myth and Reality: The Struggle for Freedom in India, 1945-47*, New Delhi, 1987, p. 478.

Communist leadership in other districts was still wavering, and consequently failed to reach the rebellious height that it did accomplish in Nalgonda.

Seeing the inefficacy of the local police forces, the Nizam's Government sent in October 1946 heavy police reinforcements from Hyderabad to Nalgonda. When even that failed to produce much effect, the State Infantry and the Cavalry were employed in November 1946. In the same month the Communist Party and the A.M.S. were declared unlawful in Hyderabad state. The military operations followed the policy of encirclement, cordoning off a village and sending in the police to make arrests.[91] The rebels put up stiff resistance against the army and police almost everywhere, especially at Dharmapuram (Janagaon), Belemula (Suryapet), Patasuryapet (Suryapet), Devaruppali (Janagaon) and Malla Reddygudem (Huzurnagar).[92] While fighting the police and the military the rebels used, for the first time, muzzle-loaders (*Bharmars*), in addition to *lathis*, sickles, slings and other agricultural implements.[93] In 35 days from the middle of November the police and the army carried out 31 raids, resulting in 10 deaths, 300 wounded and 1,500 arrested, including old men and boys.[94] According to the Communist sources, 20 persons — both men and women — were killed in the course of resisting the state forces in about 120 to 150 villages.[95] By

91. Note on Nalgonda District, Hyderabad State C.I.D., 1 December 1947, Proceedings, Ministry of States, Govt. of India, File No. 15P(S)/47, 1947, N.A.I.
92. P. Sundarayya, *Telengana People's Struggle and its Lessons*, Calcutta, 1972, pp. 41-52.
93. Note on Nalgonda District, Hyderabad State C.I.D., 1 December 1947, Proceedings, Ministry of States, Govt. of India, File No. 15P(S)/47, 1947, N.A.I. The Communists restrained their volunteers from using fire-arms for fear of elevating the struggle into "an entirely new stage". Towards the end of 1946, however, the volunteers started using muzzle-loaders rather freely. See P. Sundarayya, *Telengana People's Struggle and its Lessons*, Calcutta, 1972, p. 40.
94. From the draft statement on the proposed Adjournment Motion by Shri Vijayanand, Central Legislative Assembly, February 1947, Proceedings, Ministry of States, Govt. of India, File No. 15P(S)/47, 1947, N.A.I.
95. D.V. Rao, "Telengana Armed Struggle and the Path of Indian Revolution", *Proletarain Path* (English monthly), November 1973, Calcutta, p. 13.

January 1947 the rebels were losing ground in the face of superior arms and numbers, and their supporters and sympathisers were facing terrible repressions. The turning of the tide was heralded by the return of the landlords and the state officials to the villages, and by February 1947 the rising of *kisans* in Telengana seemed to have been over. In actuality, however, it was not, for the armed struggle was resumed vigorously by the Communist-led Telengana peasantry, following a brief interlude, and under somewhat changed circumstances.

Within a week of Komarayya's martyrdom in the hands of the *Deshmukhs*' goons in Nalgonda, Telengana, came the news from more than a thousand miles away from it of another martyr — that of Sheonath Passi, a poor peasant shot dead by the local *Zamindars* at Tamheri village of Bhabua in Shahabad.[96] Like Komarayya's death, Passi's also marked a conflagration — a rekindling, to be more precise — of the flames of *Bakasht* agitation that was originally sparked off in the Bihar countryside before the war, and whose cinders kept on burning throughout thereafter. The flare up in July 1946 had actually been born out of the Bihar *Zamindars*' concern for their *Zamindaris*, which seemed to have been threatened by the Congress election pledge of 1946, namely, "the removal of intermediaries between the peasant and the state", of course, "on payment of equitable compensation".[97] Much to the anguish of the *Zamindars*, and in spite of the long-standing reciprocity of interests between them and the Bihar Provincial Congress, the abolition of *Zamindari* could not be prevented by the Congress bosses from becoming the most important electioneering issue for obvious populist reasons. Once committed to it in the public, the Congress was not in a position after the election victory to disregard the question altogether, except that the ministry could go slow on its implementation, or even try to put it in the cold storage for the time being. This the Congress cabinet did try to do to the best of its ability, despite the Bihar Legislative Assembly's passing

96. P.M. Sen, "Epic Struggle of Bhabua Peasants", *Independent India* (English weekly), Patna, 8 December 1946.

97. All India Congress Committee, *Congress Election Manifesto*, 1946, Delhi.

a resolution in the spring of 1946 in favour of immediate steps for the abolition of the *Zamindari*. Gratified to an extent by the Congress's dilatoriness, the *Zamindars* nevertheless had neither felt reassured, nor seen any alternative to their going all-out frantically for stalling the abolition. Consequently, they started agitating against the measure within the legislature and outside it, taking recourse to the legal proceedings, contemplating deputations to the Viceroy, "as well as to the King Emperor", threatening "direct action",[98] forming armed bands (including the Zamindar Youth League) and starting a desperate offensive against the peasantry. The offensive was necessary not merely "to demoralise" the *kisans* and their leaders,[99] but also for practical reasons — for securing whatever of their landed estates could still be saved if the *Zamindaris* were finally abolished at the end of an agonisingly slow process. They were determined, therefore, not to part with the *Zirat*, which was their own, and the *Bakasht*, which they might either show to have been settled with fictitious fresh tenants (*benami*), or to have been sold away unencumbered to outside buyers. For both, the Bihar *Zamindars* were urgently required to undertake forcible occupation of as much *Bakasht* land, by dispossessing as many *Bakasht* peasants (tenants-at-will) as perhaps possible. The *Zamindars*' offensive and the *Bakasht kisans*' resistance to it occurred between 1946 and 1947 almost simultaneously in Munghyr, Gaya, Patna, Darbhanga and Saran, but the contest actually commenced in Bhabua sub-division of Shahabad district.

The Royist members of the Radical Democratic Party, who, under the leadership of its provincial secretary, Rampujan Singh, had been active among *kisans* in Shahabad district for some time, were the first to jump into the fray over the *Bakasht* lands in Bhabua. Led by Ramlal Verma, they started the agitation at Durgawati in the last week of June 1946, and by the beginning of July it spread to 75 villages, involving 20,000 *kisans*, resisting

98. "Agrarian Situation in Bihar", a report by the Central Intelligence Officer, Bihar, October 1946, Home Poll.(I), File No. 125/1946 Poll.(I) of 1946, N.A.I.

99. Arvind N. Das, *Agrarian Unrest and Socio-economic Change in Bihar, 1900-1980,* Delhi, 1983, p. 189.

the *Zamindari* bid to take over 20,000 acres.[100] Flouting the District Magistrate's suggestion of referring all the disputes to the arbitration boards, the *Zamindars* served the court notices on the *Bakasht* peasants in 24 villages, prevented them from tilling and sowing with the help of the *lathials*, and terrorised the villagers at gun points. It was in one of these villages that Passi was fired at repeatedly by a party of three *Zamindars* — Ramsurath Choudhury, Babban Singh and Tribhuvan Singh. Passi's death was the signal for the *kisans* in the neighbourhood to rise in defence of lands under their possession, and for the leftists of all hues — the Communists, the Congress Socialists, the Forward Blocists and the Swamiites — to rush to their respective fields of activity. By the middle of July 1946 the stage was fully set for the united left action, for the first time on the *kisan* front since 1942, and the *kisan* volunteers marched from village to village to ensure the tilling of the *Bakasht* lands. At the time of harvesting in October 1946 raged the battle for rights over crops and lands in Shahabad, Munghyr, Gaya, Patna, Saran and Darbhanga, and later in Muzaffarpur, Bhagalpur and Purnea. The *lathials* and the police were stubbornly resisted by the *kisan* volunteers, and whenever the men were arrested and removed from the scenes, the women came forward to take their place, and carry on the fight, as they notably did under Jadunandan Sharma in Nawadah sub-division of Gaya.[101] Deaths of *kisans* were reported from Gaya, and in a clash over harvesting, two were killed and some injured in Darbhanga in December 1946.[102] Clashes were also frequent in Munghyr — where Karyanand Sharma led the agitation — as well as in Saran where the Communists enjoyed "some influence among the peasantry".[103] Violent incidents in the Bihar countryside

100. P.M. Sen, "Epic Struggle of Bhabua Peasants", *Independent India* (English weekly), 8 December 1946.
101. *People's Age* (English weekly), 6 October 1946.
102. Fortnightly Report for 1st half of December 1946, Home Poll. File No. 18/12/46. N.A.I.
103. "Agrarian Situation in Bihar", a report by the Central Intelligence Officer, Bihar, October 1946, Home Poll.(I), File No. 125/1946 Poll.(I) of 1946, N.A.I.

increased manifold when the tillers of the *Bhowli* lands (for which the rent was paid only in grains) joined the strife in the districts of Patna and Gaya.[104] Hearing that the Bihar Congress ministry was inclined to allow the *Bhowli* tenants-at-will to approach the civil courts for permission to pay rent in cash (*nakdi*), the *kisans* started — at the instance of the leftists — removing the standing crops "to short-circuit civil litigation", as well as to present the landlords and the authorities with a *fait accompli*.[105] From the beginning of 1947 the province abounded in "agrarian riots" (such as at Nabiganj of Gaya, in Barahiya Tal and Begusarai of Munghyr, at Alwarpur of Patna, in Sasaram and Darigaon of Shahabad, to name only some), "land *satyagrahas*" (such as the one in Darbhanga where the Communist Bhogendra Jha and Gandhiite Narain Das were arrested in March 1947, along with 200 others), "acts of reprisals" (such as the burning down of the *kisan* huts, and the chopping off ears and noses of the *Zamindari Diwans*)[106], "police firings" (such as the one in Munghyr[107] in December 1946, and at Masaurah, Gaya, in March 1947) and "large scale arrests" (such as in Begusarai, Danapur, Bhagalpur and Champaran). Despite the promulgation of the Bihar Bakasht Disputes Settlement Ordinance by the provincial Government in January 1947, the attempts of the authorities at settling some of the *Bakasht* disputes summarily under it, and the euphoria that followed the Indian independence in August 1947, the *Bakasht kisans'* fight continued unabated throughout the year. Reports of clashes, deaths and injuries were pouring in from Barahiya Tal, Tikari, Sirahi, Sitamarhi and Saharsa till December 1947.[108] The acts of violence continued to recur even in the first quarter of 1948 in such storm-centres of the *Bakasht* movement as in Gaya,

104. Most of the *Bhowli* tenures existed in Patna and Gaya districts.
105. "Agrarian Situation in Bihar", Home Poll.(I), File No. 125/1946, Poll.(I) of 1946, N.A.I.
106. *The Searchlight* (English daily), 12 May 1947.
107. Fortnightly Report for 2nd half of December 1946, Home Poll., File No. 18/12/46, N.A.I.
108. See *The Searchlight* (English daily) issues of December 1947.

Munghyr, Darbhanga, Bhagalpur and Muzaffarpur, and in Gaya alone 21 were reported to have been killed in the clashes between the landlords and *kisans*.[109]

Like the *Bakasht* peasants', the Worli tribal *kisans*' agitation was a continuation of an earlier struggle, and it had been resumed in Thana district of Maharashtra in July 1946 — about the same time the *Bakasht* movement reappeared in Shahabad district of Bihar. The resumption took place over the wage dispute that the Worlis had with the *sowcars*-landlords over the cutting of grass, and with the forest lease-holders and timber merchants over the felling of trees. As regards the cutting of grass, the Worlis had already claimed under the aegis of the Communist activists of the Kisan Sabha a minimum rate of Rs. 2½ for 500 pounds of grass, and had actually fought for it in October 1945.[110] The Kisan Sabhaites similarly articulated the Worli demand for a daily rate of Re. 1¼ for the felling of trees and other forest works. Both the Worli demands being quite well-known, these were required to be sorted out before the grass-cutting and tree-felling season approached, and the mounting tension exploded. That was the reason perhaps why the District Collector of Thana, Mr. Almoula, convened in July 1946 a meeting of the representatives of the Kisan Sabha, the *sowcars*-landlords and the timber merchants. The meeting, however, was postponed, and following some dilatoriness, abandoned altogether. Instead, the Collector suddenly announced *ex-parte* the rates of Re. 1¼ to 2 for cutting 500 pounds of grass, and Re. 1 daily for felling trees. Clearly, the motivating factor behind his action was not the settlement of the wage dispute, but its aggravation, for the Worlis — who had already been reported to be receiving in many cases the rates of Re. 2½ to 3 and Rs. 1¼[111] — would not be in a position to accept less, while the landlords-timber merchants would not

109. General Secretary's Report, Annual Conference of the All-India Socialist Party, Kotwalnagar, Nasik City, 19 March 1948, Confidential C.I.D. Report, 21 March 1948, Home (Special) Dept., File No. 540-II of 1946-8, Maharashtra State Archives, Bombay.

110. See Act Two, scene III, p. 268.

111. Leslie J. Calman, "Congress Confronts Communism, Thana District, 1945-47", *Modern Asian Studies*, Vol. 21, no. 2, 1987, pp. 337-8.

be inclined to offer more than what the authorities asked them to do. It was doubtful if a District Collector should try on his own to aggravate the situation in the very district he was responsible for, without the bidding of the newly formed Congress ministry of B.G.Kher, or the nodding of its strong-armed Home minister, Morarji Desai. In the light of what happened subsequently one might even conclude that the Kher ministry did hardly wish from the beginning for a settlement of the issues, and that they rather desired for a deterioration of the conditions so that they could intervene in the name of law and order, and thereby stamp out the Communist influence among the Worlis. It was difficult to create a law and order problem if the Worli *kisans* remained as cool and restrained as they had been in 1945, and therefore, they had to be provoked, and their tempers frayed, with the help of scattered acts of offensive against them, as well as by trickery to arouse their passions. The *sowcars*-landlords started their offensive in August by lodging trumped up charges against the Worli activists in the criminal courts, and unleashing the hired hoodlums on *kisans* to brutally assault them. The one trickery attempted was similar to the one that paid some dividend in October 1945,[112] namely by giving currency to a false call that the Kisan Sabha would commemorate a "martyrs' day" on 11 October, and that all Worlis should assemble in Talwada on that day to hear the *Bai* (Godavari). Even the District Collector and the District Superintendent of Police were present in Talwada on that day with 150 armed policemen to deal with the anticipated Worli assemblage running amok. The Kisan Sabhaites were prompt to counteract the move by exposing the plot to the Worlis, and preventing a gathering at the appointed venue.[113]

Early in October 1946 the Kisan Sabha directed the Worlis not to undertake the grass-cutting and tree-felling works in the forests till their wage demands were conceded by the landlords-timber merchants. By the middle of October a massive strike began in the forests, spreading over an area of 1,000 square

112. See Act Two, scene III, p. 269.

113. S.V. Parulekar, *Revolt of the Varlis*, Bombay, 1947, p. 66.

miles, covering over 200 villages and a population of over one lakh. Not only all work came to a halt in most of this area, but even the plying of carts stopped. Later, when it was pointed out to the Worlis that the cartage had not been an issue of the dispute, they agreed to ply carts if the landlords and timber merchants obtained "permits" for such transportation from the Kisan Sabha.[114] There were stray cases of violence — according to the Government, because of the Worlis' intimidating and assaulting some of the "imported" and "loyal" labourers,[115] — and according to the Kisan Sabha, because of the *goondas*' attacking the *kisans*, holding some isolated groups of them as virtual prisoners, and forcing them to work.[116] Early in November 1946 took place a more serious clash when the policemen came to investigate a so-called case of "robbery" in a village in Dahanu *taluk*, and they were challenged, roughed up and chased away by the villagers.[117] Two days later the police reinforcement came to the spot, combed all the near about villages and arrested 55 Worlis.[118] By the first week of November the Worli strike seemed so complete that it was beginning to tell upon the nerves of the *sowcars*-landlords and the lease-holders-timber merchants. Some of the landlords in fact approached the Kisan Sabha, and expressed their willingness to pay even Rs. 3 for 500 pounds of grass, and compensate each Worli they had legally proceeded against.[119] The timber merchants went a step further, and after negotiating with the Kisan Sabha through the Special Officer for the Worli welfare (called the Prant Officer), came actually to an agreement. The agreement, which confirmed Rs. $1^1/_4$ as daily wage for felling trees and other forest works, and offered compensation to the Worlis for injuries sustained during the

114. *Ibid.*, pp. 67-8.
115. Fortnightly Reports for 1st half of October and 1st half of November 1946, Home Poll. File Nos. 18/10/46 and 18/11/46, N.A.I.
116. *People's Age* (English weekly), 27 October 1946.
117. *Times of India* (English daily), 2 November 1946.
118. S.V. Parulekar, *Revolt of the Varlis*, Bombay, 1947, p. 69.
119. Godavari Parulekar, *Revolt of the Warlis*, New Delhi, 1986, All India Kisan Sabha Golden Jubilee Series, 1936-86, no.1, p. 28.

work process, was signed on 9 November 1946 by the representatives of the Kisan Sabha, the Chairman of the North Thana Timber Merchants Association, and the Principal of the local High School in Dahanu, V.S. Karnik, who acted as an independent witness.[120] While the Prant Officer (A.H. Khan) left for showing the document to the higher authorities, the Worlis in effect called off their strike on 11 November, and the general body of the timber merchants' association ratified the settlement on 14 November.[121] It was precisely on 14 November that the Government of Bombay clamped "a state of emergency" for a month in Thana district under section 46(B) of the District Police Act,[122] on the ground of "a reign of terror" being created by the Communists and the Worlis, and it refused to be "bound by the act of a Prant Officer", or by any settlement "brought about by the Communists".[123] The imposition of a state of emergency was followed by the transfer of A.H. Khan from Dahanu, the externment of all prominent Kisan Sabhaites from Thana district and the issue of an order for detaining 200 active Worlis without trial.[124]

Once the economic battle of the Worlis was turned thus into a political one between the Government and the Communist *kisan* activists, for putting an end to "the undesirable activities of those who advocated violence to bring about ... a Communist state in India",[125] the chance for normalcy returning to Umbergaon and Dahanu *taluks* receded rudely to the background, till at least one of the contestants appeared visibly upset. Each side traded charges against the other, and while the

120. *People's Age* (English weekly), 24 November 1946.
121. Leslie J. Calman, "Congress Confronts Communism, Thana District, 1945-47", *Modern Asian Studies*, Vol. 21, no. 2, 1987, p. 339.
122. Fortnightly Report for 2nd half of November 1946, Home Poll. File No. 18/11/46, N.A.I.
123. Morarji Desai's press conference on 20 January 1947, *Times of India* (English daily), 21 January 1947.
124. S.V. Parulekar, *Revolt of the Varlis*, Bombay, 1947, p. 75.
125. The Government Press Release, *Bombay Chronicle* (English daily), 16 December 1946.

Government blamed the Kisan Sabha for inciting the Worlis to turn "violent", disturb "law and order"[126] and "obstruct" the police,[127] the Kisan Sabha accused the authorities of abetting the landlords' gangsters in acts of inhuman tortures, atrocities and assaults, and even wiping the Worli hamlets "out of existence".[128] By December 1946 the Worli strike appeared to have spread to Palghar *taluk*,[129] and continued to remain as complete as it had been from the beginning, despite the full play of direct and uninterrupted official repressions. About 400 Worlis were implicated in false cases, 250 detained without any charge, and all political activists, as well as the defence lawyers for the Worlis, meticulously externed.[130] The special court that was set up in Thana to try the Worlis would either deny bail to the under-trials so that they rotted in jails, or grant it only on condition of their agreeing not to have any track with the agitation.[131] It was mainly to avoid arrest that the Worlis started in December 1946 to take refuge in the jungles, and carry on their fight from the underground on a somewhat retaliatory temper, or what had been termed as their resorting to "guerilla tactics".[132] They organised volunteers squads, launched attacks on the landlords,[133] demolished some *awars* (farmhouses of the landlords), destroyed certain orchards, burnt stocks of grains in a few places, and ambushed a police party.[134] On 8 January 1947 occurred the most serious of the Worli clashes with the police when an aggressive mob of *kisans* in Namivali village was fired upon, resulting in the death of 5 and injury to 13.[135]

126. Fortnightly Report for November 1946, Home Poll. File No. 18/11/46, N.A.I.
127. *Ibid.*, 1st half of December 1946, Home Poll. File No. 18/12/46, N.A.I.
128. S.V. Parulekar, *Revolt of the Varlis*, Bombay, 1947, p. 84.
129. Fortnightly Report for 1st half of December 1946, Home Poll. File No. 18/12/46, N.A.I.
130. S.V. Parulekar, *Revolt of the Varlis*, Bombay, 1947, p. 83.
131. Godavari Parulekar, *Revolt of the Warlis*, New Delhi, 1986, p. 29.
132. *Ibid.*, p. 34.
133. *Times of India* (English daily), 6 January 1947.
134. *Ibid.*, 2, 4 and 6 January 1947.
135. Leslie J. Calman, "Congress Confronts Communism, Thana District, 1945-47", *Modern Asian Studies*, Vol. 21, no. 2, 1987, pp. 346-7.

The authorities were so incensed by the persistent Worli acts of defiance that they had already brought the military (a Company of Maratha Light Infantry) to the scene for maximising the use of force. Public sentiments, which had not taken very kindly to the Kher ministry's imposition of emergency on Thana, were unequivocally opposed to the despatching of military for smothering the tribal *kisans*, and so were the democratic voices within the Maharashtra Provincial Congress. The pressure of the public and democratic opinions had been so overwhelming that the military was withdrawn within two days of its arrival in Thana.[136] The Worlis' coming thus into the focus by the beginning of January 1947 also led to some refinement in the repressive Government policy towards them — it was no more the blatant and crude use of force, but a clever mixture of the determination to crush them with the display of an anxiety for their welfare, or the adoption of a strategy of "suppression and reward".[137] Simultaneously with the strengthening of the armed police forces, and the extending of the state of emergency for the second time in the area on 14 January 1947, the authorities sent "propaganda vans" into the affected villages to counter the Kisan Sabha influence,[138] energised the Congress-dominated Adivasi Seva Mandal for breaking the Communist spell on the Worlis, and supported it with funds to open new schools, set up hostels for the *Adivasi* students and distribute social welfare doles.[139] Side by side the hounding out of the Communist activists, and the indiscriminate detention of their Worli supporters and sympathisers, began the specious talks of granting land to the landless, sanctioning loans to the poor cultivators, fixing minimum rent in cash, opening grain depots in difficult terrains, making forced labour a cognisable offence and managing forest works directly by the Government, through the cooperative societies of the Worlis, and not through the *sowcars*-

136. *Ibid.*, p. 346. Also S.V. Parulekar, *Revolt of the Varlis*, Bombay, 1947, p. 84.
137. Leslie J. Calman, "Congress Confronts Communism, Thana District, 1945-47, *Modern Asian Studies*, Vol. 21, no. 2, 1987, p. 348.
138. *Times of India* (English daily), 16 January 1947.
139. Leslie J. Calman, "Congress Confronts Communism, Thana District, 1945-47", *Modern Asian Studies*, Vol. 21, no. 2, 1987, p. 346.

timber merchants.[140] But the Worli strike did not seem to have been affected very much by these in February 1947 — the timber trade still stood paralysed, and the harvesting and threshing operations were yet at a stand-still in Umbergaon, Dahanu and Palghar. By March and April, however, the agitation started showing signs of a decline, with the cessation of activities of the Worli squads, and even the suspension of the strike in certain areas.[141] By the end of July 1947 the Worli tumult was over for all practical purposes — to the great relief of the Government, and to some discomfiture of the Communists.

Howsoever much the C.P.I. central leadership tried to exaggerate the Maharashtra Provincial Congress Committee's sympathy for the Worlis, *vis-a-vis* the Congress ministry's antipathy towards them, as an "autonomous vindication" of their agitation,[142] and the Kisan Sabha similarly tried to magnify "the universal condemnation of the vested interests" in Thana to be "a victorious end of the Worli resistance",[143] the plain truths were that the *sowcar*-landlord-timber merchant combine did not formally concede to the wage demands of the Worlis, that the authorities eventually overcame the heroic Worli resistance through their policy of "suppression and reward", and that the die-hard Congress ministry under Khare and Desai succeeded in putting down finally the challenge the exuberant Communist rank and file, or the Communist *kisan* activists, had dared to throw up to the exploiters of the Worlis in Thana district. Despite all the Communist assertion from the top that what the Worlis really fought for was "a right to human existence and not a revolt against the existing order",[144] as if such a right could be secured without trying to undermine any of the bases of a

140. *Ibid.*, p. 347. Also the Report of the Special Committee on the Worlis, Maharashtra Provincial Congress Committee Meeting on 29 March 1947, *People's Age* (English weekly), 20 April 1947.
141. Fortnightly Reports for March, April and May 1947, Home Poll. File Nos. 18/3/47, 18/4/47 and 18/5/47, N.A.I.
142. "Maharashtra Congress Committee Vindicates Warlis' Struggle", P.B. Rangnekar, *People's Age* (English weekly), 20 April 1947.
143. S.V. Parulekar, *Revolt of the Varlis*, Bombay, 1947, pp. 90-1.
144. "Maharashtra Congress Committee Vindicate Warlis' Struggle", P.B. Rangnekar, *People's Age* (English weekly), 20 April 1947.

starkly exploitative society, the undoubted fact had been that the Worlis did revolt since 1945, and very gloriously so, against some of the basic modes of feudal-commercial exploitation, including the low wages in 1946-7, and that whenever revolts like theirs — the so-called "partial" ones — displayed the tendencies to become "total" (as it seemed to have done in Telengana in 1946-7), the chances of the avowed Communist objective of an "agrarian revolution" brightened up. There was nothing on record to indicate if Godavari Parulekar and others had ever thought of the over-all perspective of the Worli revolt, and planned to raise its partial character to the level of a total one by demanding the restoration of all lands the Worlis lost to the *sowcars*-landlords, or by combining a battle for lands with the fight for the wages. But even if they somehow had contemplated so doing, Godavari and her comrades would not perhaps have been able to give adequate effect to it on account of their severe organisational and infrastructural handicaps. As the splintered Communist activists who self-imported themselves in the difficult jungle lands, and functioned almost entirely on their own, with scant ideological and material support from the party and the Kisan Sabha headquarters, they were neither able, nor spared the time at any stage, to build up a sustained organisation in the location, co-ordinate and articulate the existing Worli village committees, and entrust these with the initiative of making decisions and taking actions. Crucially, therefore, as it happened so often in similar other cases, the Worli struggle developed an insurmountable crisis with the externment of Godavari and her associates, or the exit of the "outsider" agitators and ideologues from the scene, whose place in the movement could not be taken up by others. Others were also not there to play the roles, and unlike the case in Bihar during the *Bakasht* struggle, the non-Communist left political groups appeared practically to be absent in Thana district, and those rare few who might have taken some interest in the Worlis, namely, the Socialists, were so upset by the violence the Worlis and the Communists practised,[145] and the Government

145. *Janata* (English weekly) of January 1947, cited in S.V. Parulekar, *Revolt of the Varlis*, Bombay, 1947, p. 72.

indulged in,[146] that they decided to confine their activity to the task of bringing "peace" in Thana.[147] But was it possible at all for the Communist activists among the Worlis to bring "peace" by themselves, stop the agitation at a certain point, and avert the chances of any evident failure? The possibility did appear to have been very thin, indeed, from the way the Congress ministry was pre-determined to quash all negotiations, crush the rising head of a phantasmal "Communist state" and thrust a war upon the *kisans* and their leaders. Perhaps Godavari and her comrades were also not interested in calculating the losses and gains, and giving up the fight mid-way through some compromise. The mainspring of strength of persons like Godavari, as well as their weakness, lay probably in a passion for getting over the inertia of the "people's war", resuming the popular struggle that was long overdue, and rushing it on even at the expense of headlong collisions with the Government, as if to make up for the lost time.

The impatience of the Communist activists with the party's unmoving central leadership, their anxiety for giving expression to the bellicosity of the masses, and their haste for attaining the consecutive high stages of agitation were best illustrated in Kerala, mainly at Shertallai and Ambalapuzha *taluks* of Alleppey district in Travancore state, and peripherally at Karivalloor and Kuvumbayi in North Malabar. The state of Travancore — to which the district of Alleppey and the *taluks* of Shertallai and Ambalapuzha belonged — was noteworthy for its preponderance of fixed rent-paying small landholders with occupancy rights, whether as tenants of the *Sarkar* lands or of the *Jenmi* lands (the *Janmans*). Since rack-renting and evictions were not that rampant in Travancore, particularly after the amendment of the Jenmi and Kudiyan Act of 1867, the Karshaka Sanghams did not flourish there as they did in Malabar, and the Communist Party (which came clandestinely into existence in the state by the beginning of 1940) "could not rise to the position of

146. Socialist Party meeting in Palaghar, June 1947, Home (Sp.) Dept., File No. 540 -III(a) of 1947, Maharashtra State Archives, Bombay.

147. *Ibid.*

leadership" of the *kisan* masses.[148] In contrast with the limpings of the Karshaka Sanghams, however, the Karshaka Tozhilali Sanghams, or the agricultural labourers' unions of relatively recent origin, seemed to have made rapid strides under the Communist guidance. This had particularly been so because the agricultural labourers, and the similarly placed such artisanal categories as the toddy-tappers, the coconut-climbers, the fisher-folks and the boat-workers were the most exploited and oppressed in rural society in Travancore, and therefore, the keenest in awaiting their leftist and Communist deliverers. The labour in the agricultural sector was in such abundance, and so cheap in the state that the labourers employed there in proportion to the cultivators happened to be the highest in India — nearly 45 per cent of the total number of cultivators, whereas it was 19 per cent in Bengal, 16 per cent in the U.P. and 28 per cent in Bihar and Orissa.[149] The average wage per person per day in the early 1930s was approximately 6 annas,[150] or slightly more than the cost of an ordinary meal — which had roughly been 5½ annas.[151] Monetarily it increased by the mid-1940s to Rs. $1^{3}/_{8}$, but so also did the cost of an ordinary meal to Re. 1.[152] Even this meagre wage could not be demanded by the field-hands, or those attached farm workers who laboured in the landlords' lands and occupied a tiny patch therein to set up their hutments.[153] Apart from the attached farm-hands, there were also the bonded labourers (*onappanikkarans*), or those who had to work for years to repay their paltry loans (usually in grains) to the landlords and other rentiers. Their situation was most tellingly reflected in the case of an agricultural labourer in

148. E.M.S. Namboodiripad, *A History of Indian Freedom Struggle*, New Delhi, 1986, p. 883.
149. *Census of India*, Report, 1931, p. 245.
150. *Ibid.*, p. 498.
151. K.C. George, *Immortal Punnapara-Vayalar*, New Delhi, 1975, p. 25.
152. P.K.V. Kaimal, *Revolt of the Oppressed: Punnapra-Vayalar, 1946*, Delhi, 1994, pp. 43-4.
153. V.S. Achuthanandan and T.K. Ramakrishnan, *Kerala: Punnapra-Vyalar and Other Struggles*, New Delhi, 1986, All India Kisan Sabha Publications, p. 4.

the neighbouring Kuttanad *taluk*, who became an *onappa-nikkaran* in 1932 for clearing a paddy debt of 80 kilograms and who, being unable to repay it even after 10 years, — had to enlist the help of his brother as *onappanikkaran* in 1943.[154] Forced labour or *Oozhiyam* under such circumstances was bound to be abounding, and the agricultural labourers of all kinds had to bear on their backs its burden imposed not only by the landlords and the intermediaries, but also by the tenant-cultivators. A number of feudal imposts and cesses were also collected from the labourers on all conceivable pretexts, and failures to pay these invariably invited heavy penalties.

Like the agricultural labourers, the agro-industrial workers or artisans, such as the fisherfolks, the toddy-tappers, the coconut-climbers and the boat-workers were victims of stark economic exploitation. The thatched huts of the fisherfolks all along the coastal area of Travancore, especially in Punnapra, Alleppey, were situated on lands belonging to the *Jenmis*. The *Jenmis*, who included the biggest among them — the Church — were also the owners of most of the fishing boats and nets. The fisherfolks, or the *Kudians* (tenants) of the *Jenmis* for lands, boats and nets, were obliged to pay one-half of their daily catches as rent. From the remaining half, portions were kept apart as shares of "God", and of the deceased head of the family of the owners.[155] What little had been left was then divided among the crews of a fishing boat, usually 11 in number. The market mechanism was such that the fishermen and women did hardly take their shares directly to the consumers. Having taken advances beforehand, they were forced to sell at the lowest price to the intermediaries, who, in their turn, sold fish in the market at the highest. If the fisherfolks were exploited by the *Jenmis* and the intermediaries, the toddy-tappers (mostly poor Ezhavas) suffered in the hands of toddy-contractors and toddy-shopowners. Either a toddy-tapper worked for the

154. P.K.V. Kaimal, *Revolt of the Oppressed: Punnapra-Vayalar, 1946*, Delhi, 1994, p. 8.
155. K.K. Kusuman, "Punnapra-Vayalar Uprising, 1946", *Journal of Kerala Studies,* Vol. III, no. 1, p. 139.

contractor on a daily wage of annas 8 to 9, or tapped the rented trees on his own and sell the collected liquid to the shop-owners at the rate of Rs. 15 for 100 *kutti* (1 *kutti* = $1^1/_2$ litres).[156] Both kinds of earnings of the toddy-tappers were extremely low by the inflationary standards of the 1940s, and to make matters worse for them, they had to contribute towards the up-keeping of the toddy shops, pay a fee at the time of marking trees for tapping and work without payment on the last day of every month (*Muppthamtheeyathi kallu*).[157] Still the lot of the toddy-tappers was slightly better than that of the coconut-climbers, who belonged generally to the *Dalit* caste of Paravan (or Velan), and who — having no fixed wage — had to accept whatever the *Jenmis* offered for working on a certain number of coconut trees.

Over and above the commercial-feudal exploitation, the rural proletariat — the agro-industrial workers and agricultural labourers in Travancore — were subjected to the severest forms of social oppressions. Their belonging to the lowest castes in one of the most obnoxiously caste-ridden societies in India, namely the Paryas, the Pulayas and similar other categories, exposed them to social disabilities, sub-human treatments and misbehaviours. They were both "untouchables" (whose touch polluted) and "unapproachables" (with whom specified distances must be maintained to avoid pollution), forbidden to enter into public places, such as the temple precincts, the post offices and the court compounds, forced to speak in lowly terms about themselves and threatened against their putting on dresses worn usually by members of the higher castes. Their using umbrellas, sporting moustaches, having headgears, or even tying towels around their heads were frowned upon. Such a humiliating situation continued practically unabated in the 1940s, despite

156. R. Prakasam, *Keralathile Trade-Union Prasthanathinte Charitram* (Malayalam), Trivandrum, p. 139, cited in P.K.V. Kaimal, *Revolt of the Oppressed: Punnapra-Vayalar, 1946*, Delhi, 1994, p. 52.

157. *Ibid.*, p. 79.

the formation of a number of caste organisations,[158] and their creating — to a certain extent — an awareness among the socially disabled. However, the subsistence economic level of the Parayas and Pulayas seemed to have stood in the way of their building up a strong reform movement, and unlike the Ezhavas, among whom developed a substantial affluent section that simultaneously benefited from the Sree Narayana Dharma Paripalana Yogam, and contributed to its strengthening and moulding, the Sadhujana Paripalana Yogam of the agriculturally labouring Pulayas had not made any headway, but actually died a premature death. Social oppressions were not limited to the segregation and utter humiliation of a people, but extended widely to their indiscriminate physical torture. Beating, kicking and whipping of agricultural labourers, particularly of the *onappanikkarans* and the attached field-hands, for their slightest acts of supposed misdemeanour, were not only common but also considered to be the privileges of the landlord employers. When the Karshaka Tozhilali Sanghams resented the practice of physical torture, their state level President, Verghese Vaidyan, faced in 1943 a greatly dismayed landlord of Kuttanad who failed to understand why exception should at all be taken to the beating of a Pulayan — "an established tradition".[159] Therein lay the crux of the whole situation, namely, the possibility that the agricultural labourers and artisans could at a certain stage be inspired to take exception to all the established traditions of economic exploitation and social oppression.

The inspiration came mainly from the Travancore Communists, who in the phase of the "imperialist war" embarked from the underground (their party being banned in the state) upon their mission of political proselytising. Although they attained some success in spreading their ideology, and making a certain inroad

158. Mentionable among them were the South Travancore Sambavar Samajam, Mahajana Sangham, the South Travancore Aiyanavar Samajam, the Kerala Adimajana Sabha, the All-Kerala Araya Mahajana Yogam, the All-Travancore Varnavar Samajam, the Yogeswara Mahajana Sangham, the Kerala Paravan Sangham, etc.

159. P.K.V. Kaimal, *Revolt of the Oppressed: Punnapra-Vayalar, 1946*, Delhi, 1994, p. 9.

into the long established trade-union movement, especially among the coir factory workers in Alleppey and Shertallai, the Communists did not achieve much in concrete terms. There in fact was an ebbing of their political influence in the subsequent collaborationist "people's war" phase, affecting even its image in the trade-union front for treating the workers' bonus issue rather lukewarmly.[160] However, the Communists gained organisationally with the lifting of the ban on their party in 1942, and with the opportunity for moving about in the "open" while most other political activists were either behind the bars, or on the run. There were discernible increases in the number of party workers and party funds, as well as in the circulation of party organs, despite the anti-Fascist far-cry, the "grow more food" reformism and an allergy to popular agitations. Such body-building without any demonstration of strength was unlikely to satisfy the revolutionary fervours of the local Communist leaders and cadres for long, howsoever much their energies had fruitfully been channelised in the "food committees" and "de-hoarding" operations when a famine stalked over the coastal region of Travancore. They were likely, sooner or later, to be enthusiastic for stirring popular action and wresting political initiative. It was reported that as early as the end of 1943, coinciding with the turning of the war-tide in the Allies' favour, a party meeting in Alleppey planned for intensifying the labour agitation in the light of the worsening economic situation.[161] Labour disputes in fact multiplied in 1944-5, and the British intelligence appeared to be aware of the expectations of the Communist rank and file for a post-war law and order breakdown in the state and for their being able to take advantage of it.[162] It was in the middle of 1944 that the Karshaka Tozhilali Sanghams were launched by the Communists with great effect, and within ten months the Sangham at Shertallai was able to enrol 65 per cent of the total

160. Version of Sreekantan Nair, November 1977, T.J. Nossiter, *Communism in Kerala: A Study in Political Adaptation,* Delhi, 1982, p. 108, footnote 88.

161. *Ibid.*, p. 86.

162. *Ibid.*

agricultural population of the *taluk*.[163] Fish-workers' unions were fully activised by 1945, and the toddy-tappers' and the coconut-climbers' unions came into existence about the same time.

The local Communists' stepping up their activities had synchronised remarkably with the deterioration of the over-all situation in Travancore between 1943 and 1946. The rice-consuming Travancore used to produce only one-third of its total requirements of rice, and depended heavily on the supply from Burma for the rest. With the stoppage of supply from Burma, following the Japanese occupation of it, Travancore faced acute food shortage, and came under the grip of a famine that harshly affected both Shertallai and Alleppey. Although the importation of rice from the eastern part of India (and from Bengal in particular) saved the situation to an extent, the state did not recover from the scarcity of food. The state authorities' drive for procurement of rice and attempt at its public distribution failed miserably, leading to widespread hoarding and "blackmarketing" (mostly by the ration shopowners). Consequently, the prices of foodstuff in 1943-4 became three times more than the prices of 1939-40,[164] and other commodities were sold at sky-high rates. The war years also brought a crisis in the coir industry, disrupting the export of its products through the sea-routes to the European market, and consequently the Europeans' replacing them with the newly discovered synthetic materials. As a result, a large number of coir factories had closed down in Travancore, rendering multitudes of workers jobless by the end of 1945. The rank of the unemployed swelled again in 1945 when the demobilised Travancorean soldiers returned to their homes from India's north-eastern frontier. The home-coming of the demobilised men from Assam, the labour unrest, the food scarcity — "enhanced by low ration" — and the rise in the prices of essential commodities, coupled with the high-handedness of a "repressive" state Government,[165] practically brought Travancore to the very edge of a precipice.

163. K.C. George, *Immortal Punnapra-Vayalar*, New Delhi, 1975, p. 90.
164. P.K.V. Kaimal, *Revolt of the Oppressed: Punnapra-Vayalar, 1946*, Delhi, 1994, p. 58.
165. Report of the A.C.I.O. (Calicut), on the Travancore Riots, Home Poll. File No. 5/40/46 Poll.(I) of 1946, N.A.I.

The Travancore state administration was turned "repressive" by its king-pin, the *Diwan*, C.P. Ramaswamy Aiyar, known generally as "C.P.", who had been running a highly centralised, nepotist, corrupt and brutalised regime, based on a communally elected legislature (having no control over the executive, except the right to interpolate), and also a communally "reserved" bureaucracy. He had managed in 1938 with a strong arm in thwarting, on the one hand, the Travancore State Congress's agitation for his ouster, as well as for a responsible Government, and on the other, the massive industrial action by 40,000 workers in the coir district of Alleppey. Once he weathered these two storms, C.P. practically assumed the role of a ruthless dictator in Travancore, with a complete command over the royal family, clever liaison with the British authorities, and a queer linkage with the Indian National Congress. The *Diwan* suppressed the print media, banned political literature, imposed postal censorship, dispersed anti-Government rallies, and punished "objectionable" slogans and "intemperate" speeches. Whatever little of civil liberty was left in Travancore also disappeared during the second world war with the promulgation of the notorious Defence Regulations, which C.P. used indiscriminately for suppressing the popular will. But C.P. had also to swallow a bitter pill at the British instance — the anti-Fascist Communist Party of Travancore — and to legalise it, though his Government suspected its fidelity all through, and felt that the real motive behind the party's cooperation with his administration in dealing with the food situation was to extend its hold over "the working class" and "the masses".[166] This was exactly what the Travancore Communists started doing in 1945-6 by taking advantage of C.P.'s policy on strikes and agitations, namely, to permit economic struggles and trade-union activities, but not to allow political or general strikes by way of protest against "the policy

166. This had been recorded later in the Administration Report of the Police Department, Travancore State, for the year 1119 (M.E.), cited in P.K.V. Kaimal, *Revolt of the Oppressed: Punnapra-Vayalar, 1946*, Delhi, 1994, p. 123-4.

and programme" of either British Indian administration, or the administration in Travancore.[167] It was the frequent use of the legitimised economic "bargains" and the "strikes" by the local Communist activists that had disrupted the *status quo* in Travancore by the middle of 1946, and sent the vested interests and their official defenders into a hysteria. The most affected areas included Alleppey, Shertallai and Ambalapuzha — where the proportion of workers and landless labourers was the highest in the state, and where the Communists enjoyed "active control" over all sorts of trade-unionism.[168] The coir factory workers resisted retrenchment, demanded an increase in wages and clamoured for bonus. The agricultural labourers rallied against ill-treatments and forced labours, wanted better wages and working conditions, and opposed evictions from their hutments and strips of lands. The fisherfolks claimed a more equitable share of their catches, the toddy-tappers a more favourable deal from the contractors and shop-owners, the coconut-climbers a greater number from the pluck — "10 coconuts for every 100".[169]

The intensity of all these economic battles — and that too, in unison — startled the *Jenmis*, the rich peasants, the rentiers, the mercantile interests, and above all, the coir factory proprietors. Once they were able to gather their wits, they retaliated by setting their hirelings on the workers, attacking them to and fro their work places, breaking their shacks, violating their women, and framing them up before the state police. The worst of the hooligans on the rampage, however, were not employed by the vested interests, but by the state authorities — who recruited them as plain-clothed "reserve" policemen, on an allowance of Rs. 5 per month, to act as agent-provocateurs, to wreck workers' meetings, to raise counter-slogans, and to create disturbances, resulting often in looting and arsoning. The offensive could not have gone on unresisted indefinitely, and

167. "Government's Policy on Strikes", *Travancore Information Listener*, Vol. III, 1946, and also *Proceedings of the Travancore Sri Mulam Assembly*, Vol. XXVIII, no. 6, pp. 481-2, *ibid*., p. 125.

168. Report of the A.C.A.O., Calicut, on the Travancore Riots, Home Poll. File No. 5/40/46(I) of 1946, N.A.I.

169. *Ibid.*

the workers had to start confronting their opponents, engaging them into group clashes, and titing them for all the tats. On his own part personally, C.P. — who prided himself with the strength of a modern militia of 4,000 and a police force of 8,000 — was in favour of camouflaging his iron hands, so far as it was practicable, in dealing with the volatile agitation of the organised workers. He even intervened in mid-1946 when the coir workers struck work on the issue of bonus as a matter of right (and not as a part of profitability), convened a tripartite conference of the state Government, the employers and the unions, and favoured the unions' obtaining from the employers 4 per cent bonus as deferred wages.[170] His motivation apparently was to keep the activities of the Communists and their working class followers confined to the wage-battles, even by conceding some ground nominally (for the employers in many factories had already paid 4 per cent bonus on their own), and not to allow it to spread to the wider political arena. Determined to deny the substance of responsible government, as demanded by the State Congress, and sensing the British departure from India in the near future, the *Diwan* went anteriorly into his pipe-dreaming of an independent Travancore, and devised by January 1946 on the American model a constitution in which his position *vis-a-vis* the legislature and the judiciary resembled that of the President of the United States, but whose authority should rest on the Travancore Maharaja's prerogative, and not on popular election.[171] Even some of the key figures of the State Congress — those champions of responsible government in Travancore, who had been gasping for breath after being pounded by C.P. — were willing to give the American model a "fair" trial. It was only the Communist-worker combination that could prove to be a thorn in the C.P's constitutional path if it dared to dabble in "politics" and pick up the State Congress's mantle. That precisely was the most logical position the popularly committed leftists and Communists had been expected to assume — the one that C.P.

170. T.J. Nossiter, *Communism in Kerala*, Delhi, 1982, p. 90.

171. R. Ramakrishnan Nair, *Constitutional Experiments in Kerala*, Trivandrum, 1964, pp. 84-101.

forbade, but many Travancoreans anxiously awaited. Much, however, depended on the manner in which such a position was to be assumed by the Communists on their anti-feudal-mercantile capital-tyrannical strategy or strategies, and also on what they hoped to achieve locally at that given intermediary stage of the Communist revolutionary movement in India.

The Travancore Communists' urges for taking up the cause of responsible government in the state, for resisting murderous assaults on the workers, and for merging the "economic" agitation with the "political" one were not only understandable but also seemed perfectly natural. What did not appear exactly to be so, and certainly looked somewhat romantically contrived, was their forcing a premature insurrection on the toiling masses of north Travancore. In the midst of sporadic skirmishes in different places of Shertallai and Ambalapuzha *taluks* between the coir workers, agricultural labourers and artisans on the one hand, and the hoodlums of the factory-owners, *Jenmis* and liquor contractors on the other, in which the police made no mistake in siding with the latter, the Communist trade-unionists and activists met secretly at Ambalapuzha on 25 September 1946 to take a stock of the prevailing situation, and came out dramatically with the decision to intensify the resistance, and to prepare and train the workers and labourers for an imminent "large scale" struggle.[172] That the decision in effect was to plan for a rising had become apparent when "camps" (ironically for the shelter of adult male — and not female — members of the family) of workers, agricultural labourers and artisans sprang up in relatively less accessible areas of Ambalapuzha and Shertallai *taluks*, combat training centres set up in such places as Punnapra, Vayalar, Muhamma and Kalavamkodam, traditional arms (spears, knives, sticks and swords) gathered, grains and funds collected, trenches dug, army-like formations made, their commands chosen and headquarters (in Vayalar) established. There seemed in fact to be considerable self-satisfaction in the

172. Report of the Central Intelligence Officer to the Director, Intelligence Bureau, Delhi, Crown Representative Records (in microfilm, Acc. No. 133), N.A.I.

higher echelons of the local Communist Party over the "pucca military" atmosphere that was brought upon to prevail in the camps.[173] Such overflowing of insurrectionary enthusiasm was difficult to control, and there had been instances of the rebels' forcibly collecting fund, raiding the houses of known rowdies, intimidating those who did not see eye to eye with them and imposing toll tax in the area under their command.[174] On 13 October 1946 they took out a *jatha* of about 1,000 labourers from Punnamveli to Shertallai, which went berserk, attacked the houses of some landlords and manhandled the inmates.[175]

The blue-print of insurrection seemed to have been drawn from the Soviet model of Russia, calling upon the workers in both the industrial and agricultural sectors to undertake a paralysing general strike till their demands were met, backing it up with the disruption of communications, and signalling simultaneously for a civil rising in direct confrontation with the state's forces. The Travancore Communist leaders did place their blue-print before the Kerala Provincial Committee of the C.P.I. in Calicut, who (including such stalwarts like E.M.S. Namboodiripad and P. Krishna Pillai) decided — in the typical middle-level bureaucratic tradition — to pass the buck on to the C.P.I. headquarters in Bombay. K.C. George, the Travancore party boss, himself travelled to Bombay, met there on 13 October 1946 Dr. G. Adhikari of the Politbureau (the General Secretary, P.C. Joshi, being away in Calcutta at that point) and sought the green signal. Although Adhikari was "perturbed" at the "inevitability of a clash with the Government and the police",[176] he relented to the local initiative in Travancore — and not very unexpectedly so in view of the delicate balance that existed between the moderates and militants in the then C.P.I. Central Committee. According to some other version, B.T. Ranadive, the

173. The observation of T.V. Thomas, President, All Travancore Trade Union Congress to K.C. George, the chief of the Travancore Communist Party, in K.C. George, *Immortal Punnapra-Vayalar*, New Delhi, 1975, p. 63.
174. P.K.V. Kaimal, *Revolt of the Oppressed: Punnapra-Vayalar, 1946*, Delhi, 1994, p. 174.
175. Report of the A.C.I.O., Calicut, on the Travancore Riots, Home Poll., File No. 5/40/46 Poll.(I) of 1946, N.A.I.
176. K.C. George, *Immortal Punnapra-Vayalar*, New Delhi, 1975, pp. 60-1.

spokesman of militancy at the apex of the C.P.I., and a proven left adventurist by his activities later on, might have also had played a decisive role in permitting the Travancore Communists to go ahead with their plan.[177] Once the "sanction" was thus obtained, the developments started taking place in north Travancore in chaotic rapidity — the raising of the slogan to throw C.P.'s "American model into the Arabian Sea" (*Amerikkan modal Arabyan katalil*), the clamouring for the end of the *Diwan's* misrule and the restrictions on civil liberties, the combining of the workers' economic claims (for increased wages, better working conditions and prohibition on ejectments) with their political demands (for an all parties' interim Government, the formation of a Constituent Assembly and a responsible government on the basis of adult franchise), and the calling of an indefinite general strike of the workers and labourers from 22 October 1946 for the redressal of their economic and political grievances. On the third day of the general strike (24 October) the workers from the camps ran over the reserve police post in Punnapra, clashed with the military over a bridge that they wanted to sabotage in Maraikulam, and forced an army picket to abandon its post in Muhamma. On 25 October the state authorities declared martial law over the *taluks* of Ambalapuzha and Shertallai, sent out heavy military reinforcements to the affected areas on the following day, and forced the insurgents to fall back upon Vayalar — the so-called "Moscow of Travancore". The army commenced its assault on the Vayalar camp from all directions in the afternoon of 27 October 1946, and the unequal combat between rifles and wooden spears was over by the evening, leaving innumerable dead in the carnage — the party cadres, the coir workers, the agricultural and agro-industrial labourers.[178] The Travancore Communist Party and the coir workers' and fish workers' unions being declared illegal,

177. T.J. Nossiter, *Communism in Kerala*, Delhi, 1982, p. 90, footnote 90. He, however, has not disclosed the identity of his informant — "a former C.P.I. leader, no longer active in the party" from 1973.

178. According to the British Intelligence Report of the time (see Report of the A.C.A.O., Calicut, Home Poll. File No. 5/10/46 Poll.I of 1946, N.A.I.), approximately 2,000 were massacred. Recent historical enquiries into the happenings also seem, more or less, to corroborate this figure.

and the fugitives hunted down, normalcy slowly limped back to north Travancore, factories reopened and the martial law withdrawn on 10 November 1946. The state nevertheless was not the same after the Punnapra-Vayalar rising — it could not have been so, for the colossal martyrdom of thousands was bound in some way to affect the Travancoreans' making up their minds about who should rule over them, and how. Despite all his persistence, the fate of C.P.'s *Diwanship*, the "American model" and the "independence" of the state seemed to have practically been sealed by the first half of 1947. However, the blood of the martyrs — the seed of the rising left-wing — hardly had any immediate cleansing effect on the agrarian Travancore, and its feudal-commercial defilement apparently continued unabated.

Although not of such epic dimension as the Punnapra-Vayalar rising, the Communist *kisan* activists in various other places did manage locally to give vent to their militant enthusiasm for initiating popular actions. One could get a glimpse of their audacious initiative, and the rural poor's responses to it, through a reference to some of the local developments in 1946-47. The earliest one occurred in Karwar *taluk*, North Kanara, in the first quarter of 1946 when the district Kisan Sabha, under the leadership of its President, Honappa Naik, launched a movement for an increase in the crop share of the tenants-at-will, or a decrease in the produce-rent to be paid to the landlords. Despite the landlords' threats of terminating tenancies, acts of physical violence, and the formation of a "defence" organisation of their own (Shakti Sangh), the *kisans en masse* withheld the landlords' shares, withstood their attackers and guarded the harvested crops. When the landlords registered false cases against the *kisans* in the law-courts and with the police, the local Khedut Sangh started their social boycott, cut off their supply of milk and vegetables, and stopped the villagers from doing domestic jobs for them. Being forced to negotiate with the Sangh, the landlords almost gave in, agreeing apparently to a substantial reduction of their shares.[179] It was at this point in April 1946 that the district officialdom and the police intervened, detained the

179. *People's Age* (English weekly), 5 May 1946.

Sangh activists and suppressed the agitation. Almost a similar consequence followed from an agitation in Basti district of the U.P., which the Communist-*kisan* combination conducted daringly between April and September 1946 over the *Sir* lands. The *kisans,* who were evicted recently from their holdings by the Sheikh of Chatara, marched into the fields under the leadership of the local Communist *kisan* activists, recaptured these plots after fighting back the landlords' goons at Dundwa, and forcibly took away the grains produced in these by besieging the Sheikh's mansion. An identical outburst had also taken place in September 1946 at the neighbouring village of Chhatahara over the harvesting of crops in 300 *bighas* of *Sir* land of Raja Sheopati Singh. About 3,000 traditionally armed *kisans* defended their crops for sometime against the joint onslaughts of the landlord's hoodlums and the police.[180] The Basti *Shikmi Kashtkars'* examples encouraged *kisans* in other parts of the province to resist their forcible eviction by the landlords — in Azamgarh, Unnao, Jhansi, Sitapur, Badaun, Fateahpur and Ballia — leading often to deaths and injuries.[181] The local activists in south Gujarat also succeeded in reviving the *Halis'* struggle against the system of bondage in Surat, Broach and Baroda. The Kisan Sabhaites were active once again in resuming the anti-*Zamindari* agitation in Munagala, Krishna district of Andhra, in organising the *batai* cultivators against the landlords' irregular exactions in Multan and Montgomery districts of the Punjab, in mobilising the *punnaiyals* against evictions in Tanjore, Ramnad and Tinnevelli,[182] and in leading the *kisans* against the landlords' depriving them of their wood-cutting privileges in Bagribari *Zamindari*, Parbatjowar Pargana of Assam.[183] In all these happenings the *kisan* agitators had to face the coercive forces of the Government, but nowhere was the confrontation as bloody as in Malabar.

180. *Ibid.*, 13 October 1946.
181. *Ibid.*, 13 July 1947.
182. General Secretary's Report, Sikandra Rao session of the A.I.K.S., May 1947.
183. Misra, Biresh, Biswas, Pranesh and Bhattacharya, Achintya, *Struggle of the Surma Valley Peasantry*, New Delhi, May 1986, All India Kisan Sabha Publication, pp.22-3.

At Kerivalloor village of North Malabar, where the landlord (one Chirakkal Thampuram) used to take away a large part of the harvested paddy as rent, and sell it in the "black market", the *kisans* demanded during the harvesting season of 1946 either a replacement of the produce-rent by money-rent, or the landlord's selling his paddy through the local co-operative store. Since the *Jenmi* did not pay any heed to these demands, the *kisans* — under the aegis of the local Karshak Sangham — decided to prevent the landlord from having his share of crops, and to keep a round the clock vigil over the fields. The *Jenmi* sought the police help, and the authorities despatched an armed contingent from nearby Payyanoor. In the ensuing clash with the police, two *kisans* were killed in the firing, five injured and many arrested.[184] The bloodshed at Kerivalloor, however, could not stall the *kisans* from agitating against the *Jenmis*' collection of paddy as rent, and obstructing their men from touching the crop in some other neighbouring villages. The Karshak Sangham activists of the area also succeeded at this juncture in re-animating the *Punam* cultivators' agitation against the *Jenmis* over the tilling of forest lands. It reached its climax when *kisans* were led to encroach upon and plough some forest lands of the *Jenmis* near Irrikure, North Malabar. Since the police actions in defence of the landlords (such as the *lathi*-charges and detentions) could not stem the rising tide, the para-military Malabar Special Police was employed to take sterner steps against the agitationists. The *kisans* and their leaders (about 500 in number) armed themselves (with muzzle-loaders, spears, sticks, daggers etc.) and retired to the near-about Kavambayi hills, perhaps with a certain guerilla-type activity in mind. On 13 December 1946 their position was encircled by the Malabar Special Police, and in the encounter that followed, six were killed, eleven arrested, and the rest managed to disperse.[185] Clearly the instances of the *kisan* activists' anxiety for waging all

184. Home Poll. File No. 7/3/47 Poll (I) of 1946-7, N.A.I. and *People's Age* (English weekly), 29 December 1946.

185. K.R. Menon, Additional Chief Secretary, Govt. of Madras to Home Department, Govt. of India, Express Letter no. 10349/46-1 of 6 January 1947, Home Poll. File No. 7/3/47-Poll(I) of 1946-7, N.A.I.

kinds of local battles at the village, *taluk* and district levels, and the rural poor's craving for an immediate qualitative change in their existing circumstances were quite common, whether they made national newspaper headlines or not. The ones which eventually did, after being synchronised provincially by the Communists, and culminating into what was known as the Tebhaga movement, had in effect shaken the undivided Bengal for full six months (from November 1946 to April 1947).

The Tebhaga movement of the sharecroppers of Bengal was by far the most widespread of all the *kisan* upheavals in India in the recent times, engulfing 19 out of 25 districts, and involving about 6 million people. The ancient arrangement of equitable sharecropping (50 : 50), which later turned out to be an inequitable one under commodity production for the market,[186] had survived in Bengal throughout. Even in the permanently settled (1793) areas it persisted mainly because the *Zamindars*, who were negligent of agricultural improvements and extensions, often found it easy for stabilising their income to sub-let tenures to a host of intermediaries. These intermediaries saw, on their part at times, in the sharecropping arrangement the most convenient, as well as the least legally binding mode for squeezing out the agricultural surplus. The *Zamindars* themselves took recourse to sharecropping on occasions, especially after the Bengal Tenancy Act of 1885 had put an embargo on their enhancement of rent (not more than 12.5 per cent) from the secured occupancy *rayats*. To augment their income over the restricted rate, they tried to purchase the *rayati* rights of plots, and settle these outside the purview of tenancy legislation — through share contract.[187] Sharecropping, however, was very common in the reclaimed lands, or in those jungle and fallow tracts of the *Zamindars* which had been turned into cultivable lands. Such areas were given away in lots (*Jotes*) to tenants of substance (*Jotedars*) at low rates of rent for organising their reclamation through employment of landless labourers,

186. See Act One, Scene II, p. 47.
187. Adrienne Cooper, *Sharecropping and Sharecroppers' Struggles in Bengal, 1930-1950*, Calcutta, 1988, p. 22.

and their cultivation by entering into sharecropping contracts with the same toilers on the soil. It was the reclamation process that brought in sharecropping on a large scale in north Bengal — in Jalpaiguri, Rangpur, Dinajpur — and in the frontier districts of Malda and Mymensingh. Sharecropping abounded similarly beyond the *Zamindari* areas where the Government settled lands in lots temporarily with the affluent tenants (for 10, 20, 30 or 40 years) at nominal rates to encourage reclamation. These temporarily settled areas constituted altogether 15 per cent of the whole of Bengal in 1940, and included the Sundarbans stretch (covering the southern parts of the 24-Parganas, Khulna and Bakerganj), the western Duars of Jalpaiguri and the Government administered Khas Mahal estates. An account of the spread of sharecropping, however, should not carry the impression that it was the most dominant feature in the agricultural economy of the whole of Bengal, or that the *Jotedar* (the tenant-landlord)-*Bargadar* (the sharecropper) relationship was the most crucial in the agrarian politics there. It was not really so, for — unlike the *Jotedar-Bargadar* contradiction in the northern and certain southernmost parts of Bengal — the self cultivating peasant-*Zamindar* contrariety dominated the agricultural scene in east Bengal, and the *Zamindar-Khas Khamar* (personal demesne) labourer antagonism in west Bengal.[188] However, the sharecropping system was a very significant element in the agrarian life in Bengal, and it did show distinct signs of an increase during the second world war, and following the Bengal famine.[189]

The Bengali sharecroppers' circumstances — the *Bargadars*' (also the *Adhiars*' and the *Bhagchasis*') tales of woes subsequent to the great Depression, the feudal exploitation of the *Jotedars* they were subjected to, and the social oppression and torture

188. These are the findings of the recent studies of Partha Chatterji, *Bengal, 1920-47, The Land Question*, Calcutta, 1984, as well as of Sugata Bose, *Agrarian Bengal: Economy, Social Structure and Politics, 1919-1947*, Cambridge, 1986.

189. Percentage of sharecropped land increased from 21.1 per cent in 1939 to 27.0 per cent in 1944, and to 39.3 per cent in 1945. See Adrienne Cooper, *Sharecropper and Sharecroppers' Struggle in Bengal, 1930-1950*, Calcutta, 1988, table 9, p. 311.

they suffered in the hands of the *Jotedars* — have already been discussed elaborately by the political observers and historians of the Tebhaga movement.[190] Since much of these discussions relate to the sharecroppers' condition at the provincial scale in general, and to their situation in north Bengal in particular, one could perhaps refer to their state of being in one of the temporarily settled areas where the lease-holders and *Jotedars*, having relatively a short tenure, were likely to be in a hurry to exploit the sharecroppers for maximising their profit. A peep into the sharecropping arrangements and the sharecroppers' fortunes in the Sundarbans should bring out — to an extent — the *Jotedari* exploitative character at its revealing most.

When the British authorities started in the second half of the 19th century to lease out blocks of marshy forest land in the Sundarbans in lots (*lats* in the local Bengali derivative), their lease was fixed for 40 years with the concession that one-fourth of the plots would be exempted from taxation for ever, and that the rest could be held free from assessment for the first ten years. On the expiry of the ten-year period, of course, the Government would impose a rate on the lease-holders, or the *Latdars'* land, but very nominally, indeed.[191] Further, every landlord was required, under the threat of lease forfeiture, to make one-eighth of the entire *lat* fit for cultivation within the first five years, and thereafter in similar phases. This task for making the *lats* fit for cultivation, or for reclaiming it steadily, was both difficult and time-consuming. Usually after clearing a piece of forest land, a *bundh* or dyke was erected to keep out the salt water, and the plot left as fallow for about two years.[192] Only after its drying and cleaning of salt, the plot was rendered fit for the cultivation of good quality rice. Faced with such an

190. The recent, and also a very competent discussion can be found in Cooper, *ibid.*, chapter 3.
191. The rate, according to the Communist sources, became insignificant by the 1940s, or to 6 *pices* (1½ annas) per *bigha* (3¼ *bighas* = 1 acre) in Kakdwip. See the Bengali pamphlet, *Banglar Shishu Telengana — Lalganj,* 24-Parganas District Committee, C.P.I., 7 November 1949, Central Archives, C.P.I., Ajoy Bhavan, New Delhi.
192. *The Imperial Gazetteer of India*, Vol. XXIII, Oxford, 1908, pp. 144-5.

arduous process of reclamation, which involved considerable investment in labour and money, the *Latdars* commenced renting out portions of their *lats* as rightful tenancies (called *jotes* or *chaks*) to interested investors (known as *Jotedars* or *Chakdars*). It was mainly the *Jotedar* category who imported into the Sundarbans *coolies* or labourers from the inlands, the neighbouring districts and the tribal belts of Orissa and Bihar for jungle-clearing and earthwork. Following the initial phase of reclamation (i.e. deforestation and construction of *bundhs*), expert hands were required for undertaking agricultural operations. Landless cultivators from the 24-Parganas district itself, and other contiguous areas were hired on the promise of conferring on them the tenancy right over the lands they made cultivable. The lure of land attracted the lackland and the distressed to work on the difficult terrains of the Sundarbans, and bear the harsh conditions of life. Years and decades rolled by, but the toiling settlers were not given the assured tenancy right over the lands they developed and cultivated. Instead, they were pressurised to accept on an overwhelmingly large scale the sharecropping mode of agricultural production,[193] with all its accompanying ills, namely, the insecurity of tenure, the dependency on the *Jotedars* and the inadequacy of the *Adhi* (50 : 50 sharing of crops).

Apart from the fact that the produce-rent tended to be higher in real terms than the cash-rent, and that it became six to seven times more during the inflationary war years,[194] the equal sharing of crops had been shown to have resulted, even in the post-Depression period of price recovery, to small annual losses to the sharecroppers.[195] The accruing of these yearly losses, in

193. A survey made in 1979 of Budhakhali and Haripur of Kakdwip showed that 89 per cent and 65 per cent of the families, respectively, were sharecroppers in these two villages. See Krishnakant Sarkar, "Kakdwip Tebhaga Movement", in A.R. Desai (ed.), *Peasant Struggles in India*, Bombay, 1979, p. 471.
194. Adrienne Cooper, "Sharecroppers and Landlords in Bengal, 1930-50: The Dependency Web and Its Implications", *The Journal of Peasant Studies* (special issue on sharecropping and sharecroppers), Vol. X, nos. 2 and 3, January-April 1983.
195. Act One, Scene II, p. 48, footnote 115.

addition to the heavy price of dependency that they were forced to pay to the landlords, had in effect compelled the sharecroppers in Bengal to fall in perpetuity to debt-traps. The economic price of dependency consisted of *begar* (unpaid labour) at the landlord's field and house by all members of the sharecropper's family, and the extraction of *abwabs* or unlawful levies on any pretext. Over and above the payment of *nazrana* (presentation to the landlords) and *salami* (charges for the contract) at the time of renewal of the yearly settlement, the sharecroppers in the Sundarbans had to pay in the 1940s *naibana* or *hisabana* (charge for account keeping by the landlords' agents, or 3 to 6 seers of paddy per *bigha*), *kayali* (wage for those weighing the crops, or 3 to 5 seers of paddy per *bigha*), *khamar chilwani* (charge for erecting walls around the yard, or 2 to 4 seers of paddy per *bigha*), *parbani* (charge for village festivals or 2 to 5 seers of paddy per *bigha*), *golakamti* (charge for the loss of paddy-weight due to the drying in the landlords' barns, or 2 to 3 seers of paddy per *bigha*), *darwani* (charge for guarding the crops, or 1 to 3 seers of paddy per *bigha*), *kaktadani* (charge for scaring the crows away, or 2 to 4 seers of paddy per *bigha*) and *biya-shradh* (charge for a marriage or death in the landlords' families, or 2 to 4 seers of paddy per *bigha*).[196] All these were meticulously deducted at the time of divisioning the crops from the share of the *Bhagchasis*, including those who had not been able to arrange for such inputs as seeds, implements and field animals, and had, therefore, to depend on their supply by the landlords under the *krishani* arrangement, and receive only one-third share instead of the customary one-half. Deductions were also made for the return with interest of that grain-loan the sharecropper had previously incurred from the landlord voluntarily (of course, under the pressure of circumstances), and also the loan which he did not want to incur, but had to

196. See Krishnakant Sarkar, "Kakdwip Tebhaga Movement", in A.R. Desai (ed.), *Peasant Struggles in India*", Bombay, 1979, pp. 472-3, and Amit K. Gupta (mimeographed paper), "Agrarian Protest in Kakdwip of 24 Parganas", presented to the third Damodaran Memorial Symposium on Peasantry and Struggle for New India, 12-13 April 1980, Jawaharlal Nehru University, New Delhi.

take under compulsion. An example of such compulsory or enforced loan was the *Derabari* in the Sundarbans (a grain-loan advance, originally devised to encourage the destitute tillers, devoid of implements and field animals, to take to share-cropping), which the sharecroppers were required to take from the landlords on high interest, and under the threat of eviction. The heavily depleted shares of the *Bargadars*, after conceding all these deductions, were further reduced by the landlords' fraudulent practices in the weighing and measuring of the paddy stacked in the *kholans* (yards). It was the custom of stacking the entire harvest in the *Jotedars' kholans*, which gave the landlords the power to defraud the *kisans* and deduct at will from their shares at the time of division, that led the *Adhiars* of north Bengal to launch their agitation in 1940-1.[197] Whatever little remained of their shares thereafter, they retained a part for the family consumption, and the rest for sale in the market. The sale had to be immediate for obtaining ready cash to meet the cost of pressing basic necessaries (oil, salt, cloth and kerosene), and to deal with the crisis expenditures (marriage, death and illness in the family). Consequently, they had no time to wait for the prices to pick up in the grain market, and worse still, they were often obliged to hand over quickly their tiny surpluses to the *aratdars* (the grain-dealers), from whom they had taken *dadans* (advances) on the basis of the lowest possible price. The small stocks of grains for family consumption, and the smaller amount of cash in hand, usually lasted for about 3 to 4 months after the harvest, forcing the sharecroppers to approach afresh the landlords for grain-loans, and the *mahajans* for cash-loans at exorbitant rates of interest. It was the grain-loan — the most urgent for the barest subsistence — that hit them the hardest. The creditors charged them a 50 per cent or more rate of interest on the cash value of the current higher price of grains in the market, signifying that the indebted must return the cash equivalent (and not the original quantity of grains which they took as loan plus the interest) soon after the next harvesting — at the time of division. Thus the indebted sharecroppers had to

197. Act Two, Scene I, p. 155.

return about three to four times grains he actually borrowed[198] by paying in four to five months the interest of 12 months. The credit mechanism, therefore, seemed often to be more important as a means of surplus absorption than even the rent. Undoubtedly, the loans were hardly ever paid back in full, and they continued to accumulate every year till the most indebted among the sharecroppers turned *maldars* or the bonded labourers for life. Even if many of them had not formally become *maldars* because of the failure to repay debts, the majority of *Bhagchasis* in the Sundarbans were semi-serfs for all practical purposes. Conversely, if, by any chance, the fortunate few among them succeeded in clearing the loans of the previous year, and did not require fresh loans for the current, they were forced to pay *machatut*, or a compensation to the landlords.[199]

The social price of dependency that the *Bhagchasis* had to pay was based on their utterly precarious economic situation which determined for them a permanently inferior status in rural society. The hierarchical caste structure (though not as stark in Bengal as in some other parts of India), the outcasteist segregation and the religious particularity supplied a kind of ideological justification to the inferior status of the sharecroppers belonging predominantly to the scheduled castes, the tribals and the Muslim community. The socially inferior status of the sharecroppers had been quite straightforward in cases where they were members of the scheduled castes, Muslim community and tribal society, and the *Jotedars* the caste Hindus. The situation should have been somewhat different in cases where the *Jotedars* were the Muslims, the scheduled castemen and the tribals, but it was never actually so because of the axiomatic recognition of their social superiority on the grounds of economic strength. Rather, they betrayed a tendency, along with the other affluent members within their groups, for upward

198. See Act Two, Scene I, p. 155, as well as *Janajuddha* (Bengali weekly), 8 and 15 December 1943 and Sunil Sen, *Agrarian Struggle in Bengal*, Delhi, 1972, pp. 14-15.

199. A report by "Nikunja" (Asoke Bose) on the "Anti-Imperialist and Anti-Feudal Struggle of the People in the Sundarbans and the Role of the Communist Party, Kakdwip, 24 Parganas", 15 June 1951, available in Material on Kakdwipa, Central Archives, C.P.I., Ajoy Bhavan, New Delhi.

social mobility — to rise up in the caste ladder (from being the scheduled castes), to seek entry into the caste Hindu-fold (from being the tribals), and to gain the company of the elite (from being the rustic Muslims). If the poor sharecroppers were dependent "inferiors", and at the mercy of the commanding "superior" tenure-holders — who had access to the local self-governing Union Boards, and linkages with the police, the officialdom and the politicians — the former could easily be socially humiliated and physically tortured. The sharecroppers, therefore, were abusively addressed, forced to sit on the floors of the *cutcherries*, beaten with shoes for disobedience, and assaulted if they dared to defy. All acts of the *Jotedari* coercion were spearheaded by the landlords' *naibs* (managers), *gomostas* (agents) and *lathials* (*lathi*-wielding retinues), who gave effect to evictions, tortured the defiant cultivators, and , if necessary, murder them without batting an eyelid. Not only the sharecroppers, but their families — wives and children — had to be at the beck and call of the *Jotedars* for performing domestic duties, sowing seeds, husking paddy and converting it into rice flake and puffed rice on nominal wages.[200] Violating the peasant women, like the extracting of *begar*, was also considered to be a matter of right for the landlords. Those sharecroppers in the Sundarbans, who had attractive wives, would not be allotted plots till they sent their spouses to gratify the *Jotedars*.[201] The sexual intimidation they faced, and the social exploitation they suffered, as a productive force by their own right, had in fact led the women to play a pivotal role in the sharecroppers' struggle in 1946-7.

The circumstances of sharecroppers prevailing in the Sundarbans were similar (though perhaps a little less cruel) to those of

200. Adrienne Cooper, *Sharecropping and Sharecroppers' Struggles in Bengal, 1930-1950*, Calcutta, 1988, p. 88.

201. A report by "Nikunja" (Asoke Bose) on the "Anti-Imperialist and Anti-Feudal Struggle of the People in the Sundarbans and the Role of the Communist Party in Kakdwip, 24 Parganas," 15 June 1951, available in Material on Kakdwipa, Central Archives, C.P.I., Ajoy Bhavan, New Delhi.

their counterparts in the rest of Bengal.[202] None knew the sharecroppers' lot better than the Communist *kisan* activists, who had tried to organise the *Bargadars* in Bengal ever since the formation of the provincial Kisan Sabha, and led them — apart from the district level agitations — into two significant movements consecutively, the *Hattola* in 1939-40 and the Adhiar in 1940-1. Although the Adhiar movement seemed to have anticipated the developments of 1946-7 to an extent by challenging the credit mechanism and by demanding the sharecroppers' right to stack paddy in their own yards, instead of the *Jotedars*', the two most vital issues of the sharecropping arrangement, namely the proportion of the shares and the procurement of some tenurial guarantee to the tillers, had not been brought to the forefront of the sharecroppers' mobilisation in Bengal, or turned into slogans for waging battles on a wide provincial scale. It was particularly curious because the *Choudras* in south Gujarat and the sharecroppers in North Kanara had already fought in 1938 and in May 1946, respectively, and that, too, not very unsuccessfully, for a higher share of the produce, and the *Bataidars* of western Punjab, as well as the *Bhagchasis* in certain parts of Bengal itself, battled repeatedly against their indiscriminate ejectment from lands in 1938-9. All these were the Kisan Sabha-led activities, unlike the largely autonomous Santhal *Bataidars*' agitation in 1940-1 for tenurial right in Purnea district of north Bihar, and their significance should not have been missed by the Communist *kisan* activists in Bengal — those already well-entrenched in some of the distinctly sharecropping areas. Had such woeful ignorance — wilful, or not so willful — any connection with their being "outsiders", or their belonging largely to the urbane educated middle-class, whose members often gave away remnants of family lands in the villages to sharecropping as absentee rentiers? It would be difficult to give a definitive answer, but the Communist ignorance appeared to have remorselessly continued. In its historic memoranda to the Bengal Land Revenue (Floud) Commission of

202. The newer the lands brought under sharecropping, the harsher the exploitation of the sharecroppers, was the opinion of Abdulla Rasul, the eminent *kisan* leader, expressed in an interview with the author in Calcutta on 19 October 1983.

1938, the provincial Kisan Sabha, which so eloquently indicted landlordism and rent, failed to include any specific demand of the sharecroppers, and mentioned nothing about the mode of sharing crops. In fact it was the Commission, which on its own during the course of enquiry, took pity on the sharecroppers, and recommended in 1940 a two-thirds (in place of the one-half) share in their favour. Encouraged by the Commission's recommendation, the B.P.K.S. also recognised in the same year in its conference at Panjia (Jessore) that the sharecroppers should get a two-thirds share.[203] Apparently the newly learnt point was hardly discussed in the Communist circles in Bengal in the following year (1941), though the C.P.I. assiduously clung to an "imperialist war" strategy, and its *kisan* organisers committed to make militant use of any potent agrarian issue. As expected, the subject was conveniently forgotten in the subsequent four years of the "people's war" phase. Thereafter the Communist decision-makers did recollect the issue, but in a routine manner, and without attaching much importance to it. Even in the summer of 1946 the B.P.K.S., in its conference at Maubhog (Khulna), merely reiterated the sharecroppers' demand for a two-thirds share, but took no steps to back it up by contemplating an agitation.[204] And yet barely four months later, in September 1946, the Council of the B.P.K.S. decided — with scant preparation, and in an atmosphere of communal frenzy[205] — to launch a struggle for *Tebhaga* (the two-thirds) in the approaching harvesting season. The suddenness with which the B.P.K.S. discovered the

203. Bhowani Sen, a leading Communist expert on the agrarian issues, and the Secretary of the Bengal Provincial Committee of the C.P.I., 1943-8, had conceded that the *Tebhága* demand "owed more to the recommendation of the Commission of 1938 than to the ingenuity of the Sabha". See *Tebhaga Sangram Rajat Jayanti Smarak Grantha* (in Bengali), Calcutta, 1973, p. 10.

204. Sunil Sen, one of the leaders of the Tebhaga movement in Dinajpur in 1946-7, recalled his attending the conference, without, of course, having any inkling as to the immediate commencement of the movement. See his *Peasant Movements in India*, Calcutta, 1982, chapter IV, p.140, footnote 11.

205. Communal riots had already started in Calcutta in August 1946, affecting practically the whole of Bengal.

prospect of an impending agitation, and the abrupt manner in which it sprang into immediate action were, indeed, baffling, to say the least.

It has been suggested,[206] and unreservedly upheld thereafter,[207] that the Communist hue and cry in Bengal all of a sudden over the *Tebhaga* was prompted by the C.P.I.'s over-all anxiety for proving its effectiveness to the Communist Party of the Soviet Union (Bolshevik), the leader of Communist internationalism, who treated it at this point of time with "almost total disregard";[208] for showing its strength to the Congress, who denounced it for assuming an anti-"Quit India" movement and pro-Government stand during the war; and for "rehabilitating" itself in the eyes of the Indian people who had been alienated by its "people's war" policy.[209] Apart from hinting vaguely at the likely Communist moods of the time, such a far-fetched assumption (based hardly on any documentary evidence) seemed rather to be inadequate for explaining the B.P.K.S.'s haste in launching an agitation over the *Tebhaga.* Since the C.P.I. had loyally stood by the C.P.S.U.(B) at its own peril in anti-Fascism, and had not shown afterwards any inclination to do otherwise, there was no particular reason why should it be disregarded more by its mentor in 1946 than in all the preceding years, or why must it try to impress the preceptor by taking an initiative locally rather than waiting for a directive afresh from abroad. Impressing the Congress similarly could not have received high priority in the C.P.I.'s agenda once the final rupture between the two had so acrimoniously been brought about in December 1945. Even its moderate leaders, who dreamt sometimes of a role in the constitutional negotiations with the British, alongside the nationalists and the separatists, did not show after the

206. Jnanabrata Bhattacharya, "An Examination of Leudeship Entry in Bengal Peasant Revolts", *Journal of Asian Studies,* Vol. XXXVII, No. 4, August 1978.

207. Sugata Bose, *Agrarian Bengal: Economy, Social Structure and Politics, 1919-1947,* Cambridge, 1986, chapter 8.

208. G.D. Overstreet and M. Windmiller, *Communism in India,* Bombay, 1960, p. 619.

209. Sugata Bose, *Agrarian Bengal : Economy, Social Structure and Politics, 1919-1947,* Cambridge, 1986, pp. 264-5.

elections of February 1946 any of their readiness for a rapprochement with the Congress. The C.P.I. was interested, of course, in winning over the Indian public, and in coming out of the ring of isolation that its "people's war" slogan had created around itself. Its position in Bengal, however, was not as difficult and inconvenient as in some other places, and its influence over the urban working class and the rural poor there had not wholly been swept away even in the heydays of the "Quit India" movement. If one found somehow the Communists' claim of their enjoying "throughout" the "unshaken" loyalty of the *kisan* masses [210] to be too tall, he or she would concede that their need for the so-called "rehabilitation" in the countryside was certainly over during and after the famine of 1943, and following the dedicated humanitarian work of the People's Relief Committee volunteers in rural Bengal. The nationalist *Bhadralok* (the gentlemen) opinion nevertheless persisted to be hostile to the Communists, but inciting a sharecroppers' struggle — a rising of the *Chhotoloks* (the lowly men) — was by no means the best method to render it amiable, and nobody knew it better than the *Bhadralok* Communists themselves.

If their "rehabilitation" in the countryside had not been the burning issue, and their existence was not at stake over the demeanours of either the Congress or the C.P.S.U.(B), then the sudden springing into action of the Communists on the issue of the *Tebhaga* could perhaps be explained in terms of the internal and local compulsions they were faced with. The internal compulsion of the C.P.I., as it has already been referred to, was apparent from the latter half of 1945 when the militant and the moderate opinions within the party debated the urgency for taking the revolutionary initiative, and leading the post-war popular upsurges. The debate, as well as the militant-moderate contest over policy-making at the leadership level, between September 1945 (the end of the second world war) and August 1946 (the passing of the August Resolution of the C.P.I.), were tellingly experienced in the party organisation in Bengal — one

210. Interview of Abani Lahiri, a leading Kisan Sabha activist of the Tebhaga movement in Dinajpur. See *Bartrika* (Bengali periodical), Special Tebhaga Issue, July-December 1987, Calcutta, p. 147.

of the most advanced centres of the Communist movement in India. Once the August Resolution was passed, in which the militants succeeded in binding the C.P.I. Central Committee to the task of nurturing all the popular struggles, including the "more and more militant actions" of the peasants,[211] the Provincial Committee and the Kisan Sabha in Bengal could not probably avoid assuming a militant posture, if confronted with a local situation of militancy. Locally, a situation of militancy had in the meantime developed apparently by the middle of 1946 in Bengal, where the countryside was still reeling under the after-effects of the great famine. Apart from destroying 3 to 3.8 million people, the famine shattered many more physically, psychologically and economically. According to the B.P.K.S. estimate, about 2,59,300 families (mostly in the marginal peasant category) were forced to sell all their lands. While another 5,71,600 families partially sold their lands, approximately 5,10,600 families were compelled to mortgage their lands to the landlords, moneylenders and rich peasants. Besides, 3,06,000 families lost 11,47,000 plough cattle as a result of the famine.[212] As it was evident from these figures, the most affected (not really the most killed, who happened to be the agricultural labourers and artisans) had been the poor *kisans* and the sharecroppers, many of whom had to join the ranks of the rural proletariat after losing their domestic animals and agricultural implements. Although the famine was over, the food crisis continued in varying degrees, and the food-grain production of 1944-5 was far from satisfactory. So the food committees, which the Government set up during the famine for helping the distribution process, had to be continued. The *Jotedars* generally dominated these committees in the sharecropping areas (and the landlords and rich peasants in the rest), but many were taken over by the Kisan Sabha activists, and turned into instruments of their campaigns against the hoarder's and "blackmarketeer's" stocks of grains. There were also skirmishes between the cultivators

211. "Eor the Final Assault", Political Resolution of the C.P.I. Central Committee, August 1946, Central Archives, C.P.I., Ajoy Bhavan, New Delhi.
212. Memorandum from Bengal Provincial Kisan Sabha to the Govt. of Bengal on Rehabilitation, October 1945.

and *Jotedars* over the hoarded food-grain stocks, and often the *Jotedars' golas* (barns) and the grain-dealers' godowns were surrounded, with the demand for the distribution of the hoarded grains on a loan basis, or at the "control" prices. Many of these "raids" were supervised by the Kisan Sabha members, and they even participated in the seizure and distribution of the *Jotedars'* grains in the face of the police offensive.[213] In fact a predominantly anti-landlord, anti-*Jotedar* movement had actually begun in the countryside in the name of de-hoarding and peoples' relief operations by the C.P.I. cadres.[214] Only it was not recognised as an agrarian movement by the party's provincial and central leadership, despite the rank and file's insistence on intensifying the "class struggle" in the villages.[215] In 1945-6 the crop situation was bad again, forcing the sharecroppers to think in terms of resisting the collection of *abwabs* and the repayment of grain-loans, as well as to express their desire for a higher share of the produce.[216] The *Bargadars'* eagerness for demanding the *Tebhaga* was unambiguously expressed in the harvesting season of 1945,[217] and it was known to the activists in the field. Some of the Communist *kisan* leaders were also aware of the mood of the sharecroppers, but "could not correctly assess the situation".[218] They even felt in retrospect that the call of the *Tebhaga* should have been given a year earlier — during the harvesting season of 1945-6.[219] It seemed that the sharecroppers were almost certain to demand the *Tebhaga* autonomously on their own in 1946-7, irrespective of the responses of the leadership in the B.P.K.S., or in the party. The Communist *kisan* workers at the district level were also mentally prepared for

213. Abani Lahiri, "Last Battle of Bengal Peasants under British Rule" in Nisith Ranjan Ray, et al. (ed.), *Challenge: A Saga of India's Struggle for Freedom*, New Delhi, 1984, p. 376.
214. Hamza Alavi, "Peasants and Revolution" in Desai, A.R. (ed.), *Peasant Struggle for Freedom*, New Delhi, 1984, p. 376.
215. Peter Custers, *Women in the Tebhaga Uprising*, Calcutta, 1987, p. 74.
216. *Swadhinata* (Bengali daily), 9 and 11 January 1946.
217. *Ibid.*, 28 and 29 December 1945, and 11 January 1946.
218. Abdulla Rasul, interview with the author on 19 October 1983, Calcutta.
219. Abani Lahiri, "Last Battle of Bengal Peasants under British Rule" in Nisith Ranjan Ray, et al. (ed.), *Challenge: A Saga of India's Struggle for Freedom*, New Delhi, 1984, p. 386.

joining in the uproar, and heightening it to a crescendo. Their attitude was illustrative in a training camp of the Kisan Sabha activists of the three northern districts, held in Rangpur during the monsoon of 1946, where a propaganda plan for demanding the *Tebhaga*, and raising batches of volunteers for the coming agitation, had been worked out in detail.[220] In September 1946, when the harvesting season was approaching, the B.P.K.S. and the Communist Party in Bengal had no choice but to formalise the steps the peasants and the local cadres were going to take, and declare the commencement of the movement. They could not have wavered any further in view of the C.P.I. Central Committee's left militant directive to utilise any agrarian circumstance "which may develop into big local battle".[221] The launching of the Tebhaga movement was thus neither sudden nor desperate, it was simply delayed through procrastination, and therefore, unprepared to an extent.

The various developments of the Tebhaga movement of 1946-7 have already been copiously discussed, and many of the accounts — despite their being euphemistically labelled at times as mythological[222] — are so exhaustive and authoritative together[223] that they render any fresh recounting of the incidents somewhat superfluous. Even then one could not but take note of the major trends of the movement, between November 1946 and April 1947, for an overview of the Communist-rural poor interactions at one of their climactic crux. The movement had passed through three discernible phases within its time-frame of

220. The holding of this training camp was extensively discussed, on the basis of an interview with Haji Danesh, the distinguished *kisan* leader of Dinajpur, by Kamal Mesbah and Kamal Ahmed in "Dinajpur Tebhaga Andolan (Tebhaga Movement in Dinajpur), 1946-48", *Bichitra*, Dacca, cited in Peter Custers, *Women in the Tebhaga Uprising*, Calcutta, 1987, footnote 14.
221. "For the Final Assault", Political Resolution of the C.P.I. Central Committee, August 1946, Central Archives, C.P.I., Ajoy Bhavan, New Delhi.
222. Sugata Bose, *Agrarian Bengal*, Cambridge, 1986, p. 271.
223. While the briefest and the most contemporaneous of these accounts seems to be Bhowani Sen's "The Tebhaga Movement in Bengal" in *Communist* (English monthly), Vol.I, no. 3, September 1947, pp. 121-31, the latest and the most exhaustive one is Adrienne Cooper's, *Sharecropping and Sharecroppers' Struggles in Bengal, 1930-1950*, Calcutta, 1988.

six months — the first between November and December 1946, the second between January and February 1947 and the third between March and April 1947. The first phase began after about one month's preparations (such as the propagation of the *Tebhaga* demand, the holding of meetings and rallies and the formation of volunteer corps, known as the *Kisan Fauzs*), on an experimental basis in those sharecropping areas (in districts such as Jalpaiguri, Rangpur, Dinajpur, Mymensingh, Khulna, Jessore, Malda, the 24-Parganas and Midnapore) where the Kisan Sabha had previously succeeded in organising the sharecroppers and leading their local battles. The initial experiment with the mobilisation of *kisans*, and its positive outcome seemed to have greatly enthused the Communist *kisan* activists, especially in the grim background of a communal holocaust. The discovery that "those who use the ploughs and harvest the crops are neither Hindus nor Muslims, but *kisans*"[224] had enabled them to get over their nervousness about communalism being unsurmountable, or its coming disastrously in the way. That the "people's struggle" could "change the climate of rioting"[225] appeared to be the realisation of the Communists, following their immediate experiences soon after the launching of the Tebhaga movement in the villages, and not before, nor perhaps was it a "political consideration" that "influenced" their decision to start the campaign.[226] The sharecroppers' ready response to the Kisan

224. Somnath Hor, "Tebhaga Diary", written in December 1946, but published in 1981 in *Ekshan* (Bengali periodical) Autumn Issue, 1388 B.S. (1981), 15th year, nos. 1-2, pp. 15-27.

225. From the version of Krishna Benode Roy, the then Secretary of the B.P.K.S. and an important leader of the Tebhaga movement, cited in Peter Custers, *Women in the Tebhaga Uprising*, Calcutta, 1987, p. 80.

226. Binay Bhusan Choudhuri, "Organised Politics and Peasant Insurgency: The Bengal Provincial Krishak Sabha and the Sharecroppers' Struggle in Bengal, 1946-47", *The Calcutta Historical Review*, July 1988-June 1989, p. 178. There is hardly any evidence to show that the Council of the B.P.K.S., or the Provincial Committee of the Communists, had ever planned the launching of the Tebhaga movement as an antidote to the communal rioting in Bengal. Rather, they were known to have entertained an apprehension that the riotous circumstance would not be congenial for the commencement of a popular movement, and might even result in aggravating the over-all situation in the province.

Sabha's *Tebhaga* call in fact was so overwhelming that it first inspiringly surprised the Communist *kisan* activists, and then, later on, caused some consternation among them as to their ability for coping with it.

The major slogans the *kisans* raised in the first phase of the movement were *Tebhaga Chai* (we want two-thirds share) and *Nija Khamare Dhan Tolo* (stack the harvested paddy in our own yards), which resulted in the collective reaping of the crops under the strict vigilance of the *kisan* volunteers, and in the stacking of the reaped paddy either in the *panchayat khamars* (the villagers' common yards), or in the sharecroppers' individual *khamars* (yards) for division. There were clashes galore over these proceedings between the *kisans* and the landlords' goons, and in many the local bureaucracy and the police intervened in the name of "law and order", arrested *kisans* and their leaders, and imposed Section 144 Cr.P.C. over the affected areas. Some of the clashes which assumed relatively serious proportions were illustrative of the fighting mood of the *kisans* and of their determination for resistance. One such incident occurred in Shivarampur in Kakdwip, the 24-Parganas, where the landlord prevented a sharecropper from taking paddy to his own yard, and forcibly confined him in the *cutcherry*. On hearing the news, a gathering of 1,200 surrounded the *cutcherry*, threatened to burn it down and obtained the release of the *kisan*.[227] A similar act on the part of the landlord at Naotora of Nilphamari, Rangpur, resulted in the *kisans*' storming his house, and forcing him to leave the area.[228] At Rampur of Atwari, Dinajpur, a police party was chased away when they came to investigate the "theft" of grains, and make some arrests.[229] Also, the policemen, who came to Ranisankail, Dinajpur, for similar purposes, were surrounded by the *kisans*, kept captive in a local school building for 24 hours, and released after they tendered apologies.[230] At

227. *People's Age* (English weekly), 15 December 1946.
228. *Ibid.*, 5 January 1947.
229. Sunil Sen, *Agrarian Struggle in Bengal*, Delhi, 1972, p. 37.
230. *People's Age* (English weekly), 29 December 1946.

Sundardighi of Debiganj, Jalpaiguri, the *kisans* clashed with the landlord's *chowkidars* (watchmen) over the harvesting, demonstrated before the police station when some of them were arrested, and organised a boycott of the local market in protest.[231] It was, however, not scuffles and fights all the time, and there were instances of the sharecroppers' securing the *Tebhaga*, or almost the *Tebhaga*, through negotiations with the landlords, and their social ostracisation, as in Mymensingh,[232] by way of compromise, especially with the smaller landlords, as in Dinajpur,[233] and in Jessore,[234] and by presenting the landlords with a *fait accompli*, following the hurried harvesting of the paddy at record speed, as in Narail, Jessore.[235] Attempts at settlements between the sharecroppers and the landlords were also numerous, though many broke down either on account of the landlords' refusal eventually to come to terms, as in Netrakona, Mymensingh,[236] at Panchbibi and Khetal in Bogra, and at the district level in Dinajpur;[237] or because of the *Adhiars*' and the Kisan Sabhaites' insistence on the realisation of the *Tebhaga* demand in full, as in Rangpur,[238] Jalpaiguri, Phulbari of Dinajpur,[239] and in some places of Tamluk, Midnapore.[240] However, a good number of settlements did take effect, notably in Kushtia, Nadia,[241] in certain places in Dacca,[242] in Madaripur, Faridpur,[243] and even at Sutahata and Mahishadal of Tamluk,

231. *Ibid.*, 5 January 1947.
232. *Ibid.*, 15 and 22 December 1946.
233. Adrienne Cooper, *Sharecropping and Sharecroppers' Struggles in Bengal, 1930-50*, Calcutta, 1988, p, 172.
234. *Ibid.*, p. 175.
235. *Ibid.*
236. *Ibid.*
237. *Ibid.*, p. 173.
238. *Ibid.*, p. 172.
239. *Ibid.*, p. 200, footnote 40.
240. *Ibid.*, p. 178.
241. *Ibid.*, p. 176.
242. *Ibid.*, p. 177.
243. *Ibid.*

Midnapore. The most remarkable feature in the first phase, however, was not the patterns and the styles in which the *Tebhaga* had been obtained, but the enthusiasm the movement generated among the *Bhagchashis* throughout Bengal. Within a month of its commencement, the struggle had spread like wild fire beyond the locales and the districts the B.P.K.S. originally marked for its experiment with the *Tebhaga*. Such subsidiary slogans as *Bhag Jamir Rasid Chai* (we want receipts for all the sharecropping lands) and *Somosto Julum Bandho Karo* (stop all oppressions) added further fuel to the fire. Although these two slogans had no direct bearing on the *Tebhaga* demand, together they were attractive not only to the sharecroppers, but also to other sections of the *kisan* masses. The first one represented the *Bhagchashis*' anxiety for the recognition of their linkages with the lands they tilled, or of a semblance of their tenurial right. The second, the more important one, expressed the sharecroppers', as well as of all the rural poor's, age-old desire to free themselves from the oppression and humiliation at the hands of the landlords and their agents. It was the fight against *zulm* — the *kisans*' refusal to perform *begar* and to pay the *abwabs*, coupled with their defiance of the landlords' unbridled authority — that gave an emancipatory content to the movement by December 1946. The persistent talk in the villages was "liberty", as one contemporary observer noted in astonishment, that the peasants were "becoming liberated", and proclaiming, "we are free".[244] The prospect of emancipation greatly excited the sharecroppers in new localities, and attracted — significantly enough — the agricultural labourers to the movement in substantial numbers. Hereafter the agricultural labourers took a vital supportive part in the agitation, despite the fact that the *Tebhaga* demand had nothing to do with their immediate dire needs. Apart from the natural solidarity that grew between the two poverty-stricken, socially oppressed categories — the sharecroppers and agricultural labourers — a significant segment of the sharecroppers had lost their agricultural implements and cattle during the famine, and thus were compelled to join the

244. Somnath Hor, "Tebhaga Diary", *Ekshan* (Bengali periodical), Autumn Issue, 1388 B.S. (1981), 15th year, nos. 1-2, pp. 14-15.

ranks of the agricultural labourers. Emotionally, by resenting their relegation, they still remained sharecroppers in mentality. They even vaguely hoped to regain their former status, and dreamt (as all the landless always do) of securing for themselves, through the struggle, a minimum portion of land. The way the agricultural labourers involved themselves in the movement, the rapidity with which it spread in areas outside the leftists' pale, and the manner the *Bhagchasis* from obscure places besieged the district Communist Party and Kisan Sabha offices for *hukums* (commands) to rise,[245] were simply beyond all anticipations of the Communists, and it had been acknowledged to be so by the B.P.K.S. Council,[246] as well as by the Communist *kisan* activists.[247] The Communist experimentations with the *Tebhaga* were so obviously out-matched by the *Bargadars*' and the *khetmajdoors*' aspirations that only a more militant posture from January 1947 could restore the balance between the leaders and the led.

To the cautious Communist leaders, a show of increased militancy in January 1947 did not seem to pose any serious threat to the movement, rather it appeared somehow to be possible to demonstrate their empathy with the *kisans*' rising temper, without displeasing the authorities too much, or inviting a Government crackdown too soon. One would tend — as the Communist leaders perhaps did — to draw such hypothetical a conclusion from the attitude the Government of Bengal revealed till January 1947. Howsoever pro-landlord and *Jotedar*-phil were the officialdom and the police locally, the authorities at the provincial level — to begin with — had neither been overtly hostile to the sharecroppers' *Tebhaga* demand, nor excessively interested in stifling their agitation altogether. The Government, of course, was prepared for dealing with any "untoward" development affecting the law and order situation, but at the same time instructed the law-enforcing officers to ensure that their "interference" in the movement was "reduced to the

245. Krishna Benode Roy's report on north Bengal, *People's Age* (English weekly), 19 January 1947.

246. Adrienne Cooper, *Sharecropping and Sharecroppers' Struggles in Bengal, 1930-50*, Calcutta, 1988, p. 274.

247. *Ibid.*, p. 184.

minimum".[248] The tendency of the Government was to treat the *Tebhaga* dispute as an "economic" one, and advise the landlords to seek legal redress if the sharecroppers had robbed them of their shares. It felt "seriously embarrassed" sometimes, if the police were "called in [by the *Jotedars*] to use force against the Bargadars",[249] and appreciative at another, if the district officials tried to bring about negotiated settlement of the disputes.[250] Evidently the Government stand up to this point was shaped by the ruling party, the Muslim League, some of whose erstwhile Krishak Proja Party elements [251] were known to be sympathetic to the sharecroppers. Some other Muslim Leaguers, who had been bidding for a base of their party in the countryside, were also supportive of the *Tebhaga* demand in those areas where the sharecroppers happened largely to be Muslims. Even the Prime Minister of Bengal, H.S. Suhrawardy, was reported to have admitted in a meeting with the Kisan Sabha representatives "the justice of the Tebhaga demand".[252] The Revenue minister, Fazlur Rahaman, was similarly convinced, and he announced in a public meeting in Sirajganj on 4 January 1947 his determination "to prevent eviction of the Bargadars, and to make provision for them to get two-thirds of the harvest".[253] The minister in fact would have issued an Ordinance to give effect to these points had he not been persuaded by the Governor, F.J. Burrows, to

248. A secret circular from the Bengal Government to the "Officers Responsible for Law and Order", 18 January 1947, cited in Satyajit Dasgupta, "The Tebhaga Movement in Bengal, 1946-47", Occasional Paper no. 89, Centre for Studies in Social Sciences, Calcutta, December 1986.
249. Home Poll. Fortnightly Report for 1st half of December 1946, File No. 18/12/46, N.A.I.
250. Letter from F.J. Burrows, 8 January 1947, Home Poll. Fortnightly Report for 2nd half of January, 1947, File No. 18/1/47, N.A.I.
251. The members of the Krishak Proja Party, who dominated in the mid-1930s the countryside of Bengal, especially its eastern part, and more particularly its Muslim inhabitants, and many of whom joined the Muslim League thereafter, were known widely for their egalitarian agrarian commitments.
252. *People's Age* (English weekly), 12 January 1947.
253. *Amrita Bazar Patrika* (English daily), 10 January 1947.

wait a while for the meeting of the legislature, and introduce a Bill on the subject "in the normal way".[254] This he promptly did, first by publishing the Bargadars Temporary Regulation Bill in the *Calcutta Gazette* on 22 January 1947, and then by introducing it to the legislature shortly thereafter. The proposed measure stated that if the landlord supplied the in-puts (such as cattle, plough and other agricultural implements), he would receive half the crop; and if the sharecropper supplied all the in-puts, he would be entitled to the two-thirds, and the landlord to one-third. The proposal also clarified that the eviction of a sharecropper would only be possible if the landlord was going to cultivate the plot himself with the help of his family members, or if the sharecropper had failed to keep to the contract.[255] In other words, the Bill practically conceded the sharecroppers' *Tebhaga* demand, as well as some tenurial security to them, without, of course, specifying it adequately. The Communist Party and the B.P.K.S. had closely watched all these developments with some satisfaction, and sensing a victory in the offing, they thought they could venture a step further in the demonstration of militancy. What they ignored to take into account, after being lulled by the apparent discomfiture, and the defensive posture of the *Jotedars*, was the enormous leverage that landlordism enjoyed in Bengal politics — over the administration, the Muslim League and the Congress alike, barring minor aberrations — and its capability to exercise it without fail in times of great urgency.

The demonstration of militancy in January 1947 was also a physical imperative for the movement, having an intimate connection with the harvesting time. As the harvesting in Bengal did not take place all over the province together at one time, the sharecroppers in those regions harvested early — unlike their compatriots in the places harvested relatively late — could not stack the crops in the *Panchayat Kholans*. Since the harvested paddy in those areas had already reached the *Jotedars'*

254. Adrienne Cooper, *Sharecropping and Sharecroppers' Struggles in Bengal, 1930-50*, Calcutta, 1988, p. 179.
255. *The Calcutta Gazette (Extraordinary)*, 22 January 1947.

Kholans, the sharecroppers were no longer in a position to obtain their demanded *Tebhaga*, unless, of course, they managed somehow to retrieve the crops. In order to make such a retrieval possible, without which the *kisan* consolidation might adversely be affected, and for the sake of carrying all the *Bhagchasis* of the early harvested localities along with the others, the B.P.K.S. and the Communist *kisan* activists decided to raise two slogans of more militant nature, namely, *Jan Debo Tobu Dhan Debo Na* (we will give our lives, but not the paddy of our shares) and *Jotedarer Kholan Bhango* (break the granaries of the *Jotedars*). While the first of these slogans expressed a vague aggressive determination, the second one went very much further, and actually called for giving concrete effect to a bold, offensive plan of action. The storming of the *Jotedars' Kholans*, and their ransacking to snatch away what had been considered to be the rightful *kisan* shares, was qualitatively different from either the application of pressure for gaining an advantage in the sharing of the disputed crops on the fields, or the forcible transportation of the disputed crops (over which the *Bargadars'* "legal" claim was as strong as the *Jotedars'*) to the *Panchayat Kholans*, instead of the *Jotedars'*, to ensure a favourable division. It was an open call for launching concerted violent attacks directly on the properties, and, by implication, on the persons of the *Jotedars*, and therefore, its legal and political significance had been far graver than all the slogans previously raised. There was considerable debate among the Communists, and within the B.P.K.S. over the *Kholan Bhango* call — whether such "adventurism" would invite the Government repression and cripple the movement, or whether such "anticipatory" step would raise it to a new "revolutionary stage" by reflecting the mood of the peasant masses.[256] Apparently the mood of the sharecroppers and their *kisan* allies, and also of those among the rank and file Communists who reciprocated it, clinched the issue in the

256. Abani Lahiri, "Last Battle of Bengal Peasants under British Rule" in Nisith Ranjan Ray, et al. (ed.), *Challenge: A Saga of India's Struggle for Freedom*, New Delhi, 1984, p. 386.

slogan's favour. As events proved later on, the *Kholan Bhango* slogan, which in effect threatened the physical security of the *Jotedars*, and consequently prepared them for a last ditch defence of their position, both exposed the movement to all kinds of coercive police actions, and elevated it to a higher pitch of militancy.

True to the expectations of the Communists, the sharecroppers' storming of the landlords' granaries was facilitated psychologically by the talks floating about the Bargadars Bill, which sagged the spirit of the *Jotedars*[257] but boosted the morale of the *Adhiars*.[258] If the League ministry seemed favourably disposed towards their obtaining the *Tebhaga*, the *Adhiars* felt, they were as much justified in having it on the fields, as from the *Jotedars' Kholans*.[259] Since the exploitative method was invariably the same, the *Bargadars* also declined at this point to distinguish between the "big" and the "small" among their exploiters — the *Jotedars* and the petty rentiers.[260] The *Kholan Bhango* activity had spread in such a whirlwind fashion in January 1947 that it caught most of the *Jotedars* — even the usually alert ones among them — uncomfortably napping. In Rangpur it started at Bargachhi near Domar, and extended quickly to Jaldhaka, Kurigram and Nilphamari. In Thakurgaon sub- division of Dinajpur the landlords faced the *kisan* assaults at Birganj, Thumnia and Rasulpur, and then at Parbatipur, Chirir-bandar, Kotwali, Kusumandi and Itahar.[261] The "forcible taking away" of paddy and plough-cattle from the *Jotedars' Khamar* (threshing

257. Reports of S.D.O., Siliguri, no.22c of 4 March 1947, and of S.D.O., Sadar, Burdwan, no. 188c of 7 March 1947, Land and Land Revenue Dept., Govt. of Bengal, File No. 6m-38/47 of 1947, West Bengal State Archives, Calcutta.

258. Report of S.D.O., Tamluk, no. 49c of 6 March 1947, *ibid.*

259. Report of S.D.O., Sadar, Malda of 7 March 1947, *ibid.*

260. Sunil Sen, *Peasant Movements in India*, Calcutta, 1982, p. 113.

261. Report of S.D.O., Sadar, Dinajpur, no. 26c of 8 March 1947, Land and Land Revenue Dept., Govt. of Bengal, File No 6m-38/47 of 1947, West Bengal State Archives, Calcutta.

floors)[262] took place in Berubari Union of Jalpaiguri, and became quite rampant in its Boda, Debiganj, Pachagarh, Mal and Matiali areas. The landlords' *Kholans* were stormed in many parts of Chittagong, in Munshiganj sub-division of Dacca and Netrakona of Mymensingh. Similar developments took place at Delkope, Paikgachha and Fakirhat of Khulna. The police fired upon the *kisan* invaders of the landlords' *Khamars* at Jeoltala and Balabunia of Delkope on 14 and 23 January 1947, respectively, killing two and injuring some more.[263] Attacks on the landlords' granaries were widespread at Jhenidah of Jessore; at Sandeshkhali, Mathurapur and Kakdwip of the 24-Parganas; and in Contai, Ghatal and Tamluk (especially at Nandigram and Panskura) of Midnapore. In the face of intense *Kholan Bhango* offensive the *Jotedars* could do very little, except imploring — successfully at times — the police and the local officials to intervene, and registering innumerable cases against "thefts" and "robberies". Many of them in fact fled from the villages in search of safety in the nearby sub-divisional towns and district headquarters.[264] In the absence of the landlords and their agents, and with the eclipse of the traditional structure of authority, the Kisan Sabhas or the *Samitis* became the arbiters in the villages, and where their organisational base was stronger, they even managed to set up a sort of semi-liberated zones, or the *Tebhaga Elakas* as these were called. In such *Elakas*, notably in Narail of Jessore, Thakurgaon of Dinajpur, Boda-Debiganj-Pachagarh of Jalpaiguri, Tamluk of Midnapore, in about one hundred villages of Rangpur, in certain parts of Mymensingh and in a stretch of approximately 200 miles in south 24-Parganas, came about the *Tebhaga Sangram Samitis*, who controlled not only the division of crops, but also administered the village affairs, looked after the village security and acted as adjudicators in the disputes.

262. Report of S.D.O., Sadar, Jalpaiguri, no. 208c of 10 March 1947, *ibid.*
263. Home Poll. Fortnightly Reports for 1st and 2nd halves of January 1947, File No. 18/1/47, N.A.I.
264. Contrary to their apprehensions, very few landlords were killed and physically harmed by the *kisans* during the entire period of the movement.

The police sometimes had to "ask permission" for entering into the *Elakas* from the *Sangram Samitis* or the popular bodies,[265] which the Prime Minister of Bengal had described in his report to the legislature as constituting the "parallel courts".[266] Not the functioning of the parallel courts so much, but the running of the "parallel government" in the *Elakas* in practice that seemed to have actually created consternation in the Government circles by February 1947.[267]

With the addition of fresh localities into the *Elakas*, and the persistence of the *Kholan Bhango* operations in full swing, the movement reached its climax by the middle of February 1947, or at the time when the *Tebhaga* demands were renewed over the harvesting of the winter crops. The appropriation of crops straightaway from the fields, and the seizure of grains threateningly from the landlords' granaries continued simultaneously for some time. The intensity of the proceedings could be gauged from the facts that about 17 *Kholans* were broken open in Balurghat sub-division of Dinajpur, 40 to 45 in the eastern part of Jalpaiguri, and a sizable number in Malda, Midnapore and south 24-Parganas. Side by side, a "general rising" of the *kisans* in Canning forced on the landlords a compromise based on the *Tebhaga*.[268] Similar developments were reported from Gobar-danga-Maslandpur area of Barasat,[269] and at Sandesh-khali, Basirhat, a large crowd of *kisans* assembled almost everywhere to carry the entire produce from the fields, leaving in some places as little as one-fourth (*Choubhaga*) for the

265. Adrienne Cooper, *Sharecropping and Sharecroppers' Struggle in Bengal, 1930-50*, Calcutta, 1988, p.181.
266. Bhowani Sen, "The Tebhaga Movement in Bengal", *Communist* (English monthly), Vol.1, September 1947, pp. 121-31.
267. Home Poll. Fortnightly Report for 2nd half of February 1947, File No. 18/2/47, N.A.I.
268. Report of S.D.O., Alipore, no. 24c of 13 March 1947, Land and Land Revenue Dept., Govt. of Bengal, File No. 6m-38/47 of 1947, West Bengal State Archives, Calcutta.
269. Report of S.D.O., Barasat, no. 28c of 10 March 1947, *ibid.*
270. Report of S.D.O., Basirhat, no.32c of 4 March 1947, *ibid.*

landlords.[270] Such carrying away of the entire crop had taken place in many other localities, notably at Dumuria, Khulna;[271] at Nalitabari, Mymensingh;[272] at Dhalahar Union, Bogra;[273] at Badarganj, Rangpur;[274] in Tamluk, Midnapore;[275] and at Jhanguri, Khaprail and Matighara, Siliguri.[276] Both the taking away of the *aman* (winter) crops and the breaking down of the *Jotedars' Kholans* seemed to have assumed — subsequent to the publication of the Bargadars Bill — "ominous" proportions in the Sundarbans (in Kakdwip and Sagar), leading to "disorder and violence".[277] The natural corollary of such a furious show-down for crops was bound in due course to be the signalling for a desperate battle for lands. A glimpse of the possible battle for land appeared to have surfaced even in January 1947 when the sharecroppers were airing in public the belief in the lands to be theirs only.[278] Following the general cry of *Hal Jar Jami Tar* (the land belongs to the one who drives the plough), a new slogan was also being coined, namely, *Chash Karo Jami Dakhala Rekhe* (till the land by keeping it under your possession) with a view to checkmating the *Jotedars'* refusal to renew contracts with the recalcitrant *Bhagchasis* for the next

271. Report of S.D.O., Khulna, no. 112c of 10 March 1947, *ibid.*
272. Report of S.D.O., Mymensingh, no. 207c of 3 March 1947, *ibid.*
273. Report of S.D.O., Bogra, no. 113c of 10 March 1947, *ibid.*
274. Report of S.D.O., Rangpur, no. 20(1)c of 9 March 1947, *ibid.*
275. Report of S.D.O., Tamluk, no. 49c of 6 March 1947, *ibid.*
276. Bengal Police Abstract of Intelligence, no. 6 of 8 February 1947, Home (Poll.) Dept. Confidential File No. 108/1947, West Bengal State Archives, Calcutta. Similar incidents also took place in Raipura and Narasinghdi of Narayanganj, Dacca.
277. Report of S.D.O., Diamond Harbour, no. 266c of 9 March 1947, Land and Land Revenue Dept., Govt. of Bengal, File No. 6m-38/47 of 1947, West Bengal State Archives, Calcutta.
278. For instance, in a compromise meeting a *Jotedar* asked the sharecroppers: "To-day you are demanding two-thirds of the crop, and perhaps tomorrow you will demand the entire crop. How can we accept such an unreasonable demand?" Sharp but simple was the reply a *kisan* gave him: "Yes, we can do that, for the land really is mine". See Bhowani Sen, "The Tebhaga Movement: Bengal's Greatest People's Struggle Since the Indigo Rising", *People's Age* (English weekly), 12 January 1947.

cultivating season, or foiling their attempts at the *kisans'* ejectment from the lands. The local authorities were in fact seriously perturbed about the impending battle royal over the evictions the *Jotedars* were determined to put into effect.[279] The ejectment of sharecroppers was believed to have actually been started by the *Jotedars*, such as in Burdwan,[280] Feni,[281] Pabna,[282] and Sirajganj.[283] As a counterpoise — and with a view to pre-empting evictions — the sharecroppers also began either exerting pressures for the early renewals of contracts, as it was in Howrah, Hooghly and various other places,[284] or resorting to "forcible ploughing" of lands, as in Narayanganj,[285] Brahmanbaria,[286] Khulna,[287] Chittagong,[288] and Tamluk.[289]

The "forcible ploughing" of the *Jotedars'* lands was not really very different from the "seizure" of lands of the landlords, including the *Khas*, or their own. The sharecroppers were interested in it for the prospect as much of forestalling their evictions as of re-installing the recently evicted among them. The *khetmajdoors* were ecstatic about it for the probability of securing strips of land for themselves — the fulfilment of their life-long ambition. Many of the rank and file Kisan Sabhaites and Communists — who had already been in the thick of the

279. Report of S.D.O., Sadar, Jalpaiguri, no. 188c of 10 March 1947, Land and Land Revenue Dept., Govt. of West Bengal, File No. 6m-38/47 of 1947, West Bengal State Archives, Calcutta.
280. Report, S.D.O., Sadar, Burdwan, no. 188c of 7 March 1947, *ibid.*
281. Report, S.D.O., Feni, no. 173c of 8 March 1947, *ibid.*
282. Report, S.D.O., Sadar, Pabna, no. 15c of 8 March 1947, *ibid.*
283. Report, S.D.O., Sirajganj, no. 15c of 8 March 1947, *ibid.*
284. Adrienne Cooper, *Sharecropping and Sharecroppers' Struggles in Bengal, 1930-1950*, Calcutta, 1988, p. 196.
285. Report of S.D.O., Narayanganj, no. 55c of 8 March 1947, Land and Land Revenue Dept., Govt. of West Bengal, File No. 6m-38/47 of 1947, West Bengal State Archives, Calcutta.
286. Report of S.D.O., Brahmanbaria, no. 111c of 7 March 1947, *ibid.*
287. *Swadhinata* (Bengali daily), 1 April 1947.
288. Home Poll., Fortnightly Report for 1st half of April 1947, File No. 18/4/47, N.A.I.
289. Adrienne Cooper, *Sharecropping and Sharecroppers' Struggles in Bengal, 1930-1950*, Calcutta, 1988, p. 195.

Tebhaga movement in the districts — were also attracted to it for the possibility of realising a basic slogan of the agrarian revolution — the "land to the tiller". The situation in February 1947, however, did not leave much space for confabulating over how to turn the scramble for crops into a contest for land, rather it called for an immediate action, or the striking of the iron at its hottest point. As the events seem to bear out, of all the places and the *Tebhaga Elakas*, only the *kisans* and the local leaders of the Sundarbans dared to take the initiative in Kakdwip. It was roughly around the middle of February 1947 that the *Samitis* in certain villages of Kakdwip region had endeavoured hard to convert the movement for "grain seizures" into one for limited "land seizures". Some lands of the fleeing *Jotedars*, particularly those from which the actual tillers had of late been evicted, as well as the chunks of the *Khas*, were taken over by the *Samitis*, and distributed among the *kisans*. One might find it difficult to state anything definitive about the extent of lands seized, and the manner they had been distributed, mainly because of the haziness of the available accounts. But that some of these "seized" plots were restored to their evicted occupiers,[290] and some given away to the *khetmajdoors*,[291] appeared factually to be correct. The limited land seizure in Kakdwip was very significant, indeed, for not only it added a new radical dimension locally to the Tebhaga movement, but also supplied the sharecroppers and agricultural labourers with a tangible common cause, and a realisable common course of action. Consequently, their alliance became the strongest in the Sundarbans, rendering the Kakdwip *kisans'* over-all struggle perhaps more persistent and uncompromising than the ones combated in other parts of the province. The

290. A report by "Nikunja" (Asoke Bose) on the "Anti-Imperialist and Anti-Feudal Struggle of the People in the Sundarbans and the Role of the Communist Party, Kakdwip, 24 Parganas", 15 June 1951, available in Material on Kakdwipa, Central Archives, C.P.I., Ajoy Bhavan, New Delhi.

291. *Banglar Shishu Telengana — Lalganj* (a Bengali pamphlet), 24 Parganas District Committee, Communist Party of India, 7 November 1949, available in Material on Kakdwipa, Central Archives, C.P.I., Ajoy Bhavan, New Delhi.

kisans in other parts of Bengal — some of whom were certainly politically more conscious, more resourceful and better organised than their Kakdwip counterparts — could also have attempted what had been done in the Sundarbans. The intensity of feeling that drove the Kakdwip peasants to try their hands at land seizures was visibly present among the lower peasantry in the other parts. The *Bhagchasi-khetmajdoor* alliance that characterised the occurrences in the Sundarbans was likewise unmistakably evident in many other places. What the agitators in these places had presumably been lacking in was the will to risk a leap forward — the kind of will the district leaders in Nalgonda had displayed in Telengana, Hyderabad, at the beginning of 1946. Their local leaders conjecturally might also have lacked in the relative autonomy of the provincial leadership that the Jatin and Gunadhar Maitis, the Hossain Sheikhs, the Dwarakanath Sama-ntas, the Bharat Beras and the Kangsari Haldars had enjoyed in the less accessible water-logged, tiger-python-crocodile-infested forest lands of the Sundarbans. Howsoever flexible was the Kisan Sabha's approach to the local units, and its liberality towards the local initiatives,[292] liberties could hardly be taken in matters of political lines, especially in stepping out in excess of them. The provincial Communist leadership and the B.P.K.S. were politically cautious all through, from the procrastinating commencement of the Tebhaga movement in November 1946 to its tactically advantageous call for the *Kholan Bhango* in the favourable circumstances of January 1947. But the enormity with which the storming of the *Jotedars' Kholans*, as well as the wholesale seizure of the winter crops, broke loose, and the pugnacity with which the Tebhaga Sangram Samitis flourished in the various *Elakas*, were sufficient to ruffle them considerably, and give them an uncanny feeling of a grip slipping past the happenings. Not being quite clear as to what was to be done with the Tebhaga movement, whether

292. The *Kisan Handbook*, All India Kisan Sabha, 1938, conceded to the local activists "the right to choose their own practical line of action" in close conformity of the A.I.K.S. instructions, and "in harmony with the local circumstances...".

to restrict it to the bounds of a "partial" struggle, or to extricate it to the open arena of a "total" one, the Communist leadership in Bengal developed an acute hesitancy by the end of February 1947, and wavered between a tendency to dilute the local militancy by talking in generalised terms against the *Zamindari* and in favour of the civil liberties — stressing on propaganda rather than on confrontation[293] — and a disposition to concede to it by promising the seizure and the cultivation of the landlords' *Khas* lands, not immediately, but in the future, perhaps in June 1947.[294] Thus eventually in the second phase, the Communist hesitancy seemed to have outmatched the local militancy, and had allowed the Tebhaga movement at its decisive stage to drift away. The drifting of a movement, and the uncertainty of its course, were bound to favour those who wanted to block its way by any and every means.

Having failed to withstand the *kisan* offensive through the *Naib-gomosta-lathial* mechanism, and more importantly, having experienced under the League regime some difficulty in rallying their trusted allies — the district bureaucrats and the police — the *Jotedars* in their utter existential crisis had to concentrate on the mobilisation of whatever support that was available to them for bringing utmost political pressure on the Government of Bengal. For an exploiting category like the *Jotedars*, and a self-righteous society like that of the Bengalis, the support base was proved to be remarkably wide as a churchdoor, through which passed not only the feudal elements like the powerful *Zamindars*, their *amlas* and dependants — whose help could be counted upon, any way — but also the moneylenders and grain-dealers, whose operations had been disrupted by the upheaval, and a section of the rich peasants, who dealt in grain-loans, employed labour and even practiced sharecropping in

293. The finding of Adrienne Cooper on the basis of resolutions of the B.P.K.S., Panskura Conference, Midnapore, Feb.-March 1947, see her *Sharecropping and Sharecroppers' Struggles in Bengal, 1930-1950*, Calcutta, 1988, p. 280.

294. Report of the B.P.K.S. Conference in Panskura, Midnapore, Feb.-March 1947, cited in Sunil Sen, *Peasant Movements in India*, Calcutta, 1982, p. 114.

bits of excess land as "small *Jotedars*". In "small *Jotedar*" category also belonged the rentier middle classes — the epitomes of "democratic" Bengal — whose apathy, if not exactly the hostility, was discernible particularly during the second phase of the Tebhaga movement when the agitators, to the mortification of their Communist leaders,[295] did not care to make any distinction between the "big" and the "small" *Jotedar* targets. The *Jotedari* mobilisation reached its fullest extent at the time of the publication of the Bargadars Bill, startling the Muslim League ministry as much as reminding it of its social mainstay — the Muslim *Jotedars.* An urbanite H.S.Suhrawardy, the Prime Minister of Bengal, frankly admitted later on that he had no idea prior to the Bill's publicity how powerful a force the *Jotedars* were in the politics of Bengal.[296] The "implacable hostility of about 40 Muslim M.L.A.s who were rich Jotedars",[297] the Muslim League Working Committee's decision to remain neutral on the measure so that the "members could oppose it", and the pressure of landlords, especially from north Bengal for its shelving, as well as the 58 amendments the Congress M.L.A.s moved at the Select Committee stage,[298] and all these cutting across the Hindu-Muslim identities at the high noon of communal politics in Bengal, ensured that the Bill was effectually "sabotaged",[299] and never allowed to become law. Once the Muslim Leaguers had in this way been made aware of which side of the toast they ought to butter, the state repressive machinery was geared up for an all-out onslaught on the *Tebhaga* agitators. Synchronising with the *volte-face* of the Suhrawardy ministry came the British

295. Bhowani Sen, "The Tebhaga Movement in Bengal", *Communist* (English monthly), Vol. I, no. 3, September 1947, pp. 121-31.
296. M.A. Rasul, *The Tebhaga Struggle of Bengal,* All India Kisan Sabha Publication, March 1986, New Delhi, p. 8.
297. Sugata Bose, *Agrarian Bengal: Economy, Social Structure and Politics, 1919-1947,* Cambridge, 1986, p. 269.
298. Adrienne Cooper, *Sharecropping and Sharecroppers' Struggles in Bengal, 1930-1950,* Calcutta, 1988, p. 189.
299. The expression was used by the Communist M.L.A., Jyoti Basu, on the floor of the House, see Sunil Sen, *Peasant Movements in India,* Calcutta, 1982, p. 115.

announcement on 20 February 1947 of their intention to transfer political authority in India, either to the central Government, or to the provincial Governments, by June 1948. To the Muslim Leaguers, who counted heavily upon their hold over Bengal, the announcement sounded like a hooter for urgently setting the Bengal affairs in order, and more specifically, keeping them clear of such a "disorder" that the Tebhaga movement was deemed to have brought about.[300] Their coercive determination thus being reinforced, the Government of Bengal apparently lost little time in coming heavily down upon the Communists and the *kisans.* Repression in fact had already begun in a big way much before the Bengal Premier could attempt at its justification on the grounds of the *kisans*' "lawlessness and defiance of authority".[301] A police-*kisan* clash on 20 February at Khanpur village of Dinajpur resulted in the firing, and consequent killing of 20 *kisans.* On the following day (the 21st) the police fired upon the *kisans* at Thumnia, Beliadingi of Dinajpur when they resisted arrest, and killed four among them. The demonstration to protest against these firings in Thakurgaon town was declared unlawful, and fired upon by the police on 25 February, resulting in deaths and injuries.[302] The police also fired upon the sharecroppers at Chakgopal village of Panskura, Tamluk on 20 February and at Barabhita of Nilphamari, Rangpur, towards the end of February.[303] About the same time the police "severely" punished the villagers at Gajole of Malda, and at Domar, Jaldhaka and Kaurigram of Rangpur for their "lawless" acts,[304] by arresting them on false charges, by molesting their womenfolk and breaking into their homes. There were police firings in Jalpaiguri — at Mathchulka, Baradighi of Mal on

300. Bhowani, Sen, "The Tebhaga Movement in Bengal", *Communist* (English monthly), Vol. I. no. 3, September 1947, pp. 121-131. Also Sunil Sen, *Agrarian Struggle in Bengal,* Delhi, 1972, p. 68.
301. Suhrawardy's statement in the Legislative Assembly, 28 February 1947, cited in Sunil Sen, *Peasant Movements in India,* Calcutta, 1982, p. 117.
302. *Amrita Bazar Patrika* (English daily), 27 February 1947.
303. Report of S.D.O., Sadar, Rangpur, no. 27c of 9 March 1947, Land and Land Revenue Dept., Govt. of Bengal., File No. 6m-38/47 of 1947, West Bengal State Archives, Calcutta.
304. *Amrita Bazar Patrika* (English daily), 21 February and 6 March 1947.

1 March killing five, at Mahabari of Matiali on 4 April killing nine, and at Batabari on 14 April killing a dozen.[305] On 7 March took place the police firing on the *kisans* of Barmajor, Sandeshkhali in the 24-Parganas killing six, and a similar occurrence followed in Jessore, resulting in nine deaths. In the third phase of the Tebhaga movement, between 20 February and 30 April 1947, the police opened fire 22 times, killed 73 people and arrested 3,119 *kisans* and Communist workers. Innumerable police camps were set up, specific areas cordoned off to round up the activists, and prison vans brought and Civil Supply food-trucks requisitioned to transport them to jails.[306] The landlords' men and *lathials*, who had gone hitherto into the hiding to save their skin, reappeared once again to join the police in the torturing of the *kisans*, in the looting and arsoning of their households and in the assaults on their families. The combined terror of the police and the *lathials* forced not only the *kisan* activists and the local Communists everywhere to go underground, but also the inhabitants in many places to quit their villages *en masse* and leave vast stretches of their fields "untilled".[307] Yet, howsoever massive was the scale of the Government repressions, the story of the third phase of the Tebhaga movement had not wholly been one-sided, or devoid of the instances of brave resistance on the part of the *kisan* heroes and heroines.

Few samples of the *kisans*' resistance to the official acts of repression might possibly be indicative of the indomitable spirit, and the height of militancy that the Tebhaga agitators were capable of accomplishing in their struggle. The nature of resistance was symbolised at Ranisankail of Dinajpur — where a party of policemen arrived on 2 February 1947 to arrest some of the so-called "paddy-looters". The *kisans* confronted the policemen, and Bhandani — the young *kisan* woman — took the lead by snatching away the gun of the *Daroga* (police inspector), and then overpowering and detaining him in a hut

305. Adrienne Cooper, *Sharecropping and Sharecroppers' Struggles in Bengal, 1930-1950*, Calcutta, 1988, p. 194.
306. *People's Age* (English weekly), 20 April 1947.
307. *Ibid.*

for the whole night. He was released the following day, and his gun returned to him, only at the instance of the local Kisan Sabha leaders.[308] When the policemen came to arrest the *kisan* workers at Chandpur of Gajole, Malda, the villagers surrounded them and took away their uniforms and the arrest warrants. A similar encirclement of the police party was reported from a village near old Malda.[309] The encircling of the policemen was often followed by the snatching away of their fire-arms, as it happened, notably at Dhupjhora, Mal and Malbazar of Jalpaiguri, at Bagbari maidan, Raghonathpur of Jessore, at Nandigram and Panskura of Tamluk, and at Budhakhali and Layalganj of Kakdwip. *Kisans* were also anxious for undertaking some retaliatory measures against the police-*Jotedar* combine to avenge the deaths, injuries and tortures they had suffered. They insisted, for example, on counter-attacking the police after the Chirirbandar firing, sought permission of their leaders for setting fire to the landlord Singha Vahini's house at Khanpur, and demanded fire-arms following the firing in Thakurgaon — all in Dinajpur. Similarly, they were determined to attack the police pickets at Domar, Jaldhaka and Kaurigram areas of Rangpur, and prepared for the destruction of the police post at Mal, Jalpaiguri. In Sandeshkhali, the 24-Parganas, the *kisans* went a step further, and subsequent to the firing at Barmajor, they actually attacked the police camp with their traditional arms, literally overran it, and chased the policemen away.[310] All these incidents of resistance and the desires for retaliation, which had in fact been hailed in some quarters of the rank and file, did not impress the cautious provincial leadership either in the Communist Party or in the Kisan Sabha. Rather, they appeared to have caused some sort of a panic among its members — the shuddering feeling of riding a tiger — following the vacillation

308. Sunil Sen, *Peasant Movements in India*, Calcutta, 1982, p. 113 and Peter Custers, *Women in the Tebhaga Uprising*, Calcutta, 1987, p. 94.

309. Adrienne Cooper, *Sharecropping and Sharecroppers' Struggles in Bengal, 1930-1950*, Calcutta, 1988, p. 193, footnote 149.

310. A report by "Nikunja" (Asoke Bose) on the "Anti-Imperialist and Anti-Feudal Struggle of the People in the Sundarbans and the Role of the Communist Party, Kakdwip, 24 Parganas", 15 June 1951, available in Material on Kakdwipa, Central Archives, C.P.I., Ajoy Bhavan, New Delhi.

that seized them at the *Kholan Bhango* phase of the movement. The uneasiness of their being carried away by the events, the untoward shelving of the Bargadars Bill, and the unprecedented outburst of repressions in fact had already led them to think in terms of a retreat, or to look for the ways and means of an escape. It was in this escapist and retreating psychosis, bred in the half way by a misgiving as to the state of the Communist preparedness, or about their being equal to the task of "conducting the largest mass movement ... somewhat suddenly",[311] that the leadership declined to make up its mind over going further on with the movement, and tried scrupulously to avoid, even oppose, the acts of growing *kisan* resistance. That largely seemed to be the reason why the *kisans* were prevented, for instance, from snatching the police fire-arms and using them for counter-attacks at Chirirbandar,[312] refused permission to burn down Singha Vahini's house and clash frontally with the police at Khanpur, persuaded not to demand fire-arms for fighting the police in Thakurgaon, and opposed to taking up arms against the police in Rangpur.[313] The same mentality was responsible, for example, for returning the snatched gun and freeing the *Daroga* at Ranisankail, releasing with arms the 50 policemen hostages at Bagbari maidan of Raghonathpur,[314] and the throwing away of the snatched guns in the wells at Mal.[315] Once the *kisan* resistance was thus ruled out, in the name of freeing the peasantry "immediately" from the iron grip of official repression,[316] the Tebhaga agitators had been left towards the end of March 1947 only with the golden route to escape — the emergency stairway for a hurried climbdown.

311. The B.P.K.S. Council meeting discussions in January 1947, cited in Adrienne Cooper, *Sharecropping and Sharecroppers' Struggles in Bengal, 1930-1950*, Calcutta, 1988, p. 274.
312. Peter Custers, *Women in the Tebhaga Uprising*, Calcutta, 1987, p. 102.
313. Adrienne Cooper, *Sharecropping and Sharecroppers' Struggles in Bengal, 1930-1950*, Calcutta, 1988, pp 191-2 and 195.
314. *Ibid.*
315. Ranajit Das Gupta, "Peasants, Workers and Freedom Struggle, Jalpaiguri, 1945-47", Amit Kumar Gupta, (ed.), *Myth and Reality: The Struggle for Freedom in India, 1945-47*, New Delhi, 1987, p. 444.
316. Sunil Sen, *Agrarian Struggle in Bengal*, Delhi, 1972, p. 62.

The hurried retreat in fact outmatched the official repression from 27 March 1947 when the communal riot broke out afresh in Calcutta, affecting the other parts of Bengal, and providing the provincial Communist Party and the B.P.K.S. with a providential moral justification to retire from the battle arena. Asserting the party's commitment to the maintenance of Hindu-Muslim unity, and apprehending a communal turn of the Tebhaga movement in the frenzied atmosphere, the Communist leaders promptly urged their rank and file to give precedence to the stoppage of riots over the continuance of the movement — "to stop the movement for stopping the riots" (*andolan na kara, riot bandho kara*).[317] The Communist *kisan* activists could hardly defy the leaders, though their own experience in the Tebhaga movement, despite instances of occasional discomfiture,[318] taught them to treat the class struggle as the most effective antidote to the communal rioting. Besides, the Communists were not really in a position in April 1947 to stop the communal riots in Bengal, except, of course, to make an attempt at their lessening to an extent. This they might have done advantageously by trying to revivify the *kisan* struggle in the countryside, and not by withdrawing it altogether. Hypothetically perhaps the Communists could have dealt with the rising communal violence more effectively, had they not delayed the launching of the Tebhaga movement, and embarked upon it in the harvesting season of 1945-6, prior to the August killings in Calcutta, rather than in 1946-7. In the second quarter of 1947 they practically had no chance at all for reversing the historical processes in Bengal, and averting nemesis on the heroic Bengali people. Consequently, the riots did not stop in

317. Almost all the participants in the Tebhaga movement, and all those knowledgeable in the party affairs, confirmed this to be the party line from the beginning of April 1947.

318. The Kisan Sabhaites did face some difficulty, owing to the opposition of the League and the *Maulavis* in rallying the Muslim sharecroppers in Mymensingh, Faridpur, Khulna, Dacca and Jessore (see Adrienne Cooper, *Sharecropping and Sharecroppers' Struggles in Bengal, 1930-1950*, Calcutta, 1988, pp. 252-3), as well as in north Bengal (see recollections of the Kisan Sabha activists in Dhananjay Roy edited, *Uttar Banger Adhiar Vidroha O Tebhaga Andolan* in Bengali, Malda, 1984).

April 1947 — they lingered on, to the contrary, till August 1947 — but the Communist Party managed meanwhile to dismount from the tiger it was so shakenly riding. The dismounting not only hastened the retreat of the Tebhaga fighters, but also left their retreating leaders in the lurch — at the mercy of the League and the Congress, who contended for succeeding imminently to the British inheritance in Bengal. The Communists seemed suddenly to have been forced to abdicate their position on the rural scene, and leave all the agrarian issues, including the fate of their faithful followers (the *Bargadars*) to the care of the so-called "progressives" in the Congress and the League — the supposed "saviours" of the *kisan* interest in those organisations who in Bengal relied decisively on the landlords' support.[319] Such an air of helplessness does explain why the Communist spokesman in the Legislative Assembly "welcomed"[320] the League ministry's State Acquisition and Tenancy Bill — a measure which aimed at strengthening the *Jotedars*' position in the name of securing the rights of the *rayats* and under-*rayats*, and which contained not even a single provision to protect the interests of the *Bargadars*. It also clarifies why, subsequent to the actual transfer of power, the Communists consoled themselves by believing that the *Tebhaga* movement alone had put the *Zamindari* abolition "on the agenda" of the Congress ministry in West Bengal,[321] and why simultaneously they refrained themselves from raising the issue of the abolition of all kinds of landlordism, especially that of the *Jotedari* variety — the target of the entire Tebhaga exercise. Apparently stemmed from it

319. Somnath Hor in his "Tebhaga Diary" entry of 23 December 1946 noted: "wherever I have been, I have noticed how utterly contemptuous peasant masses are about the Congress and the League. Hindu *Adhiars* regard the Congress as enemy. Similar is the impression of the Muslim *Adhiars* about the Muslim League. They presume the Congress and the League are the *Jotedars'* refuge". See *Ekshan* (Bengali periodical), Autumn Issue, 1388 B.S. (1981), 15th year, nos. 1-2.

320. Jyoti Basu, the Communist M.L.A., approved of the general principles of the State Acquisition and Tenancy Bill when it was introduced in the legislature by the League ministry on 21 April 1947.

321. Bhowani Sen, "The Tebhaga Movement in Bengal", *Communist* (English monthly), Vol. I, no. 3, September 1947, pp. 121-31.

further was their concern for the political disposition of the Bengali middle class, many of whose members enjoyed a rentier interest in land, and who demonstrably dominated "our country's main political organisations". The Communists ruefully regretted the alienation of the middleclass from the Tebhaga movement, which, in the opinion of their leaders, might not have taken place at all but for the adventures of the agitators, or their failure to exempt the "petty" *Jotedars* from the sharecroppers' onslaught, by limiting it to "the biggest and the richest" of the *Jotedar* category.[322] Left adventures of the party's *kisan* activists were, therefore, roundly condemned, and the *Kholan Bhango* slogan — the alleged source of mischief behind it — was criticised in the annual conference of the Bengal Provincial Committee, C.P.I. in the first week of October 1947.[323] Soon thereafter, its General Secretary, Bhowani Sen, appealed to the peasants "not to launch direct action this year [i.e. in the harvesting season of 1947-8] as they did last year".[324] The "appeal" marked officially the end of the Tebhaga movement in Bengal, and, barring a few meetings over the *Tebhaga* in the 24-Parganas, Midnapore, Malda, Dinajpur and Jalpaiguri, the *kisan* agitators appeared generally to have given up the struggle, and accepted defeat. Even in such an over-all climate of subjugation and despair the *kisans* in two areas of Bengal, namely, in the hilly tracts of north Mymensingh and in the Sundarbans of the 24-Parganas, did not feel that they had entirely lost, and therefore decided, unyieldingly to carry on their fight.

The Kakdwip *kisans*' longing for a fight appeared to have grown out of the limited success they achieved in the head-on confrontation with the *Jotedar*-police coalesce wee. The days of the *Jotedari Zulm* in the Sundarbans were apparently over, and similarly the practice of *begar* seemed to have passed away. The *Jotedars* also found it difficult throughout 1947 to enforce the collection of illegal levies, and to evict the sharecroppers from the allotted plots. Even the Government was obliged to think in terms of according some recognition to the *Bargadars*, and start

322. *Ibid.*
323. Sunil Sen, *Peasant Movements in India*, Calcutta, 1982, p. 142, footnote 56.
324. *Ibid.*

registering their names in the 23rd column of its settlement records.[325] Although the defence of the *Panchayat Kholans* had to be given up, and the seized bits of lands surrendered, the *Bargadars* still managed in certain cases to retain the crops of 1946-7, without giving any share whatsoever to the landlords. The repayment of paddy-loans in 1947 was neither demanded, nor acceded to, and the *Jotedars* generally failed to recover any cash they had loaned to the cultivators. Besides, the unity the *kisan* masses attained in the battlegrounds had engendered their unprecedented confidence in themselves. They were also fortunate to be the least affected by the communal riots, or by the partition of the province.[326] The halting of their resistance by the police repressions had steeled rather than broken them, and they not only prized what they gained but also expected more — not only the *Tebhaga*, but also the *Choubhaga* — not only the grains but also the lands. The sharecroppers and agricultural labourers in Kakdwip, therefore, resented during the sowing season of 1947 the party and the Kisan Sabha stalwarts' decision to abstain from agitation, and were surprised that the movement was not being renewed, its scope enlarged and its operation escalated. "The party asks us to step on the tail of the cobra", the *kisans* were reported to have said, "but does not allow us to go for killing it".[327] A crucial point thereafter was reached during the harvesting time in 1947 when the Communist and the Kisan Sabha leaders, in pursuance of their official line advocated the stacking of the paddy back again to the *Jotedars' Kholans*, and then negotiating (peaceably, of course) for the

325. A report by "Nikunja" (Asoke Bose) on the "Anti-Imperialist and Anti-Feudal Struggle of the People in the Sundarbans and the Role of the Communist Party, Kakdwip, 24 Parganas", 15 June 1951, available in Material on Kakdwipa, Central Archives, C.P.I., Ajoy Bhavan, New Delhi.
326. There was no evidence of any serious communal disturbance in Kakdwip between 1946 and 1950. Its small Muslim population of 7 per cent (see *Census of India*, 1941, pp. 80-88) had no difficulty in living harmoniously with others.
327. "Nikunja" (Asoke Bose) on the "Anti-Imperialist and Anti-Feudal Struggle of the People in the Sundarbans and the Role of the Communist Party, Kakdwip, 24 Parganas, 15 June 1951.

Tebhaga. In spite of their dislike of the party line, the *Bargadars* in most parts of West Bengal reluctantly accepted it, except in Kakdwip where they and their allies favoured carrying the crops to the *Panchayat Kholans* by registering its outright rejection. Even the persuasion of high-ranking leaders of the Communist Party and the B.P.K.S.[328] had no effect on the defiant Kakdwip peasants, who were bent upon resuming the struggle. They in fact had already made up their minds without caring or waiting for the Communist and the Kisan Sabha leaders, and in November 1947 itself expressed their urge for another show-down in an open rally in the Kakdwip Dak Bungalow maidan.[329] The whole affair revealed not only the bankruptcy of the Communist line of thinking (the like of which in any case was never really rare in the party's long past), but it also demonstrated the *kisans*' unequivocal insistence on their freedom of action. Never before perhaps in the history of the *kisan* movement in India were the leaders defied so manifestly, and also compelled so obviously to be led by their followers.[330]

If Kakdwip in the Sundarbans saw in 1947 a blunt assertion of the choice of the *Bargadars*, the hilly tracts of Mymensingh witnessed the tacit refusal of the *Tanka* peasants and their

328. It is said that Krishna Benode Roy, President, and Abani Lahiri, Joint Secretary, B.P.K.S., visited Kakdwip and the surrounding areas to convince the peasants there of the justification of the party's and the Sabha's new policy, namely, the stacking of paddy in the *Jotedars' Khamars*. The peasants, however, refused to accept this policy, and sent the leaders back. See Mahasweta Devi and Maitreya Ghatak, "*Prayata Asoke Bose Smarane*" (In Memory of Asoke Bose, Who Passed Away) in Boudhayan Chattopadhyaya (ed.), *Samskriti O Samaj* (a Bengali quarterly), 1st, 2nd, and 3rd issues, Calcutta, December 1983, pp. 156-7. In a personal discussion with the author (on 15 July 1985), however, Abani Lahiri recalled his visiting Kakdwip and other places in the winter of 1947, "not for selling any new party line", but to try to read the peasant mind and to assess the situation in the area. While meeting peasants and discussing matters with them, he was struck by their militant temper and battle-readiness, and reported his findings accordingly to the party and the Kisan Sabha headquarters.
329. List of open meetings where violence was preached, in the High Court Judgment on Kangsari Haldar *vs*. the State.
330. The Kakdwip *kisans'* assertion of autonomy has no parallel in the organised sector of peasants till 1951.

leaders to listen to the provincial committees, and give up their chosen path. Although the flaring up of the Hajong, Muslim, Dalu, Garo and other *kisans'* opposition at the Garo foothills to the *Tanka* system of produce-rent coincided with the outbreak of the Tebhaga movement in 1946-7, their struggle originally commenced almost a decade before, in November 1937, and it even gained a partial success in 1939 through some reduction in the amount of rent.[331] Their demands for the abolition of the *salami*-based *Tanka* system, some tenurial security and the conversion of the produce-rent into the much lower money-rent, so that the tillers could benefit from the rising agricultural prices, had grown throughout at the subterranean level; but these were not found to have been articulated by their mentors during the "people's war" phase. When the outbreak of the Tebhaga movement electrified the Bengal countryside, the *Tanka kisans* felt greatly enthused, and decided to resume their agitation in a rally of 5,000 on 8 December 1946 in Susang by defying Cr.P.C. Section 144.[332] In the typical *Tebhaga* style they started taking the entire produce from the fields to their collective *khamar*, and refused to pay *Tanka* unless the fixity of tenure, the abolition of *salami* and the commutation of paddy-rent into cash were conceded. The *Kholan Bhango* call of the Tebhaga movement also encouraged the Hajong *kisans* to storm the landlords' granaries and intercept whatever crops the landlords had managed to collect as the *Tanka*. On 21 January 1947 a large number of them attacked a *Muharior* (the collector employed by the landlord) bringing carts full of paddy that was forcibly collected from the Garo *Tanka kisans*. The next day, on 22 January, about 4,000 Hajong *kisans* "trespassed into Durgapur thana" to get some of their arrested activists released.[333] Following the *kisan* decision to resist the police interference in favour of the landlords,[334] took place the Baheratali incident on 31 January

331. See Act One, Scene II, pp. 57-8.
332. *Stop Tanka System*, a pamphlet in Bengali, Mymensingh District Kisan Samiti, January 1947, Central Archives, C.P.I., Ajoy Bhavan, New Delhi.
333. Suhrawardy's statement in the Legislative Assembly, cited in Sunil Sen, *Peasant Movements in India*, Calcutta, 1982, p. 120.
334. *Ibid.*

1947 in which the policemen in search of the "paddy-looters" assaulted a few women of the village, and forced another to come with them. When she cried for help., the *kisan* volunteers — led by the middle-aged widow, Rashimoni — chased and confronted the policemen on the banks of the Someswari. In the resultant fierce fight between the fully armed and semi-armed groups died two policemen, as well as Rashimoni and Surendra Sarkar.[335] The clash at Baheratali was the occasion for unleashing the worst kind of official repression on the Hajongs, bringing in detachments of the Eastern Frontier Rifles, raiding village after village, beating up the *kisans* and molesting the *kisanis*, and pulling down their huts.[336] Even then it was not possible to cow down the *kisans* for paying the *Tanka*, nor to arrest their local leaders, including the legendary Moni Sinha, for detention in jail. The absconding Moni Sinha and his comrades were perhaps the first among the leftist *kisan* activists in India who succeeded in consciously preparing the ground of, or deliberately creating a prelude to, the guerilla form of struggle in north Mymensingh, in which the men were reported to "take to the hills during the day and return to the villages at night", and women to "stay on in the villages" fearlessly in defiant dignity.[337] In such a fluid situation, despite the recrudescence of communal violence, and a temporary setback in its progress in the middle of 1947, the *Tanka* movement had not only not been given up, but in actuality it was turned into a full-fledged guerilla fighting in the following year.

335. *Ibid.*, and Moni Sinha, *Jeeban Sangram* (in Bengali), Dacca, 1983, pp. 85-6.
336. Nikhil Chakravarti, "Mymensingh To-day: A Vast Concentration Camp", *People's Age* (English weekly), 2 March 1947.
337. *The Statesman* (English daily), 25 March 1947.

THE RAISONNEUR'S MONOLOGUE

In radicalised parlance the guerilla tactics in particular, and the resorting to arms in general, are the highest forms of popular struggles — depending, of course, upon whom they must discriminately be used against — since they involve the giving and the taking away of precious human lives for a cause which leaves little room for any compromise. Although they constitute a movement in themselves, in the ultimate analysis, the guerilla tactics are the means to an end — an objective the toiling masses do discover through their experiences in the "partial" struggles as realisable, irrespective of the costs. The pointing to the goal, and its attainability are, however, the tasks of the ideologues of the toilers, whose timely enterprise elevates a "partial" struggle to the level of a "total" one, and whose chronic misgiving slopes it backwards. In Bengal in the case of the Tebhaga movement, the Communist leadership could not rise to the occasion, and give the call of the battle for land at the historic point (i.e. February 1947) when the *kisan* agitators were clearly winning the battle for crops, and preparing for a forward surge. It was not that the issue had not been raised in a clear, unambiguous manner, and Bhowani Sen — the provincial secretary of the Communists — did in fact put the point squarely before the leadership and the activists as early as the middle of December 1946 by suggesting the transformation of "today's fight for crops" into "tomorrow's fight for land" — the extension of the *Tebhaga's* "first stage in the onslaught" to its successive next stage on the *Zamindari*, and on landlordism itself, by demanding "land to the tiller", as well as by arousing sympathy of all the anti-feudal elements, including, hopefully, even the well-to-do among them.[338] Even if it was anybody's guess how serious Bhowani Sen had actually been in his line of thinking,

338. *Swadhinata* (Bengali daily), 15 December 1946, cited in Sunil Sen, *Agrarian Struggle in Bengal, 1946-47*, Delhi, 1972, p. 62.

his tossing across the point nevertheless led to a lively debate, reflecting the thought processes of some, and the mood of so many. That the majority of the Communist leaders in Bengal decided eventually in favour of leashing the Tebhaga movement within its "partial" confinement, and found in their wisdom the "land to the tiller" slogan to be the "will-o'-the wisp",[339] after which they would still run in any case for playing to the gallery, betrayed a lack of confidence in themselves — an inability to get over the panic that accompanied the awesome moments of all momentous decisions. The situation apparently was quite the opposite in Telengana where the Communist rank and file and the local leadership, operating, of course, on a much smaller scale than in Bengal, seemed to be aware not only of the great significance of the "land to the tiller" slogan, but also of the immediate relevance, and the prospect of its attainment in stages. That was why, at the peak of resistance against the landlords' grabbing of lands and ejectment of *Kouludars,* the Telengana Communists did not bother to start a debate threadbare over the issue of land seizures, but simply acted on it, after getting over the initial inhibition about the use of force, or taking to arms.[340] Although the lead was taken by the *kisan* rebels, the local Communists and the revolutionary District Committee of Nalgonda itself, howsoever "groping hesitantly",[341] neither the leadership in the A.M.S., nor in the Nizam State Communist Party, nor in the Andhra Provincial Committee chose to come effectively in their way, and dissuade them from their onward thrust. It was not that the threat of state repressions, and the actual pressure of the coercive forces had proportionately been less in Telengana and more in Bengal, nor that the Nizamshahi lagged far behind in smothering the *kisan* outbreaks. Conversely also, the Tebhaga agitators in Bengal had not really been less enthusiastic in carrying on their fight than the *kisans* of

339. *Ibid.*
340. Until towards the end of 1946, the Telengana Communists were lukewarm about the use of fire-arms for fear of elevating the struggle uncertainly to "an entirely new stage". See P. Sundarayya, *Telengana People's Struggle and Its Lessons,* Calcutta, 1972, p. 40.
341. *Ibid.*, p. 54.

Telengana, judging by the development that was germinating in Kakdwip, and which might well have followed suit in other parts of the province, had it not been scrupulously discouraged by the leaders of the B.P.K.S. and the Provincial Committee. What was it then that really hampered the more experienced of the Communists in Bengal to rise to the height the less experienced among them had reached in Telengana? Was their urbanite and semi-urbanite upbringing by and large — unlike the rural background of the Telengana Communists generally — responsible for the Bengal Communists' being insufficiently "de-classed" from the middle class fold,[342] inadequately appreciative of the full potential of the *kisan* masses, and in consequence, increasingly unsure of the rural poor's, and the local activists' ability for taking the initiative?

While practising revolutionism — whether in the urban centres, or in the countryside — the revolutionists were found to have been left with very little alternative to their relying responsibly on the vast multitude of those whom they wished to lead, on the local initiative of their cadres and followers. Responsible reliance on the local initiative could not, however, mean leaving the proceedings to their spontaneous course, and getting rudderlessly carried away by its momentum. The maintenance of a certain equilibrium between the over-all perspective and the local initiative seemed, therefore, to be the most desirable one for any revolutionary leadership at its national, provincial, district and even village levels. If in the context of an agrarian revolution in India, the Communists failed to maintain such an equilibrium in Bengal in 1946-7 by discouraging the *kisans* and the rank and file locally — quite unlike what their timely interventions had succeeded substantially in achieving about the same time in Telengana — they appeared to have thoroughly disrupted it in October 1946 in Travancore, in somewhat different backdrop, by surrendering to a sentimentally worked up local initiative. The perspective of the Communists in Travancore had hardly been one of agrarian revolution, since they did not really make much of a headway in the anti-landlord movement, and

342. Badruddin Umar, *Chirasthayee Bandobaste Bangla Desher Krishak* (In Bengali), Dacca, 1381 B.S., pp. 28-9, 35-7 and 88-90.

resultantly, they were not exactly in a position to think in terms of "land to the tiller". Their forte was trade-unionism, initially of the coir industry workers, and thereafter of the agricultural and agro-industrial labourers, whom they had organised with a lot of care. This successful uniting together of the industrial and agricultural workers over such issues as high prices, better wages and retrenchments, howsoever competently performed, did not actually throw up a serious challenge to the *Jenmi* and moneylender-dominated, rent and forced labour-based, and caste and community-ridden feudal structure of Travancore. Even the primacy that the agricultural labourers' trade-unionistic tendencies received in the Travancore Communist circles over their capabilities as the proletarian opponents of feudal exploiters, to an extent, diluted the consolidation of the anti-feudal forces, alienated the rich peasants, and confused all others. If feudalism had not thus been put severely under strain in Travancore, the repressive Government that reclined on it there, and stood up to defend it and its privileges, was not easy to be restrained, and very difficult, indeed, to be dislodged. It did not follow from this, however, that the workers and agricultural labourers would hesitate to repel their attackers, resist repressions tooth and nail, and join wholeheartedly the popular movement for responsible government and civil liberties in the state. The Communists in Travancore in fact were perfectly justified in deciding to pick up the standard of civil liberties that had been slipping past the hands of the State Congress, and resolving to intensify the battle for responsible government in whatever way they could, using popular pressure in the main, but not ruling out even the skilful use of arms. Since the perspective in Travancore apparently was one of responsible government, to be achieved through the involvement and movement of diverse sections of the Travancoreans, and that, too, without the advantage of a stride towards the agrarian revolution in intrinsically an agrarian society, how could the Communists think they would be able to short-circuit the entire process merely by inventing all on a sudden an insurrection, and thrusting it upon their semi-armed proletarian following? Or, was it that they entertained in their flight of imagination — and as suggested by the preparations they made on a miniature

Bolshevik revolutionary fashion, and the high-strung disposition they impatiently demonstrated — an altogether different perspective of the capture of power in the state, of setting up the Soviets, and perhaps of socialism, irrespective of the state of affairs in the rest of the country? Revolutionaries are essentially romantics, and there is no bar in their romanticising a situation, provided it does not go drastically beyond all the basic realities. In Punnapra-Vayalar it certainly did, and what was worse, neither the Kerala Provincial Committee, nor the Politbureau of the C.P.I. had the sense of responsibility for questioning the misadventurous plan before giving it the way in the name of upholding the "local initiative". All these issues and sundries had naturally been relegated to the background after the occurrences, and in the glory of the unparalleled scale of martyrdom of the thousands, whether it included some of the front-ranking Travancore Communists or not. The tragedy was that the immensity of martyrdom did not qualitatively change the circumstances of Travancore in 1947 in the manner the immeasurably less of it did in Telengana.

In the context of the "land to the tiller" slogan, which seemed realisable in Telengana, and not wholly unrealisable in Bengal, the "local initiative" might also have developed in Ratnagiri of Maharashtra, and could have even flourished in many parts of Bihar. That it did not take shape in the course of the Worli rising was possibly because of the organisational handicap of the Kisan Sabhaites, and the steamrolling capacity of their adversaries, which pressed the *Bai* and her associates almost always to a corner, and denied them the space and time to plan in terms of "land seizures", or of restoring land to their original owners. Such, however, was not the case in Bihar where the Kisan Sabha had not only been one of the most organised in the entire country, but it had also the longest experience of conducting, practically without a break from 1937, the massive volatile movement like that of the *Bakasht* peasants. Since the leftists and the *Bakasht kisans* had been engaged in semi-armed bloody conflicts with the landlords for about a decade over the issues of the ejectment from lands and the possession of the standing crops, they were in the fittest condition to demand "land to the tiller", and sound the death-knell of landlordism in

Bihar. It was not clear why they could not move from the defence of lands and crops to the next logical step of the seizure of crops and lands — as a means either of their recovery, or of their distribution, or both. Were they so naive as to misread in the immediate prospect of the *Zamindari* abolition a kind of writ to end automatically all other forms of landlordism, and that of feudalism altogether? Was it the lack of perceptional and programmatic unity among the Communists, Socialists, Swamiites, Forward Blocists and Royists in Bihar, and not their failing to act in unison — certainly not exemplarily in 1946-7 — that had stood by any chance in the way of further advancement? And most crucially, had they been able to make any serious attempt at organising the agricultural labourers, and mobilising them in support of the *Bakasht kisans*' "do or die" struggle? Could the agricultural labourers be suitably mobilised in a feudal society without the scope for their visualising some chance of owning lands for themselves? Did the caste-conscious *kisans*' mentality to avoid touching the cause of the "untouchable" agricultural labourers play at all any role? The unevenness of the progress, following a certain amount of steady growth, was the common predicament of the agrarian revolutionaries in most countries under the colonial domination. If the agricultural and bonded labourers had been raised together to an extent in Ratnagiri, and even at the expense of being rather lukewarm towards the other anti-feudal categories — such as it was in Travancore — the rural proletariat seemed to have somehow been neglected, as in Bihar, in the over-enthusiasm for fostering resistance among the categories slightly above them. If the local initiative appeared on account of some misapprehension to be almost unmountable in places like Bengal, it was responsibly rode upon in Telengana, though allowed to gallop reinlessly in Travancore. Since the revolutionists were not really the natural scientists, nor even the social scientists, despite their obsession with the scientific approaches, they hardly ever needed to go into the shells awaiting the meticulous unfolding of an ideal situation — a perfectly balanced position of all the circumstances — provided their own forces, and those of whom they had harnessed, had no hesitation in springing realistically into action. Judging by such symptomatic occurrences as had taken place in

Maharashtra, Gujarat, Hyderabad, Travancore, Malabar, Bengal and Bihar, and by the articulated style in which the rural poor had thrown up their own brave forerunners, it appeared that the Communist rank and file and the *kisan* masses were impatiently in readiness for an all-out struggle at the transitional point in 1947. The firing, or the misfiring, of the readied guns and the dried up gun-powders, however, depended largely on those who were supposed to handle them efficiently and, of course, somewhat imaginatively.

SCENE II
1948-49
Another Setting

Whatever the revolutionists and the rural poor did, or tried to do in 1948-9, was shaped essentially by the ways they viewed the most significant occurrence of Indian history in the twentieth century, namely, India's attainment of political independence in August 1947, and the price it paid for by partitioning itself. Any overviewing of the developments that led by stages to the 15th of August 1947 must in all propriety have as its starting point the July of 1945 when the British Labour Party took over the reins of government in Britain. Known for their sympathies with the nationalist cause in India, the Labour leaders had already committed themselves to freeing India, if and when they were voted to power. As early as 24 June 1938, in fact, such front-ranking Labourites as Clement Attlee, Aneurin Bevan, Stafford Cripps and Harold Laski met Jawaharlal Nehru and V.K. Krishna Menon at Filkins near London, and agreed — in the case of their forming a Government in Britain — to accept the future constitution of India as decided by an Indian Constituent Assembly, elected on "universal suffrage", and to transfer authority in India from the British to the Indian hands. So unequivocal appeared to be the Labour Party's position on the issue of Indian independence, and so complete was its victory in the British elections that even the Viceroy of India shuddered at the prospect of the new British rulers' handing over India "to their Congress friends as soon as possible".[343] What Wavell, as well as the nationalists in India did not know, but both came to

343. Wavell, *The Viceroy's Journal*, Oxford, 1973, p. 159.

understand in the due course, was that the Labourite enthusiasm for making a promise without being in office could not be the same for keeping it when in office. If the Whigs and Tories in Britain, or for that matter the Tories and Liberals there, did not drastically differ in their over-all attitudes towards the maintenance of the Indian empire, despite the differences in ideology, why should the Labours not agree — in spite of their socialist affectations — with many of the Conservatives, bureaucrats and the vested interests on the most advantageous way of dismantling it. After all, the act of freeing an unmanageable colony could by no stretch of imagination be termed as imperialistic, howsoever the disuniting and dividing its people exposed it ever so weakeningly to fresh neo-colonialist designs. Apparently the Labours had no particular qualms about such an exposure, for they were almost as willing as the Tories and the imperial bureaucracy in letting the separatists enjoy a pre-eminence in all discussions as to the future of India, in silencing the popular outbursts in the country by the use of brute force, and defending obstinately through thick and thin most of the British overseas interests. Even the Conservatives would not have been able to match the anxiety they had shown for propping up the French and the Dutch colonialists, through the employment of the British-Indian troops in Indo-China and Java. Consistent with the responsibilities of guardianship for the British interests, the first moves that the Attlee cabinet made in India were hardly earth-shaking, or which a non-Labour Government could not have made. It asked the Viceroy to announce on 21 August 1945 the decision to hold under the Act of 1935 fresh elections for the Indian legislatures in the approaching winter of 1945-6. The elections were not only overdue for the centre (last elected in 1934) and for the provinces (last elected in 1937), but also necessary for reopening the constitutional game — the bitter wrangles and squabbles — in the name of negotiations for a peaceful transfer of power. The Viceroy was further prompted to renew on 19 September 1945 the promises of early "self-government" (refraining thoughtfully from using the term "independence"), and of discussing with the elected legislators and the representatives of the Indian princes on the formation of a Constituent Assembly for undertaking constitutional arrangements (forgetting conveniently the earlier Labourite assurance to elect a Constituent Assembly on "universal suffrage").[344]

By the time the elections took place in 1945-6, the League — following the official recognition (by the consecutive Viceroys, Linlithgow and Wavell) of its monopoly to represent the Muslim opinion, and the dangling of the carrot of Pakistan, or of *Musalmanon-ki-hukumat*, before the Muslim public — was in a favourable situation to deal effectively with its separate Muslim electorate. The task was rendered easier when it decided to whip up religious passions, use mosques for the election meetings and persuaded the *Pirs* and *Maulavis* (the Muslim religious leaders) to issue *Fatwas* (directives) in its favour — "a vote for the League and Pakistan as a vote for Islam". In such a religiously built up atmosphere the Congress was hardly able to carry the bulk of the Muslim voters with it, despite its riding at the crest of popular enthusiasm over the intimations of independence. It did perform spectacularly in the elections, securing 91.3 per cent votes in the General non-Muslim constituencies, and winning majorities at the centre and in all the provinces, except Sind, Punjab and Bengal, but it was not able to diminish the significance the Government had already thrust upon the Muslim electorate. From the British point of view, and at the negotiation table to be presided over by them, what mattered more in 1946 than the massive national mandate for the Congress was the League's ability to goad the Muslim voters to its side. Apparently in this the League attained remarkable success by polling 86.6 per cent of the Muslim votes, winning all the Muslim seats at the centre, and almost all of them in the provinces. But in spite of achieving so much, the League could not establish its sway on those Muslim majority provinces which it was demanding for Pakistan. It lost North-West Frontier Province and Assam to the Congress, and failed to dislodge the Unionists from the Punjab. Even the League ministries that were set up in Bengal and Sind hinged perilously

344. Sumit Sarkar, *Modern India, 1885-1947*, Delhi, 1983, p. 418.

on the official and European support.[345] It was, however, the face-value of the League, and not so much its intrinsic worth, that the British authorities hoped for using as a trump card at the negotiating round. Since India had reached the boiling point by March 1946, and the Congress the threshold of another countrywide "mass movement or revolution", which the Viceroy was not certain that the authorities could "control",[346] the Attlee Government lost no time in initiating constitutional discussions mainly with the Congress and the League — the two freshly elected in their respective strength. Any initiative for a peaceful and negotiated transfer of power must proceed — if the sub-continent had to be left to its disjointed and disunited fate — on the lines either of a loose Indian federation or of the partition of India. As the events eventually turned out, the British tried their hands at both — first unsuccessfully at the country's destabilisation, and then successfully at its division. There could be a debate among the India observers, and there was one within the Congress, as to which of the two — between the destabilisation and the division — had been less evilsome from the nationalist viewpoint as a choice than the other. That the choice had been made by the British to look like the solitary one between the two alternatives, and seemed genuinely promising to the League, was by no means so excruciatingly limited as far as the Congress had been concerned. The Congress always had a third choice, that of going to the people, and stirring up an upheaval, purely because it did not ever stake its very existence

345. The fact was that the League's claim for absolute Muslim support had not adequately been tested in undivided India. The elections of 1945-6 were held not only on the basis of separate electorates, which had been devised to keep the Muslims away from the national mainstream, but also on the strength of severely restricted franchise — barely 10 per cent of the total population. Had the elections been contested on the adult franchise, as Sumit Sarkar felt in his book, *Modern India*, Delhi, 1983, pp. 438-9, it is difficult to say what might have happened, in view especially of the Congress's success in such elections in India in 1952, and the League's reverses in east Pakistan in 1954, as well as of its failure to control affairs in west Pakistan.

346. Wavell, *The Viceroy's Journal*, Oxford, 1973, p. 232.

only on the "negotiations" for a transfer of power, nor accept the constitutional method as its strongest point, nor face difficulty in reaching and leaving the stages of the parleys in between engagements in the popular struggles.

The Cabinet Mission, whom the Labour Government sent to India in February 1946, and who conferred with the Indian leaders till June 1946, formulated the scheme for a loose union of all the Indian territories under a centre that would look merely after the defences, the foreign affairs and the communications, and leave all other subjects to the provinces. The provincial legislatures would then elect a Constituent Assembly, with each province having been allotted a specified number of seats proportionate to its population, and distributed strength-wise among its various communities. The members so elected would "divide up in three sections" — Section A for the non-Muslim majority provinces (Bombay, the U.P., the C.P., Bihar, Orissa and Madras), Section B for the Muslim majority provinces in the north-west (Baluchistan, Sind, N.W.F.P. and the Punjab) and Section C for the same in the north-east (Bengal and Assam). All these sections would have the authority to draw up provincial constitutions, and if necessary, group constitutions, and set up thereby provincial and sectional legislatures and executives. As the completion of all these long-term arrangements was likely to take considerable time, the Mission proposed a short-term measure — the formation of an Interim Government at the centre, enjoying the support of the major political parties, and leaving all the portfolios to the Indian members. Clearly the Mission's plan was intended to be a compromise, by placating the Congress through the rejection of the Pakistan plan, and mollifying the League through the creation of autonomous Muslim majority areas in some proximity. At the outset, therefore, both the League and the Congress were inclined to accept the plan, including the limited and the indirect election of the Constituent Assembly, which so blatantly contradicted the previous Congress demand for such an election on the basis of adult franchise. But soon a difficulty surfaced over the provisions for sections or groups, which the League interpreted to be compulsory, for that might brighten up the possibility of a future wholesome Pakistan by steamrolling the Congress-governed

Muslim majority provinces of N.W.F.P. (in Section B) and Assam (Section C) into it (by reducing them in their respective sections to helpless minority). It was precisely because of the opposition of the N.W.F.P. and Assam to their being forced into a minority position in Sections B and C that the Congress wanted the groupings to be optional. By July 1946 the Cabinet Mission plan for putting up a disarranged India under a nominal centre, and with the communally segregated autonomous units, had in effect collapsed over the League-Congress difference on the issue of groupings. Thereafter, in their haste to leave the ground to the neo-colonialist experimentation, the British had not even discussed seriously of the necessity for maintaining the pretence of a weak Indian union.

The setback over the Mission's plan so exasperated the League that it wanted forthwith to force the situation through "Direct Action", or give concrete expression to its post-election slogan: *Ladke Lenge Pakistan* ("we shall have Pakistan by force"). The outcome was the communal carnage that began first on the Direct Action Day (16 August 1946) in Calcutta, and then spread in a chain of reactions over the other parts of the country, notably in Bombay, eastern Bengal, Bihar, a certain part of the U.P., N.W.F.P. and the Punjab. Coinciding practically with the outbreak of communal violence that an Interim Government at the centre — the one the Mission proposed as a short-term measure in its plan — came into existence, despite the problem of keeping a "parity" in it between the Congress and the League nominees, and the resultant League refusal to take part in its formation. It was a threat to law and order, either in the shape of a mutiny of the armed forces of the recent past, or in the cast of the agrarian unrest then prevailing, or in the form of strikes by the post and railway employees in their imminence, that compelled the Viceroy to go ahead with the erection of an Interim Government, for the time being, constituted even solely by the Congress — the party which enjoyed the greatest influence generally over the public mind. "If the Congress will take responsibility, they will realise that firm control of unruly elements is necessary, and that they put down the Communists and try to end their own left-wing", felt Wavell, who also hoped "to keep them [the Congress] so busy with administration that they had much less time for politics".[347] Elated by the Viceregal gesture of giving them precedence over their League counterparts, and expecting the Interim Government to be to their advantage in the peacefully negotiated transfer of power, the Congress leaders opted on 2 September 1946 for the making of a cabinet under Jawaharlal Nehru's leadership. As the situation unfolded itself later on, the Congress-dominated functioning of the Interim Government became on the whole an expensive exercise in futility. In spite of all its concerns, it was in practice helpless — in the face of the communal holocaust — to move the leisurely army, under the British Commander-in-Chief, into the riot-afflicted areas. Being presided over by the Viceroy, the Interim Government was also not able to withstand the pressure of his vetoing power. And its position worsened when Wavell persuaded the League leaders to join it on 26 October 1946, overlooking their persistence with the "Direct Action", and by agreeing symbolically to uphold "parity". Thereafter the Interim Government, obstructed by its League members, and divided sharply into the Congress and League camps, backed up by their warring followings within the bureaucracy, was reduced for all practical purposes to a figure-head.

If the Government of a country at the centre was thus torn asunder, and the major communities of its people were led maniacally to cut each other's throats, could it still hope to remain united, and yet be independent? The senior and venerable Congress leaders — those already rendered a battle-weary, haggle-harassed and riot-wrecked lot by the beginning of 1947 — were no longer hopeful. Rather, they were too keen to come out of the labyrinth and reach the corridors of power (of course, with the pious desire for building a new India) at any and every cost, if necessary by putting their life-long nationalist dreams at an auction, and selling them for a transfer of power at the exorbitant price of partitioning the nation. The alternative course was to refuse to serve a sham Interim Government, to take to the streets for confronting both the Muslim and the Hindu communalists, to go all-out for waging the last battle against the Raj, and to attempt

347. Wavell to the Secretary of State, 31 July 1946, N. Mansergh (ed.), *Transfer of Power*, Vol. VII, p. 154.

at forging popular unity on the battle-lines. It was clearly hazardous, extremely uncertain and immensely daunting, but not absolutely beyond the realms of possibility in the first quarter of 1947. Else a pacifistic realist like Gandhiji would not have thought of suggesting the Congress exit from the Interim Government, recommending its re-constitution with Jinnah as the head, forcing the British to quit India unconditionally first,[348] and then deciding the issue of Pakistan, or the division of the country, by the Indians themselves, "as a result of understanding between the parties, or of an armed conflict".[349] The option was so obviously divergent from the path of "negotiated settlement" with the British, and so strikingly inconvenient to pursue in comparison, that those Congress "stalwarts", who had suddenly turned overzealous to shoulder the responsibility for "administering the affairs of millions",[350] were unwilling to give it even the slightest of serious consideration. Once the religion, and the religious community-based partition of India had been practically agreed to, particularly after the pressure the Attlee cabinet exerted upon the negotiating parties on 20 February 1947 by resolving to transfer power to whosoever exercised authority wherever in India by June 1948, nothing much really remained, except determining whether Jinnah could get the Pakistan he bargained for, or the Pakistan he considered "truncated and moth-eaten". The settlement of this and the other details — the *modus operandi* for the "divide and quit" — were left to the care of the new Viceroy, Lord Mountbatten, who replaced Wavell in March 1947. Following hectic negotiations, Mountbatten was able to evolve his plan of 3 June 1947, in accordance with which the British partitioned the country and transferred power to India and Pakistan simultaneously in the middle of August 1947.

348. Bimal Prasad, "Gandhiji and India's Partition", Amit Kumar Gupta (ed.), *Myth and Reality: The Struggle for Freedom in India, 1945-7*, Delhi, 1987, pp. 106-9.
349. Gandhi to Mountbatten, 8 May 1947, N. Mansergh (ed.), *Transfer of Power*, Vol.X, p. 667.
350. *Collected Works of Mahatma Gandhi*, Vol. LXXVII, pp. 254-7.

Play On

The coming of the independence and the setting up of a Congress Government in India under Jawaharlal Nehru, through hard bargains and prolonged negotiations — not so much between the British and the Indians, but among the differing Indians themselves under the British arbitratorship — and that, too, after the communal vivisection of the country, did not satisfy many, and caused uneasiness in the mind of almost everyone. Apparently the most dissatisfied, and even displeased, were the leftists of practically all varieties, and if the Socialist Party described the Mountabatten's plan as an "act of surrender",[351] the Forward Bloc took it as "a bogus transfer of power",[352] the R.S.P. as "a backdoor deal between the treacherous bourgeois leadership of the Congress and imperialism",[353] the R.C.P.I. as the result of "political conspiracy hatched by British imperialism and the Indian bourgeoisie",[354] and the Bolshevik Party as an "act of betrayal" by the Indian bourgeoisie.[355] Apart from the Royists, who stoically accepted the development as it emerged, only the C.P.I. was remarkably benign in its estimate of the situation. While the party regretted the British's setting in motion, through a "double-faced" policy, the disruptive and reactionary forces "to obstruct the realisation of a real independence", it acknowledged the Mountbatten plan to have made "important concessions" to the Indians, and opened up "new opportunities for national advance".[356] The logical corollary of such an estimate being a Congress-Communist

351. *Indian Annual Register*, N. Mitra (ed.), 1947, Vol.1, p. 259.
352. *Ibid*., p. 197.
353. L.P. Sinha, *Left Wing in India*, Muzaffarpur, 1965, pp. 552-3.
354. Soumyendranath Tagore, *The Hour Has Struck*, Calcutta, 1949.
355. Satyabrata Ray Chowdhuri, *Leftist Movements in India, 1917-47*, Calcutta, 1977, p. 232.
356. "Mountbatten and After", Resolution, Central Committee, C.P.I., June 1947, Party Documents, Central Archives, Ajoy Bhavan, New Delhi.

unity for "the achievement of full independence", and for the "fulfilment of the economic and social demands" of the toiling masses of India,[357] the C.P.I. came out in the immediate post-independence days with the slogans of "all support to Nehru Government", and of "a united front between the Government and the people".[358] Even if the slogans had been proved convincingly to be correct, and the "national bourgeoisie" (or those bourgeoisie of the colonised countries who took interest in nation-building) and their Congress Government shown to be progressively against neo- colonialism, comparatively free from the monopoly capitalistic influences and sympathetically disposed towards many of the popular causes, it was doubtful if they would have satisfied the pent-up militancy the Communist rank and file had rapidly gathered from 1944-5, and the revolutionism they rehearsed in 1946-7. The slogans were bound to be suspect in their eyes, and hence not acceptable to them if the "national bourgeoisie" and the Congress Government were unable to lay bare a promise for living up to the popular egalitarian and anti-neo-colonial expectations. There could be a serious debate whether the period of a mere four months and a half had been adequate at all for the Congress Government to establish its progressive credentials, and in case it had not been so, whether it was visibly disillusioning its loyal supporters, and losing its massive all-India support-base. Since no yardstick was yet available to measure up the Congress's position, except the wailings over a partitioned and drought-ravaged country, and whisperings over the dislocated, fluid state of affairs — a condition that offered unlimited opportunities to all kinds of freebooters — the militant leaders in the C.P.I., in their own anxiety for carrying the belligerent party cadres with them, jumped in the latter half of 1947 to the abrupt conclusion that the "native bourgeoisie" (or those bourgeoisie of the colonised

357. R.P. Dutt, "The Mountbatten Plan for India", *Labour Monthly*, London, July 1947, pp. 210-19.

358. "Review of the Second Congress of the Communist Party of India", M.B. Rao (ed.), *Documents of the History of the Communist Party of India*, Vol.VII (1948-50), New Delhi, 1976, p. 184.

countries who reclined on imperialism against the interests of nation-building)[359] and the Congress leaders had been discredited in the eyes of the people for the way they had retreated from their anti-imperialist "oppositional" role to that of a "collaborationist" one with imperialism.[360] If this was the true surmise, as it might well have appeared to be so to many from the manner the Congress leaders assumed power through negotiations conducted by the imperialists, or, as it had in the later days been believed, with the help of a neo-colonialist design, then "the struggle for real freedom and democracy" in India, according to the militant leaders, had to be waged afresh "in opposition to the collaborationist policy of the Congress leaders".[361] Since the Congress leaders' collaboration with the imperialist domination was not feasible without the wholesale collusion of the forces perpetuating the retardation of the colonised society, such "tails" of imperialism as the monopolists, the big business houses and the feudal exploiters, the struggle in opposition to the Congress leadership was anticipated to attain, sooner or later, the proportions of a popular, revolutionary one.

The militant Communist leaders, who started questioning the position of the moderate leadership in the C.P.I. from December 1945, and seriously challenged it in August 1946, had finally registered a decisive victory over it at the end of 1947 by reversing the earlier party line on Indian independence. Following its deliberations between 7 and 10 December 1947, the Central Committee of the party under the militant influence dubbed the 15th of August as a day of "betrayal by the Bourgeoisie",[362] and the transfer of power as a "surrender" to imperialism — a British manoeuvre to "share power" with their junior partners.[363] The Central Committee also appointed a

359. It was assumed that the "national bourgeoisie" had fallen to the status of "native bourgeoisie" in 1947.
360. "Report on Revisionist Deviation", presented by B.T. Ranadive to the Second Congress, M.B. Rao (ed.), *Documents of the History of the Communist Party of India*, Vol. VII (1948-50), pp. 161-3.
361. "Review of the Second Congress of the Communist Party of India", Politbureau, March 1948, *ibid.*, p. 185.
362. "Report on Reformist Deviation", *ibid.*, p. 163.
363. "Political Thesis", adopted at the Second Congress, 28 February to 6 March 1948, *ibid.*, pp. 39-50.

commission to prepare some draft political thesis — on the basis of the newly found wisdom — for adoption in a party congress. The second Congress of the C.P.I. met in Calcutta between 26 February and 6 march 1948, replaced P.C. Joshi by B.T.Ranadive as the General Secretary, and opted for ardent "revolutionism" in place of rank "reformism". According to the political resolution passed in the Congress, the bourgeois class as a whole (irrespective of its "national", "native" and "big" categories) had "turned its face from the masses, and gone over to collaboration" with imperialism and feudalism. Consequently, the Nehru Government representing it had linked itself with the Anglo-American bloc of imperialist powers — "a bloc which seeks to crush all democratic revolutions to create satellite states".[364] The march of democratic revolution in India, therefore, was to proceed — in the view propounded in it — "directly in opposition to the bourgeois Government and its policies, and the bourgeois leadership of the Congress", along the "path of armed struggle against imperialists and their allies"[365] — the path that had been cleared in the colonies in the post-war revolutionary epoch.[366] Led by the proletarians, and set in motion by all other forces in alliance with them, the democratic revolution would bring about a "people's democratic" state, by establishing a Government "representing the workers, toiling peasants and the oppressed petty bourgeoisie"; by confiscating foreign capital in banks, industries and transport concerns; by

364. *Ibid.*, p. 41.
365. *Ibid.*, p. 10.
366. Concepts, such as the division of the globe into the Anglo-American bloc of imperialists and the rest, the bourgeoisie's becoming entirely counter-revolutionary and pro-imperialistic world over, and the rising prospect of anti-bourgeois and anti-imperialist armed struggles in the colonies — were the hints the militant Communist leaders in India chose to exaggerate from their reading of Andrei Zhdanov's Report (which had been published in the *People's Age*, 25 January 1948) in the Nine Parties' or the Cominform's inaugural session in late September 1947. Their exaggeration was reinforced by the writings of the Soviet Russian experts on Indian affairs, V. Balavushevich and A. Dyakov, who tried to interpret Zhdanov's report slantingly to mark the return of the international Communist movement to the "left" strategy, and that the "left" strategy must necessarily be thoroughly anti-bourgeoisie.

nationalising "big industries, big banks and insurance companies"; by abolishing landlordism and distributing land to the tiller; and by undertaking "socialist construction".[367] The people's democracy was contemplated as a detour for by-passing the stage of bourgeois revolution on way to socialism, or the "intertwining" of the phases of bourgeois and socialist revolutions — "without an intermediary stage of capitalism".[368] Clearly in its second Congress, the C.P.I. — under the leadership of B.T. Ranadive — was raising a call to overturn the existing state of affairs, overthrow the Congress Government at the centre and in the provinces, and commence a revolutionary armed struggle all over the country. In the extreme heat of the moment nobody seemed to bother not only about such startling discoveries as the entire Indian bourgeoisie's going over — bag and baggage — to the camp of neo-colonialists, or the Nehru Government's complete desertion of, and by the Indian people, but also about the barest necessity (even for the sake of self preservation) for preparing oneself minimally for any armed struggle. Thus when the axe fell, as it was bound to fall on those who threatened the existence of a national Government, and declared a state of civil war for its ouster, the entire party and all its mass organisations were proved to be easy victims. The authorities reacted to the second Congress of the C.P.I. ruthlessly and swiftly, declaring the party illegal on 26 March 1948, raiding and sealing its trade-union and Kisan Sabha offices, and hounding on its leaders and activists at every level. Thousands of Communists had been rounded up by April 1948, and their leaders were either detained in the jails or forced to go into the underground. Thus the party, bubbling with a revolutionary fervour disproportionate to its organisational

367. "Political Thesis", M.B. Rao (ed.), *Documents of the History of the Communist Party of India*, Vol. VII (1948-50), New Delhi, 1976, pp. 86-8 and 117.

368. *Ibid.*, p. 117. The "intertwining" theory was stated originally by Edvard Kardelj, the Yugoslav Communist theorist, at the Cominform's inaugural meeting in late September 1947. His speech, entitled, "Communist Party in Yugoslavia in the Struggle for Independence of Her Peoples, for the People's Power and Socialist Reconstruction of Economy" was published in the *People's Age* of 22 February 1948.

readiness, was wholly "caught unawares", and some leading centres of it, like Bengal, took a long time (April to September 1948) in settling down to serious underground political business.[369]

It was from the underground in the third quarter of 1948 that the Ranadive-led C.P.I.'s most startling of discoveries sprang up — the formulation of drastically altering the strategy of agrarian revolution, and fitting it into the party's obsessively all-pervasive anti-bourgeois line of action. The new militant Communist leaders could not wholly deny the primacy of the feudal exploitative and oppressive relations in the country's agrarian sector, and hence they had to reiterate their previous commitment to the causes of anti-feudal struggle. What, however, they also noted, and tried energetically to play up, was the recently growing ascendancy of the capitalist relationship "inside the feudal framework", and at such a "great speed" with the passage of each day that "the struggle against feudal relations" became, in their opinion, "linked with the struggle against the new capitalist exploiters in the countryside".[370] It was Bhowani Sen, the winsome salesman of any Communist concept, be it ultra-revolutionary or rank-reformist, who anticipated Ranadive's crusading zeal against anything capitalistic, and raised in style the bogey against agricultural capitalism. In his booklet, *Banglar Krishite Dhanatantrer Vikash* (the growth of capitalism in the agriculture of Bengal), written under the pseudonym, "Rabindra Gupta", and published in Calcutta in October 1948, Sen tried to measure capitalism in the agriculture of Bengal in terms of the expanding volume of agricultural wage labour. With the help of the Government statistics between 1940 (the year the Floud Commission submitted its report) and 1945 (the year the Ishaq Commission enumerated the agricultural data in Bengal), he

369. Draft Report of the West Bengal Party, 1948-51, File No. 1948/52, P.C. Joshi Archives, J.N.U., New Delhi.
370. "The Agrarian Question in India", Politbureau Resolution, December 1948, M.B. Rao (ed.), *Documents of the History of the Communist Party of India*, Vol VII (1948-50), New Delhi, 1976, pp. 495-6.

contended that the employment of agricultural wage labour had doubled, the self-cultivating total area had decreased by one-fourth, and the area under sharecropping had increased by one-tenth.[371] He also noted in the official data a steady loss of peasant lands, especially of those belonging to the "middle" category (possessing 5 to 10 acres), whose holding of about 25.4 per cent of the total in 1940 slided down to 14.3 per cent in 1945.[372] Sen asserted, without clarifying his source of information, that the beneficiaries of such substantial loss of the "middle" peasants' lands were the rich peasants — the perpetrators of market-based capitalism in Indian agriculture. He accused the wage labour-employing rich peasants of producing mainly for the market and for profit, of "black-marketing" in food grains in collaboration with the *aratdars* (grain-dealers), of taking over a huge chunk of the *mahajani* dealings in the villages, of acquiring lands by manipulating the credit mechanism, and of trying to step into the shoes of the *Jotedars*. The *Jotedars*, Sen hastened to add, were not all unadulterated feudal exploiters, and he asserted, again without any qualification, that those among them who emerged from the rich peasant category, and took to sharecropping by investing in the in-puts, were theoretically the capitalist exploiters, pure and simple.[373] The mantle of the exploitative system in the countryside, in Sen's opinion, was passing from the hands of the *Zamindars* to the hands of the rich peasants and the *Jotedars*. According to him, therefore, the historic task of the Communists was to resist simultaneously both the feudal and the capitalist forms of exploitation in agriculture, and to confront not only the *Zamindars* and the *Jotedars*, but also the rich peasants.[374] Sen believed that what had been true of Bengal was truer in case of many other parts of India, particularly in the non-*Zamindari* areas like Madras, Bombay, the Punjab and

371. Rabindra Gupta, *Banglar Krishite Dhanatantrer Vikash* (in Bengali), Calcutta, October 1948, pp. 28-9.

372. *Ibid.*, pp. 43-4.

373. *Ibid.*, p. 10.

374. *Ibid.*, pp. 47-9.

Assam, which facilitated the growth of profit-oriented capitalism, but did not obstruct the progress of the rent-based landlordism.[375] Two months later in December 1948, the Politbureau, led by Ranadive, and probably guided by Sen himself, chose to follow in its entirety the path charted out in *Banglar Krishite Dhanatantrer Vikash.* Although it lacked Sen's finesse to select statistical data out of context, and juggle skilfully with them, the Politbureau's resolution, "On the Agrarian Question of India", did attempt very similarly at emphasising in a countrywide scale on the rise in the number of agricultural labourers, the increase in the importance of capitalist commodity production in agriculture, the high rate of land transfer to the upper section of the peasantry and the consolidation of the socio-economic power of the class of rich peasants that benefited from the war-time high prices, that produced surplus from the market, "that hires labour, that buys land and that regards agriculture as a source of profit, and not a source of livelihood".[376] The Politbureau under Ranadive was in fact of the opinion that the old feudal exploitative system of agriculture was being replaced with a new capitalistic one, that the persistence of the feudal relations in agrarian society was merely on account of the sluggish industrialisation in the colonial period, and that the "middle" peasant category was under pressure from both the landlords and the "peasant bourgeoisie".[377] The prescriptions of both Sen and the Politbureau against the feudal-bourgeois ills in the countryside were exactly the same, namely, to mark the rich peasants and the landlords-usurers as the "main" enemies of the *kisan* masses, to identify the "middle" of the peasantry as vacillating — who would join the rich unless they were prevented from it, to commence an offensive against the main enemies by organising the semi-proletarians (the poor peasants and the sharecroppers) under the proletarian leadership of the

375. *Ibid.*, pp. 35-40.
376. "The Agrarian Question in India", M.B. Rao (ed.), *Documents of the History of the Communist Party in India*, Vol.VII (1948-50), New Delhi, 1976, p. 484.
377. *Ibid.*, p. 492.

agricultural labourers, and to achieve not merely the "land to the tiller", but also the "nationalisation", and at a later stage, the "socialisation" or the "collectivisation" of land.[378]

The prescriptions did mark a qualitative change not only in the Communist approach towards the attainment of an agrarian revolution in India, but also in their perception of the agrarian revolution itself. Since the mid-1930s the Communist ideologues and *kisan* activists considered the agrarian revolution to mean in the colonial Indian context as freeing the toiling rural masses from the feudal system of extortion and oppression, and freeing lands from the clutches of the landlord-usurer combine, so that these could be distributed among their actual tillers — the multitudes of the landless. If these ideals were to be achieved, and if feudalism was found to be the basic and the most retrograde of all the contradictions in rural society, then the strategy for an agrarian revolution had to be the intensification of the anti-feudal struggle by isolating the primary enemies of the *kisan* masses in the countryside, and by building up the solidarity of all *kisan* categories against them. The solidarity of the *kisan* categories suffering under landlordism, both of the landed and landless varieties, against their common enemies, was possible to realise not so much by threatening the lands of the landed as by demanding an equitable dispersal of the landlords' and the Government's lands among the landless. To all those who had more or less been trampled by the landlord-usurer combine, including the affluent sections of the peasantry, the "land to the tiller" was such an egalitarian call which they could not conscientiously, or otherwise, oppose. Hence the two major slogans of the Communist-conceived agrarian revolution prior to 1948, namely the "abolition of landlordism" and the "land to the tiller" seemed justifiable battlecries against feudalism, even if one conceded them — to an extent — to be

378. While Sen was quite emphatic about "collectivisation" in his *Banglar Krishite Dhanatantrer Vikash* (in Bengali), Calcutta, October 1948, p. 56, the Politbureau — out of a concern perhaps for the landed poor *kisans*' support — remained more careful, and merely hinted at it in the resolution, "The Agrarian Question in India", M.B. Rao (ed.), *Documents of the History of the Communist Party of India*, Vol VII (1948-50), New Delhi, 1976, pp. 502-4.

concessions to the "rich and middle peasant psychology", and for not offending the "property-holding" *kisans*.[379] It was not wholly true that the Communists of the pre-1948 days were totally unaware of, at least theoretically, the significance of the commercialisation of agriculture and of its capitalistic trends, of the limited role the well-to-do peasantry might play in the anti-feudal struggle, of its exploitative class contradiction with the agricultural labourers. But since the agrarian revolution in India was thought essentially to be undertaken against feudalism and not for the establishment of full-fledged socialism, nor for the opposition of all tendencies of capitalism in agriculture, and since feudalism was felt to be obstructive and stifling to their entrepreneurial growth, the rich peasants were expected to act as allies of the agrarian revolutionaries, passive and unreliable at least, if not active and reliable. Even if one accepted the rich peasants' emergence after the second world war, as the wholesale capitalist farmers, by brushing aside such relevant suspicions as to their really using new techniques of agricultural production, having irrigational facilities (except in the Punjab, certain parts of Madras province and western U.P.), getting easy credit from the Government and the commercial banks,[380] and being able to raise the per acre yield of food grains and other crops,[381] he or she would find the moot issue of 1948 to be two-fold — whether the contradiction with the feudal forces had still remained the main one in the rural India, and whether the so-called capitalist farmers had yet been experiencing the feudal presence as a thorn in their path of advancement. None of these two issues were comprehensively dealt with either by Bhowani Sen or by Ranadive's Central Committee, but both — in their anxiety to conform to the novelty of "interlacing" the people's democratic and socialistic revolutions — committed the Indian

379. *Ibid.*, p. 501.

380. According to the Rural Credit Survey Report of 1954, the Government and commercial banks supplied barely 6 per cent of the total borrowings of the peasants, leaving the rest to the usurers.

381. It is well known that the per acre yield in India declined from 1900 onwards, despite the acreage expansion between the two world wars.

Communists in the agrarian sector to "the struggle against feudal exploitation, as well as capitalist exploitation",[382] against the landlords-usurers, and more so against the rich peasants,—"one of the main enemies in the rural areas".[383] Clearly the strategy for such a dual struggle could no longer be as broad as the solidarity of *kisans* of all categories, but somewhat sectarian — a formation only of the rural semi-proletariat, led doctrinally by the rural proletariat or the agricultural workers. Besides, the dual struggle had to be waged by keeping the "vacillating" "middle" peasants at some distance, and for achieving the obviously orthodox socialist objectives of the "nationalisation", and the eventual "collectivisation" of lands, irrespective, of course, of the panic they might cause even among the peasants of barest holdings. While a grand theory, such as this one, was being day-dreamingly propounded in the underground seclusion of Calcutta and Bombay, and enforced regimentally into practice, the actual practices in the field about the same time or slightly earlier in another part of the country, namely in Telengana and Andhra, had been leading to the enunciation of an equally significant theory. Without a reference to the Andhra thesis — the parallel to the one advocated by Sen and Ranadive — any understanding of the post-independence Communist movement in India is bound to be incomplete. Similarly, an appreciation of the Andhra thesis will not be complete without a peep into what was taking place in Telengana.

The agrarian situation in Telengana boiled up once again from August 1947, subsequent to the creation of the independent states of India and Pakistan, and in conjunction with the rising nationalist temper of the vast majority of the Hyderabadi people. Despite such facts that the Raj failed to make any special constitutional arrangement for its princely allies, that Hyderabad like any other Indian state must merge itself with either India or Pakistan, and that — because of the contiguity of its territories to India, and the majority of its people being overwhelmingly

382. "The Agrarian Question in India", M.B. Rao (ed.), *Documents of the History of the Communist Party of India*, Vol. VII (1948-50), New Delhi, 1976, p. 509.

383. *Ibid.*, p. 511.

non-Muslims — it was practically left with no other alternative than to join India, the Nizamshahi continued to feel excited over the possibility of an independent Hyderabad, following the termination of British paramountcy, and to talk tall about "the treaty rights", "the outlets to sea" (for an access to the sea-routes of its own) and "the greater Hyderabad" (anticipating the return from the erstwhile British India of the Ceded Districts, Berar and the Northern Circars). It went further in the sub-continental atmosphere of communal tension, and encouraged its longtime beneficiary, the rabid Ittehad-ul-Muslimin, who believed in the concept of *An-ul-Malik* (or in each Hyderabadi Muslims' claim to the rulership of Hyderabad since the Nizam symbolised in himself the sovereignty of the entire Muslim community in the state) to demand the establishment of an Islamic state under the Nizam, and raise its armed brigands, the Razakars or the so-called "patriotic homeguards". In reality the Razakars were organised to act Fascistically for asserting the revivalist content of the Nizam's rule, and taking charge of the political destiny of the state. Apparently the Nizam, his aristocracy and the bureaucracy found in the Razakar-based Ittehad a crude, but nevertheless a useful weapon for the defence of their position and the survival of the privileges, and they, therefore, had no serious objection to its assuming political power in the state in 1947. Consequently, the Ittehad did manage to oust one Prime Minister of the state (the Nawab of Chhatari), dominate the newly set up cabinet of another (Mir Laik Ali), and took over the negotiations with India on the constitutional future of Hyderabad. Although it could not prevent a "stand-still" agreement from coming into force from 29 November 1947 between Hyderabad and India, as per Sardar Vallabhbhai Patel's policy on the integration of the Indian states (by giving the Government of India an authority over the defences, foreign affairs and communications of Hyderabad, but allowing it a *status quo* for one year to enable the Nizam to make up his mind over the eventual accession), the Ittehad hoped to make the best of this breathing space for stamping out its dissenters among the Hindus, as well as from the Muslims, for spreading the Razakar depredations all over Hyderabad, for embittering the relations with the Indian authorities (by banning the export of precious metals to India, and by ceasing the Indian rupee to be a legal tender in Hyderabad),[384] and for going all-out for the establishment of an independent state under the Nizam.

As expected, the independence of Hyderabad did not seem acceptable to most of the Hyderabadis, and the opposition to it became very widespread, indeed, ranging from the Communist and Socialist ranks to the nationalist and the Hindu communalist line-ups. Some of the leading opponents, the Communists, saw in the "independence" move not only a perpetuation of the feudal dominance, but also a British imperialist plot to use Hyderabad as a base for policing India, and the countries beyond.[385] Some others, the nationalists in the Hyderabad State Congress, also thought similarly, and considered an "independent" Hyderabad to be "a positive danger to the unity and freedom of India".[386] Their attitudes towards the Nizamshahi, the Ittehad and the Razakars being practically identical, and the Indian reaction outside Hyderabad being somewhat in their favour, the State Communist Party and the State Congress strongly opposed the Nizamshahi ban on the flying of the Indian flag within the state, and combined together in an agitation for Hyderabad's merger with India.[387] The educational institutions and the law-courts were boycotted, the Government offices picketed, the *Patel-Patwaris* called upon to resign and the customs barriers between India and the Nizam's territories broken. Having had the previous experience of resisting the Nizam's forces in the countryside, the Communists did better in withstanding the counter-offensive of the state authorities and the Razakars than the nationalist State Congress could manage. The State Congress's agitation in fact wilted under the pressure of the Nizamshahi repression by October 1947, with the

384. V.P. Menon, *The Story of the Integration of the Indian States*, Calcutta, 1956, p. 338.
385. Barry Pavier, *The Telengana Movement, 1944-51*, New Delhi, 1981, p. 106.
386. Durga Das, *Sardar Patel's Correspondence*, New Delhi, 1973, p. 9.
387. The Communists participated in the agitation on their own, and not as an outcome of any agreement or understanding with the State Congress. See Swami Ramanand Tirtha, *Memoirs of Hyderabad Freedom Struggle*, Bombay, 1967, pp. 196-7.

detention of its leader, Swami Ramanand Tirtha, and the arrest of 21,000 of its followers.[388] Although he was released towards the end of 1947, Tirtha could not revive the movement any longer, and he had to abandon the *satyagraha* within the state in favour of sporadic border "raids" from the camps "outside", or from the Indian territories. Contrarily, the Communists — who attempted at escalating "whatever programme the [State] Congress chalked out",[389] and who succeeded in re-grouping their forces retreating between April and July 1947 — not only survived the Nizamshahi onslaught in August and September 1947, but also were able to take the fight thereafter to the rural sector, or to the agrarian front of their own choice and advantage. Again the Nalgonda District Committee of the Communists showed the way as it did in July 1946, first by forcibly destroying the land records in the possession of the *Patel-Patwaris* in the name of pressurising (in accordance with the State Congress programme) them to resign, and then by organising the *Jaitra Yatras* (victory marches) of *kisans* which hoisted the national and the red flags in the villages they passed by, broke open the granaries of the landlords they came across, and distributed the grains among the local populace on their way. Thus in consecutive masterly strokes by October 1947 the Communists in Nalgonda united the nationalist and the agrarian campaigns, and dramatically elevated the popular struggle to its outstanding revolutionary phase.

The architects of the Telengana outbreak of 1946-7 took astonishingly little time in spreading the destruction of the *Patel-Patwaris'* land records to that of the rural creditors' debt records, in transforming the seizure of grains into the seizure of lands, and in turning the *guttapalu* (*lathi*-weilding) "volunteer corps" in the villages into the regular *taluk* "squads" with "whatever fire-arms that could be obtained".[390] The armed "squads", or the "company squads" as they were called then, came into formation in the wake of the post-*Jaitra Yatra* phase of the Razakars' and the Nizamshahi forces' retaliatory counter-

388. *Ibid.*, p. 198.
389. P. Sundarayya, *Telengana People's Struggle and its Lessons*, Calcutta, 1972, p. 56.
390. *Ibid.*, p. 59.

attacks. The Razakars, who had secured modern weapons from the Nizam's Government, and whose headquarters remained by and large in the urban centres, often undertook incursions into the countryside for steamrolling the rising of the people, and rescuing the landlords groaning under popular pressures. Since such incursions combined loot, arson, physical torture, rape and murder, their repulsions necessitated as much use of force as was feasible on the part of A.M.S., and despite the Ittehad's fanatical talk of Islam, both the Razakar raids in favour of the landlords (mostly Hindus) and the Sangham resistances against them were surprisingly free from all religious articulations. Repulsion of the Razakar-police-army attacks started furiously in Suryapet (notably in Balemula, Kandagatta, Thimmarapuram, Patasuryapet, Mamillagudem and Kotapadu), Huzurnagar (notably at Pedaveedu), Janagaon (notably at Chitrakalura and Akunoor), Warangal (notably at Eraballi and Bairanpalli), Bhongir (notably at Kalanupaka), Nalgonda (notably at Nomula and Pardala), Miryalagudem (notably at Pamulapadu), Madhira (notably at Allinagaram, Meenavolu and Rayanapeta) and Khammam. The "company squad" membership being somewhat large in number, and the squads themselves being less mobile and prone to heavy casualties, the Communist-led Telengana peasants learnt by their experience to organise small "village squads", procure fire-arms for them by snatching the guns of the chased away enemies, as well as by forcing the village officials and the *Deshmukhs* to part with their muzzle-loaders, bore-guns and shot-guns, and adopt the method of "hit and run", of quick engagements and

391. "Guerilla warfare is not so much a military technique as it is a political condition. It does not depend primarily on favourable geography, or mobility at the expense of supply trains, or the most adroit employment of commando tactics, rather guerilla warfare is civilian warfare — that is conflict between a professional army pressing the advantage of superior training and equipment, and an irregular force, less well-trained, less well-equipped, but actively supported by the population of the area occupied by the army. It is precisely this mass backing for the full-time guerillas that gives rise to characteristic tactics employed by the guerillas: surprise attack or ambush, extreme mobility, and fighting only at times and places of their own choosing". Chalmers A. Johnson, *Peasant Nationalism and the Communist Power: The Emergence of Revolutionary China, 1937-45*, Stanford, 1962, p. 186.

quicker dispersals.[391] Once an indigenous mode of guerilla technique was thus imbibed in the hard, naive way — a manner which impressed even the experts of guerilla actions[392] — the "village squads" were so organised as to be able to change their defensive postures (of face to face confrontations and armed resistances) to attacking positions (for dislocating communications and destroying the Razakars' and the state forces' camps).[393] The "guerilla squads" systematically pounced upon the Razakar and the police-military camps, and destroyed a large number of them, including the ones at Almakur (Suryapet), Errapadu and Kodakandla (Janagaon), Mushtiyalapalli (Bhongir), Wardhannapet and Rayaparthi (Warangal) and Gunnavaran and Malkalapalli (Khammam). They also ran over many of the local police and army pickets, and successfully attacked the Nizamshahi patrols on the Kodada-Khammam-Seelempet road. Since many of the Razakar, police and army camps were set up in the fortified residences of those whom they had come to protect — the landlords — some of the *Deshmukhs'* and *Jagirdars'* mansions were also attacked and raged to the ground, personal retinues challenged and scared away, livestock seized and distributed. Such developments continued to take place till August 1948, spreading the rising territorially from Nalgonda, Warangal and Khammam districts to parts of Adilabad, Karimnagar and Medak districts. The A.M.S. and the Communist organisational structures were also altered suitably to meet the guerilla operational requirements, and the administrative unit-based committees (such as the district, the *taluk* and the village ones) gave way to the actual battle-based area committees — each divided into several zonal committees. More than 3,000 villages under these area committees were practically freed from the Nizam's rule, forcing its militarymen and policemen, as well as the Razakars, to retreat, and to leave behind their weapons and arsenals, bags

392. Major Jaipal, Singh, *In the Battle for Liberation*, New Delhi, 1990, pp. 101-2.
393. From this point onwards two types of small squads functioned in co-operation with each other in the Telengana countryside: the "village squad" in charge of the defence of the village, and of propaganda work within its limits, and the "guerilla squad" in charge of the surprise armed action against the enemies, and of the disruption of communications.

and baggages. The Communists in the deltaic Andhra also came forcefully at this juncture to the support of the Telengana guerillas, by setting headquarters at the storm centre of Munagalla, and by offering them shelters and medical facilities, arms and ammunitions, and funds and propaganda materials. Peasants in Telengana had in fact been able to throw up already a powerful militia, comprising about 10 thousand strong "village squads" and 2 thousand strong "guerilla squads", to shake the Nizamshahi to its roots. Militarily, by the end of August 1948, the Nizam's Government in effect was collapsing all over Telengana, and the peasant rebels had actually been taking over the greater parts of the region, and establishing their sway.

What, however, had been happening in Telengana was not just the military collapse of the Nizam's regime there, but — most significantly — a serious Communist experimentation in agrarian revolution, in the capturing of lands from the landlords, and giving these away to their actual tillers. Like the crystallising process in the peasant guerilla formations in Telengana, the concretisation of the snatching, as well as the giving away of lands, also occurred in the aftermath of the *Jaitra Yatras.* Having had the acquaintance in 1946-7 of seizing the landlords' unjustly occupied lands, and of restoring these to their original *kisan* holders, the Communists succeeded in coinciding the seizures of the *Deshmukhs'* and the *Jagirdars'* lands with the ongoing peasant onslaughts on the Razakars' and the Nizamshahi forces' positions. The military reverses of the state had panicked the landlords very thoroughly, and as most of them had either fled, or lived in isolation at the mercy of the villagers, the land seizures by the "village and guerilla squads" did not assume the violent proportions that they might otherwise have. The large scale taking over of the landlords' lands (including of those heavy-weights among the landed magnates like Jana Reddy, the Kollura family, the Nagulancha landlord, the Kalakota landlord, the Edunutala landlord, the Telladarupal *Jagirdar*, the Aswarpet landlord, etc.), and bringing them under the newly formed *Gramraj* or the village *Panch* Committees, actually commenced in the last quarter of 1947, and proceeded at a whirlwind speed in the accumulation approximately of 10 lakhs of acres in about 3 thousand villages by the middle of 1948.[394] What the Communists and the rural poor did with this vast amount of "seized" lands, and also, what they thought to be the land-holding limit (ceiling) of a single or joint family, beyond which the lands became "seizable", constituted the essence — the very basis of Telengana's attempt at agrarian revolution.

When the land "seizures" began in October 1947 the Telengana Communists decided to take over only those lands of the landlords which were in excess of the limit of 500 acres per family. As some of the landlords appeared in the middle of 1947 to be somewhat anti-Nizam in their approach, the Telengana party was inclined to be liberal towards them, and to act in such a way as not to alienate them.[395] Thereafter, at the time of distributing the seized lands among the landless, and during the phase of setting up the village *Panch* Committees to undertake the distribution, the Communists found the quantity of the seizures to be too inadequate to quench even partially the *kisans'* land thirst. By the first quarter of 1948, therefore, they decided to bring down the limit from 500 to 200 acres per family, and readied themselves for facing the wrath of the entire landlord class without exception. The scaling down, however, did not really go very much further in meeting the demand for land. The poor peasants and the agricultural labourers also started questioning at this point the justifiability of leaving so much land with the landlords, and demanded a fairer, a more equitable distribution of land.[396] Resultantly, in the middle of

394. P. Sundarayya, *Telengana People's Struggle and Its Lessons*, Calcutta, 1972, p. 2, and Chandra Pulla Reddy, *The Great Heroic Telengana Struggle*, C.P.I.(M-L) Publication, September 1968, p. 20. The Government of India, who was very keen, indeed, to dispute the Communist claim, had eventually to acknowledge that the rebels' having distributed "one million acres may be quite true". L.J. Rajwade, Secy. Gen. Admn. Dept., Govt. of Hyderabad, D.O. No. 398/GAD-C/182/51 of 12 Feb. 1952 to S. Narayanaswamy, Dy. Secy., Min. of States, Govt. of India, Hyd. Section, Proc. Min. of States, File No. 6(5)-H/52, 1952,N.A.I.

395. Sundarayya, *ibid.*, p. 117.

396. "Political and Organisational Report", Andhra-Telengana After the Police Action, Inner C.C. No. 6, 1949, P.C.J. Archives, File No. 1949/56, J.N.U. p. 20.

1948, coinciding with the climax of the Communist-led anti-Nizam and the anti-feudal campaign, the ceiling was lowered once again to 10 acres of *tari* (wet) and 100 acres of *khushki* (dry) land per family or joint family. This limit, however, would not include the lands under the occupation of *kouludars* of 5 years' standing, who were declared *Pattadars*, or permanent occupants, and who were freed from the liability of paying any rent. Any family in possession of 10 acres of wet and 100 acres of dry lands could still get them cultivated under the *kouludari* arrangement, but only on the basis of a "just rent" to be fixed by the *Panch* Committees, and without any right to eject the new *kouludars.*[397] Even after resolving to pass over lands to all the *kouludars*, whether at once or after 5 years, restoring to *kisans* most of the lands they had lost in the recent past to the landlords, and distributing whatever surplus land of the landlords that could be seized, the Communists were not able — and quite understandably so in the prevailing paucity of cultivable lands — to give effect adequately to the "land to the tiller" slogan, or to satisfy substantially the multitude of the lackland. Consequently, they encouraged the tillers, on the one hand, to occupy lakhs of acres of waste lands (the *banjara* and *banchari* lands under the Government and the landlords) and the village community and grazing lands, with a view to render them cultivable,[398] and tried, on the other, to increase the agricultural labour wages, roughly from 60 to 70 seer*s* of paddy to 90-120 seer*s* per month.[399] Since the village records had already been destroyed in many cases, and the *Patel-Patwaris* ceased to maintain them, the collection of both land revenue and the levy of grains stopped for all practical purposes. Similarly

397. "Land Distribution in Telengana: Mistakes and Future Programme", Circular of the State Fraction of the Andhra Committee of the C.P.I., 1 June 1950.
398. P. Sundarayya, *Telengana People's Struggle and its Lessons*, Calcutta, 1972, p. 116.
399. "Political and Organisational Report", Andhra-Telengana After the Police Action, Inner C.C. No.6, 1949, P.C. Joshi Archives, File No. 1949/56, p. 21. In practice, however, even the minimum of 90 seers per month could not always be implemented on account mainly of the rich peasants' reluctance to pay more.

stopped the collection of debt re-payments from *kisans*, for most of the landlords and moneylenders either had left the villages, or had decided not to operate during the "troubled times". The agricultural credit nevertheless continued to flow primarily from the rich and the affluent section of rural society, or from those who had been allowed to keep up to 10 acres of wet and 100 acres of dry lands. All the old debts were eventually annulled, and the *Panch* Committees asked *kisans* to contract and pay up the current debts at an annual interest of 6 per cent.[400] Like the exercising of some control over the rural credit, the Telengana Communists also tried to regulate the grain trade, to fix the grain prices,[401] and to stop generally the movement of grains towards the towns, so that it did not continue "feeding the enemy". They had to relent, however, when they learnt by experience that some of the essential commodities like salt, cloth, oil etc. could not be procured in the villages without selling a certain amount of grains in the town markets. In consequence, therefore, the Communists did allow, under a system of "permits", and along with the cash crops, some paddy and jowar to reach the markets.[402]

Proportionately in effect, the largest beneficiary of the "permit" system, and the marketing of cash and food crops, happened to be the rich among the Telengana peasants, as well as some marginal landlords, whose properties had been protected by the ceiling the Communists fixed. The well-to-do peasants were also allowed a certain flexibility in their operations over the credit and the wage labour-employment scenario, and the agricultural labourers' clamours had deliberately been kept on a low key so as not to antagonise their employers "by raising impossible demands."[403] To the Communists in Telengana, whose primary object was to wipe out landlordism — "the main method of exploiting our people, and for supporting the autocratic Nizam"[404] — and who wanted to achieve it by combining

400. *Ibid.*, pp. 22-3. Actually *kisans* had to contract current debts at 10 per cent interest or more for "fear of loss of credit in the future".
401. The price of jowar was kept 4-6 seer*s* and that of paddy within 5-6 seer*s* per rupee, *ibid.*, p. 24.
402. *Ibid* ., p. 24.
403. *Ibid.*, p. 22.
404. "Land Distribution in Telengana: Mistakes and Future Programme", Circular of the State Fraction of the Andhra Committee of the C.P.I., 1 June 1950.

all the opponents of the feudal system, the category of the rich peasants appeared clearly to be an ally to the struggles of the poor and the landless peasants. It was, according to them, not a passive ally who should be kept under close observation, but an active one who ought to be encouraged to take part in the agrarian revolution. The concessions to the rich and the "middle" peasants, the Telengana Communists felt, represented together the encouragement they deserved, and the cost of such encouragement — so far as the poor and the landless were concerned — had not been proved to be too high, and debilitating. A very large number of the rural poor had in fact benefited within one year (from August 1947 to August 1948) from the restoration and distribution of lands, the conferment of *Pattadari* rights, the annulment of accumulated debts, the cessation of revenue and levy collections, and the increment, howsoever modest, in the wages. A huge quantity of paddy and jowar that had been taken away from the granaries of the landlords, the stores of the Razakar camps and the godowns of the Government, amounting approximately to 15,000 - 20,000 *putties* (or 1,20,000-1,60,000 bags),[405] was distributed among the poor and the needy. Similarly were allotted to them "tens of thousands" of the confiscated cattle, goats and sheep "in good numbers", and also a considerable quantity of agricultural implements from the landlords.[406] Throughout this year of turmoils and disturbances, the agricultural operations continued practically unabated, and more significantly, without any drastic fall in the over-all productivity. For the first time in their lives perhaps, the poor peasants and the agricultural labourers had managed to take two square meals daily during the whole year, despite the backward techniques of agriculture and the constant depredations of the Razakars and the Nizamshahi forces. "This is one of the biggest gains of the struggle", noted the Telengana leaders with some satisfaction, for "it is for the first time the village poor have seen and realised that they can have their stomachs full if they do not pay rents, taxes, debts, and if they divide the lands of the

405. "Political and Organisational Report" etc., P.C. Joshi Archives, File No. 1949/56, p. 24, J.N.U., New Delhi.

406. P. Sundarayya, *Telengana People's Struggle and its Lessons*, Calcutta, 1972, pp. 124-5.

landlords and fight for the wages".[407] So, on the balance, as the Telengana Communists seemed to believe at that point of time (August 1948), the rural poor's progress in the agrarian revolution had not really been impaired by the concessions to the rich, rather these allowances appeared to have stabilised the economic process of a sudden change, and strengthened the solidarities of the peasant categories. Out of the Communists' experimentation with the rich peasants, and their experience of fierce anti-feudal and anti-Nizam campaigns in Telengana, was born in the Telugu-speaking area of the country a new political thesis for the consideration of all the Indian Communists — an alternative to what the Ranadive-led Central Committee had already succeeded in imposing.

It was how the rural poor should, in the midst of their struggle, view the role of the rich peasants under the prevailing over-all Indian circumstances that marked the starting point of the much talked about Andhra thesis, or the Andhra Letter — a resolution drafted by the Andhra Provincial Committee of the C.P.I. for discussion among all the Communist ranks.[408] Since the reality in

407. "Political and Organisational Report" etc., P.C. Joshi Archives, File No. 1949/56, p. 25, J.N.U., New Delhi.

408. The historic document, entitled, "The Present Stage and the Strategy of the Indian Revolution: Is it Socialist or New Democratic?" had been written and sent in the month of June 1948 to the Politbureau, which seemed to have received it on 9 July 1948. Although a vague knowledge of such a communication evoked a lot of speculative interest in it among the Communists throughout India, it was never circulated for discussion, and had deliberately been shelved for all practical purposes. It was only at the time of the reconstitution of the C.P.I. Central Committee, in which C. Rajeshwar Rao of Andhra briefly became the General Secretary, that some copies of the document was cyclostyled on 29 April 1950, perhaps with a view to its circulation, but promptly forgotten soon thereafter. Scholars on the Communist movement in India later on did realise the importance of the Andhra Letter, but not being persistent enough to make a search for the document, decided to refer invariably to its formulation on the basis of a caricatured and distorted version of it from B.T. Ranadive's report of December 1948 to the Politbureau, entitled, "Strategy and Tactics in the Struggle for People's Democratic Revolution in India". By some coincidence, M.B. Rao edited *Documents of the Communist Party of India*, Vol.VII, 1948-50, New Delhi, 1976 — otherwise an authoritative collection — has also not included the Andhra Letter, though a few cyclostyled copies of it can still be located among the C.P.I. records preserved in Ajoy Bhavan, New Delhi.

Telengana "demonstrated" as a "concrete proof" that a large number of the rich peasants were anti-feudal, and "coming with us in the liberation struggle" against landlordism and the Nizamshahi,[409] the Andhra leaders opposed their being treated in the Ranadivean way as enemies and counter-revolutionaries, and favoured their inclusion generally among the ranks of the agrarian revolutionaries, at least as the "immediate reserve".[410] Similarly, they opposed the Ranadivean idea of "neutralising" the "middle" peasants, laid stress on their character as allies of the agrarian revolution, and emphasised on the urgency for "solidly uniting" them with the rural poor. The Andhra Provincial Committee confirmed, with the sole exception of one who pinned his hopes loyally on everything that Ranadive stood for,[411] what the Communists believed so far to be true, namely, that the objectives of the agrarian revolution in India were to "smash landlordism", or to "completely wipe out all the features of feudalism", and to give "land to the tiller", allowing the individual proprietors and the capitalist farmers to operate simultaneously.[412] The Andhra Letter also upheld the hitherto accepted belief that the agrarian revolution of the rural masses in India would be spearheaded by the agricultural proletariat (agricultural labourers) and the semi-proletariat (sharecroppers and poor peasants) in alliance "in particular" with the "middle" peasants, but also with the rich peasants. It did not find anything wrong in the agrarian revolutionary situation with the rich peasants' producing for the market, and profiting by the use of wage labour, except having a strong reservation against some among them who had not been able to shake off their "tails of feudalism" — the tendencies to take to sharecropping and usury, and to assume the high-brow feudal attitude of social domination. The committee wanted to be on guard against a minority of such "old type rich peasants", and

409. Andhra Letter, June 1948, Party Documents, Central Archives, C.P.I., Ajoy Bhavan, New Delhi.

410. *Ibid.*

411. The lone dissenter was identified as "Comrade P.S." (P. Sundarayya?) by the Secretary, P.C. Andhra C.P.I., in his lengthy forwarding note to the Andhra Letter.

412. Andhra Letter, June 1948, Party Documents, Central Archives, C.P.I., Ajoy Bhavan, New Delhi.

to try to isolate them politically, but not to think in terms of their economic extermination. To think of their economic extermination, as well as that of the great majority of the wage labour-employing rich peasants, together with the plot for the neutralisation of the "middle" peasants, would not only jeopardise the prospect of an anti-feudal bourgeois democratic revolution, but impose surreptitiously the "utopian" task of carrying out a highly advanced socialist revolution, and force upon it by "backdoor methods" the grossly unrealistic socialist strategy for establishing "the dictatorship of the proletariat and the poor peasants". One should not employ the socialist strategies for attaining the bourgeois democratic gains, and that was why the Andhra leaders alleged that the Ranadive-led Central Committee's plan for the so-called "people's democratic revolution", in which the bourgeois democratic and the socialist phases had cleverly been lumped together, was a theoretical camouflage for giving the fantasised and opportunistic call for a socialist revolution in India on the model of Bolshevik insurrectionary civil war, i.e. led in the front by the workers' strikes, and backed up at the rear by the poor peasants' risings.

The Andhra leaders were convinced that the phase of the socialist transformation could not be achieved without attaining the stage of thorough-going bourgeois democracy, or that the striding into the second step would not be possible without a foothold on the first. "It is to suffer from the worst illusion", they felt, "to give assent to the suggestion that the Democratic stage of the revolution has not got its own specific tasks and time-schedule, and that it is possible to accomplish in one stage the tasks of an entirely different stage — a later stage".[413] They refused to share in the Ranadivean discovery that the Indian economy, though retarded, had become, more or less, bourgeoised, and that the bourgeoisie had turned into a class of "collaborators" with imperialism and feudalism against the democratic aspirations of the Indian people. To the contrary, the Andhra Provincial Committee tended to believe that the India of 1948 was not an independent capitalist country but a semi-colony, and that the Indian economy still remained basically

413. *Ibid.*

under the domination of a concert of colonial, feudal and monopoly capital vested interests. Apparently, its members did not feel that the "entire capitalist class", the "middle" and the "lower" bourgeoisie, the "upper middle-class" and the large section of the rich peasantry, or taken together, the "national bourgeoisie" (if one might have taken the liberty of the Andhra leaders to use the term), had gone over to the camp of the reactionaries. They were of the opinion, therefore, that in an essential semi-colony like India, the stage of the Indian revolution was primarily bourgeois democratic against the feudal oppressors, their imperialist benefactors and their monopoly capitalist collaborators. Since the bourgeois democratic revolution must achieve the exercise of popular political rights in the nation, the utilisation of all national resources, the increment in the national income and the expansion of nation's internal market, it could aim neither at the liquidation of capitalism, nor at the dictatorship of the proletariat. Rather, it must "smash" the feudal-imperialist-monopolist combine, bring in modernisation, foster entrepreneurship and set up "the democratic dictatorship of several classes", and of course, in doctrinaire exuberance, "under the hegemony of the proletariat".[414] The success of such a bourgeois democratic revolution in a predominantly agricultural country like India, according to them, depended fundamentally on the successful completion of its agrarian revolution, and on the decisive role of its peasantry — in fact "on the political transfer of power to the peasantry".[415]

Whether its formulations were correct, or not wholly so, the Andhra Letter did mark an attempt at realistically estimating the Indian situation from a substantially original, and indigenously experienced (in Telengana) Indian Communist viewpoint. It was so good so far, but the Andhra leaders started suddenly suffering at this point of their political thinking from the same disease that the Ranadiveans so acutely suffered, namely, from the psychosis of frantically searching out a model of revolution which they must somehow copy — irrespective of its relevance — as if they could not rise above the role of mere copyists, or

414. *Ibid.*
415. *Ibid.*

as if the Telengana experience did not show them any glimpse of an independent Indian model by itself. It was while defining the stage of bourgeois democratic revolution in India, and deciding upon the tactics to be adopted for achieving it, that they seemed to have seriously tripped, and fell into simplistic conclusions. They took a lot of pains in showing at length how the objective conditions in the Russian and the prospective Indian revolutions were "entirely different", and why the Soviet Russian example could not be followed in India. Once they did that, it was incumbent upon them to explain the characteristics of a typically Indian bourgeois democratic revolution that they had in mind, rather than taking refuge totally in the Maoist concept of New Democracy[416] on the ground of the old western type bourgeois democratic revolutions' becoming "outdated",[417] and then preferring for the employment of the Chinese Communist line *in toto* for attaining it in India, merely because of such apparent closeness of the generalities between China and India as their both being predominantly agricultural in economy, and semi-colonial and semi-feudal in the exploitation of their people. It was not really that the broad objective of the New Democracy was incongruous in India, since it stood for the enjoyment of all the fruits of a bourgeois democracy "under the united dictatorship of several classes", and since the peoples of China and India must fight for the bourgeois democratic revolutions against all those whose interest it was to keep both the countries in perpetual semi-colonial and semi-feudal state. Despite such resemblances, the objective conditions prevailing in India and China were vastly dissimilar in their respective social structures, growth of economy, strength of their

416. In January 1940 Mao Zhe Dong first conceived (and later developed) a phase of New Democracy for transforming a semi-colonial and semi-feudal Chinese society into an independent democratic society through a bourgeois democratic revolution of a new type, by setting aside the landlords, the colonialists and the "reactionary" bourgeoisie (categorised eventually as the "bureaucrat" bourgeoisie), and by setting up the "combined" dictatorship (instead of the old type dictatorship of a single bourgeois class) of several classes, including workers, peasants and petty and "national" bourgeoisie.

417. Andhra Letter, June 1948, Party Documents, Central Archives, C.P.I., Ajoy Bhavan, New Delhi.

bourgeoisie, *status quo* of the feudal order, experience of colonialism, perception of national politics, nature of the state and government and the persistence of anarchy and civil war. Clearly if the bourgeois democracy had to take a New Democratic shape in India, it was to be fashioned on the Indian requirements, and not on the Chinese requisites. Contrarily, if in the Chinese fashion it was tried to be thrust upon India, such oversimplifications as equalising the Chinese war-lords with the Indian princes and landlords, the Kuomintung with the Congress, the Chiang Government with the Nehru Government, the Chinese bourgeoisie's anti-democratic and anti-working class offensive in 1927 with the disposition of "dominant" Indian bourgeoisie in 1948 — as had been made by the Andhra leaders in their document[418] — were bound to take place. Once these had cropped up somehow, then the echoing of the Maoist slogans could hardly be restrained, such as dubbing the coming of independence as the "dominant" Indian bourgeoisie's sharing power with the landed magnates, "under the wings of imperialism",[419] the Nehru Government as the stooge of the colonialists, monopolists and landlords only, and not the representative of the national bourgeoisie, and the state action against the civil war-waging C.P.I. as part of the international offensive against "the progressive and democratic forces of the world". The only way to defeat the offensive of the counter-revolutionaries, therefore, appeared to the Andhra leaders to be a long-drawn civil war on the Chinese Communist style, to resist the enemies "inch by inch" through "guerilla warfare", and to form "two Governments" or dual authorities in the so-called "liberated zones" over as many parts of India as possible, leading finally to "the general rising and capture of power by the people".[420] Thus by a different route — through the rejection of the Soviet Russian model for an insurrectionary civil war, but through the adoption of the Chinese model for a protracted guerillaite civil war — the Andhra leaders came practically to

418. *Ibid.*
419. *Ibid.*
420. *Ibid.*

the same slippery spot the Ranadiveans had already reached, and hoped similarly to hit the jackpot the Ranadiveans did, with almost the identical kind of tragic downfall in store.

The Ranadivean line in fact dramatically collapsed within one year of its historic propounding when the Central Committee's grandiose Bolshevik scheme for turning the intended railway strike of 9 March 1949 into an all-India general strike, and then to an "all-parties struggle" with "new and high revolutionary forms",[421] failed palpably to work. Comparatively, however, the decline of the Andhra line — the one that had eventually been taken out of its contextual realities to conform to the Maoist tradition — was a long-drawn affair, though serious cracks in it appeared within the two months of its enun- ciation, from 13 September 1948 to be more accurate. The 13th of September saw the boiling point of the relations between the Nizam and the Government of India which had steadily been heating up since the day they signed the "stand-still" agreement. The Nizam apparently staked almost everything for forestalling the accession of Hyderabad to India, and for achieving its independence. The Ittehad and the Razakars, though on the run from Telengana, were still tirelessly terrorising the Hyderabadis in other regions of the state, especially in the border areas, fanning up blind communal fury, particularly among those who took refuge in Hyderabad from the riot-ridden parts of India, and silencing all opposition — whether from the Hindus or the Muslims — as symbolised in the brutal murder of the *Imroz* editor, Sheobullah Khan, on 22 April 1948. Since the Communists seemed indomitable in Telengana, and also as anti-Nehru Government as their compatriots in all other parts of India, the Nizamshahi even tried to mollify them by withdrawing its ban on their organisations on 16 May 1948, and attempting at rallying them behind an "independent Hyderabad". Contrary to all canards spread against them, the Telengana Communists did not appear

421. "Railway Strike and Our Tasks", Central Committee Circular of 22 February 1949, M.B. Rao (ed.), *Documents of the History of the Communist Party of India*, Vol. VII (1948-50), New Delhi, 1976, p. 535.

at any stage to have truck with the Nizamshahi or the Razakars,[422] although they might have benefited in their "open" rebellion from the withdrawal of the ban. Meanwhile the Nehru Government — already embittered by the dilatoriness of negotiations with the Nizam, and by the sufferings of the Hyderabadis in areas falling "geographically" and otherwise within India — was determined not to allow any longer "the campaign of murder, arson and loot" in the Nizam's territories to rouse "communal passions in India", and to jeopardise "the peace of the Dominion".[423] Diplomatically also the Nehru Government was not in a position to delay matters indefinitely further in view of the Nizam's desperate bid for international recognition of independent Hyderabad, his all-out exertion for getting Britain's and the United States' support in the placement of the Hyderabad case before the United Nations' Security Council, and his frantic communication of 19 July 1948 to the British Crown praying for assistance in the United Nations.[424] It had to act swiftly when the Nizam's delegation actually left for the United Nations, and to issue an ultimatum on 10 September 1948, demanding the suppression of the Razakars, the restoration of the internal security and the re-occupation by the Indian troops of the cantonments in Hyderabad which they vacated in August 1947. On 13 September 1948 — a day after Jinnah's death had incapacitated Pakistan to raise a furore — began the march of the Indian Army into Hyderabad. The tinselled Nizamshahi soldiers and the hordes of demoralised Ittehadi Razakars could hardly offer some resistance, and the so-called "police action" by India was over within four days when a military Government took charge of the Hyderabad administration on 17 September 1948 under General J.N. Choudhury. Any drastic alteration of Hyderabad's fortune in the year 1948,

422. General J.N. Choudhury's interview with the press in Secundrabad, 2 December 1948, as reported in the *Hitavad* (English daily), 3 December 1948.

423. Patel's submission to the Constituent Assembly on Hyderabad, Durga Das, *Sardar Patel's Correspondence*, New Delhi, 1973, pp. 236-7.

424. The originals of the letters sent by the Nizam, Mir Usman Khan, to the Premier Attlee and King George VI are available in the India Office Library and Records, London.

however, was inconceivable without a reference to the Telengana Communists — as to what happened to be their view of the momentous enactment — and also how they themselves had been viewed at the time of its enacting.

Evidently Nehru's Government viewed the Communist activity and the peasant rising in Telengana with great concern — greater perhaps than what it felt about the Razakar brutalities and the Nizam's moves for independence. It was only natural for the central authority in India, who had been challenged by the Communists in a civil war, and who had also been trying hard for the last six months to nip it in the bud, to be alarmed at the way the Nizam's rule demonstrably crumbled in the Communist-dominated south-eastern Hyderabad. K.M. Munshi, the Indian Agent-General in Hyderabad during the "stand-still" period, was clear about it when he discussed in his report at the beginning of August 1948 the threat to the internal security that the deteriorating situation in Hyderabad seemed to have posed to India. The threat, in his opinion, represented a "double problem" of "liquidating" the Razakars, as well as the Communists in Hyderabad. The Razakar problem seemed "easy" to him, but not so the problem of the Communists, who could affect the entire southern part of India, and turn out to be "a danger to the National Government".[425] Munshi's anxiety was suitably shared by the policy-makers on Hyderabad in New Delhi, Sardar Vallabhbhai Patel, the Deputy Prime Minister, and H.V.R Iengar, the Home Secretary, both of whom were apprehensive of Telengana's contaminating the whole of the Andhra region, and then even the places beyond.[426] Their line of thinking in fact fitted well with the hysterical framework of mind in which the Government of India talked one year later (in September 1949) about the possibility of a Communist take over in the heart of the Indian territories.[427] It was no wonder, therefore, that in the

425. Munshi's Note, Durga Das, *Sardar Patel's Correspondence*, New Delhi, 1973, p. 201.

426. B.N. Mullick, *My Years With Nehru, 1948-1964*, New Delhi, 1972, p. 243

427. *Communist Violence in Hyderabad*, Government of India, New Delhi, September 1949, p. 243.

"police action" in Hyderabad the authorities at the centre would ask the Indian forces "(a) to round up the Communists in the South-eastern districts; (b) to go round *taluk* by *taluk*, tracing out the Razakars and disarming the population ...".[428] That they were the prime targets of the Indian army in Hyderabad, once it managed to hit the Nizam and the Razakars, had not wholly been a mystery to the Telengana Communists themselves. It could not have been so after their having opted for the Maoist mode of creating liberated zones in the country through the "partially armed Chinese way of resistance",[429] and a prolonged civil war against a Government representing the imperialist, feudal and monopolist forces. The Telengana Communists certainly did not hope for the Nehru Government, whose class character was as reactionary as they formulaically imagined, to become friendly towards those who wanted to impose a civil war on it — whether of Bolshevik or of Maoist variety — merely for their being anti-Nizam and anti-Razakars. Rather, they vaguely anticipated the Indian authorities, following an armed intervention, to join hands with the Nizam, to restore lands to the landlords, to destroy the village *Panch* administration, and to commence repressions on the rebels — a situation calling for their utmost vigilance and assumption of defensive posture.[430] Even if they felt that all these fears of theirs would come true, the Telengana Communists ought to have thought a little more as to what they must do, if — apart from realising the main objective of an agrarian revolution — the other causes they stood for, such as the fall of the autocratic Nizamshahi, the suppression of the Razakars, and the accession of Hyderabad to India, were fulfilled through the military intervention. Would they not avail themselves of the rare opportunity of "police

428. Government of India, Information Department, File No.25/8 (India Office Library and Records, London), Inward Telegrams to Commonwealth Relations Office, no. 937: 2, cited in D.N. Dhanagare, *Peasant Movements in India, 1920-1950*, Delhi, 1983, p. 211, footnote 79.
429. Andhra Letter, June 1948, Party Documents, Central Archives, C.P.I., Ajoy Bhavan, New Delhi.
430. "Political and Organisational Report", Andhra-Telengana After the Police Action, Inner C.C. No. 6, 1949, File No. 1949/56, p. 1, P.C. Joshi Archives, J.N.U., New Delhi.

action" for unhesitatingly reconsidering their political and military strategies, various other supplementary tactics of struggle, and above all, their ideological formulations? The Telengana rebels might have done their introspection better had they not been thoroughly surprised by the timing of the "police action", and consequently "unprepared" for reading its significance. None of them "expected it to come so soon", and worse still, "to end so soon",[431] and therefore, was not in a position to take a decisive stand on it. They not only failed to make full use of the chance for examining their own placement once again *vis-a-vis* the Indian army and the Nehru Government, but also allowed the rising to drift towards spontaneity — as it was likely to happen in any unstable circumstance.

When the "police action" was actually taking place, and the Nizam was succumbing to his fate, many of the Communist rank and file in Telengana sprang instantaneously into action, seeing the peasantry's spontaneous advance "in thousands" to make the best of the turmoils. A very large number of the landlords' *garhis* were attacked and razed to the ground (such as, those of Jana Reddy Pratapa Reddy in Suryapet, of Kummarakuntla at Manukota, of Ramasahayam Damodara Reddy at Maripeda, of the Suryapet *Deshmukh* at Kakarayi, of the Visunuri *Deshmukh* in Janagaon, of the *Matkadar* of Betavel), the torturers of people apprehended and killed (such as Jaganmohan Reddy, his son and son-in-law at Tadikonda, Warangal; the landlords' agents at Motukar, Bhuvanagiri; the landlord of Kaṣarlapedu in Suryapet), the Razakar and police camps destroyed and arms taken (such as, Nellikoduru of Manukota, Koppal at Miryalaguda; Motukar, Rajapet, Kotanupaka and Kurraram in Bhuvanagiri; Laddanur and Maddur in Janagaon; Anwaropet in Pavalancha; Tadikondo and Japargad in Warangal; Koyada in Huzurabad) and huge quantities of grains seized and distributed (such as, at Manukota in Suryapet, at Dornakal railway station, at Garla in Huzurnagar). The "police action" also encouraged the peasants to take possession of the *Deshmukhs'* lands in these areas where they previously hesitated — in Karimnagar, Medak, and even far off Nizamabad. Seeing that the Nizam's rule had ended, and thinking

431. *Ibid.*

all their lost lands could now be taken back, they — on their own — started re-occupying those of the landlords' lands they originally held.[432] Since hardly any coordination could be effected, and "centralised directions" be given, "the people took [the] initiative themselves"[433] leaving the Telengana Communists startled by what was happening around them. It was not easy for them in a situation of such rupturous fluidity to try to understand the full meaning of the "police action" in its all-India context. Had the Telengana Communists been able to do so they would perhaps have known that the so-called "liberation" of the Telengis and other Hyderabadis from the Nizamshahi did not automatically make it incumbent on them to think in terms of waging a titanic struggle for liberating all the Indians, until and unless they managed to secure their own agrarian revolution in Telengana, and exhorted their comrades simultaneously to emulate the example in other parts of India. It was the liquidation of landlordism and usury — the shedding of the unbearable feudal burdens — that represented the burning problem as much in Telangana as in most other parts of India, and that appeared to be the urgent need for all the toiling Indians. The "liberation" of the whole of India, and the founding of a sort of Indian "New Democracy" depended entirely on the successful completion of this task, and no body knew it better than the Telengana or the Andhra Communists themselves, who seemed to have no doubt whatsoever that "our Revolution is in the main agrarian revolution".[434] If that really was the case, the Telengana Communists ought to have tried first to safeguard the unparalleled gains that they had so heroically achieved together with the entire peasantry, but mainly at the initiative of the rural poor, and then advance further with them in other areas, especially in those where the agrarian situation seemed depressingly similar, like Rayalseema,

432. "Political and Organisational Report", Andhra-Telengana After the Police Action, Inner C.C. No. 6, 1949, File No. 1949/56, p. 21, P.C. Joshi Archives, J.N.U., New Delhi.

433. P. Sundarayya, *Telengana People's Struggle and Its Lessons*, Calcutta, 1972, p. 188.

434. Andhra Letter, June 1948, Party Documents, Central Archives, C.P.I., Ajoy Bhavan, New Delhi.

or Andhra localities bordering Telengana, and in places where the Communist *kisan* activists enjoyed some influence over "a good proportion in the masses", such as the deltaic Andhra, Kerala, Bengal, etc.[435] Could all these pioneering activities be undertaken at all by confronting exclusively within Telengana the mighty Indian army, who had so swiftly swept away the Nizamshahi, and whose success generated so "great [a] jubilation and a sense of freedom" among the majority of the population?[436] Did even some of the peasant guerilla squad members not dump their arms and return to homes in view of the ushering in of a "far better" and a "free and democratic" future?[437] Contrarily, was it possible for the Communists in Telengana at the point of the "police action" to withdraw unconditionally their armed struggle by disbanding the *Panch* Committees and the Gramraj they had set up, surrendering the fire-arms they had so assiduously collected, and giving up the lands they had already distributed? To do that, as had been advocated by some of the prominent among the Telengana leaders (Ravi Narayan Reddy, Baddami Ella Reddy, Arutla Ramachandra Reddy etc.); or to think that the seizure and distribution of land had been a mistake, as Ravi Narayan felt in retrospection, would have been an act of betrayal to the cause of the agrarian revolution, a sheer treachery to the interests of the rural poor — the backbone of the Telengana rising.

To preserve the important gains of agrarian revolutionary strides, for which the stubborn armed actions had already been successfully resorted to, the continuation of the armed struggle — clandestinely and otherwise — or the pursuing of the "partisan struggle" in the Marxist-Leninist terminology, should have been perfectly justifiable by the Communist standard, provided the Telengana Communists did not confuse it with the

435. *Ibid.*

436. "Political and Organisational Report", Andhra-Telengana After the Police Action, Inner C.C. No. 6, 1949, File No. 1949/56, p. 47, P.C. Joshi Archives, J.N.U., New Delhi.

437. P. Sundarayya, *Telengana People's Struggle and Its Lessons,* Calcutta, 1972, p. 190.

"liberation struggle" for all the Indian people. The only insurance against such a confusion, or the only way to differentiate the "partisan" from the "liberation" struggle, was to take a hard look afresh at those whom the Communists thought they must fight in Telengana, and convince themselves of the veracity of their enemies' character. With the military intervention of the Government of India in September 1948, a thorough understanding of the Indian rulers' class characterisation had become so pressing a matter of life and death for the rebels that it could not fashionably be left to the care of the Maoist formulations, and it had to be resolved only by their own realisations. Was the Congress Government in New Delhi, like the Chiang Government in Nanking, merely a puppet in the colonial-feudal-monopoly capital hands? Did it represent at all any section of the petty and national bourgeoisie by any chance? Had it by any stretch of imagination even fondly wished to respond (after the drafting of a constitution for the Republic of India) to the democratic and reconstructive aspirations of the people? Had the bulk of the Indians turned so disillusioned within a year of its being in office as to desert it altogether? Was the motivation for puting an end to the Communist "menace" entirely its own, or had the second Congress of the C.P.I. substantially contributed to the build-up? And again, when the Telengana and the Andhra Communists differed so diametrically in their political position from the one the second Congress adopted and pursued, to the apparent detriment of the Communist movement in India, why could they not publicise their own views, and break formally away from the Ranadiveans? In other words, what the Telengana Communists could perhaps have done in September 1948 was to suitably amend their stand *vis-a-vis* the Nehru Government, if, of course, they had developed some doubt about their original, militantly off-balanced characterisation of it in June 1948, and to let the act of amending be known to all, including the Ranadiveans and the Nehru Government. The possibility that the enemy was not perhaps as inimical towards the theme of agrarian transformation (at least in the public, and in view of its fumblingly moving towards a sort of *Zamindari* abolition) as it was initially made out to be, might have turned the defence of the Telengana rebels' gains more elaborate, through the mobilisation of public opinion in their favour, and through an invocation of popular interference in their support. The defence could have been reinforced by utilising the difference within the Indian Government between the Nehruvian and the Patelite-Rajajian viewpoints,[438] by sympathising with the "mass following"[439] of Swami Ramanand Tirtha in the State Congress against the rival reactionary faction set up by K.M. Munshi and company, and by withholding the arms, keeping them for use, if need be, in the last ditch. The rebels' inability, for whatever reason, to review the ideological and programmatic stand at a crucial juncture, and their floating, howsoever anxiously, on the course of collision with the Indian army and the Government, were certain to expose the agrarian revolution in Telengana to its greatest peril. The revolutionary achievements there seemed too precious to be risked Bonapartistically in a contest with the vastly superior opponents, and consequently in a predictable politico-military rout. But this was precisely what the Telengana Communists selected to do by continuing the "partisan struggle" in the name not only for the defence of their gains, but also for the "liberation" of the Indian people, or for the establishment of a "New Democracy" in India.[440]

The more one tended to become sectarian, the more he or she was likely to lose the followings, whether of the trusted or the not-so-trusted, and this seemed to have happened to an extent

438. It was well-known that unlike Patel, the Home Minister, who wanted a wholesale annulment of the Communist land distribution in Telengana in favour of the landlords, Nehru, the Prime Minister, was against restoring to them those lands which the Communists had already distributed among the landless. Nehru was also known to have adopted a lenient view of the Communists in Telengana, and, despite opposition from Patel's successor, Rajagopalachari, he desired to commute the death sentences passed on many among them. His inclination for opening a dialogue with the Telengana Communists, privately through Dr. Jayasoorya, and publicly through Vinoba Bhave's peace mission (which included Mridula Sarabhai), was hardly any secret.

439. "Political and Organisational Report", Andhra-Telengana After the Police Action, Inner C.C. No. 6, 1949, File No. 1949/56, p. 44, P.C. Joshi Archives, J.N.U., New Delhi.

440. "Land Distribution in Telengana: Mistakes and Future Programme", Circular of the State Fraction of the Andhra Committee of the C.P.I., 1 June 1950.

in Telengana, coinciding with the pressures the Indian army brought upon the populace. The Telengana rebels started experiencing the Indian army's full weight roughly from the end of September 1948, or soon after it had meticulously snuffed out all the Nizamshahi and the Razakari flickerings in Hyderabad. The Military Governor concentrated his attention almost entirely on the "Communist menace" in Telengana, and despite the Telengana peasantry's being "not altogether cooperative", the army succeeded as early as the end of October 1948 in capturing 347 rebels in Nalgonda, about 50 in Karimnagar and quite a sizable number in Warangal, along with large quantities of arms and ammunitions.[441] The account of the Telengana Communists themselves corroborated the intensity of the military offensive, and the atrocities committed on them and their sympathisers. According to them, by the end of the year 1948, "more than 1000 villages" had been raided, "tens of thousands of people beaten, hundreds of women raped, and tens of people killed".[442] As the military offensive was taking place in an atmosphere of general approbation in favour of Hyderabad's accession to India, and as the rural rich by and large shared in this nationalist euphoria, the Telengana Communists' attitude towards the *kisan* solidarity — towards the upper crust of the peasantry — started getting hardened. For the first time at the beginning of 1949 the rebels appeared to be smelling a strong stench of landlordism within the ranks of the rich peasants, discovering police agents and military informers among them, accusing them of plots to dominate village *Panch* Committees, criticising them for systematic delays in land distribution, and then lowering down — to the evident dismay of the village affluent — the land ceiling in certain places from 10 acres of *tari* and 100 acres of *khushki* to 7 acres of *tari* and 70 acres of *khushki*, as in Suryapet, and 5 acres of *tari* and 50 acres of *khushki* as in Janagaon-

441. "A Report on Certain Aspects of the Situation in Hyderabad", by Maj. Gen. Choudhury, Military Governor, Hyderabad State, 19 November 1948. Proceedings, Ministry of States, Government of India, File No. 1(11)-H of 1948, N.A.I.

442. "Political and Organisational Report", Andhra-Telengana After the Police Action, Inner C.C. No. 6, 1949, File No. 1949/56, p. 9, P.C. Joshi Archives, J.N.U., New Delhi.

Warangal area. They in fact planned to scale down the land ceilings further in different categories of lands, namely, (1) 2 acres of *tari* and 20 acres of *khushki* in the high-yielding black soil, (2) 3 acres of *tari* and 30 acres of *khuski* in the ordinary yielding red soil, and (3) 4 acres of *tari* and 40 acres of *khushki* in the poor-yielding sandy soil.[443] Although the Telengana Communists were still theoretically agreeable not to alienate the so-called "middle" peasants, they could do precious little to stop the snatching away — in the name of "illegality" — those bits of lands from the semi-substantial peasantry which it had been suspected of procuring against the debt-arrears of the poor. For inculcating a "proper class outlook", or acquiring a proletarian perspective in the typical Ranadivean style, the Telengana Communists now decided to banish the entire rich peasantry from among the forces of the Indian New Democratic Revolution, from the revolutionary consolidation of "the working class in the towns, the oppressed middleclass, petty employees and traders, the unemployed intellectuals, agricultural labourers and poor and middle peasants led by the working class and its party — the Communist Party".[444] The rich peasants, it was thunderingly announced, had "no place in this democratic front", and the Telengana Communists themselves began lumping together — as had already been done by the Ranadiveans, very questionably, according to the Andhra Letter — all the bourgeois categories under the broad classification of the "Indian bourgeoisie", and emphasizing almost axiomatically on their enemy character without any substantiation afresh that they had "joined hands" with the imperialist and feudal forces.[445] The rebels in Telengana were willing even to go as far as Bhowani Sen went in West Bengal, i.e. to talk "boldly", and "without hesitation", of the taking away of lands the rich peasants were presently cultivating with the help of wage-labour, and about "collective farming" for building socialism in the future.[446] There

443. "Land Distribution in Telengana: Mistakes and Future Programme", Circular of the State Fraction of the Andhra Committee of the C.P.I., 1 June 1950.
444. *Ibid.*
445. *Ibid.*
446. *Ibid.*

could not be a surer way than such a threatening assertion to isolate the agrarian revolution from all categories of the landholding peasantry — the rich, the "middle" and even some among the poor. It was amazing how the divergent viewpoints of the Ranadiveans and the Andhra Letterites eventually seemed to converge in 1949 in a similarly contrived, make-believe, ultra-revolutionary world of their own. Apart from a degree of emphasis here and relaxation there, and the distinction of nomenclatures of a "New Democratic Revolution" and a "People's Democratic Revolution", the only major, and material, difference that persisted between them in 1949 and thereafter was essentially one of military technique — whether to persevere for an insurrection engulfing the whole country (which the Ranadiveans still did even after the miscarriage of the industrial action of 9 March 1949), or to pursue a guerilla war liberating the nation in doses (which the Telengana Communists were already engaged in). In the ultimate analysis, the history of the great Telengana rising boiled simply down in 1949 to a straightforward and a tragic chronicle of military engagements of guerilla actions and anti-guerilla counter-actions.

The military offensive, and the encirclement of a certain village or villages for apprehending the rebels, had already cornered the Telengana guerilla and village squads to an extent in their own spheres of influence in Nalgonda, Warangal and Karimnagar, despite their efforts to wriggle out of the combing operations, break up in agile tiny groups (of five),[447] and merge completely with the village folk.[448] The military authorities also sealed the Telengana-Andhra border with the help of the Madras Government, drafted special armed police from the Indian

447. P. Sundarayya, *Telengana People's Struggle and Its Lessons*, Calcutta, 1972, p. 197.

448. "It is difficult to distinguish the Communist from either the peasant or the State Congress worker, and the Communists are naturally taking advantage of this difficulty in identification." Summary of the Situation and Events in Hyderabad since 10.10.48, Military Governor's Office, Bolaram, Deccan, Proc. Ministry of States, Government of India, File no. 318-H/48, Part II, 1948, N.A.I.

territories to supplement the troops in Telengana, and succeeded in claiming by March 1949 about "50 per cent reduction" in the over-all Communist activities in Nalgonda and Warangal.[449] Obviously at a disadvantage, the Communists and the peasant guerillas courageously fought back the Government forces, distinctively at Ellampet and Bommanapalli of Manukota; Patasurya-pet and Nasimpeta of Suryapet; Lavvala on the Nagaram-Mulugu road; Gudur of Narsampeta and Rayamadaram of Illendu. They also launched direct assaults on the military and police camps, for instance at Gundal of Palvancha, Jangadu of Parkhala, Kamaram and Miryalapenta of Narsampeta, Karepalli of Illendu, Suddarevu in Khammam-Palvancha area, Arutla and Chittapuram in the Bagata-Devairakonda-Amrabad area, Buchhanpeta, Akkanapet, Akunoor and Sircilla in the Karimnagar-Janagaon area. There were cases of sniping galore at the army and police personnel, and the number of ambushes they encountered had similarly been very considerable. There were also innumerable clashes when the landlords returned at the back of the Indian army and police, and started — under their protection — forcibly reoccupying the lands the Telengana Communists had already distributed. In the grimly fought local contests for lands, a large number (perhaps the largest in any phase of the Telengana rising) of landlords lost their lives, such as Rallakanti Venkata Reddy at Edulapusapalli, Musipalli Narasayya at Jangalapalli, Challa Rajayya at Suravaram (in Manukota area), Venkata Ranga Rao at Produttur, Khommineni Prakash Rao at Kurnavelli (in the Khammam-Madhira area), Kandibandh Janakirama Rao in Huzurnagar, Patel Ananta Ramulu at Malkacharia, Potu Venkatanarasayya at Rangapuram (in the Huzurnagar-Mirya-lagudem area), Patel Pomula Kistayya at Madapuram, Hanamantu at Brahmanapalli, Ramachandra Reddy at Bhattugudem, and Chalama Reddy at Artula (in the Bhongir-Ibrahimpatnam area). In spite of all their desperate bids for stemming the rot, the rebellious peasants and their Communist leaders were nevertheless losing the ground. From the official

449. Report from Hyderabad till March 1949, Proc. Ministry of States, Government of India, Hyderabad Branch, File No. 10(105)-H/49, 1949, N.A.I.

point of view, the general situation in Telengana had "improved" so much that the Military Governor even contemplated the withdrawal of a certain number of troops "as an experiment".[450]

The "improvement", most significantly, was not merely the consequence of the overwhelming superiority of the Governmental forces in sophisticated arms and highly trained men (belonging to the considerable number of combat battalions of the Indian army, the Hyderabad army, which had not yet been disbanded, the Hyderabadi police and the special armed police raised from various parts of India, and consisted of 8,500 men and officers), but the outcome of the rapidity with which they were overcoming their previous "lack of intelligence" about the rebel whereabouts, or getting over the "problem of identifying" the Communist peasant guerillas. There were frequent references in the official circles from February 1949 to the villagers' — the previous harbourers of the Communists — "cooperating" with the army and the police,[451] to their "helping" the Government to an extent,[452] to their "supporting the local authorities",[453] and also to the party cadres' "giving out information".[454] Intelligence continued to flow regularly to the Indian army and police, in spite of the *kisan* guerillas' systematically annihilating the village officials, the Government agents and the informers.[455] The authorities also took solace from such facts as the "larger cultivators" being greatly "panicked" by the Communist decree of permitting a maximum of "3 acres of irrigated and 30 acres of unirrigated lands" per family, or the Communist support-base getting shrunk only to those among whom the *Panch*

450. Military Governor, Hyderabad, to Secretary, Ministry of States, Government of India, D.O. No. 48/384/MG of 25 August 1949, Proc. Ministry of States, Government of India, File No. 10(60)-H/49, 1949, N.A.I.

451. Hyderabad Fortnightly Report, 1st half of February 1949, Ministry of States, Hyderabad Branch, Government of India, File No. 11(3)-H/49, 1949, N.A.I.

452. "Forecast of Law and Order Situation in Hyderabad State and Its Control", Gen. J.N. Choudhury, 27 September 1949, Proc. Ministry of States, Government of India, File No. 1(80)-H/49, 1949, N.A.I.

453. Hyderabad Fortnightly Report, 1st half of October 1949, Ministry of States, Hyderabad Branch, Government of India, File No. 11(3)-/H 49, 1949, N.A.I.

454. *Ibid.*, 1st half of April 1949.

455. *Ibid.*, 1st half of May 1949.

Committees had distributed the confiscated lands.[456] Even those of the landless agricultural labourers, who did not receive yet their shares of the confiscated lands, felt disheartened, despite the "intense Communist propaganda" to arouse them again.[457] Unmistakably the Telengana Communists had lost by the end of 1949 the whole-hearted support they previously enjoyed from the substantial chunk of the peasantry, and it had become increasingly difficult for the peasant guerillas to operate among a civil population whose certain components — either under the Governmental repression, or by their ideologistic side-lining — could no longer remain as dedicated to them as before. According to the official sources, some of the guerillas themselves were somewhat perturbed about the failure of the guerilla tactics, and pondered over "a change in the *modus operandi*".[458] The rebel ranks also revealed a tendency for desertion and inactivity, a clear fall in the number of the guerilla squads and a depletion in their organisational strength.[459] Acts of heroism, defiance and self-sacrifice were not enough to break the ring of isolation that had been closing in 1949 around the Telengana Communists. It was no wonder that by the end of the year they had been compelled by the military circumstances to move out of their chosen battle-front of four years' standing to get into the Koya and the Chenchuri inhabited Krishna forest area in the southern tip of Nalgonda and Mahboobnagar districts, as well as into the Gond, the Kalamalu and the Naikapadu-populated Godavari forest region in parts of Adilabad, and the eastern fringes of Warangal and Karimnagar districts. Howsoever much it had been made out to be "an extension" of the struggle to "new areas",[460] the rebels' taking refuge in the forests was

456. *Ibid.*, 1st half of June 1949.
457. *Ibid.*, 2nd half of December 1949.
458. *Ibid.*, 1st half of August 1949.
459. In the second Congress of the C.P.I. early in 1948, the Telengana Communists claimed, perhaps exaggeratedly, a strength of 8,000 party members. A year later, they had found it to have come down to about 3,000 party members. See "Political and Organisational Report", Andhra-Telengana After the Police Action, etc.
460. P. Sundarayya, *Telengana People's Struggle and Its Lessons*, Calcutta, 1972, pp. 285 & 295.

evidently a retreat, of course, with the undiminished resolution for continuing the guerilla struggle either in search of yet another Yenan in the Maoist fashion, or in pursuit of a national legend in Alluri Sitaramayyan style.

If the Andhra Letterites found immense difficulty at the end of 1949 in their exclusive area of dazzling performances — in Telengana itself — the Ranadiveans were already deep in trouble on the *kisan* front by that time in the rest of the country. Throughout 1948 they had remarkably succeeded in shifting the weight of all agrarian struggles from anti-feudalism to anti-rich peasantry, in hostilely keeping at a distance the so-called "middle" peasants, and even creating confusion within the ranks of the poor peasants, sharecroppers and agricultural labourers through an obsessive assertion of the "proletarian" leadership. Proletarianism became such an obsession with them that they went so far as to neglect the *kisans*' own organisation and betrayed a distinct preference for putting up the militant party units among the *kisans* with a view to extending and strengthening the Kisan Sabhas.[461] It was hardly possible for individual Communist heroes, who distanced themselves in effect from various segments of peasant society, and who continued to be on the run almost ceaselessly, to make much headway in their socialist revolutionary activities in the countryside. They did nevertheless make serious attempts at taking up the *khetmajdoors*' cudgels practically everywhere, notably at Mahasamund (Raipur) and Chandur (Amraoti) of the C.P. and Berar;[462] at Narsarapeta (Nellore), Razole and Ramachandrapuram (East Godavari), Divi (Krishna) and Kamasamudram (Cuddapah) of Andhra;[463] at Sidhapur (Ghazipur), Singhpur (Aligarh) and a few places in Agra of the U.P.;[464] among the *Halis* (Surat and

461. E.M.S. Namboodiripad, *Agrarian Problem of India*, Calcutta, June 1952, pp. 58-63.
462. Fortnightly Reports, C.P. & Berar, 2nd half of February and 2nd half of May 1949, Ministry of States, Government of India, File No. 9(24)-P/49, 1949, N.A.I.
463. P. Sundarayya, *Telengana People's Struggle and Its Lessons*, Calcutta, 1972, chapter V, and also Fortnightly Report, Madras, 2nd half of October 1949, Ministry of States, Government of India, File No. 9(40)-P/49, 1949, N.A.I.
464. *Crossroads* (English weekly), 30 December 1949.

Broach) and the landless (Kanara) of Bombay[465] in support of the Majdoor Khet Sabha (Jullundur) of East Punjab;[466] in a number of places in Birbhum, Midnapore, Bankura, the 24-Parganas and West Dinajpur of West Bengal;[467] at Korome, Thilankari and Manayakannu (North Malabar) of Kerala; and in certain places (belonging to South Arcot, Ramnad and Coimbatore) of Tamil Nadu.[468] The Communists also stirred up a passionate agitation of the landless refugee *kisans* from West Punjab in Jullundur, Ludhiana and Ferozepur of East Punjab over the issue of their eviction from lands they were temporarily permitted to occupy.[469] Almost a similar emotionally charged movement they tried to build up in different parts of the country over the forcible procurement of grains from *kisans*, at a nominal price under the levy system, notably in Anantapur and Krishna of Andhra,[470] Rae Bareli, Aligarh and Meerut of the U.P.,[471] Bhilwara of Rajasthan — where more than 15 died on 22 May 1949 at Sawana village in a single clash with the police,[472] and in Nasik and Ahmadnagar of Maharashtra, especially at Erandgaon village in Shevagaon (Ahmadnagar) where *kisans* were subjected

465. Fortnightly Reports, Bombay, 1st half of February and 2nd half of March 1949, Ministry of States, Government of India, File No. 9(17)-F/49, N.A.I.
466. Fortnightly Report, East Punjab, 1st half of January 1949, Ministry of States, Government of India, File No. 9(45)-P/49, 1949, N.A.I.
467. Fortnightly Reports, West Bengal, 1st half of February and 1st half of March 1949, Ministry of States, Government of India, File No. 9(18)-P/49, 1949, N.A.I.
468. Fortnightly Report, Madras, 2nd half of March 1949, Ministry of States, Government of India, File No. 9(40)-P/49, 1949, N.A.I.
469. Fortnightly Reports, East Punjab, 2nd half of August, 1st half of October and 1st half of December 1949, Ministry of States, Government of India, File No. 9(45)-P/49, 1949, N.A.I.
470. Fortnightly Reports, U.P. 2nd half of February and 1st half of March 1949, File No. 9(40)-P/49, Ministry of States, Government of India, 1949, N.A.I.
471. Fortnightly Reports, Madras, 1st half of March, 2nd half of April, Ist half of May, 1st half of June and 1st half of July 1949, Ministry of States, Government of India, File No. 9(44)-P/49, 1949, N.A.I.
472. Fortnightly Report, Rajasthan Union, 1st half of June, 1949, Ministry of States, Government of India, File No. 9(19)-P/49, 1949, N.A.I.

to repeated police acts of repression and firings.[473] Since in many places the villagers were "more inclined to help the underground [Communist] workers than the administration",[474] a large number of bloody clashes occurred over the taking of Communist prisoners by the police, and at the instance of the landlords, prominently in Aligarh and Ghazipur of the U.P.;[475] in Muzaffarpur of Bihar;[476] in Ramnad, Salem, Coim-batore and Tiruchirapalli of Tamil Nadu; in West Godavari, Guntur, Cuddapah and Krishna (at Velivelu village of Divi *taluk* in particular) of Andhra;[477] at Onchiyam and Padikkunu of Kerala;[478] in Midnapore (at Kalagachhia village for example),[479] Hooghly (at Bada Kamalapur and Dubir Bhedi), Bankura (at Jaipur and Bandhgaba) and Burdwan (at Agradwip)[480] of West Bengal. Apart from conducting some stray cases of "land seizures", such as the forcible possession of *Sir* lands in Sultanpur of the U.P.,[481] of forest lands by Santhals in Purnea of Bihar,[482] of *hota* lands in Ganjam of Orissa,[483] of *Punam* lands in Koothali of

473. Fortnightly Report, Bombay, 1st half of April 1949, Ministry of States, Government of India, File No. 9(17)-P/49, 1949, N.A.I.
474. Fortnightly Report, East Punjab, 1st half of May 1949, Ministry of States, Government of India, File No. 9(45)-P/49, 1949, N.A.I.
475. Fortnightly Reports, U.P., 1st half of June and 1st half of August 1949, Ministry of States, Government of India, File No. 9(44)-P/49, 1949, N.A.I.
476. Fortnightly Report, Bihar, 2nd half of January 1949, Ministry of States, Government of India, File No. 9(68)-P(s)/49, 1949, N.A.I.
477. Fortnightly Reports, Madras, 2nd half of April, 1st half of October, 1st half of November and 2nd half of November 1949, Ministry of States, Government of India, File No. 1949, N.A.I.
478. Achuthanandan and Ramakrishna, *Kerala: Punnapra-Vayalar and Other Struggles*, A.I.K.S. publication, New Delhi, 1986, pp. 32-3.
479. Fortnightly Report, West Bengal, 1st half of March 1949, Ministry of States, Government of India, File No. 9(18)-P/49, 1949, N.A.I.
480. Sengupta, Amalendu, *Uttal Challish* (in Bengali), Calcutta, 1989, pp. 365-7 and 377-82.
481. Fortnightly Report, U.P., 2nd half of June 1949, Ministry of States, Government of India, File No. 9(68)-P(S)/49, 1949, N.A.I.
482. Fortnightly Report, Bihar, 1st half of January 1949, Ministry of States, Government of India, File No. 9(25)-P/49, 1949, N.A.I.
483. Fortnightly Reports, Orissa, 1st and 2nd halves of January 1949, Ministry of States, Government of India, File No. 9(25)-P/49, 1949, N.A.I.

Kerala,[484] and of wastelands in Cuddapah of Andhra,[485] the Communists also managed in certain places to carry on the Tebhaga pattern "crop seizures" by leading the sharecroppers, for example, in Cachar of Assam,[486] in Cuttack (Jajpur) and Ganjam (Sherguda) of Orissa,[487] in Jullundur of East Punjab,[488] in Tellicherry and Arool of Kerala,[489] and in Midnapore (Contai and Tamluk), Hooghly, Howrah (notably at Sankrail), Burdwan, Bankura, the 24-Parganas, Nadia and Jalpaiguri of West Bengal.[490] There was even an abortive attempt with the help of the *khetmajdoors* and tenants at creating "a Telengana in Azamgarh" of the U.P. in 1948-9, by planning to drive out the *Zamindars* from the villages, seizing and distributing their lands and properties, and establishing the "village power".[491] Despite the valiant efforts from a Communist point of view, all such enactments on the Ranadive-led party line were brief, disconcerted and highly localised occurrences without any long-lasting and wide-ranging significance. There were, however, exceptions which had outgrown the general run of incidents — both in persistence and in intensity, namely the ones that took place in the Sundarbans of West Bengal, in Patiala of PEPSU (Patiala and East Punjab States Union) and in Tanjore of Tamil Nadu.

484. Achuthanandan and Ramakishnan, *Kerala: Punnapra-Vayalar and Other Struggles*, A.I.K.S. publication, New Delhi, 1986, p. 28.
485. P. Sundarayya, *Telengana People's Struggle and Its Lessons*, Calcutta, 1972, p. 162.
486. Fortnightly Report, Assam, 1st half of February 1949, Ministry of States, Government of India, File No. 9(70)-P(S)/49, 1949, N.A.I.
487. Fortnightly Reports, Orissa, 1st and 2nd halves of January 1949, Ministry of States, Government of India, File No. 9(25)-P/49, N.A.I.
488. Fortnightly Report, East Punjab, 2nd half of April 1949, Ministry of States, Government of India, File No. N(18)-P/49, N.A.I.
489. *The Hindu* (English daily), 10 May 1948.
490. Fortnightly Reports, West Bengal, 1st and 2nd halves of February 1949, Ministry of States, Government of India, File No. N(18)-P/49, N.A.I.
491. "Strategies and Tactics in the Struggle for People's Democratic Revolution in India", Politbureau, C.P.I., December 1948, in M.B. Rao (ed.), *Documents of the History of the Communist Party in India*, Vol. VII, New Delhi, 1976, pp. 354-63.

A Kisan Sabha-led agitation among the *varam* peasants and the agricultural labourers and farm-hands or the *punnaiyals* was gaining momentum in Tanjore district of Tamil Nadu from 1946. The *varam* sharecroppers, who had to cultivate lands under the worst of terms in the whole of India, i.e. by surrendering to the landlords more than three-fifths of the net produce, were clamouring for a two-thirds share (or the *tebhaga*), and agitating against periodic ejectments.[492] The agricultural labourers were demanding an increase of 50 per cent in their daily paddy wages, and the farm-hands (who were settled in strips of the landlords' lands) an increase of 25 per cent.[493] The *varam kisans*' resistance to the *Mirasdars*' taking away the crops, and the *punnaiyals'* refusal to till the lands unless the demands of both of them were met, often resulted in violent clashes. In one such clash at Alathur village two of the *Mirasdars'* men were killed on 23 December 1946, in which Kuppuswamy — one of the dynamic and popular *kisan* leaders of Tanjore district — was implicated.[494] Apart from a number of agricultural labourers' strikes, Tanjore recorded by the earlier part of 1947 about 50 cases of "paddy looting", five cases of "agrarian riots" and one case of murder.[495] The number of wage-labourers' strikes and the sharecroppers' resistances so steadily increased in the latter half of 1947 that the authorities brought certain areas under Section 144 Cr.P.C. (notably in Pattukottai and Arangtangi *taluks*) and prosecuted peasants for "trespassing into the Mirasdari lands" (notably at Tiruvalaputur).[496] The

492. Confidential Report of Inspector General of Police, Madras, to Chief Secretary, Government of Madras, No. Sec. 161 of 5 February 1948, Under-Secretary's Safe Sec. Files, Deposit No. 31 of 7/7/48, Tamil Nadu State Archives, Madras.

493. *Jana Shakti* (Tamil weekly), 1 February 1948.

494. Kuppuswamy was later sentenced to death in a trial on "unsubstantiated" charges, and while the Communists started a movement throughout the province for his release, he was found dead in Trichi jail under mysterious circumstances on 18 April 1948.

495. Questions and Answers in Madras Legislative Assembly, Public (General) Dept., G.O. No. 1959 of 27/6/47, Tamil Nadu State Archives, Madras.

496. Inspector General of Police, Madras, to Chief Secretary, Govt. of Madras, No. Sec. 161 of 5 February 1948, Under-Secretary's Safe Sec. Files, Deposit No. 31, of 7/7/48, Tamil Nadu State Archives, Madras.

Mirasdars, on their part, frequently instituted "false" criminal cases against the *varam kisans* and *punnaiyals* to teach them the necessary lessons, which they exemplarily did at Arunthavapuram early in 1947,[497] harassed the *kisans* and disturbed their gatherings,[498] maintained armed retinues or "private levies", and liberally gratified the police for pulling them to their side.[499] Following the Calcutta Congress of the C.P.I., the Communists in Tanjore tried to raise promptly the struggle of the *varam kisans* and *punnaiyals*, who constituted roughly 40 per cent of the total rural population of the district, to a new height of militancy in the first half of 1948. There were widespread agricultural labourers' strikes, such as at Tiruthiraipundi, Mannargudi, Pathukottai and Mayavaram,[500] the share-croppers' .forcibly retaining two-thirds of crops, such as in Sirkazhi, Nagapattinam, Aranthanki and Thiruvaduthudai,[501] and the villagers' taking back the common lands from the *Mirasdari* occupation, such as at Thiruth-uraipundi.[502] The *Mirasdars* fought back with the help of their retainers, burnt down the *kisan* huts, threw out the farm-hands from the fringes of their lands, and successfully persuaded the authorities to come to their rescue. The Government responded by banning the *kisan* volunteer force, extending Section 144 Cr.P.C. practically to the whole of the eastern part of Tanjore district, employing a large number of the Special Armed Police, and making thousands of arrests. The police and the *kisans* clashed in many places, notably at Karapaganathargulam,[503] Singamangalam, Senthamaraiken,

497. District Magistrate, Tanjore, to Secretary, Public (Gen.) Dept., Govt. of Madras, No. 2162-956/47-CL of 7/5/47, Public (Gen.) Dept. G.O. No. 2160 of 15/7/47, Tamil Nadu State Archives, Madras.
498. Questions and Answers in Madras Legislative Assembly, Public (Gen.) Dept., G.O. No. 1938 of 24/6/47, Tamil Nadu State Archives, Madras.
499. *Ibid.*, Public (Gen.) Dept., G.O. No. 1416 of 9/6/48, Tamil Nadu Archives, Madras.
500. *Jana Shakti* (Tamil weekly), issues between February and May 1948, and the *Cross Roads* (English weekly), 23 June 1950.
501. *Jana Shakti* (Tamil weekly), issues of February and March 1948.
502. *Ibid.*
503. Questions and Answers in Madras Legislative Assembly, Public (Gen) Dept., G.O. No. 1416 of 9/6/48, Tamil Nadu State Archives, Madras.

Vedakku-Manalur and Pattamanglam,[504] resulting in injuries and deaths of the *kisan* activists (like Raju Vaaikarau, Shivaraman, Hiranayan and Murugayan). By the middle of 1948 the repressive machinery of the Government seemed more or less to be in control of the affairs in Tanjore, and the rural poor's resistance apparently subsided towards the end of the year, though it had not wholly died down at places like in Kallugudi, Thiruthiraipundi and Mannargudi.[505]

Despite their militant tempers and acts of heroism, the sharecroppers and agricultural labourers in Tanjore could neither raise their "partial" struggle to the level of a "total" one by building up an anti-landlord joint front with the *Kuthakai* "middle" and poor peasants or the ordinary tenants, nor turn their battle for "crop seizures" into "land seizures" by pursuing the "land to the tiller" slogan. It was not easy to try to achieve both these by staying strictly within the parameters of the Ranadivean political line. That the *Muzaras* or the occupant sharecroppers could manage to launch at all in 1948-49 an assault on the *Biswedari* landlordism and its lands in Patiala was on account of their being led without restraint by the Lal Communist Party,[506] who sympathised with the Ranadivean politics, but who had been free from the dictates of the official Communist Party. The *Muzaraṣ* had also been placed in a certain position of agitational advantage on account of the nature of the Patiala state administration, and their own moral standing *vis-a-vis* the *Biswedars*. The character of the Maharaja's rule in Patiala state, unlike other modernistic Indian states like Hyderabad, Mysore and even Travancore, was not only oppressively autocratic, but also personal, and hence increasingly weak, and practically irresponsible. It was by influencing and

504. *The Hindu* (English daily), 24 and 26 June 1948.

505. Fortnightly Reports, Madras, 2nd half of May and 1st half of August, Ministry of States, Government of India, File No. 9(40)-P/49, 1949, N.A.I.

506. A section of the militant Communists in the Punjab, particularly those belonging to the "Kirti" group of *kisan* activists, who resented the moderate policies of the P.C. Joshi-led Central Committee, and its stand on the Muslim nationality question and the partition of India, broke away from the C.P.I. late in 1947 and formed the Lal Communist Party to step up the *kisan* movement through armed struggles.

manipulating a whimsical, infirm state administration that the *Biswedars* or landlords succeeded in gaining the proprietary rights over lands under the possession of the *Muzaras*. Since their sudden demotion from the status of the owners of lands to the position of the occupancy tenants thereon was completed by the beginning of the twentieth century, or within their living memory, the *Muzaras* rightly considered the *Biswedars* as usurpers, devoid of all legitimacy.[507] Besides, as they were subjected to a produce-rent under the *Kankut* system,[508] to various forms of irregular grain deductions, such as the "privilege" charges, and the charges for the "services" of the landlords' servants and retinues,[509] as well as to evictions for any failure to pay rent, the *Muzaras* had also turned *bataidars*, or feudalistically exploited sharecroppers. From the very beginning the *Muzaras* refused to take the injustice lying down, and resisted the *Biswedars* whenever it was possible, even by resorting to physical violence. Organised agitation started sometime later, and in the late 1930s a lively movement against the payment of *batai* took off the ground at the instance of the Communist-dominated Kisan Muzara Committee. Following the lull during the war period, the agitation against *batai* picked up again from 1945, resulting in the *Biswedars'* attempts at evictions for the non-payment of rent, and the *kisans'* efforts at foiling these at any cost. There were frequent court cases and open clashes between the *Biswedars* and the *Muzaras*, with the *riyasat* (state) authorities intervening at times in favour of the landlords, till the biginning of 1946. From 1946 the *Muzara* movement was elevated sharply to a new height under the guidance of leaders like Dharam Singh Fakkar and Jagir Singh Jogga, when it added

507. See Mridula Mukherjee's articles: "Peasant Movement in Patiala State, 1937-48" in *Studies in History*, Vol.1, no. 2, July-December 1979, pp. 215-83; and "Communists and Peasants in Punjab: A Focus on the Muzara Movement in Patiala, 1937-53" in Bipan Chandra (ed.), *The Indian Left: Critical Appraisals*, New Delhi, 1983, pp. 401-46.

508. According to this system, the standing crops in the fields were assessed before each harvest by a *Kankut* committee, consisting of the state functionaries, who decided the amount the *Muzaras* must pay as rent.

509. *Kishengarh: The Peasants' Heroic Defence of His Land*, PEPSU Kisan Sabha, Sangrur, 1951, pp. 1-51.

to the refusal to pay *batai* the demand for the restoration of lands to the tillers — their just claimants.[510] The violent encounters which continued throughout 1947 were given a further boost in 1948 with the formation of the Lal Communist Party, and the creation of a small "armed force" to deal mainly with the *Biswedars'* hirelings.

The battles for *batai* or crop-share turned at this point in 1948 so furiously into the battles for re-occupation of lands that the Patiala administration had to come up with an ordinance in January 1949 which allowed the *Muzaras* to take possession of two-thirds of the lands they were cultivating, provided they surrendered one-third to the *Biswedars*, and cleared the arrears of *batai* and "other dues". The climb-down by the authorities, though substantial, did not satisfy the *Muzaras*, who saw in it the prospect for obtaining more — all the lands they had lost — and consequently the Patiala Kisan Sabha, under the leadership of Teja Singh Swatantar and G.S. Randhawa, decided to oppose the ordinance.[511] Meanwhile PEPSU had been formed under a care-taker ministry headed by G.S. Rarewala, the Maharaja's uncle, and it decided to give effect to the ordinance by sending the revenue staff and the police to the villages for partitioning the plots. When one such official party, consisting of about 100 policemen, the *Biswedars* and their hired *goondas*, arrived on 16 March 1949 in Kishengarh — a centre of the *Muzara* activities — the *kisans* stubbornly resisted their proceedings. In the ensuing clash some of the landlords' men and a Sub-Inspector of Police were killed, and the rest chased away. The next morning (on the 17th) the police returned with a greater force under a Deputy Commissioner, surrounded the village with the help of about 400 regular troops in armoured cars, demanded the surrender of the *kisan* activists and opened fire, killing five and injuring 12. Houses were razed to the ground, inmates beaten up and tortured, and hundreds (including Dharam Singh Fakkar and Mahinder Singh) detained and taken to Faridkot

510. *Ibid.*
511. *Ibid.*

jail.[512] Far from demoralising the *kisans*, the Kishengarh atrocities inflamed the *Muzaras* further, led to their gaining support among the agricultural labourers, and resulted in their renewed combined aggression on the *Biswedars*. Even another instalment of the Government concession in September 1949, namely, the scaling down the ownership of land from one-third and two-thirds in favour of the *Biswedars* and *Muzaras*, respectively, to one-fourth and three-fourths, did not improve matters much. Feeling insecure, most of the *Biswedars* left the villages, and some of their one-fourth shares of lands (amounting to about 750 acres) had been taken away by the Patiala Kisan Sabha and distributed among the landless.[513]

Like the *Muzaras* in Patiala, the *Bhagchasis* in the Sundar-bans were also able, and with greater intensity, to elevate their contests for "grain-seizures" to those for "land-seizures". The *kisans* of Kakdwip in particular — who not only refused to give up their movement for the *tebhaga* (the two-thirds crop share) in 1947, but resolved to continue it, irrespective of the stand of the provincial Communist leadership — again rallied round their local leaders over the issue at Haripur-Layalganj and Budhakhali on 8 and 9 February 1948, respectively, and started stacking the entire winter crops in their own yards instead of the landlords'. The skirmishes with the *Jotedars* and their men began once again, and the armed policemen hurriedly returned to the villages to maintain "law and order". The *kisans* of Budhakhali especially had to confront the police almost continually,[514] and the *tebhaga* was obtained in most cases in Kakdwip, while in some the

512. Of the arrested, 85 were charged with obstructing the operation of law, and 25 with murder and resistance against the authorities. Their trial drew a lot of public attention, leading to the formation of Kishengarh Defence Committee, a legal contest for a year and a half, and the eventual acquittal of all in September 1950.

513. *Kishengarh: The Peasants Heroic Defence of His Land*, PEPSU Kisan Sabha, Sungrur, 1951, pp. 1-51.

514. "Sukhen's report, 6 November 1948, M.B. Rao (ed.), *Documents of the History of the Communist Party of India*, Vol.VII (1948-50), New Delhi, 1976, pp. 340-1.

Bargadars even refused to concede any share to the *Jotedars*, claiming *choubhaga* or all the four parts of the shares. The *Latdars* and *Jotedars* also lost very little time in retaliating, and dealing the heavy blows. Flanked by policemen, they re-grouped their *lathials*, called in the mercenaries and organised the volunteer corps or *Seva Dals*. Exercising their influence in the corridors of political and administrative powers, they managed to stop all special settlement work for registering the *Bargadars'* names. At the beginning of the sowing season of 1948 the landlords issued thousands of ejectment notices against the sharecroppers, and obtained innumerable court orders prohibiting *kisans* from tilling lands. Disturbances were, therefore, let loose at the commencement of the sowing season in 1948 itself when the ejected *Bhagchasis* — those debarred by the court orders — went for tilling the lands they had previously cultivated. They aggressively raised a new slogan in the wake of the second C.P.I. Congress, namely, *chas karo jami dakhale rekhe* (till the land by keeping it under your occupation), which instantly became popular throughout the Sundarbans, and the *Bargardars* forcibly occupied and tilled about 7,000 acres in Kakdwip in the sowing season of 1948.[515] As anticipated by both the warring sides, pitched battles were fought in Kakadwip very furiously, indeed, with the beginning of the harvesting. The pattern was the same in all the villages: the *Jotedar* would come to the field with his men, *lathials* and the police to take away the crops. The *Bhagchasis* would prevent the landlord from appropriating the crops, and defend the produce with as much force as they could master. But victory in the field did not always decide the issue conclusively, and the fight continued even after the victorious party had succeeded in taking away the paddy and stacking it in the yard. If the victory was of the *Jotedars*, the sharecroppers would try later on to raid their yards. In case it was the other way round, which seemed to have

515. A report by "Nikunja" (Asoke Bose) on the "Anti-Imperialist and Anti-Feudal Struggle of the People in Sundarbans and the Role of the Communist Party", Kakdwip, 24 Parganas, 15 June 1951, available in Material on Kakdwipa, Central Archives, C.P.I., Ajoy Bhavan, New Delhi.

generally happened, the *Jotedars'* men would attack the *Bargadars'* huts with the support of the police and ransack their hamlets. One such battle was fought frenziedly at Chandanpiri village on 6 November 1948.

It was decided at a meeting of the *kisans* of Chandanpiri on 4 November that the sharecroppers would go to the fields to harvest the crops in the morning of 6 November. At the appointed hour on this day, men (with *lathis* and agricultural implements) and women (with *jhantas* and *bontis*[516]) collected on the fields and began to reap the crop. Soon the *Naib* (manager) of the landlord appeared with a dozen *lathials* and some policemen to stop them. In the scuffle that followed, the *kisans* roughed up the *lathials* and the policemen, and took away their weapons, including a few rifles. The policemen and the *lathials* were allowed to leave the place, but the *Naib* was kept as a hostage to ensure good conduct from the police. A couple of hours later, a police reinforcement marched out of the landlord's *cutcherry*, clashed with the assembly of men and women and opened fire, killing eight (four men and four women) on the spot. The dead women included Ahalya, the mother of an adolescent son and a leading figure in the village, who was more than eight months' pregnant. After the incident the police party carried away six of the dead bodies, but they were not allowed to take away the bodies of Ahalya and another woman, Batasi. The *Naib*, who had been kept as a hostage by the *kisans*, was tried and executed soon thereafter. The following morning the body of Ahalya was taken around the village in a procession before placing it on the funeral pyre.[517] From Chandanpiri, the tale of Ahalya's death travelled to all the

516. Broomsticks and fish-cutting knives
517. Maitreya Ghatak reconstructed an account of the incident by interviewing the observers and participants at Chandanpiri in November 1978. See Mahasweta Devi and Maitreya Ghatak, "*Prayata Asoke Bose Smarane*" (In Memory of Asoke Bose, Who Passed Away) in Boudhayan Chattopadhyaya (ed.) *Samskriti O Samaj* (a Bengali quarterly), 1st, 2nd and 3rd issues, Calcutta, December 1983, pp. 156-7.

villages of the Sundarbans, and she became a legend overnight,[518] as well as a symbol of both the heroic peasant resistance and the brutality of police repression.[519] Harvesting and resistance continued simultaneously with renewed vigour at Chandanpiri, and the lead of its sharecroppers was soon emulated at Buḍhakhali, Haripur and Layalganj. The *Jotedar*-police-*Seva Dal* combine did try to stem the tide by attacking the sharecroppers' common yards, burning their huts, and arresting and torturing them. The peasant men and women promptly retaliated by throwing out the landlords' mercenaries, challenging the police pickets and snatching away the police rifles. Sometimes the villagers captured the *Jotedars* and their officials, tried them in open meetings for their misdeeds and inflicted punishments on them, including the capital one. Despite the increase in the number of police camps in the area between December and April 1949, and the stationing of regular troops at Namkhana, the rural poor in Kakdwip appeared to have gained an upper-hand in the contest and brought crops from thousands of acres to their own yards.[520] Naturally, during the upsurge, cultivation was thoroughly neglected, and the winter crops could not be raised. Normal trade and communication with the urban centres were also seriously disturbed. By the summer of 1949 an acute food shortage developed in Kakdwip, and it was against this background of worsening food situation that a spurt of *kisan* attacks on the *Jotedars' golas* (granaries) and *cutcherries* began in May 1949. The *kisans* of Layalganj showed the way by occupying the *cutcherries* and granaries of four prominent *Jotedars* of the locality,[521] and by seizing their

518. The circumstances and impact of Ahalya's death resemble those of the martyrdom of Doddi Komarayya on 4 July 1946 at Kaduvendi village, Janagaon *taluk*, Nalgonda district, Hyderabad.
519. Folklore grew in the Sundarbans over Ahalya's legend, and a popular song by the late Benoy Roy was broadcast by Radio Moscow.
520. Amit Kumar Gupta, "Forest Fire in the Sundarbans: The Communists and the Kakdwip Rising, 1946-50", *The Indian Historical Review*, vol. XII, nos 1-2, New Delhi, 1986, pp. 338-72.
521. They were Dwarik Samanta, Aditya Samanta, Pulin Das and Krishnapada Mazumdar.

grains, livestock and agricultural implements.[522] The entire operation in Layalganj was conducted by an Action Committee formed by the Communists, which declared on 1 May 1949 its intention to take over all lands surrounding the village, and distribute them afresh among the agricultural labourers and sharecroppers. In the first week of August 1949 the Committee re-named Layalganj as Lalganj (the Red locality) and declared the place as a "liberated zone" to be administered directly by it. It announced the formation of an armed village volunteer corps, or a "liberation army" and took upon itself the responsibility of a revolutionary tribunal for the settlement of village disputes. The Committee also warned the enemies of *majoor-chasi raj* — the *Jotedars, mahajans* and rich peasants — of dire consequences.[523]

From the "liberated" centre of Lalganj the Communist-led rebels extended the upsurge to Radhanagar and Rajnagar. About 150 to 200 volunteers were sent to these villages to assist the sharecroppers in fighting the *Jotedars* and the police, as well as to lend a hand in harvesting the crops. Serious clashes took place in both these villages on 18 and 20 August 1949, and in spite of the police party's resorting to firing on 4 September at Radhanagar, killing one and injuring many, it was unable to quell the disturbances.[524] The developments at Radhanagar were followed by similar incidents at Haripur and Maharajganj, where the armed *kisans* had beaten up and chased away the *Jotedars' lathials* and the *Seva Dal* members, occupied the *cutcherries*, broke into the *Jotedars'* granaries and distributed paddy, agricultural implements and other articles among the poor. The examples in Kakdwip were soon followed in other parts of the Sundarbans — at Bishnupur, Jaynagar, Dhapdhapi, Sandeshkhali and Canning. The trend in all these places remained the same,

522. *Shibir* (Bengali weekly), 12 October 1949. Also *Banglar Shishu Telengana — Lalganj* (a Bengali pamphlet), 24 Parganas District Committee, Communist Party of India, 7 November 1949, available in Material on Kakdwipa, Central Archives, C.P.I., Ajoy Bhavan, New Delhi.

523. *Ibid.*

524. *Shibir* (Bengali weekly), 12 October 1949.

namely, the forcible harvesting and stacking of crops, the attacks on the *Jotedars' golas* and *cutcherries*, the distribution of the seized grains and other movable properties, and the destruction of the loan documents and hand-notes (*hatchithas*) preserved by the *Jotedars*. Approximately 2,000 acres of land were confiscated in Kakdwip (mainly in Lalganj, Haripur, Budha-khali, Radhanagar and Rajnagar) and distributed among the landless. About 33 establishments of the *Jotedars* (which included *cutcherries, golas* and houses) were destroyed and burnt, four *Jotedars* were killed and seven seriously injured.[525] The rest of the *Jotedars* had either fled to the nearby towns, or lived under strict police protection. A sizable number of the *Jotedars' lathials* and the *Seva Dal* members, as well as some policemen, were also killed and injured. Apart from using conventional weapons (such as *lathis*, spears, bows and arrows), peasants also used fire-arms — mostly rifles taken away from the police. Bombs, or locally produced grenades, were also freely used, and there was evidence of the use of a few revolvers and sten-guns.[526]

With the spread of the rising at Chandranagar and Sibarampur in December 1949, the Communist-led *kisan* rebels seemed to have reached the highest point in the campaign. They had to pay, however, a heavy price for their remarkable advance, and although the exact number of casualties was not known, about a hundred persons were believed to have died, hundreds injured and several hundreds arrested.[527] Many more persons were detained and tortured from time to time in the *Jotedars' cutcherries* and police camps to extract information about the actors of the rising. Villages were raided, huts of *kisans* devastated and their belongings taken away or destroyed. The rural masses endured all these in the first flush of success, and hailed the martyrs among them by saying: *rane jiban dichhe,*

525. *Matamat* (Bengali weekly), 15 January 1950.
526. Secret Fortnightly Report, Home Poll. Dept., Government of West Bengal, 2nd half of December 1949, West Bengal State Archives, Calcutta.
527. This is the rough estimate of those who participated in the Kakdwip rising.

sagge jaichhe (died in battle, so must have reached the heaven).[528] But such sufferings and losses could not be sustained by a small population in a limited area for very long. The loss of lives might have been substantially reduced if the peasants had been introduced to the rudiments of armed resistance. The Communists, who had led by this time a full-fledged peasant war in Telengana, and employed guerilla tactics there with great effect, failed to make any use of their experiences in the Sundarbans. This happened even after their commitment to the "Telengana Way",[529] and their assertion of Kakdwip being a "miniature Telengana" or a *shishu* Telengana. Hearing tit bits of the Telengana movement from their leaders, the Kakdwip *kisans* expressed a distinct desire to learn from the military experiences of their Telengana brethren.[530] The leaders, however, could not arrange for their military training in partisan struggle, and consequently, the *kisan* masses had to go into frontal clashes with the police and the landlords' hirelings almost without preparation. Their defence of the crops or attack on the *cutcherries* was like the surge of an angry crowd — often the easiest target of their enemies' bullets. It was not, however, the military aspect that exposed the widest chink in the Kakdwip rebels' armour. Their real difficulty was how to extend the battle areas beyond certain pockets in the Sundarbans, for unless a number of Kakdwips were created in the 24-Parganas and other adjacent districts — on the line the *Tebhaga Elakas* propped up in various parts of Bengal in 1946-7 — they were not likely to

528. *Banglar Shishu Telengana — Lalganj* (A Bengali pamphlet), the 24-Parganas District Committee, Communist Party of India, 7 November 1949, pp. 22-3, available in Material on Kakdwipa, Central Archives, C.P.I., Ajoy Bhavan, New Delhi.

529. "For Telengana today means Communists and Communists mean Telengana", Review of the Second Congress of the C.P.I., Politbureau, March 1948, in M.B. Rao (ed.), *Documents of the History of the Communist Party of India*, Vol.VII, (1948-50), New Delhi, 1976, p. 197.

530. A report by "Nikunja" (Asoke Bose) on the "Anti-Imperialist and Anti-Feudal Struggle" etc., 15 June 1951, available in Material on Kakdwipa, Central Archives, C.P.I., Ajoy Bhavan, New Delhi.

survive for long the increasing pressure of a strong-arm provincial Government. There was no reason at the inspirational level, and following the readiness the *kisans* had shown in many places during the Tebhaga agitation, why the Kakdwip rebels' demands for the *Choubhaga* and the "land to the tiller" would not have been echoed in most parts of West Bengal, provided, of course, the peasantry as a whole, or the majority of its categories sympathised with these. In the latter half of 1949 such anti-feudal moral support was difficult to obtain outside the Sundarbans by branding the rich peasant as "enemy" and the "middle" peasant as "not a firm ally".[531] Even in the Sundarbans, where the substantial peasants (the rich and the "middle" taken together) did not count numerically and politically as a force to be reckoned with, unlike in the other parts of the 24-Parganas, the anti-*Jotedar* camp in each village was a house divided between them and the *Bhagchasis* and *khetmajdoors*, practically without any interaction.[532] What turned out to be worse in the Sundarbans was the Communist *kisan* activists' dogmatic insistence — in accordance with the Ranadivean politics — on the leadership of the proletariat in the struggle which had in the main been one of the sharecroppers'. This was bound to create an amount of confusion among the ranks of the rural poor themselves, especially over the distribution of the seized grains, agricultural implements, domestic animals and lands. Such emphasis on the "proletarian leadership" did clearly result in the sapping of the organisational strength of the movement, and in the ebbing of the participants' passionate involvement. The manner the "Action Committees" became more a kind of the party branch committees than the chosen popular bodies, and the way they reflected the Communist idiosyncrasies more than the articulations of the rebellious *kisans*, led quickly to an

531. "Strategy and Tactics in the Struggle for People's Democratic Revolution in India", Politbureau, December 1948, in M.B. Rao (ed.), *Documents of the History of the Communist Party of India*, Vol. VII (1948-50), New Delhi, 1976, p. 221.

532. A report by "Nikunja" (Asoke Bose) on the "Anti-Imperialist and Anti-Feudal Struggle" etc., 15 June 1951, available in Material on Kakdwipa, Central Archives, C.P.I., Ajoy Bhavan, New Delhi.

inanition, reducing the peasant participation to the level of mere soldiery, and leaving too much initiative, and too many of the responsibilities to the care of too few party members. The arrest and detention of a single Communist Party member often caused serious disturbances, creating crisis in specific locales. Behind a facade of victorious militancy in 1949 thus the defeat was lurking at the back of the rebels marooned in Kakdwip and its neighbourhood.

THE RAISONNEUR'S MONOLOGUE

The rebellious Kakdwip of the 24-Parganas, Kishengarh of Patiala and Tanjore of Tamil Nadu were all glaring instances of the rural poor's engagements in the Communist-led partisan struggles. While it had not been possible for the rebels in Tanjore to go beyond "partial" partisanship (or the extracting of their partial demand for increase in wages and crop-shares), they did attain in Kakdwip, as well as in Patiala, a kind of "total" partisanship (or the claiming of the entire crop and land, to the detriment of the landlord system). But even then, and despite their indomitable spirit and endeavour, they managed in their respective small pockets to reach only the threshold of an agrarian revolution — the avowed destination of all the agrarian revolutionaries. It was exclusively in Telengana, however, that they not only succeeded in entering into the stage of agrarian revolution, but were in practice in the thick of it, and also within the close range of realising its completion. Qualitatively, and density-wise, the Telengana rising was the most distinguished of all the peasant outbreaks in the annals of modern India. It was also the most outstanding from the viewpoint of the intensity of involvement on the part of its participants, including that of about half the peasant humanity — the women. The wide scale in which the *kisanis* often took the lead in mobilising the menfolk and children in the struggle, defended the crops and lands side by side the others, faced the Razakars, the police and the army, fought against the rapes and tortures practised on them, were in fact unprecedented. Their performance during the guerilla phase of the Telengana rising as trained squad members and political organisers, their ceaseless opposition against gender inequalities and male chauvinism, their persistent defence of the rights of marriage, divorce and re-mariage, clearly had no parallel in the

533. The subject matters have attracted some scholarly attention of late, though not adequately enough in an all-India perspective.

history of any popular movement.[533] Similarly unparalleled was the depth of popular support for the rising, not only among the workers (at Ballampalli and Kothagudem, and in Hyderabad city and Warangal town) but also among certain sections of the petty bourgeoisie and the students (in Warangal, Karimganj and Hyderabad city). Besides, in proportion to what the Telengana rebels had actually achieved, and such achievements were very significant, indeed, by any radical standard, they had immense potentiality for setting up an Indian model, along side the Russian, the Chinese and the Yugoslav ones, for the indigenous revolutionary experimentations in other colonised and semi-colonised parts of the world. That the potentiality did not eventually come true, and betrayed — to the contrary — unmistakable signs of its dissipation by the end of 1949, was decisively due to the Andhra and the Telengana Communists' ideology-based programmatic bungle.

Whatever the Communists and the *kisan* rebels had inspiringly attained in Telengana by September 1948 would not perhaps have been possible but for the soundness of their agrarian formulations. Relying largely on these, they arrived at some of their strategic conclusions and political convictions which were later enumerated in the Andhra Letter, such as, the Indian bourgeois categories' — with the exception of the monopoly capitalists — remaining outside the enemy camp, the stage of the Indian revolution being one of anti-feudal bourgeois democracy, the socialist strategies' transpiring unsuitable for the realisation of bourgeois democratic gains, and even the ideal of a New Democracy becoming the goal for India, appear in the main to be correct by the Marxist standards. But all this partial correctness of the Andhra Letter was heavily outweighed by such incorrectness as its assertion of the similarity between the Chinese and the Indian circumstances, its opting wholeheartedly for a Chinese model of revolution, its obsession for thrusting a long-drawn guerilla warfare on the toiling masses of India, and above all, its characterising the Nehru Government in India, like the Chiang Government in China, as a stooge of the imperialists, monopolists and landlords. It was the incorrectness in the Andhra Letter on which the Telengana rebels seemed to have increasingly reclined when faced with a new situation, following the "police action", and under the pressure of the Indian Army. The heavier was the pressure, more sectarian and adventurous they became, by replacing the Nizamshahi with the Nehrushahi as the target of attack, by trying to turn the liberation of Hyderabad into the liberation of the whole of India as the politico-military objective, by substituting the liberal treatment of the substantial agrarian categories with a hardened, hostile attitude towards them, by supplanting all the differentiations among the bourgeoisie with their lumping together in the "enemy camp", and by relegating the task of carrying out an agrarian revolution into the background of a larger aim for the establishment of a "New Democracy" under proletarian leadership. By the end of 1949, therefore, the Andhra-Telengana Communists came so close to the position of the Ranadive-led Central Committee of the C.P.I. that they could not possibly escape its disastrous destiny.

The fate of the Ranadivean C.P.I. was practically decided soon after its declaring in effect an insurrectionary civil war against the bourgeois Congress Government — the puppetry which, in its opinion, had conspiratorially been foisted upon the Indian people by the imperialist-bourgeois-feudal combine — and its fabricating in theory the shortest route to socialism by circumventing all the intermediary stages. The Government counter-offensive that the party thus invited from March-April 1948, the lack of popular empathy it experienced for its unbridled revolutionism,[534] and the narrowing down of the ring of isolation that it asphyxiately felt to its utter dismay — thoroughly dampened its ebullient spirit and severely maimed its spreading organisation. The total membership of the party staggeringly dwindled from 89,000 at the time of the second Party Congress to 20,000 two years later,[535] with thousands languishing in jails, sources of party funds drying up, and the trade-unions and

534. B.T. Ranadive, at the fag end of his life, acknowledged that the basic mistake in 1948 was to assume the Congress and its leadership to have lost all their influences on the mass of the Indian people. See his interview of October 1987 with Bipan Chandra, Mridula and Aditya Mukherjee in *The Telegraph* (English daily), 19 and 20 April 1990.

535. M.B. Rao, (ed.), *Documents of the History of the Communist Party of India*, Vol.VII, (1948-50), New Delhi, 1976, p. XIV.

Kisan Sabhas reaching almost a moribund state. The fate of the Ranadive line, which relied heavily on the revolutionary action of the working class, was sealed for all practical purposes in March 1949 when the authorities succeeded in foiling the Communist plan for an all-India general strike, of course, with the fiercest use of force — the *lathi*-charges, the tear-gassings and the firings — and with the detention of 25,000, over and above the 50,000 undertrial.[536] The Ranadiveans did nevertheless wage battles on the *kisan* front in a scattered manner, and in keen theoretical bigotry, with the help of *khetmajdoors*, sharecroppers and marginal peasants, shifting the main emphasis from anti-landlordism to an offensive against the "bourgeoised" rich peasants, or the "Kulaks". Even the "middle" peasants were not spared, and the Communists in West Bengal admitted that "in actual practice our movement in many places ... went directly against the middle peasants".[537] Since their line of demarcation with the so-called "middle" peasants was often very thin, the poor peasants — who barely existed from hand to mouth — also felt insecure. Forsaken thus by the important chunks of peasantry, and deviated deliberately from the path of agrarian revolution, the Ranadivean Communists and *kisan* militants could not make any significant headway, except, of course, in the forlornly Kakdwip and Patiala. This, however, they were able to do — one must emphasise — only by taking up the age-old agrarian revolutionary tasks for attacking landlordism, and giving "land to the tiller", and not by straying into the novel search for enemies among the substantial peasants. Even the significance of Kakdwip was limited to the *kisans*' dogged persistence with the battle in hand — their refusal to accept defeat — and did not go much further in terms of innovating tactics and styles of resistance. To an extent, however, the resistance did go beyond it in Patiala, though not very noticeably so, because of the

536. *Cross Roads* (English weekly), 13 May 1949.

537. The section on Sectarianism and Adventurism in the Kisan Front, "Draft Report of the West Bengal Provincial Organisation Committee, C.P.I., from the 2nd Congress till September 1951" (cyclo.), File No. 1948/52, P.C. Joshi Archives, J.N.U., New Delhi.

relative obscurity of the tumult there. The *kisan* volunteers of the Lal Communist Party managed to evade in Patiala all direct confrontations with the police and the army, and succeeded in concentrating their attacks only on the landlords and their hired *goondas*. This was a matter of policy for them, as Jagir Singh Jagga, one of the distinguished leaders elaborated: "Our volunteers had strict instructions not to confront the police. They were only to confront the landlords' guards and armed gangs, but not the Government forces," and whenever the police came in hot pursuit of the volunteers, the latter were directed to simply vanish from the scene.[538] That was the reason why, "apart from Kishengarh, there was no major clash with the police,"[539] no serious reverses leading to large scale casualties, and resultantly no great demoralisation. There was not much evidence to show that such tactics of selective confrontations were patiently and consistently applied for a considerable length of time in Kakdwip, or in Telengana (barring, of course, for "a few weeks" subsequent to the "police action")[540] where, no doubt, the landed magnates' position of strength had been greater, and their influence on the authorities stronger than that of the *Biswedars* in Patiala, and the capacity of the West Bengal Government and of the Military Governor of Hyderabad for stamping out rebellion vastly superior to that of the weak-kneed Patiala *riyasat* and the dishevelled PEPSU ministry. In the second place, the long-standing camaraderie of the Communists and the progressive nationalists, led by Brish Bhan, both in the *Muzara* and the Prajamandal movements in Patiala, stood the former in good stead in articulating wider popular support in favour of the *Muzaras*, especially centring round the Kishengarh trial. Although the Congress in the Sundarbans under Charuchandra Bhandari had not contained the similar progressive elements, and it was frankly pro-*Jotedar*, as well as instrumental

538. Mridula Mukherjee, "Communists and Peasants in Punjab: A Focus on the Muzara Movement in Patiala, 1937-53" in Bipan Chandra (ed.), *The Indian Left : Critical Appraisals*, New Delhi, 1983, pp. 411-12, footnote 12.

539. *Ibid.*

540. P. Sundarayya, *Telengana People's Struggle and Its Lessons*, Calcutta, 1972, p. 181.

in creating the *Seva Dal* against the *kisan* rebels, such did not seem exactly to be the case with the left-minded rank and file of the Hyderabad State Congress, particularly those who followed Swami Ramanand Tirtha and Govind Das, and who — despite their anti-Communism — were known to be interested in the Telengana *kisans'* causes, and curious about the Communist land distribution. The Sundarbans also had a distinct R.C.P.I. presence among peasants in certain localities, and so had Telengana of the Socialists' — though more prominently in Marathawada. In spite of their exaggerated hostility towards the Communists, which had grown in leaps and bounds over the "Quit India" movement, the Socialists were nevertheless well-entrenched in left-wing politics, and many among them more firmly so after independence. It was not wholly impossible for the Communist activists, locally at least in the fields of actions, and behind the barricades, to make overtures to them, on the basis of such leftist fundamentals as the abolition of landlordism and giving "land to the tiller". Would one pursue the cause of the agrarian revolution, or for that matter the ideals of the "New Democracy" and the "People's Democracy", fastidiously alone, without caring for any attempt at forging some kind of working unity with other seemingly anti-feudal forces, especially with some of those who appeared still to be active among the *kisan* masses in their own ways?

The Socialists did appear to be active on the *kisan* front throughout the period which the Communists dominated, and try their hands at the *kisan* mobilisation. A typical example was that of a *kisan* non-cooperation movement that they launched under the leadership of B.G. Durve in Akola *taluk* of Ahmadnagar (Rajur and Balvendi villages to be more specific) in May 1947 against the *sowcars'* taking over the mortgaged lands of peasants. The *kisans* refused to work for the *sowcars*, declined to supply milk and vegetables to them, and ostracised them in all other ways till the mortgaged lands were restored to their occupiers.[541] The agitation continued for some time, and seemed

541. Home (Sp.) Dept., Govt. of Bombay, File No. 540 (III) of 1947, Maharashtra State Archives, Bombay.

to have yielded the desired results when the majority of the *sowcars* found it convenient to agree to return the mortgaged lands.[542] In Bihar, where they always enjoyed a pre-eminence, the Socialist *kisan* activists took a prominent part in the resurgence of the *Bakasht* peasants' struggle either by setting up new *gram panchayats*, or by activising the existing ones. In one such *gram panchayat* in Jamui, Munghyr distict, they in fact were running at the beginning of 1948 some sort of a *gram sarkar* (village administration), effectively looking after the village affairs, settling the village disputes and imposing fines on the guilty.[543] Following their break-up with the Congress in March 1948 at the 6th national conference in Nasik, the Socialists seemed to have stepped up their agrarian agitational activities in leaps and bounds. By the middle of 1948 the Socialist *kisan* activists organised the *Bataidars* in Patna, Bihar, and the *Bhagchashis* in certain parts of Orissa for demanding increased crop-shares from the landlords.[544] They were also seen by the middle of 1949 to be rallying *kisans* in a number of places in the U.P. against the authorities' forcible grain procurement, and in Mayurbhanj in Orissa against the estate's forest, fishing and *Chowkidari* charges.[545] Similar agitations over the forest rights, as well as against rack-renting, were led by the Socialists in Betul and Bilaspur districts of the C.P. and Berar,[546] and against the Government drive for the procurement of grains in Madurai and Coimbatore in Tamil Nadu.[547] A more serious occurrence

542. *Ibid.*
543. Intelligence Branch Report on the Activities of the All India Socialist Party for the period, July 1947 to April 1948, Proc. Ministry of States, Government of India, File No. 373-P/48, 1948, N.A.I.
544. Intelligence Branch Report on the activities of the All India Socialist Party for the period, May to November 1948, Proc. Ministry of States, Government of India, File No. 16(1)-p/49, 1948, N.A.I.
545. Intelligence Branch Report on the activities of the All India Socialist Party for the period December 1948 to May 1949, Proc. Ministry of States, Government of India, File No. 1(79)-D/49, 1949, N.A.I.
546. Fortnightly Report, C.P. and Berar, 2nd half of May 1949, Ministry of States, Government of India, File No. 9(24)-P/49, 1949, N.A.I.
547. Fortnightly Reports, Madras, 1st half of January and 2nd half of February 1949, Ministry of States, Government of India, File No. 9(40)-P/49, 1949, N.A.I.

took place in Hissar district of East Punjab, where the Socialist *kisan* activists led the *Bataidars* to refuse crop-shares to the landlords, organised land *satyagrahas* to forestall ejectment proceedings against the *kisans*, courted arrests in large numbers, and eventually forced the authorities to look into the *kisan* grievances.[548]

Despite their differences at the leadership level with the Communists, and their setting up at the apex the Hind Kisan Panchayat in March 1949 as a parallel to the Communist-controlled All India Kisan Sabha, the Socialist *kisan* activists were in effect treading the same path that the Communists had trodden by taking up such issues as crop-shares, evictions, forcible grain procurements, recovery of mortgaged lands, and all this, too, by aspiring to organise the same *kisan* masses — the poor peasants, sharecroppers and agricultural labourers. What seemed to be true of the Communists and the Socialists on the *kisan* front, was also true to an extent in the case of the Forward Blocists, though their activities were limited to few pockets in Bihar, the C.P. and Berar, West Bengal and the U.P. There did not seem to be any reason why their *kisan* workers would not respond to the exhortations, if they were made at all for joining the Communist rank and file at the ground wrath level, and rather against the common opponents. Even if a certain unity was inconvenient at the "top" of the respective political parties, it was not impossible to achieve at the "bottom" — among the actual fighters in the battle-lines. If, hypothetically, an agrarian revolution was seriously attempted, in whatever manner, and wherever possible, by either the Socialists, or the Revolutionary Communists, or the Revolutionary Socialists, would the Communists not participate in it, whether their participation was liked or not, and try to escalate and intensify it? It seemed highly unlikely that those who had followed the "united front" line for full five years (1937-41), howsoever controversially, were innocent of the efficacy of building up a joint left front. Obviously the Communists decided to ignore the point between

548. Fortnightly Reports, East Punjab, 1st half of January, 1st half of February, 2nd half of February and 2nd half of June 1949, Ministry of States, Government of India, File No. 9(45)-P/49, 1949, N.A.I.

1947 and 1949 in their undue sectarian haste, in the mid-way in Andhra-Telengana, and from the very outset in the rest of the country. It was the sectarian brinkmanship — deduced dogmatically, and adventurously, from a concocted and jaundiced world view — that had ensured by the end of 1949 the stillborn Communist delivery of an agrarian revolution in India. It would perhaps not be utterly unjustifiable if one seemed reluctant to share Rabindranath Tagore's apparent faith in the shedding of "the valiant's flow of blood and the mother's roll of tears", not being lost ever in "the dust of our earth".[549] Had the intricate sense of confused emptiness, the complex feeling of sublimated futility, not been the post-Tagorean, and the post-world war phenomena for the Indian sensibilities?

549. Rabindranath Tagore's poem no. 37 of *Balaka* in *Vishwabharati Rabindra Rachanabali*, Vol.12, 1966, Calcutta, p. 7.

SCENE III
1950-51

The chronic political instability in PEPSU, in course of which the Rarewala ministry was replaced by a care-taker Government till May 1951, and by the Raghbir Singh ministry thereafter up to the general election of 1952, enabled the PEPSU Kisan Sabha to continue with the *Muzara* movement in comparative freedom. The *kisans'* refusal to pay *batai,* and determination to foil the landlords' attempts at their evictions persisted in Patiala, Sangrur and Barnala practically throughout 1950-1. Since very little effective support was forthcoming from a tottering administration, the *Biswedars* found it extremely difficult to defend their weak position, despite the bogey of the Communist "lawlessness" and of "parallel Communist Government" they raised,[550] the criminals they hired, and the arms and ammunitions they collected in "enormous quantity" for dealing with the *kisan* resistance.[551] A number of *Biswedars* had in fact come to the decision for making up with the *Muzaras* by voluntarily surrendering lands to the Kisan Sabhas, after being allowed to retain some for themselves.[552] Such a state of fluidity and confusion in PEPSU ran on even after the general elections of 1952 and till the President's rule was proclaimed over it in March 1953, eventually abolishing the *Biswedari* system with compensation.

In comparison with their comrades-in-arms in Patiala, the rebels in the Sundarbans were less fortunate against a strong and efficient West Bengal Government, who meticulously prepared from the beginning of 1950 for the suppression of the Kakdwip

550. Proceedings, Ministry of States, Government of India, File No. 15(36) PA/51 of 1951, N.A.I.

551. *Milap* (Urdu daily), 15 November 1951.

552. *Kishengarh: The Peasant's Heroic Defence of His Lands*, PEPSU Kisan Sabha, Sangrur, 1951, pp. 1-51.

rising. The Deputy Inspector General of Police, Intelligence Branch, H.N. Sarkar, was first sent to the Sundarbans to make a detailed survey of the affected area, and submit a report on counter-insurgency. On receiving his report, a high level committee, presided over by the Chief Minister, Dr. B.C. Roy himself, drew up an elaborate plan of action.[553] The over-all charge of the military operation was given to a military officer, one Major Chatterjee, whose services were lent to the Government of West Bengal as Additional District Magistrate of the 24-Parganas.[554] Strong police contingents were rushed to Kakdwip as reinforcements, and troops moved simultaneously to encircle an area of 40 square miles. Curfew was clamped on the volatile spots, and combing operations began in the "disturbed" villages on the lines on which the Malcolm Mcdonald regime had reportedly been proceeding against the Communist insurgents in Malaya. A large number of suspects were rounded up, the inhabitants tortured to give out information about the absconders, and forced to carry "passes" issued by the authorities. By the first quarter of 1950, the condition in Kakdwip was believed in the Governmental circles to have vastly improved. In the succeeding months the *Jotedars*, who had fled from the villages, gradually started returning. The local Congress also became active in the area, and set up under the police protection a volunteer organisation to work for "peace" in the region. The rich and the "middle" peasants, being rather anxious to see the return of normalcy, did not appear to resent the Government measures very much. Even the *Bargadars* and the *khetmajdoors*, who had developed a certain mute misunderstanding between themselves over the issue of "proletarian leadership", appeared to have considerably lost their previous enthusiasm for a fight with vastly superior and ruthless Government forces. The Action Committees, packed mainly with the Communist Party members, lost control generally, and the arrest

553. *Matamat* (Bengali weekly), 15 January 1950.

554. Secret Fortnightly Report, 1st half of January 1950, Home Poll. Dept., Government of West Bengal, File No. 109/1950, West Bengal State Archives, Calcutta.

of the key committee members tended to paralyse the local organisations. Barring stray incidents of resistance, essentially of adventurist and individualist nature, the Kakdwip rising subsided by the middle of 1950. The last minute effort of the Communists to impart guerilla training to the Kakdwip rebels could not produce any result.[555] It had already been too late, and the police and the army were in full command of the Sundarbans. By August 1950, all resistance in Kakdwip apparently petered out, though some fugitive Communist local leaders were still at large, desperately trying to re-group their straggly followers. Their exercise naturally remained a sterile one, though the rural poor lovingly protected, and fondly remembered them for long.

Unlike the authorities' suppression of the rising in Kakdwip, their crack-down on the rebels in Telengana could by no stretch of imagination be a certain walk-over. It never really was for full two years (between October 1949 and October 1951), costing the Hyderabad and the central Governments very dearly, indeed, in terms of men and money. About Rs. $8^1/_2$ crores, or 85 millions (6 for the military[556] and $2^1/_2$ for the special armed police[557]) had to be spent over and above the normal expenses for maintaining law and order in Hyderabad. About 800 were killed on the official side (18 policemen, 92 employees of the civil departments and 694 other employees),[558] excluding, of course, the casualty figure of the military. On the Telengana rebels' side 765 had been killed,[559] 4,000 arrested (of which 2,658 seemed to have been released from time to time) and 66 condemned to death[560]

555. Major Jaipal Singh was brought to Kakdwip at this point to organise and train guerilla squads. The visit, however, was not very productive.
556. Note by S. Narayanaswamy of 23.11.50, Proc. Ministry of States, Government of India, File No. 18(52)-H/50, 1950, N.A.I.
557. Home Ministry's reply to the question of Shri Ramacher in Parliament, dated 18.12.50, Proc. Ministry of States, Government of India, File No. 18(73)-H, 1950, N.A.I.
558. *Ibid.*
559. Proc. Ministry of States, Government of India, 1 August 1950, Proc. Ministry of States, Govt. of India, File No. 5(31)-H/50, 1950, N.A.I.
560. Proc. Ministry of States, Govt. of India, File No. 5(31)-H/50, N.A.I. The Communists, however claimed that death sentences were passed originally against 108. See *Cross Roads* (English weekly), 5 May 1950.

by the Special Tribunals set up by the Hyderabad Government towards the end of 1948. The Telengana death sentences, as well as the 45 years' prison sentence on Dilli Venkadu of Nalgonda, aged 13 years, created a furore not only in India, but also abroad, including protests from the British M.P.s, the International Association of Democratic Lawyers and the Parisi-based Women's International Democratic Federation. Appeals against all these sentences were upheld by the High Court and the Supreme Court, and the authorities eventually decided to send Venkadu to a reformatory.[561] Although the army rule in Hyderabad was replaced with a civil administration in February 1950, its stark occupational military nature, as well as its military way of functioning in Telengana, remained practically intact. Despite the fanfare over the withdrawal of troops, the garrisons continued to operate at centres like Nalgonda and Warangal, and at least 5 battalions and 1 company of the Indian army did appear to have taken part in the campaigns against the peasant guerillas in Telengana throughout 1950-51.[562] The campaigns were conducted by a troika of Nanjappa (who had been inducted into the civil service from the army, and made Special Commissioner of the affected Telengana districts), Khot (who had been appointed the Deputy Inspector General of Police of Hyderabad) and Venkatavardhan (who had been promoted to the post of Central Intelligence Officer in Hyderabad) on the lines the British followed under General Briggs in Malaya against the Communist guerillas. Nanjappa had no doubt that the Communist problem in Hyderabad was "comparable to that of Malaya", and called for similar remedies.[563] The remedies included extraction of intelligence about the guerillas from the villagers, breaking the contacts between the villagers and the guerillas, commanding the communication routes through which the guerillas linked themselves with each other and the outside

561. Govt. of Hyderabad to Ministry of States, Govt. of India, 1 August 1950, Proc. Ministry of States, File No. 5(31)-H/50, 1950, N.A.I.

562. Answer to Question by Shri Ramcher in Parliament on 18.12.50, Proc. Ministry of States, Government of India, File No. 18(73)-H/50, 1950, N.A.I.

563. *The Statesman* (English daily), 9 May 1950.

world, and establishing concentration camps for shifting a particular local population in its entirety, such as the Lambadis and Koyas from the hilly and forest tracts where the guerillas had taken refuge, and leading incursions into the rebels' jungle hide-outs. Along with this relentless use of the sticks, the authorities were also able to dangle a few carrots before the peasantry for enticing it away from the Communists — the Jagir Abolition Regulation in August 1949, the appointment of an Agrarian Enquiry Commission soon thereafter, and a liberal Hyderabad tenancy legislation in 1951. Simultaneously the *Patel-Patwaris* and the *Deshmukhs* were directed to assume a low profile, the schools and health centres to start their normal working, and the local administration to appear as if nothing had happened in the meantime. It was between April and June 1951 came Vinoba Bhave on his mission to apply the balm of peace for healing the wounds of rural Telengana. The outcome of his mission not only pleased the Indian Prime Minister,[564] but also satisfied the troika in Telengana for "having useful effect from the propaganda point of view".[565]

To begin with, the peasant guerillas' retreat in 1949-50 into the forest areas of Mahboobnagar, Adilabad and Warangal districts seemed not only safe, but also sound for building up strategic bases. The tribal masses enthusiastically veered round them, attacked the landlords of the areas, and seized their grains and lands. But once the Government forces followed the rebels there, as they were bound to do sooner or later, and the police and military camps sprang up on the forest outskirts, the upsurge gradually receded, forcing the guerillas to fall back upon defensive positions. Defending themselves in the jungle terrains did not prove to be difficult for the rebels, and their existence was not really at stake among the hard-pressed yet sympathetic population. Their actual difficulty apparently lay in the invisibility of a silver-lining, either in political mobility or in military break-through. Outnumbered and out-gunned, as well as closely

564. Nehru to Gopalaswamy Ayyangar, Minister of States, 12 May 1951, Proc.. Ministry of States, Government of India, File No. 16(8)-H/51, 1951, N.A.I.

565. Nanjappa's Fortnightly Report for 2nd half of April 1951, Hyderabad, *ibid.*

marked by the opponents, their military exploits gradually shrank in the hills and dales to small operational zones. It could not have been otherwise after their retreat from the plains of Nalgonda, Warangal and Khammam, where they might have operated *in cognito* like "fishes in the water", among a populace already steeled under repression. Since military offensive was extremely hazardous against the heavily manned camps of the Government forces, the guerilla squad actions were limited to attacks on the enemy agents and individual landlords. Too many attacks on individuals with too few participating in them, were bound to affect the popular character of the guerilla movement adversely, and bring it down from the height of the toiling masses' partisanship to the level of individual terrorism. Even in such unenviable position, the peasant guerillas might have avoided the mire of individual terror if their political directions had been abundantly clear, and they knew what exactly should be done. Unfortunately for them, the C.P.I. was in a state of utter ideological and organisational quandary throughout 1950, following the international Communist movement's denunciation of the Ranadive-led C.P.I.'s political line in an editorial of the 27 January 1951 issue of *For a Lasting Peace, For a People's Democracy*, the organ of the Information Bureau of the Communist and Workers' Parties. Consequently, by May 1950, B.T. Ranadive had to make room for C. Rajeshwar Rao as the General Secretary of the C.P.I. and the old Politbureau was replaced with a new one. The change-over, however, did not resolve the vexatious issues confronting the party, rather it opened up the floodgates of controversies, parallel political lines and factional activities. The impasse was so grave that the Indian Communists had to approach the great arbiter — the C.P.S.U.(B) — in Moscow for political guidance. Following the Moscow deliberations, the C.P.I. leadership was changed again in May 1951 by the reconstitution of the Politbureau and the replacement of C.Rajeshwar Rao by Ajoy Kumar Ghosh as General Secretary, to give effect to a new policy. A very vague knowledge of some of these dramatic developments at the top, and that, too, under the smokescreen of secrecy, further confused the peasant guerillas in their Telengana wilderness. With the stooping down of their morale, the deserting out of their ranks and the creeping in doubt about their future, the Communist peasant guerillas in Telengana were not in a position to continue the unequal fight much longer. On 21 October 1951 the Telengana armed struggle was withdrawn unconditionally in the elusive hope perhaps that "Tomorrow is another day," and that "wherever life has not died out, it staggers to its feet again".[566]

CURTAINS

566. Bertolt Brecht, *Mother Courage and Her Children*, London (Methuen Student Edition), 1983, p. 88.

EPILOGUE

This drama is woven around the theme of an agrarian revolution in India which the leftists and their rural poor followers wished to bring about simultaneously with the victory of the popular forces against imperialism. The final output of the anti-imperialist struggle, or the Indian independence movement, along with the partitioning of the subcontinent, did not satisfy many, and had actually annoyed the leftists and their sympathisers. They were sore not only because of what they perceived to be the neo-colonialist conspiracy between imperialism and the Indian vested interests for a negotiated transference of power in August 1947, but also on account of their being unable to meaningfully influence the crucial course of events, and to extract some kind of a say in the negotiations, despite the selfless devotion with which they tried for quarter of a century to serve the causes of the people. The gradual building up in their general mood of frustration coincided throughout with the leftists' falling short in particular of the avowed target of radical agrarian transformation — the culmination of the "total" struggles, instead of the mere "partial" ones. The daring and somewhat desperate bid of some of them for setting the agrarian revolution in motion did take off the ground at times and in certain places, but only to be crashed eventually in the performance of aerobatics through hazardous techniques. The hope for revolutionising agrarian society that the leftists raised in the countryside, the care that they took in mobilising the poor *kisan* categories for its pursuance, the combat that they undertook alongside the rural poor for its achievement, and finally the demoralising setback that they encountered at the end of a hectic period of 18 years, had a deep tragical poignancy about them — akin to nemesis the valiant must suffer in the Attic tragedies. Since this narration of dramatic agrarian politics is a product of some historical enquiries which do not count on nemesis, it becomes obligatory for the enquirer to try to understand why occurrences occurred the way they in fact did, what prevented an agrarian revolution on the leftist model from taking place in India, and who had been responsible for the splendid fiasco, and to what extent. The social and economic power the landlordism and usurious capital exercised, the political and administrative support the colonial set-up offered to them, the intervention and dislocation the external exigencies so often effected within the country, the compulsion and contrariness the Indian independence movement brought to bear upon at various levels — had all contributed to the common fortunes of the left and the rural poor, and therefore, these have been noted as far as practicable. In the ultimate analysis, however, it is the conduct of the revolutionaries that has been found to have played the most decisive role in any revolutionary endeavour — in its success as much as in its failure. Consequently, the functioning of the agrarian revolutionaries in India between 1934 and 1951 deserved the enquirer's stringent scrutiny, and received perhaps the scrutiniser's hardest observation on the basis of the discernible facts and the programmatic standards the leftists set for themselves. It could not have been otherwise, for any observer of historical developments ought to try to rise above his or her predispositions and predilections in order to attain a reasonable degree of objectivity, which is essential for an enquiry worth its name.

Any attempt to critically review the leftists' advances and reverses on the *kisan* front is to put their revolutionary belligerency in its overall perspective, and not to take away from them the credit for demonstrating the basic heroic quality — the passion to fight for the just causes. Heroes, however, do fail and falter, and despite all their heroism, they are unable sometimes to cope with the societal, familial and existential crises, leading to the enactment of tragedies of various proportions. The dramatic effect of tragedy of the major characters is considerably more than that of the minor ones, and the distinction between the two types depends on the values they represent in the drama and the limelight they enjoy on the stage. Considering the egalitarian image in popular perception, and judging by the public attention they succeeded in inviting on themselves — of course, in due proportion to their more formidable competitors on the Indian political stage — the leftists do appear generally in the highly complicated colonial setting to have made the grade of the major characters. Contrary to certain beliefs that their position often turned difficult because they conçeded either too little to Gandhian nationalism,[1] or too much to it, and diluted the speciality,[2] one finds the leftists to have steadily gained in influence from 1936 onwards, especially among the rural poor — their genuine constituency. Their organisation seemed in the countryside to be expanding, activities increasing and militant tempers rising, except for an interregnum between 1942 and 1944 when they preferred the "Quit India" and the "people's war" slogans to the anti-feudal war-cries, and during which the scarcities and famines struck India. The leftists apparently had not faced any particular difficulty in reviving their agrarian revolutionary endeavours in 1944, and neither the post-"Quit India" isolation, nor the sniffing governmental hounding could prevent them from rallying the rural poor. Even the abrupt worsening of the communal situation did not prove to be insurmountably obstructive to the poor peasants' mobilisation against the landlord-*mahajan*-bureaucrat combine's tyranny. There is also no evidence that the class based leftist *kisan* consolidation had run into any serious trouble in the community and caste-based rural societies, or that the principle of class struggle — the leftist panacea for all human disorders — floundered palpably in tiding over the locally divisive trends. It will, of course, be hypothetical to consider what might have happened if the leftists harped between 1936 and 1951 on the social reality of caste and class convergences in the Indian countryside — whether such articulations could have led to the density of the agrarian revolution, or its diffusion. Rather it will be worth his or her while to take note of the fact that the leftists usually tried — in accordance with their

1. See "Conclusion", Bhagwan Josh, *Struggle for Hegemony : The Colonial State, The Left and the National Movement*, Vol. II (1934-41), New Delhi, 1992.
2 See "Conclusion", Sanjay Seth, *Marxist Theory and Nationalist Politics: The Case of Colonial India*, New Delhi, 1995.

ideology — as much to rise above the caste considerations as to go beyond the class interests. In both these they apparently made considerable progress, notwithstanding such utterly unfounded allegation of "upper-casteism" against the Bihar Swamiites,[3] or such closely suspected weakness of the U.P. Congress Socialists' for the "small" *Zamindars*, the Punjab Communists' for the "middle" peasants,[4] and the Bengal radicals' for the rentier middle class. Their exertions to de-caste and de-class themselves seemed in fact to have constituted the vital clue to the left-wing leadership entry into the rural poor's tormented, claustrophobic social space.

The breaking in of leftism upon the countryside was largely facilitated by its practitioners' frequent self-banishment from urbanity to rusticity, readiness to share in the rugged life of the lowly and the outcaste, contentment in the "forbidden" partake of their food and drinks, constancy to treat them with the hitherto unheard of civility, and above all, conviction in their ability to mould a promising future. Appreciating all these, the rural masses were also struck by the leftist volunteers' anxiety for organising relief, howsoever meagre in extent, at times of obvious physical peril — during droughts, scarcities, floods and famines. But what impressed the poor *kisans* most in their constricted rural world were the messages the radicals brought from outside, the hopes they raised, the expectations they nurtured and the dreams they peddled. Since the dreams appeared to be realistic, the hopes and expectations well within reach, and the messages loud and clear, the rural poor hardly

3. This hallucination has found expression in two articles by "D.N.", "Swami Sahajanand and the Kisan Sabha" and "Iconoclasm is Necessary" in the *Economic and Political Weekly*, 1 April and 19 August 1989, pp. 660-2 and 1921-3, respectively.
4. This was what Sohan Singh Josh, the eminent Communist leader of Punjab, thought to be true during a discussion with the author on 24 April 1982.

hesitated in following the lead wherever the leftists succeeded in giving it. Intrigued initially at the prospective liberators' nonchalance and non-conformism,[5] the rural masses started admiring and loving them, and they soon got carried away by the novelty and the *force majeure* of leftism. The trend explains how the "outsiders" — the predominantly upper caste, petty bourgeois, school and college educated, urbane and semi-urbane political activists — were readily accepted by the "insiders" and why, while working together, the former's sway had become so complete over the latter. The "outsiders", whether they originated in the villages, or in the towns and cities, were the transmitters of fresh ideas from the world beyond the *kisans*' relatively closed domain. Their superiority as political ideologues, and as carriers of unrestful urban defiance was so overwhelming that the illiterate or semi-literate poor *kisans* — under the grinding of the colonial system, and with a nebulosity of yearnin -- hardly had any alternative but to rely on their gorgeous promises and abide by their spirited commands. The scope for any autonomous action under this circumstance, at the conjunction of radical undertakings and popular perceptions,[6] was severely limited, and barring the lone case of the Kakdwip peasants in

5. An account of Moni Sinha, the renowned *kisan* leader of Bengal, is pointingly illustrative. While addressing a gathering of the *Tanka* cultivators in November 1937, he laid stress on the unity of *kisans*, without which no resistance against their exploiters could be organised. His repeated use of the term "*kisan* unity" evoked derisive laughter from his *kisan* listeners. They noisily pointed out to him that the unity of *kisans* of various sorts, from different villages, castes and communities was simply not possible, as it would never be possible to keep in one bucket frogs from different ponds and marshy plots. "What do you think the frogs will do"? they asked Sinha, and assertively observed: "The frogs will jump out of the bucket, and run in different directions". Sinha thunderingly retorted: "But the *kisans* are not frogs, they are human beings". This his listeners did not remember, that human beings could do a lot which frogs could not. The meeting thereafter maintained a profound silence for sometime. See Moni Sinha, *Jeeban Sangram* (in Bengali), Dacca, 1983, pp. 48-9.
6. Inukonda Thirumali, has dealt with the popular perceptions — the socio-cultural angles more than the economic viewpoints — in his "Lords and Peasants in Telengana, 1920-48: An Enquiry into the People's Uprising in Nalgonda and Warangal Districts", Ph.D. thesis, Centre for Historical Studies, School of Social Sciences, Jawaharlal Nehru University, New Delhi, 1991.

November 1947, only the tribal poor in the remote corners, and that, too, beyond the pale of leftist influence, had revealed some streaks of autonomy. The indomitable Worlis' free play to a certain extent in Thana, in the midst of their following the Communist line, was a distinctive exception to the general run of the *kisan* masses' dependence on the leftist ideologues and mobilisers. The wholesale reliance apparently was responsible for much of the rural poor's predicament between 1942 and 1944 when their leftist mentors unilaterally withdrew from the battle scenes. Called upon to fend for themselves at that juncture, they did not seem to know exactly how to deal with the adversities and adversaries, to figure out the plan of action on the basis of the lessons already learnt, and rise above the desperate acts of sporadic social brigandage. The situation, however, drastically changed with the left political activists' return to the front-lines in 1944-5 and the resumption of the leftist-led battles in which the rural poor energetically joined and resolutely fought. Their handicap in theoretical skill, and dazzlement under demagogic brilliance did not, however, mean that the poor *kisans* were incapable either of producing their own leaders at the grass-roots, or of taking the initiative at the local levels. Instances of such initiative and leadership quality, as had been shown by the poor *kisans*, as well as the rank and file of the left, are proofs of the vibrant, dynamic nature of the agrarian revolutionary movement.

The dynamism of the participants that a movement generates, the feasibility of realising the goal it projects, and the dedication of the organisers that it reveals, do contribute richly to its onward march, but they do not by themselves guarantee its result. The outcome of a movement — whether it turns out to be inspiring, or despairing — is equity-wise the moral and political responsibility of those who have built it up, and who have committed themselves and their following to its cause. Fortunately for the agrarian revolutionaries in India between 1934 and 1951, the historical enquiries into all the significant human enterprises always try to take cognisance of both their achievements and aspirations, their victories and defeats — the heroic losses in particular.

SELECT BIBLIOGRAPHY

A. OFFICIAL PAPERS

I. National Archives of India, New Delhi:

1. Home Political Department Files (including Fortnightly Reports), 1932-1947.
2. Home Department Public Files, 1933-1947.
3. Proceedings of the Ministry of States (including Fort-nightly Reports), 1948-1952.
4. Proceedings of the Political Department, Ministry of States, 1947-1952.
5. Proceedings of the Ministry of Home Affairs, 1948-1952.
6. Crown Representative Records (microfilm), 1946-1947.

II. State Archives, West Bengal, Calcutta:

1. Home (Political) Department Files (including Fortnightly Reports), 1934-1950.
2. Revenue Department (Land Revenue Branch) Files, 1935-1947.

III. State Archives, Uttar Pradesh, Lucknow:

1. Political Department Files, 1935-1947.
2. General Administration Department Files, 1935-1947.
3. Police Department Files, 1935-1947.

IV. State Archives, Maharashtra, Bombay:

1. Home (Special) Department Files, 1934-1948.
2. Home (Political) Department Files, 1934-1940.

V. State Archives, Tamil Nadu, Madras:

1. Public Department Files (including Fortnightly Reports), 1934-1951.
2. R.I. (Confidential) Section, Under-Secretary's Safe Secret Files, 1934-1951.

VI. State Archives, Bihar, Patna:

1. Home Political Department (Special Section) Files, 1934-1948.

VII. State Archives, Andhra Pradesh, Hyderabad:

1. Proceedings of the Revenue Department, 1940-47.
2. The Report on the Administration of H.E.H. the Nizam's Dominions, Hyderabad, 1940-1942.

B. NON-OFFICIAL PAPERS

I. Central Archives, Communist Party of India, Ajoy Bhavan, New Delhi:

1. Party Documents, 1934-1951.
2. Printed Reports of the All India Kisan Sabha Sessions, 1936-1947.
3. Leftist Political Pamphlets, 1934-1951.
4. Some Cyclostyled, as well as Printed, Copies of *Communist* (English monthly), 1937-1941.

II. P.C. Joshi Archives, Jawaharlal Nehru University, New Delhi:

1. Documents on the Communist Movement in India, 1935-1951.
2. Pamphlets of the Left Political Parties, 1936-1951.

III. Nehru Memorial Museum and Library, New Delhi:

1. Institutional Papers

a. All India Congress Committee, 1934-1947.
b. Bombay Provincial Congress Committee, 1934-1947.
c. Tamil Nadu Congress Committee , 1934-1947.
d. Uttar Pradesh Congress Committee (microfilm), 1934-1947.
e. Peasant Movement, 1929-1949 (copies of 28 pamphlets and reports).

2. Individual Papers

a. Jayaprakash Narayan, 1934-1947.
b. Swami Sahajanand Saraswati, 1930-1951 (major part in microfilm)
c M.N. Roy (microfilm), 1934-1950.
d. Jainarayan Vyas, 1930-1947.
e. Dr Rajendra Prasad, 1934-1941 (microfilm), and the period thereafter at the National Archives of India, New Delhi.
f. Sri Prakasa, 1937-1947.
g. Anugraha Narayan Sinha, 1937-1940.
h. Ramnandan Mishra, 1936-1951.
i. Indulal Yajnik, 1936-1947.

3. Oral History Transcripts

a. Dr Gangadhar Adhikari.
b. B.P.L. Bedi.
c. S.V. Ghate.
d. Dr Sampurnanand.
e. Achyut Patwardhan.
f. P. Sundarayya.
g. Ramanand Tiwari.
h. Sazzad Zaheer.

C. NEWSPAPERS AND PERIODICALS

Advance (English daily), 1933-1934.
Amrita Bazar Patrika (English daily), 1945-1948.
Ananda Bazar Patrika (Bengali daily), 1939-1950.
Bombay Chronicle (English daily), 1945-1947.
Bombay Sentinel (English daily), 1940-1948.
Communist (English weekly), 1947-50.
Congress Socialist (English weekly), 1934-1938.
Cross Roads (English weekly), 1949-1952.
Harijan (English weekly), 1936-1947.
Hindu (English daily), 1937-1951.
Hindustan Times (English daily), 1934-1947.
Hitavad (English tri-weekly up to 1936 and daily from 1943), 1940-1950.
Hunkar (Hindi weekly), 1942-1950.
Independent India (English weekly), 1938-1947.
International Press Correspondence (English weekly), 1933-1937.
Jana Juddha (Bengali weekly), 1943-1945.
Jana Shakti (Tamil weekly), 1947-1948.
Janta (Hindi weekly), 1938-1945.
Janata (English weekly), 1946-1948.
Jugantar (Bengali daily), 1942-1945.
Kisan Bulletins (issued by the All India Kisan Sabha bi-weekly in English as supplementaries to the *Congress Socialist* between 16 April 1936 and 22 July 1938, and occasionally as reprints in the *People's War* from 4 July 1942).

Krishna Patrika (Telugu weekly), 1937-1940.
Labour Monthly (English monthly), 1946-1947.
Manjil (Bengali weekly), 1949.
Matamat (Bengali weekly), 1950-1951.
Milap (Urdu daily), 1950-1951.
Modern Review (English monthly), 1936-1947.
National Front (English weekly), 1938-1940.
National Herald (English daily), 1938-1942.
New Age (English monthly), 1936-1939.
Pacific Affairs (English monthly), 1951.
People's Age (English weekly), 1945-1947.
People's War (English daily), 1941-1945.
Sangharsh (Hindi weekly), 1937-1941.
Searchlight (English daily), 1936-1947.
Shibir (Bengali weekly), 1949.
Socialist (English monthly), 1939.
Statesman (English daily), 1945-1947.
Swadhinata (Bengali daily), 1945-1947 and 1951.
Times of India (English daily), 1940-1947.
Tribune (English daily), 1937-1947.
Zamin Ryot (English weekly), 1937-1939.

D. REPORTS AND COMPILATIONS

The Imperial Gazetteer of India, Vols. IX, XXIII and XXIV, Oxford, 1908.
The Report of the Agricultural Commission, 1927, Government of India, Vol.1, Delhi, 1928.
Economic Investigations in the Hyderabad State, 1929-1930, Vols. I-III, S.K. Iyengar, Hyderabad Government of the Nizam, Hyderabad, 1930.
Census of India, 1931, 1941 and 1951.
Indian Annual Register, N. Mitra (ed.), 1933-1947.
Annual Reports of the Punjab Administration, 1934-35 to 1938-39.
Report on the General Administration of the United Provinces, 1934-1947.

Annual Report of the Director of Agriculture, Bombay Presidency, 1934-1947.

Administration Report of the Government of Madras, 1935-1947.

Report of the United Provinces Congress Agrarian Reforms Enquiry Committee, 1936.

Agricultural Indebtedness in H.E.H. the Nizam's Dominions, S.M. Bharucha, Hyderabad, 1937.

Report on the Administration of Bengal, 1937-1947.

Report on the Administration of the Police in the Madras Presidency, 1937-1947.

Report on the Administration of the Department of Agriculture in the Madras Presidency, 1937-1947.

Report on the Administration of the Bombay Presidency, 1937-1947.

The U.P. Government at Work, July 1937-June 1938, Department of Public Information, Government of the U.P., no date.

Provincial Autonomy: Ministers and Parties in Assam (1937-1945), Bureau of Public Information, Government of India, 1946.

Annual Report of Land Revenue Administration in the Punjab, 1938-39 to 1944-45.

Report of the Land Revenue (Floud) Commission, Bengal, 1938-1940, Alipore, 1940.

Annual Report of the All India Kisan Sabha, 1939-1940, Bombay.

Five Years of Provincial Autonomy, Punjab Information Bureau, Punjab Government, Lahore, 1942.

Congress Responsibility for the Disturbances of 1942-43, R. Tottenham, Government of India, Delhi, 1943.

Famine Enquiry (Woodhead) Commission Report on Bengal, Delhi, 1945.

Agricultural Statistics by Plot to Plot Enumeration, H.S.M. Ishaque, Calcutta, 1945.

Sample Survey of the After-Effects of the Bengal Famine of 1943, Indian Statistical Institute, Calcutta, 1946.

Report of the U.P. Zamindari Abolition Committee, Vol.1, Allahabad, 1948.

White Paper on Hyderabad, Government of India, Hyderabad, 1948.

Communist Violence in India, Government of India, New Delhi, September 1949.

Communist Crimes in Hyderabad, Government of India, Hyderabad, 1950.

Rural Economic Enquiries in the Hyderabad State, 1949-1951, S.K. Iyengar, Hyderabad Government, Hyderabad, 1951.

Report of All India Rural Credit Survey, Delhi, 1954.

Operation Polo: The Police Action in Hyderabad, 1948, S.N. Prasad (ed.), Historical Section, Ministry of Defence, Government of India, Delhi, 1972.

North-West Frontier Province Legislative Assembly Debates, Peshawar, 1938, Vol. IV.

E. CONTEMPORARY TRACTS AND BOOKLETS

Bihar Prantiya Kisan Sabha ki Report (Hindi), November 1929-November 1935.

Kisan Sabha Aur Kashtkari Kanoon Samsodhan (Hindi), Awadheshwar Prasad Sinha, 1935.

Swaraj Kiun Aur Keise (Hindi), Dr. Rammanohar Lohia's Presidential Address at the Second Bihar Provincial Socialist Conference, 5 December 1936.

Presidential Address by N.G. Ranga, 2nd session, All India Kisan Sabha, Faizpur, December 1936.

Peasants and Congress, N.G. Ranga, 1938.

The Other Side of the Shield, Swami Sahajanand Saraswati, 1938.

Presidential Address by Swami Sahajanand Saraswati, 3rd session, All India Kisan Sabha, Comilla, May 1938.

Kisan Handbook, All India Kisan Sabha, 1938.

Peasants' Struggle at Kalipatnam (Andhra), 1939.

Rent Reduction in Bihar : How It Works, Swami Sahajanand Saraswati, 1939.

Memorandum on the Permanent Settlement, Bengal ProvincialKisan Sabha to the Land Revenue (Floud) Commission, 1939.

The League of Radical Congressmen: Declaration of Objects and the Constitution, Bombay 1939.

History of Kisan Movement, N.G. Ranga and Swami Sahajanand Saraswati, 1939.

Speech of Jadunandan Sharma, Chairman, Reception Committee, 4th session, All India Kisan Sabha, Gaya, April 1939.

Presidential Address by Narendra Deva, 4th session, All India Kisan Sabha, Gaya, April 1939.

All India Kisan Sabha Constitution as Adopted in June 1939 and April 1943.

Istehar (in Bengali), Bangiya Pradeshik Krishak Sabha, 1940.

Political Line Adopted at the 2nd Party Congress, Communist League of India (Soumyendra Nath Tagore), March 1940.

Intensify National Struggle : On the Revolutionary Defence of U.S.S.R. (Revolutionary Socialist Party), Calcutta, 1941.

Jagirulaloni Sthitigatulu (Telugu), Suravaram Pratapa Reddy, Hyderabad, 1941.

Is the War Indivisible, "A Congress Socialist", Patna, 1942.

The War: Imperialist or People's? Narendra Deva, Bombay, 1942.

Jang Aur Rastriya Ladai (Hindi), Swami Sahajanand Saraswati, 1942.

Presidential Address by Swami Sahajanand Saraswati, Bihar Provincial Kisan Conference, 9th session, Sherghati, Gaya, April 1942.

Bihar Prantiya Kisan Sabha Ki Report (Hindi), Mathura Prasad Tiwari, 1942.

Presidential Address by Indulal Yajnik, 6th session, All India Kisan Sabha, Bihta, May 1942.

The Congress and the Kisan Sabha, Swami Sahajanand Saraswati, Patna, 1942.

Report of Provincial Kisan Conference (Bengali), Bangiya Pradeshik Krishak Sabha, 6th session, Nalitabari, May 1943.

A Short History of Peasant Movement in Kerala, E.M.S. Namboodiripad, 1943.

With Ploughshare and Sickle : Kisan Sabha in the Campaign for Food, E.M.S. Namboodiripad, 1943.

Kisans March For Food and Freedom, E.M.S. Namboodiripad, 1943.

Kranti Aur Samyukta Morcha (Hindi), Swami Sahajanand Saraswati, 1943.

Presidential Address by Bankim Mukherji, 7th session, All India Kisan Sabha, Bhakra-Kalan, April 1943.

Save Bengal's Two Crores, People's Relief Committee, 1943-44.

Congress-Leaguer Milan Chai (Bengali), Pradeshik Krishak Sabha, 1944.

Speech of Shri Vasudeva Rao, Chairman, Reception Committee, 8th session, All India Kisan Sabha, Bezwada, March 1994.

Slogans of Netrakona : Report of the 9th Annual session of the All India Kisan Sabha, Mymensingh, April 1945.

Presidential Address by Muzaffar Ahmad, 9th session, All India Kisan Sabha, Netrakona, April 1945.

Rural Bengal in Ruins, Bhowani Sen, Bombay, 1945.

Bengal Today, Speech of Moni Sinha, Chairman, Reception Committee, 9th session, All India Congress Committee, Netrakona, April 1945.

New Charter of Kisan Demands, All India Kisan Sabha, October 1945.

Conditions of Telengana and Deshmukhs' Exploitation in Nalgonda and Warangal, Telengana Communist Party, Bezwada(?), 1945(?)

A Move For the Formation of an All India Organisation for the Kisan at the Initiative of Purushottam Das Tandon, August 1945.

Memorandum of Bengal Provincial Kisan Sabha to the Government of Bengal on Rehabilitation, Calcutta, October 1945.

Langal Jar Jami Tar, and *Krishak Kahake Vote Dibe* (Bengali), Pradeshik Krishak Sabha, 1946.

Sangathanik Patra (Bengali), Bangiya Pradeshik Krishak Sabha, October 1946.

Abolition of Zamindari: How to Achieve It, Sawmi Sahajananad Saraswati, 1946.

Forward Bloc: Programme and Post-War Revolution, Bombay, 1946.

Hyderabadu Samasthanamlo Vettichakiri (Telugu), D.V. Rao, Bezwada, 1946.

Andhralo Rayatu Udyamam (Telugu), N. Prasada Rao, Hyderabad, 1946.

Warangallu Zilla Rayatu Poratalu (Telugu), P. Venkataramanaya, Bezwada, 1946.

Janagaon Prajala Virochita Poratalu (Telugu), D.V. Rao, Bezwada, 1946.

Fighting Famine and Landlordism, All India Kisan Sabha, January 1947

Jamir Ladai (Bengali), Krishna Benode Roy, Calcutta, 1947.

Bakasht Mahamari Aur Uska Achook Ilaaz (Hindi), Jadunandan Sharma, Allahabad, 1947.

Kisan Sabha Ke Sansmaran (Hindi), Swami Sahajanand Saraswati, Patna, 1947.

Ab Kya Ho (Hindi), Swami Sahajanand Saraswati, Patna, 1947.

A.I.K.S. Organisational Reportage, No.1, 1947-48, Sikandra Rao Decisions, 10th session of All India Kisan Sabha.

Arrah Summons to Struggle, All India Forward Bloc, Bombay, January 1947.

Programme, Socialist Party, Bombay, 1947.

How to Abolish Landlordism, All India Kisan Sabha, January 1947.

Tebhagar Dabi Kayem Karo (Bengali), Bangiya Pradeshik Krishak Sabha, Calcutta, 1947.

Tebhaga O Maddhabitta, and *Krishak O Bhagchashi Ladai Jitilo* (Bengali), Bangiya Pradeshik Krishak Sabha, Calcutta, October 1948.

Banglar Krishite Dhanatantrer Vikash (Bengali), "Rabindra Gupta", Calcutta, October 1948.

The Hour Has Struck, Soumyendra Nath Tagore, Calcutta, 1949.

Kisans and Communists, N.G. Ranga, 1949.

The Programme to End Poverty, Rammanohar Lohia, Bombay, 1950.

Kisan Sabhani Sawari (Gujarati), Indulal Yajnik, Bombay, 1951.

The Third camp in World Affairs, Rammanohar Lohia, Bombay, 1950.

Peasant Question in Kerala, S. Parameswaran, 1951.
Kishengarh: The Peasant's Heroic Defence of His Land, PEPSU Kisan Sabha, Sangrur, 1951.
Agrarian Problem in India, E.M.S. Namboodiripad, Calcutta, June 1952.

F. UNPUBLISHED MONOGRAPHS

Rusch, Thomas A., "Role of the Congress Socialist Party in the Indian National Congress", Unpublished Ph.D thesis, Chicago University, Chicago, 1955 (microfilm).

Hauser, Walter, "The Bihar Provincial Kisan Sabha, 1929-1942: A Study of an Indian Peasant Movement", Unpublished Ph.D thesis, Chicago University, Chicago, 1961 (microfilm).

Bedford, Ian, "The Telengana Insurrection", Unpublished Ph.D thesis, Australian National University, Canberra, 1967 (microfilm).

Gopalankutty, K., "The Rise and Growth of the Communist Party in Malabar, 1934-1947", Unpublished M. Phil. thesis, Centre for Historical Studies, School of Social Sciences, Jawaharlal Nehru University, New Delhi, 1978.

Thirumali, Inukonda, "Aspect of Agrarian Relations in Telengana, 1928-1948", Unpublished M. Phil thesis, Centre for Historical Studies, School of Social Sciences, Jawaharlal Nehru University, New Delhi, 1979.

Nambiar, Gangadharan, T.K., "Growth of Class Consciousness Among the Peasantry of North Malabar (Kerala),1934-1942", Unpublished thesis, Centre for Historical Studies, School of Social Sciences, Jawaharlal Nehru University, New Delhi, 1982.

Singha, Radhika, "Aspects of the Quit India Movement in Eastern U.P.", Unpublished M.Phil. thesis, Centre for Historical Studies, School of Social Sciences, Jawaharlal Nehru University, New Delhi, 1986.

Subbarao, C.V., "Hyderabad : Social Context of Industrialisation, 1875-1948", Unpublished dissertation, Indian Council of Social Science Research, New Delhi, 1990.

Thirumali, I., "Lords and Peasants in Telengana, 1920-48: An Enquiry into the People's Uprising in Nalgonda and Warangal Districts", Unpublished Ph. D. thesis, Centre for Historical Studies, School of Social Science, Jawaharlal Nehru University, New Delhi, 1991.

G. INTERVIEWS

Sohan Singh Josh, 24 April 1982, in New Delhi.
Abdulla Rasul, 19 October 1983, in Calcutta.
Abani Lahiri, 15 July 1985, in New Delhi.
N.G. Ranga, 28 March 1986, in New Delhi.
Dr. Chandan Mitra, 27 July 1990, in New Delhi.
Arun Bose, 27 December 1990, in Calcutta.

Mention must also be made of Debabrata Chattopadhyaya, who replied to the author's queries by writing three incisive letters (dated 27 November 1991, 6 March and 12 April 1992), and analysed his experiences as a leading local Communist activist between 1948 and 1951 in Bankura district of West Bengal.

H. BOOKS AND ARTICLES

A very large number of printed books and articles, as well as mimeographed research papers and seminar presentations, has been consulted for this study. Since their list is unduly lengthy, and also unlikely to be of much use to the general readers, the author has decided against its inclusion here. However, he has provided in the footnotes full references of those secondary works which are related directly to the text.

INDEX